CW01263613

T&T Clark Critical Readings in Biblical Studies

Other titles in the series:

The Son of Man Problem: Critical Readings
The Letter to the Hebrews: Critical Readings

The Hebrew Bible and History

Critical Readings

Edited by
Lester L. Grabbe

t&tclark
LONDON • NEW YORK • OXFORD • NEW DELHI • SYDNEY

T&T CLARK
Bloomsbury Publishing Plc
50 Bedford Square, London, WC1B 3DP, UK
1385 Broadway, New York, NY 10018, USA

BLOOMSBURY, T&T CLARK and the T&T Clark logo are trademarks of Bloomsbury Publishing Plc

First published 2019

© Lester L. Grabbe, 2019

Lester L. Grabbe has asserted his right under the Copyright, Designs and Patents Act, 1988, to be identified as Editor of this work.

Cover image © Petr Strnad/Shutterstock

All rights reserved. No part of this publication may be reproduced or transmitted in any form or by any means, electronic or mechanical, including photocopying, recording, or any information storage or retrieval system, without prior permission in writing from the publishers.

Bloomsbury Publishing Plc does not have any control over, or responsibility for, any third-party websites referred to or in this book. All internet addresses given in this book were correct at the time of going to press. The author and publisher regret any inconvenience caused if addresses have changed or sites have ceased to exist, but can accept no responsibility for any such changes.

A catalogue record for this book is available from the British Library.

Library of Congress Cataloging-in-Publication Data
Names: Grabbe, Lester L., editor.
Title: The Hebrew Bible and history : critical readings / edited by Lester L. Grabbe.
Description: 1 [edition]. | New York : T&T Clark-Bloomsbury Academic, 2018. |
Series: T&T Clark Critical Readings in Biblical Studies |
Includes bibliographical references and index.
Identifiers: LCCN 2018009756 (print) | LCCN 2018031009 (ebook) |
ISBN 9780567672681 (ePDF) | ISBN 9780567672674 (hardback : alk. paper)
Subjects: LCSH: Bible. Old Testament--History of Biblical events. |
Jews--History--To 70 A.D. | Bible. Old Testament--Criticism, interpretation, etc.
Classification: LCC BS1197 (ebook) | LCC BS1197 .H35 2018 (print) |
DDC 221.9/5--dc23
LC record available at https://lccn.loc.gov/2018009756

ISBN: HB: 978-0-5676-7267-4
       ePDF: 978-0-5676-7268-1

Typeset by Forthcoming Publications (www.forthpub.com)
Printed and bound in Great Britain

To find out more about our authors and books visit www.bloomsbury.com and sign up for our newsletters.

Dedicated to
Professor Philip R. Davies
(1945–2018)

Colleague and Friend

Contents

Abbreviations	xi
Original Publications	xv
Introduction	xix

Part 1
Studies in Methodology

Introduction to Part 1	3
Some Aspects of Working with the Textual Sources Herbert Niehr	15
The Strange Fear of the Bible: Some Reflections on the 'Bibliophobia' in Recent Ancient Israelite Historiography Hans M. Barstad	24
Is It Possible to Write a History of Israel without Relying on the Hebrew Bible? J. Maxwell Miller	31
Reading the Bible Historically: The Historian's Approach J. Maxwell Miller	39
Does Archaeology Really Deserve the Status of a 'High Court' in Biblical Historical Research? Nadav Na'aman	56
Malleability and its Limits: Sennacherib's Campaign against Judah as a Case-Study Ehud Ben Zvi	72
On the Problems of Reconstructing Pre-Hellenistic Israelite (Palestinian) History Niels Peter Lemche	100

Text, Context and Referent in Israelite Historiography
    Thomas L. Thompson   116

The Big Max: Review of *A Biblical History of Israel*, by Iain Provan, V. Philips Long, and Tremper Longman, III
    Lester L. Grabbe   138

"Who Is the Prophet Talking about, Himself or Someone Else?" (Acts 8:34): A Response to Lester Grabbe's Review of *A Biblical History of Israel*
    Iain Provan, V. Philips Long, and Tremper Longman, III   156

Part 2
The Beginnings of Israel and the Rise of the Monarchy

Introduction to Part 2   171

The Geography of the Exodus
    John Van Seters   185

History in Joshua
    Ernst Axel Knauf   203

History in Judges
    Ernst Axel Knauf   213

Saul ben Kish in History and Tradition
    Diana Edelman   222

The Mighty Men of Israel: 1–2 Samuel and Historicity
    Lester L. Grabbe   236

Sources and Composition in the History of David
    Nadav Na'aman   256

David and the Philistines: Literature and History
    Walter Dietrich   270

King Solomon's Copper Supply
    Ernst Axel Knauf   293

The Socio-Political Shadow Cast by the Biblical Solomon
Hermann Michael Niemann   311

Biblical Jerusalem: An Archaeological Assessment
Anne E. Killebrew   352

Secondary Sources Also Deserve to Be Historically Evaluated: The Case of the United Monarchy
Rainer Albertz   367

Part 3
Case Study:
The Question of the Reform under Josiah

Introduction to Part 3   383

Josiah and the Law Book
Philip R. Davies   391

Why a Reform Like Josiah's Must Have Happened
Rainer Albertz   404

Was There a Cult Reform under King Josiah? The Case for a Well-Grounded Minimum
Christoph Uehlinger   425

Part 4
Case Study:
The Problem of Nehemiah's Wall

Introduction to Part 4   467

Geographical Lists in Ezra and Nehemiah in the Light of Archaeology: Persian or Hellenistic?
Israel Finkelstein   475

Jerusalem between Two Periods of Greatness: The Size and Status of the City in the Babylonian, Persian and Early Hellenistic Periods
Oded Lipschits   499

Part 5
Conclusions

Introduction to Part 5   519

Seventeen Years of the European Seminar
in Historical Methodology: The Results
    Lester L. Grabbe   521

Index of References   534
Index of Authors   546
Index of Subjects   555

Abbreviations

AASOR / *AASOR*	Annual of the American Schools of Oriental Research
ÄAT	Agypten und Altes Testament
AB	Anchor Bible
ABD	*Anchor Bible Dictionary.* Edited by David Noel Freedman. 6 vols. New York: Doubleday, 1992
ABRL	Anchor Bible Reference Library
ADPV	Abhandlungen des Deutschen Palastina-Vereins
AfO Beiheft	Archiv fur Orientforschung: Beiheft
AHI	Graham I. Davies. *Ancient Hebrew Inscriptions.* New York: Cambridge University Press, 1991.
ALASPM	Abhandlungen zur Literatur Alt-Syrien-Palastinas und Mesopotamiens
AnBib	Analecta Biblica
ANET / ANET³	*Ancient Near Eastern Texts Relating to the Old Testament.* Edited by James B. Pritchard. 3rd ed. Princeton: Princeton University Press, 1969
AOAT	Alter Orient und Altes Testament
ATANT / AThANT	Abhandlungen zur Theologie des Alten und Neuen Testaments
ATD	Das Alte Testament Deutsch
ATSAT	Arbeiten zu Text und Sprache im Alten Testament
AUSS	*Andrews University Seminary Studies*
BA	*Biblical Archaeologist*
BAR / BARev	*Biblical Archaeology Review*
BASOR	*Bulletin of the American Schools of Oriental Research*
BBB	*Bulletin de bibliographie biblique*
BeO	*Bibbia e oriente*
BETL	Bibliotheca Ephemeridum Theologicarum Lovaniensium
BHS	*Biblia Hebraica Stuttgartensia.* Edited by Karl Elliger and Wilhelm Rudolph. Stuttgart: Deutsche Bibelgesellschaft, 1983
Bib	*Biblica*
BibEnz	Biblische Enzyklopädie
BKAT	Biblischer Kommentar, Altes Testament
BM	British Museum
BN	*Biblische Notizen*
BO	*Bibliotheca Orientalis*
BSOAS	*Bulletin of the School of Oriental and African Studies*
BTAVO	Beihefte zum Tübinger Atlas des Vorderen Orient
BWANT	Beitrage zur Wissenschaft vom Alten (und Neuen) Testament

BZ	*Biblische Zeitschrift*
BZAW	Beihefte zur Zeitschrift fur die alttestamentliche Wissenschaft
CBQ	*Catholic Biblical Quarterly*
CBQMS	Catholic Biblical Quarterly Monograph Series
CIS	Comparative Islamic Studies
ConBOT	Coniectanea Biblica: Old Testament Series
CR:BS	*Currents in Research: Biblical Studies*
DBAT	Dielheimer Blatter zum Alten Testament und seiner Rezeption in der Alten Kirche
EB	Echter Bibel
EHST	Europäische Hochschulschriften
ErIs / EI	*Eretz-Israel*
ESHM	European Seminar in Historical Methodology
EThSt	Erfurter theologische Studien
EvT	*Evangelische Theologie*
FAT	Forschungen zum Alten Testament
FBE	Forum for Bibelsk Eksegese
FOTL	Forms of the Old Testament Literature
FRLANT	Forschungen zur Religion und Literatur des Alten und Neuen Testaments
GGG	Othmar Keel and Christoph Uehlinger. *Göttinnen, Götter und Gottessymbole : neue Erkenntnisse zur Religionsgeschichte Kanaans und Israels aufgrund bislang unerschlossener ikonographischer Quellen*. Freiburg: Herder, 1992.
GGIG	*Gods, Goddesses and Images of God in Ancient Israel*. Translated by Thomas H. Trapp. Minneapolis: Fortress Press, 1998.
HALOT	*The Hebrew and Aramaic Lexicon of the Old Testament*. Ludwig Koehler, Walter Baumgartner, and Johann J. Stamm. Translated and edited under the supervision of Mervyn E. J. Richardson. 4 vols. Leiden: Brill, 1994–99
HAT	Handbuch zum Alten Testament
HBT	*Horizons in Biblical Theology*
HSM	Harvard Semitic Monographs
HSS	Harvard Semitic Studies
HUCA	*Hebrew Union College Annual*
IEJ	*Israel Exploration Journal*
Int	*Interpretation*
JANES	*Journal of the Ancient Near Eastern Society of Columbia University*
JAOS	*Journal of the American Oriental Society*
JBL	*Journal of Biblical Literature*
JCS	*Journal of Cuneiform Studies*
JEA	*Journal of Egyptian Archaeology*
JESHO	*Journal of the Economic and Social History of the Orient*
JNES	*Journal of Near Eastern Studies*
JQR	*Jewish Quarterly Review*

JSOT	*Journal for the Study of the Old Testament*
JSOTSup / SupplJSOT	Journal for the Study of the Old Testament Supplement Series
JSS Supplement	Journal of Semitic Studies Supplement
KAT	Kommentar zum Alten Testament
LAPO	Litteratures anciennes du Proche-Orient
LHBOTS / LHB/OTS	The Library of Hebrew Bible/Old Testament Studies
LSTS	The Library of Second Temple Studies
NCB	New Century Bible
NCBC	New Century Bible Commentary
NEAEHL	*The New Encyclopedia of Archaeological Excavations in the Holy Land.* Edited by Ephraim Stern. 4 vols. Jerusalem: Israel Exploration Society & Carta; New York: Simon & Schuster, 1993
NTT	*Norsk Teologisk Tidsskrift*
OBO	Orbis Biblicus et Orientalis
OIP	Oriental Institute Publications
OLA	Orientalia Lovaniensia Analecta
OLP	Orientalia Lovaniensia Periodica
OLZ	*Orientalistische Literaturzeitung*
Or	*Orientalia*
OTG	Old Testament Guides
OTL	Old Testament Library
PEFQST	*Palestine Exploration Fund, Quarterly Statement*
PEQ	*Palestine Exploration Quarterly*
Phil-hist K	Philologisch-Historische Klasse
PJ	*Palastina-Jahrbuch*
PTMS	Pittsburgh Theological Monograph Series
Qad	*Qadmoniot*
QDAP	*Quarterly of the Department of Antiquities in Palestine*
RA	*Revue d'assyriologie et d'archeologie orientale*
RB	*Revue biblique*
RBL	*Review of Biblical Literature*
*RGG*⁴	*Religion in Geschichte und Gegenwart.* Edited by Hans Dieter Betz. 4th ed. Tubingen: Mohr Siebeck, 1998–2007
RLA	*Reallexikon der Assyriologie*
RM	Die Religionen der Menschheit
RSR	*Recherches de science religieuse*
RUB	Reclams Universal-Bibliothek
SAA	State Archives of Assyria
SAAS	State Archives of Assyria Studies
SAM	Sheffield Archaeological Monographs
SBA	Studies in Biblical Archaeology
SBAW	Sitzungsberichte der bayerischen Akademie der Wissenschaften
SBLDS	Society of Biblical Literature Dissertation Series
SBLSS	Society of Biblical Literature Symposium Series
SBT / SBTSS	Studies in Biblical Theology (Second Series)
ScrH	Scripta Hierosolymitana

SESJ	Suomen Eksegeettisen Seuran julkaisuja
SHANE / SHCANE	Studies in the History of the Ancient Near East
SJOT	*Scandinavian Journal of the Old Testament*
SOTSMS	Society for Old Testament Studies Monograph Series
SR	*Studies in Religion*
SSEA	Society for the Study of Egyptian Antiquities
SVT / *SVT*	Supplements to Vetus Testamentum
SWBA	Social World of Biblical Antiquity
SWBAS	Social World of Biblical Antiquity Series
TA	*Tel Aviv*
TCEI	Territorial Concept of Eretz Israel
ThB	Theologische Bücherei
TLZ	*Theologische Literaturzeitung*
TRu	*Theologische Rundschau*
TZ	*Theologische Zeitschrift*
UF	*Ugarit-Forschungen*
VT	*Vetus Testamentum*
VTSup / SupplVT	Supplements to Vetus Testamentum
VWGTh	Veröffentlichungen der Wissenschaftlichen Gesellschaft für Theologie
WdO	*Die Welt des Orients*
WMANT	Wissenschaftliche Monographien zum Alten und Neuen Testament
WSS	*Corpus of West Semitic Stamps and Seals*
WUB	*Welt und Umwelt der Bibel*
ZAH	*Zeitschrift für Althebraistik*
ZAW	*Zeitschrift für die alttestamentliche Wissenschaft*
ZBKAT	Zurcher Bibelkommentare. Alten Testament
ZDPV	*Zeitschrift des deutschen Palastina-Vereins*
ZTK	*Zeitschrift für Theologie und Kirche*

Original Publications

Albertz, Rainer, 'Why a Reform like Josiah's Must Have Happened', in Lester L. Grabbe (ed.), *Good Kings and Bad Kings: The Kingdom of Judah in the Seventh Century BCE*, JSOTSup 393 = European Seminar in Historical Methodology 5 (London/New York: T&T Clark International, 2005), 27–46.

Albertz, Rainer, 'Secondary Sources also Deserve to Be Historically Evaluated: The Case of the United Monarchy', in Philip R. Davies and Diana V. Edelman (eds), *The Historian and the Bible: Essays in Honour of Lester L. Grabbe*, LHBOTS 530 (New York and London: T&T Clark International, 2010), 31–45.

Barstad, Hans M., 'The Strange Fear of the Bible: Some Reflections on the "Bibliophobia" in Recent Ancient Israelite Historiography', in Lester L. Grabbe (ed.), *Leading Captivity Captive: 'The Exile' as History and Ideology*, JSOTSup 278 = European Seminar in Historical Methodology 2 (Sheffield: Sheffield Academic Press, 1998), 120–27.

Ben Zvi, Ehud, 'Malleability and its Limits: Sennacherib's Campaign against Judah as a Case-Study', in Lester L. Grabbe (ed.), *'Like a Bird in a Cage': The Invasion of Sennacherib in 701 BCE*, JSOTSup 363 = European Seminar in Historical Methodology 4 (Sheffield: Sheffield Academic Press, 2003), 73–105.

Davies, Philip R., 'Josiah and the Law Book', in Lester L. Grabbe (ed.), *Good Kings and Bad Kings: The Kingdom of Judah in the Seventh Century BCE*, JSOTSup 393 = European Seminar in Historical Methodology 5 (London/New York: T&T Clark International, 2005), 65–77.

Dietrich, Walter, 'David and the Philistines: Literature and History', in Gershon Galil, Ayelet Gilboa, Aren M. Maeir, and Dan'el Kahn (eds), *The Ancient Near East in the 12th-10th Centuries BCE: Culture and History: Proceedings of the International Conference Held at the University of Haifa, 2-5 May, 2010*, AOAT 392 (Münster: Ugarit-Verlag, 2012), 79–98.

Edelman, Diana, 'Saul ben Kish in History and Tradition', in Volkmar Fritz and Philip R. Davies (eds), *The Origins of the Ancient Israelite States*, JSOTSup 228 (Sheffield: Sheffield Academic Press, 1996), 142–59.

Finkelstein, Israel, 'Geographical Lists in Ezra and Nehemiah in the Light of Archaeology: Persian or Hellenistic?', in Lester L. Grabbe and Oded Lipschits (eds), *Judah between East and West: The Transition from Persian to Greek Rule* (ca. 400–200 BCE), LSTS 75 (London/New York: T&T Clark International, 2011), 49–69.

Grabbe, Lester L., 'The Big Max: Review of *A Biblical History of Israel* by Iain Provan, V. Philips Long, and Tremper Longman III', in Lester L. Grabbe (ed.), *Enquire of the Former Age: Ancient Historiography and Writing the History of Israel*, LHBOTS 554; European Seminar in Historical Methodology 9 (London/New York: T&T Clark International, 2011), 215–34.

Grabbe, Lester L., 'The Mighty Men of Israel: 1–2 Samuel and History', in Walter Dietrich, Cynthia Edenburg, and Philippe Hugo (eds), *The Books of Samuel: Stories - History - Reception History*, Bibliotheca Ephemeridum Theologicarum Lovaniensium 284 (Leuven: Peeters, 2016), 83–104.

Grabbe, Lester L., 'Seventeen Years of the European Seminar in Historical Methodology: The Results', an adaptation of the concluding essay in Lester L. Grabbe (ed.), *'Not Even God Can Alter the Past': Reflections on 17 Years of the European Seminar in Historical Methodology*, LHBOTS; European Seminar in Historical Methodology 11 (London and New York: Bloomsbury T&T Clark, 2018), 215–31.

Killebrew, Ann E., 'Biblical Jerusalem: An Archaeological Assessment', in Andrew G. Vaughn and Ann E. Killebrew (eds), *Jerusalem in Bible and Archaeology: The First Temple Period*, SBLSymS 18 (Atlanta: Society of Biblical Literature), 329–45.

Knauf, Ernst Axel, 'King Solomon's Copper Supply', in Edward Lipiński (ed.), *Phoenicia and the Bible*, Studia Phoenicia 11 (Leuven: Peeters, 1991), 167–86; reprinted in Ernst Axel Knauf, *Data and Debates: Essays in the History and Culture of Israel and Its Neighbors in Antiquity/Daten und Debatten: Aufsätze zur Kulturgeschichte des antiken Israel und seiner Nachbarn*, ed. Hermann Michael Niemann, Konrad Schmid and Silvia Schroer, AOAT 418 (Münster: Ugarit-Verlag, 2015), 85–100.

Knauf, Ernst Axel, 'History in Joshua', in Lester L. Grabbe (ed.), *Israel in Transition: From Late Bronze II to Iron IIA (c. 1250–850 BCE)*. Volume 2, *The Text*, LHBOTS 521 = European Seminar in Historical Methodology 8 (London/New York: T&T Clark International, 2010), 130–39.

Knauf, Ernst Axel, 'History in Judges', in Lester L. Grabbe (ed.), *Israel in Transition: From Late Bronze II to Iron IIA (c. 1250–850 BCE)*. Volume 2, *The Text*, LHBOTS 521 = European Seminar in Historical Methodology 8 (London/New York: T&T Clark International, 2010), 140–49.

Lemche, Niels Peter, 'On the Problems of Reconstructing Pre-Hellenistic Israelite (Palestinian) History', in Lester L. Grabbe (ed.), *'Like a Bird in a Cage': The Invasion of Sennacherib in 701 BCE*, JSOTSup 363 = European Seminar in Historical Methodology 4 (Sheffield: Sheffield Academic Press, 2003), 150–67.

Lipschits, Oded, 'Jerusalem between Two Periods of Greatness: The Size and Status of the City in the Babylonian, Persian and Early Hellenistic Periods', in Lester L. Grabbe and Oded Lipschits (eds), *Judah between East and West: The Transition from Persian to Greek Rule (ca. 400–200 BCE)*, LSTS 75 (London/New York: T&T Clark International, 2011), 163–75.

Miller, J. Maxwell, 'Is it Possible to Write a History of Israel without Relying on the Hebrew Bible?' in Diana V. Edelman (ed.), *The Fabric of History: Text, Artifact and Israel's Past*, JSOTSup 127 (Sheffield: Sheffield Academic Press, 1991), 93–102.

Miller, Max [J. Maxwell], 'Reading the Bible Historically: The Historian's Approach', in Stephen R. Haynes and Steven L. McKenzie (eds), *To Each Its Own Meaning: An Introduction to Biblical Criticisms and their Application* (Louisville, KY: Westminster John Knox Press, 1993), 11–28.

Na'aman, Nadav, 'Sources and Composition in the History of David', in Volkmar Fritz and Philip R. Davies (eds), *The Origins of the Ancient Israelite States*, JSOTSup 228 (Sheffield: Sheffield Academic Press, 1996), 170–86; reprinted in Nadav Na'aman, *Ancient Israel's History and Historiography: The First Temple Period: Collected Essays*, Volume 3 (Winona Lake, IN: Eisenbrauns, 2006), 23–37.

Na'aman, Nadav, 'Does Archaeology Really Deserve the Status of a "High Court" in Biblical Historical Research?' in Bob Becking and Lester L. Grabbe (eds), *Between Evidence and Ideology: Essays on the History of Ancient Israel read at the Joint Meeting of the Society for Old Testament Study and the Oud Testamentisch Werkgezelschap Lincoln, July 2009*, OTS 59 (Leiden: Brill, 2011), 165–83.

Niehr, Herbert, 'Some Aspects of Working with the Textual Sources', in Lester L. Grabbe (ed.), *Can a 'History of Israel' Be Written?*, JSOTSup 245 = European Seminar in Historical Methodology 1 (Sheffield: Sheffield Academic Press, 1997), 37–64.

Niemann, Hermann Michael, 'The Socio-Political Shadow Cast by the Biblical Solomon', in L. K. Handy (ed.), *The Age of Solomon: Scholarship at the Turn of the Millennium*, Studies in the History and Culture of the Ancient Near East 11 (Leiden: Brill, 1997); reprinted in Hermann Michael Niemann, *History of Ancient Israel, Archaeology, and Bible: Collected Essays/Geschichte Israels, Archäologie und Bibel: Gesammelte Aufsätze*, ed. Meik Gerhards, AOAT 418 (Münster: Ugarit-Verlag, 2015), 91–126.

Provan, Iain, V. Philips Long, and Tremper Longman III, '"Who Is the Prophet Talking about, Himself or Someone Else?" (Acts 8.34): A Response to Lester Grabbe's Review of A Biblical History of Israel', in Lester L. Grabbe (ed.), *Enquire of the Former Age: Ancient Historiography and Writing the History of Israel*, LHBOTS 554; European Seminar in Historical Methodology 9 (London/New York: T&T Clark International, 2011), 235–52.

Thompson, Thomas L., 'Text, Context, and Referent in Israelite Historiography', in Diana V. Edelman (ed.), *The Fabric of History: Text, Artifact and Israel's Past*, JSOTSup 127 (Sheffield: Sheffield Academic Press, 1991), 65–92; reprinted in Thomas L. Thompson, *Biblical Narrative and Palestine's History: Changing Perspectives 2*, Copenhagen International Seminar (Sheffield: Equinox, 2013), 163–81.

Uehlinger, Christoph, 'Was There a Cult Reform under King Josiah? The Case for a Well-Grounded Minimum', in Lester L. Grabbe (ed.), *Good Kings and Bad Kings: The Kingdom of Judah in the Seventh Century BCE*, JSOTSup 393 = European Seminar in Historical Methodology 5 (London/New York: T&T Clark International, 2005), 279–316.

Van Seters, John, 'The Geography of the Exodus', in J. Andrew Dearman and M. Patrick Graham (eds), *The Land that I Will Show You: Essays on the History and Archaeology of the Ancient Near East in Honour of J. Maxwell Miller*, JSOTSup 343 (Sheffield: Sheffield Academic Press, 2001), 255–76; reprinted in John Van Seters, *Changing Perspectives I: Studies in the History, Literature and Religion of Biblical Israel*, Copenhagen International Seminar (London: Equinox, 2011), 115–33.

Introduction

In keeping with the aims of the series, Critical Readings, this volume proposes to present a number of articles that have addressed the problem of history in ancient Israel and discussed it from a variety of perspectives. Not all the articles are definitive but many are. In any case, they all address the question from a particular perspective which will be clear from the article itself but will also be commented on in the preface to the section in question.

No single volume can address all the issues that are important for the history of ancient Israel. What the present volume hopes to do, however, is deal with some of the main issues. This will be partly through articles dealing directly with such issues in the first or methodology part of the volume (Part 1) but partly through 'case studies', in which several articles are brought together to address the question from different, even contradictory, perspectives (Parts 3 and 4). This includes two main case studies: the supposed reform of Josiah in the second half of the seventh century BCE, and the question of Nehemiah's wall in the fifth century BCE. A good deal of emphasis (especially in Part 2) is also placed on illustrating and exemplifying the principles of writing a history of Israel by means of articles on specific aspects of Israel's history.

As will be obvious, a number of the articles collected here were originally printed in volumes arising out of meetings of the European Seminar on Methodology in Israel's History. This is because our discussions covered not only many questions of historical methodology but also wrestled with them in debate over specific periods and problems in the history of Israel (or Palestine or Southern Levant). For those not familiar with the work of the European Seminar, the final essay explains how it originated and discusses its work over 17 years and 11 volumes. However, the essays can be read on their own and do not require knowledge of their origins or original context to be understood.

More information about individual articles and case studies will be given in the introductions to the individual parts of this book. Also, an Annotated Bibliography relating to other studies of potential value will be included in each of these introductions.

Principles for Writing History

A number of principles for writing history will emerge from the conclusions of different articles but also through engaging in current debate about the history of ancient Israel. Various of these principles will be discussed in the articles in Part 1 and, especially, in the concluding article in Part 5 when a more systematic presentation of my own views about the principles of writing history are given. There are two issues that will be flagged up here but which will be taken up in more detail in the individual articles and in my final concluding chapter.

Two terms that are thrown about quite promiscuously in current discussion are 'minimalists' and 'maximalists'. These were originally meant as descriptive terms but have more recently been used as slogans or weapons—often inaccurately—to promote or denigrate particular positions. Strictly speaking, minimalism means that everything which is not corroborated by evidence contemporary with the events to be reconstructed is dismissed, while maximalism operates on the principle that everything in the sources that could not be proved wrong has to be accepted as historical (see further in the final essay in Part 5). That means there are few real minimalists and even fewer maximalists. There are a few scholars who fall into one or the other category, sometimes by self-designation. This will be noted in the discussion, but for the most part we should try to move beyond these labels.

Another term often bandied about is 'postmodernism', a term that is hard to define since most definitions engage in telling us what it is not rather than what it is. Most of those working as historians are not postmodernists, even if many accept that postmodernism can teach us a few lessons in our work. By its nature postmodernism tends to be a-historical or even anti-historical. More on this in Part 5.

Contents of the Volume

This volume is divided into four parts. This is only a rough-and-ready organization, since the essays in the different parts often overlap the contents of those in other parts and, especially, because the essays often have material relevant to the discussion in other sections. Therefore, the discussion at the beginning of the individual parts might very well refer to essays that are actually placed in another section.

Part 1 gives a focus to the question of historical methodology. Several of the essays talk about historical methodology in general or perhaps about some specific aspect of historical research and the Bible. Several of the essays give specific examples that help to illustrate how historical method works 'at the coal face', as it were. The essays are written from a variety of perspectives and help to show how different researchers conceive of the task of writing the history of ancient Palestine. Part 2 has essays that especially relate to the earlier period of the history of ancient Israel. They range from the exodus and Joshua/Judges but especially discuss the early kings Saul, David and Solomon. One essay talks about the archaeology of Jerusalem.

Parts 3 and 4 are case studies that help to orient the reader to historical problems by giving discussion and debate on specific issues from different perspectives. Part 3 is on Josiah's reform, an event once widely accepted as historical without too much debate but one which has become a major source of interest and scepticism. Part 4 is another topic once widely accepted as historical but now queried by a leading archaeologist, the existence of Nehemiah's wall. This time we move into the 'post-exilic' period, which was once neglected but is now a major focus for the development of scripture and Judaic religion. Finally, Part 5 is a single essay but one outlining much that has been debated in the past 20 years. It also suggests the main categories of historical method to be applied in researching the history of ancient Israel.

The number of essays in this volume could be multiplied many times over. Especially in the area of case studies, many more examples could be presented. The reader is encouraged to explore the subject further by following up the suggestions for further reading about specific episodes in the history of Israel given in the annotated bibliographies.

Part 1

Studies in Methodology

Introduction to Part 1

The purpose of the present section is to present a number of articles that have attempted to articulate methodological principles with regard to writing a history of ancient Israel. This could have been expanded almost without limit, since all sorts of considerations come up when trying to develop a proper method for writing history. Yet these essays illustrate some of the main points to think about, especially those that are the subject of current debate. Much can be learned by example, through considering the work of historians who have wrestled with the issues and seeing how they have resolved or at least dealt with various historical problems.[1]

The section begins with comments by HERBERT NIEHR on sources and the methodological problems in that arise in dealing with them. One can start with what he calls 'historical anthropology' (though others use the term *longue durée*, borrowed from Braudel), which means things like climate, geography, sociology and economics. Next are the 'primary sources', which means those close in time and space to the event(s) being described. 'Secondary sources' are those removed from the events by time, editing and rewriting, and includes most of the biblical text. Yet secondary (and tertiary) sources have their place. Also, secondary sources are primary sources to the extent that they reflect the mentality of the editors and writers who create them and also for their times. J. MAXWELL MILLER also discusses some general points about writing history, including how the historical method works (using the court-room analogy). He comments as well on how writers of the Bible approached their task. (Note that some of these points about writing history are discussed in more detail by GRABBE in the final essay in Part 5.)

That the biblical text is not to be neglected in writing a history of Israel is also one of the points made by HANS BARSTAD when he talks about the 'strange fear of the Bible' in certain historical circles. The biblical text is usually a secondary source, but it does not differ from such important historical sources as Herodotus or the *Sumerian King List*. We have to treat the Bible like other ancient Near Eastern secondary sources, and the biblical text has been shown to have useful information at times. GRABBE also makes this point (see Part 5), that classical historians often must use sources that have some of the same problems as the biblical text (not only Herodotus but also Arrian, Livy, Cassius Dio and even

---

[1] Note that the names of the authors of articles reprinted in this volume are given in small caps. Other references relate either to the Annotated Bibliography or are given in a footnote.

Polybius). Indeed, as MILLER makes clear we depend heavily on the Bible for certain background information that we take for granted when doing our research on ancient Palestine, including such basic information as the existence of certain place names in the region or even certain figures of the ancient Near East. Any discussion of Palestine is suffused with data that ultimately derives from the Bible.

One of the primary historical sources is archaeology, and its importance is paramount. Yet NADAV NA'AMAN reminds us that we always rely on a variety of sources, only one of which is archaeology. Archaeology has two lacks: it does not necessarily give us complete data, and it is always interpretative. There are times that we know of the existence of certain settlements because they are mentioned in the text, even though archaeologists have not found them. Archaeologists may also have sincere disagreements about how to interpret the same set of data from the material culture. Our recognition of the value of archaeology must not allow us to elevate it to the position of ultimate arbiter of historical events.

Further views about the historical method are given in the next three essays. EHUD BEN ZVI uses the analogy of the Sennacherib's invasion to illustrate his point that this account of an event in 701 BCE was written a century or more later in the sixth century BCE and to show the parallels between what happened under Sennacherib and under Nebuchadnezzar. Nevertheless, the writer was constrained by his knowledge of the earlier event and by the beliefs of the intended audience. Thus, although the account of events under Sennacherib could be shaped to fit the author's needs, they were not infinitely malleable but had limits. NIELS PETER LEMCHE also uses Sennacherib's invasion, which he contrasts with the actions of Mesha of Moab. The main events of Sennacherib are clear, especially because of the Assyrian records, but little in 2 Kings 3 is confirmed by the Moabite inscription. Although some might dispute LEMCHE's conclusions about Mesha, his point is to avoid circular reasoning when trying to write the history of Israel. The biblical writers were providing examples of good and bad behaviour, not writing history in the modern sense. THOMAS L. THOMPSON also comments on the nature of the biblical narrative. He notes how the biblical writers do not distinguish between narratives that we would regard as more mythical (e.g., in the early chapters of Genesis) and those that are considered more historiographical (as in 1 and 2 Kings). There is also the time gap between when the events took place and the narrative of those events which is from a much later time. The picture of society given in the Bible is often very different from that derived from archaeology.

These conclusions about the nature of the biblical accounts will be debated by scholars. Major differences in interpretation are illustrated by LESTER L. GRABBE's review of IAN PROVEN, PHILIPS LONG and TREMPER LONGMAN's *A Biblical History of Israel* (2003). Whereas their history gives great credence to the biblical text, GRABBE challenges their conclusions in certain areas, primarily those relating to the book of Joshua and the Israelite settlement. One hopes that the reader is familiar with *A Biblical History of Israel*. In this case, the aim is for the reader to peruse GRABBE's review and the response by the three authors of *A Biblical History of Israel*, and make some judgments about how to go about writing a history. Again, more information on his approach to historical method is given by GRABBE in the final essay of the volume (Part 5).

Summary of Articles

1. HERBERT NIEHR ('Some Aspects of Working with the Textual Sources') looks at the question of the various types of sources and the methodological problems with using each of them. The basic level of study is 'historical anthropology', which makes use of non-written sources including climatology, geography, archaeology, agriculture, sociology and economics. Primary sources, those written close to the event, are the second level of investigation. Secondary sources are copies, interpretations, rewritings, and re-editings of the original. The biblical text is clearly a secondary source in most cases, because it is removed in time from the events it purports to describe. In some cases (e.g., the books of Chronicles) the biblical text is only a tertiary source. Yet it still has a function in the task of writing a history and cannot just be dismissed, for it serves to integrate primary written and unwritten data. Also, the text is a primary source for the mentality of the (re)writers or editors. A critical history of ancient Israel can begin with the time of Jeroboam and Omri. History is not what is in the sources; history is what historians write, though it is based on a critical evaluation of all sources.

2. HANS M. BARSTAD ('The Strange Fear of the Bible: Some Reflections on the "Bibliophobia" in Recent Ancient Israelite Historiography') discusses an issue which has bedeviled our discussions in many ways. Recognizing that the use of the Hebrew Bible in historical reconstruction is highly uncertain, he points out that it is not a unique problem to ancient historians. The same applies to Herodotus, for instance. A very useful example is that of the 'Sumerian King List' the problems of whose use are similar to those of the biblical text. For example, it was composed quite some time after the events it proposes to describe, and the text has many lacunae; it also has an ideological aim. Nevertheless, Assyriologists have found it to contain useful information about Sumerian history. The Deuteronomistic history has details about many named kings whose existence has been confirmed by extra-biblical sources; in particular, 2 Kings 24–25 on the last days of Jerusalem provides sufficient verified data to assume that it is correct in general for areas where it cannot be checked. To reject the biblical text beforehand as fictitious without due consideration is as incompatible to a scholarly mind as to accept it uncritically. We have to treat the Bible, for better or for worse, as we do other ancient Near Eastern sources.

3. J. MAXWELL MILLER ('Is it Possible to Write a History of Israel without Relying on the Hebrew Bible?') begins by noting the different information conveyed by texts and artifacts: for the names of people and details of history we need a text; on the other hand, texts are often biased. There is also the tendency to give precedence to the written evidence over that from artifacts in the sense of letting the texts determine how the artifacts are interpreted. Nevertheless, there is much that we could not glean from the material culture, only from texts. But even within texts from the neighbouring regions of Egypt and Mesopotamia many references make sense only when read in the light of the Bible. Would we be able to make much sense of the 'Israel' of Merenptah without the biblical text? Some authors have given the impression that they can write a history of the Palestinian area without the Bible, but their statements often presuppose data that comes first and foremost from the biblical text. For example, we continually refer to Judahites and Israelites, even though these are people known mainly from the biblical text, not other sources, and certainly not from artifacts. Their rhetoric often implies that we can decide whether the Bible is a reliable source for historical information but ignores the fact that archaeological research for Syro-Palestine is suffused with assumptions and data from the Bible. There are also the problems associated with any reconstruction of history from the material culture. Ultimately, the question is not *whether* we should use the Hebrew Bible in our attempts to understand the history of Israel but *how* we should use it.

4. In a second contribution ('Reading the Bible Historically: The Historian's Approach'), J. MAXWELL MILLER first discusses the definition of 'history' and 'historiography', before going on to discuss that method. The only method of note is that of *analogy*: historians judge the past by their experience in the present. Thus, since the supernatural does not intrude into the present day, historians generally reject scenarios that presuppose supernatural intervention in the past. Also, analogy serves to help explain the situation in ancient Israel by comparison with better-known societies or events in the past, such as Egypt or Mesopotamia. Otherwise, the historical method is very much like an investigative legal expert who examines and weighs the evidence, comes up with an explanation (hypothesis) of what this evidence means and presents it to a jury (the body of other historians) to see whether it is convincing. History is, therefore, not just 'what happened' but 'what can you convince your peers happened'. The writers of the Bible were more theologians but were conscious of history and presented a good deal of the text in the form of a historical narrative. The historicity of the Bible has been much debated in modern times, with views ranging from giving great credence to the biblical account to an extremely sceptical perspective. Most biblical scholars do not adhere to either extreme, but even in the middle ground there is a wide range of views. Analysis of the biblical text generally necessitates some knowledge—and a view—of the history of ancient Israel, and many such histories have been written over the years, but a significant shift in approach came about in the 1970s. This was partly because of new evidence (such as data

from epigraphic finds and archaeological excavations and surveys) but especially because of new methodologies (such as application of insights from the fields of sociology and anthropology). [The essay gives a survey of histories of Israel available in the 1960s, 1970s and 1980s, which is very helpful, but could not discuss anything published after about 1990 because of the essay's publication date. Some of the histories mentioned indeed had later editions that appeared after 1990. Two of these—Miller/Hayes and Soggin—are listed in the bibliography, along with some more recent histories by Frevel, Knauf/Guillaume, and Grabbe.]

5. **NADAV NA'AMAN** asks, 'Does Archaeology Really Deserve the Status of a "High Court" in Biblical Historical Research?' While recognizing the advances in archaeology, he wants to know whether some researchers are justified in giving preference to archaeology when it differs from the textual data, and looks at a number of case studies: the Amarna letters and cities in Palestine; Jerusalem in the Iron IIa; the walls of Jerusalem in the ninth–eighth centuries; Jerusalem in the Persian period; Gibeah of Benjamin; and Bethel. He notes several reasons why the archaeology may not show settlements that in fact existed: the problem of dating the beginnings of archaeological strata, the destruction of evidence by later building activity and the high bedrock in the highlands which meant that new builds often removed previous levels down to bedrock. From Mesopotamia we know of important cultic sites (such as Nippar and Eridu) for which the city settlement declined and came to include only cult personnel. Thus, without in any way detracting from the importance of archaeology, it should be treated with caution when dealing with multi-strata highland sites in times of the supposed 'united monarchy' and the Babylonian and Persian periods. The limitations of both text and archaeology need to be recognized.

6. **EHUD BEN ZVI** ('Malleability and its Limits: Sennacherib's Campaign against Judah as a Case-Study') uses the episode to investigate historical method. His detailed survey of the sources argues that the 2 Kings account was written to be read by Jews in the post-exilic period, who would notice the parallels between the events in the time of Hezekiah and those a century later in the time of Zedekiah, but would also notice the contrasting fates. Hezekiah (unlike Zedekiah) tried to submit, but Sennacherib invaded anyway; hence, it was an attack on Yhwh himself, putting Sennacherib in a different category from Nebuchadnezzar. The account in 2 Chronicles is quite different, being only a small unit within a literary complex lionizing Hezekiah for his piety. Together with Josephus's version, these illustrate how malleable the tradition was in the various sources, depending on the interests and ideology of the composer, the context in which it was composed and the intended message for a particular audience. Yet there are limits to this malleability, for we do not find unrestrained creativity. One constraint is what the intended audience already believes and is prepared to believe. It is not stated anywhere, e.g., that Hezekiah was deposed. Being closer to the event does not mean that the sources are less interpretative or found in a more accurate form, as modern accounts of recent military campaigns show; their historical accuracy

still has to be tested. One test is whether diametrically separate groups share perceptions or representations; if so, this may point to something outside their representation, i.e., a 'historical event'.

7. **NIELS PETER LEMCHE**'s contribution ('On the Problems of Reconstructing Pre-Hellenistic Israelite [Palestinian] History') addresses directly the question of historical method, using two main examples: the invasion of Sennacherib and the actions of Mesha king of Moab. The 'historical-critical' method developed two centuries ago distinguished between *Bericht* ('story, interpretation') and *Überreste* ('remains of historical data') on the assumption that it could differentiate between the two. Because of the information from the Assyrian annals, it is not so difficult to draw a line between *Überreste* and *Bericht* in 2 Kings 18–19 since the main outlines of what happened are clear. The speech and letter of the Rabshakeh are invented (though some would wish to defend their genuineness), but much of the story reflects an actual campaign of Sennacherib. The picture of King Mesha in 2 Kings 3 is rather different. Although the Moabite inscription shows a King Mesha of Moab who lived close to the time of Omri, there is little in 2 Kings 3 that is confirmed by the inscription. Contrary to expectations, Ahab is not mentioned by name, and Omri could be the eponymous figure of *Bit Ḫumri*, 'house of Omri', of the Assyrian inscriptions. The piece of assured data is the name Mesha plus a bit on Moab of the time. The problem is historical reconstruction because most of ancient Israel's history is based on the biblical text alone and forms a 'hermeneutical circle', i.e., a logical circle. We have some external data, and the history of Israel and Judah as told by biblical historians is not totally devoid of historical information. There are historical remains in the biblical text, as well as an approximate chronological framework. The problem is how to determine what is *Überreste* without use of circular reasoning. The first step is to establish the genres of historiography in the ancient Near East. The biblical writers were not trying to write history in the modern sense; the past was of interest mainly for examples of good and bad behaviour. Thus, Omri's achievements are suppressed because the writer was not interested in giving a comprehensive account of the past as we might expect of a modern historian. There is history in the narrative, but it is mainly short notes. Recent study has shown that the patriarchal narratives are not history, that the exodus and conquest are a fiction, that the 'judges period' is a series of hero tales, and that the empires of David and Solomon and the 'united monarchy' are a fictional representation. There were certainly the two kingdoms of Israel and Judah, but the other 'actors' of the region are mostly ignored or their part distorted. During the so-called exile, most of the population remained in the land. The Persian period is mainly a dark spot, while Ezra is probably a late invention. We should give up hope of reconstructing pre-Hellenistic history on the basis of the Old Testament; it is simply an invented history with only a few referents to things that really happened.

8. THOMAS L. THOMPSON ('Text, Context, and Referent in Israelite Historiography') refers to Wellhausen's dictum that texts reflect the historical context in which they were written rather than a more distant past to which they ostensibly refer. He surveys the consensus view that biblical texts were rooted in the historical events to which they refer. Yet the biblical narratives begin at the earliest in the Persian period, and historical criticism is fundamental to reading these narratives. Canon criticism anachronistically projects a social construct into the early Persian period, since there was no canon at this time. Reading the text as directly relevant to today's audience is more uncritical than simply ahistorical. Any examination of the origins of Israel is forced to examine the development of Israelite tradition. The great divide between Genesis 11 and 12, once seen as demarcating the shift from myth to history in the Bible, has finally disappeared from the textbooks. The tales of Kings are traditions, not history. Plausibility and verisimilitude cannot be recognized as valid criteria for historicity, since they are also characteristic of good fiction. We cannot seek an origin of literature in Palestine prior to the eighth or even the seventh century BCE. The collection of literature in Genesis to 2 Kings survived because it was popular or because it found meaning in the lives of those preserving it. It has been linked by redactors but has only the appearance of history. Both historiographic and antiquarian concerns sought to preserve traditions after the collapse of the old order. The biblical traditions reflect on incoherent, part-fictive remnants of a past that the survivors were able to put together and give meaning to. As survival literature the traditions render a composite ideological understanding to the periods in which they were compiled, which may well preclude their use for any historical reconstruction based on assumed events from a greater past. Only a very few Israelite narratives involved historiography at a primary level of the tradition. The hypothesis of a Saulide chieftainship serves as an example. Difficulties of accepting it as historically viable are the fact that there is a gap of several centuries between the tradition and the supposed events; the origins of the state are assumed to equate to sedentarization of the central hills in Iron I, even though identifying this as Israelite is unwarranted: direct evidence for regional centralization before the foundation of Samaria in Iron II is lacking; to assert the existence of a historico-political entity 'Israel' as early as Iron I creates enormous difficulties for political continuity and unity; and the effervescent relationship between biblical literature and historical research, since this Saulide state is a hybrid bearing little resemblance to either the Israel of tradition or historical reconstructions derived from archaeology. The synthetic approach to historiography which has dominated our field since Eduard Meyer must be abandoned.

9. **LESTER L. GRABBE** considers Iain Provan, V. Philips Long and Tremper Longman III, *A Biblical History of Israel* (2003): this is one of the few true 'maximialist' histories. Strangely a full third of the text is given over to an introduction that deals with principles of historiography. It becomes clear that this is a smokescreen to make it appear that to give priority to the biblical text is a perfectly respectable historical method. An argument is made for depending on 'tradition', but it is never made clear what constitutes 'tradition'; in any case, the concern is not really with wider historical study but purely with the history of ancient Israel. An apparent openness to consider various possible reconstructions always concludes in favour of the biblical text. But to write a 'biblical history of Israel' is no different in principle from writing a 'Book of Mormon history of Mesoamerica'. What would historians think about a history of the Olmecs that talked about the migration of 'Jeredites' and included horses, cattle and elephants, but ignored typical Central American plants and animals? Interestingly, the techniques of Mormon apologists are basically the same as those used to defend a 'biblical history of Israel'. What seems to be overlooked is that if, for example, you withhold negative judgment because archaeology might eventually turn up something supportive, you are bound to withhold positive judgment where the archaeology presently seems to support the biblical text. This history gives no new insights and is essentially a boring paraphrase of the biblical text. It may reassure many readers without the knowledge or understanding to recognize its lack of contribution to the field, but it does not differ from the many 'biblical' sermons given across America every week.

10. **IAIN PROVAN, V. PHILIPS LONG and TREMPER LONGMAN III** respond to Lester L. Grabbe's review in '"Who Is the Prophet Talking about, Himself or Someone Else?" (Acts 8.34): A Response to Lester Grabbe's Review of *A Biblical History of Israel*'. Provan, Long and Longman [PLL] begin by summarizing their own book, and then part of Grabbe's 2007 book, in which he laid out his own view of how we should approach the history of Israel and how we should discuss it with others. One of his stated principles was to avoid ad hominem argumentations and comments. Therefore, it was to be expected that Grabbe would engage seriously with PLL's arguments in an objective way; instead he has not lived up to these reasonable expectations, including prose which is often mocking in tone. Moreover, he has not in fact accurately represented their arguments in the book:

1. They do not accept themselves as 'maximalists' but accept as historical exactly that amount of material in the sources that appears to be historical.
2. The first chapter of *A Biblical History of Israel* is not confused when discussing the history of historiography, especially over the question of positivistic historiography.
3. They do not argue 'that historians cannot be objective', nor that history is just another form of fiction. Recent qualifications to the idea that a purely objective reconstruction of the past is possible were discussed in a form quite different from what Grabbe claims.

4. They do explain what is meant by 'testimony' in the book, though Grabbe had denied that he could find an explanation. They do not believe that any account of an event, no matter how late or ignorant, has historical value. Rather, they argue that we cannot decide in advance whether an account has historical value simply by noting its closeness to or distance from an event.
5. They do not wish to debunk eye-witness sources, only to give them their appropriate weight.
6. *A Biblical History of Israel* is not 'essentially a paraphrase of the biblical account'. They do take the biblical account seriously as a major source, but also spend considerable amounts of space bringing the text into conjunction with all kinds of other historical evidence.

Most disturbing in this first part of the review is Grabbe's lack of engagement with PLL's arguments, for example on testimony and on archaeology, and his recourse instead to what 'most/real historians' think. This most unsatisfactory (and brief) set of reflections on Part I of the book then gives way to a substantial discussion of only one section of Part II, where Grabbe portrays PLL's reading of Joshua and Judges as an attempt to get away from scholarly consensus. He does not present an argument against PLL's reading here, however, but only the reassertion of a traditional view. Grabbe's subsequent summary of their overall position is disgracefully misleading. PLL's intended readership is not evangelical, but anyone who is interested in thinking seriously about matters of history and historiography in general, and about the history of Israel in particular. The term 'biblical' history of Israel does not mean that the Bible is given a privileged position, but only that nonbiblical texts are not taken more seriously (or less seriously) than the biblical text. There is not much to say about the strange and unduly long third section of Grabbe's review, which draws an analogy between the *Book of Mormon* and the Bible; the analogy is a ridiculous one. In sum, PLL assert, in this review of *A Biblical History of Israel* Grabbe evades, rather than engaging with, their arguments; misrepresents, rather than listening to, their words; ridicules, rather than conversing. In many ways, his essay is not a dialogue with the authors of this book at all, but with quite other conversation partners.

Annotated Bibliography

This section has dealt with questions of methodology. Naturally, many other articles—not to mention books—could have been included in this bibliography. However, questions of methodology are also summarized and discussed in the concluding essay (Part 5), with bibliography. Therefore, the items listed here are primarily histories of Israel but also some other works that have had a major influence on the development of the debate on history.

Davies, Philip R. (1992), *In Search of 'Ancient Israel'*, JSOTSup 148 (Sheffield: JSOT Press).
   This was an important book, not because of its original ideas—it did not claim to offer anything original—but because it disseminated (especially to students and non-specialists) a number of ideas about ancient Israel. Davies especially credited Niels Peter Lemche and Thomas L. Thompson, though he himself also originated some of the critical thinking that was summarized in the book. Its main contribution was distinguishing between the picture of 'Israel' as described in the Bible from the one that historians reconstruct from archaeology and primary sources. This distinction has been widely accepted and forms an important presupposition in much of the debate.

Frevel, Christian (2016), *Geschichte Israels*, Kohlhammer Studienbücher Theologie (Stuttgart: Kohlhammer).
   This is the first history of Israel in German to take into account much of the recent debate on the subject. It covers the lengthy period from the second millennium BCE to the fall of Jerusalem in 70 and the Bar Kokhba Revolt in 132 CE, though it must be said that the period of seven centuries from Nebuchadnezzar's conquest of Jerusalem to the Bar Kokhba Revolt is treated much more briefly than the six centuries before and during the Kingdoms of Israel and Judah. It has a good coverage of both primary and secondary literature (much of it in English! though it naturally lists what is available in German).

Gottwald, Norman (1979), *The Tribes of Yahweh: A Sociology of the religion of Liberated Israel, 1250–1050 B.C.E.* (Maryknoll, NY: Orbis Books).
   Following on the success of Thompson and Van Seters (see below) in breaking the Albrightean hold on much English-speaking biblical historical scholarship, Gottwald offered an alternative view of the origins of Israel. The idea was not new: it had already been presented in outline by the Albright student George Mendenhall, and the hypothesis became known as the 'Mendenhall-Gottwald' thesis. Yet this book was very influential for a number of years and started a new debate about the origins of Israel. The thesis in its original form is now widely rejected, but it has been drawn on and modified by and had an influence on many succeeding writers, which is the test of a good theory.

Grabbe, Lester L. (2017), *Ancient Israel: What Do We Know and How Do We Know It?*, 2nd edn (London/New York: Bloomsbury T&T Clark).
   The original 2007 edition was designed as 'prolegomena to a history of Israel' rather than aiming at being a complete history in the normal sense. Its purpose was primarily to draw attention to some of the main issues in the debate and the different approaches to them by different scholars (though the author generally made a judgment as to which views were more likely to be aligned with proper historical method and the available sources). The revised 2017 edition has expanded certain sections, as well as updating the text, so that it is more like a full history of Israel (down to the fall of Jerusalem in 587/586 BCE).

Hayes, John H., and J. Maxwell Miller (eds) (1977), *Israelite and Judaean History*, OTL (Philadelphia: Westminster Press).
   A collection of essays rather than a synthetic history as such but a discussion of the scholarship, historical problems and original sources for each period from the earliest settlement in Palestine to the destruction of the Second Temple. This volume really began the process of questioning the traditional positions over the history of Israel, especially for the early period but not exclusively there.

Knauf, Ernst Axel, and Philippe Guillaume (2016), *A History of Biblical Israel: The Fate of the Tribes and Kingdoms from Merenptah to Bar Kochba*, Worlds of the Ancient Near East and Mediterranean (London: Equinox).

This is a short history of Israel from the second millennium BCE to the end of the Second Temple period (rather briefer than Frevel above). Knauf is one of the leading scholars working in the history of Israel on the Continent (Guillaume is Knauf's former student and now assistant). This benefits from long experience in wrestling with historical problems and with analyzing the biblical text.

Miller, J. Maxwell, and John H. Hayes (2011), *A History of Ancient Israel and Judah*, 2nd edn (Minneapolis: Fortress Press; London: SCM Press).

This was a classic account of the 1980s that went against the conservative picture of the rather popular history of Israel by John Bright in the Albright mould. In its time it was the most up-to-date one-volume synthetic history. However, in the present context it has a good deal of competition, in spite of an updated edition in 2011, and now appears to be on the conservative end of the spectrum. Although individual statements are not always documented, the bibliographies are useful and the scholarship generally good. Needs to be supplemented by Frevel, Grabbe and Knauf/Guillaume.

Soggin, J. Alberto (1999), *An Introduction to the History of Israel and Judah*, 3rd edn (London: SCM Press; Valley Forge: Trinity Press International).

Soggin, J. Alberto (2002), *Storia d'Israele: Introduzione alla storia d'Israele e Giuda dalle origini alla rivolta di Bar-Kochbà*, 2nd edn revised and expanded, Bibliotteca di cultura religiosa 44 (Brescia: Paideia Editrice).

From the first Italian edition in 1983 to the last Italian edition in 2002, Soggin's history responded to the on-going debate on writing the history of ancient Israel perhaps more closely than any other author, with the English translations following along. For an evaluation of Soggin's important development in this area, see Grabbe, 'Alberto Soggin's *Storia d'Israele*: Exemplifying Twenty Years of Debate and Changing Trends in Thinking', in Lester L. Grabbe (ed.), *Enquire of the Former Age: Ancient Historiography and Writing the History of Israel*, LHBOTS 554; European Seminar in Historical Methodology 9 (London/New York: T&T Clark International, 2011), 253–60.

Thompson, Thomas L. (1974), *The Historicity of the Patriarchal Narratives: The Quest for the Historical Abraham*, BZAW 133 (Berlin/New York: W. de Gruyter).

Van Seters, John (1975), *Abraham in History and Tradition* (New Haven: Yale University Press).

These are two seminal works which mark the beginning of a new quest for the historical Israel, using the patriarchal period as the main focus. They began to erode the Albrightean hold over much of biblical scholarship in North America and Anglophone biblical scholarship more broadly. The result was that the patriarchal period was quickly dropped as a historical period in much of biblical scholarship (except among conservative evangelicals). Both authors went on to critique other areas of history, though the results there are sometimes more controversial.

Some Aspects of Working with the Textual Sources*

Herbert Niehr

1. Introduction

The intention of this paper is to position the evaluation of textual sources within a greater and more comprehensive set of approaches necessary for reconstructing the history of Israel.

In writing a history of Israel different levels of approach have to be distinguished. The basic level can be termed *historical anthropology*. On this level we work without written evidence. The second level is made up by evaluating written *primary sources* from outside and inside Palestine. Archaeological evidence is also a *primary source*. The third level is given by the evaluation of biblical sources which have to be judged as *secondary* or even *tertiary sources*. The gap between these sources has to be taken seriously. Only then can attempts to bridge this gap be cautiously made. This work with the sources has to be followed by a trial to integrate the results into hypotheses.

2. The Levels of Approach

a. Historical Anthropology

By the term *historical anthropology* is meant all data delivered by climatology, geography, landscape formation, settlement archaeology, agriculture, sociology and economy. These data can be separately assembled for the central hills of Ephraim and Manasseh and for Judah.[1] Working within this level we get a picture

---

* I am indebted to Lester Grabbe for improving my English.
[1] R.B. Coote and K.W. Whitelam, 'The Emergence of Early Israel' (SWBA, 5; Sheffield: Almond Press, 1987), pp. 27-116; T. Thompson, *Early History of the Israelite People* (SHANE, 4; Leiden: Brill, 1992), pp. 215-412.

of the *longue durée* (Braudel), or in other words, we obtain a general frame which in the subsequent stages has to be filled with the events which have taken place within this frame.

b. Primary Sources

Generally a primary source can be defined as 'written at a time close to the event. It can be a report, a royal annal, a letter or an original story.'[2] Or to put it differently: primary sources are more or less contemporary or close to the events they narrate or testify.[3] It is useful to distinguish several classes of primary sources.

As regards the aim of writing a history of Israel it is important to see that primary sources are independent of the Old Testament. They did not undergo the censorship exercised by, for example, the Deuteronomistic theologians nor were they submitted to the process of canonization. That is why the clear distinction between primary and secondary sources has to be upheld.[4]

Written sources from outside Palestine

Data for constituting a history of Israel begin with the appearance of a Palestinian kingdom *bit ḫumri* in Assyrian inscriptions of the ninth century BCE and the mention of the Omrides and their kingdom in a Moabite source (about 850 BCE). The data given in these inscriptions are followed by the mention of Israelite and Judaean kings in Assyrian, Babylonian and Aramaic inscriptions. Not only kings but also events (battles, conquests, coalitions, tributes) are listed in these sources. There are even things reported in the sources which are not mentioned in the Old Testament, for example the battle of Qarqar and Ahab's participation in it (853 BCE) or the siege and conquest of Lachish (701 BCE). By reading these sources we get a very rough outline of Israel's and Judah's past.

There has been some discussion about the historical reliability of the Assyrian annals. Their reliability had been put into question because of the topoi, exaggerations, ideologies and propaganda contained in them. Nevertheless, the historical

---

[2] G.W. Ahlström, 'The History of Ancient Palestine from the Palaeolithic Period to Alexander's Conquest' (JSOTSup, 146; Sheffield: Sheffield Academic Press, 1993), p. 21; cf. also *idem*, 'The Role of Archaeological and Literary Remains in Reconstructing Israel's History', in D.V. Edelman (ed.), *The Fabric of History* (JSOTSup, 127; Sheffield: Sheffield Academic Press, 1991), p. 117; J.M. Miller, 'Is it Possible to Write a History of Israel without Relying on the Hebrew Bible?', in Edelman (ed.), *The Fabric of History*, p. 94; E.A. Knauf, 'From History to Interpretation', in Edelman (ed.), *The Fabric of History*, p. 46.
[3] N.P. Lemche, 'On the Problems of Studying Israelite History', *Biblische Notizen* 23 (1984), p. 115.
[4] Contra I.W. Provan, 'Ideologies, Literary and Critical: Reflections on Recent Writing on the History of Israel', *JBL* 114 (1995), p. 598 with n. 61.

reliability of these sources was recently shown to be very high.[5] Further topics with special relevance for the histories of Israel and Judah which have also been investigated thoroughly are the western expansion of the neo-Assyrian Empire[6] and the tributes imposed.[7]

Written sources from inside Palestine

Further primary texts come from Israel and Judah themselves. This is the place for the evaluation of all kinds of epigraphical texts within the frame of historical dates obtained on the base of written sources from outside Palestine. In the case of epigraphical texts we are dealing with inscriptions on stone, metal, wood, leather and other materials and ostraca, seals and papyri.[8]

So far we have very careful analyses of writing techniques[9] and palaeographical development[10] of the Northwest Semitic scripts which are important for dating the primary written sources.

In this context the question of writing, scribes and scribal schools in Palestine deserves a special interest because the primary sources can be dated on palaeographic and archaeological evidence. The insights gained in this field are also influential for the political history of Judah and Israel, including administrative considerations and also the dating of Old Testament texts.[11]

Archaeological evidence from Palestine

Archaeological evidence (e.g. buildings, artefacts) is also to be judged as a primary source, but compared to the written primary sources this evidence is a mute one so that deciphering these sources is still more open to misunderstanding than is the case with written sources.[12] But the deciphering and reading of archaeological

---

[5]   Cf. W. Mayer, *Politik und Kriegskunst der Assyrer* (Abhandlungen zur Literatur Alt-Syrien-Palästinas und Mesopotamians, 9; Münster: Ugarit-Verlag, 1995), pp. 21-60.
[6]   Cf. R. Lamprichs, *Die Westexpansion des neuassyrischen Reiches* (AOAT, 239; Neukirchen-Vluyn: Neukirchener Verlag, 1995).
[7]   Cf. J. Bär, *Der assyrische Tribut und seine Darstellung* (AOAT, 243; Neukirchen-Vluyn: Neukirchener Verlag, 1996).
[8]   Cf. the enumeration of the material in H. Weippert, *Palästina in vorhellenistischer Zeit* (Handbuch der Archäologie, II.1; Munich: C.H. Beck, 1988), pp. 578-87 and the edition of all epigraphical texts from the royal periods in Israel and Judah by J. Renz and W. Röllig, *Handbuch der althebräischen Epigraphik* (3 vols.; Darmstadt: Wissenschaftliche Buchgesellschaft, 1995–96).
[9]   Cf. G. van der Kooij, *Early North-West Semitic Script Traditions* (Leiden: Brill, 1986).
[10] Cf. Renz and Röllig, *Handbuch der althebräischen Epigraphik*, II.1, pp. 95-208.
[11] Cf. D.W. Jamieson-Drake, *Scribes and Schools in Monarchic Judah* (JSOTSup, 109; Sheffield: Sheffield Academic Press, 1991).
[12] Ahlström, 'The Role of Archaeological and Literary Remains', p. 117.

sources can be learned[13] and important results have been achieved for the history of Israel and Judah,[14] especially for Jerusalem.[15] The special meaning of archaeology is that it shows us the everyday life of ancient people.[16]

This is also valid for the realm of iconography which in Palestine is mainly represented by seals. Their codes of understanding can be solved and thus much for the cultural and religious history can be learned from this kind of miniature art.[17]

c. Secondary and Tertiary Sources

A secondary source 'may be a copy of an original, an interpretive text, a rewriting, re-editing, distortion, falsification or the like.'[18] Because of its dating the Old Testament text falls into this category of secondary sources at least for the time of the kingdoms of Israel and Judah.

As concerns the Old Testament sources it has already been seen correctly that 'the Bible is presented from a Judahistic, Jerusalemite point of view. The historiography reflects the ideology of a certain group in Judah who believed that the kingdom of Israel should never have existed as a separate kingdom, because it was "sinful". Its cardinal sin was to have split the United Monarchy. At the same time this polemical attitude defends the political supremacy of the kingdom of Judah'.[19] This leads to the fact that our knowledge of the kingdom of Israel is even less than our knowledge of Judah. With respect to the history and the religion of Israel we have to reckon with an influential *damnatio memoriae*. This remark is valid, for example, for the existence of a Yahweh-temple in Samaria and for the historical roles of Omri and Ahab which cannot be fully recognized from the Old Testament alone because the roles of both of them are seriously minimized and thus distorted in the secondary sources.[20]

---

[13] Cf. Knauf, 'From History to Interpretation', pp. 28-41.
[14] Cf. e.g. Weippert, *Palästina in vorhellensitischer Zeit*; H.-P. Kuhnen, *Palästina in griechisch-römischer Zeit* (Handbuch der Archäologie, II.2; Munich: C.H. Beck, 1990).
[15] Cf. K. Bieberstein and H. Bloedhorn, *Jerusalem. Grundzüge der Baugeschichte vom Chalkolithikum bis zur Frühzeit der osmanischen Herrschaft I–III* (Beihefte zum Tübingen Atlas des Vorderen Orients, 100.1-3; Wiesbaden: L. Reichert, 1994).
[16] Cf. M. Weippert, 'Geschichte Israels am Scheideweg', *TRu* 58 (1993), pp. 84-85.
[17] Cf. especially O. Keel, *Studien zu den Stempelsiegeln aus Palästina/Israel* (4 vols.; OBO 67, 88, 100, 135; Freiburg: Universitätsverlag; Göttingen: Vandenhoeck & Ruprecht, 1985–94).
[18] Ahlström, 'The History of Ancient Palestine', p. 21; cf. also Knauf, 'From History to Interpretation', p. 46.
[19] Ahlström, 'The Role of Archaeological and Literary Remains', pp. 129-30.
[20] Cf. G.W. Ahlström, *Royal Administration and National Religion in Ancient Palestine* (SHANE, 1; Leiden: Brill, 1982), pp. 60-63; *idem*, 'The Role of Archaeological and Literary Remains', p. 131.

This does not exclude the possibility that Old Testament texts contain older materials, for example, from royal annals. But the existence of such older material in younger texts can only be reconstructed hypothetically. These hypotheses are open to debate as is shown by the example of the temple consecration prayer (1 Kgs 8.12-13) or the Cyrus edict (Ezra 1.2-4; 6.2-5). In both cases the historicity of the documents is highly debated and nowadays judged as unlikely. Even in those cases we judge more probable we have to admit that we 'simply do not have the documents; all we can do is in some cases reasonably assume that we may have copies of copies.'[21]

On the other hand the basic reliability of the royal successions and datings from Jeroboam to Hosea in Israel and from Azariah/Uzziah to Zedekiah in Judah, as verified by Assyrian and Babylonian primary sources, points to the existence of royal annals at the courts of Samaria and Jerusalem and their use by the Deuteronomistic Historian.[22]

An example of a tertiary source is that of the books of Chronicles which rework the Torah and the Deuteronomistic History during the second century BCE. It is not to be overlooked that the Old Testament can also serve as a primary source for the *histoire de la mentalité* of the time when it was written. This was already recognized by J. Wellhausen who wrote about the patriarchal narratives: 'Freilich über die Patriarchen ist hier kein historisches Wissen zu gewinnen, sondern nur über die Zeit, in welcher die Erzählungen über sie im israelitischen Volke entstanden'.[23]

As in the realm of epigraphic texts we have also to ask about the circles responsible for writing the Old Testament texts. Here it can only be mentioned that these circles of scribes and priests are not identical to 'Israel' as a whole.[24]

d. The Gap between Primary and Secondary Sources

A difference has to be made between those secondary sources which are mainly fictitious and those which contain older data. In the early history of research, until the end of the last and the beginning of our century, all Old Testament texts from Genesis 1 to 2 Chronicles 36 were regarded as historical. Later on Old Testament scholars saw a frontier between the stories of the prehistory in Genesis 1–11, on one hand, and the history of the patriarchs from Genesis 11/12 onwards, on the

---

[21] E.A. Knauf, 'King Solomon's Copper Supply', in E. Lipiński (ed.), *Phoenicia and the Bible* (Studia Phoenicia, 11; Leuven: Peeters Press, 1991), p. 47 n. 1.
[22] Knauf, 'King Solomon's Copper Supply', p. 173.
[23] J. Wellhausen, *Prolegomena zur Geschichte Israels* (Berlin: de Gruyter, 6th edn, 1981 [1927]), p. 316; ET *Prolegomena to the History of Israel* (trans. J.S. Black and A. Menzies; Edinburgh: Black, 1985), pp. 318-19: 'It is true, we attain to no historical knowledge of the patriarchs, but only of the time when the stories about them arose in the Israelite people'.
[24] Cf. P.R. Davies, *In Search of 'Ancient Israel'* (JSOTSup, 148; Sheffield: Sheffield Academic Press, 1992), pp. 44-48, 94-112.

other hand. But in the course of time this frontier moved beyond the patriarchal narratives, then beyond the exodus narrative or even beyond the times of Moses, Joshua and the judges. Others nowadays do not see any frontiers, declaring all texts from Genesis 1 to 2 Kings 24 as more or less historically unreliable. That is why it has correctly been stressed that there 'is no way in which history automatically reveals itself in a biblical text'.[25] The criterion to establish this frontier can only be an external one.

To my mind a frontier between unhistorical mythological narratives and historically reliable texts can only be seen between the narratives of Saul, David and Solomon, on the one side, and the history of the separated kingdoms on the other side. That is to say that we can start a critical reconstruction of the history of Israel only with the time of Jeroboam and Omri. This is possible because we thus begin shortly before Omri, who founded the state of Israel mentioned in the Assyrian sources, and who is himself mentioned in other primary sources, that is, in the stela of Mesha. From Omri's time on we have primary written sources verifying at least some aspects of the secondary sources.[26] From the time before Omri we have a seal which perhaps mentions a servant of Jerobeam I.[27]

Furthermore, with Omri the lineage of the kings of Israel begins. The basic correctness of this lineage as concerns its succession and rough chronology is proved by primary evidence. In this case it is possible to bridge the gap between primary and secondary evidence.

At this point biblical data can be evaluated and integrated into the picture thus far achieved. In rough outline the biblical data can match the aforementioned data as concerns the lineage and successions of the kings from Omri to Hosea in Israel and from Azariah/Uzziah to Zedekiah in Judah.

But there can also be several contradictions between the data given in the primary sources, especially those from outside Palestine, and those in the secondary or even tertiary sources.

Further, the Old Testament also contains information which cannot (not yet?) be verified by external sources. That is why its historicity cannot be proven and must at least be left open to further debate unless its historicity is rejected for other reasons.

Biblical sources being judged as secondary or tertiary sources, at least for the kingdoms of Israel and Judah, cannot be taken at face value but should be examined critically in light of the criteria discussed in the preceding levels.

---

[25] Davies, *In Search of 'Ancient Israel'*, p. 12.
[26] Cf. Knauf, 'King Solomon's Copper Supply', pp. 172-80; M. Ottoson, 'Ideology, History and Archaeology in the Old Testament', *SJOT* 8 (1994), pp. 213-18.
[27] Cf. L.G. Herr, *The Scripts of Ancient Northwest Semitic Seals* (HSM, 18; Missoula: Scholars Press, 1978), p. 82,1 who instead pleads for a date during the reign of Jerobeam II, but cf. now G.W. Ahlström, 'The Seal of Shemac', *SJOT* 7 (1993), pp. 208-15, with arguments in favour of the time of Jerobeam I.

3. Trying to Integrate the Sources

The main task of the historian consists in working within these levels of evidence. This evaluation tends to give a connection of events indicated by and narrated in the primary and secondary sources as *history*.

That is to say, history is not in the sources but history is constituted by the work of the historian. This work is essentially a reconstructive one, a reconstruction achieved by hypotheses.[28] The plausibility of its results depends on what kind and what amount of sources the historian has at his disposal. Furthermore it also depends on the historian's reconstructive ideas and his ability at argumentation.

As concerns the evaluation of the sources, especially the secondary sources of the Old Testament, a maximalist view 'which implies that everything in the sources that could not be proved wrong has to be accepted as historical',[29] thus relying heavily and uncritically on the Hebrew Bible, is to be distinguished from a minimalist view 'which means that everything which is not corroborated by evidence contemporary with the events to be reconstructed is dismissed',[30] which is in danger of being hypercritical. Both views seem to be radical and one-sided and call for finding a balance.

That those radical and irreconcilable extremes are on the market (the maximalist view still dominating) is due to the history of research in this realm.

The first stage of this history of research is given with uncritical summaries of what the Old Testament texts tell about the history of Israel. This naive and pre-critical approach consists in paraphrasing, harmonizing and combining the contents of the so-called historical books from Genesis to 2 Chronicles. All texts were taken at face value. This stage has not yet fully disappeared from modern books which often turn out to be rationalistic paraphrases of Old Testament narratives.

A second stage was inaugurated by J. Wellhausen's *Prolegomena*. Here we find a source critical approach which no longer takes the texts at face value but looks for tendencies in the texts. So in a revolutionary manner the Pentateuchal traditions of the sacred tent (P) were taken as exilic or post-exilic traditions reflecting the existence and the service of the Second Temple. It is important to state that Wellhausen developed his views on the basis of the Old Testament texts alone without drawing on external sources. Thus he tried to get a diachrony of Old Testament texts for his aim of establishing a religious history of Israel on this basis.[31]

---

[28] Cf. Knauf, 'From History to Interpretation', pp. 27-34; *idem*, 'The Cultural Impact of Secondary State Formation: The Cases of the Edomites and Moabites', in P. Bienkowski (ed.), *Early Edom and Moab* (Sheffield: J.R. Collins Publications, 1992), p. 47; Weippert, 'Geschichte Israels am Scheideweg', pp. 71-72.
[29] Knauf, 'King Solomon's Copper Supply', p. 171.
[30] Knauf, 'King Solomon's Copper Supply', p. 171.
[31] Cf. H.-J. Kraus, *Geschichte der historisch-kritischen Erforschung des Alten Testaments* (Neukirchen: Neukirchener Verlag, 3rd edn, 1982), pp. 257-58, 260-69.

Concomitantly to Wellhausen's work more and more ancient Oriental texts (Egyptian, Akkadian, Phoenician, Aramaic and later also Hittite) were published and threw light on Egypt, Mesopotamia, Syria-Palestine and Anatolia. It is interesting to know that Wellhausen himself refused to work with this external evidence because it would have changed his romantically-based picture of Israel's religious history.[32] This progress can be called the third stage of writing a history of Israel. From this stage on an integration of the history of Israel into the histories of the ancient Near East had to be undertaken. The difficulties associated with the attempt were demonstrated by the 'Babel-Bibel-Streit'.[33] This task given by the primary evidence has not yet been completed.

During the nineteenth century the scientific exploration of Palestine began, thus adding lots of topographical and archaeological insights to all reconstructive efforts.

A fourth stage is marked by a late dating of the Old Testament sources into mainly the exilic and postexilic times. The Old Testament is seen more and more as a secondary source the historical value of which is very much in debate. If we had no Old Testament text we would not be able to integrate the primary written and unwritten data into a history of Israel.[34] The Old Testament text is valuable and irreplaceable for an outline sketch of the history of Israel. Or in other words, the Old Testament 'primarily sets the parameters'[35] and 'when one combines artifactual and written evidence to produce a historical scenario, usually the written evidence takes precedence'.[36]

Finding this balance is a task to be undertaken ever anew. From the methodological point of view the difference between primary and secondary and even tertiary sources has first to be respected. Then all these texts adduced for reconstruction work are to be examined as concerns their literary genera, their *Sitz im Leben*, their intentions and tendencies. Concerning the secondary evidence of the Old Testament sources the question whether these texts contain older material (e.g. annals, folk tales) has to be put. Last but not least, as it has already been underlined, secondary texts are sources for the time in which they have been written.

4. Summary and Conclusion

From the preceding paragraphs it follows that all kinds of written and unwritten sources have to be adduced and evaluated for establishing the goal of writing a history of Israel. The range of written sources goes from neo-Assyrian and

---

[32] Kraus, *Geschichte der historisch-kritischen Erforschung*, p. 298.
[33] Cf. R.G. Lehmann, *Friedrich Delitzsch und der Babel-Bibel-Streit* (OBO, 133; Freiburg: Universitätsverlag; Göttingen: Vandenhoeck & Ruprecht, 1994).
[34] Cf. Miller, 'Is it Possible to Write a History of Israel'.
[35] Miller, 'Is it Possible to Write a History of Israel', p. 95; cf. also p. 99.
[36] Miller, 'Is it Possible to Write a History of Israel', p. 99.

neo-Babylonian inscriptions, Phoenician Moabite and Aramaic inscriptions to the Old Testament texts. But it also has to be stated that those sources are not on one and the same level. That is why they have to be evaluated according to their status as primary or secondary sources in their own right. Only in this case a *circulus vitiosus* of getting Old Testament texts 'proved' by archaeological findings and getting archaeological findings 'interpreted' by Old Testament texts can be avoided.

As a result of all this we can only achieve tentative sketches of a history of Israel and Judah which are always subject to a continuing process of alteration. In so far as more and more primary evidence will be detected and become available for scholarly evaluation, there will undoubtedly be a need to reduce the influence of the Old Testament texts and thus to change the hypotheses and paradigms by which we try to grasp the history of Israel and Judah.

That there will always be a subjective range of different opinions in this reconstructive work of history writing should be neither denied nor overlooked. The choice between those different opinions has to rely on the specific kind of method and argumentation which has been followed for establishing this opinion.

The Strange Fear of the Bible: Some Reflections on the 'Bibliophobia' in Recent Ancient Israelite Historiography*

Hans M. Barstad

I

Several times during the discussions on 'ancient Israel' in Dublin and Lausanne objections were raised by some of the members of our Seminar whenever attempts were made to refer to historical information taken from the Hebrew Bible. Since I have always felt this to be a somewhat strange attitude for someone who claims to be a historian of Iron Age Palestine, I would like to make a few comments on this particular point of view.

Obviously, the matter in question is far too comprehensive for a short response like the present one. For this reason I shall limit myself to a few general points. I take it for granted that all the members of our Seminar (more or less) believe that knowledge of the past of some sort is possible. It is, of course, quite legitimate to be a sceptic and to deny the possibility of 'historical' knowledge altogether. However, from our discussions I did not quite get the impression that this is the case (then again I may be wrong in my assumption).

There is no need to deny that the use of the Hebrew Bible for historical (re)construction is highly uncertain (to say the least). This, however, is a problem shared by everyone who is engaged in ancient historiography.[1] My main point here must be that we cannot treat the Bible *any differently* from other historical (or rather literary) sources from the ancient world, like, for instance, those of ancient

---

* This response was not read during any of the sessions at Lausanne. Also, it does not concern itself directly with any of the papers that were read there. Instead I have chosen to comment briefly upon one particular issue that turned up during our discussions both in Dublin and Lausanne and which, to some, appears to have become an important heuristic and methodological principle, namely, that the Hebrew Bible cannot be used as a source for any reconstruction of 'historical events' relating to the 'kingdoms' of Israel and Judah during the 'Iron Age'

[1] I use the word 'historiography' in two ways throughout this article: (1) stories about past events in sources used for historical reconstruction; (2) modern attempts to write 'history', that is, attempts to find out what in these same sources may be 'historically' true in a positivistic fashion.

Greek or ancient Mesopotamian historiography. This is a highly important point. If someone wants to claim that the Hebrew Bible is less suitable as a basis for historical reconstruction than (say) Herodotus's *Historiae* or the 'Sumerian King List', I have no problems with this (even if I do not hold this view myself). I should, however, *need to know the grounds* for such a claim. No such grounds have sufficiently been put forward in our discussions so far. Thus, it is not enough to say that we cannot use the Bible as a historical source because it is 'unhistorical', 'unreliable', 'ideological', and so on; and moreover, that it is late (from the Hellenistic period), and that it, as a literary product far removed from the historical periods it describes, has no value for attempts to reconstruct historical reality prior to its composition.[2] All of this is something that the Hebrew Bible also shares with other ancient literary sources used for historical reconstruction. If these grounds alone should be the reason behind the claim that we cannot use the Bible for historical reconstruction, we should, consequently, have no ancient history at all. There would, in fact, be no history of ancient Egypt, of Mesopotamia, the Levant, Anatolia, Persia, Greece or Rome. Since this would represent a major upheaval in intellectual history, I believe that it is imperiously required that those scholars who plead such a special case for the cultural, compositional and cognitive status of the Hebrew Bible as compared to other ancient sources inform us why this is so. In the meantime we shall have to treat the Bible in a similar way as we treat other ancient literature.

II

It is not uncommon to find among orientalists and classicists who are dealing with historical issues a highly negative attitude towards the historical truthfulness of the sources with which they are working. Sometimes, this attitude goes a long way back. The reliability of Herodotus, for instance, has in varying degree been called into question ever since antiquity. At present, the (re?)discovery that the source evaluation of the 'father of history' (with its 'tripartite' ὄψις, γνώμη and ἱστορίη) has more to do with literary genres than with historical source criticism in our meaning of the word, has resulted in a heated debate over Herodotus's

---

[2] One significant problem that cannot be dealt with in this short response, but that will need considerable attention in all future discussion, concerns the question of the linguistic nature of the texts. To put it very simply: Can the Hebrew Bible be said to represent some kind of a 'linguistic museum' with a diversity bearing witness to centuries of diachronic history, or is the lack of linguistic uniformity a result of circumstances other than chronological developments? See, for instance, I. Young, *Diversity in Pre-Exilic Hebrew* (Forschungen zum Alten Testament, 5; Tübingen: J.C.B. Mohr, 1993). The most recent contribution to the debate is that of A. Hurvitz, 'The Historical Quest for "Ancient Israel" and the Linguistic Evidence of the Hebrew Bible: Some Methodological Observations', *VT* 47 (1997), pp. 301-15.

trustworthiness, not dissimilar to what is going on in biblical studies for the moment. The recent discussion in Greek historiography has in particular followed the publication of Detlev Fehling's *Die Quellenangaben bei Herodot* from 1971.³ The consequence of these discussions is not that we shall have to stop using Herodotus (or other ancient sources) for historical reconstruction, but that we shall have to be even more aware of the problems we are facing when doing so. Obviously, every single piece of information will have to be examined with close scrutiny.⁴

Even if Herodotus is no doubt of great interest, and much can be learnt from studying his works,⁵ ancient Near Eastern historiography must be regarded as even more relevant to historians of ancient Israel. In the present context I am thinking above all of Mesopotamian history.⁶ Not only are we dealing here with literature that is closely related both from a cultural and geographical point of view, we are also dealing with a history that, for some of its periods, is closely intermingled with the history of Iron Age Palestine in a quite direct manner.

---

3   D. Fehling, *Die Quellenangaben bei Herodot: Studien zur Erzählkunst Herodots* (Untersuchungen zur antiken Literatur und Geschichte, 9; Berlin: W. de Gruyter, 1971). See also the English translation by J.G. Howie: *Herodotus and his 'Sources': Citation, Invention and Narrative Art* (ARCA Classical and Medieval Texts, Papers and Monographs, 21; Leeds: F. Cairns, 1989). A major attack on Fehling is found in W.K. Pritchett, *The Liar School of Herodotos* (Amsterdam: J.G. Gieben, 1993). Cf. also in general the useful volume by C. Gill and T.P. Wiseman (eds.), *Lies and Fiction in the Ancient World* (Exeter: Exeter University Press, 1993).

4   For an example of how one may go about when wanting to extract historical information from Herodotus, one may compare the article by F. Thordarson ('Herodotus and the Iranians: ὄψις, ἀκοή, ψεῦδος'), the first part of which has been published in *Symbolae osloenses* 71 (1996), pp. 42-58 (I am grateful to Professor Hugo Montgomery for drawing my attention to this work). In his article Thordarson discusses the historical foundation for Herodotus's description of Scythian funeral rites in Book IV, 71-75 and demonstrates how Herodotus must have had access to genuine Scythian mythological traditions. In my view, Thordarson's work provides us with an excellent example of how to deal with the problematic field of historical reliability in ancient literary sources.

5   See, for instance, the useful survey in J. Van Seters, *In Search of History: Historiography in the Ancient World and the Origins of Biblical History* (New Haven: Yale University Press, 1984), in particular pp. 31-54. Since it has not yet appeared as I write these lines, I have not had access to the most recent contribution to this field: F.A.J. Nielsen, *The Tragedy in History: Herodotus and the Deuteronomistic History* (Copenhagen International Seminar, 4; JSOTSup, 251; Sheffield: Sheffield Academic Press, 1997).

6   The book by Van Seters, *In Search of History*, also gives a survey (pp. 55-99) of Mesopotamian historiography (Van Seters also deals in his book with other ancient Near Eastern historiographical texts). For a more complete survey of Mesopotamian historiographical texts, see A.K. Grayson, 'Assyria and Babylonia', *Or* 49 (1980), pp. 140-94. The recent, substantial volumes by A. Kuhrt, *The Ancient Near East c. 3000–330 BC, I–II* (London: Routledge, 1995), have large sections on Mesopotamian historiography. A most useful work, dealing with history of research and methodological problems, is O. Carena, *History of the Near Eastern Historiography and its Problems: 1852–1985* (AOAT, 218.1; Neukirchen-Vluyn: Neukirchener Verlag, 1989). Only the first volume (dealing with the period from 1852 to 1945) has appeared so far.

The 'Sumerian King List' may illustrate our problem. Clearly, many other texts from the vast historiographical literature of ancient Mesopotamia could have been mentioned. I have chosen the 'Sumerian King List' as an example because this is one of the texts whose historical value has been under attack. The debate is in many ways reminiscent of the discussion over the 'trustworthiness' of the Hebrew Bible.[7]

It is believed that the final composition of the 'Sumerian King List' took place in the late nineteenth century BCE (after the fall of the Ur III Dynasty). We are, consequently, dealing with a text that, similar to the literature of the Hebrew Bible, got its final shape considerably later than the events it describes. It is assumed that the purpose of the present form of the 'Sumerian King List' is to legitimize the rule of the kings of the Isin dynasty as the appropriate successors to the Ur III kings.[8] We are, in other words, dealing with a text that is heavily wrapped in a shroud of ideology. Also, the text is full of lacunae. Despite the many problems involved, students of early Mesopotamian history still consider the 'Sumerian King List' as a valuable source for historical information about Sumerian history. For instance, most scholars assume that the names of the kings and cities of the Agade and Ur III kings are historically correct.[9]

---

[7] Nevertheless, critical Mesopotamian historiography must still be considered a field of research that is still in its very beginning. Whereas most Assyriologists are, as a rule, widely engaged with the publishing and editing of texts, they have paid less attention to the methodological, literary and ideological aspects of these texts in relation to historiography. Dealing with method are W.W. Hallo, 'Biblical History in its Near Eastern Setting: The Contextual Approach', in C.D. Evans, W.W. Hallo and J.B. White (eds.), *Scripture in Context: Essays on the Comparative Method* (PTMS, 34; Pittsburgh: The Pickwick Press, 1980), pp. 1-26; *idem*, 'Sumerian Historiography', in H. Tadmor and M. Weinfeld (eds.), *History, Historiography and Interpretation: Studies in Biblical and Cuneiform Literatures* (repr. Jerusalem: Magnes Press, 1984 [1983]), pp. 9-20. A rare article dealing with theory is K. Pomian, 'La reconstruction historique: point de vue réaliste', in *Historie et conscience historique dans les civilisations du Proche-Orient Ancient* (Les cahiers du CEPOA, 5; Leuven: Editions Peeters, 1989), pp. 93-107. During recent years there has been an increasing interest also in the ideological nature of Mesopotamian historiography. See F.M. Fales (ed.), *Assyrian Royal Inscriptions: New Horizons in Literary, Ideological, and Historical Analysis* (Orientis Antiqui Collectio, 17; Rome: Istituto per l'Oriente, Centro per le Antichità e la Storia dell'arte del Vicino Oriente, 1981); and F.M. Fales, 'Narrative and Ideological Variations in the Account of Sargon's Eighth Campaign', in M. Cogan and I. Eph'al (eds.), *Ah, Assyria ... Studies in Assyrian History and Ancient Near Eastern Historiography Presented to Hayim Tadmor* (Scripta Hierosolymitana, 33; Jerusalem: Magnes Press, 1991), pp. 129-47.

[8] Kuhrt, *The Ancient Near East*, I, p. 77.

[9] Kuhrt, *The Ancient Near East*, I, p. 30; J.N. Postgate, *Early Mesopotamia: Society and Economy at the Dawn of History* (London: Routledge, 1992; rev. edn, 1994), pp. 28-32; H. Crawford, *Sumer and the Sumerians* (repr. Cambridge: Cambridge University Press, 1994 [1991]), pp. 19-20. Thorkild Jacobsen's suggestion that the 'Sumerian King List' also contains reliable historical information for the Early Dynastic period does, however, not have many followers today. Cf. Thorkild Jacobsen, *The Sumerian King List* (Assyriological Studies, 11; Chicago: University of Chicago Press, 1939), pp. 166-67.

In the 'Sumerian King List' we have an example of a text whose status is quite similar to that of the Hebrew Bible ('late', 'ideological', 'literary'), but which may still be used by historians to reconstruct historical circumstances prior to its final composition. I am not saying that this is either a good or a bad thing. The point of issue is only to claim that when scholars do use Mesopotamian literary texts for historical reconstructions, it is important that those who deny that this is possible with regard to the Hebrew Bible would also have to apply the very same procedures towards the 'Sumerian King List' (and other historiographical ancient Near Eastern sources). If not, they will most certainly have to make allowances for what it is that is so special to the Hebrew Bible that it, unlike other sources, is totally unfit for historical reconstruction. I have not seen that anything of this kind has sufficiently been done in our debate.

III

When it comes to details, each piece of information will have to be investigated separately. Here, many examples could have been mentioned. With the names of the Sumerian kings and their cities from the 'Sumerian King List' fresh in mind, it is not difficult to see here a parallel to the kings mentioned in the Deuteronomistic history. Moreover, when so many of the kings mentioned in that work (Omri, Ahab, Jehu, Joash, Ahaz, Menahem, Pekah, Hoshea, Hezekiah, Manasseh, Jehoiachin) are also referred to in sources outside the Hebrew Bible, it becomes methodologically obscure to claim that the Hebrew Bible does not yield historical information concerning periods prior to its creation. We shall, however, have to go further than that. When the historian finds that the names of all these kings are confirmed by other sources, he or she will also know something about the reliability of the Hebrew Bible, at least in this particular matter, and may also safely assume that other names of kings mentioned in the Deuteronomistic history may be historically correct.[10]

I shall briefly mention just one more example. Several other, equally well-known texts could have been mentioned,[11] but the story of the last days of Judah in 2 Kings 24–25 was specifically referred to during our discussion in Lausanne. In this text we may read how Jerusalem is besieged by Nebuchadnezzar and the king, Jehoiachin, replaced by the king of Babylon with his uncle Mattaniah, who was given the name Zedekiah. Since this event is reflected also in Mesopotamian

---

[10] Which, of course, is precisely what many historians of ancient Israel in fact do; cf. Lester L. Grabbe, 'Are Historians of Ancient Palestine Fellow Creatures—Or Different Animals?', in *idem* (ed.), *Can a 'History of Ancient Israel' be Written?* (European Seminar in Historical Methodology, 1; JSOTSup, 245; Sheffield: Sheffield Academic Press, 1997), pp. 19-36.

[11] See the survey by F. Deist, 'The Yehud Bible: A Belated Divine Miracle?', *Journal of Northwest Semitic Languages* 23.1 (1997), pp. 117-42.

texts,[12] we have here yet another example of how the Hebrew Bible does yield reliable historical information. Again the historian, I would have thought, should say to him- or herself: This is interesting; perhaps at some time we shall have access to further extra-biblical evidence bearing witness also to other historical details found in 2 Kings 24–25. In the meantime, there is little cause not to suspect that the Hebrew Bible is correct, and that the story in 2 Kings gives us reliable information about the last days of the kingdom of Judah.[13] If one is at all interested in the historical circumstances surrounding the fall of Judah, it is very difficult to see how one can avoid using the Hebrew Bible as a historical source for the reconstruction of the history of Palestine during this particular period.

When dealing with ancient historiography, our sources will quite often have to be given the benefit of the doubt. Whether we like it or not, the pre-modern, narrative historiography of the Hebrew Bible does not provide us with verifiable historical 'facts'. Since we cannot any longer ask for historical facts the way we used to do,[14] we shall instead have to ask for what is likely (very likely, quite likely, not likely). 'Factual historical truth' must be replaced with 'narrative historical truth', which is related to 'factual truth', but not identical with it. It is, of course, always nice when historical statements are 'validated' by those of other sources. This, however, due to the very accidental nature of our sources, will always be the exception rather than the rule.

However, when reading some of the historiographical literature today one is left with the feeling that some scholars have made up their minds *beforehand* about the reliability of the historical information which we may find in the Hebrew Bible. Being convinced that they are 'fictitious', they are unwilling to discuss these texts in a scholarly manner. Instead, they waste a lot of energy attempting to prove what they already believe that they know. Others, again, have apparently decided beforehand that more or less everything we find in the Hebrew Bible is 'historically correct'. This other extreme, of course, must be judged as equally incompatible with the ideal of an open, scholarly mind.

IV

To conclude: As a historical source the Hebrew Bible is of the 'same' nature and quality as other ancient Near Eastern literary texts. This has the somewhat drastic consequence that if we renounce the use of the Hebrew Bible on the basis that it

---

[12] E.F. Weidner, 'Jojachin, König von Juda in babylonischen Keilinschriften', in *Mélanges syriens offerts à René Dussaud* (Paris: Paul Geuthner, 1939), pp. 923-35. Three different texts mention 'Jehoiachin, king of Judah'. In a fourth text he is referred to as 'the son of the king of Judah' (see pp. 925-26).
[13] See the outline in L.L. Grabbe, pp. 87-88 above.
[14] See my paper referred to in n. 17 below.

is late and fictional, we shall also have to do so with regard to most of the ancient sources. If we do not want to do this, we shall have to accept, for better or for worse, the Hebrew Bible not only as necessary, but also as by far the most important source for our knowledge of *the history* of Iron Age Palestine. To deny this is not only unduly hypercritical, but it is also based on a positivistic view of history that today is deplorably outdated.[15]

---

[15] Cf. H.M. Barstad, 'History and the Hebrew Bible', in Lester L. Grabbe (ed.), *Can a 'History of Ancient Israel' be Written?* (European Seminar in Historical Methodology, 1; JSOTSup, 245; Sheffield: Sheffield Academic Press, 1997), pp. 37-64 *passim*.

Is It Possible to Write a History of Israel without Relying on the Hebrew Bible?

J. Maxwell Miller

In several publications over the past years, I have explored the complex methodological problems involved when one attempts to interrelate nonwritten evidence (artifacts) with written sources for purposes of historical reconstruction.[1] I have observed, for example, that while nonwritten artifacts provide information about general socioeconomic conditions, settlement patterns, life styles and the like, they are silent regarding specific people and events. If we are to know the names of the people who left the artifacts or any specific details about their history, we must rely on written records. Written records are also limited in the kind of information they provide and often give a biased or one-sided impression of things.

I have observed further that, when historians combine artifactual and written evidence to produce historical scenarios, the written evidence tends to take precedence, and there is always some degree of circular argumentation involved. On the first point, that the written evidence tends to take precedence, I mean that it tends to set the definitions and parameters of the scenario and thus determine the way the artifacts will be interpreted in that context, more so than the other way around. Regarding the inevitable circularity, the best a historian can do is try to hold it to a minimum; and one way to do this is to analyze each type of evidence separately, with the tools and methods appropriate to it, and determine what can be learned from this particular kind of evidence alone, before interweaving it with other kinds of evidence.

Consider for a moment the kinds of evidence available for dealing with the origin and early history of Israel. From the artifactual, nonverbal evidence alone (all the foundation walls, potsherds, and what have you, excavated to this point) one

---

[1] Cf. esp. *The Old Testament and the Historian* (Philadelphia/London: Fortress Press/SPCK, 1976), pp. 40-48; 'Archaeology and the Israelite Conquest of Canaan: Some Methodological Considerations', *PEQ* 109 (1977), pp. 87-93; and 'Old Testament History and Archaeology', *BA* 49 (1987), pp. 51-62.

would never even surmise that the people known as Israel appeared on the scene in ancient Palestine. Simply to use the name 'Israel' in association with the Iron Age means to draw on written sources. The written sources pertinent for dealing with ancient Israel fall into two categories: materials of various sorts collected in the Hebrew Bible and certain nonbiblical documents (royal inscriptions, for the most part). Most of the nonbiblical documents may be considered first-hand evidence in that they were written soon after the events which they report. Unfortunately, they provide only occasional references to Israel, and without prompting from the Hebrew Bible these references would not tell us much.

Without prompting from the Hebrew Bible, for example, do you suppose it would occur to historians to read the hieroglyphic name of Merneptah's foe in his so-called Israel Inscription as 'Israel' and to recognize it as the equivalent of the Moabite and Assyrian renditions of the name that do not turn up until 350 years later? I doubt it. And what would they make of these later references? Our hypothetical historians (still working entirely with the inscriptional sources and without prompting from the Hebrew Bible) probably would make the connection between 'Omri king of Israel' mentioned in the Mesha Inscription, 'Jehu *mar Humri*' in three of Shalmaneser's inscriptions, and the references to the 'land of *bit-Humria*' in Tiglath-pileser's records. But would they read 'Ahab of *Sir-'i-la-a-a*' in Shalmaneser's Monolith Inscription as 'Ahab the Israelite' or recognize that Samaria, which also turns up occasionally in other Assyrian contexts, was the capital of 'Omri land' rather than some other place altogether? Probably not. And if they did, the general impression derived would be that Israel was a small kingdom, located somewhere in the vicinity of Damascus or the Phoenician coast, apparently founded by one Omri during the first half of the ninth century and surviving to the latter half of the eighth century. I am confident, moreover, that any efforts to isolate the material culture of ancient Israel would follow the lead of these written sources. Rather than talk about Early Iron Age settlement patterns in the central Palestinian hill country, the search would focus on Iron Age II, on southern Lebanon or perhaps Galilee, and would involve widely divergent views regarding the location of Samaria.

Obviously this is not where things stand now in our research, and it is because we rely heavily on the Hebrew Bible. Not the archaeological evidence, nor the extrabiblical sources, nor a combination of the two, but the Hebrew Bible primarily sets the parameters of the ongoing discussion regarding the origin and early history of Israel. Whether this *should* be the case, whether we *should* rely so heavily on the Hebrew Bible is another question that I will address briefly below. For the moment, I am concerned only to observe that this is what we are doing. Any time historians, archaeologists, sociologists, or whoever speak of Israelite tribes in the central Palestinian hill country at the beginning of Iron Age I, or about the Davidic–Solomonic monarchy, or about two contemporary kingdoms emerging from this early monarchy, they are presupposing information that comes from, and only from, the Hebrew Bible.

Now I would have thought that this is self-evident, but apparently it is not, since several recent papers and monographs make rather a lot of the fact that the Bible is an unreliable source of historical information. They take a condescending attitude toward historians who bother with it and they insist that we can deduce a great deal about the origin and early history of Israel quite apart from it.

Coote and Whitelam's recent book, *The Emergence of Early Israel*,[2] is perhaps the best example. Pointing out the inadequacies of histories of Israel that rely on the Hebrew Bible and old-time literary-critical methodologies, they proposed 'an alternative approach ... which assigns priority to interpreting archaeological data within a broad interdisciplinary framework' (p. 8). Thereupon, without involving themselves with the biblical materials in any direct way, they set about clarifying the socioeconomic circumstances in Palestine during the early Iron Age, explaining how the Israelite tribes emerged under these circumstances and then describing the process by which the tribes were transformed into a centralized, Davidic state. How do they know that Israel's origins are to be associated with the early Iron Age in the first place, or that the tribes were soon transformed into a centralized Davidic state? They appeal to scholarly consensus: 'The most commonly agreed datum to mark the emergence of Israel is the extension of village and agricultural settlement in the central highland of Palestine from the thirteenth to the eleventh centuries BCE' (pp. 27-28). And this is the pattern throughout; either they assume information that can only have come from the Hebrew Bible, or they appeal to scholarly consensus, which itself rests on the Bible. In short, their study does not bypass the Hebrew Bible, it only bypasses any critical evaluation of it. While remaining aloof from the Bible of literary analysis, they assume the essential historicity of the Bible story as they heard it in Sunday school.

Thomas Thompson, in his *The Origin Tradition of Ancient Israel*,[3] characterized the recent history which I coauthored with John Hayes as 'essentially a theological and apologetic work'[4] because of its heavy involvement with the biblical materials and announced that we are on the threshold of a new era with respect to the study of Israelite history. Theological histories such as ours are about to be replaced with scientifically objective ones that rely instead on revolutionary new archaeological evidence and on epigraphical sources.

---

[2] R.B. Coote and K.W. Whitelam, *The Emergence of Early Israel in Historical Perspective* (SWBAS, 5; Sheffield: Almond Press, 1987).

[3] T.L. Thompson, *The Origin Tradition of Ancient Israel*. I. *The Literary Formation of Genesis and Exodus 1-23* (JSOTSup, 55; Sheffield: JSOT Press, 1987), p. 26.

[4] *A History of Ancient Israel and Judah* (Philadelphia/London: Westminster Press/SCM Press, 1986).

It is ... the independence of Syro-Palestinian archaeology that now makes it possible for the first time to begin to write a history of Israel's origins. Rather than the Bible, it is in the field of Syro-Palestinian archaeology, and the adjunct fields of ancient Near Eastern studies, that we find our primary sources for Israel's earliest history (p. 27).

Presumably Thompson will demonstrate what he has in mind in his next book.

In the meantime William Dever assures us that archaeologists can now isolate the earliest Israelite settlements and tell us a great deal about these earliest Israelites entirely from the material remains. As for my observation that artifacts are silent and remain 'anonymous unless interpreted in the light of written records', he quipped that 'the archaeological data are not mute; but the historian is often deaf'.[5] Dever, of course, like Coote, Whitelam, and presumably Thompson, is associating the Israelites with the early Iron I hill-country settlements. How does he know that these are Israelite settlements? Is there anything about the potsherds or wall lines that cries out 'Israelite'? Certainly not. Dever also is relying on the current scholarly consensus, which itself rests on clues from the Hebrew Bible that have been interpreted to suggest that Israelite tribes must have been settling in that area at about that time. The artifacts are still silent unless interpreted in the light of written documents. And the interpreting document in this case is the Bible.

When claiming that a revolutionary new kind of archaeological evidence is available now for tracing the roots of Israel, our colleagues apparently have in mind the sort of research pioneered by Israel Finkelstein and set forth in his recent book *The Archaeology of the Israelite Settlement*.[6] All of them emphasize the value of comprehensive regional surveys (as opposed to the earlier archaeological work that tended to focus on the stratigraphy of major 'tells'), and all of them are vague on what exactly they mean by 'Israelite'. How, for example, are we to distinguish an Israelite village from a Hivite, Gibeonite, or Kenizzite village? In the final analysis, they beg the question by using 'Israelite' as an all inclusive term for anyone living in a hill-country village during Iron I. According to Finkelstein,

> even a person who may have considered himself a Hivite, Gibeonite, Kenizzite, etc., in the 12th century, but whose descendants in the same village a few generations later thought of themselves as Israelite will, in like manner, also be considered here as an Israelite (p. 28).

Finkelstein proceeds then to describe the material culture of the Iron I villages and trace their spread—which, given his question-begging definition, is the same as tracing the spread of the early Israelite tribes. Tracing the spread requires

---

[5] W.G. Dever, 'Unresolved Issues: Toward a Synthesis of Textual and Archaeological Reconstructions?' (Presented in a SBL-ASOR jointly sponsored symposium on the topic 'New Perspectives on the Emergence of Israel in Canaan' at the 1987 annual meeting in Boston).
[6] I. Finkelstein, *The Archaeology of the Israelite Settlement* (Jerusalem: Israel Exploration Society, 1988).

distinguishing early Iron I sites from later Iron I sites. He mentions several criteria for this purpose, but the only really tangible ones involve the so-called Ark Narrative in 1 Samuel 4–6 and 2 Samuel 6. This narrative describes a Philistine victory over Israel in the vicinity of Aphek and Ebenezer, and Finkelstein's program requires (a) that the story be accepted as historical; (b) that the battle be dated to the mid-eleventh century BCE; (c) that Aphek be identified with present-day Ras el-'Ain; (d) that Aphek/ Ras el-'Ain be seen as a Philistine frontier city; (e) that nearby 'Izbet Ṣarṭah be seen, accordingly, as an Israelite village (possibly Ebenezer); and (f) that as a follow up to their victory at Aphek the Philistines overran the central hill country, destroyed Shiloh, and perhaps also Ai and Khirbet Raddana. Assuming all of this, 'Izbet Ṣarṭah III and Shiloh become type-sites for recognizing early Iron I villages (i.e. pre-mid-eleventhth century/pre-battle of Aphek), while the existence of Philistine pottery in a hill-country site marks it as a later Iron I village (post-battle of Aphek).

What if there is a fallacy somewhere in Finkelstein's chain of assumptions? Suppose, for example (just for the sake of argument, if nothing else), that virtually all of the critical commentators who have worked with the Ark Narrative are correct in warning that it is a tendentious literary piece that plays very loose with history at best.[7] Suppose that my interpretation of the narrative is correct, which I have elaborated elsewhere; namely, that this story represents a duplicate account and distorted memory of the Aphek battle that occurred near Mount Gilboa at the end of Saul's reign.[8] This would undercut the Aphek/Ras el-'Ain equation (which is uncertain in any case, as Robert North pointed out years ago[9]), make it very difficult (even with Finkelstein's sweeping definition) to secure 'Izbet Ṣarṭah III as an early-stage Israelite settlement, and lower the date of any village destructions associated with the Aphek battle (Shiloh in particular) from the middle of the 11th to at least the end of the eleventh century BCE.

But whether you accept Finkelstein's interpretation of the Ark Narrative or mine, the situation illustrates again my point that when one combines artifactual

---

[7] Cf. esp. L. Rost, *Die Überlieferung von der Thronnachfolge Davids* (BWANT, 3; Stuttgart: Kohlhammer, 1926) = L. Rost, *Das kleine Credo und anderer Studien zum Alten Testament* (Heidelberg: Quelle und Meyer, 1856), pp. 119-253; A.F. Campbell, *The Ark Narrative* (SBLDS, 16; Missoula, MT: Scholars Press, 1975); P.D. Miller and J.J.M. Roberts, *The Hand of the Lord: A Reassessment of the 'Ark Narrative'* (Johns Hopkins Near Eastern Studies; Baltimore, MD: Johns Hopkins University Press, 1977); and P.K. McCarter, Jr, *I Samuel* (AB, 8; Garden City, NY: Doubleday, 1980), pp. 23-26. Even Miller and Roberts, who dated the narrative prior to David's victories over the Philistines, recognized that 'it is a thoroughly theological narrative at its very core' (p. 60). 'The whole narrative was not created immediately after the return of the ark. One must assume that the legend grew and developed in response both to doubt and to the storyteller's art, and it was probably affected as well by the growing distance from the historical events' (p. 75).

[8] *History of Ancient Israel*, pp. 127, 130; 'Site Locations in the Saul Narratives of I Samuel' (Presented at the southeastern regional meeting of the Society of Biblical Literature, Chattanooga, 1986).

[9] Robert North, 'Ap(h)eq(a) and 'Azeqa', *Bib* 41 (1960), pp. 41-63.

and written evidence to produce a historical scenario, usually the written evidence takes precedence. It identifies the people who left the artifacts: Finkelstein calls them 'Israelites', not Iron I people. It establishes the historical parameters: these Israelites are understood to have been in the early stages of an expansion and consolidation process, which would result in an Israelite monarchy, which occupied a definable region, which in turn serves to identify the Iron I villages in that region as 'Israelite'. Finally, having established these historical parameters, the written evidence influences significantly the way that the archaeological details are interpreted. Begin with the potsherds, and Khirbet Seilun is an anonymous site with a reasonably impressive building complex that was destroyed sometime during Iron I. Interpreted in the context provided by the Hebrew Bible, it becomes ancient Shiloh, an important Israelite cultic center destroyed by the Philistines in the mid-eleventh century BCE and thus, a type-site for tracing the earliest stages of Israelite settlement.

Please understand. It is not my intention to belittle the importance of archaeology for historical research. Neither is it my intention (in this presentation) to challenge the assumptions of specific conclusions reached by these colleagues. I also suspect, as a matter of fact, that the early Israelites are to be associated in some way with the early Iron I villages of central Palestine.[10] My purpose rather is to call attention to their indirect (thus uncritical and often muddled) use of the Hebrew Bible and object to their condescending remarks regarding historians who attempt to work with the biblical materials more directly and critically. In my own case, rather than being a biblical apologist, I would say that it is precisely my critical work with the biblical materials that has led me to be more cautious than they regarding its historical reliability, apparently more aware than they of the biblically based assumptions that underlie current scholarly consensus, and more hesitant than they to spin out scenarios that involve interweaving Bible and archaeology. More than anything else, I object to the methodological implications of some of their rhetoric.

In the first place, their rhetoric suggests that now, after generations of false starts, we can finally reconstruct with scientific objectivity what really happened in ancient Israel. Theirs, in short, is the talk of positivistic historians. I am more of a relativist, for reasons that I have explained on earlier occasions.[11] When it comes to the origin and early history of Israel, I think the best we can ever hope to do is make some guesses and offer some hypothetical scenarios. These scenarios, moreover, will reveal as much about how we understand our own historical circumstances as what we know about ancient Israel.[12]

---

[10] *History of Ancient Israel*, p. 85.
[11] 'New Directions in the Study of Israelite History', *Teologiese Tydskrif* 30 (1989), pp. 152-60; 'In Defense of Writing a History of Israel', *JSOT* 39 (1987), pp. 53-57.
[12] Cf., e.g., J.M. Sasson, 'On Choosing Models for Recreating Israelite Pre-Monarchic History', *JSOT* 21 (1981), pp. 3-24.

Secondly, their rhetoric implies that it is a simple question of deciding whether the Hebrew Bible is a reliable source of historical information and, correspondingly, whether or not to use it in historical research. Of course it is not a reliable source, taken at face value. But neither should it be dismissed as totally irrelevant. Its very existence is a historical fact to be reckoned with. The appropriate question is not *whether* we should use the Hebrew Bible in historical research, but *how* we should use it.

Thirdly, while declaring the Hebrew Bible an unreliable source and depreciating the relevance of literary-critical research for historical investigation, these colleagues ignore the problems and limitations of the other kinds of evidence and the alternative methodologies that they espouse. Having conducted one of the regional archaeological surveys, I must tell you that surveys are not entirely reliable either. The data collected represent a highly selective sampling at best and are usually open to a range of interpretations. As for alternative methodologies, perhaps we need to be reminded that methodologies are ways of examining evidence and never should be mistaken for evidence itself. Coote and Whitelam may have fallen into this trap. Much of their scenario for the origin of Israel, which they advertise as the result of applying new methodology, strikes me as just another hypothesis dressed up in sociological jargon.

Finally, by declaring that archaeology is more reliable than the Hebrew Bible for dealing with the origin and early history of Israel, the rhetoric ignores the extent to which Syro-Palestinian archaeology itself is infused with assumptions derived from the Bible. To put it bluntly, Thompson's remark about the independence of Syro-Palestinian archaeology reflects a misunderstanding of how archaeology works. Regarding ceramic typology, for example, archaeologists can work out a relative chronology from the potsherds alone, but when they assign dates they rely directly or indirectly on other kinds of evidence. For Syro-Palestinian pottery this usually means written records, and for Palestinian Iron Age pottery, the Hebrew Bible plays a major role in the process. Consider, for example, the famous 'collared-rim jar'. Is there anything about its shape or form that cries out twelfth–eleventh century BCE? Of course not. Albright identified this ceramic type at Tell el-Fûl, which he believed to be Gibeah of Benjamin, and dated the jars accordingly. They have since turned up at other sites and in contexts that confirm his dating. But at these other sites also, the confirmation relies ultimately on written records, including the Hebrew Bible.

Summary and Conclusion

While it is theoretically possible to write a history of early Israel without relying on the Hebrew Bible, the result would be a very thin volume indeed and would have little in common with the current discussion. Any time historians, archaeologists, sociologists, or whoever speak of Israelite tribes settling the central Palestinian hill country during Iron I or of any sort of Israelite monarchy before the ninth century BCE, they are assuming information derived from the Hebrew Bible. The important question is not whether we should use the Hebrew Bible in our attempts to understand the origin and early history of Israel, but how we should use it. In my opinion, it should be approached critically, examined with the same careful attention to its internal typology and stratigraphy that archaeologists give to their data, and then used very cautiously, alongside other kinds of evidence, always with a conscious effort to avoid excessive circular argumentation. This process involves judgment calls every step of the way and will never lead to scientifically provable conclusions. But such is the nature of historiography.

Reading the Bible Historically: The Historian's Approach

J. Maxwell Miller

History and Historical Methodology

Although "history" is a much-used term, it is not easily defined. Is history the sum total of past people and events? Or does it include only those people and events whose memory is preserved in written records? The available written evidence from ancient times is uneven in coverage, with some peoples and periods better represented than others. Moreover, the ancient documents provide very selective kinds of information. This information often is ambivalent, and sometimes the ancient sources make unbelievable or conflicting claims. Would it be more accurate, then, to say that history is the past as understood by historians, based on their analysis and interpretation of the available evidence but not necessarily identical with the claims made by ancient documents? What if the historians disagree? And does history belong to the professional historians anyhow? Perhaps history should be equated instead with the common consensus notions about the past held by the general public. These notions might be influenced by what professional historians say as well as by other factors, such as prevailing political, social, and religious attitudes. For that matter, are not professional historians themselves deeply influenced by prevailing attitudes?

It may be said, in any case, that historians seek to understand the human past and that they depend heavily on written sources for their information. Heavy reliance on written evidence is perhaps the main distinguishing characteristic of historical research as compared with other disciplines that also seek to understand the human past. This does not mean, of course, that contemporary historians concentrate solely on written evidence or that historical research is conducted independently of other disciplines. Contemporary scholars exploring the history of ancient Israel find themselves necessarily involved, for example, in Palestinian archaeology and sociology.

Historians seek objectivity. They are interested in discovering and reporting what really happened in the past, as opposed to collecting and passing on fanciful stories, writing "docudramas," or producing "revisionist" accounts of the past for propagandistic or ideological purposes. However, complete objectivity is a goal never reached. The historian's own presuppositions, ideology, and attitudes inevitably influence his or her research and reporting. Perhaps it is not an overstatement to say that any history book reveals as much about its author as it does about the period of time treated. If so, then a proper definition of history would suggest that it consists neither of the totality of past people and events on the one hand, nor of what we contemporaries know (or think we know) about the past on the other, but of an ongoing conversation between the past and the present. As we humans, individually and collectively, seek to understand the present, we naturally look to the past for bearings. At the same time, we constantly revise our understanding of the past in light of current developments, understandings, and attitudes.

Basic to modern historiography is the principle of "analogy." Historians assume, consciously or unconsciously, that the past is analogous to the present and that one human society is analogous to another. Thus a historian's understanding of present reality serves as an overriding guide for evaluating evidence and interpreting the past, and the cultural patterns of a better-known society may be used as a guide for clarifying those of a lesser-known society. As an example of how this works in modern treatments of ancient Israelite history, note that the Bible presupposes a dynamic natural world into which God intrudes overtly upon human affairs from time to time. It is a world with waters rolling back so that the Israelites can escape Pharaoh's army, a world of burning bushes and floating ax heads. God hands down laws on Mount Sinai and sends angels to defend Jerusalem against the massive Assyrian army. Modern Western historians tend to perceive the world as being more orderly, however, and one of the standard tenets of modern historiography is that a natural explanation for a given historical phenomenon or event is preferable to an explanation that involves overt divine intervention. When speculating about the "actual historical events" behind the biblical account of Israel's past, therefore, what historians often do, in effect, is bring the biblical story into line with reality as we moderns perceive it. Surely the Assyrian army was not routed by angels, because angels, if they exist at all, do not play this sort of role in the world as we experience it. What other "more reasonable" explanation might there be for the rout of the Assyrians—"more reasonable" in the sense that it is more in keeping with our modern Western perception of reality? Possibly a plague broke out among the Assyrian troops, or maybe the narrator of the biblical account embellished the report. Either of these possibilities would be analogous to the world as we perceive it. But angels are not. In effect, then, the modern historian offers explanations that do not involve miracles or "God talk" for historical developments reported in the Bible.

The analogy principle also is at work when historians draw upon knowledge of other societies, ancient and modern, in attempts to clarify aspects of Israelite and early Christian history. The Bible reports the names of court officials who served under David and Solomon, for example, but does not describe the duties of these various officials. Historians, assuming that the royal court in Jerusalem would have been similar to other royal courts of the day, search the records of neighboring kingdoms for information regarding the duties and responsibilities of such officials.

Another example pertains to the chronological data provided in the Bible for each of the Israelite and Judean kings following Solomon. Specifically, each king's accession to the throne is dated relative to the reign of his contemporary on the other throne; and also the length of each king's reign is recorded. The following verses are typical.

> In the twentieth year of King Jeroboam of Israel Asa began to reign over Judah; he reigned forty-one years in Jerusalem. (1 Kings 15:9)

> Nadab son of Jeroboam began to reign over Israel in the second year of King Asa of Judah; he reigned over Israel two years. (1 Kings 15:25)

> In the third year of King Asa of Judah, Baasha son of Ahijah began to reign over all Israel at Tirzah; he reigned twenty-four years. (1 Kings 15:33)

However, the figures provided do not always "add up." This may be due in part to copyists's mistakes in the transmission of the ancient manuscripts. But there are also other factors to be considered in view of the records of other ancient Middle Eastern kingdoms. It is known, for example, that some of these records presuppose a fall-to-fall calendar year while others presuppose a spring-to-spring calendar year. Some designate as the first year of a king's reign the year during which he ascended to the throne; others count only his first full year (i.e., the first full fall-to-fall or spring-to-spring year, depending on the calendar used). The possibility arises, therefore, on analogy with the practices of neighboring peoples, that the two Hebrew kingdoms, Israel and Judah, used separate and different calendars, employed different methods of reckoning their respective kings' reigns, and may even have changed calendars or methods of reckoning at one time or another. One or more of these factors may explain why the biblical figures seem to be internally inconsistent. It is hardly surprising, moreover, in view of the confusing biblical figures and the various factors to be taken into account, that historians rarely agree on exact dates for the Israelite and Judean kings.

Other than this principle of analogy, which is basic also to the other approaches treated in this volume, there is no specific methodology for historical research. Rather, the historian might be compared to an investigative lawyer who searches out and examines whatever evidence is available and relevant to a particular case, employs whatever techniques and methods of analysis apply to the evidence (often relying on the opinion of specialists), constructs a hypothetical scenario as to what probably happened, and then presents the case for this scenario to other historians and the public. The last step is as important as the first. The leading historians who have been able to influence academic and public opinion regarding the past have not only been outstanding scholars who demonstrated amazing coverage, competence, and creativity in research, but have also been able to present their ideas in an understandable and convincing fashion. Thus history is a search for "what really happened," but it is also what the historians can convince us really happened.

The Bible as History

The opening books of the Hebrew Bible, Genesis through 2 Kings, present a narrative account of people and events that extends from creation to the end of the Judean monarchy. Another sequence of books, 1–2 Chronicles, Ezra, and Nehemiah, presents an overlapping account that begins with Adam and concludes with Nehemiah's activities in Jerusalem under Persian rule. The so-called prophetical books (Isaiah, Jeremiah, Ezekiel, Hosea, etc.) make numerous references to national and international circumstances. The first part of the book of Daniel (chapters 1–6) describes events that supposedly occurred in the Babylonian court while Daniel and other Jews were exiled there. The latter part (chapters 7–12) reports a dream-vision that organizes world history into a sequence of four great empires and anticipates the culmination of history during the fourth. The Gospel of Luke dates Jesus' birth in relation to Roman history (Luke 2:1), and all four of the Gospels narrate episodes in Jesus' ministry in what the reader is left to suppose is an essentially chronological sequence. The book of Acts describes the emergence of Christianity from the immediate aftermath of Jesus' crucifixion to Paul's arrival in Rome for trial. Finally, the book of Revelation reports dream-visions similar to those of the book of Daniel and also presupposing a schematic view of history.

In short, the biblical writers were very conscious of history, and the Bible itself may be looked upon as largely historical in format and content. It is not history written for the sake of history, of course, and not history of the sort one would read in a modern history book. One might argue, in fact, that the biblical writers were more akin to contemporary theologians than to historians. Nevertheless, the theological messages that the biblical writers sought to convey are so thoroughly intermeshed with their perceptions of history that it is difficult to separate one from the other. The Bible itself, in other words, confronts us with history and raises historical questions that are difficult to ignore. It is only natural, therefore, that biblical scholarship through the ages has involved attention to historical matters.

Reflected to some degree in earlier biblical research, but becoming especially intense during the twentieth century, are differences of opinion regarding the trustworthiness and accuracy of the Bible as a source of historical information. At one extreme are those who, usually on theological grounds, insist that the Bible is literally accurate in all historical details, including the chronological data provided in Genesis–2 Kings that place the creation of the world approximately 6000 years ago. Historical research for those who hold this extreme position involves harmonizing the information provided in different parts of the Bible—for example, the overlapping accounts of Genesis–2 Kings and 1 Chronicles–Nehemiah—and interpreting evidence from extrabiblical sources (other ancient documents and archaeology) to fit. Apparent contradictions within the Bible are viewed as being only "apparent," usually the result of the modern reader's failure to understand all of the surrounding circumstances. Conflicts between the Bible and extrabiblical sources also are explained away in one way or another.

At the opposite extreme are those who regard the biblical accounts as being so theologically and nationalistically tendentious and composed of such a hodgepodge of literary genera (myths, legends, etc.) that, except where extrabiblical sources shed some light, any attempt to reconstruct the history of ancient Israel is fruitless. This extreme is sometimes stated or implied by scholars who take essentially ahistorical approaches to the text, such as structuralist, narrative, or reader-response criticisms (see especially Part 3 of this volume).

However, it is very difficult to hold consistently to either of these extreme positions. The first, that of unwavering confidence in the historical accuracy of the biblical materials, is difficult to maintain in view of (1) the obvious tension between the dynamic and theocentric view of nature and history presupposed by the biblical writers and the more "scientific" or positivistic approach to reality that characterizes modern Western thought, (2) the mental gymnastics required to harmonize some of the apparent contradictions within the biblical narratives and to bring extrabiblical evidence into line, and (3) the results of close analysis of the biblical materials in accordance with source criticism, form criticism, tradition history, and other historical-critical methods.

As for the second position, that of extreme skepticism, it can hardly be doubted that there was an ancient Israel, that Israel had a history, or that the Bible is somehow relevant for understanding that history. Indeed, the very existence of the Bible, regardless of what one makes of its historical claims, is an undeniable item of historical evidence pointing to ancient Israel. It is difficult, moreover, regardless of the theory behind one's methodology, to approach an ancient document totally free of the influence of notions regarding the historical context from which it emerged. This is especially true with the Bible, which, as indicated above, is overtly attentive to history and makes such forceful historical claims. Close attention to the wording of their comments, therefore, often reveals that scholars who seem to take totally ahistorical approaches to the biblical materials nevertheless work with presuppositions regarding the history of ancient Israel that influence their overall understanding of the Bible if not their individual research.

Most biblical scholars, therefore, fall somewhere between the two extremes described above. On the one hand, they proceed in confidence that the Bible preserves authentic historical memory. On the other hand, they recognize that the Bible is not a monolithic document, that its different voices reflect different perceptions of ancient Israel's history, that these perceptions usually are heavily influenced by theological and nationalistic interests, and that some of the biblical materials were not intended to be read as literal history in the first place. The historian's task, therefore, is to separate the authentic historical memory from its highly theological and often legendary context.

Naturally, there is a wide range of views even within this middle ground between the extreme positions, with some scholars tending to place greater confidence in the historical accuracy of the biblical materials regardless of the theological, nationalistic, or legendary overtones and others tending to place less confidence in them. To see how this works out on a passage-by-passage basis, one might compare the *NIV Study Bible* (1985) with *The New Oxford Annotated Bible* (1991). The commentary and explanatory notes of the former were prepared by scholars who, although not biblical literalists, tend to take the biblical accounts of Israel's past as essentially historically accurate. Those of the latter were prepared by scholars who tend to be much more cautious on the matter.

Biblical Scholarship and the Study of Ancient Israelite History

Biblical scholarship and the study of ancient Israelite history are integrally related. On the one hand, most of our information about the history of ancient Israel prior to Roman times comes from the Bible. There are, to be sure, certain other ancient written sources and an ever-increasing amount of archaeological data to take into account. As will become apparent below, however, these extra-biblical sources are useful primarily in that they shed light on the general cultural, social, and international circumstances of biblical times. Usually they tell us very little specifically about the people and events of Israelite history, except when interpreted in light of the biblical record. On the other hand, as observed above, analysis of biblical literature generally involves some knowledge of (or at least some notions about) the history of ancient Israel. This is particularly true insofar as the analysis is historical-critical in approach. Historical-critical analysis (including such specialized approaches as source criticism, form criticism, tradition-historical criticism and redaction criticism) seeks to determine the historical contexts out of which the various biblical materials emerged, and what changes occurred in these materials as they were transmitted from ancient times to the present. Even to speculate on such matters presupposes some knowledge of the history of biblical times.

It is not surprising, therefore, that modern histories of ancient Israel typically have been written by scholars also deeply involved in biblical research, and that their application of historical-critical methodology to the biblical materials has significantly influenced their treatments of Israelite history. This is noticeable especially when one compares histories of Israel written during the nineteenth century. H. H. Milman's *History of the Jews* (1829) represents the emerging spirit of critical biblical scholarship during the first half of the century. H. G. A. Ewald's *Geschichte des Volkes Israel bis Christus* (1843–1855)[1] was based on a systematic source analysis of the Pentateuch, although not yet the classical "documentary hypothesis." While recognizing that the biblical traditions derive from a much later time than the period they describe and include imaginative elements, Ewald went to great lengths to explain that these traditions nevertheless preserve historical memory. He never clearly committed himself on what, if any, historical memory is preserved in the opening chapters of Genesis (which describe creation, the great flood, and the spread of population following the Tower of Babel episode), but he regarded the patriarchs (Abraham, Isaac, Jacob) as personifications of tribal groups. Ewald was also noncommittal regarding the specific circumstances of the exodus but believed that it was a historical event in connection with which Moses inaugurated a Hebrew monotheistic theocracy that set the direction for the future of Israelite history.

Julius Wellhausen, so closely identified with the documentary hypothesis in its classical form, spelled out the radical implications of this and other late nineteenth-century historical-critical developments in his compelling *Prolegomena zur Geschichte Israels* (1878).[2] Since, according to the documentary hypothesis, none of the four sources that compose the Pentateuch predates the Israelite monarchy, neither these individual sources nor the Pentateuch as a whole is trustworthy for reconstructing history prior to that time. According to the hypothesis, moreover, the "Priestly" source, which accounts for the bulk of the narrative and legal instructions associated with Moses, actually reflects circumstances at the end of Judah's history, the time of the Babylonian exile and following. In Wellhausen's treatment of Israel's history, therefore, Moses becomes a very shadowy and virtually unknown figure, and the characteristic features of the Mosaic era as presented in the Pentateuch (monotheism, a highly developed priesthood, elaborate legal and cultic practices, etc.) are seen instead as characteristic of exilic and postexilic times.

During the present century, as other historical-critical methodologies (especially form criticism, tradition history, and redaction criticism) have added their voices to source criticism, usually it has not been a question of whether treatments of

---

[1] English edition, *The History of Israel*, 3rd ed. (London: Longmans, Green & Co., 1871–1876).
[2] English edition, *Prolegomena to the History of Ancient Israel* (Gloucester, Mass.: Peter Smith, 1973).

Israelite history should presuppose a historical-critical approach to the Bible but of how much emphasis to place on the results of the analysis of the biblical literature itself as opposed to those of Palestinian archaeology or sociological models. This is illustrated by two widely used histories of Israel that were written during the 1950s and became very influential during the 1960s and 1970s—Martin Noth's *Geschichte Israels* (1950)[3] and John Bright's *A History of Israel* (1959).

Noth was one of the pioneers of tradition history, published comprehensive studies of the Pentateuch and the Deuteronomistic History,[4] and agreed with Wellhausen's conclusion that the Pentateuchal account of Israel's origins is an artificial literary construct composed largely of legendary materials. Thus Noth's history of Israel does not treat the patriarchs as historical figures, nor does he regard the exodus from Egypt or the conquest of Canaan as historical events. Drawing instead upon the sociological theories of Max Weber, the creative ideas of his teacher Albrecht Alt, clues from his own extensive tradition-historical studies of the Pentateuch, and what he thought were close parallels between early Israelite society and that of ancient Greek and Italian tribal leagues (known as amphictyonies), Noth argued that the ancestors of Israel probably were seminomads who ranged between the desert fringe and Canaan in search of pasture until they gradually settled down and took up agriculture. In stages, for which Noth believed there are clues in the Pentateuchal traditions, these tribal settlers formed an amphictyonic cultic league. Finally, under Saul and David, there emerged the Israelite monarchy, and it was only with the expansion of this monarchy under David that it is appropriate to speak of an Israelite conquest of Canaan.

Bright, while not ignoring the implications of historical-critical analysis, was inclined to give the biblical presentation of Israel's origins the benefit of the doubt except where it seemed to be in serious conflict with extrabiblical evidence. Also, he was much influenced by the ideas of his teacher W. F. Albright, who had been one of the pioneers in Palestinian archaeology and had advanced some rather appealing correlations between the biblical account of Israel's origins and archaeology. Thus Bright's *History* began with the patriarchs and followed the biblical outline fairly closely from that point on. Following Albright, he saw these as historical figures who lived approximately 2000 B.C.E. and probably were associated with Amorite movements that were believed to have been under way at the time. The exodus from Egypt occurred during the reign of Ramses II (ca. 1304–1237 B.C.E.), and the Israelite conquest of Canaan, which occurred near the close of the thirteenth century, was reflected in the pattern of city destructions that brought the Late Bronze Age to an end in Palestine.

---

[3] English edition, *History of Israel*, trans. Peter Ackroyd (New York: Harper & Row, 1960).
[4] The Deuteronomistic History is a term for the books of Deuteronomy, Joshua, Judges, 1–2 Samuel, and 1–2 Kings, which scholars generally regard as originally a single work.

While Noth's and Bright's histories of Israel still are widely read, the 1970s witnessed a decided shift in the discussion. This is reflected, for example, in a series of essays by an international team of scholars published under the title *Israelite and Judean History* (Hayes and Miller, 1977). Before turning our attention to recent developments in this discussion, however, some observations are in order regarding epigraphy, archaeology, and sociology.

Epigraphical Evidence

In its broadest sense, epigraphy is the study of written documents recovered from ancient times. Over the past two centuries, thousands of such documents have been recovered and numerous languages of the peoples of the ancient Middle East deciphered. Among the major developments are the decipherment, beginning in 1822, of Egyptian hieroglyphic writing; the decipherment, beginning in 1846, of the cuneiform scripts of several Mesopotamian languages; the discovery in 1887, in the el-Amarna district of Egypt, of correspondence between Egypt and various Syro-Palestinian rulers during the late fifteenth–early fourteenth centuries B.C.E.; the decipherment in 1915 of royal Hittite archives discovered at Boghazköy (ancient Hattusas) in central Turkey; the discovery in 1929 at Ras Shamra (ancient Ugarit) on the Syrian coast of a mid-fourteenth- to early twelfth-century B.C.E. archive of Canaanite documents, including mythical texts concerning the Canaanite god, Baal; the discovery, beginning in 1947, in caves along the northwest shore of the Dead Sea, of Hebrew documents from the first centuries B.C.E. and C.E., including manuscript fragments of most of the books of the Hebrew Bible; and finally, in 1975, the discovery at Tell Mardikh in Syria of royal archives of the ancient city of Ebla.

The recovery and decipherment of extrabiblical documents from the ancient Middle East understandably has had a major impact on biblical studies. The Israelites are not mentioned very often in these documents, however, which probably is to be explained on two grounds. First, epigraphical evidence from ancient Palestine is meager compared to the extensive archives that have been discovered in Egypt, Mesopotamia, Syria, and Asia Minor. Second, the Israelites rarely played a significant role in international affairs outside of Palestine, so that there was little occasion for them to be mentioned in the documents from ancient Egypt, Mesopotamia, and so forth.

A hieroglyphic inscription from the reign of Merneptah, an Egyptian pharaoh of dynasty XIX (thirteenth century B.C.E.), provides the earliest epigraphical reference to "Israel." Unfortunately, we learn very little about Israel from this inscription, and no other such references turn up in the epigraphical sources for the next three and a half centuries, until the time of Omri and Ahab in the ninth century B.C.E. This means that none of the characters or events that appear earlier than Omri and Ahab in the biblical narrative (Abraham, Isaac, Jacob, Joseph,

Moses, the exodus from Egypt, Joshua, the conquest of Canaan, Saul, David, Solomon, etc.) are mentioned in any ancient sources outside the Bible. Another Egyptian inscription from the tenth century reports Pharaoh Sheshonk's military campaign into Palestine, an event that is mentioned also in 1 Kings 14:25–28 (where he is called Shishak). But while Sheshonk claims to have conquered some cities in Palestine, some of which presumably belonged at that time to the separate kingdoms of Israel and Judah, his inscription is conspicuously silent regarding these kingdoms.

Israel (the northern kingdom) seems to have enjoyed a brief period of national strength during the reigns of Omri and Ahab in the ninth century. But Assyria was beginning to expand westward during the same century and continued to grow in strength and to dominate much of the ancient Middle East for the next two centuries. Thus several kings of Israel and Judah are mentioned in the records of the Assyrian kings as having been subjugated by them or having paid tribute to them. Since these Assyrian rulers can be dated fairly securely, the points of contact between their records and the biblical account serve as valuable benchmarks for working out the chronology of the Israelite and Judean kings. With the collapse of Assyria and the rise of Babylon, the Palestinian kingdoms (including Judah) that had survived Assyrian domination fell into Babylonian hands. One of the Babylonian Chronicles reports Nebuchadrezzar's conquest of Jerusalem in March of 597 B.C.E., and King Jehoiachin of Judah is mentioned in Babylonian lists of exiles in Babylon during Nebuchadrezzar's reign (604–561).

Of the epigraphical evidence from Palestine that pertains to the time of the Israelite and Judean monarchies, the following items are especially noteworthy. The *Mesha Inscription* reports the accomplishments of Mesha, king of Moab in the ninth century B.C.E. Mesha boasts that he rid Moab of Israelite domination and identifies Omri as the Israelite king who subjugated Moab in the first place. Mesha himself figures in the narrative of 2 Kings 3:4–28. The Siloam Inscription commemorates the completion of a tunnel hewed out of solid rock for the purpose of transferring water from the Gihon Spring to the Siloam Pool in Jerusalem. Most scholars associate it with Hezekiah (cf. 2 Kings 20:20; 2 Chron. 32:30), although no king is mentioned by name on the surviving, legible portion of the inscription. Groups of *ostraca* (inscribed pottery fragments) from the ruins of several ancient cities in Israel and Judah contain administrative records and military correspondence.

There are no specific references to either the province of Samaria or Judah in surviving records of the Persian rulers (who succeeded the Babylonians as masters of Syria-Palestine in 539 B.C.E.) or of the Ptolemaic and Seleucid rulers who dominated Syria-Palestine following Alexander the Great's conquest of the East. For the period following Alexander, the writings of Josephus, a Jewish historian in the latter half of the first century C.E., become our chief source of information for Samaritan and Judean affairs. Other Greek and Roman writers add further details and perspectives on the history of Palestine following Alexander. Also, occasional papyrus and manuscript discoveries from this time are useful for historical research. Included among these are the Dead Sea Scrolls, which provide insight into a Jewish sect around the time of the emergence of Christianity in the first centuries B.C.E. and C.E.

Archaeological Evidence

Artifactual evidence—that is, material remains of the sort usually associated with archaeology (city and village ruins, architectural remains, remnants of tools, potsherds, etc.)—is to be distinguished from epigraphical evidence, even though artifacts occasionally bear written messages (ostraca, scarabs, seal impressions, etc.), and many of the epigraphical texts discussed above were discovered in the course of archaeological excavations. With systematic analysis of the artifactual evidence surviving in a given area, archaeologists can learn a great deal about the settlement patterns and life-styles of the people who lived there in times past. Since artifactual evidence typically is nonverbal, however, it usually is neither ethnic-specific nor very useful for clarifying matters of historical detail. If the people who lived in the cities, used the tools, and produced the pottery are to be identified in terms of their ethnic identity, in other words, or if any details are to be known about specific individuals and events of their history, the artifactual record must be coordinated with and interpreted in the light of written sources. The following is an example of how this works in the case of Palestinian archaeology and Israelite history.

Palestinian archaeologists recognize the end of the thirteenth century as a time of transition between two major cultural phases—that is, the end of the Late Bronze Age (ca. 1550–1200 B.C.E.) and the beginning of the Iron Age (ca. 1200–332 B.C.E.). Among the changes that marked the transition was the appearance of numerous Early Iron Age villages in the central Palestinian hill country, an area that had been only sparsely settled during the Late Bronze Age. Nothing has been discovered in any of the Early Iron Age village ruins that identifies the settlers by name. Taking into account Merneptah's Inscription, however, which places Israel on the scene in Palestine at the end of the thirteenth century, and also the biblical narratives that associate the Israelite tribes specifically with the central hill country, it makes sense to suppose that the Israelites and the Early Iron Age settlements were connected in some way.

It is not always a simple task to locate the archaeological ruins of particular cities and villages mentioned in the Bible, or, from the other direction, to identify archaeological sites in terms of their ancient names. Places like Jerusalem, which have been occupied continuously since ancient times, pose no problem. But for many abandoned sites whose ancient names have long since been forgotten, archaeologists must turn to the Bible and epigraphical sources for clues as to which ruins represent which ancient cities. The following are some of the cities that figure prominently in the biblical narratives and, in parentheses, the modern Arabic names of their respective ruins: Jericho (Tell es-Sultan), Ai (et-Tell), Gibeon (el-Jib), Samaria (Sebastiyeh), and Megiddo-Armageddon (Tell el-Mutesellim). When the ruins of biblical cities are excavated, naturally it is of interest to archaeologists and biblical scholars alike whether the archaeological findings corroborate the biblical record. In some cases, there seems to be a confirming fit. In other cases, there is obvious conflict. Often it is a matter of interpretation and debate. Research pertaining to the interface between biblical studies and archaeology sometimes is referred to as biblical archaeology.

Sociology

Historians necessarily work with conceptual models—hypothetical notions about how human society functions and what patterns of change tend to occur and under what circumstances. The Bible presents some very pronounced conceptual models and notions—for example, the idea that ethnic groups (Israelites, Moabites, Edomites, etc.) are extended families descended from individual male ancestors, that the direction of human history is guided by divine intervention, that Yahweh selected the Israelites as his special people and gave them the land of Canaan, and that the course of Israelite history was determined by Israel's fidelity or infidelity to Yahweh. These notions undergird the Genesis–2 Kings narrative, which in turn has provided the basic outline for postbiblical treatments of Israel's history throughout the centuries, all the way from Josephus to Bright.

As mentioned above, the Alt-Noth reconstruction of Israel's origins and early history relied heavily on the sociological theories of Max Weber. Specifically, Weber distinguished four basic social structures in ancient Palestine (nomadic bedouin, seminomadic herders, peasant farmers, and city dwellers) and three basic types of societal authority (legal, traditional, and charismatic). The conceptual models undergirding the Alt-Noth scenario have been seriously challenged in recent years. Several studies have suggested that seminomadic herding normally exists in symbiotic relationship with a village farming economy rather than in competition with it and that seminomadic herding is more likely to have derived from sedentary agriculture in ancient Palestine than to have intruded from the desert fringe.

The most aggressive challenge to Alt and Noth argued that the early Israelite tribes did not enter Palestine from elsewhere but emerged from a revolt within the indigenous Canaanite population. This would have been a peasant uprising against the oppressive Canaanite city-states that resulted in an egalitarian tribal society. This notion of a peasant revolt also is influenced by a sociological model, specifically Marxism. The peasant revolt model was very influential from the late 1960s through the 1970s but receives little attention now. But two aspects of this model remain influential—the idea that the early Israelite tribes emerged from the Canaanite population rather than entering the land from elsewhere and the recognition that any satisfactory explanation as to how this occurred must be well grounded in sociological research.

Recent Developments

Three major histories of Israel were published during the last decade, all of them appearing about the same time. H. Donner's *Geschichte des Volkes Israel und seiner Nachbarn in Grundzugen* (1984–1985) falls well within the Alt-Noth tradition. J. A. Soggin, in his *A History of Ancient Israel* (1984), finds the biblical presentation of Israel's history prior to the time of David as untrustworthy for the historian's purposes. Beginning with David, however, he places considerable confidence in the biblical narrative and follows it fairly closely. *A History of Ancient Israel and Judah* (1986) by J. M. Miller and J. H. Hayes also declines any attempt to reconstruct events prior to the establishment of the monarchy. Miller and Hayes are neither as reluctant as Soggin to speculate on the sociopolitical circumstances of the Israelite tribes from which the monarchy emerged nor as trusting of the biblical materials pertaining to monarchical times. Specifically, Miller and Hayes argue that

1. The clan was probably the basic sociopolitical unit among the early Israelite tribes, with the tribes themselves being essentially territorial groupings of clans whose sense of identity and mutual kinship developed in Palestine over a period of time.
2. The name "Israel" in premonarchical times probably referred specifically to the tribe of Ephraim and certain neighboring clans/tribes, such as Benjamin and Gilead, which Ephraim dominated.
3. This Ephraim-Israel tribal domain became the core of Saul's "kingdom," which itself remained essentially tribal in character.
4. Both Saul and David began their careers as military adventurers of a sort that may not have been typical of Ephraim-Israel but for which there was precedent nevertheless—that is, Saul and David followed in the tradition of Abimelech and Jephthah, who also had organized private armies with which they provided protection to their kinfolk in return for material support and engaged in raids on surrounding peoples.
5. David succeeded in carving out a territorial state that included as its core a southern grouping of tribes dominated by Judah, the city-state of Jerusalem, and the Ephraim-Israel tribes.
6. The biblical presentation of Solomon's "empire" is largely a literary fiction. Actually, his territorial domain probably was not any larger than David's, which did not even include some parts of Palestine (such as Philistia), much less all the lands between Egypt and the Euphrates.

7. Of the two kingdoms that resulted from the split at Solomon's death, the northern kingdom—which included the old Ephraim-Israel tribal domain and took the name Israel—emerged as the more powerful. Under the Omride dynasty, in fact, Israel achieved a level of commercial strength and international prestige superior to that achieved by either David or Solomon.
8. Beginning with the Omride period, moreover, and until Israel's defeat and annexation by the Assyrians, Judah often was little more than an Israelite vassal.

In yet more recent discussions about Israel's history the following positions have emerged. Some conservative biblical scholars continue to correlate an essentially literal reading of the biblical account of the Israelite conquest of Canaan with the available epigraphical and archaeological evidence. However, Albright's solution, which called for a thirteenth-century conquest, has been largely abandoned in favor of a conquest at the end of the fifteenth century. An opposite perspective is represented by scholars who regard the biblical materials as products almost entirely of exilic and postexilic Judaism and thus irrelevant for reconstructing the history of earlier periods. This means that we can know little about the history of earlier Israel beyond whatever information can be derived from epigraphy and archaeology and that, for all practical purposes, therefore, the history of Israel begins in the ninth century B.C.E.

Certain archaeologists have raised hopes that data from recent archaeological surveys and excavations will clarify such questions as whether the Israelites entered Palestine from elsewhere or emerged from the indigenous population, whether they were agriculturalists or pastoralists when they first settled in the hill country, and by what stages they spread throughout the land. Obviously, these new data are extremely important, but they are still inconclusive. For one thing, these archaeologists treat all of the Early Iron Age hill country settlements as Israelite and thus beg the question of what would have been meant by "Israelite" during premonarchical times and why the biblical narratives pertaining to this period distinguish between Israelite and non-Israelite villages in the hill country (cf. Judg. 19:12). Also, the chief proponents of this approach have not yet reached agreement on their interpretation of the new data with respect to Israel's origins.

Yet other scholars are calling for a highly multidisciplinary approach to ancient Israelite history, involving close attention to the geographical features of Palestine, its various ecological zones, long-range settlement patterns as indicated by archaeological surveys, agricultural techniques and potentials, international trade patterns, and so on. Informed by the most up-to-date anthropological and sociological theories and models, archaeologists utilize all of these various data to explain the process by which Israel came into being and gradually was transformed from tribal society into monarchy. One can only affirm the theoretical appropriateness of this approach; certainly all of the factors that these studies bring into consideration are relevant for understanding the history of ancient Israel. Perhaps their main contribution to this point, however, is that they raise new kinds of questions and warn against oversimplified answers. Thus far, in other words, it can hardly be said that this multidisciplinary approach has produced any notable breakthroughs or compelling clarifications—at least none that does not depend as much on the researcher's methodological presuppositions and working models as upon the various data compiled. An unfortunate characteristic of these studies is that they tend to use very jargonistic language—sometimes, it seems, belaboring the obvious. Also, they discuss such a wide range of factors at such an abstract and theoretical level that it is often difficult to understand what it all means with respect to the specific people and events of ancient Israel. The proponents of this approach tend to be deterministic in their social philosophy—that is, history unfolds in predictable fashion as determined largely by environmental circumstances; individual initiative plays a minor role in the course of human affairs, and specific events are incidental items in the broad sweep of social change.

Finally, the charge is being heard from several quarters that biblical studies in general, including historical-critical methodologies and treatments of ancient Israelite history, are biased to the core and should be approached from totally different perspectives. This bias begins, so the argument goes, with the ancient written sources, which tend to be male and elitist—that is, written records normally were produced by and for the powerful in ancient times (kings, priests, etc.). Even archaeology tends to present an elitist picture, since the substantial structures of the politically powerful naturally survive in greater proportion than the humble dwellings of the lower classes. This bias in the ancient sources has only been exacerbated by religious leaders in the Judeo-Christian tradition, it is charged, who usually have been men. Moreover, contemporary biblical scholarship in Western universities is decidedly Eurocentric—that is, culturally biased—in approach.

An increasing number of studies are appearing that attempt to redress the situation. Some attempt to do this by uncovering and correcting the old biases. Others, apparently liberated by the recognition of modern historians that complete objectivity is an unattainable goal anyhow, put aside even any effort in that direction and write essays on historical topics that unabashedly replace the old biases and ideologies with new ones.

For Further Reading

Avi-Yonah, M. *The Holy Land, from the Persian to the Arab Conquests (536 b.c. to a.d. 640): A Historical Geography.* Rev. ed. Grand Rapids: Baker, 1977. A well-documented summary of the political chronology and geographical boundaries of Samaria and Judea under the Persians, Greeks, and Romans.
Bartlett, J. R. *Jews in the Hellenistic World.* Cambridge Commentaries on Writings of the Jewish and Christian World 200 B.C. to A.D. 200, vol. 1, part 1. Cambridge: Cambridge University Press, 1985. An introductory discussion of Josephus and other selected Jewish sources from the Roman period.

Bimson, J. *Redating the Exodus and Conquest.* Sheffield: Journal for the Study of the Old Testament, 1978. Taking the biblical account of Israel's exodus from Egypt and conquest of Canaan essentially at face value, Bimson seeks to demonstrate that this account is corroborated by archaeology. Read this as a balance to Van Seters's *In Search of History.*

Bowersock, G. W. *Roman Arabia.* Cambridge: Harvard University Press, 1983. Although it focuses on the Transjordan, this book is especially helpful for understanding the political context of Palestine during the Roman period.

Clements, R. E., ed. *The World of Ancient Israel: Sociological, Anthropological, and Political Perspectives.* Cambridge: Cambridge University Press, 1989. A very useful collection of essays that explores the influence of sociology and anthropology on biblical studies in general and on the study of ancient Israelite history in particular.

Edelman, D. *The Fabric of History: Text, Artifact, and Israel's Past.* Sheffield: Journal for the Study of the Old Testament, 1991. Essays on historiography and archaeology as related to the study of ancient Israelite history by six contemporary scholars.

Finkelstein, I. *The Archaeology of the Israelite Settlement.* Jerusalem: Israel Exploration Society, 1988. Provides a wealth of archaeological information about the Early Iron Age settlements in the central Palestinian hill country. However, readers should be cautious of the author's underlying assumption, reflected in the title of his book, that all of these Early Iron Age settlements were Israelite.

Hayes, J. H., and Miller, J. M., eds. *Israelite and Judean History.* Philadelphia: Westminster, 1977. Reprinted London/Philadelphia: SCM/Trinity Press International, 1990. Essays by an international group of scholars that signaled a move away from the Albright-Bright and Alt-Noth approaches to Israelite history. Especially useful is the opening chapter by Hayes, which surveys approaches and trends in the study of Israelite history from ancient to modern times.

Knight, D. A., and Tucker, G. M., eds. *The Hebrew Bible and Its Modern Interpreters.* Philadelphia/Chico, Calif.: Fortress/Scholars, 1985. A collection of essays that reviews scholarship pertaining to the Hebrew Bible since 1945. See especially the first three essays on "Israelite History" (J. M. Miller), "Syro-Palestinian and Biblical Archaeology" (W. G. Dever), and "The Ancient Near Eastern Environment" (J.J.M. Roberts).

Mazar, Amihai. *Archaeology of the Land of the Bible, 10,000–586 B.C.E.* The Anchor Bible Reference Library. Garden City, N.Y.: Doubleday, 1990. An up-to-date introduction to Palestinian archaeology (with coverage from prehistoric times through most of the Iron Age), with close attention to possible connections between Palestinian archaeology and Israelite history.

Meyers, C. *Discovering Eve.* New York: Oxford University Press, 1988. Seeks to give more adequate attention than do standard histories to the role and circumstances of women in ancient Israel. See also in this regard the collection of essays edited by P. L. Day, *Gender and Difference in Ancient Israel* (Minneapolis: Fortress, 1989).

Miller J. M. *The Old Testament and the Historian.* Guides to Biblical Scholarship. Philadelphia: Fortress, 1976. Discusses more fully several of the issues raised in this chapter.

Miller, J. M., and Hayes, J. H. *A History of Ancient Israel and Judah.* London/Philadelphia: SCM/Westminster, 1986. A recent attempt to reconstruct the history of ancient Israel, which is concerned also to inform readers about the issues and uncertainties involved.

Pritchard, J. B., ed. *Ancient Near Eastern Texts Relating to the Old Testament.* Princeton: Princeton University Press, 1955. See also the companion volume, *The Ancient Near East in Pictures Relating to the Old Testament* (Princeton: Princeton University Press, 1954), and the supplement to both, *The Ancient Near East Supplement Relating to the Old*

Testament (Princeton: Princeton University Press, 1969). Still the most widely available and easily accessible collection of translated epigraphical texts relating to the Hebrew Bible.

Rogerson, J. *Atlas of the Bible*. New York: Facts on File, 1985. Useful for getting a grasp of the physical setting in which the history of ancient Israel and Judah unfolded and from which the Bible emerged. Another good atlas, written from a more conservative perspective, is B. J. Beitzel, *The Moody Atlas of Bible Lands* (Chicago: Moody, 1985).

Van Seters, J. *In Search of History: Historiography in the Ancient World and the Origins of Biblical History*. New Haven, Conn.: Yale University Press, 1983. An analysis of the biblical materials in comparison with other similar literature from the ancient world leading to a very skeptical view regarding its trustworthiness as a source for historical information. Read this as a balance to Bimson's *Redating the Exodus and Conquest*.

Does Archaeology Really Deserve the Status of a 'High Court' in Biblical Historical Research?

Nadav Na'aman

1. Introduction

From its earliest days, modern research archaeology has played an important role in biblical-historical studies. Many of the places mentioned in the Bible were identified in the early stage of research, and it was assumed that excavating them would complement the limited information conveyed in the Bible. In those years, archaeology was seen as an important instrument in the struggle against the 'higher criticism'—the approach that questioned the historicity of some parts of biblical historiography. Since archaeology is an external, 'objective' scientific tool, it was believed that it could disprove the modern literary critical approach. These hopes were shared by fundamentalist Christians and orthodox Jews, and so archaeology gained a highly favourite place in the early biblical historical research.[1]

Since the late nineteenth century, major biblical sites—such as Jerusalem, Gezer, Taanach, Megiddo, Samaria and Jericho—have been excavated. However, the technical skills and pottery knowledge of the early excavators was very limited, and it took many years before archaeology developed a proper methodology for excavating the ancient mounds. Likewise, the accurate sequence of pottery and its chronology were only gradually established, and today these are the key to all modern excavations and the point of departure for discussing the results of the excavations.

In addition to site excavations, archaeology has developed other research tools. These include surveys, in which beside the urban centres, the surrounding hinterland as well as the peripheral zones are systematically studied. The material remains of the societies that inhabited Palestine became the key for reconstructing the history of settlement throughout the country. In addition, scientists in various

---

[1] Y. Shavit, M. Eran, *The Hebrew Bible Reborn: From Holy Scripture to the Book of Books. A History of Biblical Culture and the Battles over the Bible in Modern Judaism* (Studia Judaica, 38), Berlin/New York 2007, 17–191.

fields (such as nuclear physics, archaeozoology, archaeobotany, geomorphology, etc.) became increasingly involved in the archaeological research. An example of the usefulness of these new scientific tools is the growing application of radiocarbon measures to the results of the archaeological excavations. Compared to the dates obtained by the traditional pottery analysis, radiocarbon supplies much more accurate dating for the destroyed strata, and helps refine the date of the pottery. The increasing use of scientific tools in archaeology has given it an aura of exact science and increased the trust in its results.

By contrast with the progress made in the field of archaeology, the study of the Bible as an historical source has lost many of its former safe anchors. For example, for many years scholars believed that biblical historiography was written as early as the time of the United Monarchy; and that two generations after the establishment of the monarchy, the history of the United Monarchy, and even works of the early history of Israel, were put in writing. Today, however, there is a fairly broad consensus that biblical historiography did not emerge before the eighth century BCE, and that the extensive historiographical works were written at the earliest in the seventh century BCE, while most of the biblical literature was composed during the Babylonian exile and the Persian period. Thus it is evident that biblical historiography was written hundreds of years after many of the events it describes. Scholars also grew more aware of the many other difficulties of treating the Bible as historical source—such as its literary nature, its marked ideological and theological nature, and the central part played by God in the events described.

We see then that biblical history and archaeology moved in different, almost opposite, directions. Whereas archaeology gained the status of quasi-scientific research, dealing in solid scientific evidence, biblical history has been increasingly considered an unreliable field, full of uncertainties and question-marks. No wonder that many biblical scholars tend to accept the conclusions drawn from archaeology, and in light of these conclusions dismiss the historicity of many biblical descriptions.

But is archaeology such an accurate scientific discipline that its conclusions must always be preferred to those of the written sources? This is the opinion of the archaeologist David Ussishkin who, upon discussing the excavations of Jerusalem, wrote as follows:[2]

> The corpus of archaeological data should be the starting-point for the study of Jerusalem, its borders, history, and material culture in the biblical period. This source of information should take preference, whenever possible, over the written sources, which are largely biased, incomplete, and open to different interpretations.

---

[2] D. Ussishkin, 'The Borders and De Facto Size of Jerusalem in the Persian Period', in: O. Lipschits, M. Oeming (eds.), *Judah and the Judeans in the Persian period*, Winona Lake 2006, 147–148.

The artificial contrast that this statement poses between the written sources, which are 'open to different interpretations', and the results of the archaeological research, which by inference are free from such problems, is doubtful. Like the written sources, the results of the archaeological excavations are open to different, sometimes even contradictory, interpretations. The archaeological literature is replete with controversies on an endless number of issues, including stratigraphy and pottery typology, the function of the excavated buildings and artefacts, settlement hierarchy, population estimate, among many others. Archaeological data do not speak for themselves and its interpretation is fraught with difficulties.[3]

It goes without saying that in many cases, archaeology is an excellent research tool and supplies solid evidence. But is archaeology as accurate as some archaeologists claim it to be? Should we always prefer the results of the archaeological research over the biblical evidence? In what follows I will examine a series of test-cases in which the documentary evidence disagrees with the results of the archaeological research. In the light of this comparison, I will point out the circumstances in which the archaeological research is quite limited and should be treated with great caution.

2. Archaeology and the Amarna Letters

Let me start with the Amarna letters. The great advantage of the Amarna period (the fourteenth century BCE) for examining the potential and the limitations of the archaeological research is that here we have the evidence of both the archaeological excavations and surveys and of primary written sources. Amarna was a time of great decline in urban culture in Canaan, hence an ideal case for comparing text and archaeology. Since I have discussed this problem in detail elsewhere,[4] I will summarize the results of my research of four sites, two in the highlands (Jerusalem and Shechem), and two in the lowlands (Gezer and Lachish).

There is a striking discrepancy between the testimony of the Amarna letters concerning these four cities, which present them as strong and flourishing kingdoms, playing an important role in the affairs in southern and central Canaan and having considerable influence over other city-states near and far, and the finding of the archaeological excavations at their sites. To illustrate it, we need only ask what kind of picture would the archaeologists have visualised if the

---

[3] For the issue of text and archaeology, see D.V. Edelman (ed.), *The Fabric of History. Text, Artifact and Israel's Past* (JSOTSup, 127), Sheffield 1991.

[4] N. Na'aman, 'The Contribution of the Amarna Letters to the Debate on Jerusalem's Political Position in the Tenth Century BCE', *BASOR* 304 (1996), 17–27; N. Na'aman, 'The Trowel vs. the Text: How the Amarna Letters Challenge Archaeology', *BARev* 35/1 (2009), 52–56, 70–71; N. Na'aman, 'Text and Archaeology in a Period of Great Decline: The Contribution of the Amarna Letters to the Debate on the Historicity of Nehemiah's Wall', in: P.R. Davies (ed.), *The Historian and the Bible: Essays in Honour of Lester L. Grabbe* (forthcoming).

settlement strata and the findings dated to the Amarna period were associated with a time for which we had no written documentation? In that case they would have concluded that in the entire mountain region between the Jezreel Valley and the Beersheba Valley there was only one ruling centre, that of Shechem, which controlled the northern part of the hill country; the rest was a kind of no-man's-land. Jerusalem would have been thought of as a village in a sparsely-inhabited highland region. Sites like Gezer and Lachish would have been defined as either unimportant city-states, or as provincial towns in the territories of the neighbouring kingdoms. Some scholars might even have suggested that at that time the enormous, strong and prosperous kingdom of Hazor ruled over most of the inner regions of Canaan, and that all the cities in this vast area were secondary centres in its territory.

How can we explain the discrepancy between the documentary and archaeological evidence? Following the utter destruction of the prosperous Middle Bronze III urban culture, the country underwent a serious decline, and this is indicated in the excavations and surveys of the Late Bronze Age I–II. When urban culture is at a low ebb, structures of lesser strength and quality are often built on the foundations of solid structures from an earlier time. In multi-strata tells, these feeble structures are easily obliterated by later building operations. This is especially true of highland sites, where the bedrock is high and late construction and levelling can remove almost all traces of the earlier buildings and artefacts. Archaeological research can identify the fragmented remains and establish their date and function. Yet often the erosion and obliteration of much of the evidence by later operations, the fragmented state of the structures and the dispersal of the artefacts, hinder the reconstruction of the ancient reality. In this situation, only the documentary evidence can indicate the political situation in a broader territory and the relative status of cities vis à vis their neighbours.

3. Jerusalem in the Iron Age IIA

In the Amarna period the results of the archaeological research can be checked against the written sources, but the situation is quite different in other periods of urban culture decline, such as the times of the so-called United Monarchy (tenth century BCE) and the Persian period. There are no primary written sources for those periods, and the Bible, the single written text available for comparison with the results of the archaeological excavations, has well-known limitations. Given the many problems inherent in the historical study of the biblical texts, biblical scholars tend to accept uncritically the conclusions drawn from archaeological research. However, as we have noted, in periods of decline, the archaeological research, particularly in highland mounds, also suffers from severe limitations. This is especially true of Jerusalem, which was continuously inhabited for thousands of years and many of the ancient remains disappeared completely over time.

To illustrate the problems entailed in the excavations of Jerusalem, let me present a recent discovery from the excavations of the City of David.[5] A few scattered and fragmented pottery vessels from Iron Age IIA, and hardly any pictorial artefacts have been found in 150 years of excavations at Jerusalem; our archaeological knowledge of ninth century BCE Jerusalem was severely limited. Recently, however, Ronny Reich and Eli Shukron excavated a rock-cut pool near the spring, and in the fill they found a large number of pottery vessels from Iron Age IIA, dated to the late ninth century BCE. When sifting the earth of the fill, they found ten seals and scarabs, about 170 broken clay bullae bearing seal impressions with different motifs, and a large amount of fish bones. None of the seals, scarabs or bullae found bears any alphabetical writing, but the reverse side of some of the bullae bears the imprint of papyrus, indicating that they were used to seal letters. Other bullae bear imprints of woven fabrics, straw and canes, indicating that they sealed packaged commodities. An analysis of the fish bones showed that the bulk originated in the Mediterranean, but some were from the Nile.

This accidental find makes it possible to re-evaluate the society, economy and culture of Jerusalem in the ninth century BCE. The importation of a large amount of fish from the Mediterranean and the Nile testifies that a network of commerce with the coast of Philistia was already developed at that time. The papyrus imprints on the bullae indicate extensive writing, though it may have been used only by the royal palace and the elite. The many different designs on the bullae, each representing the seal's owner, show that seals were used by many court officials and private citizens. The absence of writing on the seal impressions shows that the fashion of inscribing the owner's name on a seal was introduced later, in the second half of the eighth century BCE. The sealed artefacts must have been commercial commodities, or taxes, brought to the court from the surrounding districts.

In sum, this accidental discovery shows how little we still know about Jerusalem in the early first millennium, after 150 years of excavations, and how risky it is to draw conclusions from negative evidence (namely, the not-found = never-existed dictum). The reconstruction of tenth-ninth century Jerusalem made on the basis of the archaeological evidence alone, while ignoring the biblical text, might be misleading, because it fails to take into account the great limitation of the archaeological research while ignoring the historical potential of the biblical text.

4. Jerusalem's Walls in the Late Ninth-Eighth Centuries BCE

Almost all the scholars who discussed the description of the wall built by Nehemiah in Jerusalem (Neh. 3:1–32) assumed that it surrounded only the City of David, but a few argued that it surrounded both the Western Hill and the City of

---

[5] R. Reich, E. Shukron, O. Lernau, 'Recent Discoveries in the City of David, Jerusalem', *IEJ* 47 (2007), 153–160.

David.⁶ The latter position was recently defended by my colleague, Prof. David Ussishkin, on the basis of the archaeological evidence alone.⁷ His discussion rests on the finding of the archaeological excavations conducted along the western slope of the City of David. No city wall was discovered along this line. He thus concluded that during the First Temple period, the City of David was not fortified along its western slope.⁸ It led him to the conclusion that Iron Age Jerusalem was fortified for the first time in the late eighth century, when the wall surrounding the Western Hill was built. Since there was no Iron Age wall along the western slope of the City of David, and Nehemiah restored the destroyed Iron Age city wall, he suggested that Nehemiah's wall surrounded both the Western Hill and the City of David.

This bold reconstruction has many flaws. First, all Syro-Palestinian capital cities and all the major Judahite cities were fortified during the ninth century BCE (e.g., Beth-shemesh, Lachish, Tel Beersheba). It is highly unlikely that Jerusalem alone was left unfortified until the late eighth century. Second, according to 2 Kgs. 14:13, following his victory in the battle of Beth-shemesh, King Joash of Israel conquered Jerusalem, 'and he made a breach of four hundred cubits in the wall of Jerusalem, from the Ephraim Gate to the Corner Gate'. Also, when Rezin, king of Aram, and Pekah ben Remaliah advanced on Jerusalem, 'They besieged Ahaz, but they were not able to attack' (2 Kgs. 16:5; see Isa. 7:1). The two accounts show that Jerusalem was already fortified throughout the eighth century BCE. Third, Neh. 3:8b reads as follows: 'and they left out Jerusalem as far as the broad wall'. As noted by Williamson,⁹ 'Taking the words at face value, the clause will offer further evidence for the view that Nehemiah's wall cut inside part of the pre-exilic city'. According to Neh. 12:38–39, the second procession marched on the wall, 'above the Tower of Ovens to the Broad Wall; and above the Gate of Ephraim.' The 'Broad Wall' can safely be identified as the 'wall outside it', whose construction is attributed to Hezekiah according to 2 Chr. 32:5.¹⁰ Thus the description of the building of Nehemiah's wall suggests that 'the Broad Wall' surrounding the Western Hill was left out of the fortifications built by Nehemiah.

Although the remains of the western wall of the City of David have never been found, we may safely assume that Jerusalem was fortified along its western side in the early eighth century, probably earlier. The wall must have been removed or eroded in the course of time, so that no fragment of it was discovered until now in the excavations. Nehemiah's wall must have surrounded the City of David, whereas the Western Hill remained unfortified and deserted in the Persian and early Hellenistic period, and was first fortified in the Hasmonaean period.

---

6 See the list of references in Ussishkin, 'De Facto Size of Jerusalem', 147.
7 Ussishkin, 'De Facto Size of Jerusalem', 147–166.
8 Ussishkin, 'De Facto Size of Jerusalem', 153.
9 H.G.M. Williamson, *Ezra, Nehemiah* (WBC, 16), Waco 1985, 205.
10 N. Na'aman, 'When and How Did Jerusalem Become a Great City? The Rise of Jerusalem as Judah's Premier City in the Eighth-Seventh Centuries BCE', *BASOR* 347 (2007), 44–45.

5. Jerusalem in the Persian Period

No wall dated to the Persian period has ever been found, and very few remains from this period have been assembled in the many excavations conducted in the City of David. The number of sites with archaeological remains in the immediate environs of Jerusalem is very small, and there is a drastic demographic depletion in the area of the province of Yehud in the Persian period.[11] Based on this and other negative evidence, my colleague Prof. Israel Finkelstein rejected the authenticity of the detailed description of Nehemiah's building of a city wall,[12] In his opinion,

> The finds indicate that in the Persian and early Hellenistic periods Jerusalem was a small unfortified village that stretched over an area of about twenty dunams, with a population of a few hundred people—that is, not much more than one hundred adult men. This population—and the depleted population of the Jerusalem countryside in particular and the entire territory of Yehud in general—could not have supported a major reconstruction effort of the ruined Iron II fortifications of the city.

The earliest Second Temple city wall unearthed in the excavations of Jerusalem is dated to the Hasmonaean period. Many buildings, too, as well as substantial quantities of pottery and other artefacts uncovered in the excavations, are dated to this period.[13] Finkelstein therefore suggests that the description of the building of Nehemiah's wall was written in the second century BCE and was inspired by the construction of the Hasmonaean city-wall.[14]

Wolfgang Zwickel calculated the population of the province of Yehud in the Persian period to about 2000–4000 men. On this basis he estimated the population of Jerusalem to about 200–400 or 400–600 men, 10% to 15% of the overall population of the province.[15] Zwickel's rough estimation of the population of Jerusalem is close to Finkelstein's calculation, as against Hillel Geva, who estimated the number of inhabitants in the late Persian period to about 1000 men.[16]

Was fifth century BCE Jerusalem so small, and was its population so tiny as Finkelstein and Zwickel suggest on the basis of the archaeological evidence? A

---

[11] I. Finkelstein, 'Jerusalem in the Persian (and Early Hellenistic) Period and the Wall of Nehemiah', *JSOT* 32 (2008), 504–507.

[12] Finkelstein, 'Jerusalem in the Persian Period', 501–520.

[13] Finkelstein, 'Jerusalem in the Persian Period', 510–514.

[14] We may question Finkelstein's assumption that biblical authors were free to manipulate the evidence even when it contradicted the reality of their own time. It is inconceivable that scribes, who lived in the Hasmonaean period and knew very well that the wall was built at that time, ignored it altogether and attributed the building to Nehemiah, who lived three hundred years before their time.

[15] W. Zwickel, 'Jerusalem und Samaria zur Zeit Nehemias—Ein Vergleich', *BZ* 52 (2008), 204–218.

[16] H. Geva, 'Estimating Jerusalem's Population in Antiquity: A Minimalist View', *Eretz Israel* 28 (2007), 56–57 (Hebrew).

letter from Elephantine addressed by Jedaniah, the priests, and all the Jews of Elephantine, to Bagavahya, governor of Judah in the late fifth century, includes the following passage:[17]

> Moreover, before this, at the time that this evil was done to us, a letter we sent to our lord [namely, Bagavahya], and to Jehohanan the High Priest and his colleagues the priests who are in Jerusalem, and to Avastana the brother of Anani and the nobles of the Jews. A letter they did not send us.

The original letter was sent by the community of Elephantine to the heads of the religious and civil institutions of Jerusalem, asking them to intervene on their behalf to the Persian authorities of the 'Satrapy Beyond the River'. The picture of an established city with its local institutions that emerges from this late fifth century letter stands in marked contrast to the image of Jerusalem, as a small unfortified village that stretched over an area of about twenty dunams, with a population of not much more than one hundred adult men.

Calculating the inhabited area and the size of the population in multi-layered mounds, on the basis of the distribution and quantity of pottery, is always problematic. We should recall that Jerusalem was continuously inhabited from the late sixth–early fifth century BCE down to the Roman conquest and destruction of 70 CE, and that in the course of these centuries the fragile buildings of the Persian period were destroyed and obliterated and the pottery broken and dispersed. Estimating the inhabited area and the size of the population in the fifth century BCE on the basis of the archaeological evidence alone is highly uncertain. In my opinion, it cannot be used as a premise for judging the authenticity of the description of Nehemiah's building operations.

Taking into account the relatively small number of people who built the wall, and that it took only fifty-two days to build (Neh. 6:15), Nehemiah's wall must have been thin, an enclosure rather than a city wall. On three sides it was built on the foundations of the First Temple city wall, so these upper courses on top of the early wall simply could not have survived. I agree with scholars who have suggested—on the basis of the description—that on the eastern side Nehemiah deviated from the line of the early wall and constructed a new wall near the eastern edge of the city.[18] This must have been a thin, fragmentary wall, rising on top of a steep slope. Such a thin wall could hardly survive the erosion and extensive

---

[17] B. Porten, 'Request for Letter of Recommendation', in: W.W. Hallo, K.L. Younger (eds.), *The Context of Scripture*, III: *Archival Documents from the Biblical World*. Leiden/Boston 2003, 128.

[18] H.G.M. Williamson, 'Nehemiah's Walls Revisited', *PEQ* 116 (1977), 82; H.G.M. Williamson, *Ezra, Nehemiah*, 200, 208; J. Blenkinsopp, *Ezra-Nehemiah—A Commentary* (OTL), London 1989, 231–232, 237; H. Eshel, 'Jerusalem under Persian Rule: The City's Layout and the Historic Background', in: S. Ahituv, A. Mazar (eds.), *The History of Jerusalem in the First Temple Period*, Jerusalem 2000, 339 (Hebrew).

building operations that took place on that slope in later years. It is therefore unlikely that the enclosure wall built by Nehemiah in the City of David would last, and it is not surprising that it has not been found.

6. Gibeah of Benjamin

Another case in point is biblical Gibeah (Tell el-Fûl). The site was first excavated by Albright (1922–1923, 1933)[19] and later by Paul Lapp (1964).[20] The destruction of the Iron Age I fortress (Stratum II) was followed by a long gap in the site's occupation. Only late Iron II pottery was found in the excavations (Stratum IIIA). Lapp therefore suggested that the late Iron site, with its casemate walls, was built no earlier than the second half of the seventh century BCE.[21] He thus corrected the earlier, eighth century date, proposed by Albright for the foundation of this stratum.

However, fourteen lmlk seal impressions were discovered in the site.[22] The impressions are dated to the late eighth and early seventh century BCE, indicating that stratum IIIA was founded no later than the early seventh century. Moreover, Gibeah is mentioned three times in the Book of Hosea: once in the call, 'Blow the horn in Gibeah, the trumpet in Ramah' (Hos. 5:8), which may possibly be dated to the Syro-Ephraimite war;[23] and twice in the combination 'the days of Gibeah' (Hos. 9:9; 10:9). Gibeah of Saul is also mentioned in the prophecy of Isaiah (10:28–32) side by side with Ramah. These four prophetic texts seem to

---

[19] W.F. Albright, *Excavation and Results at Tell el-Fûl (Gibeah of Saul)* (AASOR, 4), New Haven 1924; W.F. Albright, 'A New Campaign of Excavations at Gibeah of Saul', *BASOR* 52 (1933), 6–12. See L.A. Sinclair, 'An Archaeological Study of Gibeah (Tell el-Ful)', *AASOR* 34–35 (1960), 1–52; L.A. Sinclair, 'An Archaeological Study of Gibeah (Tell el-Ful)', *BA* 27 (1964), 52–64.

[20] P.W. Lapp, 'Tell el-Fûl', *BA* 28 (1965), 2–10; N. Lapp, 'Casemate Walls in Palestine and the Late Iron II Casemate at Tell el-Fûl (Gibeah)', *BASOR* 223 (1976), 25, 36–42; N. Lapp, *The Third Campaign at Tell el-Fûl: The Excavations of 1964* (AASOR, 45), Cambridge, Mass. 1981; N. Lapp, 'Fûl, Tell el-', in: E. Stern (ed.), *The New Encyclopedia of Archaeological Excavations in the Holy Land*, vol. 2, Jerusalem 1993, 445–448, with earlier literature.

[21] P. Lapp, 'Tell el-Fûl', 3; N. Lapp, 'Casemate Walls', 40; P. Lapp, 'Fûl, Tell el-', 446.

[22] A.G. Vaughn, *Theology, History and Archaeology in the Chronicler's Account of Hezekiah* (SBL, Archaeology and Biblical Studies, 4), Atlanta 1999, 192.

[23] A. Alt, 'Hosea 5,8–6,6: Ein Krieg und seine Folgen in prophetischer Beleuchten', *Kleine Schriften zur Geschichte des Volkes Israel*, II, München 1953, 163–174 (originally published in *Neue kirchlische Zeitschrift* 30 [1919], 537–568). Alt's analysis was accepted by many scholars; see the list of literature cited in H.W. Wolff, *Hosea. A Commentary on the Book of the Prophet Hosea* (Hermeneia), Philadelphia 1982, 110–114 (original publication: *Dodekapropheton. 1: Hosea* [BKAT, 14/1], Neukirchen-Vluyn 1965); H. Donner, *Israel unter den Völkern: die Stellung der klassischen Propheten des 8. Jahrhunderts v. Chr. zur Aussenpolitik der Könige von Israel und Juda* (SVT, 11), Leiden 1964, 47–48; W. Rudolph, *Hosea* (KAT, 13/1), Gütersloh 1966, 122–129; J.L. Mays, *Hosea—A Commentary* (OTL). Philadelphia 1969, 85–90; F.I. Andersen and D.N. Freedman, *Hosea* (AB, 24). New York 1980, 399–416; J. Jeremias, *Der Prophet Hosea übersetzt und erklärt* (ATD, 24/1). Göttingen 1983, 78–81; G.I. Davies, *Hosea* (NCBC), Grand Rapids 1992, 145–148.

indicate that Gibeah was inhabited in the second half of the eighth century BCE. There is thus a marked discrepancy between the biblical evidence and the results of the archaeological excavations at Tell el-Fûl. It brings us to the question, which set of evidence should be preferred?

Whereas fixing the date of the destruction of archaeological strata is relatively easy, as it is based on the pottery unearthed on the floors, establishing the date of strata's foundations is notoriously difficult. I have already mentioned the problem of detecting pottery of intermediate stages in multi-layered highlands sites, which existed uninterruptedly for a long time. Stratum IIIA at Tel el-Fûl was settled from its foundation down to the Babylonian destruction of 587, and resettled in the sixth–early fifth century BCE (stratum IIIB). Detecting the pottery of the earliest stage of this stratum is difficult, as the bedrock is high and there is little accumulation of strata on top of it. Moreover, the site was settled in the Hellenistic period, and the late settlement must have damaged the underlying strata. The pottery of the earliest stage of Stratum IIIA must have been scattered and most of it completely disappeared.

Some years ago I discussed a similar contradiction in the excavations of Tel Miqne (Ekron), where the cuneiform documents demonstrate that it was already an important city in the late eighth century BCE, though only pottery of the seventh century has been discovered in the excavations of the lower city.[24] I believe that the case of Tell el-Fûl is similar. Stratum IIIA was probably founded in the second half of the eighth century, as indicated by the prophecies of Hosea and Isaiah, whereas the unearthed pottery indicate only the date of the site's destruction, not that of its foundation.

7. Bethel in the Sixth Century BCE

The city of Bethel is well attested in biblical historiography and prophetic books of the eighth-seventh centuries.[25] A settlement at Bethel in the sixth century is not mentioned explicitly in the Bible,[26] but a fifth century settlement is presupposed

---

[24] N. Na'aman, 'Ekron under the Assyrian and Egyptian Empires', *BASOR* 332 (2003), 81–91. For a similar date reached on the basis of the archaeological evidence, see D. Ussishkin, 'The Fortifications of Philistine Ekron', *IEJ* 55 (2005), 35–65.

[25] Four monographs devoted to the history and archaeology of Bethel have been published in the last decade. See H. Pfeiffer, *Das Heiligtum von Bethel im Spiegel des Hoseabuches* (FRLANT, 183), Göttingen 1999; K. Koenen, *Bethel: Geschichte, Kult und Theologie* (OBO, 192), Freiburg/Göttingen 2003; J.F. Gomes, *The Sanctuary of Bethel and the Configuration of Israelite Identity* (BZAW, 368), Berlin/New York 2006; M. Köhlmoos, *Bet-El—Erinnerungen an eine Stadt. Perspektiven der alttestamentlichen Bet-El-Überlieferung* (FAT, 49), Tübingen 2006 (the book of Köhlmoos is not available to me).

[26] The interpretation of Zech. 7:2 is debated among scholars. Some understand 'Bethel' as the destination ('had sent to Bethel'), others as the subject of the sentence, either as part of a composite

by the lists of returnees in Ezra (2:28) and Nehemiah (7:31; see 11:31). However, Finkelstein, who systematically examined the sites named in these lists, suggested that they reflected the reality of the Hasmonaean period, and that Bethel was deserted in the Persian period.[27]

Four seasons of excavations were carried out at Bethel (in the years 1934, 1954, 1957 and 1960) and the final results of the excavations were published by James Kelso.[28] In the historical chapter he concluded that 'Bethel was destroyed in a great conflagration either at the hands of the Babylonian Nabonidus or shortly afterwards at the hands of the Persians, perhaps in the chaotic period preceding Darius'.[29] Lawrence Sinclair, who analyzed the pottery unearthed at Bethel, suggested that there was continuity in the site from the early Iron Age down to the second half of the sixth century.[30] Yet John Holladay, who examined the published pottery, claimed that pottery of the sixth century was missing from the archaeological reports and that the site was deserted at that time.[31] Recently, Finkelstein and Singer-Avitz published a detailed article in which they examined the results of the excavations at Bethel.[32] They analysed the published pottery of the sixth–fourth centuries BCE and concluded that material evidence for activity at Bethel in the Babylonian, Persian and early Hellenistic period is very meagre, if it exists at all. They thus dismissed the idea that Bethel served as a prominent cult place in the Babylonian period, and that significant scribal activity at Bethel in this time is not a viable option.[33]

---

proper name (Bethel-sharezer) or as a personified place name ('Bethel sent Sharezer'). In addition to the commentaries see: J.P. Hyatt, 'A Neo-Babylonian Parallel to Bethel-sar-eser, Zech. 7:2', *JBL* 56 (1937), 387–394; P.R. Ackroyd, *Exile and Restoration, A Study of Hebrew Thought of the Sixth Century BC*, London 1968, 206–208; T. Veijola, *Verheissung in der Krise. Studien zur Literatur und Theologie der Exilzeit anhand des 89. Psalms*, Helsinki 1982, 194–196; J. Blenkinsopp, 'The Judaean Priesthood during the Neo-Babylonian and Achaemenid Periods: A Hypothetical Reconstruction', *CBQ* 60 (1998), 32–33; E.A. Knauf, 'Bethel: The Israelite Impact on Judean Language and Literature', in: Lipschits, Oeming (eds.), *Judah and the Judeans*, 306 n. 77; Y. Hoffmann, 'The Fasts in the Book of Zechariah and the Fashioning of National Identity', in: O. Lipschits and J. Blenkinsopp (ed.), *Judah and the Judeans in the Neo-Babylonian Period*, Winona Lake 2003, 200–202; Koenen, *Bethel*, 62–64; J. Middlemas, *The Troubles of Templeless Judah* (Oxford Theological Monographs), Oxford/New York 2005, 134–136.

[27] I. Finkelstein, 'Archaeology and the List of Returnees in the Books of Ezra and Nehemiah', *PEQ* 140 (2008), 1–10.

[28] J.L. Kelso, *The Excavation of Bethel (1934–1960)* (AASOR, 39), Cambridge, Mass. 1968.

[29] Kelso, *Excavation of Bethel*, 51; cf. p. 37.

[30] L.A. Sinclair suggested that there was a substantial continuity of occupation in Bethel in the 6th century BCE. Sec L.A. Sinclair, 'Bethel Pottery of the Sixth Century bc', in Kelso, *Excavation of Bethel*, 70–76; cf. O. Lipschits, 'The History of the Benjamin Region under Babylonian Rule', *Tel Aviv* 26 (1999), 171–172, with earlier literature.

[31] J.S. Holladay, in W.G. Dever, 'Archaeological Methods and Results: A Review of Two Recent Publications', *Or* 40 (1971), 468–469.

[32] I. Finkelstein, L. Singer-Avitz, 'Reevaluating Bethel', *ZDPV* 125 (2009), 33–48.

[33] Finkelstein, Singer-Avitz, 'Reevaluating Bethel', 47–48.

In spite of the scanty archaeological evidence of the sixth century BCE, some scholars recently suggested that after the destruction of Jerusalem, the administrative centre moved to Mizpah, and Bethel became the central cult place of either the Babylonian province of Yehud, or the southern district of the province of Samerina.[34] According to this assumption, Bethel, in particular the temple, continued to be inhabited in the sixth century. These scholars further suggested that part of the biblical historiography was composed at Bethel, which served as a crossroad for Israelite and Judahite literature and literary traditions. Later, when Jerusalem was rebuilt and restored as the capital of the province of Yehud, the scrolls produced at Bethel were transferred to the new capital and formed the nucleus of the growing corpus of scrolls assembled in the temple.

Richard Steiner suggested that Papyrus Amherst 63 is a liturgy of a New Year's Akitu festival and was written by people deported by Ashurbanipal from the land of Rashi, on the Babylonian-Elamite border, and settled in Bethel.[35] In his opinion, this is the deportation that is mentioned in Ezra 4:9–10. The deportees lived in Bethel for an unknown period, but severe drought forced them to leave the place, and they migrated to Syene, on the southern border of Egypt, and settled there. However, his interpretation of the papyrus is controversial and remains uncertain.[36]

---

[34] For the suggestion that Bethel was an important cult and scribal centre in the exilic and early post-exilic periods, see Veijola, *Verheissung*, 176–210; J. Schwartz, 'Jubilees, Bethel and the Temple of Jacob', *HUCA* 56 (1985), 74–81; Blenkinsopp, 'Judaean Priesthood', 25–43; Blenkinsopp, 'Bethel in the Neo-Babylonian Period', in: Lipschits, Blenkinsopp (eds.), *Judah and the Judeans*, 93–107; A. de Pury, 'Le cycle de Jacob comme légende autonome des origins d'Israël', *SVT* 43 (1991), 237–241; A. Rofé, 'The History of Israelite Religion and the Biblical Text. Corrections Due to the Unification of Worship', in: S.M. Paul, R.A., Kraft, L.H. Schiffman (eds.), *Emanuel. Studies in Hebrew Bible, Septuagint and Dead Sea Scrolls in Honor of Emanuel Tov*, Leiden 2003, 781–793; Gomes, *Sanctuary of Bethel*, 185–223; Knauf, 'Bethel', 291–349; Middleman, *Templeless Judah*, 133–144; P.R. Davies, *The Origins of Biblical Israel* (Library of Hebrew Bible/Old Testament Studies, 485), New York, London 2007, 159–171, with earlier literature.

[35] R.C. Steiner, 'The Aramaic Text in Demotic Script: The Liturgy of a New Year's Festival Imported from Bethel to Syene by Exiles from Rash', *JAOS* 111 (1991), 362–363; R.C. Steiner, 'Papyrus Amherst 63: A New Source for the Language, Literature, Religion, and History of the Aramaeans', in: M.J. Geller, J.C. Greenfield, M.P. Weitzman (eds.), *Studia Aramaica. New Sources and New Approaches* (JSS Supplement 4). Oxford 1995, 204–207.

[36] For discussions, see e.g., R.C. Steiner, C.F. Nimms, 'You Can't Offer Your Sacrifice and Eat It Too: A Polemical Poem from the Aramaic Text in Demotic Script', *JNES* 43 (1984), 89–114; R.C. Steiner, C.F. Nimms, 'Ashurbanipal and Shamash-shum-ukin: A Tale of Two Brothers from the Aramaic Text in Demotic Script', *RB* 92 (1985), 60–81; S.P. Vleeming, J.W. Wesselius, *Studies in Papyrus Amherst* 63. *Essays on the Aramaic Texts in Aramaic/Demotic Papyrus Amherst* 63, vol. I, Amsterdam 1985; Steiner, 'The Aramaic Text', 362–363; Steiner, 'Papyrus Amherst 63', 199–207; R.C. Steiner, 'The Aramaic Text in Demotic Script (1.99)', in: W.W. Hallo, K.L. Younger (eds.), *The Context of Scripture*, I: *Canonical Compositions from the Biblical World*. Leiden/Boston 2003, 309–327; I. Kottsieper, 'Anmerkungen zu Pap. Amherst 63 Teil II–V', *UF* 29 (1997), 385–434; I. Kottsieper, 'Zum Hintergrund des Schriftsystems im Pap. Amherst 63', *Dutch Studies* 5/1–2 (2003), 89–115; N. Na'aman, R. Zadok, 'Assyrian Deportations to the Province of Samerina in the Light of Two Cuneiform Tablets from Tel Hadid', *Tel Aviv* 27 (2000), 179.

The documentary evidence proposed by these scholars for the rise of Bethel as a cult centre after the downfall of Jerusalem is of varying strength and nature, but remains inconclusive. To this evidence I would like to add new, and in my opinion crucial, data. Scholars have long realized that elements in the story of Jacob's dream at Luz (Gen. 28:10–22) have remarkable Babylonian comparisons.[37] In a recently published article, Victor Hurowitz compared the story of Jacob's dream at Bethel to Mesopotamian sources connected specifically with Babylon, in particular Nabopolassar's construction of the wall Imgur Enlil at Babylon and the fifth tablet of the Babylonian Epic of Creation (Enūma Eliš).[38] By meticulous examinations of these compositions he demonstrated that 'the account of Jacob's dream contains hardly a detail without some prominent linguistic or thematic parallel to Babylon in general and the myth of its primeval foundation in particular'. On this basis he concluded that the Bethel legend is a clear example of appropriating traditions of one city and applying them to another.[39] Hurowitz logically dated the composition of Jacob's dream to the time when the Babylonian empire dominated the ancient Near East, and Babylon, with Marduk's temple of Esagil at its centre, was the most prominent city in the empire. The transfer of the literary motifs from Babylon to Bethel indicates its importance at that time, and should be seen as decisive evidence of the importance of the place and its temple in the sixth century BCE.

Upon returning to the results of the excavations at Bethel, first we should recall that unlike at many other Judahite sites, where clear destruction layers were exposed in the excavations, at Iron Age Bethel no destruction layers were detected. This indicates that the process of desertion and abandonment was gradual and took place over a long period of time. Second, the location of the temple remains unknown, so the sixth century settlement and cult place may be located in other parts of the mound. Third, Bethel is located in the highlands, where the bedrock is high and later construction and levelling works in the Hellenistic to the Byzantine periods might have removed the remains of older buildings and scattered the pottery away from its original location.

---

[37] C. Houtman, 'What Did Jacob see in His Dream at Bethel? Some Remarks on Genesis xxviii 10–22', *VT* 27 (1977), 337–351, with earlier literature; M. Weinfeld, 'Zion and Jerusalem as Religious and Political Capital: Ideology and Utopia', in: R.E. Friedman (ed.), *The Poet and the Historian. Essays in Literary and Historical Biblical Criticism* (HSS, 26), Chico 1983, 104–108; F.E. Greenspahn, 'A Mesopotamian Proverb and Its Biblical Reverberations', *JAOS* 114 (1994), 36–37 and n. 25; C. Cohen, 'The Literary Motif of Jacob's Ladder (Gen 28:12) according to the Interpretation of Ibn-Ezra and in Light of Parallels in Akkadian Literature', in: Y. Bentolila (ed.), *Hadassah Shy Jubilee Book. Research Papers on Hebrew Linguistics and Jewish Languages* (Eshel Beer-Sheva, 5), Beer-Sheva 1997, 21–26 (Hebrew); D. Lipton, *Revisions of the Night: Politics and Promises in the Patriarchal Dreams of Genesis* (JSOTSup, 288), Sheffield 1999, 80–92, 99–104.

[38] V.A. Hurowitz, 'Babylon in Bethel—New Light on Jacob's Dream', in: S.W. Holloway (ed.), *Orientalism, Assyriology and the Bible*, Sheffield 2006, 436–448.

[39] Hurowitz, 'Babylon in Bethel', 443.

Nevertheless, several relatively sizeable fields were excavated at Bethel. Since a large amount of Iron Age II A–B pottery was unearthed at the site, it is difficult to assume that late Iron IIC pottery disappeared almost completely. The paucity of sixth century pottery at Bethel is in marked contrast to the textual evidence presented above, so the lack of accord between text and archaeology requires explanation.[40] To overcome the difficulty I will bring analogies drawn from Mesopotamia, which might suggest a solution to the impasse.

According to the Sumerian King List, Eridu was the first city on which kingship descended, and this is confirmed by the Sumerian flood story.[41] Whereas the city was abandoned after the 'Ubaid period (late fifth millennium BCE), E-abzu, the great cult centre of the god Enki (Babylonian Ea), continued to function for a long time.[42] Several south Mesopotamian rulers of the second half of the third and the early second millennium BCE mention the restoration of the temple, the final restorer being Hammurabi, king of Babylonia in the 18th century. Babylon then absorbed the mythology and cosmological identity of Eridu and Marduk took the place of Ea, the god of Eridu.[43] The combined historical-archaeological picture that emerges is clear: 'Throughout the historical period the picture is thus one of a single venerable temple whose cult was entirely dependant on the patronage of pious kings. During all this time the local population of the site perhaps comprised only the personnel of this ancient cult-centre'.[44]

Nippur was the religious centre of Sumer in the third millennium and held the supreme religious position in Mesopotamia throughout most of the second millennium BCE. Enlil, the city's god, was considered the supreme deity in the Sumerian pantheon, and Ekur, his temple, the most important sanctuary in the country. The city carried the epithet Duranki, 'the bond of heaven and earth/underworld', and was considered the cosmic centre of the universe.[45] As far as we know, Nippur was never an important political capital, but was a thriving city in the third and

---

[40] Koenen (*Bethel*, 62) concluded that 'Bethel nach den archäologischen Quellen in exilischer und persischer Zeit als Stadt oder nennenswerte Siedlung nicht nachgewiesen ist'. Nevertheless, he suggested that Bethel was settled in the exilic period and did not decide whether it was settled in the Persian period (p. 64).

[41] W.W. Hallo, 'Antediluvian Cities', *JCS* 23 (1970), 60–63; T. Jacobsen, 'The Eridu Genesis', *JBL* 100 (1981), 513–527.

[42] For Eridu in the 'Ubaid period, see M.E.L. Mallowan, 'The Development of Cities: From Al-'Ubaid to the End of Uruk 5', in: I.E.S. Edwards, C.J. Gadd, N.G.L. Hammond (eds.), *Cambridge Ancient History* (3rd ed.), 1/1, Cambridge 1970, 330–350.

[43] A.R. George, '"Bond of the Lands": Babylon, the Cosmic Capital', in: G. Wilhelm (ed.), *Die orientalische Stadt: Kontinuität, Wandel, Bruch* (1. Internationales Colloquium der Deutschen Orient-Gesellschaft), Saarbrücker 1997, 129–133.

[44] George, "Bond of the Lands", 132.

[45] W.G. Lambert, 'Nippur in Ancient Ideology', in: M. de Jong Ellis (ed.), *Nippur in the Centennial. Papers Read at the XXXVe Rencontre Assyriologique Internationale*, Philadelphia 1992, 119–120; J.G. Westenholz, 'The Theological Foundation of the City, the Capital City and Babylon', in: *idem* (ed.), *Capital Cities: Urban Planning and Spiritual Dimensions* (Proceedings of the symposium

early second millennium BCE. The city suffered great decline in the 17th century and was almost completely deserted in the 16th–15th centuries.[46] It was restored in the 14th century and its temple rebuilt.[47] In the late 13th century the city declined once again and by the end of the first millennium it had diminished to a village flanking Enlil's temple.

In spite of the city's great decline in the 17th–15th centuries, the god Enlil was considered the head of the Mesopotamian pantheon and Ekur, his temple, the navel of the earth. Enlil's and Ekur's places were appropriated by Babylon and Marduk only in the time of Nebuchadnezzar I (1125–1104), following his victory over Elam and the restoration of Marduk's image to Babylon.[48] However, the literary-theological conflict between the Babylonian priests and authors and their opposite members in Nippur continued for about a century, and literary works were composed in the struggle for religious seniority between the two gods, their temples and cities.[49] It is evident that the pre-eminent position of Nippur and its god was the acknowledged ideology in Mesopotamia until the late second millennium. Like E-abzu at Eridu, in time of decline and desertion the Ekur temple and its personnel formed the nucleus of the settlement at the site, and pious Mesopotamian kings continued to support the temple throughout the second millennium BCE.

Likewise, the temple of Bethel was the most important sanctuary in the Kingdom of Israel and must have kept its elevated status under the Assyrian empire (note the legendary story in 2 Kgs 17:25–28). Following Josiah's conquest of Bethel and its despoliation, the city probably suffered serious decline and even partial desertion. But the venerated temple was restored and formed the nucleus of the place, being supported by the government of the province, similar to the E-abzu temple at Eridu and the Ekur temple at Nippur. Since the location of the temple is

---

Held on May 27–29, 1996, Jerusalem, Israel), Jerusalem 1996, 45–46; W. Sallaberger, 'Nippur als religiöse Zentrum Mesopotamiens im historischen Wandel', in: Wilhelm (ed.), *Die orientalische Stadt*, 147–168.

[46] S.W. Cole, *Nippur in Late Assyrian Times* c. 755–612 BC (SAAS 4), Helsinki 1996, 7–12; George, 'Bond of the Lands', 132–133.

[47] E.C. Stone, 'Economic Crisis and Social Upheaval in Old Babylonian Nippur', in: L.D. Levine, T. Cuyler Young (eds.), *Mountains and Lowlands: Essays in the Archaeology of Greater Mesopotamia* (Bibliotheca Mesopotamica, 7), Malibu 1977, 267–289; Cole, *ibid.*, 7–12; George, 'Bond of the Lands', 132–133.

[48] W.G. Lambert, 'The Reign of Nebuchadnezzar I: A Turning Point in the History of Ancient Mesopotamian Religion', in: W.S. McCullough (ed.), *The Seed of Wisdom. Essays in Honour of T.J. Meek*, Toronto 1964, 3–13; W.G. Lambert, 'Studies in Marduk', *BSOAS* 47 (1984), 2–5; W. Sommerfeld, *Der Aufstieg Marduks. Die Stellung Marduks in der babylonischen Religion des zweiten Jahrtausends v. Chr.* (AOAT, 213), Kevelaer/Neukirchen-Vluyn 1982, 182–189; A.R. George, 'Marduk and the Cult of the Gods of Nippur at Babylon', *Or* 66 (1997) 65–70.

[49] V.A. Hurowitz, *Divine Service and Its Rewards. Ideology and Poetics in the Hinke Kudurru* (Beer-Sheva 10), Beer-Sheva 1997, 16–19; V.A. Hurowitz, 'Reading a Votive Inscription: Simbar-shipak and the Ellilification of Marduk', *RA* 91 (1997), 39–47.

unknown, it is impossible to evaluate the scope of settlement that was built around it. The sanctuary's elevated religious status was propagandized by the priests, who composed literary works that emphasized its great antiquity, its consecration by the Patriarch Jacob, and its religious importance as a bond between heaven and earth—parallel to the status of Esagil in Babylon.

The case of Bethel shows once again that we must be cautious in drawing conclusions on the basis of negative evidence. In view of the documentary evidence we had better assume that Bethel was an important cult centre in the sixth century BCE, and that its decline in the late sixth to early fifth century should not be separated from the rise of Jerusalem at that time.

8. Summary Notes

In conclusion, it seems that in multi-strata mounds, especially in periods when the urban culture is at a low ebb and only a few poor structures are built, and these often on the foundations of earlier structures, the archaeological research can draw erroneous conclusions from the findings in the dig. This is especially true in the old city of Jerusalem, which was built on terraces and settled for thousands of years, each new city resting its foundations on the bedrock, destroying what had stood on it. In sites of a single stratum, or just a few strata, even poor, scattered structures may be well preserved. However, in multi-layered highland mounds, even the public and private buildings in periods of decline may disappear completely due to the extensive construction and developments carried out on the site in later periods. The old truth, 'absence of evidence is not evidence of absence', is particularly applicable for multi-layered highland sites and should always be taken into consideration.

I don't mean to belittle the importance of archaeology, which can shed light not only on aspects of the material culture, but also on other significant areas, such as economy and society, imports and exports, religion and the cult, among others. But in regard to multi-strata highland sites in such times as the 'United Monarchy' and the Babylonian and Persian periods, the results of the archaeological excavations should be treated with great caution.

The discussion of the documents and the archaeological finding vividly demonstrates the dangers of ignoring the limitations of either of these disciplines. Exclusive reliance on one of them alone can produce a distorted picture. Only the skilful use of both can lead to a balanced evaluation of the ancient reality.

Malleability and its Limits: Sennacherib's Campaign against Judah as a Case-Study*

Ehud Ben Zvi

Introduction

As per its title, the purpose of this paper is to deal with the campaign of Sennacherib against Judah as a case study for the more general issue of malleability *and* its limits in ancient historical reporting and particularly Israelite historiographical writings. This issue raises important questions for the study of ancient historical writing in general, and in particular for the study of its dependence on outside-the-narrative referents and on the question of representation.[1]

Several of the features of this campaign contribute to its being a good case study for this purpose. First, one has to deal with a single, clearly defined campaign[2]

---

* May this paper serve as a token of appreciation for Professor John Van Seters. I have learned much from John, and enjoyed greatly our talks and meals together. It is with a deep sense of gratitude that I dedicate this paper to him.

[1] To be sure, conclusions based on a particular case should not be assumed to hold true for the general case, but still they raise good heuristic issues and concerns for its study.

Discussions on the question of representation, external referentiality and the like are becoming more common, and increasingly 'passionate' in theoretical discussions about history and history writing. See, for instance, the following exchange of articles, Perez Zagorin, 'History, the Referent, and the Narrative: Reflections on Postmodernism Now', *History and Theory* 38 (1999), pp. 1-24; K. Jenkins, 'A Postmodern Reply to Perez Zagorin', *History and Theory* 39 (2000), pp. 181-200; Perez Zagorin, 'Rejoinder to a Postmodernist', *History and Theory* 39 (2000), pp. 201-209.

Unlike these works on the theory of history, however, the present one discusses the inferences that may be reasonably gleaned from a study of different constructions of a particular historical event, and focuses particularly on these that contribute to our understanding of the work and limitations of ancient historians. As such, this article does not attempt at all to be a contribution to meta-history, but to the study of ancient Israelite historiography.

[2] Two-campaign models have been advocated for more than a century. But there is no clear evidence that either Sargon or Sennacherib much later in his reign (e.g., 688–687 BCE) campaigned against Judah. Moreover, all the accounts of Sennacherib's campaign—in their present form at least—describe only one campaign, and as usual, one should not multiply hypothesis without necessity. These issues have been debated at length many times. Regarding the proposal of two campaigns by Sennacherib, see, for instance, W.H. Shea, 'Sennacherib's Second Palestinian Campaign', *JBL* 104 (1985), pp. 401-18 but see also the response to his proposals in F.J. Yurco, 'The Shabaka-Shebiktu

whose historical outcome was a stable situation that lasted for a relatively long period. This being the case, there is no room for telescoping of subsequent military campaigns and military outcomes.[3] Second, archaeological data—and other information from the area—allows a good historical-critical reconstruction of the political (and demographic) outcome of the campaign. This reconstruction is, at least in its main lines, not dependent on either the neo-Assyrian or any biblical description of the events.[4] This being the case, one can compare the actual historical outcome with the ideological outcomes of Sennacherib's campaign to Judah in diverse literary constructions of the event.[5] Such comparisons may contribute

---

Coregency and the Supposed Second Campaign of Sennacherib against Judah: A Critical Assessment', *JBL* 110 (1991), pp. 35-45. On the proposal of an early campaign by Sargon and second one by Sennacherib, see A.K. Jenkins, 'Hezekiah's Fourteenth Year: A New Interpretation of 2 Kings xviii 13-xix 37', *VT* 26 (1976), pp. 284-98; Bob Becking, *The Fall of Samaria: An Historical & Archaeological Study* (SHANE, 2, Leiden: E.J. Brill, 1992), pp. 54-55. But see also N. Na'aman, 'Hezekiah and the Kings of Assyria', *TA* 21 (1994), pp. 235-54, esp. 235-47. A detailed analysis of the arguments involved is beyond the scope of this paper. However, it is perhaps worth mentioning that recent contributions to the study of the 25th dynasty and its chronology in no way require or support a double campaign model. As for these contributions, see D.B. Redford, 'Taharqa in Western Asia and Libya', *Eretz Yisrael* 24 (1993), pp. 188-91, A. Fuchs, *Die Annalen des Jahres 711 v. Chr.* (SAAS 8; Helsinki: The Neo-Assyrian Text Corpus Project, 1998), pp. 124-31; G. Frame, 'The Inscription of Sargon II at Tang-i Var', *Or* 68 (1999), pp. 31-57; D.B. Redford, 'A Note on the Chronology of Dynasty 25 and the Inscription of Sargon II at Tang-i Var', *Or* 68 (1999), pp. 58-60. For the purpose of this study, it will suffice to state that the account of the third campaign in the annalistic sources, those in Kings and Chronicles—at least in their present form—the reports in Josephus and the archaeological evidence pointing to massive destruction in Judah either reflect or attempt to represent the events of 701 BCE (see also n. 4).

[3] This is certainly an issue for the study of Sennacherib's southern campaigns. See L.D. Levine, 'Sennacherib's Southern Front: 704–689 B.C.', *JCS* 34 (1982), pp. 28-55. It is worth stressing that because the past is always becoming past, reports of events may reflect and vary according to changes later than the described events. These variations are at times very large; see, for instance, the accounts of the fate of Merodach Baladan at the hands of Sennacherib or the issue of the appointment of Bel-Ibni as King of Babylon. On these matters, see M. Liverani, 'Critique of Variants and the Titulary of Sennacherib', in F.M. Fales (ed.), *Assyrian Royal Inscriptions: New Horizons in Literary, Ideological, and Historical Analysis: Papers of a Symposium Held in Cetona (Siena), June 26–28, 1980* (Orientis antiqui collectio, 17; Rome: Istituto per l'Oriente, Centro per le antichita e la storia dell'arte del vicino Oriente, 1981), pp. 253-57.

[4] D. Edelman recently claimed that 'in spite of the important information contained in the various accounts of Sennacherib's campaign and the reliefs of his conquest of Lachish that were on the palace wall at Nineveh, their absence would have little effect upon the recreation of the events in the reign of Hezekiah by historians of Judah'. See D. Edelman, 'What If We Had No Accounts of Sennacherib's Third Campaign or the Palace Reliefs Depicting the Capture of Lachish?', in J. Cheryl Exum (ed.), *Virtual History and the Bible* (Leiden: E.J. Brill, 2000), pp. 88-103, quotation from p. 102 (= D. Edelman, 'What If We Had No Accounts of Sennacherib's Third Campaign or the Palace Reliefs Depicting the Capture of Lachish?', *Bib Int* 8 [2000], pp. 88-103).

[5] It might be argued from some corners that this or similar critical reconstructions are nothing more than another 'narrative' created by a certain group (i.e., critical historians) at a particular time, and as such essentially not different in value from the account in Kings, or some paraphrases of it.

to study of the nature and extent of malleability in historical reports. Third, it is possible to compare two accounts of the campaign written from substantially different perspectives and social locations. One can compare (a) the account in Kings, within its own ideological and literary context, with (b) the account of the campaign against Judah in Sennacherib's annals within its own ideological and literary context. Such comparison may contribute to assess how ideological backgrounds and literary contexts enable and further malleability in ancient historical

---

It seems to me that the 'nothing more' in this type of claims is highly misleading. This and similar reconstructions are the best approximation that present historians have now to what may called 'temporary historical truth'. The latter term requires some explanation. This and similar reconstructions account better for the facts that are agreed upon by critical historians at this time than any other possible reconstructions. Given that the facts agreed upon by critical historians at a particular time are the best possible approximation for their time to the historical facts and if by 'historical truth' one means correspondence with facts, then reconstructions like the one mentioned above are the best approximation to truth that exists at this moment, and as such they can be considered a 'temporary historical truth'.

The alternative to an approach that evaluates the claims of different reconstructions against the best possible approximations to historical fact, has to be based either on a denial of factual reality or of any possibility to refer to it. Very few historians seem willing to follow that path. After all, most historians (and not only professional historians) would maintain that there is a difference between the following statements: (a) During WWII Nazis murdered numerous Jews (and people from other target groups) in Auschwitz as part of a general policy of extermination against them, and (b) during WWII Jews murdered numerous Nazis in Auschwitz as part of a general policy of extermination against them. To be sure, the obvious difference between the statements is that the first one is true, but the other is blatantly false. How do we know that? Because whereas statement (a) corresponds to historical facts, (b) does not. These historical facts are surely not dependent on whatever narrative/text/discourse the references to the events in Auschwitz may be embedded in. If so, they have to stand outside (or beyond) purely narrative or textual worlds. For a theory of history approach to some of the issues raised here and on the implied notion of progress in historical research that they advance, cf. R. Martin, 'Progress in Historical Studies', *History and Theory* 38 (1998), pp. 14-39. Cf. Perez Zagorin, 'History, the Referent, and the Narrative'.

One may also approach the difference between the mentioned reconstructions of the Assyrian campaign and alternative ancient reconstructions from the perspective of whether they qualify as a 'scientific theory'. By the latter I mean here a well-substantiated explanation of a particular set of related events (including particular actions and outcomes) that incorporates known/agreed-upon facts, historical 'laws' (i.e., usual relations between causes and effects within a particular society/ies), inferences and tested hypotheses better than any of its proposed alternatives and that has not yet been falsified. (This definition is a substantial adaptation of the definition of theory advanced by the National Academy of Sciences.) If this terminology is accepted, then the reconstruction mentioned above is not only 'another narrative', but the current 'theory of Sennacherib's campaign'. To be sure, theories may be falsified later, but until they are, they represent the best approximation to 'methodological truth' that is possible under the circumstances in which they are tested. The narratives in Kings, Chronicles, Josephus and the annalistic account cannot be considered as 'theories' because they contradict known (or agreed-upon) facts, and are therefore falsified to some extent or another.

On the possibility of testing hypotheses in relation to this particular matter see D. Edelman, 'What If'.

writings, but it may also point to some of the limitations for malleability that they also create. Fourth, the construction of this event in Kings led to subsequent constructions in later pieces of Israelite/Judean historical writing, namely Chronicles and Josephus.[6] What kind of malleability does appear in successive, partially dependent constructions of the event?[7]

Given the genre limitations of an academic paper, the scope of the discussion has to be narrowed from the outset. First, it is consistent with the focus of this paper—namely questions of ancient historiography—to focus mainly on narrative accounts of the campaign as they appear in works that shape and reconstruct a larger image of the past,[8] rather than all possible sources for the study of Sennacherib's campaign against Judah. Second, despite the fact that neo-Assyrian material is and must be discussed—and that occasionally some observations will be made—the focus is on Israelite historiography.[9] Third, the basic aim of this paper is neither to advance the most likely historical reconstruction of the events nor to provide a full analysis of its representation in historical writings (e.g. the book of Kings, Chronicles), nor to study the potential sources that could be reflected in the account in 2 Kings.[10] The goal of the paper is to explore the issue of malleability and its limits in a particular set of accounts all of which (a) claim to refer to a single historical event and (b) are an integral part of larger historical narratives. This being the case, the paper will explore the relation between ideologically oriented narratives and referents that stand outside the world created by each narrative. Numerous matters that are directly pertinent to the study of the campaign itself but not necessary to achieve the purposed mentioned above will not be covered.[11]

---

[6] See 2 Chron. 32.1-23; *Ant.* 10.1-23 and cf. *War* 5.386-88, 404-408.

[7] It goes without saying that there are very substantial differences among these constructions of the campaign, as one may expect from writings written from very different perspectives, for diverse purposes, in more than one language or sociolect and with different public in mind. Yet there are also similarities. The issue is whether similarities and differences may be clustered and explained in general terms.

[8] There is no need to enter here into the question of how to define 'historical writings'. If would suffice to say that the Book of Kings and the Book of Chronicles, but not the Book of Isaiah, qualify as works of ancient historiography.

[9] Although this is simply a study case, it may be advisable to take note of the danger of 'universal' explanations. Conventions found in Israelite historiography may or may not work in neo-Assyrian historiography. It is worth noting that different conventions about what can and cannot be changed, and accordingly on malleability and its limitations seem to appear within the Mesopotamian tradition itself (cf. the Synchronistic History and Chronicle P).

[10] Possible but hypothetical pieces of ancient historiography, such as proposed editions of the Book of Kings prior to the present form are also not considered given the uncertain character of these hypothetical texts.

[11] I am confident that other contributions will more than make up for what is not, and cannot be discussed here.

Malleability in Historical Writing:
Shape and Purpose of Reports of the Campaign
within their Own Contexts. Meaning/Significance
in Historical Narratives

Survey of Evidence: The Annalistic Account

The neo-Assyrian account of the campaign against Judah that suits the purpose of this study is the one present in the annalistic tradition.[12] Its literary context is clear. It is part and parcel of the account of Sennacherib's third campaign, namely the one against the land of Hatti. In other words, the third campaign is one among others, and the campaign against Judah is a subset of this third campaign. Thus, the geographical horizon of the campaigns in the annals as a whole is imperial.[13] The particular horizon of the third campaign is clearly regional; it focuses on the land of Hatti rather than on Judah. Further, both the annals in general and each of

---

[12] The account of the third campaign itself is basically stable in the different versions of the annals of Sennacherib since the Rassam Cylinder (700). The main difference is that the Rassam Cylinder shows a longer description of the booty. For the 'traditional' edition of the annals in the Oriental Institute Inscription (the Chicago Prism), see D.D. Luckenbill, *The Annals of Sennacherib* (The University of Chicago Oriental Institute Publications, 2; Chicago: University of Chicago Press, 1924), pp. 23-47. The account of the third campaign is in OIP II, 37-III, 49 (Luckenbill, *Annals*, pp. 29-34). The text in the Rassam Cylinder that is omitted in the later editions can be found in Luckenbill, *Annals*, pp. 60-61. For a comparison of the relevant texts, one may consult R. Borger, *Babylonisch-Assyrische Lesestücke* (Rome: Pontificium Istitutum Biblicum, 2nd edn, 1979), I, pp. 73-77. The Rassam Cylinder has been published recently, see E. Frahm, *Einleitung in die Sanherib-Inschriften* (AfO Beiheft, 26; Horn: Selbstverlag des Instituts für Orientalistik der Universität Wien, Druk F. Berger & Söhne, 1997), pp. 47-61. In this work, it is referred to as T4. The relevant sections of the text of the Rassam Cylinder are discussed at some length in W.R. Gallagher, *Sennacherib's Campaign to Judah* (SHCANE, 18; Leiden: E.J. Brill, 1999). The 'annalistic' tradition includes also a generally shortened, but at points slightly different version in Bull IV. See, for instance, Gallagher, *Sennacherib's Campaign*, pp. 12, 99-101, 105-10, 135.

The mentioned, basic textual stability is due in part to the tendency of the authors of these texts to use previous versions when dealing with the same subject matter and to the lack of major differences in ideological or rhetorical requirements (contrast with, for instance, Nabonidus' inscriptions concerning the building of the temple of Sin at Harran). On these matters, see J. Van Seters, *In Search of History* (New Haven: Yale University Press, 1983), esp. pp. 62-64.

[13] This is true, despite the weight of the reports about Sennacherib's actions in the Southern front—six out of the eight campaigns described in the annals deal with this area. Here, beyond-the-narrative events pre-shape the possible ways in which the narrative may evolve. In other words the historical emphasis on the 'southern problem' in Sennacherib's day results in an annalistic narrative that has no alternative but to reflect such emphasis in a literary manner. On Sennacherib's southern front, see, for instance, L.D. Levine, 'Sennacherib's Southern Front: 704-689 B.C.', *JCS* 34 (1982), pp. 28-55. Further, the imperial approach is true already in the first appearance of this account, in the Rassam Cylinder (700 BCE).

the reported campaigns in particular construct time as imperial, sequential time based on successive royal campaigns carried out by a particular Assyrian (/world) king.[14] The account of the campaign against Judah and its literary context are fully embedded in the discourse of, and convey the ideology of the Assyrian center of power.

The account of the third campaign carried numerous messages, but one that is surely central can be summarized as follows: The Assyrian king succeeded—as expected—to return the land of Hatti to its normative, 'godly' order.[15] Because of his actions, rebellion is no more in the area.[16] In a nutshell, he defeated and punished those who did not submit, and accepted homage and tribute from those who submitted. Those who opposed him suffered the expected and well-deserved defeat, and severe punishment. Hezekiah, who is described as one of the main enemies of the victorious Assyrian king, is portrayed as a pathetic anti-hero who is unable to defend his country, his people and even his own household and palace before the proper ruler, Sennacherib. The latter destroys forty-six cities, numerous villages, exiles a multitude, and takes a large booty. He later receives Hezekiah's tribute, which includes not only his army but his daughters and the women of the palace.[17] As for Hezekiah, he was terrified by the radiant splendor of Sennacherib's lordship, so accepted servitude and sent him his extraordinary 'gift'. True, he was left as king over Judah, but those who were exiled did not return after his servitude, and his kingdom did not return to its former border. Sennacherib diminished his land and raised his tribute. Hezekiah was left as king because he became a servant of the Assyrian king, but he did not go unpunished, nor his land, nor his people.

In sum, the account of the third campaign is presented as 'empiric proof' supporting the ideology of the Assyrian center of power (including the persona of the reigning king) in a multitude of ways.

Survey of Evidence: The Account in Kings

The account in 2 Kgs 18.13–19.37 is an integral part of the book of Kings and of what may be called the deuteronomistic collection of historical books (as

---

[14] The way (or usually ways) in which an historiographical work constructs time communicates much of the (often implied) worldview advanced and reflected by the work. Cf. E. Ben Zvi, 'About Time: Observations about the Construction of Time in the Book of Chronicles', *HBT* 22 (2000), pp. 17-31.

[15] For a detailed study of the account see, among others, H. Tadmor, 'Sennacherib's Campaign to Judah: Historical and Historiographical Considerations', *Zion* 50 (1985), pp. 65-80 (71-78) (in Hebrew).

[16] This includes agents of rebellion beyond-the-region forces. The Egyptian-Nubian expedition is rooted out the area, and its allies are no more.

[17] Needless to say, the text communicates not only a transfer of 'goods', but also a clear 'transfer' of honor and markers of honor from Hezekiah to Sennacherib.

opposed to the 'chronistic' collection of historical books).[18] The account in Kings is not only an extended one, but it is also far from simple. Numerous studies have focused on its possible sources, its redactional history, and its relation to Isa. 36–37. For the purpose of this study it would suffice to point to some of the main lines of this account.[19]

First, the narrative in Kings moves straight from the fall of the Northern Kingdom at the hands of the Assyrians (2 Kgs 18.9-12) to Sennacherib's campaign against Judah. Further, the latter is presented as fully successful at first,[20] as the text reports that all fortified cities of Judah were conquered (2 Kgs 18.13). The narrative was clearly written so as to convey a sense that what remained of Judah

---

[18] The account is paralleled, in the main, in Isa. 36.1–37.38. It bears note, however, that the literary context of the account is clearly not the same. The book of Isaiah is not a historiographical work; the book of Kings is.

[19] There are numerous studies on this account. It is usually divided in accounts A (2 Kgs 18.13-16) and B (2 Kgs 18.17–19.37). Account B is often divided in B_1 (2 Kgs 18.17–19.9a+36-37 and B_2 (2 Kgs 19b–35), with vv. 19a+36-37 usually, but not always, considered to be the fulfillment of the promise in v. 7. The extent and the relations between these proposed sources or traditions, the editorial processes that led to the present form in Kings, their degree of 'historicity', as well as its relation to the parallel account in the Book of Isaiah have been discussed extensively, though no full agreement is in sight. See, among many others, B.S. Childs, *Isaiah and the Assyrian Crisis* (SBT, Second Series 3; London: SCM Press, 1967), pp. 69-103; R.E. Clements, *Isaiah and the Deliverance of Jerusalem* (JSOTSup, 13; Sheffield: JSOT Press, 1980); P.E. Dion, 'Sennacherib's Expedition to Palestine', *Bulletin of the Canadian Society of Biblical Studies* (presidential address; 1989), pp. 3-25; F.J. Gonçalves, *L'expédition de Sennachérib en Palestine dans la littérature hébraïque ancienne* (EB NS 7; Paris: Gabalda, 1986), esp. pp. 331-487; and more recently, *idem*, 'Senaquerib na Palestina et a tradiçao bíblica. Da grande derrota de Judá à maravilhosa salvaçao de Jerusalén', *Didaskalia* 20 (1990), pp. 5-32; C. Hardmeier, *Prophetie in Streit vor dem Untergang Judas* (BZAW, 187, Berlin: W. de Gruyter, 1990); Antti Laato, 'Hezekiah and the Assyrian Crisis in 701 B.C.', *SJOT* 2 (1987), pp. 49-68; I. Provan, *Hezekiah and the Books of Kings: A Contribution to the Debate About the Composition of the Deuteronomistic History* (BZAW, 172, Berlin: W. de Gruyter, 1988), pp. 118-30; C.R. Seitz, *Zion's Final Destiny. The Developments of the Book of Isaiah, A Reassessment of Isaiah 36–38* (Philadelphia: Fortress Press, 1991); *idem*, 'Account A and the Annals of Sennacherib: A Reassessment', *JSOT* 58 (1993), pp. 47-57; M.A. Sweeney, *Isaiah 1–39 with an Introduction to Prophetic Literature* (FOTL XVI; Grand Rapids, MI: Eerdmans, 1996), pp. 454-88; J. Vermeylen, 'Hypothèses sur l'origine d'Isaïe 36–39', J. Van Ruiten and M. Vervenne (eds.) *Studies in the Book of Isaiah, Festschrift Willem A.M. Beuken* (BETL, 132; Leuven: Leuven University Press, 1997), pp. 95-118.

There are also numerous contributions to the study of particular portions or aspects of these accounts. See, for instance, H. Tadmor, 'Rab-saris and Rab-shakeh in 2 Kings 18', C.L. Meyers and M. O'Connor (eds.) *The Word of the Lord Shall Go Forth: Essays in Honor of David Noel Freedman in Celebration of his Sixtieth Birthday* (Winona Lake, IN: Eisenbrauns, 1983), pp. 279-86; E. Ben Zvi, 'Who Wrote the Speech of Rabshakeh and When?', *JBL* 109 (1990), pp. 79-92; D. Rudman, 'Is the Rabshakeh Also Among the Prophets? A Rhetorical Study of 2 Kings XVIII 17-35', *VT* 50 (2000), pp. 100-110.

[20] Of course, none of this holds true for Isa. 36–37, but this is another book with a different story to tell.

(Jerusalem?[21]) was about to fall just as the Northern Kingdom.[22] At this moment, the text brings forward what, on the surface, seems to be the turning point of the narrative, namely Hezekiah proclaims his 'sin' (compare and contrast with 2 Sam. 24.17),[23] and decides to pay tribute to Sennacherib. The latter accepts the tribute given by Hezekiah, but contrary to all expectations this extreme anti-hero decides to continue the campaign, to exile the people and destroy Jerusalem.[24] In other words, the text creates a literary (and ideological) scenario that leads to clear anticipations and then frustrates them to negatively characterize Sennacherib. To be sure, this is not the worst that the implied author ascribes to Sennacherib. Much of the rest of the account serves now to characterize Sennacherib as a blasphemer who confronted YHWH. This characterization is carried out through (reported) citations from his words, and it is explicitly reinforced by the evaluation placed twice in the mouth of Hezekiah (see 2 Kgs 19.4; 16) and four times in YHWH's (see 2 Kgs 19.6, 22, 23, 28).[25] The extremely negative characterization of Sennacherib stands in sharp contrast to those of Hezekiah, Isaiah and a number of minor Jerusalemite characters, including the people in general (see, for instance, 2 Kgs 18.36).

---

[21] It is worth noting that the language of text already communicates a strong Jerusalem-centered ideology. Jerusalem is not among all the fortified cities of Judah; it stands in a category of its own.
[22] To be sure, the intended readership knew well that this was not to be. They knew well the end of the story before reading it. The purpose of the text was never to inform the literati able to read the Book of Kings that Jerusalem was not destroyed by Sennacherib, but rather to explain why and how lessons relevant to them may be learned. For that purpose the narrative had to be read as such. People could approach and recreate the ideological and theological messages conveyed by the text by closely following the narrative, its plot and the characterization of the main protagonists.
[23] The precise language of the text bears note. Hezekiah is not described as saying חטאתי לך (cf. Judg 10.10). The text as it stands allows a multiplicity of meanings. To be sure, in the narrative Sennacherib is supposed to understand that Hezekiah sinned against him, but the character Hezekiah and above all the intended readers may have understood that the king thought he has sinned against YHWH by rebelling against Sennacherib (cf. 2 Kgs 18.7, 24.20; Jer 52.3 and see Ezek 17.16). This impression is supported by the fact that his actions directly led to the removal of all the silver treasures of the temple and to its physical downgrading (2 Kgs 18.15-16) which are acts that convey dishonor of the temple (contrast with Hag. 2.7-9). It is worth noting that the book of Chronicles, which has a very different version of the events and omits completely any report about this matter, in a subtle way turns the entire issue upside down (2 Chron. 32.23). Alternatively, the reader may think that Hezekiah's confession of 'sin' is not reliable. But if this were the case, then Sennacherib's fault will be lessened. This reading is less likely, see below.
[24] Cf. Josephus, *War* 5.405. It is worth noting that Josephus faced a situation comparable to that of the intended readership of the book of Kings. He had to explain why Jerusalem was saved in Hezekiah's days but not in his, why the correct response to the crisis in his time would have been submission to Rome rather than confrontation whereas Hezekiah was right in standing against Assyria (2 Kgs 18.17–19.37). In this regard, Josephus, in whose writing the destruction of Jerusalem looms large, can be considered close to the intended readers of the book of Kings. See below.
[25] Both of whom are reliable and authoritative characters in the narrative.

Once all these characterizations are well-established, the text moves to describe the (by now anticipated) salvation for Jerusalem, the dramatic destruction of the army of the sinful anti-hero—involving a nocturnal attack carried out by מלאך יהוה—and his shameful death.[26] Further, since the Assyrians are never mentioned again in Kings, the implication is that the yoke of Assyria was removed from Israel forever.[27]

The perspective of the account—and of the book of Kings as a whole as well as the mentioned collection of historical books—is clearly Judah- and Jerusalem-centered, and to be sure, it is YHWH-centric. It also communicates support for centralization, Hezekiah's reform, for stressing the futility of relying on mighty worldly powers (e.g. Egypt) rather than YHWH, and, for other central biblical messages.[28]

The account does exist within the book of Kings. The events that it creates are part and parcel of the world created by the book of Kings. Thus particular contextual meanings deserve much attention. The introduction to the report on this campaign (i.e. the account in 2 Kgs 18.9-12) serves, on the surface, to compare and contrast the fate of the Northern Kingdom and Judah. But, as with similar references to the Northern Kingdom in the context of either destruction or threatened destruction against Judah in other works in the Hebrew Bible (e.g. Mic. 1), the goal is to sharpen the focus on the ensuing description of the fate of Judah in the text, and—from the postmonarchic perspective of the readership of the book of Kings—the actual destruction of Jerusalem and the underlying reasons that led to it.[29]

From the perspective of this postmonarchic readership, the report about the Assyrian campaign against Judah and Jerusalem could not have been read but in a way that was strongly informed by their knowledge of the outcome of the Babylonian campaign against Judah and Jerusalem in the days of Zedekiah.[30] In fact, it is highly plausible that the obvious contrast between the two campaigns is one of the reasons for the unusually extended coverage of Sennacherib's campaign in Kings. (No military or political crisis of the divided monarchy received so much narrative space in the book, including the story of the fall of Jerusalem.)

This being so, a most salient issue is the acute dissimilarity in the outcomes of these campaigns. To be sure this book provides, directly and indirectly, several explanations for the fall of monarchic Jerusalem. These explanations, which on

---

[26] 2 Kgs 19.35, 37.
[27] This implication influenced some constructions of the past in rabbinic times. See b. Pesahim 119a. It is worth noting that Chronicles contradicts Kings at this point.
[28] I discussed some of these issues in Ben Zvi, 'Who Wrote the Speech'.
[29] The destruction of monarchic Judah and of Jerusalem looms heavily on the book of Kings as a whole, and on its intended readership.
[30] Cf. Seitz, 'Account A'.

the surface may contradict each other, in fact inform each other and contribute to the creation of a more sophisticated multivocal approach to this ideologically central issue.[31]

The account of Sennacherib's campaign in Kings contributes to this set of ideological responses, among others, by explicitly pointing to the difference between the situation in Hezekiah's days and that in Zedekiah's. According to the book, the Jerusalemites are pious in the former but not the latter period. But piety alone does not cover all the differences between the two cases.

From the perspective of the mentioned readers, it is obvious that Zedekiah should not have rebelled against the Babylonian king in the first place, and once he has rebelled, he should have tried to come to terms with the Babylonian king, just as Jehoiachin did (2 Kgs 24.12).[32] On the surface, the same holds true for Hezekiah.[33] He did rebel, but here is the first pointed difference, as a good king, and unlike Zedekiah, he was willing to submit, and pay even a very high tribute to the foreign king when the fate of Jerusalem was at stake, and he actually

---

[31] If all the difference had been that Hezekiah lived before Manasseh (cf. 2 Kgs 24.3) there would be no need for the expanded narrative about Sennacherib nor the description of the sins of Northern Israel in 2 Kgs 17. If Jerusalem was saved because YHWH will never let YHWH's city to fall into the hands of its enemies, as a non-contingent understanding of 2 Kgs 19.34 may suggest, then there is a priori no explanation for the destruction of Jerusalem. Clearly such a reading is falsified in the context of the book of Kings.

The presence of networks of positions on some ideologically (or theologically) significant matter in which each position interacts and intermingles with others, and all shed light on each other and as a whole provide and reflect a more comprehensive and balanced response is clearly attested in other books (e.g. Micah, Chronicles, Jonah). I wrote on these issues elsewhere. See, for instance, E. Ben Zvi, *Micah* (FOTL XXIB, Grand Rapids, MI: Eerdmans, 2000), passim; *idem*, 'A Sense of Proportion: An Aspect of the Theology of the Chronicler', *SJOT* 9 (1995), pp. 37-51.

[32] Of course, they were well aware of the consequences of that rebellion, but see also Jer. 38.17-23; Ezek. 17.11-21. One may also compare the ending of the story of Jehoiachin (2 Kgs 25.27-30) and that of Zedekiah in the light of the (perceived and actual) fact that Jerusalem was saved by Jehoiachin's surrender (cf. Jer. 38.17-23) and destroyed by Zedekiah's defiance.

It is true that the book of Kings characterizes negatively those who willingly submit to a foreign power (see N. Na'aman, 'The Deuteronomist and Voluntary Servitude to Foreign Powers', *JSOT* 65 [1995], pp. 37-53), but from this observation it does not follow at all that the book characterizes positively those who rebelled against a suzerain king.

[33] To be sure, according to Kings, when Sennacherib decided to continue his campaign and mock YHWH, then Hezekiah was right to stand firm against the Assyrian king, but his actions at that point do not necessarily express retroactive approval for his decision to rebel against Assyria in the first place, nor an evaluation that he was right to rebel before he knew the actual goals and character of Sennacherib.

(One may argue that, because of its context, the reference in 2 Kgs 18.7 is positive, although it is not necessarily the case. In any event, the note stands within a general summary of his reign and it performs a double duty. On the one hand, as an evaluative note in a general summary it looks at the entire enterprise from a holistic perspective that was influenced by 'the end of the story'. On the other hand, it provides the reader with information needed to understand the reasons for Sennacherib's arrival.)

did so.³⁴ However, Hezekiah's actions did not produce the expected result, because Sennacherib was not any other king, not even Nebuchadnezzar. Hezekiah states, 'Withdraw from me, whatever you impose on me I will bear'. Sennacherib makes clear what it is he wants, and Hezekiah pays. Despite the fact that Sennacherib took the large tribute (2 Kgs 18.14-15), he still continued to attack Jerusalem—unlike the Babylonian king, or any other king, in Kings, for that matter. The reason for this unexpected behavior according to the text is that Sennacherib's real target is not Hezekiah—nor the tribute he may pay—but YHWH, whom he mocks.³⁵ The lengthy account in 2 Kings 18–19 strongly communicates that Nebuchadnezzar, certainly not a beloved character in the book, was still far from being Sennacherib. The 'demonization' of Sennacherib is *not* a peripheral element in the account of the Assyrian campaign against Judah in Kings, rather it strongly contributes to an understanding of the difference between the events in Hezekiah's and Zedekiah's days, and as such contributes to an understanding of the destruction of Jerusalem.³⁶

In addition, the account contributes to the understanding of the dissimilarity between the two events from a second perspective. It stresses and elaborates at some length the (proper) relation between a true prophet and a king in monarchic Judah. The contrast between the relation between Hezekiah and Isaiah, on the one hand, and that between Jehoiakim/Zedekiah and Jeremiah is obvious. Significantly, just as the 'demonization' of Sennacherib is allocated substantial narrative space in the account in Kings, so is the prophet–king interaction.

Survey of Evidence: The Account in Chronicles

The account of Sennacherib's campaign against Judah in the book of Chronicles (2 Chron. 32.1-23) is dependent on the one in Kings. To some extent it is a streamlined version of the latter. Minor characters are erased and so are even main

---

34. Of course, it would have been better if he had not rebelled at all. Neither of the cities would have been destroyed nor the tribute taken from temple and palace, which is not considered a positive result. But Hezekiah's rebellion was already a given. What was left open was how to deal/describe Hezekiah and his rebellion.
35. On this matter see also D. Rudman, 'Is the Rabshakeh Also Among the Prophets?'.
36. Nebuchadnezzar is not 'demonized' in Kings. He is, however, in later literature. Sennacherib, however, was very negatively characterized particularly in Babylonian circles because of his destruction of Babylon, a sacrilege. See Nabonidus' stela, *ANET* 309a; and the implicit, but strong negative characterization in Chronicle 1, iii l. 28 (see A.K. Grayson, *Assyrian and Babylonian Chronicles* [Locust Valley, NY: J.J. Augustin, 1975], pp. 81, 240). It bears note that unlike other cases involving Assyrian kings (e.g. Sargon), the biblical rendition of the name Sennacherib seems to be influenced by Babylonian—rather than Assyrian—phonology. See A.R. Millard, 'Assyrian Royal Names in Biblical Hebrew', *JSS* 21 (1976), pp. 1-14.

It is worth noting that the same double argument that the foreign king is not Sennacherib-like and that the Jerusalemites are not pious is used by Josephus in *War* 5.404-8. On Josephus, see below.

narrative detours.[37] While doing so, the (implied) author of Chronicles shows a high degree of reading competence, if by this one means a reading position close to that of the intended reader. This author does not miss the strong message in support of the centralization of the cult, nor the main issue that Sennacherib's speech brought up, namely his mocking of Yhwh. The basic plot of both stories is also similar, namely Sennacherib comes, commits a sacrilege with his derisive comments about Yhwh, and is miraculously defeated.

All this said, the account in Chronicles is not, and cannot be considered an abbreviated and simplified version of that in Kings. It is a different account, and it stands on its own. Although as a whole it is much shorter than its source in Kings, it expands on certain issues and raises others that are not mentioned at all. It is set in an ideological and literary context that is unlike that of its predecessor, and serves different ideological and rhetorical purposes.

To begin with, the account is not preceded by the report of the fall of the Northern Kingdom, but by an unusually extended description of Hezekiah's pious deeds (2 Chron. 29–31). Even the language of the text strongly suggests to the (intended) readership that they should read this description and the campaign as two associated events.[38] In fact, the account of the campaign of Sennacherib is only a subunit of the general account of Hezekiah in Chronicles (2 Chron. 29–32). In fact, it is not even the most elaborated of the subunits that together constitute this account.

A closer reading of the report of the campaign shows a number of differences between Chronicles and Kings. For instance, in Chronicles there was a siege of Jerusalem (2 Chron. 32.10), and the number of casualties in the Assyrian army goes unmentioned.[39] More importantly, there is no reference to Hezekiah's revolt, no reason is given or suggested for Sennacherib's invasion: Hezekiah never rebelled,[40] nor are his cities conquered (see 2 Chron. 32.1), nor is there any reference to his submission to Assyria, and his 'sin' is nowhere mentioned.[41] As a result

---

[37] See H.J. Tertel, *Text and Transmission. An Empirical Model for the Literary Development of Old Testament Narratives* (Berlin: W. de Gruyter, 1994), pp. 156-71.

[38] One may notice that the campaign is not dated to the fourteenth year of Hezekiah but 'after these things and these acts of faithfulness' (2 Chron. 32.1) which explicitly link this unit to the preceding, and see the language of 2 Chron. 31.20. On this matter see, for instance, S. Japhet, *I and II Chronicles. A Commentary* (OTL, Louisville, KY: Westminster/John Knox Press, 1993), pp. 980-81.

[39] The former attempts to strengthen the sense of peril for Jerusalem, which is diminished by the lack of reference to the conquered cities and by the certitude about the character of the king expressed in Chronicles. The latter may be due to a sense that the great miracle mentioned there is diminished by a reference to 185,000 people (2 Kgs 19.35). Chronicles prefers 'all mighty warriors, and commanders and officers' (2 Chron. 32.21).

[40] This absence of a report about Hezekiah's revolt may suggest that the Chronicler too was troubled about this characterization of Hezekiah.

[41] The image of Hezekiah as a rebel is problematic for Kings—see above. Significantly, it disappears completely in Chronicles—a text in which Hezekiah is lionized. It is problematic again in Josephus (see below). Most likely at least some of the reasons for this tendency are related to the

the ideological and literary links that bind this unit in Kings to the report about the fate of the Northern Kingdom are fully removed.[42] Moreover, some significant aspects of the comparability between the events in Hezekiah's and Zedekiah's days are either minimized or removed altogether.

Sennacherib remains a strongly negative character, but whereas the narrative space allocated to his characterization is much larger in 2 Kings than in Chronicles, the opposite holds true for the *positive* characterization of Hezekiah. Hezekiah is characterized as the best king of Judah since Solomon. His characterization takes most of the literary space not only in 2 Chron. 29–32 as a whole, but also in 2 Chron. 32.1-23. Hezekiah is described as trusting in YHWH, busy organizing the defense of Jerusalem, encouraging people, giving excellent theological speeches, serving in this capacity as an *ad hoc* prophet and working together with Isaiah.[43] In other words, Hezekiah is doing what an ideal Chronicler's king[44] would have done in such circumstances. Significantly, the narrative space allocated to the interaction between prophet and king in Kings is removed, since the distance between the two is minimized (see 2 Chron. 32.20; and note also the quasi-prophetic speech of Hezekiah in 32.7-8; cf. 2 Chron. 15.1-7). As a result, the relation between this unit and the Zedekiah/Jehoiakim-Jeremiah story loses salience.

Hezekiah is not only, or even mainly, a positive counterpart to either Sennacherib or to Zedekiah but rather a peerless example. The choice of words at the beginning of the account not only suggests a comparison with Josiah—the best king of the divided monarchy according to Kings—but also Hezekiah's superiority (see 2 Chron. 32.1 and cf. 35.20).[45] The extended description of Hezekiah's Passover in Chronicles (not present in Kings) is consistent with this tendency (and cf. with the extent of the 'coverage' of Josiah's Passover in Chronicles; also cf. 2 Kgs 23.22 with 2 Chron. 35.18).[46]

---

social and political circumstances at the time of the writing and first reception of these historiographical works. It is worth noting that whereas Hezekiah does not rebel, Zedekiah does in Chronicles (see 2 Chron. 32.13).

[42] This is consistent with the ideology of the Chronicler on this matter. Note the omission of a parallel account to 2 Kgs 17 in Chronicles.

[43] Y. Amit, 'The Role of Prophecy and the Prophets in the Teaching of Chronicles', *Beth Mikra* 28 (1982/83), pp. 113-33 (117, 121-22) (in Hebrew).

[44] By Chronicler, I mean here and elsewhere in this paper, the implied author of the book of Chronicles.

[45] Cf. I. Kalimi, *The Book of Chronicles. Historical Writing and Literary Devices* (Jerusalem: Mosad Bialik, 2000), pp. 28, 50 (in Hebrew).

[46] All in all this is the beginning of a tendency to lionize Hezekiah that leads eventually to the traditions reflected in b. Sanh. 94a. One has to take into account also that the characterization of Hezekiah in Chronicles is strongly associated through opposition with that of Ahaz. See P.R. Ackroyd, 'The Biblical Interpretation of the Reigns of Ahaz and Zedekiah', in W.B. Barrick and J.R. Spencer (eds.), *In the Shelter of Elyon. Essays on Ancient Palestinian Life and Literature in Honor of G.W. Ahlström* (JSOTSup, 31; Sheffield: JSOT Press, 1984), pp. 247-59.

One may attempt to reconstruct the thought of the Chronicler at this point. Since YHWH defeated the Assyrians in the days of Hezekiah according to the world of knowledge shared by authorship and primary readership, the Chronicler most likely assumed that such a great event must have been associated with Hezekiah's approach to YHWH.[47] The greater the deliverance, and this was a great deliverance, the greater the piety of Hezekiah.

But the greater the piety of Hezekiah, the less suitable he is for a meaningful comparison with Zedekiah. His account may easily evoke now meaningful comparisons between him and Solomon[48] or Josiah, but not with Zedekiah or Jehoiakim. Moreover, the greater his figure is, the more the account of his actions (2 Chron. 29–32) as a whole may serve to communicate the Chronicler's understanding of the role of a worthy king in monarchic Judah to the readership of the book.

As a final comment, in Kings the account of Sennacherib's campaign serves several rhetorical purposes. One of the most important of them is to contribute to its readership's understanding of the fall of Jerusalem. But explanations of that particular event are less important in Chronicles. This book focuses less on the (traumatic) experience of the temporary fall of Jerusalem and, in any case looks (a) for general explanatory rules of the divine economy and (b) beyond the destruction of 586 BCE and the 'exile'.[49]

Survey of Evidence: Josephus

For the purpose of this paper, a few words about Josephus's construction of Sennacherib's campaign will suffice. His main sources were biblical. The reference to Berossus and Herodotus in *Ant.* 10.18-23 serve in the main to authenticate his reconstruction of the events to the intended readership of *Antiquities*. Except for the reference to Herodotus the plot follows the basic biblical story and particularly its Kings' version.[50]

Josephus's rhetorical situation was closer to that of the readership (and authorship) of Kings than Chronicles. His focus was, however, not on the Babylonian destruction of Jerusalem, but rather the Roman. As mentioned above, within his opus in general but particularly and explicitly in *War*, his dealing with Sennacherib's campaign allows him to dwell on why Jerusalem was saved in Hezekiah's days but not in his. Why was the correct response to the crisis in his time submission to Rome rather than confrontation, whereas Hezekiah was right to stand against Assyria? Following the lead of Kings, Josephus stresses the difference between the Romans (who stand now instead of the Babylonians of Kings) and the

---

[47] This assumption is fully consistent with the theology/ideology expressed in the book of Chronicles.
[48] See H.G.M. Williamson, *Israel in the Books of Chronicles* (Cambridge: Cambridge University Press, 1977), pp. 119-25.
[49] Cf. J. Dyck, *The Theocratic Ideology of the Chronicler* (Leiden: E.J. Brill, 1998), esp. pp. 80-81.
[50] The citation from Berossus serves to communicate the report in 2 Kgs 19.35-37.

Assyrians.[51] Although a positive characterization of Hezekiah is pre-shaped by the traditions he inherited, he is also worried about being a rebel and subtly attempts to tarnish somewhat Hezekiah's image.[52]

Malleability, Meaning/Significance, Narratives, and Ideological Constraints

The preceding considerations are positive proof that ancient constructions of Sennacherib's campaign against Judah were highly malleable. In other words, ancient writers could mould their account of the campaign to serve particular theological, ideological, literary and rhetorical purposes, as required by their own situation.

It should be stressed that their actions should not be constructed as hypocritical or cynical, that is the work of a group of literati who knowingly *lied* to helpless readers to pursue their own good and the good of those who supported them. For ideology to be successful—and those represented in the neo-Assyrian account, and in Kings' and Chronicles' ideologies were successful—not only the 'consumers' of the ideology but also those constructing and propagating it should be believers.[53] In fact, it is much better to place the entire issue *not* under heuristic questions such as who deviated from the truth, when and why, but rather to view it in terms of the particular significance of certain historical events for particular groups.[54]

The significance of an historical event—be it ancient or modern—can be discerned only in terms of a particular historical narrative.[55] This significance is deeply dependent on expectations or consequences associated with the event. To use examples of recent events, one may think of 'the meaning' of disparate events such as the fall of the Berlin Wall, the election of Franklin D. Roosevelt or Ronald Reagan, the Oslo agreements between Israel and the PLO, the use of an atomic bomb on Hiroshima, or WWI; or one may think of earlier historical events such as the one in 1492 CE referred to as either 'the discovery of America' or 'the First Encounter'. Whatever significance a historian—or any person for

---

[51] See Josephus, *War* 5.404-8; *Ant*. 10.1-23. See also *War* 5.386-88.
[52] See L.H. Feldman, 'Josephus's Portrait of Hezekiah', *JBL* 111 (1992), pp. 597-610.
[53] Cf. M. Liverani, 'The Ideology of the Assyrian Empire', in Mogens Trolle Larsen (ed.), *Power and Propaganda. A Symposium on Ancient Empires* (Mesopotamia, 7; Copenhagen: Akademisk Forlag, 1979), pp. 297-317 (299).
[54] To be sure there was much inventiveness and literary creativity among the literati—a group that includes ancient historians—but the outcome of their works was pre-shaped to some degree by their understanding of the particular significance of the event they are writing (and reading) about. This holds true whether they were aware or unaware that such is the case. On creativity and particularly creative imitation in the Hebrew Bible, see J. Van Seters, 'Creative Imitation in the Hebrew Bible', *SR* 29 (2000), pp. 395-409.
[55] 'Narrative' is here understood in a broad sense.

that matter—would ascribe to these events depends on the set of consequences (and at times expectations) that such a historian associates with them. Needless to say, these sets reflect (and indirectly communicate) information about events, or construction of events later—and at times much later—than the event being discussed. Thus these sets and the significance ascribed to events in the past are influenced by ideological frames and considerations.[56]

This being so, differences of viewpoints on consequences (and at times, expectations) lead to different meanings ascribed to events, and to different narratives of them. For instance, an account of the '*third* campaign' already connotes and reflects a viewpoint that construes this campaign as one in a set of successive successful campaigns, and carries an expectation of further victorious campaigns against any possible group that may defy the king and the gods.[57]

Since the meaning of the event is expressed by means of an historical narrative, and both are dependent on the discourse and potential repertoire of the writers and readers ('producers' and 'consumers') of this literature, it is only to be expected that the narrative construction of the account will be strongly influenced by the significance ascribed to the event. The present discussion has shown that differences in the narratives that result from these considerations affect not only 'the lesson to be learned' but also involve very basic issues such as how the event came about and how it ended, as well as narrative details. These conclusions hold true for Kings and the Annals and their inversions of the story. They also hold true even when a clear line of dependence and of pre-shaping traditions links separate works (see Kings, Chronicles and Josephus).

---

[56] This type of issues has been discussed, in one way or another, numerous times in articles on *History and Theory*. See, for instance, L. Hölscher, 'The New Annalistic: A Sketch of a Theory of History', *History and Theory* 36 (1997), pp. 317-35; R. Martin, 'Progress in Historical Studies'. To be sure, from the mentioned observations it certainly does *not* follow that 'anything goes'. See, for instance, the mentioned bibliography and the results of the present examination of this case study.

[57] The only scenario that would allow a rejection of that expectation is one in which there will be no 'sinners' ever, so there will be no need for the heroic military actions of the king, but this was not a likely scenario, either historically nor ideologically. The king is expected to demonstrate his heroism, his outstanding prowess as a warrior. See B. Oded, *War, Peace and Empire. Justification for War in Assyrian Royal Inscriptions* (Wiesbaden: Dr Ludwig Reichert Verlag, 1992), pp. 145-62. Moreover, there is the ideological construction that the king is supposed to enlarge the borders of Assyria. As expected, this construction created some difficulties to the authors of Sennacherib's inscriptions, because one of their constraints was that he—unlike his predecessors and successors—did not expand the territory of Assyria, i.e., there was tension between the expected characterization of the king and facts that were agreed upon by the society within which these texts were composed and displayed. On these ideological characterizations of the king and on how Sennacherib's scribes actually coped with this issue, see H. Tadmor, 'World Dominion: The Expansion Horizon of the Assyrian Empire', in L. Martino, S. de Martino, F.M. Fales and G.B. Lanfranchi (eds.), *Landscapes. Territories, Frontiers and Horizons in the Ancient Near East* (Part I, History of the Ancient Near East/Monographs-III/1, Padova: Sargon srl, 1999), pp. 54-62. On the general issue of constraints on (historical) writing due to facts agreed upon by the producers and consumers of texts, see discussion below.

One final observation, the mentioned malleability is strongly contingent on the general discourse of the producers and intended consumers of these historical narratives. Malleability here does not mean that 'everything goes', or that inner demands of the world of the narrative are the only factors to be taken into account. There is a social reality 'out there' in the world of the producers and consumers that includes their respective ideologies, expectations, ranges of potentially acceptable meanings and significances, as well as worlds of knowledge. The following section will approach the issue of the potential extent of malleability from a somewhat different perspective.

Possible Extent of Malleability: Some Considerations Based on Historical Events as Reconstructed Today and Ideological Quests for Meaning/Significance

The accounts differ not only among themselves, but also from what 'most likely happened' according to contemporaneous, historical-critical analysis. This is true also of the two that were the closest to the events, among those studied here.

There is no doubt from a historical-critical approach that Sennacherib's campaign to the West in 701 BCE was a great strategic success. First, without having to expend the enormous resources that would have been required to conquer Tyre, Sennacherib brought the entire Phoenician coastland under his control and began a process that led to the steady decline of Tyre and its replacement as the main city of the area by Sidon.[58] The Philistines were under clear control after the campaign and did not rebel again. The southern commercial routes remained open to Assyria, and Ekron developed into a major industrial/commercial city. Judah, the ringleader of the rebellion, was so weakened that it became a 'faithful' vassal to the end of the Assyrian dominion and was never again to be any kind of threat to the imperial suzerain. As for the Egyptians, they did not send armies to the area until much later, under very different circumstances. In fact, Sennacherib created a new and stable regional balance of power that allowed Assyria to control the area (except Phoenicia) successfully for more than a century—in fact, till the downfall of Assyria—with minimal costs.[59]

---

[58] See J. Elayi, 'Les relations entre les cites phéniciennes et l'empire assyrien sous le règne de Sennachérib', *Semitica* 35 (1985), pp. 19-26. One may notice that—all things equal—a regional center of power around Sidon (as opposed to Tyre) was strategically preferable from an Assyrian perspective. It was far easier to subdue Sidon—if the need arose—than to subdue Tyre.

[59] It is noteworthy that this successful combination of strategic achievements was the result of one campaign and did not require significant direct administrative involvement on Assyria's part, but rather an effective use of local leaders. This is consistent with Sennacherib's policy, not to annex territories.

It is obvious that this description of the events is substantially different from the one in Kings and later writings in that tradition, but it is also different from the story in the Assyrian annals too. Strategic wisdom and careful use of (large, but always limited) military resources was not something to be glorified in Assyrian royal ideology. The latter emphasized the king as a successful military leader, as a mighty hero and builder. So, for instance, although one may conclude that Sennacherib's decision not to invest his military and logistic resources in an attack on Tyre itself or its Cypriot territories, and consequently to allow Luli to remain as its king was correct in strategic terms, the annals do not report about it. In the annalistic narrative, Luli is referred to as the king of Sidon—rather than Tyre[60]—so he can be replaced with a 'proper king'.[61] Further, the strategically irrelevant fact that Luli died a few years after the campaign becomes an important ideological fact in later versions of the annalistic narrative/s of Sennacherib's campaign to Phoenicia, because it brings a superior (ideological) closure to the

---

For a similar historical reconstruction and for an evaluation of Sennacherib's campaign to the West as an overwhelming success, see, among others, N. Na'aman, 'Hezekiah and the Kings of Assyria'; *idem*, 'Forced Participation in Alliances in the Course of the Assyrian Campaigns to the West', in M. Cogan and I. Eph'al (eds.), *Ah, Assyria! Studies in Assyrian History and Ancient Near Eastern Historiography Presented to Hayim Tadmor* (ScrH, 33; Jerusalem: Magnes Press, 1991), pp. 80-98 (94-97).

To be sure, it might be argued from some corners that this reconstruction is nothing more than another 'narrative' created and adopted by a certain group/s of scholars at a particular time, for their own reasons, and according to their own perspectives and expectations, and that this being the case, their narrative is not *essentially* different from, for instance, the account in Kings, or paraphrases of it. But there is a difference between this, or substantially similar reconstructions of the events on the one hand, and noncritical—by present historiographical standards—reconstructions on the other. See n. 5.

[60] N. Na'aman who maintains that Luli was indeed the king of Sidon, and not the king of Tyre, has recently questioned the consensus on this matter. See N. Na'aman, 'Sargon II and the Rebellion of the Cypriote Kings against Shilta of Tyre', *Or* 67 (1998), pp. 239-47 (245-47). But a number of considerations suggest that the consensus position is still preferable. Thus, for instance, Luli is explicitly associated with Tyre in the inscriptions in Bulls 2, 3 and 4 that mention that he fled to Cyprus—which was Tyrian territory; this is the first reference to Cyprus in Assyrian material since the days of Sargon; see Gallagher, *Sennacherib's Campaign*, p. 99). Moreover, Tyre was the regional center of power, rather than Sidon at the time of the campaign. Although one may question the tactical wisdom of Luli's decision to move from Tyre to his Cypriot territories in 701 BCE, good reasons for that move may be envisioned too, particularly given Tyre's control of the sea, the importance of supplies, and the previous rebellion of Cypriote kings against Tyre, a few years earlier, when Shilta reigned over Tyre. On these matters, see Elayi, 'Les relations', and Gallagher, *Sennacherib's Campaign*, pp. 91-104. On Bulls 2, 3, 4 (T 26, 27, 29) see Frahm, *Einleitung*, pp. 115-18.

[61] This observation raises already an interesting issue regarding factual constraints on the narrative. Luli could be, and was characterized as the king of Sidon since his dominion included the city, but his replacement, Tuba'lu could not and was not characterized as king of Tyre because the city was not under his control. See below.

story of Luli.⁶² Similarly, although the decision to leave Hezekiah on the throne of a substantially weakened Judah and not to conquer Jerusalem was proven to serve well Assyrian interests, the narrative had to allocate a relatively substantial space to the defeat of Hezekiah,⁶³ not only because of his political importance in the anti-Assyrian coalition, but also to compensate for the lack of reference to the conquest of Jerusalem and for his being left sitting on his throne.⁶⁴ This problem was developed by the logic of the narrative and the ideological construction of the character of the king, as the successful, powerful military leader. The text implies a tripartite division of the Judahite cities: (a) main cities (and they were numbered, 46) (b) minor (and they go unnumbered) cities that surround the main cities, and (c) a capital city. Since Sennacherib is described as one who conquered the first two categories of cities, the text has to avoid any potential implication that the lack of completion of the series might suggest that he was unable to conquer the capital city and, accordingly, tarnish his characterization.

---

⁶² He probably died only a few years after 700 BCE. See Gallagher, *Sennacherib's Campaign*, pp. 93-96; Elayi, 'Les relations', pp. 22-23. References to his death appear in T10 (697 BCE; Frahm, *Einleitung*, p. 66); T12 (BM 103.000; 694 BCE; Frahm, *Einleitung*, pp. 87-89), the inscriptions in Bulls 2, 3 and 4 (694 BCE), and later versions of the annals (e.g. OIP). A comparable reference to the (late) death of a king within a narrative that suggests immediacy and some correlation between sinful behavior and death occurs in 2 Kgs 19.37. The villain there is, however, Sennacherib.

(It seems that by 694 BCE some kind of compromise between Assyria and Tyre—including the Cypriot territories—was worked out. Such arrangement would have included vassal status for Tyre.)

These observations imply again some factual constraints on the narrative. It seems that Luli could not be described as dead in the annalistic narratives until he actually was. On this matter, see below. This being so, the lack of reference to Hezekiah's death in this literature may suggest that he was alive by the time it was composed.

⁶³ This claim has to be set also in some general proportion. Despite the fact that within the ideological constrains of the annals, the submission of Hezekiah was likely the greatest deed Sennacherib could boast in the Western front, the account itself is relatively minor in terms of the full version of the annals.

Yet, the conquest of Lachish still stood as a significant symbol of Assyria's power—and of its rhetoric of terror at Sennacherib's palace, in a room that had some architectural prominence, room XXXVI. It bears notice that the 'story' told by the reliefs there is clearly not identical with that of the annalistic sources (where Lachish is not even mentioned), and that the latter could not have been the source for the reliefs, nor do these sources and the reliefs share—in the main—a common audience. Reliefs that may be associated with the third campaign were likely present in other rooms in the palace (e.g. I, X, XII, XXIV). On these matters, see J.M. Russell, *Sennacherib's Palace without Rival at Nineveh* (Chicago: University of Chicago Press, 1991), pp. 28-31, 64, 160-64, 200-209, 245-57, and passim; D. Ussishkin, *The Conquest of Lachish by Sennacherib* (Tel Aviv: The Institute of Archaeology, 1982), pp. 59-126.

⁶⁴ Cf. H. Tadmor, 'Sennacherib's Campaign', esp. p. 77; J.M. Russell, *Sennacherib's Palace*, p. 256. On the tripartite division, here and in other texts, see M. de Odorico, *The Use of Numbers and Quantifications in the Assyrian Royal Inscriptions* (SAAS III; Helsinki: The Neo-Assyrian Text Corpus Project, 1995), p. 15.

Thus, the differences that do exist between the account and the events as reconstructed today by critical historians involve much more than some form of frame that conveys meaning to the events themselves. It directly affects and shapes details in the narrative, such as the basic material concerning the Luli-Tyre episode, the number of Judahite exiles, which is obviously an exaggeration,[65] the ideological characterization of Hezekiah, and how much narrative space will be allocated to each episode. (One may also note that the narrative omits any reference to events such as the likely takeover [conquest?] of Gaza by the enemies of Assyria.[66])

There is nothing surprising about these conclusions. A plethora of examples of military, political and social crises in recent years show that very soon after the events—or even at the time they actually occur—clearly different descriptions of them do arise. These descriptions vary according to the expectations, rhetorical and ideological perspectives and needs of the opposing sides. They describe and construe (or wish to others to construe) the events and their consequences in a way that reflects their 'true' significance or meaning, from their own viewpoint. The Gulf War, numerous events and clashes in the Palestinian–Israeli conflict, and even the case of one Cuban child rescued from the sea in the USA (Elian Gonzalez) to mention only a few examples, provide positive proof that such is the case.

To be sure, these considerations strongly undermine the principle that the closer to the events, the higher the historical accuracy of a document. Each document reflects the worldview, expectation and goals of those who write them and those for whom they are intended, if the writer is proficient. Its level of historical accuracy has to be tested rather than privileged 'by default'.[67] Although close-to-the-event reports tend to show more details, these do not necessarily contribute to the larger historical picture and may well serve rhetorical needs for verisimilitude than 'factual' observations. Needless to say, this conclusion cannot be construed in any way or manner as a veiled preference for later documents.[68]

---

[65] The number of Judahite exiles—i.e. 200,150—is impossible. On the use of this 'very high+exact' number see M. de Odorico, *Use of Numbers and Quantifications*, pp. 114-16 and 171-74. These numbers 'represent the attempt to associate the sense of emphasis given by the "high round number"…with the (appearance) of truthfulness given by their "exact" form' (p. 172).

[66] The Egyptian army reached as far north as Eltekeh, so it is unlikely that Gaza remained a pro-Assyrian island in the area till the final victory of Sennacherib. In addition, there is also the strong tendency towards force participation in regional alliances. Significantly, there is no reference to the king of Gaza among the faithful kings of the Amurru who 'willingly' brought their tribute to Sennacherib (Rassam, pp. 36-38; OIP, II, 50-60). A similar event, the takeover of Ekron is mentioned, however, but within a context that glorifies the Assyrian king as the restorer of the proper order and as the one who overwhelmed Hezekiah, the agent of 'chaos'.

[67] One may note that whereas Kings implies that the Assyrian domination came to an end with Sennacherib's defeat, Chronicles suggests that this is not the case, as the story of Manasseh demonstrates. In this particular instance, Chronicles' picture is more consistent with our knowledge of the period than the one offered in Kings.

[68] At times, some 'historical perspective' is gained and some telescoping might be useful, but there are numerous examples that show how reports in later narratives may share little with the actual events.

All this said, it is worth noting that the account of the third campaign does not claim that Sennacherib conquered Jerusalem, or that he deposed Hezekiah, or that Luli—or the city of Tyre for that matter—was captured, or that Tub'alu was made king of Tyre, or that the Hezekiah—rather than Luli—passed away, implicitly because of his sins, nor does the account contain any reports of Luli's death prior to the event itself. In other words, despite the fact that such claims would have been supportive of the ideology and genre of the report, they were not made. There seems to be a grammar of writing that does not allow unrestrained creativity with some matters.[69] These considerations lead us directly to the discussion of limits to malleability.

Limits to Malleability: Questions of Representation and Historical Referents

The preceding considerations have also hinted at some limitations imposed on these narratives, of some pre-shaped elements that condition the narratives. These pre-shaped elements are of a variety of kinds. The ideological and literary constraints discussed above certainly constrain and control the potential malleability of the narrative.

There is a second type of constraints: What the authorship/intended readership group may consider acceptable in a historiographical work. To be sure, the standard by which something is or is not considered to be acceptable cannot be a feature of the narrative itself. It is a standard by which different historical narratives created in the world of various works are evaluated. As such, it stands outside the world created by any particular book or historical narrative embedded in it. The existence of the standard creates a situation in which certain accounts do pass the test and become plausible narratives from this perspective, whereas others fail and accordingly, become potential but implausible historical narratives. As such they are unlikely to be written, and if they are written at all, the 'consumers' will reject them.

---

[69] To be sure, there is much ideologically-oriented creativity in other matters. Some battles in which the Assyrians, at least, did not achieve complete victory were described as unequivocal successes, e.g. Der, Halulei; see A.K. Grayson, 'Problematic Battles in Mesopotamian History', in H.G. Güttersbock and Th. Jacobsen (eds.), *Studies in Honor of Benno Landsberger on his Seventy-Fifth Birthday, April 25, 1965* (Oriental Institute, Assyriological Studies, 16; Chicago: Chicago University Press, 1965), pp. 337-42; A. Laato, Assyrian Propaganda and the Falsification of History in the Royal Inscriptions of Sennacherib', *VT* 45 (1995), pp. 198-226 (199-213). Even if this or that example may be debatable, the fact that no neo-Assyrian king reported a defeat in his annals is positive proof of a strong principle of selection. It is disputable, however, whether the highly loaded, evaluative term 'falsification of history' is appropriate for these and similar cases (e.g. the account of Sennacherib's campaign in Kings and Chronicles).

Given that these narratives shape history, it stands to reason that at least some of these standards are directly related to the question of the plausibility of historical representation. In other words, on whether the narrative's description/ construction of an event, as a whole, may be considered a plausible representation of what the authorship and intended readership of the work assumed is being represented, that is, the historical event as they construe it.[70]

This construction of the historical event may be based directly or indirectly on some witnesses of the event, or on narratives that are directly related to these witnesses, or on accepted narratives that may be quite remote from the event itself and are only vaguely related to any direct or indirect witness. Thus, for instance, it is clear that the Assyrian narrative of the third campaign was written close to the events—it existed in 700 BCE—and it is reasonable to assume that the mentioned standard of representation had to do, at least to some extent, with Assyrian recollections of the events of the campaign.[71] If this is so, then the question is what was required to qualify as plausible by this representation standard? And given the focus of this paper on the extent of malleability, what could the account *not* claim about the campaign against Judah lest it becomes implausible to its readership, from the perspective of this particular standard?[72]

One has to admit that there is no sure answer to these questions. But in light of the considerations advanced above and given that the account was considered plausible by an Assyrian readership that had some knowledge of the historical events, the range of answers to these question seems to consist of a subset of the set created by the overlap between the Assyrian account and the most likely reconstruction of the events. In the case of the campaign against Judah this set includes: (a) the names of the two kings involved in the Assyrian campaign against Judah, and, of course, the existence of such a campaign; (b) some basic elements of the order imposed by Assyria on the area, namely the removal of lands from Judah's domain, the 'transformation' of Hezekiah into a loyal vassal king, the payment of tribute; (c) the destruction of the main cities of Judah along with the lack of conquest of its capital; and (d) the failure of the Egyptian expedition. In all these cases, the world of the narrative points to referents outside this narrative and represents them in what was considered to be a plausible manner.

To be sure, reference to all these elements was not necessary to maintain the general plausibility of a reference to the campaign as a representation of the

---

[70] In other words, the description should correspond to at least some degree with what the authorship and readership think that the historical facts were.
[71] Cf. J.M. Russell, *Sennacherib's Palace*, pp. 28-31.
[72] To be sure, there are other standards too, such as consistency with the accepted ideology, meaning conveyed, genre considerations, and the like. For instance, a reference to the king's defeat would have rendered the account as an implausible representation of the events. On these issues, see above.

historical events, for the Assyrian readership.⁷³ But, significantly, there is no account of this campaign in Assyrian sources in which the names of the kings are changed, nor one in which Jerusalem was conquered, or in which Hezekiah did not become (eventually) a vassal king who submitted to Assyria,⁷⁴ or for that matter one in which Hezekiah passed away, when he was still alive.

These considerations raise an important point: to omit references to the agreed-upon facts of the time is possible, and at times may be desirable for different reasons (e.g. genre, ideological bent, rhetorical needs), but to contradict them openly and maintain plausibility is a much more difficult task. Moreover, this task becomes impossible if the agreed-upon facts that are contradicted by the potential account were considered not peripheral but 'core' facts for the understanding of the historical event (e.g. the name of Hezekiah, his being a Judahite king, etc.)

If a similar analysis is carried out for the account of Sennacherib's campaign in the book of Kings, which is an account much later than the events themselves and much later than the annalistic account, then the set created by the overlap between this account *as a whole*—that is when the full outcome of the campaign is taken into consideration⁷⁵—and the most likely reconstruction of the events includes: (a) the names of the two kings involved in the Assyrian campaign against Judah, and, of course, the existence of such a campaign; (b) the conquest of the main cities of Judah—including Lachish—along with the lack of conquest of Jerusalem; and (c) the murder of Sennacherib.⁷⁶ It is difficult to see the references to the conquest of the main cities of Judah and to the death of Sennacherib as a *sine qua non* component for the plausibility of the representation for the producers and consumers of the book of Kings in its present form. In fact, they seem to be present in the text mainly for narrative purposes. If this is the case then the plausibility of the account—from the perspective of these standards—required only that there was a campaign and that it involved Kings Sennacherib and Hezekiah. One may reach similar conclusions if the accounts in Chronicles and in Josephus are examined in this way.⁷⁷

---

⁷³ See the Nebi Yunus Inscription (Frahm's T 61; Luckenbill's H4), l. 15; Luckenbill, *Annals*, p. 86. The minimal reference there includes the name of the king of Judah, his submission to Sennacherib and the substantial damage that the latter inflicted on Judah.

⁷⁴ To be sure, the latter would also be implausible for ideological reasons, if Hezekiah is left on the throne.

⁷⁵ The narrative reference to Hezekiah's paying tribute does not show a good overlap with the historical reconstruction of the events, because in Kings it did not lead to a stable position of servitude. Similarly, the narrative reference to the Tirhakah does not qualify because it does not directly point to the failure of the Egyptian expedition. In fact, if 2 Kgs 19.9a is to be read in a way informed by 2 Kgs 19.36, then Tirhakah's expedition cannot be considered a failure. The connection between the two verses is, however, debated, see n. 19.

⁷⁶ Perhaps one may add also the presence of Sennacherib at Lachish, but this is somewhat implied in item (b).

⁷⁷ The difference between the account in Kings and the annalistic account may be associated with their temporal distance from the events they are narrating, and with the actual outcome of the events that was at the time of the events more suitable for direct Assyrian than Judahite ideological appropriation.

It must be stressed that this conclusion is true only within the limits of the frame from which it emerges, that is, comparisons between the different account of the event in the mentioned texts and the most likely reconstruction of the events, as agreed by the majority of critical historians of the ancient Near East. But this conclusion shows an inherent and severe limitation: Referents do not have to point to the historical events, but to what the producers and intended consumers of the reports thought happened, in other words, to the system of agreed-upon facts held by a particular social group. For instance, Josephus did not and *could not* have advanced a case for the plausibility of his narrative on the basis of a correspondence between the historical events as known to critical historians today and his representation of them in the narrative. For him, the limitation raised by the demand for plausibility involved the correspondence between his knowledge of the events (i.e. the facts agreed upon by him and his peers) and his narrative. His knowledge of the Assyrian period in Judah was based on Kings and Chronicles. For Josephus (and his intended readership), a plausible representation of the events is one that can be judged favorably by some basic standards set by the accounts in Chronicles and Kings.[78]

Chronicles, as it is well-known, departs from Kings and Samuel on numerous occasions. But the presence of these departures does *not* mean, 'anything goes'. The study of the limitations on malleability that strongly influenced the work of the Chronicler deserves a separate study.[79] It will suffice here to state that its historical plausibility was contingent on the acceptance of a core construction of the past (e.g. David could not have been described as the actual builder of the Temple, since the authorship and readership of the book were well aware that Solomon, and only Solomon, built it—again an issue of main,—or core,—facts agreed upon by the community and the necessity of correspondence).[80] Turning

---

[78] On Josephus and his use of Kings and Chronicles, see I. Kalimi, 'History of Interpretation: The Book of Chronicles in Jewish Tradition. From Daniel to Spinoza', *RB* 105 (1998), pp. 5-51 (17-19).

[79] See my 'Shifting the Gaze: Historiographic Constraints in Chronicles and their Implications', in J.A. Dearman and M.P. Graham (eds.), *The Land that I Will Show You: Essays on the History and Archaeology of the Ancient Near East in Honor of J. Maxwell Miller* (JSOTSup, 343; Sheffield: Sheffield Academic Press, 2001), pp. 38-60. A substantial outline of Israel's story of its past was already fixed, 'canonical' one may say, by the time of the composition of Chronicles. Although there was never a 'true' canonical history (i.e. a single, authoritative version) the authority of the book of Kings—and narratives about the past in other authoritative books—reflected and shaped a kind of communally agreed basic history of the past. This history served to create a sense of (mythical) unity with the past, and contributed to social solidarity and identity in the present.

[80] To put it simply, had the Chronicler claimed that David actually built the temple and not Solomon, the book would not have been accepted by the intended readership. Of course, this fact does not mean that the Chronicler could not shape the story in very particular, and inventive ways. Thus, for instance, David is described as responsible for the planning of the temple and for its construction, for preliminary actions towards its building, and even for aspects of its work when it was built. Yet he cannot actually build it. Since, as it is well-known, Chronicles did not maintain a full correspondence with all facts that could have been agreed upon by the community on the basis

to our particular case, the question is what aspects of this core construction of the past had the Chronicler to abide by in the account of Sennacherib's campaign?

Given the considerations mentioned above, and assuming that the main source of Chronicles is the account in Kings, the range of answers to these questions consists of a subset of the set of claims created by the overlap between the account in Kings and that in Chronicles. The set includes: (a) the names of the two kings involved in the Assyrian campaign against Judah; (b) the salvation of Jerusalem; (c) the piety of Hezekiah; (d) the collaboration between a pious king and the prophet Isaiah; and (e) the blasphemy of Sennacherib and his punishment. To be sure, Kings and Chronicles shape different meanings in their respective accounts and each deal with the issues in the set in (slightly) different ways. But for the narrative in Chronicles to be considered a plausible representation of the events and outcomes of Sennacherib's campaign against Judah, all these basic elements had to be present in some way and be incorporated in the narrative, due to the social reality and world of knowledge within which (and for which) Chronicles was composed

To be sure, the plausibility of the account of the campaign in the book of Kings was also contingent on its acceptance of a traditional reconstruction of the past. It is unlikely that the authors of the present form of the book in the postmonarchic period invented, out of nothing, a full tradition about the miraculous salvation of Jerusalem or the related tradition on Sennacherib's sinfulness, or even the link between prophet and king. It is much more likely that they reflected what was believed by Judahites at the time of the composition of the book to be core elements of a plausible representation of the campaign.

This observation may lead to a move towards the study of hypothetical written sources of the account in Kings and to attempts to analyze their dependence on the degree of plausibility of their own representation of the events within the discourse of their time and social-ideological group, and so on. But a study of hypothetical sources stands beyond the intent of this paper. Still, there is an important point here. The significant lack of correspondence between the historical facts and the facts agreed upon by the social group within which one finds the authorship and first readership of the book of Kings demands an explanation.[81] A process in which the significance or meaning of the event begins to shape the communal understanding of the event, and along with it the facts that are agreed upon by the community, seems to bridge the gap between these two sets of facts. To illustrate, an emphasis on the 'salvation of Jerusalem' possibly led to a construction

---

of Kings, the question is one of a hierarchy of facts. Some facts can be challenged, but others—e.g. that Solomon built the temple—are so central that challenge is impossible. The latter may be considered 'core facts' within the world of the writers and intended and primary readers of the book. These issues stand beyond the scope of this paper and are discussed in the article mentioned in the preceding note.

[81] If this were not the case, then the book would not have been accepted as a plausible representation of the past.

of accepted facts such as the destruction of the Assyrian army, and eventually the implied full independence of Judah from Assyria.

These are a few final considerations. The discussion has shown that narratives as separate as the accounts of the campaign in Kings and in Sennacherib's annals share a few claims: there was a campaign, it involved Hezekiah and Sennacherib, Jerusalem was not conquered—though the main cities of Judah were, Hezekiah remained in power, and there was an Egyptian expedition. In other words, both texts, despite all their differences, point to similar referents, however they may be represented (and evaluated). A referent that belongs to more than one narrative *cannot* exist only in the world of any one of its narratives, and so it has to be present in a world that exists beyond any of them individually.[82] This world is the general discourse—including the world of knowledge—shared by the writers and readers of this type of literature; it certainly includes their own understanding/s of the past, and along with it a set of facts they agree upon. This discourse is an integral part of the social reality within which ancient historical works were written and read.

Both the Chronicler and Josephus lived within their own social reality and accordingly they wrote within the limits created by shared core facts derived from the report of Sennacherib's campaign in Kings. In sum, they were not constrained by the historical facts themselves—or as known to us—but by the facts agreed upon by their respective groups, and the expectations that were raised in these discourses by these particular facts.

But what about Kings and the annalistic traditions? There are very few shared elements and traditions that could have strongly informed both the discourse of the writers and readers of Kings and those of the Assyrian Annals. The authors of the Annals certainly did not have the book of Kings, nor any of the possible sources of this book. It is very unlikely that the authors of Kings—or any of the mentioned sources for that matter—based their account of the campaign on the Annals, or certainly they did not assume that their readers will have any reason to accept the annalistic version of the events as a norm from which deviation is possible but certainly limited. If so, how to explain claims shared by the two accounts? Shared claims between these two independent discursive constructions most likely reflect shared core attributes ascribed to the events themselves as they were perceived or represented by those involved at the time they happened and immediately after. In turn, shared perceptions or representations by diametrically separate groups must point to something that stands beyond or outside their own perceptions or representations, although these perceptions or representations surely point at it. If these perceptions or representations are independent, this 'something' is likely to be what we usually call the historical event.[83]

---

[82] Cf. L. Hölscher, 'New Annalistic', esp. pp. 318-20.
[83] Which, of course, is immediately appropriated and given significance in a way that is consistent with particular discourses, ideologies, worlds of knowledge, expectations and the like.

Summary

The different accounts of Sennacherib's campaign against Judah serve as a good case study for the extent and limitations of malleability in ancient Israelite historiography. The significance of the event as communicated (and shaped) by different accounts varies significantly. This variation in turn strongly influences the accounts since their narratives are the means by which this significance is shaped and communicated, and since there was ample—but not limitless—room for innovation and creation. These significances directly relate to and are contingent on social and ideological expectations, worlds of knowledge—including constructions of the past—and the like. Moreover, they lead to a process in which the sets of facts that are agreed upon about the past may change. The creation of new facts agreed upon by the relevant community/ies leads in turn to future pre-shaped accounts.

There are also limitations on the malleability of the narratives. These limitations are associated with the contingencies mentioned above, but also with the conditions for plausibility of historical representations that exist among different groups. These conditions may depend on an accepted, pre-shaped understanding of the past or on perceptions of historical events. The latter are to some extent pre-shaped directly or indirectly by the historical events,[84] and by whatever facts are agreed by the community/ies within which the authorship and readership of the work were situated. Historical events and historical facts agreed upon by

---

It is to be stressed that the independence of the representations is a *sine qua non* condition. If the representations are not independent they point to a shared discourse or a shared world knowledge. For instance, Manetho and biblical tradition (and later Jewish traditions influenced by the latter; e.g., Jewish-Hellenistic writers, Josephus, etc.) refer to a clash between the ancestors of the Jewish settlers in Judea and Jerusalem and the ('true') Egyptians that took place in Egypt and that led to the exit of the former from Egypt. The presence of the motif in two clearly different discursive worlds points to a shared referent, namely a 'core fact' agreed upon by both discursive communities, namely that there was such a clash. Needless to say, this 'core fact' is given very different significance in these two cases and is embedded in different general metanarratives. This 'core fact' does go back to an historical event, but to a point in which constructions of the past share a particular element. One cannot learn from the dual attestation of this 'core fact' that it points to an historical exodus from Egypt, because either Manetho or the sources behind Manetho's knowledge of this particular clash are not totally independent from biblical or related traditions. Manetho's knowledge does not go back to a series of referents and representations that eventually reaches representations emerging out of the experiences of those involved in the events, nor is it 'untouched' by biblical or related traditions on these matters.

On Manetho and the texts relevant to the discussion here, see M. Stern, *Greek and Latin Authors on Jews and Judaism* (Jerusalem: The Israel Academy of Sciences and Humanities, 1976), pp. 62-86; cf. P.R. Davies, 'Judaeans in Egypt: Hebrew and Greek Stories', in L.L. Grabbe (ed.), *Did Moses Speak Attic? Jewish Historiography and Scripture in the Hellenistic Period* (JSOTSup, 317; Sheffield: Sheffield Academic Press, 2001), pp. 108-28.

On general matters discussed in these final considerations, cf. Hölscher, 'The New Annalistic'.

[84] Insofar as it influences the communal set of agreed facts about the past.

communities stand outside and beyond the particular narrative in which a representation of the historical event is embedded. Some of the mentioned agreed facts are less changeable than others; they represent a 'core' of facts strongly ascribed to the understanding of the event in the relevant community/ies.

This line of analysis has the potential to contribute to the understanding of the texts themselves as social productions that involve writers and intended readers who live within particular social realities and because of that had to deal, and in most cases follow, a certain socio-cultural grammar of historical writing.[85] This grammar deserves much attention.

---

[85] To some extent compare with several of the 'grammatical' claims advanced in D.H. Akenson, *Surpassing Wonder: The Invention of the Bible and the Talmuds* (New York: Harcourt, Brace & Company; Montreal/Kingston: McGill-Queen's University Press, 1998).

On the Problems of Reconstructing Pre-Hellenistic Israelite (Palestinian) History*

Niels Peter Lemche

The so-called 'historical-critical' school that created a universe of its own, dubbed 'ancient Israel', has dominated the last two hundred years of biblical studies. The texts of the Old Testament—in some circles called 'the Hebrew Bible'—were believed to refer to an 'ancient Israel' thought to be a historical reality. Already at an early stage of the development of historical-critical methodology scholars accepted that the Old Testament was not simply a history book—or textbook—that told the truth and nothing but the truth about ancient Israel. In accordance with developments within the field of general history this was not considered an insurmountable problem to biblical scholars. Historians began in the early nineteenth century to develop methods of source criticism that enabled them—or so they believed—to make a distinction between real information and secondary expansion. In the words of the leading historian of this period, Johann Gustav Droysen (1808–84), the historian had to distinguish between 'Bericht', that is story or interpretation, and 'Überreste', that is, what is left of historical information. In every part of the historical narrative in the Old Testament, it would, according to this view, be possible to make a distinction between information that originates in the past, and additions and commentaries to this information from a later period.[1]

Let me quote as an example of such a source analysis the story about Sennacherib's attack on Jerusalem in 701 BCE:

> Now in the fourteenth year of king Hezekiah did Sennacherib king of Assyria come up against all the fenced cities of Judah, and took them. And Hezekiah king of Judah sent to the king of Assyria to Lachish, saying, I have offended; return from me: that which you puttest on me will I bear. And the king of Assyria appointed unto Hezekiah king of Judah three hundred talents of silver and thirty talents of gold. And Hezekiah gave *him* all the silver that was found in the house of the Lord, and in the treasures of the king's

---

* Originally published in *Journal of Hebrew Scriptures* 3/1 (2000); available at http://purl.org/jhs and http://www.jhsonline.org.
[1] More about this in my *The Israelites in History and Tradition* (Library of Ancient Israel; Louisville, KY: Westminster/John Knox, 1998), pp. 1-21, 22-34.

house. At that time did Hezekiah cut off *the gold from* the doors of the temple of the Lord, and *from* the pillars which Hezekiah king of Judah had overlaid, and gave it to the king of Assyria (2 Kgs 18.13-16; KJV).

This story that can be found in 2 Kgs 18–19 opens with notes about King Hezekiah's reign, how he behaved well in the eyes of the Lord and how he revolted against the Assyrians and smote the Philistines. The narrative about King Hezekiah is broken off by a short interlude explaining how King Shalmanasser of Assyria besieged and conquered the city of Samaria—an event already mentioned in the preceding chapter. After this break, the narrative continues with a description of Sennacherib's attack on Hezekiah's fortified cities. While the Assyrian king rests at Lachish, King Hezekiah gives in and surrenders to the Assyrians and pays a handsome tribute to mollify his overlord, the king of Assur. After this tribute has been paid, the Assyrian king sends his general to Jerusalem. There is the famous Rabshakeh incident, when the Assyrian officer stands in front of the gates of Jerusalem and delivers a harsh speech that intends to scare the inhabitants of Jerusalem and its king that they may surrender to the Assyrians. Hezekiah in great distress turns to the prophet Isaiah who promises the assistance of God against the Assyrians. The Assyrian general returns to his master now with his army at Libnah in order to move against an Egyptian army trying to outflank the Assyrian army. Rabshakeh sends a letter to Hezekiah repeating many of the threats against Judah already delivered in his speech in front of Jerusalem. When he receives this letter, Hezekiah approaches the Lord in order that he might help him against the Assyrian army. As a result the avenging angel of the Lord kills 185,000 Assyrian soldiers during the night, whereupon Sennacherib returns to Assyria in dismay, only to be murdered some time later.

Already a casual reading of these chapters makes it certain that the narrative does not constitute a homogenous description of the events of the fateful year of 701 BCE. The Rabshakeh incident is clearly superfluous as Hezekiah had already surrendered and paid his tribute to the king of Assyria, before Rabshakeh moved to Jerusalem in order to deliver his speech. There was no reason for the Assyrian king not to return home since he already achieved his goal, to stop the rebellion in southwestern Palestine. In the text, however, a letter from Rabshakeh to Hezekiah that includes the same themes as his speech provokes the intervention of Isaiah and leads to God destroying the Assyrian army. It is as if the author of this narrative prefers to present his scenes in pairs. However, from the modern historian's point of view, it should be possible in 2 Kgs 18–19 to distinguish between—in Droysen's words—*Bericht* and *Überreste*. Such a historian would primarily look for historical information in the short description of Sennacherib's campaign at the beginning of the narrative in 2 Kgs 18–19 rather than in the literarily elaborated passages which follow. Most historians would say that after the paying of Hezekiah's tribute, the remaining part is a *Bericht*, i.e. a reflection from a later date of the events of 701 BCE.

Now we actually possess another version of this campaign of Sennacherib, in Sennacherib's royal annalistic report of the campaign.² In Sennacherib's version, the campaign opens with a diversion to Phoenicia, to Sidon, in order to clear any obstacles that may arise behind the frontline and to safeguard the route of retreat. The Sidonian king flees before the Assyrians. The main aim of the campaign is, however, to settle matters in Palestine where the Judaean Hezekiah (Sennacherib's wording) has interfered with loyal Assyrian vassals including Padi, the king of Ekron, who is kept as a prisoner by Hezekiah. Hezekiah and his allies had also approached the king of Egypt and an Egyptian army had already arrived and had prepared for a battle at Elteqeh. The Egyptian army was no match for the Assyrians and Sennacherib could, after having dismissed the threat from Egypt, continue to settle matters along the coast of Palestine. Here he conquers the cities of Elteqeh and Timnah and attacks and occupies Ekron. Hezekiah is evidently (Sennacherib does not say how it happened but we may guess why) persuaded to set Padi of Ekron free and return him to his city, where he is reinstalled as an Assyrian vassal. Hezekiah does not yield any further but Sennacherib devastates his country, destroys 46 fortified cities and shuts Hezekiah in his city of Jerusalem, like a bird in a cage. The devastated parts of Hezekiah's kingdom are handed over to the Philistine cities. Hezekiah gives up the hope of fighting the Assyrians and pays a heavy tribute that is delivered by his envoys to the Assyrian king in Nineveh.

There can be no doubt that the biblical narrative and Sennacherib's annalistic report are two reflections of the campaign of Sennacherib that ended when Hezekiah gave in and paid the tribute which the Assyrians demanded including his daughters. There are many differences between the biblical and the Assyrian version, but they also agree on several important points. Hezekiah rebelled against the Assyrians. Sennacherib attacked his country and destroyed many cities. At the end Hezekiah paid a tribute, but Jerusalem remained in his hand unharmed. The astonishing fact claimed by 2 Kings that the Assyrians did not conquer Jerusalem is obviously a historical fact. Otherwise the differences have mostly to do with chronological details and numbers such as when and where did Hezekiah send his tribute and how big was this tribute. These are minor points. Basically the two accounts are in agreement.

When these two versions are compared it is obvious that the Rabshakeh incident may have been invented by the author of 2 Kings in order to create the impression that Sennacherib did not conquer Jerusalem because the holy city was saved by its God.³ Rabshakeh's actions follow the payment of the tribute. The Assyrians

---

[2] *ANET* 3, pp. 287-88.
[3] For a different look on the Rabshakeh incident as historical cf. among others Brevard S. Childs, *Isaiah and the Assyrian Crisis* (SBTSS, 3; London: SCM Press, 1967), pp. 76-93, and more recently Mordechai Cogan and Hayim Tadmor, *II Kings: A New Translation with Introduction and Commentary* (AB, 11; Garden City, NY: Doubleday, 1988), pp. 240-44.

had already closed the case of the rebellion. Although this section includes one piece of historical information: the appearance of an Egyptian army in Palestine, it is a safe guess to conclude that there is nothing historical about the Rabshakeh incident. The biblical narrative that follows the payment of the tribute is invented history or simply fiction.

This example may count as an easy one. Other examples are less obvious. Among them, we may mention the story about the campaign of the kings of Israel and Judah against King Mesha of Moab in 2 Kgs 3. The story opens with a note saying that Mesha paid a heavy tribute to Israel but also that he had revolted against his master after the death of Ahab. The king of Israel accordingly invited his colleague in Jerusalem to join him in a war party against Moab. The party also included the King of Edom. The campaign opens with a seven-day-long march but it is halted because of lack of water. The kings turn to the prophet for help, and on the prophet's instructions rites are performed and water made available by a miracle. The prophet also delivers an oracle predicting the fall of all of Moab. The following battle between the Israelites and Moabites ends in disaster for the Moabite army, and Mesha retreats to his city of Kir-hareseth. After an unsuccessful breakout from Kir-hareseth, Mesha sacrifices his son on the wall of his city, 'and there was great indignation against Israel' (KJV) or better 'there was such great consternation among the Israelites' (REB) that the Israelites lifted the siege and returned home.

Now is this a historical report? The central part of the story has to do with the water miracle and the Moabite misinterpretation of it that brings disaster upon their heads. Miracles are certainly out of focus in a historical report of events that really happened, and very impractical for the historical analysis. It is safe to say—from a historian's point of view—that it never happened. Does it mean that this narrative in 2 Kgs 3 is totally devoid of historical information? Hardly, because we are in possession of not only one but also two inscriptions carrying the name of Mesha, king of Moab. One of them is only a short fragment, the second probably the most important royal inscription from the southern Levant ever found.[4]

Also Mesha has a story to tell. In his version, he describes how Omri oppressed Moab for forty years in all of his time and the half of his son's time. Mesha, however, attacked Israel and destroyed it forever. Most of the inscription is devoted to a description of the cities retaken—in Mesha's words—from Israel and the rearrangement prepared for them by Mesha, all of this made possible by Kemosh, the god of Moab.

---

[4] Cf. John C.L. Gibson, *Textbook of Syrian Semitic Inscriptions*. I. *Hebrew and Moabite Inscriptions* (Oxford: Clarendon Press, 1971), pp. 71-84. For an extensive analysis of the main text, cf. Andrew Dearman (ed.), *Studies in the Mesha Inscription and Moab* (ASOR/SBL Archaeology and Biblical Studies, 2; Atlanta: Scholars Press, 1989). Although the second inscription from Kerak is broken at the beginning where we find Mesha's name, the name of his father (*kmšyt*) has been so well preserved that it is beyond doubt that this is a second inscription by Mesha king of Moab.

If we compare the biblical story in 2 Kgs 3 with the inscription of Mesha of Moab, there may be a slight degree of communality between them. Both texts explain how Mesha revolted against Israel and reckon Mesha to be king of Moab. Otherwise it is a hopeless affair to try to unite the information in the biblical text with the information provided by Mesha himself. Although the biblical text includes maybe one or two pieces of information that are historical, it has nothing to do with Mesha's text. Mesha has a totally different story to tell. Mesha's story may constitute a historical report, but it is far from certain. Maybe it is just as much literature as the version in 2 Kgs 3. Mesha is not telling the truth and nothing but the truth. It is clear that his inscription is also to a large degree fictional and propagandistic and includes such elements from popular literature as the proverbial period of oppression of forty years. Mesha somehow makes a show of not knowing the name of any king of Israel except Omri. He 'forgets' to mention Omri's successor, Ahab—after all, a very important king in his time and who is mentioned by the Assyrians—and therefore makes Omri the oppressor of Moab also in his son's time.

By introducing these two texts, 2 Kgs 3 and the Moabite royal inscription of Mesha, we have penetrated further into the problem of studying the history of ancient Israel. There are some general similarities between Mesha's version and the biblical one. Mesha was really the king of Moab and Moab was, before Mesha's revolt, a vassal of Israel. Furthermore, Israel was not able to subdue Moab again. Apart from this, no extra-biblical evidence can substantiate the plot of the narrative in 2 Kgs 3. The text might well be an invented and fictional piece of work that only includes a name and a few other things to act as its historical credentials. We cannot harmonize the information. Not even the chronology fits. According to 2 Kgs 3, Mesha revolts after the death of Ahab, while Mesha speaks about Israelite oppression that lasted for half the reign of Omri's son who only appears without a name in the Moabite text. Although the Mesha inscription is usually dated to c. 850 BCE, the vagueness of the information included here does not preclude that it could be later than that date. The argument in favor of such a position is the mentioning of Omri who oppressed Moab in the time of his son. This indicates that in this text Omri may not be Omri the king of Israel but the eponymous king of *Bet Omri*, the 'house of Omri', which in Assyrian documents of the ninth and eighth century BCE is the usual name of the state otherwise known as Israel.[5] Omri and Israel in the Mesha inscription are synonymous.

To conclude: The Mesha inscription does not make 2 Kgs 3 a reliable historical source, nor changes its basic genre. 2 Kgs 3 remains as miraculous and fictional as ever although it mentions a historical king of Moab and refers to a general political situation that may have some historical nucleus.

---

[5] For a recent review of this evidence, cf. my *The Israelites in History and Tradition*, pp. 51-55.

It is nevertheless often assumed that 2 Kgs 3 has a historical nucleus that can be reconstructed by modern historians. Such historians may be of the conviction that a distinction can be made also in this text between *Bericht* and *Überreste*. This is a very imprudent position to take. The only piece of *Überreste* in this chapter is a name and some general knowledge of the status of Moab in Mesha's time. It is hardly enough to make a narrative historical. This should not surprise us. Ancient history writing is very different from modern historical reconstruction. When reconstructing the past, the modern historian must reject many sorts of information found in an ancient source. To illustrate my point, I only have to quote from Danish 'national' history as told by Saxo Grammaticus who includes a long tale about the Viking king Regner Lodbrog, who killed a dragon to find a wife.[6] All kinds of legendary material are included in Saxo's version of Regner's life. Such tales can easily be dismissed when we try to write a history of Denmark's beginnings. However, the name of Regner is historical, as this Viking king appears in a Frankish chronicle from the ninth century CE as a contemporary of the writer of this chronicle.[7] It is, alas, hardly evident that this historical Regner ever killed a dragon.

In biblical studies the problem is that it is almost impossible to decide which part of a biblical narrative belongs to the genre of *Bericht*, and which part includes *Überreste* if we have no other information than that which is included in the biblical texts. If we do not possess external evidence, it is the individual scholar who decides what is history and what fiction, and this scholar will only have his or her common sense as a guideline. This is clearly a logical problem that has to do with historical-critical studies at large.

Historical-critical biblical scholarship operates within a hermeneutical circle that is really a logical circle. The source of information is more often than not the biblical text that stands alone. The conversation goes between the scholar who studies the text and the text itself. The scholar presents a theory that is based on the text and the text confirms the theory. It is an amazing fact that in biblical studies this has worked for almost 200 years, since the early days of modern scholarship at the beginning of the nineteenth century. Although every historical-critical scholar explains that there is a problem, it has to a large degree been ignored when it comes to history writing. The standard procedure is—to quote Bernd Jørg Diebner—that although we cannot prove it, it is a fact! We cannot prove that Moses ever existed but as we cannot explain the development of Israelite monotheism without a Moses, he must have existed. Otherwise we would have to invent him … disregarding the possibility that ancient writers did exactly that! When in a

---

[6] Saxo, a monk in the service of the bishop Absalon, the founder of Copenhagen, wrote his *Res gestae danorum* towards the end of the 12th century CE.

[7] The reference dates to 845 CE when Regner's army of Normans at the Seine was destroyed by a plague. He may also be mentioned in other contemporary sources as one of the main figures in the Danish process of conquering England in the second half of the 9th century CE.

bad mood, one may be willing to say that historical-critical scholarship is nothing but a bluff. The procedure—the hermeneutical circle—is from a scientific point of view false, and a false procedure in science will automatically tell you that the results obtained by this method are false and can be discarded without further ado. The conclusion that historical-critical scholarship is based on a false methodology and leads to false conclusions simply means that we can disregard 200 years of biblical scholarship and commit it to the dustbin. It is hardly worth the paper on which it is printed.

It is no excuse to say that this is the only way we may obtain historical information from the Bible. That is only a bad excuse for laziness. It has also to do with greediness: scholars want to say more than they can possibly do. Since the Bible has to do with religion and most scholars have been and still are religious people, there has been a constant pressure on biblical scholars to produce results that concur with results obtained in other fields such as general history. And biblical scholars have readily lived up to such expectations. In my dissertation on 'Early Israel' (1985) I presented a number of maxims, the first of which said that the most important thing is to acknowledge your ignorance. The second added that when you know the extent of your ignorance, you also have an idea about what you really know.[8] These maxims form a kind of Procrustes' bed on which to place all kinds of biblical studies, because the demand is that we start our investigation by accepting that we know almost nothing about the past and that we should begin with the little we know.

Now, some people might object, is it really true that we know so little about ancient Israel that we cannot reconstruct the history and religion of this society? The truth is that from the time that precedes the introduction of the so-called 'Hebrew Monarchy' we only possess one external source mentioning Israel. This Israel is included among a host of vanquished foes placed in Palestine in an Egyptian inscription dating to the time of Pharaoh Merenptah c. 1210 BCE.[9] It is likely that this inscription refers to Israel as a population group of some kind. Apart from this, nothing is known about the circumstances referred to in this inscription, which uses a lot of traditional language and might have less to say about historical events in Palestine at the end of the thirteenth century BCE than often believed.

There is a gap of more than 300 years from the Merenptah inscription to the next references to Israel. One of these has already been mentioned, namely the Mesha-inscription from Moab. A second inscription contains an Assyrian reference to a battle in 853 BCE in which Ahab of Sirla'a—it is definitely a corrupted form of Israel—participated.[10] The third one mentions an anonymous king of

---

[8] *Early Israel: Anthropological and Historical Studies on the Israelite Society before the Monarchy* (VTSup, 37; Leiden: E.J. Brill, 1985), p. 414.
[9] *ANET3*, pp. 376-78.
[10] *ANET3*, p. 279.

Israel who is supposed to have been killed by the author of the recently found so-called 'Bet David' inscription from Tel Dan in northern Palestine.[11] From the eighth century BCE a small number of Assyrian texts refers to Israel either as 'the house of Omri' or simply as Samaria, i.e. the capital of the kingdom of Israel in northern Palestine until 722 BCE. Most of these inscriptions include rather short references to Israel; a few can directly be related to information contained in the Old Testament such as Tiglatpileser III's regulations in northern Palestine a few years before the fall of Samaria.[12]

This Israel of the inscriptions from the 1st millennium BCE is, however, not ancient Israel but the state of Israel that existed between c. 900 BCE and 722 BCE. In the Old Testament this state appears as one of the two successor states to David's and Solomon's empire.

The second successor-state is referred to as Judah. Not before the eighth century do Assyrian inscriptions refer to this Judah. Again most of the texts include rather limited information, the most important being without doubt the already mentioned report of Sennacherib's campaign to Palestine. After the fall of Nineveh a few Babylonian inscriptions include references to Judah or to events that can be related to the fate of Judah in the sixth century BCE, the most important being the Neo-Babylonian Chronicle that includes a report of the Babylonian conquest of Jerusalem in 597 BCE.[13]

The ancient Near Eastern inscriptions that refer to Israel and Judah are limited in number but are nevertheless important evidence. They tell us that the names of Israel and Judah are not invented—fictitious—names, but refer to political structures that really existed. They also mention a selection of kings otherwise known from the Old Testament. They show that so far as we can control the evidence the succession of these kings as well as the synchronisms that can be established between the kings of Israel and Judah and Assyrian and Babylonian kings are not totally misleading. Sennacherib really attacked Judah in the days of Hezekiah and Nebuchadnezzar really conquered Jerusalem and installed Zedekiah on the throne of Judah more than a century later.

To conclude this section, it is obvious that the history of Israel and Judah as told by biblical historians is not totally devoid of historical information. The people who wrote the historical narratives of the Old Testament did at least know some facts about Israelite and Judaean history. We might even say that there is a certain number of *Überreste*—i.e. historical remains—included in the texts of the Old Testament. There might even be a kind of coherency that binds this information together and creates a kind of chronological framework for the historical narrative.

---

[11] Avraham Biran and Joseph Naveh, 'An Aramaic Stele Fragment from Tel Dan,' *IEJ* 43 (1993), pp. 81-98 and 'The Tel Dan Inscription: A New Fragment', *IEJ* 45 (1995), pp. 1-18. As to this writer's present position on the inscription, cf. his *The Israelites in History and Tradition*, pp. 38-43.
[12] *ANET3*, pp. 282-84; cf. 2 Kgs 15.29-30.
[13] *ANET3*, pp. 563-64.

All this is rather unproblematic. The problematic part is when we are confronted with the task of deciding what is *Überreste* and what *Bericht* when we read about events in ancient Israel that cannot be compared to external evidence. How do we solve this problem without ending in the famous hermeneutical circle already described?

One way would be to approach ancient near eastern historiography in general in order to perceive how it worked and how far it can be trusted. The first step would be to establish the genres of historiography in the Near East in antiquity. Here two genres dominate the field, on one hand the year-chronicle system that lists for every year its most important events in a kind of shorthand, and on the other, more extensive royal inscriptions such as the Assyrian royal annals claiming another Assyrian conquest of the world.

Sometimes the authors of 1 and 2 Kings refer to the chronicles of Israel or of Judah.[14] If we are to trust these notes as references to something that really existed (we must never forget that it was not uncommon in literature from ancient times to include fictitious references in order to create confidence), these chronicles would most likely be of the shorthand type. Such annals only included short references to past events. They would probably not have contained extensive narrative, not to say long reports. If we turn to the chronicles of Assyrian and Babylonian kings, it might be possible here to gain an impression of exactly what kind of information we should look after in order to reconstruct this source. Again, we should not forget that the biblical author might have invented the reference while at the same time writing in a chronistic style when it suited his purpose.[15]

When it comes to royal literature of the kind found, for example, in Assyrian inscriptions, it is much more difficult to establish the presence of such sources in the Old Testament. A large part of the Assyrian inscriptions contain war reports. Although it cannot be excluded that such literature also existed in Israel and Judah in the Iron Age, we cannot say for sure on the basis of the extant books of Kings that it did. It must be realized that as soon as we approach this genre, we move into literature, into the world of fiction and invention. This is certainly the case in many Assyrian inscriptions where the acts of the king are embellished—defeats hardly acknowledged. Such reports are always written with a purpose and are often composed to make an impression on the gods who were to approve the acts of the king in question. Some might call it propaganda!

---

[14] E.g. 2 Kgs 15.6-11, 21-26, 31-36.

[15] Cf. on the possibility of information coming from royal Israelite and Judaean archives, J.A. Montgomery, 'Archival Data in the Books of Kings', *JBL* 53 (1934), pp. 46-52. The question by Gösta W. Ahlström is, however, very relevant: 'But where have these archives been preserved so that the material could be used by later scribes or historiographers?' See *The History of Ancient Palestine from the Palaeolithic Period to Alexander's Conquest* (ed. D. Edelman; JSOTSup, 146; Sheffield: Sheffield Academic Press, 1993), p. 661 n. 9.

Returning to the books of Kings, it is safe to say that although minor sections may have an annalistic background in royal chronicles, most of the literature there neither belongs to this genre nor to that of the royal inscriptions of the Assyrian and later Babylonian type. This is a natural consequence of the aim and scope of the books of Kings, which are not written in order to praise the institution of kingship in Israel and Judah or to establish an exalted position for their kings. On the contrary, the impression gained from reading these biblical books is the opposite, that a human kingdom represented a departure from the just rule of God and that its human exponents were hardly heroes of the Yahwistic faith. Only very few among the kings of Judah are praised for their piety—all of the kings of Israel are condemned. Royal laudatory inscriptions would simply be the wrong type of literature to quote and are hardly present among the narratives of 1 and 2 Kings. Rather than tracing non-existing historical events, we should study the *topoi* of the authors of the books of Kings. It would be the goal of such an investigation to find out whether some kind of a pattern can be found. Already several years ago scholars realized that the biblical books of 1 and 2 Chronicles are dominated by a series of stereotypical *topoi*—each of them having a special purpose, either to recommend a king loved by God or reject a godforsaken king.[16] The very character of the narrative in 1 and 2 Kings speaks against extensive use of royal inscriptions as the base of this narrative. The authors of Kings used some extant annalistic information but only selected what suited their purpose. Their selection was dominated by the wish to create a generally negative impression of the period of the Hebrew kingdom.

When a modern author writes historical fiction, for example books like Robert Graves's *I Claudius*, we do not expect such a writer to be faithful to history. We allow this author the liberty to reformulate history in such a way that it supports the author's intention to make history conform to his intended goal. Although we may be in possession of the interpretation of the past also by professional historians, we can enjoy and appreciate historical fiction. Now, this is quite extraordinary and contrary to the belief of many scholars. Also people of the modern age can be more interested in literature than in historical facts. Hollywood would a long time ago have gone bankrupt without this human ability to disregard historical facts.

If we—having in a scientific way studied history for 200 years—do not always think that historical exactitude is a virtue that cannot be counterbalanced by morally acceptable fiction literature, what about people of ancient times who never shared our sense of history? Would they have paid attention to the historical correctness of a narrative about the past or would they have placed more emphasis on its aesthetical and probably moral values? The answer is provided not by ancient Near Eastern literature—we know very little about the reception

---

[16] Cf. the interesting study by Peter Welten, *Geschichte und Geschichtsdarstellung in den Chronikbüchern* (WMANT, 42; Neukirchen-Vluyn: Neukirchener Verlag, 1973).

of this literature among ordinary people—but by the discussion among classical intellectuals about the value of history. Here Cicero's famous characterization of history as the 'teacher of life' is important, as Cicero on the basis of Hellenistic philosophy regards history not as a literary genre dealing with the past but as a genre that uses the past to educate the present and future generations.[17]

We should not limit our interest in, say, 1 and 2 Kings in order to find historical information. Such information may only be present in short notes. We should pay attention to the purpose of this literature, because it is a safe guess to assume that the literature was composed to impress the present, and not to save recollections from the past for its own sake. It is a long story that exceeds the limits of one short article.[18] However, it is my thesis that the authors of ancient literature of the kind found in the Old Testament did not care much about the historical exactitude of their description of the past. The past was not very interesting except for the examples of good and bad behaviour it provided for the present and future. The past was interesting because it explained the present—even sometimes made present arrangements seem legitimate or natural. Otherwise let the dead bury the dead!

This is one side of the coin. The other has to do with the claim that we should not expect ancient historical narrative to be precise about the past or even related to it except in a superficial way. How can I prove my case? The easy solution to this problem is to say that it is sometimes possible to point at passages where the authors of Kings directly say that they are not interested in history. The already mentioned references to the chronicles of the kings of Israel and Judah actually tell us this. Thus King Omri is dismissed in a few verses in 1 Kgs 16. We are informed that he assumed power by a *coup d'état*, and that he ruled Israel for twelve years and built Samaria. After this, focus changes and we hear about his sins against Yahweh. The author of 1 Kgs 16, however, knows that Omri was a great king but says, 'Go and look for yourself in the chronicles of the kings of Israel!' (1 Kgs 16.27). The biblical historiographer has no intention of providing his reader with an exact report of Omri's reign. Although he accepts that Omri was a great king—after all, after his death his kingdom carried his name for more than a hundred years—this is from the perspective of the ancient history writer absolutely immaterial. Thus this historiographer does not deny Omri's greatness; he silences it.

A more complicated way to solve the problem presented here will be to establish whether or not the history of ancient Israel as told by biblical writers is exact in any comprehensive way. I mean, this history can be split into several succeeding periods, the period of the patriarchs, the time of the exodus, the Israelites

---

[17] Cicero, *De oratore*, 2.9.36.
[18] Cf. also my forthcoming article, 'Good and Bad in History. The Purpose of historiography', in Steven McKenzie and Thomas Römer (eds.), *Rethinking the Foundations: Historiography in the Ancient World and in the Bible: Essays in Honor of John Van Seters* (BZAW, 294; Berlin: W. de Gruyter, 2000), pp. 127-40.

travelling in the desert for forty years, the conquest of Canaan, the heroic exploits of the hero-judges of Israel, the period of national greatness under David and Solomon, impending disaster under the kings of Israel and Judah, and so on. Has this anything to do with the real past of this geographical region otherwise known as the southern Levant or Palestine?

I have no intention of reviewing this history in any detail in this place. I have already presented such reviews in several publications.[19] Other scholars have contributed. The history of Israel as told by the Old Testament begins with the patriarchal age. It continues with the sojourn in Egypt followed by the Exodus and the wanderings in the desert. Then follows in succession the conquest of Canaan, the period of the Judges, the empire of David and Solomon, the era of the Hebrew kings, the exile, and the Persian period. This history officially ends with Ezra's promulgation of the *Torah*, the Law of Moses, in front of the assembled inhabitants of Jerusalem and Judah.

1999 represents the silver anniversary of the final settlement—represented by the contributions by Thomas L. Thompson and John Van Seters—with the idea that there ever was a patriarchal period.[20] This is based on family stories, sagas and legends about the past, and has nothing to do with history. The idea once formulated by Albrecht Alt that there was a special patriarchal religion based on the belief in *der Gott der Väter*, 'the God of the fathers', is simply nonsense as Alt based his argument on Nabataean evidence from the second century BCE through the second century CE.[21]

The exodus has a long time ago passed from history into fiction. It never happened. Neither did the conquest ever happen. Several biblical scholars including myself have made this clear. From an historical point of view, the Israelites could not have conquered Canaan by destroying Canaanite forces, for the simple reason that the Egyptians still ruled Canaan when Joshua is supposed to have arrived, that is shortly before 1200 BCE.[22] Secondly, there is no trace of foreign immigration, and thirdly, even the biblical account about the conquest is contradictory (compare Joshua to Judg. 1).

---

[19] For convenience, *Ancient Israel: A New History of Israelite Society* (The Biblical Seminar, 5; Sheffield: JSOT Press, 1988) (which is after all not so new anymore).

[20] Cf. Thomas L. Thompson, *The Historicity of the Patriarchal Narratives: The Quest for the Historical Abraham* (BZAW, 133; Berlin: W. de Gruyter, 1974), and John Van Seters, *Abraham in History and Tradition* (New Haven: Yale, 1975).

[21] Albrecht Alt, *Der Gott der Väter. Ein Beitrag zur Vorgeschichte der israelitischen Religion* (BWANT, 48; Stuttgart: W. Kohlhammer, 1929; ET [R.A. Wilson] 'The God of the Fathers', in Albrecht Alt, *Essays on Old Testament History and Religion* [The Biblical Seminar; Sheffield: JSOT Press, 1989], pp. 1-77).

[22] For a recent evaluation of the duration of the Egyptian empire in Asia, cf. Donald B. Redford, *Egypt, Canaan, and Israel in Ancient Times* (Princeton, NJ: Princeton University Press, 1992), pp. 283-97. Redford dates the Egyptian withdrawal to c. 1150 BCE.

In my original monograph on the period of the judges that appeared almost thirty years ago, I argued that the narratives in Judges about the heroic exploits of the Israelite judges were coloured by later experience.[23] They were also dominated by the wish, in a paradigmatic meaning, to demonstrate how Israel should fight its enemies, the Canaanites, the Moabites, Ammonites, Philistines, Aramaeans etc. These narratives do not allow us to reconstruct the history of the period between the (non-existing) conquest and the (likewise non-existing) empire of David and Solomon. The stories about the judges of Israel belong among the genre of heroic tales that most civilizations include among their memories of the past.

The empire of David and Solomon believed to have existed in the tenth century BCE is evidently based on a fictional representation of the past. Many things speak in favour of this conclusion. One of them has to do with the status of Jerusalem in the tenth century BCE when Jerusalem was at most a village or a small town.[24]

We have already discussed the period of the Hebrew kings. Although the two kingdoms of Israel and Judah are historical facts, we are in possession of very little in the way of solid knowledge about them. Furthermore, when reviewing the evidence we have in the Old Testament and in other sources, it is evident that the Old Testament has totally distorted our view of ancient Palestinian history. This was far more complicated and included many more actors than just these two kingdoms. Thus the Old Testament never explains why and how this territory got the name of Palestine ('the land of the Philistines'). Foreigners including Assyrian authors of royal annals and Herodotus knew the name of Palestine. Herodotus simply states that Palestine is the part of Syria that is situated between Lebanon and Egypt.[25]

There is hardly time to discuss the historicity of the exile, which might not have been as important as described by the Old Testament. Recent investigations have shown that the 'land of Israel' was not deserted in the time of the exile and that it only affected very few among the population of Palestine. There was no

---

[23] *Israel i dommertiden: En oversigt over diskussionen om Martin Noths 'Das System der zwölf Stämme Israels'* (Tekst og Tolkning, 4; Copehagen: C.E.G. Gad, 1972), pp. 86-87.

[24] I have no intention in this place to go into a detailed discussion about the historicity or non-historicity of David and Solomon. The idea of an united monarchy of Israel/Judah died as terminology changed. Now, it is preferable to see the period from c. 1250 to c. 900 as one long intermediary period, a 'transitionary period', and the way to approach this period has been demonstrated by e.g. Israel Finkelstein, 'The Emergence of Israel: A Phase in the Cyclic History of Canaan in the Third and Second Millennia BCE', in Israel Finkelstein and Nadav Na'aman (eds.), *From Nomadism to Monarchy: Archaeological and Historical Aspects of Early Israel* (Jerusalem: Israel Exploration Society, 1994), pp. 150-78, and Shlomo Bunimowitz, 'Socio-Political Transformations in the Central Hill Country in the Late Bronze-Iron I Transition', in Finkelstein and Na'aman (eds.), *From Nomadism to Monarchy*, pp. 179-203.

[25] Cf. Herodotus, *The Histories*, 1.105; 2.104; 3.5.91; 4.39; 7.89.

'empty land' as postulated by the biblical books of Chronicles and other biblical literature.[26]

The Persian period is, finally, a dark spot on the historical map of Palestine. We know almost nothing about this period. Ezra, the great hero of postexilic Judaism, is probably a late invention (by Pharisaic authors?), probably 200 years old when he arrived (his father was killed by Nebuchadnezzar's general, Nebuzaradan, in 587 BCE—according to the biblical evidence).[27]

Although this review is in some ways 'reductionist', it is nevertheless very much to the point. It is based on a review of all kinds of evidence, not least the results of extensive archaeological excavations in Palestine that have lasted for more than a hundred years. I need not say that archaeology is not an exact science like mathematics and never will be. Any result obtained by an archaeologist will include a number of hypotheses made by this archaeologist based on the material he or she has found. Furthermore the basis on which the archaeologist founded his or her theories can never be revisited. All excavations include—in Kathleen Kenyon's words—destruction. The archaeologist destroys the evidence when it is excavated. The original archaeological situation can never be re-established.

However, archaeologists continually formulate general hypotheses about the development of this geographic area in ancient times that speak against the evidence of a late-written source such as the Old Testament (which according to me and the members of my school hardly predates the Graeco-Roman Period). It is therefore a safe guess to argue that this late source—although written—does not constitute a historical source. It is not—to recall Droysen—*Überreste*, it is definitely *Bericht*, a tale about the past.

The development in Palestine between, say 1250 and 900 BCE is an example of this. Archaeology as well as other non-biblical information about ancient Palestine will tell us that Palestine in the late Bronze Age (roughly the second half of the second millennium BCE) was an Egyptian province ruled by local princes who looked upon themselves as faithful vassals of their patron, the Pharaoh. For most of the time, Palestine was left alone. Only occasionally did the Egyptians interfere directly with the mundane problems of Palestine. The everlasting internecine war-games played by the local chieftains who saw themselves as 'kings'

---

[26] Cf. Hans M. Barstad, *The Myth of the Empty Land: A Study in the History and Archaeology of Judah during the 'Exilic' Period* (Oslo: Scandinavian University Press, 1996). See, however, also Ehud Ben Zvi, 'Inclusion in and Exclusion from Israel as Conveyed by the Use of the Term "Israel" in Post-Monarchic Biblical Texts', in Steven W. Holloway and Lowell K. Handy (eds.), *The Pitcher is Broken. Memorial Essays for Gösta W. Ahlström* (JSOTSup, 190; Sheffield: Sheffield Academic Press, 1995), pp. 95-149, and the discussion in Lester L. Grabbe (ed.), *Leading Captivity Captive: The 'Exile' as History and Ideology* (JSOTSup, 278; Sheffield: Sheffield Academic Press, 1998).
[27] Cf. Ezra's pedigree, Ezra 7.1: Ezra, son of Seraiah, son of Azariah, son of Hilkiah, son of Shallum, etc. On Seraiah's death, cf. 2 Kgs 25.18. Hilkiah was high priest in the days of Josiah, 2 Kgs 22.4. Of course many scholars will maintain that the genealogy is either false or telescoped.

(the Egyptians had other ideas about their importance and called them *hazanu*; i.e. 'mayors') had a devastating effect on the well-being of the country. It was not before the so-called 'Ramesside restoration' of the Egyptian presence in Western Asia after the debacle that ended the 18th dynasty, that matters changed and the Egyptian presence became more dominating. Some could say that Ramesses II created a kind of 'Pax Egyptiaca' in Palestine. Now, the Egyptian masters limited the devastating effects of the 'free-for-all' politics of the local Palestinian chieftains. The Egyptians created a situation of relative peace in the country that might have had a positive demographic effect as people moved from the cities to the countryside to live closer to their fields. The late thirteenth, the twelfth and the early eleventh centuries BCE were witnessing the foundations of scores if not hundreds of insignificant and unprotected village settlements, not least in the mountains of Palestine. Life must have become pretty safe. From at least the eleventh century BCE, a certain reduction of the number of villages took place. This demographic chance was counterbalanced by the rise of certain settlements to the status of sometimes heavily fortified townships. Tel Beersheva with its circular walls and planned layout is a typical example of such a settlement that may look more like a mediaeval fortress than a proper city or town.

This stage may have occurred as a consequence of an at least partial Egyptian withdrawal from Palestine (although it now seems likely that at least in Bet She'an an Egyptian garrison was present as late as the beginning of the tenth century BCE[28]). Life became more dangerous and the socio-political system of the past (local patrons fighting other local patrons) emerged again. I have once described this development as a move from one patronage society to another patronage society, from an old political system to a new system that was an exact copy of the former system.[29] This period lasted until probably the middle of the ninth century when some of the local chieftains were able to create large political structures that exceeded the boundaries of those present in the Late Bronze Age, a time when most Palestinian political systems were extremely small. Such large political structures might have existed before the Iron Age, for example in the Early Bronze Age (third millennium). Here remains of considerable cities are found. The Middle Bronze Age might be another period that included comprehensive political organizations although we know very little about the exact political structure of the Palestinian society before the Late Bronze Age.

---

[28] Cf. the short discussion by Patrick E. McGovern, 'Beth-Shean', *ABD* I, pp. 694-95. The LBA phase of occupation continued to about 1000 BCE. Only after that date a new stratum reveals different layouts and culture. The city was hardly Philistine (the author of 1 Sam. 31 got it totally wrong); only a single piece of Philistine pottery has been found at the tell (McGovern, same place).

[29] 'From Patronage Society to Patronage Society', in Volkmar Fritz and Philip R. Davies (eds.), *The Origins of the Ancient Israelite States* (JSOTSup, 228; Sheffield: Sheffield Academic Press, 1996), pp. 106-20.

The biblical picture of ancient Israel does not fit in but is contrary to any image of ancient Palestinian society that can be established on the basis of ancient sources from Palestine or referring to Palestine. There is no way this image in the Bible can be reconciled with the historical past of the region. And if this is the case, we should give up the hope that we can reconstruct pre-Hellenistic history on the basis of the Old Testament. It is simply an invented history with only a few referents to things that really happened or existed. From an historian's point of view, ancient Israel is a monstrous creature. It is something sprung out of the fantasy of biblical historiographers and their modern paraphrasers, that is, the historical-critical scholars of the last two hundred years.

Text, Context and Referent in Israelite Historiography*

Thomas L. Thompson

The dictum of Wellhausen that a biblical document reflects the historical context of its own formation rather than the social milieu of its explicit referents to a more distant past[1] is one that has hardly been overcome by any of the attempts to synthesize traditio-historical and archaeological research during the past century. The Altean and Albrightean syntheses of biblical and extrabiblical research,[2] especially when viewed in the light of the encyclopedic accomplishments of a Galling or a de Vaux,[3] have only intensified the Wellhausen impasse. From another direction, the analysis of the prehistory of the Pentateuch's documentary traditions, following the leads of Gunkel, Eissfeldt, Noth and Nielsen,[4] has substantially modified perceptions of the historical contexts of traditions and redactions. Such analysis has lent support particularly to the now axiomatic assumption, strongly influenced by the 'biblical theology' movement, that the traditions originated in events.

These post-Wellhausen scholarly movements have shared a common goal and common presuppositions. The goal was to reconstruct the history of Israel's past and of its origins through a historical-critical appraisal of the complex biblical

---

* Diana Edelman is to be thanked for many substantial improvements in the style and content of this paper. However, faithfulness to its context in the discussion at Anaheim prevents me from making any extensive revisions.

[1] J. Wellhausen, *Prolegomena zur Geschichte Israels* (Berlin: de Gruyter, 1905), p. 316. This dictum played a central role in the development of his evolutionary history of Israelite religion.

[2] Cf. A. Alt, *Kleine Schriften* (3 vols.; Munich: Beck, 1953); W.F. Albright, *From the Stone Age to Christianity* (Baltimore: Johns Hopkins University Press, 1940; 3rd edn, 1957).

[3] Cf. K. Galling, *Biblisches Reallexikon* (Tübingen: Mohr, 1977); R. de Vaux, *L'histoire d'Israel* (2 vols.; Paris: Gabalda, 1971).

[4] Cf. H. Gunkel, *Das Märchen im alten Testament* (Tübingen: Mohr, 1921); *idem*, *Genesis* (ATD; Göttingen: Vandenhoeck & Ruprecht, 1966); O. Eissfeldt, *Einleitung in das alte Testament* (Tübingen: Mohr, 1965); *idem*, 'Stammessage und Novelle in den Geschichten von Jakob, und von seinen Söhnen', in *Eucharisterion, Gunkel Festschrift*, I (Göttingen: Vandenhoeck & Ruprecht, 1923), pp. 56-77; M. Noth, *Uberlieferungsgeschichte des Pentateuchs* (Stuttgart: Kohlhammer, 1948); *idem*, *Uberlieferungsgeschichtliche Studien*, I (Königsberg: Niemeyer, 1943); E. Nielsen, *Oral Tradition* (London: SCM Press, 1954).

tradition. It was commonly assumed that the tradition's literary fixation first came about during the time of the United Monarchy or slightly later. The existence of a considerable oral prehistory of the texts that leads back to the central core of the tradition's referents in a yet more distant past was taken for granted. This assumption that the traditions maintained an 'essential historicity', or that they were 'rooted' in historical events of the past, is fundamental to an understanding of a historical period of the Judges, and, for some, of even more distant 'Mosaic' or 'patriarchal periods'.

In spite of these substantial changes, the essential thrust of Wellhausen's axiom continues to haunt us, illustrating a perspective necessary to an understanding of the biblical traditions through their historical context. As archaeologically oriented historical scholarship has finally adjusted its assumption that biblical and extrabiblical research are open to direct synthesis, mutual confirmation and conjectural harmonization, much progress in the secular history of Palestine for the Bronze and Iron Ages has become possible.[5] Moreover, as traditio-historical assumptions of a historical core to biblical traditions have been questioned and gradually abandoned, this direction of research has found value and legitimacy as an aspect of compositional theory.[6] It has also become a viable method for one significant aspect of Israel's history; for the development of the tradition reflects the historically significant formative process by which 'Israel', through its use of tradition, was created out of the political and historical disasters of the Assyrian and neo-Babylonian periods. The formation of biblical narrative—this ideologically motivated, originating process that makes Israel—begins at the earliest during the course of Assyria's domination of Palestine. At the latest, the Israel we know from the tradition comes to be during the pre-Hellenistic postexilic period.[7] In the twilight and destructions of the states of Samaria and Jerusalem, the Israel of tradition first presents itself to history, like the phoenix, ever in the form of an *Israel redivivus*, whose true essence and significance—and future glory—is traced in the legends of the patriarchs, of the wilderness and the Judges, and of the golden age of the United Monarchy. Idealistic sentiments of futuristic incipient messianism ring throughout this revisionist tradition with the recurrent affirmation of one people and one God. It is this God, the only true king and emperor, who will some day, finally, really rule from his throne in the temple of the future Jerusalem and who will draw all nations to him through his chosen remnant. This is the Israel of tradition.

---

[5] Cf. H. Weippert, *Palästina in vorhellenistischer Zeit* (Munich: Beck, 1988); G.W. Ahlström, *A History of Ancient Palestine* (Sheffield: JSOT Press, forthcoming).

[6] T.L. Thompson, *The Origin Tradition of Ancient Israel*, I (JSOTSup, 55; Sheffield: JSOT Press, 1987); idem, *The Early History of the Israelite People* (Leiden: Brill, forthcoming).

[7] See also on this E.A. Knauf, 'The Archaeology of Literature, and the Reality of Fictitious Heroes', *Scandinavian Journal for the Old Testament* 6 (forthcoming); idem, *Midian: Untersuchungen zur Geschichte Palästinas und Nordarabiens am Ende des 2. Jahrtausends* (ADPV; Wiesbaden: Otto Harrassowitz, 1988).

To understand the orientation of this literature to any real world of history, renewed focus needs to be given to the context and referent of the text. This is Burke Long's challenge: Does this sacred book render history?[8] I have often argued that it does not. Nevertheless, I agree with Axel Knauf's recent objection to the tendency of my 1987 volume *Origin Tradition* to deny that the literary figure of Abraham 'betray(s) any historical traits'. In fact it does; or perhaps more accurately, at least it must. How it does is not yet clear. Yet Knauf is most certainly correct: the text cannot be divorced from its historical context without loss or grave distortion. Certainly, the near-generational hemorrhaging of literary critics from any serious effort at historical criticism is a huge disaster, diminishing biblical studies through growing ignorance of the world from which our text comes.

Knauf points to a strong tendency, to a categorical error, and reasserts the obvious for all of us who are inclined to the easy road of ahistorical exegesis: even totally 'fictional heroes...reflect the time, place, and conceptual world of their authors'. This is axiomatic for any serious study of literature from the past. No text is understood apart from its context. However difficult historical criticism may be and however uncertain its conclusions, the questions it asks are adamantly fundamental to reading and have no alternative. Only a text that we ourselves write, and even that for only a brief fleeting time, can be read univocally and simplistically as a coherent, signifying, holistic entity created fully—whole and entire—in itself in its final form. And this is so, not because we are aware of the process of its formation and may be ignorant of that process in the work of another, but rather, more sacramentally, because we, as authors, in its final form, signify it as such. It is that final form that we own and not its sources, nor its many drafts.

If a text, however, presents itself to us as a composite, a holistic and univocal reading of its final form significantly distorts that text unless we can reasonably believe that the final form was a significant and inherently functional construct of that given text's composition and not a unity and reality given to it externally. Such an external unity and reality could arise, for example, through its inclusion centuries after its composition in an extraneous, and to its world foreign, canon. We must always ask about those structural unities of a text that signify meaning. All meaning-bearing structures, to the extent that they are translatable, have a historical contingency or context that must be unlocked if we are to make it ours. Meaning does not signify apart from a historical context, real or assumed. Historical-critical thought is nothing more than the systematic task of reducing the blindness and ignorance of our assumptions.

The final form of most biblical texts rarely purports to be a unit whole in itself. Within a canon, biblical texts never do. Anthological, historiographic and archival motives and functions are so common that the signification of much of what the extant form brings together bears meaning primarily in marked independence from the context in which it is collected and only secondarily as an element of a

---

[8] B.O. Long, 'On Finding the Hidden Premises', *JSOT* 39 (1987), pp. 10-14.

larger context. I submit that this distinctive peculiarity of so many of the units of biblical tradition is the result of their having been collected as meaningful traditions in themselves. They are voices apart from the collector, historiographer, or archivist, that spoke to them, as they do to us, from the past.

An insistence on analysis from the perspective of the final form of the tradition is valid insofar as what is meant is that our point of departure is the extant biblical texts. This is valid because it requires us to read the texts we have and not some other more imaginary traditions. This is an issue of authenticity and the directness of our observation of evidence; it is the issue of objectivity.

However, what is at times spoken of as a canonical reading of biblical tradition is essentially misleading to anyone who wishes to discover the signification of the tradition that was Israel's. Such reading distorts the tradition from the perspective of a theologically biased ideological orthodoxy of late antiquity. Such canonical context has no relevance either to the biblical tradition's original signification, nor does it bear any intrinsic meaning of the text for us. The value added to these texts by their canonical context is extraneous and intrinsically separate from them. The wishful thinking of this socalled criticism may have its place in formulating theological *desiderata*. Canonical criticism certainly has an important role to play in early church history—but it does not belong in a field that purports to speak critically about ancient Israel and about the literature of that ancient people,[9] who had neither a canon nor anything that can be described as a 'biblical community'.

The assumption that the process of the formation of the canon was already an aspect in the process of Torah composition[10] not only takes far too much for granted in Pentateuchal composition theory, but anachronistically projects a social construct such as a rabbinate back into the early Persian period. Even an assumption of such a social reality dominating the early Palestinian Judaism of R. Akiba (110–135 CE) stretches credulity unnaturally. The coercive essence of canonicity reflects a historical contingency that goes well beyond mere literary context or favored lists of divinely favored manuscripts. It is normative in character and, as such, necessitates a norm-producing and sustaining context, a situation that did not

---

[9] The understanding of Brevard Childs (*Introduction to the Old Testament as Scripture* [London: SCM Press, 1979]) that canon began already in the early Israelite period is certainly anachronistic, as is the assumption of James Sanders (*Torah and Canon* [Philadelphia: Fortress Press, 1972]) about a 'biblical community' in the early and pre-Persian periods. T. Sheppard's presentations (*Wisdom as a Hermeneutical Construct: A Study in the Sapientializing of the Old Testament* [Berlin: de Gruyter, 1980], and esp. *idem*, 'Canonization: Hearing the Voice of the Same God through Historically Dissimilar Traditions', *Int* 36 [1982], pp. 21-33) are substantially more sophisticated. N.K. Gottwald's incisive criticism of Childs's tendencies to dehistoricize theology and the reading of scripture ('Social Matrix and Canonical Shape', *Theology Today* 42 [1985], p. 320) cannot be overstressed. However, his attempts to trace an analogy to the 'canonical process' in a legendary revolutionary tribal confederation (p. 313) totally lacks historical warrant.

[10] As presented by S.Z. Leiman, *The Canonization of Hebrew Scripture: The Talmudic and Midrashic Evidence* (Hamden: Ktav, 1976).

pertain either in Judaism or Christianity before the 4th-6th century CE. It is hardly before the late 1st and 2nd centuries CE that competing lists and the validity of the now Christian LXX for Judaism might be seen to focus attention on the limits of the sacred. A more likely period—subsequent to the unanimity of so-called canonical lists—for canonical coerciveness of Akiba-like intensity would be the doctrinal and gnostic controversies of the following 3rd to 5th centuries in which both Judaism and Christianity first began to form their distinctive orthodoxies. It is in this context of incipient orthodoxy that origin legends about Yavneh such as those of Yohanan ben Zakkai and Vespasian[11] and, on the Christian side, about the LXX such as the 'Letter of Aristeas' helped establish the foundations of a new conservative traditionalism. Similarly, perspectives such as 'audience-response' criticism have a tremendously important historical-critical role to play, not only in regard to Knauf's essential historical context of narrations and their successive revisions, but also throughout subsequent stages in the text's history of interpretation, where audience and eventually canonical context became two foci of one continuing project of interpretation.

An example might be useful. To understand the LXX as translation is a thoroughly profitable orientation when a scholar is attempting to reconstruct the various possibilities of Hebrew *Vorlage* that may have existed in the 2nd-1st centuries BCE. Such a perspective would provide an invaluable and necessary historical context for questions asked of the text. Similarly, to read the LXX as literature requires the assumption—and hopefully the explication—of the historical context of that text in the 2nd century BCE. However, to read the LXX as Luke–Acts' Bible requires an understanding of an entirely different historical context, the explication of which involves such issues as the similarities of Luke's Bible to extant manuscripts of the LXX, as well as an investigation of the enormous differences that exist between Hellenistic Alexandria and the Greco-Roman world of the New Testament.

To confuse such thoroughly historical-critical subgenres of both tradition and church history with the reading of a literature that is understood as directly relevant to today's audience (i.e. the Bible of Judaism and Christianity) is to make a historically contingent blunder. That is religion, not biblical scholarship. Such a blunder is comparable to the anachronistic metaphysics of many sociological approaches to Israel's history.

It is wholly unacceptable to assume even for a moment that the text, metaphysically transcending historical context, is not of a very specific past. The past context of a text must always form a part of any contemporary understanding. It was written in a now dead language within a culture that ceased to exist more than two millennia ago. Although a substantial core of Israelite tradition has survived until today in the form of our much later extant manuscripts, any perspective, theological or literary, that starts from the mythical premise that biblical texts exist in

---

[11] Cf. J. Neusner, 'Beyond Historicism after Structuralism: Story as History in Ancient Judaism', *Henoch* 3 (1981), pp. 171-99, esp. pp. 189, 194-95.

themselves or speak directly to us, having us for their audience, is more uncritical than simply ahistorical.[12] That some of these efforts, such as 'structuralism', claim to seek an objectivity in their research compounds our problems. What is 'objective' is the extant text that exists apart from any contemporary reader. Old texts hold images, meanings and intentions that are as historically contingent as the images, meanings, and intentions of very specific individuals now long dead. To discover their signification is the task of exegesis. The neofundamentalistic rejections of historical criticism I have mentioned, while bypassing its problems, leave little hope of understanding texts of the sort we find in the Bible. The primary point of departure for critical exegesis is and always remains historical context, which enables us to recreate the conceptual world of the tradition's authors.[13]

The specific manner in which we find this historical context and conceptual world refracted by the tradition requires yet further discussion. Unfortunately, Pentateuchal scholarship, and traditio-historical literary criticism generally, are not yet at the point at which we can reconstruct history directly from tradition. The interpretive problem involving the historical changes that moved the people of ancient Palestine to forge a sense of ethnicity out of the political and military disasters that overtook the indigenous states of Samaria and Jerusalem at the hands of the Assyrians and Babylonians is one that can hardly be dealt with apart from an understanding of the initial formulation and development of the specific traditions and ideologies that first gave expression to this ethnicity. These traditions and ideologically motivated perspectives are not so much direct refractions of ancient Israel's past as they are themselves intrinsically and substantially causative forces in the development of what, in spite of our dependence on these perceptions, we today understand as Israel.[14] As Max Miller has clearly and convincingly argued, any examination of the origins of Israel is forced to move in lock step with an examination of the development of Israelite tradition.[15] Apart from biblical tradition, this Israel never existed as a historical reality open to independent historical research and judgment. It was in the formation of the tradition as such that—to borrow a phrase from Malamat—Israel of tradition, for the first time, became a

---

[12] Such a perspective is to be expected in theologically oriented exegesis and may even be understood as legitimate in the context of homiletics. I have rather in mind such efforts as those of R. Alter (*The Art of Biblical Narrative* [New York: Basic Books, 1983]) on one hand, and of D. Jobling (*The Sense of Biblical Narrative* [JSOTSup, 7; Sheffield: JSOT Press, 1978]) on the other. An interesting discussion of some of these issues is found in R.N. Whybray, 'On Robert Alter's, *The Art of Biblical Narrative*', *JSOT* 27 (1983), pp. 75-86, esp. pp. 77-78, and in D. Jobling, 'Robert Alter's, *The Art of Biblical Narrative*', *JSOT* 27 (1983), pp. 87-99.
[13] Similarly, Neusner, 'Beyond Historicism', p. 196.
[14] This does not involve a judgment about the historicity of many aspects of the biblical tradition, especially of 2 Kings, but addresses only the process by which older narratives and historiographical sources are understood as traditions about an Israel, which, transcending its pre-exilic status as the state of Samaria, takes on the contours of the Israel of tradition (cf. also G. Garbini, *History and Ideology in Ancient Israel* [trans. J. Bowden; New York: Crossroad, 1988]).
[15] Orally at the annual convention, SBL, Chicago, 1988.

dominant reality in the history of ancient Palestine.[16] From this perspective, one must agree with Miller's conviction that Israel's tradition is in a radical and fundamental way our starting point for the history of Israel.[17] Without it, we cannot write a history of Israel, because, within the context of the Persian renaissance, the tradition itself created the population of Palestine as Israel out of the ashes of the Assyrian and Babylonian empires.

Biblical tradition is related to Israelite history when we use it teleologically and understand Israel as the end result of a literary trajectory. If, however, we use the tradition as historical evidence for a history prior to the historical context of the tradition, such a history can hardly avoid being anachronistic in its essence. Nevertheless, when understood teleologically, the tradition gives focus and direction to our research; for it is the Israel of tradition that we need to explain historically.

I hope it is true that the great divide between Genesis 11 and 12, demarcating myth from history or heroic epic, has finally disappeared from our textbooks. Nowhere in the narrative tradition of Genesis–2 Kings do we have such a watershed.[18] The stories within this extended tradition generally bear the character of 'traditional narratives' that stand somewhat apart from both history and historiography.[19] Chronicles, Ezra and Nehemiah also do not stand substantially closer to a recoverable 'history', for they too took their shape long after the events of which they might be thought to speak. The purported referents of these later works are also distinct from their contexts. Nor is the intent underlying their collection so obviously a historiographic one, however much they have been structured chronologically.[20] Any interpretive matrices, which we may be tempted to draw from the biblical story itself, render for us only hypothetical historical contexts, events, and situations whereby our texts only seem to take on meaning as literary responses. The matrix, however, remains imbedded in the literary vision and is not historical.

This danger of eisegesis is particularly serious when assumptions akin to Eissfeldt's imaginary *Stammesgeschichte* are present,[21] where fictional stories

---

[16] A. Malamat, 'Die Frühgeschichte Israels: eine methodologische Studie', *TZ* 39 (1983), pp. 1-16.
[17] J.M. Miller and J.H. Hayes, *A History of Ancient Israel and Judah* (Philadelphia: Westminster Press, 1986).
[18] *Contra* J.A. Soggin, 'The Davidic and Solomonic Kingdom', in *Israelite and Judaean History* (ed. J.H. Hayes and J.M. Miller; Philadelphia: Westminster Press, 1977), p. 332. Cf. my 'History and Tradition: A Response to J.B. Geyer', *JSOT* 15 (1980), pp. 57-61, esp. pp. 59-60. See also J. Rogerson, *Myth in Old Testament Interpretation* (BZAW, 134; Berlin: de Gruyter, 1974).
[19] Following here D. Gunn, *The Stories of King David* (JSOTSup, 4; Sheffield: JSOT Press, 1976).
[20] Cf. P. Welten, *Geschichte und Geschichtsdarstellung in den Chronikbüchern* (WMANT, 42; Neukirchen-Vluyn: Neukirchener Verlag, 1973); H.G.M. Williamson, *Israel in the Book of Chronicles* (Cambridge: Cambridge University Press, 1977); R.L. Braun, 'Chronicles, Ezra and Nehemiah: Theology and Literary History', in *Studies in the Historical Books of the Old Testament* (ed. J.A. Emerton; Leiden: Brill, 1979), pp. 52-64.
[21] O. Eissfeldt, 'Stammessage und Menscheitserzählung in der Genesis', in *Sitzungsberichte der Sächsischen Akademie der Wissenschaften zu Leipzig* (Phil-hist Kl 110, 4; Berlin: Akademic-Verlag, 1965), pp. 5-21.

are understood as refracted pantomimes of supposedly real political and social struggles. As with other forms of allegorical interpretation, these efforts bypass all critical evaluation.[22] Fairly mainstream historical-critical exegetical efforts are implicated in this criticism. For example, recent scholarly efforts have tried to associate such a central tradition-complex like Numbers 16–18 with a presumed historical Levitical conflict in the pre-exilic period or to an equally imaginary postexilic Aaronide hegemony over the cult.[23] Both options are unverified fictions, created wholly from the traditions themselves. They share the common categorical error of assuming the very history they seek to reconstruct. Similarly, the increasingly common temptation to associate the Abraham wandering tales or the Exodus stories with a historical context in the exile, interpreting these stories as implicit reflections of the return and of the exiles' self-understanding as *gērîm*, is equally suspect.[24]

Not even the Pentateuch's golden calf story or Bezalel's construction of the Ark and tent of meeting can, with any reasonable security, be related to any alleged historical matrices by making them retrojections of presumably reliable depictions of cultic innovations undertaken by the Jeroboam and Solomon of 2 Kings. The tales of 2 Kings are also traditions, not history, and as traditions they are fully equivalent to their variants set in yet more hoary antiquity.

One does well to reflect on both the multivalent and distinctive nature of so many of the traditions found within biblical historiography. We find parallel patterning of narration in such tradition variants as the two crossings of the sea in Exodus and the comparable miracle at the Jordan in Joshua, or in the recurrent use of common motifs as in Genesis 16 and 21 or 12, 20, and 26, Genesis 19 and Judges 19, Gen. 12.10 and Ruth 1.1. Equally importantly, however, are the variant traditions of 'events' such as in Genesis 10 and in 11.1-9; or in the accounts of the three distinct conquests of Jerusalem and of Lachish. Similarly, there are variant persons of biblical heroes—not only the many Abrahams, or the two or more Moseses of the prewilderness narratives, but also the two Judahs: the son of Jacob and the first of the Judges. Apart from a consideration of the many lost traditions unavailable to us, the immense complexity involved in the history of the extant traditions alone must give pause to any scholar employing a method of historical research that prefers one element of the tradition as more viable historically than another. Without concrete external evidence, such selective preference is not critical. As long as we continue to work with historical contexts that are not based on independent evidence, plausibility and verisimilitude cannot be recognized as

---

[22] See my 'Conflict Themes in the Jacob Narratives', *Semeia* 15 (1979), pp. 5-26.

[23] Cf. J. Milgrom, 'The Rebellion of Korah, Numbers 16-18: A Study in Tradition History', in *SBL Seminar Papers* (ed. K.H. Richards; Atlanta: Scholars Press, 1988), pp. 570-73 and E. Rivkin, 'The Story of Korah's Rebellion: Key to the Formation of the Pentateuch', in *SBL Seminar Papers* (ed. K.H. Richards; Atlanta: Scholars Press, 1988), pp. 574-81.

[24] Here I am reacting to my own inclination to reinterpret these traditions as stories *originating* in an exilic or early postexilic context. Cf. my *Origin Tradition*, pp. 194-98.

valid criteria for historicity. Plausibility and verisimilitude are characteristics that are to be attributed even more to good fiction. Reasonableness is far more a characteristic of the fictional genres of literature than it is of history. History happens; meaning and coherence are created.

When we are dealing with univocal traditions without extant variants we have precious few[25] means which enable us to recognize and confirm positively a reference to a real past[26] or to measure in any significant way the manner and extent to which the tradition reflects its own historical context. Valid negative conclusions are many, come immediately to hand, and certainly do not need emphasis in this forum.[27] Knauf's suggestions for the analysis of the various discrete social contexts in our tales certainly carry us in the right direction. However, our need to situate such potentially relevant contexts geographically and chronologically is, given the known variability and constant flux in human societal forms, all the greater if the suggestions and the methods involved are ever to be trusted.

Moreover, the recognition and clarification of explicit and implicit referents and conceptual contexts do not define the limits of the positive contributions to be expected from a study of the historical world of our narratives. Of equal importance is the growing realization that the redactional techniques of the comprehensive traditions of the Pentateuch, of the so-called deuteronomistic tradition and of their variants in Chronicles–Ezra–Nehemiah reflect not merely the occasional historiographical intentions of the redactors, but also and more frequently the pedantic, antiquarian efforts of curiosity and preservation.[28] These are not only distinct from historiography but at times inimical to it. Historians ask the question of historicity and critically distinguish and evaluate their sources. They 'understand' history and therefore often slip into tendentious ideologies and theologies—so Thucydides.[29]

---

[25] This lack is rapidly diminishing in recent years, not only through the dozens of monographs and hundreds of articles that have revolutionized the history of Palestine, but also through the recent comprehensive handbooks of Helga Weippert, *Archäologie Palästina* and Gösta Ahlström, *History of Ancient Palestine*.

[26] For an earlier discussion of some of these issues, cf. my 'Conflict Themes', pp. 5-26.

[27] One might note the discussions in M. Weippert, *Die Landnahme der israelitischen Stämme in Palästina* (Göttingen: Vandenhoeck & Ruprecht, 1967); T.L. Thompson, *The Historicity of the Patriarchal Narratives* (BZAW, 133; Berlin: de Gruyter, 1974); J.H. Hayes and J.M. Miller (eds.), *Israelite and Judaean History* (Philadelphia: Westminster Press, 1977); J.A. Soggin, *The History of Israel* (Philadelphia: Westminster Press, 1984); N.P. Lemche, *Early Israel* (VTSup, 37; Leiden: Brill, 1985); Miller and Hayes, *A History of Israel and Judah*; Garbini, *History and Ideology*.

[28] Recent comparisons of biblical narrative with Greek authors, especially Herodotus (cf. J. Van Seters, *In Search of History* [New Haven: Yale University Press, 1983] and R.N. Whybray, *The Making of the Pentateuch* [JSOTSup, 54; Sheffield: JSOT Press, 1987]), underscore the importance of this more detached scholarly aspect of our traditions. *Pace* Van Seters, such detachment is to be contrasted to the more politically and ideologically motivated genre of historiography. Cf. further on this, my article 'Historiography' in the forthcoming *Anchor Bible Dictionary*.

[29] The issue here is not one of historicity but of historiography and pertains to the intention of the author, not his success. On this, see the interesting discussion of W.R. Connor, 'Narrative Discourse in Thucydides', in *The Greek Historians: Literature and History, A.E. Raubitschek Festschrift* (ed.

The antiquarian, on the other hand, shares the more ecumenically pluralistic motivations of the librarian (not without significant discrimination and occasional critical control) classifying, associating, and arranging a cultural heritage that is greater than both the compiler and any single historiographical explanation—so perhaps Herodotus,[30] Philo of Byblos,[31] and certainly the Pentateuch![32]

W.R. Connor; Saratoga: Saratoga University Press, 1985), pp. 1-17; P. Robinson, 'Why Do We Believe Thucydides? A Comment on W.R. Connor's "Narrative Discourse in Thucydides" ', in *Greek Historians*, pp. 19-23; and S.W. Hirsch, '1001 Iranian Nights: History and Fiction in Xenophon's Cyropaedia', in *Greek Historians*, pp. 65-86.

[30] For recent discussions of historiography in Herodotus, cf. H.R. Immerwahr, *Form and Thought in Herodotus* (Philological Monographs, 23; Cleveland: Western Reserve University Press, 1966); H. Fahr, *Herodot und altes Testament* (EHST 23, 266; Frankfurt: Lang, 1985); P.R. Helm, 'Herodotus' Medikos Logos and Median History', *Iran* 19 (1981), pp. 85-90; K.D. Bratt, 'Herodotus' Oriental Monarchs and Their Counsellors' (dissertation, Princeton University, 1985); J.M. Balcer, *Herodotus and Bisitun* (Historia, 49; Stuttgart: Steiner, 1987); H. Sancisi-Weerdenburg, 'Decadence in the Empire or Decadence in the Sources?', in *Achaemenid History*, I (ed. H. Sancisi-Weerdenburg; Leiden: Brill, 1987), pp. 33-45; F. Hartog, *The Mirror of Herodotus: The Representation of the Other in the Writing of History* (trans. J. Lloyd; The New Historicism: Studies in Cultural Poetics, 5; Berkeley: University of California Press, 1988).

[31] Cf. H.W. Attridge and R.A. Oden, *Philo of Byblos: The Phoenician History* (CBQMS, 9; Washington, DC: Catholic Biblical Association, 1981). Other ancient Near Eastern historiographic ethnographies and related genres might profitably be compared with Old Testament literature and themes. Cf., e.g., W.W. Hallo, 'Assyrian Historiography Revisited', *Eretz Israel* 14 (1978), pp. 1*-7*; *idem*, 'Sumerian Historiography', in *History, Historiography, and Interpretation* (ed. H. Tadmor and M. Weinfeld; Leiden: Brill, 1984), pp. 9-20; *idem*, 'Biblical History in its Near Eastern Setting: A Contextual Approach', in *Scripture in Context* (ed. W.W. Hallo, C.D. Evans and J.B. White; Pittsburgh: Pickwick Press, 1980), pp. 1-26; N.E. Andersen, 'Genesis 14 in its Near Eastern Context', in *Scripture in Context*, pp. 59-78; P. Veyne, *Did the Greeks Believe in Their Myths?* (Chicago: Chicago University Press, 1988); F. Rochberg-Halton, 'Fate and Divination in Mesopotamia', *Archiv für Orientforschung* 19 (1982), pp. 363-71; M. Liverani, 'The Ideology of the Assyrian Empire', in *Power and Propaganda*, (ed. M.T. Larsen; Mesopotamia, 7; Copenhagen: Academisk 1979), pp. 297-317; P. Michalowski, *The Lamentation over the Destruction of Sumer and Ur* (Winona Lake, IN: Eisenbrauns, 1989); M. Weinfeld, 'Divine Intervention in War in Ancient Israel and in the Ancient Near East', in *History, Historiography and Interpretation*, pp. 121-47; H. Tadmor, 'Autobiographical Apology in the Royal Assyrian Literature', in *History, Historiography and Interpretation*, pp. 36-57; H. Cancik, *Mythische und Historische Wahrheit* (SBS, 48; Stuttgart: Katholische Bibelwerk, 1970); *idem*, *Grundzüge der Hethitischen und alttestamentlichen Geschichtsschreibung* (ADPV; Wiesbaden: Otto Harrassowitz, 1976).

[32] Cf. Van Seters, *In Search of History*; Whybray, *Making of the Pentateuch*; Thompson, *Origin Tradition*. For a dissenting voice on the comparison between the Pentateuch and Herodotus, cf. R.E. Friedman, 'The Prophet and the Historian: The Acquisition of Historical Information from Literary Sources', in *The Past and the Historian* (HSS, 26; ed. R.E. Friedman; Cambridge, MA: Harvard University Press, 1983), pp. 1-12. Some important recent studies of Israelite historiography are: H. Schulte, *Die Entstehung der Geschichtsschreibung im alten Israel* (BZAW, 128; Berlin: de Gruyter, 1972); M. Weippert, 'Fragen des israelitischen Geschichtsbewusstseins', *VT* 23 (1973), pp. 415-41; G.W. Trompf, 'Notions of Historical Recurrence in Classical Hebrew Historiography', in *Studies in the Historical Books of the Old Testament* (VTSup, 30; ed. J.A. Emerton; Leiden: Brill, 1979), pp. 213-29; D.I. Block, 'The Foundations of National Identity: A Study in

The recent discussions by Giovanni Garbini, Axel Knauf, and especially by David Jamieson-Drake[33] of the ancient scribal profession, issues involved in book formation and library collections have all agreed that we cannot seek an origin of literature in Palestine prior to the 8th, or perhaps even better, the 7th century BCE at the height of Judah's influence in the hill country north of Jerusalem that had formerly been part of the state of Samaria. An 8th or 7th century historical context pertains not only to the conceptual world of the narrators of biblical tradition, but equally as powerfully to the world of the collectors of those narrations.[34]

In a world that knows libraries, not only does the nonutilitarian function of writing find room to expand and proliferate, but the genre of the collected literature itself undergoes structural alteration. Tales are linked and become chains of narration, which in turn, can extend in a theoretically infinite succession of chains. In the broad conceptual context of a library, chronology, the linear progression of a series of heroic persons or the great periods and epochs of the past steps outside of the semantic and historiographic nuances of past, present and future and provides an order and structure that is uniquely external to the literature itself. Chronology becomes capable of relating a multiplicity of literature within a comprehensive framework. The resulting succession of episodes and narratives has only the appearance of history.

The collection of literature from Genesis–2 Kings was expanded in the late Persian or early Hellenistic period with Chronicles, Ezra, and Nehemiah and even later with the Megilloth. Many of the extended traditions contained in this library have survived because they were 'popular' or because they were 'in demand'; that is, they found echo and meaning in the lives of their possessors, the handful of collectors and those limited few who used books for leisure. For them, these traditions held relevance for both their political and social worlds, often lending these fragmented worlds of experience interpretive contexts of their own.

Ancient Northwest Semitic Perceptions' (dissertation, University of Liverpool, 1981); R. Schmitt, *Abschied der Heilsgeschichte?* (EHST, 195; Frankfurt: Lang, 1982); J.A. Soggin, 'Le Origini D'Israele Problema per lo Storiografo?' in *Le Origini di Israele* (Rome: Accademia nazionale dei lincei, 1987), pp. 5-14; B. Halpern, *The First Historians* (New York: Harper & Row, 1988); Garbini, *History and Ideology*.

[33] Garbini, *History and Ideology*; Knauf, *Midian*; and D. Jamieson-Drake, *Scribes and Schools in Monarchic Judah: A Socio-Archaeological Approach* (SWBAS, 9; Sheffield; Almond Press, 1991). Cf. further on this the earlier related studies of Rogerson, *Myth in Old Testament Interpretation*; A. Lemaire, *Les écoles et la formation de la Bible dans l'ancien Israel* (OBO, 39; Göttingen: Vandenhoeck & Ruprecht, 1981); and Halpern, *First Historians*.

[34] That the Old Testament is a 'collection' or even a library of literature, authored by many different persons, is a commonplace of biblical studies. The perception, however, that this description also accurately describes the *function* of the collection of traditions of Genesis–Ezra–Nehemiah as library, substantially explaining the textual context of the works included in this collection, was first granted me by the observations of S.E. Janke in a seminar in Jerusalem in 1985. That there is not a normative role in such collections or anything at all similar to a canon is obvious.

One ought not to assume, however, that such *Sitze im Leben* lie *im Leben des Volkes*. Rather, we are dealing only with a small handful of scholarly bibliophiles.[35]

We cannot then assume that the traditions as such necessarily reflect either indirectly or explicitly the real world of their tradents and collectors. They are only meaningful to that world either in terms of contemporary signification or of a more distant future projection. The issue of the sources for the final compositions and collections is of critical importance in understanding our text. It is in the context of the discrete traditions themselves being from the past that we come to deal for the first time with the originating signification of their historical context. Our understanding of collectors and redactors, such as the author of the *tôlᵉdôt* structures of Genesis or the collector of the wilderness variants found in the second half of Exodus and in Numbers does not supply us with that primary context which can be understood as a historical matrix of tradition. Nor can the world of such compilers be understood as the referent of the tradition, that is, the situations or events which the tradition is about. Rather, research into the historical context of such redactions, even of a 'final' redaction, renders only a secondary usage and perspective, only a world in which our traditions have become meaningful or useful. This world was earlier than, but nonetheless comparable to, the much later *Sitz im Leben* of the traditions in one or another canon of the early church or synagogue.

From the perspective of the world of the collectors, we do not understand the historical referent. Nor are we able to reconstruct specific historical and sociopolitical contexts that somehow (with Knauf) must be reflected in such traditions from the past, whether or not they have been fragmented and transformed by these secondary contexts. In addition, the more the narrator or collector of such composite traditions is convinced that the 'realities' of such traditions represent the distant past or more recent events, or are significant to his world-view, the less we will be able to understand his sources in their own context and signification. To the extent, on the other hand, that they have not been transformed by their inclusion in this 'library' and by their association with the other discrete works that surround them—each with its own context, referent and intention—to that extent they become amenable to a historical-critical analysis of both their originating context and their historicity. In addition, the traditions become open to being understood in their own terms, meanings and intentions, apart from what they have been made to mean in the accumulating, distinct contexts of their tradents.

---

[35] These, however, do not form a class of 'elite'. Uncritical assumptions such as B. Lang's (*Monotheism and the Prophetic Minority* [SWBAS, 1; Sheffield: Almond Press, 1983]) seeming equation of literacy and political and economic dominance is without historical justification—anywhere or anytime.

The issues of whether or not the biblical traditions of Genesis–2 Kings and Chronicles–Ezra–Nehemiah are literarily unified, dealing with Israel's past *ex novo*, whether they are primarily tendentious, ideological and/or theological historiographic redactions of traditions, whether they are oral or literary, or whether they are the gatherings of a bibliophile or librarian are of immense interpretive importance. That they are traditions of the past is the primary *raison d'être* for their inclusion. How past they are is a subject of examination for each recognizably distinct tradition collected.

The nature of both the manner of composition and the tendentiousness of historiography, however, renders it exceedingly difficult to recognize and distinguish the discrete sources of historiography. What we can know is largely restricted to the understanding of the world and of tradition at the time of the writing of the historiography. Even when a more ancient source is claimed by the putative historian, our judgment regarding the veracity of such claims must derive almost totally from the world we understand to be contemporary with the historiography. The pursuit of a specific *Traditionsgeschichte* must by necessity be limited to the analysis of changes that are specifically observable in the text, and even such observable transitions may reflect a variety of contemporary understandings rather than an evolutionary development that might carry us into a prehistory of the text. The unproven assumption that the Pentateuch tradition is historiographical and the creation of a single literary hand—perhaps undergoing successive revisions and editions by subsequent authors[36]—can speak only to the successive secondary contexts within which the growing tradition finds a home. In only a limited fashion does it speak to our tradition's originating matrices or significant referents. Such historiographic traditions must be seen as largely irrelevant to critical historical reconstruction because any questions regarding the sources or bases of the successive author's assumptions and perspectives are essentially closed to us. Also lacking is any criterion for establishing either a relative or absolute chronology for strata within the tradition. Indeed, we lack criteria for confirming the existence of any distinctive strata at all, since the basis for the recognition of distinctive ideologies is itself derived primarily from internal considerations without any demonstrable relationship to any realities apart from the text, which at least *prima facie*, is a unit. To assume that J2, for example, is to be dated to the exilic period because it is easier to interpret it within that context is wholly inconsequent as a historical-critical evaluation. However much the process of this tradition formation might presumably reflect the worlds of the redactors or collectors, each with their distinctive political, social and religious realities, it can hardly be used directly for reconstructing these worlds that are largely unknown to us. Even less can they be used for a reconstruction of the circumstances and

---

[36] I am thinking here for instance of such as the revisionist hypothesis of Van Seters (*Abraham in History and Tradition* [New Haven: Yale University Press, 1975]).

events of the tradition's past referent. The tradition, within its field of semantic references, lives within both a real and a literary world. Without a detailed and independent understanding of the historical contexts within which a tradition has relevance, our ability to distinguish or even identify the historical contexts of the tradition is fleeting and sporadic. Furthermore, both the historiographic and antiquarian concerns that sought to preserve traditions after the collapse of the old order do not pretend to present any coherent or univocal truth about the past.[37] Unlike the collections of laws at Qumran, but comparable perhaps to the seemingly omnivorous collections of tradition found in Greek literature or those attributed to Yavneh, the efforts at tradition collection and preservation reflected in the Pentateuchal and deuteronomistic corpora grew out of the collapse and destruction of the societies of Samaria and Jerusalem. It was these disasters that gave the traditions and tradition fragments a historical context as collection and meaning as revered tradition.

However, the specific content of the narratives that have been suspended out of their own time and held as meaningful to these late pre-exilic, exilic, and postexilic tradents does not directly reflect either the exilic or the postexilic world in which the traditions have found their final form. The narratives do not even reflect the pre-exilic world they so desperately tried to preserve. Like the traditions of Yavneh, the biblical traditions reflect only incoherent, part-fictive remnants of a past that the survivors of the destruction and their descendants were able to put together and give meaning to in the radically new worlds into which they were thrown.

It is their significance as meaningful expressions of the old order, giving hope and direction to the new that affected these traditions' preservation, not their dependability in preserving past realities, so painful and ineffective as they were. Both the form and the content of the preserved past have been strongly affected—I hesitate to use the word determined—by the needs of the tradents. Understandably, the realities of the referents were often perceived as having less significance.

It is indisputable that many elements of the received tradition reflect the exigencies of the exilic and early postexilic periods. Yet other elements refer to what has become a fictionalized or literary past. Clear examples of a past existing in literature only are the referents of the immensely instructive phrases in Exod. 15.26d and 23.21. The appeal to 'Yahweh, your healer', in 15.26d is out of context in the tale episode of 15.22-26, wherein Yahweh neither plays nor is called upon to play the role of healer. Nor does this divine title derive from the larger context of Exodus 1–23, where Yahweh provides and protects, guides and saves, but never heals. On the other hand, the close variant tradition found in Num. 21.4-9

---

[37] One might note an analogous indifference to a thoroughgoing ideology in the efforts made to collect the traditions of the schools of Hillel and Shammai by Hillelites after the fall of Jerusalem in AD 70. Cf. J. Neusner, *From Politics to Piety* (New York: Orbis, 1979), p. 100.

presents a deity with whom the motif of healing might be associated, and another variant in Deut. 7.12-15 not only presents Yahweh as healer, but also refers to a now lost account of an episode in Egypt in which Israel, too, suffered disease. It is noteworthy that Yahweh's healing is presented as a reward for obedience to his ordinances in both Exod. 15.22-24 and Deut. 7.12-15. A process of literary allusion, not historical reference, is apparent here.

Even more striking is Yahweh's speech to Moses in Exodus 23. In its context of the early constitutional tradition of Exodus 1–24.8, the speech by Yahweh who is sending his angel to lead Moses and his people against his enemies in 'the place [he] has prepared' refers to a future transgression, which Yahweh will not forgive (v. 21). The immediate and original context (23.1–24.8) makes it very clear that the unforgivable transgression to which this speech directs us is Israel's entering into covenants with the peoples and gods of *Eretz Israel*. The referent then is historiographical and external to the tradition. The threatened punishment for this unforgivable transgression refers to the destruction of either Jerusalem or Samaria, understood theologically and ideologically as having been caused by their own God as a result of what is here attested as Israel's fault. The suggested historical context of this original narration is obviously then the post-destruction period, either the 7th or the 6th centuries. This context is perhaps *pre*-Persian since the potential transgression is understood as unforgivable. Yet this must remain uncertain as the remnant ideology of postexilic prophetic tradition epitomizes Yahweh's mercy with the forgiveness of the unforgivable.

Within the context of the whole of the Pentateuch our pericope of Exod. 23.20–24.8 radically alters its referent. No longer does Yahweh's speech reflect immediate preparations for the conquest of Palestine. Rather, it serves as an opening to the wilderness wandering. The book of the covenant that Moses wrote (Exod. 24.4, 7) is quickly displaced by Yahweh's tablets (Exod. 24.12), themselves displaced by Moses' copy (Exod. 34.4-6, 27-29) as he runs up and down the mountain for successive variations on the traditions of Exodus 19 and 20. Within this context, the referent is literary and internal. It is the transgression of continued murmuring and the sins of Miriam and Aaron, and of Aaron and Moses, in the growing conglomerate of narrative, explaining the entrance into the Promised Land of a new generation rather than the generation addressed by Yahweh in Exodus 23. The historical context of this literary referent is apparently the postexilic situation in which the tradition supports the hope of a new generation in Palestine who have identified with the return from the 'wilderness' of exile to the Promised Land. This hope is born, or promises to find its fulfillment, in their lives in the Persian period.

Although many primary elements of the tradition reflect the historical contexts of periods earlier than the received tradition's formation, their narrative contexts, both primary and secondary, imply a historical context associated with the complex secondary level of the tradition. This suggests in turn that the compilation of the extant tradition is, in terms of intellectual history, clearly distinct from its sources. Such a distinction between an originating historical context (i.e. historical matrix) and a secondary historical context is particularly pertinent when dealing with traditions that appear to be largely irrelevant to their received contexts, yet assumed by this secondary context to derive from hoary antiquity. Here one might well think of Leviticus 16, but perhaps also those tales introduced into larger narratives by means of 'postintroductory inclusion'[38] such as Gen. 12.10-20, Genesis 26 and Genesis 38. It is equally necessary for the historical critic to sort out the potentially distinctive literary and historical referents and contexts of narratives that appear to exhibit historiographical or literary harmony (e.g. Gen. 11.26–12.4)[39] or an editorial dovetailing of successive variant narrations of what was perceived as an equivocal episode or tale (e.g. Gen. 6–9; Exod. 5–13; and Exod. 14).[40]

Given the complex manner in which the tradition has functioned as survival literature, our ability to relate the historical context of various redactive moments to the late pre-exilic, the exilic, or the postexilic periods does not substantially help our arriving at either the specific historical and intellectual milieu of their received form or, ultimately, the specific sociohistorical matrix of their origins, except in the grossest and most general terms. As survival literature, the traditions render a composite ideological understanding to these periods. The traditions are not so much a direct reflection of or reference to their periods of origin and composition as they are an explanation that gives meaning to them. That is, the ideological and theological *Tendenz* of the received or extant traditions, to the degree that they are oriented to the world of the final stages of the tradition's formation, may well preclude their use for any historical reconstruction based on assumed events from a greater past. For such past worlds refracted from the redactions are constructs of a world contemporary to the redaction. Indeed, they stand outside of any historical field of reference other than intellectual history. The historical significance of the received tradition, holistically perceived, lies primarily in its dual functions as meaningful literature and as library in post-compositional times.

One must indeed incline towards the Persian period for the historical context in which our narratives have their significance as a tradition of Israel. At such a late date considerable portions of the tradition's original contextual content have already lost much of their intrinsic relevance. While these traditions have been transvalued in the process of transmission and have acquired an even wider meaning than they bore as reflections of the often opaque world of their original historical context, they have also lost much cohesion with their specific origins in antiquity.

---

[38] Cf. Thompson, *Origin Tradition*, p. 169.
[39] Thompson, *Historicity of the Patriarchal Narratives*, pp. 308-11.
[40] Cf. Thompson, *Origin Tradition*, pp. 74-77, 139-46.

Unlike the problems surrounding the historical context of a literary unit, the problem dealing with their intentional referent involves one immediately with the many variant degrees of fictional and historiographical intent as well as with the externally oriented issues of accuracy and historicity. Internally, one necessarily distinguishes a number of discrete formal categories as relevant: (a) aetiologies, (b) traditional tales, (c) *Standesgeschichte*, (d) *Stammesgeschichte*, (e) genealogical tales, (f) romances, (g) ethnographies, and (h) historiographies.[41] Their intentional referent distinguishes them. For instance, aetiology is different from historiography in that the referent of an aetiology is typically some contemporary reality, while historiography refers to the perceived past. Historiographical narrative is distinct from the often literarily comparable traditional tale in that historiography involves a critical reflection on sources for the past with the intention of presenting the reality of the past, while traditional narratives are preserved either for antiquarian motives (because they are from the past) or because of their hermeneutical and heuristic value to the tradent. Propaganda, on the other hand, and other ideologically tendentious literature are essentially anticritical, intending to distort or to create a past for extraneous reasons. *Stammesgeschichte*, *Standesgeschichte*, and genealogical tales, with their signification born of attraction to the tradents, are all essentially subvarieties of historiography, propaganda or romances. Romances are distinct from traditional tales in that they are fictional histories and literary expressions of the aura surrounding the heroes and events of the past. Certainly Genesis 14 fits this category (*pacem* Cancik!), perhaps the song of Deborah in Judges 5, and with little doubt the song in Exodus 15.

Only very few Israelite narratives involve historiography at a primary level of the tradition.[42] This genre is most notably present in the larger redactions and final forms of composition. Even there, a comprehensive, historiographically motivated critical perspective rarely surfaces in our literature. The sweeping assertions common today that boldly refer to 'historians' and the like existing long before Thucydides[43] say much more than they properly can.

---

[41] Cf. further my article 'Conflict Themes', pp. 5-26.

[42] On this particular issue, see the early chapters of either Miller and Hayes, *History of Israel and Judah* or Soggin, *History of Israel*. The more recent and more radical presentations of N.P. Lemche (*Ancient Israel: A New History of Israelite Society* [Sheffield: JSOT Press, 1988]) and Garbini (*History and Ideology*), though less comprehensive, are closer to the writer's position; cf. my *Early History of the Israelite People* (forthcoming).

[43] I am thinking here of such otherwise helpful studies as Van Seters's *In Search of History*. One might also refer to similar assumptions of B. Long ('Historical Narrative and the Fictionalizing Imagination', *VT* 35 [1985], pp. 405-16) and C. Meyers ('The Israelite Empire: In Defense of King Solomon', in *Backgrounds for the Bible* [ed. M.P. O'Connor and D.N. Freedman; Winona Lake, IN: Eisenbrauns, 1987], pp. 181-97). See, on the other hand, the very interesting discussion of H.M. Barstad ('On the History and Archaeology of Judah during the Exilic Period: A Reminder', *Orientalia Louvaniensa Periodica* 19 [1988], pp. 25-36).

The hard times that have come upon historical-critical research in its effort to write a history of Israel reflect a positive growth in awareness of the biblical tradition's lack of historicity and historiography. Much of the historical-critical research of the past that has been written in reaction against Wellhausen has been committed to the preservation of these two endangered species and has supported the now defunct dogma that a critical history of Israel is rendered through a synthesis of biblical archaeology and biblical criticism.

Very recent efforts to write a history of the United Monarchy as a development from the sedentarization of the central hill country in terms of Saulide and Davidic 'chieftainships' are to be commended for many reasons. They attempt a new synthesis of archaeological evidence and biblical tradition, while at the same time dealing competently and critically with the issues of historiography and historicity.[44] The hypothesis of the existence of 'chieftainships' in the central hills of Palestine during the Iron I period, identified as the historical reality from which the biblical traditions sprang, is useful for illustrating the benefits and pitfalls of synthetic reconstructions of the history of Palestine. This is particularly true of the hypothesis of a 'Saulide chieftainship'. Not only are some, perhaps primary episodes of the biblical narrative isolated, but the historical reality of such a political structure, limited to the central hills of Palestine as J.M. Miller has long argued,[45] can be justified as possible with considerable persuasiveness.[46] The arguments for such a synthesis, however, must, given the lack of specificity in our archaeological sources, proceed along the lines of verisimilitude—what is often perceived as 'probability'. The strength of such a model, based as it is on historical-like observations of a Finkelstein-like archaeological summary of surveys and excavations in the hill country,[47] is considerable as long as a close

---

[44] Most notable among these studies are: Lemche, *Ancient Israel* and I. Finkelstein, *The Archaeology of the Israelite Settlement* (Jerusalem: Israel Exploration Society, 1988). The Chicago dissertation of D. Edelman ('The Rise of the Israelite State under Saul' [1986]; see also especially her 'Saul's Rescue of Jabesh Gilead [1 Sam 11:1-11]: Sorting Story from History', *ZAW* 96 [1984], pp. 195-209; and her 1989 paper, 'The Deuteronomist's Story of King Saul: Narrative Art or Editorial Product?', in *Pentateuchal and Deuteronomistic Studies* [BETL, 94; ed. C. Brekelmans and J. Lust; Leuven: Leuven University Press, 1990], pp. 207-20) deserves particular focus both because of its critical control of much of the recent progress in Palestinian archaeology, but also because of its detailed concentration on the tales of the 'United Monarchy' that are historically the most viable. Because of this heuristic value, the following remarks have Edelman's dissertation most in mind. The recent 'holistic' interpretation of the David stories by J. Flanagan (*David's Social Drama: A Hologram of Israel's Early Iron Age* [SWBAS, 7 and JSOTSup, 73; Sheffield: Almond Press, 1989]) on the other hand, does not share Edelman's control of the archaeological material and takes a largely uncritical perspective of the biblical tradition. Consequently, it is of less value for a theoretical and methodological discussion.

[45] J.M. Miller, 'The Israelite Occupation of Canaan', in *Israelite and Judaean History*, esp. pp. 213-45.

[46] Edelman, 'Rise of the Israelite State', who, however, argues for a Saulide kingship, not a chieftainship.

[47] Finkelstein, *Archaeology*.

association between Iron I Ephraim and the Israel of tradition can be maintained. The validity of such a comprehensive hypothesis, however, does not directly relate to these issues, even when the archaeologically oriented discussion appears most persuasive. The validity of any such synthetic hypothesis, even when carried out with detail and care, stands or falls on issues of historiography and historicity. Some of the difficulties of accepting a Saulide chieftainship as a historically viable reality, in spite of the truly impressive archaeological illustration of such hypotheses are as follows.

1. Given the more recent datings of 1–2 Samuel, there exists a three-to-four-century gap between the biblical tradition and the reconstructed events to which the 'primary' traditions supposedly refer. This weakness is particularly awkward since the necessary continuity between a hypothetical Saulide chieftainship and the royal dynasties of the state of Samaria, and through them with the Israel of tradition, is essentially supported by an obviously fictional, or at least fictionalized association with the legendary Davidic dynasty of a neighboring state.[48]

2. Secondly, following the line of argument developed in Israeli scholarship by B. Mazar, Y. Aharoni and M. Kochavi, there is an assumed equation of the sedentarization of the central hills of Iron I with the origins of the state, which is later known in both tradition and international politics as Israel.[49] In spite of objections to a simplistic identification of the pre-Saulide Iron I settlements as 'Israelite', this equation allows an association of the Saulide chieftainship with the Iron I settlements of this region, in spite of the lack of historical warrant for that identification.

3. This caution is intensified by the observation that we are also lacking any direct evidence for a process of regional centralization in the central hills before the foundation of Samaria during Iron II. Thus, such an association in the Iron I period remains in the realm of mere possibility.

---

[48] I am thinking here, for example, of the well-worn numerical motif of 40 for the number of kings between Saul and the Judean exile.

[49] Cf. esp. B. Mazar, *Canaan and Israel* (Jerusalem: Mošad Bialik, 1974); *idem*, 'The Early Israelite Settlement in the Hill Country', *BASOR* 241 (1981), pp. 75-87; Y. Aharoni, *The Settlement of the Israelite Tribes in Upper Galilee* (dissertation, Jerusalem, 1957); *idem*, 'New Aspects of the Israelite Occupation in the North', in *Near Eastern Archaeology in the Twentieth Century, Glueck Festschrift* (ed. J.A. Sanders; New York: Doubleday, 1970), pp. 254-65; *idem*, 'Nothing Early and Nothing Late: Rewriting Israel's Conquest', *BA* 39 (1976), pp. 55-67; M. Kochavi, 'The Period of Israelite Settlement', in *The History of Eretz Israel*. II. *Israel and Judah in the Biblical Period* (ed. I. Eph'al; Jerusalem: Israel Exploration Society, 1984), pp. 19-84; *idem*, 'The Land of Israel in the 13th-12th Centuries B.C.E. Historical Conclusions from Archaeological Data', in *Eleventh Archaeological Conference in Israel* (Jerusalem: Israel Exploration Society, 1985), p. 16; Finkelstein, *Archaeology*. In his paper at the 1990 SBL Convention in New Orleans Finkelstein rejected the necessity of this association.

4. To assert the existence of a historico-political entity 'Israel' as early as Iron I—however small a 'chieftainship' or 'kingship' that might be—seems to create enormous difficulties for illustrating political continuity and unity: continuity with the state of Samaria in Iron II and unity with the early settlements of other regions, including the Jezreel Upper Galilee and the Iron II sedentarization of Judah. To relate, for example, a hypothetical Davidic chieftainship with the Hebron and northern Negev region does not lighten the problem of continuity, however judiciously these associations might be expressed and however much it may help bypass issues of historicity with arguments of comprehensiveness bolstered by plausibility.

5. The greatest problem of such synthetic reconstruction touches upon the paramount issue of the effervescent relationship between biblical literature and historical research. One cannot but question any alleged 'reliable pool of information'. Reminiscent of the syntheses of the Albright school in the fifties and sixties, the concept of a Saulide or Davidic state or chieftainship is a hybrid, bearing little resemblance to either the Israel of tradition or the historical associations potentially derived from archaeology. Real historical issues are not those infinite ones of possibility and necessity (history is *Wissenschaft*, not metaphysics), but rather those of reconstruction, related to evidence established. If historicity cannot be granted to the biblical tradition as a whole or even to very specifically defined parts of it, why should we be tempted to adopt a perspective that is derivative from the comprehensive tradition? Why should we assume that Saul's kingdom was a precursor to the Davidic monarchy and had its roots in the divinely rejected northern hills? And if such anachronistic reconstruction cannot be supported, what benefit is derived from attributing such political unification to Saul? These efforts to harmonize archaeological evidence and biblical tradition reminds me of a poem by Milne:

> Halfway up the stairs
> Isn't up, and isn't down.
> It isn't in the nursery
> It isn't in the town.
> And all sorts of funny thoughts
> Run round my head:
> It isn't really anywhere!
> It's somewhere else instead.[50]

In suggesting that the essential interpretive context of the narrative tradition of Genesis–2 Kings is that period during which the tradition achieved its role as survival literature, a perspective is recommended which is quite different from that

---

[50] A.A. Milne, *When We Were Very Young* (London: Dutton, 1972), p. 83.

usually taken by tradition history. Again as Miller has argued, it is unlikely that we will be able to correlate adequately the earlier strata of the tradition with concrete historical events in Israel's past, or even with any of the episodes of the tradition, as if they were, somehow, memories of a real past. Determining the potential historical referents of the tradition and determining that tradition's relevance to the writing of a history of Israel is theoretically more possible the closer we are to the extant form of the tradition. However, this is true only to the extent that these latest formulations and revisions relate to or are identical with those issues and events informing these ultimate redactions.

The hypothesis that the received traditions once existed in antiquity in substantial form at a time prior to these latest redactions needs reinvestigation. Certainly Wellhausen forms of 'documents' dating from as early as the United Monarchy must now be abandoned—if only because of the tenuous hold on existence the period of the United Monarchy has. Furthermore, much recent scholarship has questioned the existence of such extensive and coherent portions of the received text at such an early period and variously recommends a historical context in the late pre-exilic, exilic, or the early postexilic periods.[51] An early date certainly seems impossible now. However, too specific, late dates appear arbitrary and seem based on circular arguments.

Our understanding of the Josianic reform and of the prophetic and convenantal ideologies that presumably supported it is essentially based on a historicistic and naïve reading of 2 Kings,[52] which is, after all, a product of the same spectra of traditions that use 2 Kings for their referential context. Similarly, in dating the prophets—Amos, Hosea, 1 Isaiah–Ezekiel—we too quickly assume that the prophetic traditions had original nuclei deriving from the events and persons alleged by the traditions themselves, which continued to have significance in a postdestruction world. In fact, however, we know historically little of such events or persons.

The external confirmatory evidence we have for these assumptions is both fragmentary and oblique. The very knowledge we have of the exilic and postexilic periods rests on the presupposition that Chronicles, Ezra and Nehemiah can somehow be translated into refractions of historical reality. Yet we know that these

---

[51] H. Vorländer, *Die Entstehungszeit des Jehowistischen Geschichtswerkes* (EHST, 23.109; Frankfurt: Lang, 1978); Van Seters, *Abraham in History and Tradition*; idem, *In Search of History*; H.H. Schmid, *Der Sogenannte Jahwist: Beobachtungen und Fragen zur Pentateuchforschung* (Zurich: Theologischer Verlag, 1976); Lemche, *Early Israel*; E. Blum, 'Die Komplexität der Uberlieferung: Zur synchronen und diachronen Analyse von Gen 32:23-33', *DBAT* 15 (1980), pp. 2-55; idem, *Die Komposition der Vätergeschichte* (WMANT, 57; Neukirchen-Vluyn: Neukirchener Verlag, 1984); M. Rose, *Deuteronomist und Jahwist* (ATANT, 67; Zurich: Theologischer Verlag 1981); and F. Kohata, *Jaw hist und Priesterschrift in Exodus 3–14* (BZAW, 166; Berlin: de Gruyter, 1986).

[52] Lowell Handy's recent paper to the SBL Midwest regional convention in February 1990 at Madison is a serious effort to redress this perspective ('Assyro-Babylonian Cult Narratives and Historical Probability for Josiah's Reform').

traditions were also written and edited as substantial traditions of Israel's past long after the exilic and early postexilic periods. Because of this, the assumption that they can render history is no longer obvious and has to be tested with each unit of tradition.

The synthetic approach to historiography, which has dominated our field at least since Eduard Meyer, must now be abandoned. If we are ever to achieve our exegetical goal of allowing the biblical narrative to be heard and understood within the modern context of our discipline, the first and primary need is to establish, in all the fullness and detail possible, an independent history of early Palestine and Israel that might serve as the historical context from which these narratives speak. Without such an interpretive matrix, we continue to read the biblical tradition in faith—as through a glass darkly.

The Big Max: Review of *A Biblical History of Israel*, by Iain Provan, V. Philips Long, and Tremper Longman, III

Lester L. Grabbe

The terms "maximalist" and "minimalist" get thrown around a lot in contemporary discussions about the history of ancient Israel. It seems to me that they are often employed inappropriately, if we accept a widely used definition of the terms.[1] By that description, only a few minimalists exist and hardly any maximalists, at least in mainstream scholarship. Yet now, in *A Biblical History of Israel*, by Iain Provan, V. Philips Long, and Tremper Longman III (PLL),[2] we see what looks to me like a genuine maximalist work. What sort of history do we get when maximalists write it?

The first thing that strikes the reader on opening the book is that out of a text of approximately three hundred pages, one hundred—a full 34 percent—are devoted to the question of how to write history. We should expect a preface or introductory chapter explaining the authors' approach, general principles, and the like—the book would be deficient without such an explanation. But why should only 66 percent of the text be devoted to the actual history? This seems strange.

This long introductory chapter includes a survey of how history has been written in the past two centuries. The discussion is prolix, turgid, and meandering, but does it accomplish its purpose? The point that seems to be emphasized is that the "scientific" approach dominated history writing from the Enlightenment until recent times. Sometimes this is expressed as "positivism," though the use of this

---

[1] William W. Hallo claims to have coined this definition: Hallo (2005, 50), citing Hallo (1980, 3–5, nn. 4, 11, 12, 23, 55). E. A. Knauf defined the "minimalist approach" as "everything which is not corroborated by evidence contemporary with the events to be reconstructed is dismissed" and "the maximalist approach which implies that everything in the sources that could not be proved wrong has to be accepted as historical" (Knauf 1991, 171).

[2] The authors and their book will be collectively referred to as "PLL" in the rest of this review. While not entirely satisfactory, it seems preferable to more cumbersome abbreviations.

term is potentially confusing: surveys of the development of historiography tend to use "positivism" mainly of those historians in the tradition of Comte, such as Henry Thomas Buckle, Hippolyte Taine, and perhaps John Bagnall Bury. PLL have acknowledged using E. Breisach's overview as the basis for their survey (p. 306 n. 35). Yet when Breisach speaks of positivists in the twentieth century, he seems to use the term primarily of such individuals as Carl Hemper and Carl Popper, who were philosophers of science, though they made pronouncements on history (1994, 327–29). Other standard surveys seem to want to avoid the term "positivism" (e.g. Iggers 1975, 1997; Evans 1997), while the reference *Encyclopedia of Historians and Historical Writings* (Boyd 1999) does not have an entry on positivism.

When I read the historiographic surveys of Breisach (1994), Iggers (1975, 1997), Evans (1997), and other professional historians,[3] I do not recognize the PLL characterization of historiographical development in the nineteenth and twentieth centuries, expressed in such statements as,

> By the end of the 1880s, this history-as-science had replaced philosophy as the discipline to which many educated people in Europe and elsewhere in the Western world turned as the key that would unlock the mysteries of human life. (p. 21)

I began to wonder whether they are using "positivist" simply as a synonym for "objective," since Ranke is described by the term "quasi-positivism," even though he "stopped well short of a full-blown scientific positivism" (p. 22). But then various objectors to positivism are described, including J. G. Droysen, W. Dilthey, and B. Croce (pp. 39–43), and they hardly rejected the concept of objectivity in history writing. Also, the contrast of "science" and "philosophy" in relation to history, made by PLL (see the quote above), seems an artificial one, since the application of science to history is couched in a particular philosophy of history. But then I became completely flummoxed when I read further (on p. 42):

> We may with confidence say, then, that the whole movement of the last century was in general a movement away from the notion that history is a science and back towards the notion that history is an art.

How does this square with the earlier statement quoted above? Did "science"/ "positivism" dominate history writing from the late nineteenth century or did it not?

I think most working historians would see what they do as both science and art. But the fact is that most contemporary historians are not overly concerned with historical theory; at least, that has been my firm impression. When I talk to members of the History Department in my own university, they do not usually

---

[3] See my own survey of trends in writing history in Grabbe 2004.

agonize over whether to use postmodernism or follow some particular philosopher of history. Indeed, it is difficult to find anyone interested in discussing historical theory or method: apart from an introductory class or two, it seems to be taken for granted. Their concern is in having resources to visit archives or to develop the library collection in their specialist area and in having the time away from teaching and administration to do their research. This impression is reinforced by a comment by Allen Megill, "Even in the late 20th century, most historians are largely unconcerned with the theory of their discipline" (1999, 1:540).

PLL's discussion leads up to the presentation of contemporary history as choosing between being an intellectual ostrich, a postmodernist, or taking their own approach. Since most contemporary historians do not take the PLL approach, does this mean they either "deny reality" or base their work on postmodernist principles? An emphasis seems to be placed on the view that historians cannot be objective. This applies not just to textual sources but also to archaeology. Artifacts do not speak for themselves; they have to be interpreted. Archaeology is no more objective than any other source. Again, one is somewhat surprised at their discussion. Postmodernism has certainly had its influence, but it is fair to say that there is only a handful of truly postmodernist historians. While most historians recognize that some of the issues raised by postmodernists are relevant to writing history, most also believe that the historian can maintain a certain objectivity and that some access to the past is possible. Most believe that some approaches are preferable to others and that even though there is an inevitable subjectivity in the process, proper writing of history is not the same as writing fiction. (Mis)quotation of Hayden White does not make history just another form of fiction.

PLL do give one innovation, however: the appeal to the importance of "testimony." It is difficult to pretend that real historians accept this view, and most space is given over to defending the concept rather than suggesting that other historians would agree. This is a difficult concept to defend, in large part because it is never made clear what is meant by "testimony." The idea seems first to have been raised by Provan (see Provan 2000), but neither his original discussion nor the discussion in PLL really clarifies what is meant.[4] For example, is archaeology a form of testimony? A statement on p. 55 seems to say so, but the statement on p. 63 seems to say the opposite. If I am anywhere close to understanding what they are getting at, then any account of an event—no matter how late or how ignorant the author—has historical value. It does not seem to be eye-witness knowledge, which is castigated (p. 49). Indeed, a secondary source centuries after the event seems to have as much value as an eye-witness primary source.

---

[4] Those dealing in oral history sometimes use the term "testimony" to refer to the statements made in an oral context. See, for example, the various contributions to Perks and Thomson 1998. Yet I do not believe that this is the way that PLL are using "testimony." Also, it should be noted that the term "written testimony" can be used as well as "oral testimony" (Perks and Thomson 1998, 41).

What is more, eye-witness testimony has no preference because it can be unreliable. They are quite right about the problems with eye witnesses and the possible distortions that eye-witness accounts may contain, but if there were no eye witnesses, how do we know anything about an event? In their enthusiasm to debunk eye-witness sources, they seem to have missed that without eye witnesses, we are unlikely to know anything about many sorts of historical incidents, at a time when photography, sound recordings, and the like were not available. PLL should have given some thought to that before getting carried away in discounting the importance of eye witnesses.

When PLL finally get to the actual question of history, they do indeed write a "biblical" history of Israel—in the sense of giving a version of events that is essentially a paraphrase of the biblical account. Two questions arise: first, why is the amount of space given to certain events out of proportion to their value as history? This seems to depend in part on the amount of biblical material available, but not necessarily. For example, the 350 years between the time of Solomon and the fall of Jerusalem to Nebuchadnezzar receives only 25 pages (pp. 259–84)—or 8 percent of the text. Secondly, while the biblical outline is evident, the details are often skipped over. There is not enough space, of course, to treat all the details, but this means that many problematic and embarrassing details are simply ignored.

At this point, I want to focus on one major example to illustrate some of the problems I see with their approach. This example is PLL's discussion of the settlement of Israel in the land of Canaan (pp. 138–92). Not only is this an important area where standard scholarship argues against the biblical picture, but PLL also spend a considerable amount of space discussing the topic. At first blush, there are a number of positive features in this discussion: difficulties with the biblical picture are acknowledged, caution in interpretation and drawing conclusions is encouraged, both biblical and extra-biblical material are discussed, and conclusions are presented as a personal view rather than a dogmatic assertion (but see below).

After a survey of current theories, PLL begin by analyzing Joshua and Judges. This is an understandable place to begin (though I would have begun with the primary sources, a concept they reject[5]). Time and again the authors assert that the text has to be properly read, and castigating references are made to "flat, literalistic (mis)readings of biblical texts" (p. 149). PLL advise "caution against simplistic, literalistic readings" (p. 153) and "avoidance of a simplistic approach" (p. 167). Texts "should not be read in a flat, literalistic way" (p. 153) or given a "wooden reading" (p. 196).

---

[5] See pp. 64–65.

A good example of this involves numbers. When the Bible says that "600,000 men on foot" (besides women and children: Exod 12:37; Num 10:21) went out of Egypt, and a census gives the figure of 603,550 men (not counting Levites: Num 1:46; 2:32), an alternative explanation is quoted (p. 130). No judgment is made ("space does not permit a full presentation...and it may not in the final analysis be correct"—p. 131), but the conclusion is: "Numbers in the biblical narrative frequently have purposes other than merely to communicate literal fact" (p. 131). Similarly, the chronological figures in the book of Judges:

> All these figures added together would yield some 573 years (plus the unspecified years of the elders who outlived Joshua), a sum far in excess of 1 Kings 6:1's 480 years. Obviously, simply adding figures together wreaks havoc with a fifteenth-century exodus, to say nothing of a thirteenth-century one. Are we to conclude that the biblical data are simply confused?... Taking all this into account, we can easily see the difficulty (perhaps impossibility) of establishing a precise chronology of the period of the judges; there are simply too many open variables. This conclusion does not mean that the book of Judges is unreliable, only that it must be taken on its own terms. (pp. 163–64)

So how is the text to be read? Apparently, texts cannot be taken at face value because this would be reading them in a flat, wooden, literalistic way. It is admitted that some texts are expressed "in hyperbolic terms" (p. 153); reference is made to the "hyperbolic character of the summary" (p. 153); another passage mentions "more hyperbole" (p. 154). Sometimes the text sounds "exaggerated" (p. 154). There might even be—would you believe it?—a not "total absence of anachronism" (p. 116). But all of this is presented with a slightly indulgent air— like a father shaking his head at the antics of a favourite son. For it soon becomes clear that in the eyes of PLL, the text can never simply be mistaken: we just need to understand it "on its own terms." If you or I made such statements, other scholars—including PLL—would point out that we were misleading, inaccurate, or just plain wrong. But never the biblical text: it may be "hyperbolic," "exaggerated," not free of "anachronism"—but never wrong. For example:

> If, for instance, one were to overlook the hyperbolic character of the summary of Joshua's southern campaign found in Joshua 10:40—Joshua "left no one remaining, but utterly destroyed all that breathed"—then the discovery...that many Canaanites survived would appear to constitute a contradiction. The problem, however, would lie not with the text but with the inappropriate construal of the texts. (p. 153)

> The first part of the summary (11:16–20) is an intriguing combination of generalities and specifics, of history and theology, of hyperbole and restraint. In one sense, the claim that "Joshua took all that land" (v. 16) sounds exaggerated, because he clearly did not take every city (some were not taken until David's day) and even some whole regions, such as the coastal plain, are not mentioned in the description that follows. In another sense, however, the statement may be quite accurate, claiming only that Joshua gained the upper hand throughout the land as a whole. (p. 154)

> ...we must approach the territorial allotments listed in Joshua 13–19 with circumspection. In his helpful discussion of the allotments, Hess points out that the lists, which were originally family allotments, would have soon become administrative documents and, as such, would likely have been subject to updating as new towns emerged. Any late monarchic features found in the lists, therefore, might best be understood not as establishing the origin of the lists but as demonstrating their continued use. (p. 156)

PLL later refer to "the second half of the book of Joshua, which includes also proleptic references to the varied successes of the tribes in actually occupying their allotments" (p. 189).

The question is asked, "Or might avoidance of a simplistic approach, closer attention to the distinction between initial conquest and eventual occupation... indeed yield a better understanding of the conquest and occupation?" (p. 167). The answer is quickly given: "The basic point is that misreading Joshua's initial campaigns—central, south, and north—as 'permanent conquests' and setting these in opposition to the slower 'occupations' described in Judges 1 are fundamental errors" (p. 167). To support this, it is asserted,

> Simply put, an important difference exists between subjugation and occupation... The land has been given, it lies subdued, but Israel must still take possession of it and occupy it... In chapter 23, Joshua juxtaposes without embarrassment assertions of the success of the conquest...with clear admissions that work remains to be done... All things considered, the oft-cited contradiction between Joshua and Judges is ill-conceived in a number of ways... In broad strokes, then, and taking Joshua and Judges together, the biblical depiction of Israel's emergence in Canaan is internally coherent: Israel entered and gained an initial ascendancy..., but was far less successful in consolidating its victories by fully occupying its territories. (pp. 167–68)

Can PLL so easily get away from the scholarly consensus that Judg 1 paints a rather different picture of the occupation of the land from that ending Joshua? Or is this distinction between "subjugation" and "occupation" an artificial creation to get out of a bind? Apparently, it would be "simplistic" to draw attention to passages in Joshua that say the work of conquest had been finished by the time of Joshua's death, but I shall do so nonetheless:

Josh 11:23; 14:15: "And the land had rest from war."

Joshua 13:1–7: Yhwh tells Joshua that a good deal of land remains to be taken possession of (or "subdued/subjugated"). What is this land? It is the area of the Philistines, the area of the Phoenicians, Lebanon, and north into Syria. It is clear that Joshua and the Israelites have conquered most of Cis-Jordan except for Philistia.

Joshua 21:41–43:

> Yhwh gave to Israel all the land which he had sworn to give to their fathers, and they subdued it and settled in it. And Yhwh gave rest to them on every side according to all that he had sworn to their fathers: no man stood before their face from all their enemies—Yhwh had given all their enemies in their hand. Not one word failed from all the good words that Yhwh had spoken to the House of Israel—all had come to pass.

Try as one might, one cannot get away from the overall picture of Joshua: the Israelites under Joshua's leadership came from across the Jordan and conquered the land and the indigenous peoples in what was basically a five-year campaign and then divided the country up. Those Canaanites who had not been destroyed or driven out were put into servitude. By the time of Joshua's death the work was accomplished and the promises fulfilled. If any land remained unconquered, it was that outside the traditional borders of Israel, that is, the Philistine, Phoenician, and Lebanon regions. The idea that the land was "subdued/subjugated" but that the indigenous Canaanites still had to be "subdued/subjugated" is absurd—and it accords little respect to the biblical text.

Of course, some passages do not agree with the picture: there are passages such as Josh 17:14–17 that suggest the Canaanites still had control of extensive areas, in agreement with Judg 1. There are also territorial lists that contradict each other: for example, Jerusalem is assigned both to the inheritance of Judah (Josh 15:63) and Benjamin (Josh 18:28); both Judah and Dan are said to be assigned the cities of Ekron and Timnah (Josh 15:45, 47; 19:43). According to the standard scholarly understanding of the biblical books, these discrepancies present no surprises. The usual explanation is that Joshua was written by a Deuteronomistic editor or editors who made use of a variety of traditions. The main message of the Deuteronomist did not always jibe with the message of the traditions, nor did the various traditions necessarily agree with each other. The tradition(s) lying behind Judg 1 and perhaps some passages in Joshua did not accord with the message incorporated into Joshua by the editor/compiler. If one is not committed to an artificial compulsion to deny any conflict or contradictions in the text, everything falls into place. But it does require you to read the text for what it says (disdainfully dismissed as "simplistic"), not in some convoluted ("unsimplistic") way.

Moving from textual analysis to material remains, we are immediately informed that "contrary to popular (and sometimes scholarly) opinion, actual property damage caused by the conquest may have been quite modest, so that Israel's arrival may have left little or no archaeological mark" (p. 173). Why? Deuteronomy 6:10–12 is quoted to the effect that the Israelites would take over the houses, vineyards, and olive groves of the Canaanites, so "we have no reason to expect archaeological evidence of widespread city destructions in the wake of an Israelite conquest" (p. 173). Furthermore, "only three sites are explicitly said to have been burned in the course of Joshua's campaigns" (p. 173).

But wait: are these the same people who were warning us against flat, literalistic readings? Apparently, it is all right to read "literalistically, simplistically, woodenly" if it suits your purpose. Numbers can apparently "communicate literal fact" when you decide it helps your case. So when Joshua says that "not one was left alive" of the Canaanites, we should not read that literally, but if Deuteronomy says that the Israelites will inherit the houses, cisterns, vineyards, etc., of their enemies, we can take that literally. As for the three cities burned, Joshua is not quite as precise as PLL imply: the fact is that only three towns are *explicitly stated* to have been burned, but is "absence of evidence evidence of absence"? They deny that it is (p. 228); have they changed their mind here?[6] A similar appeal to "absence of evidence" is made with regard to other sites:

> In the brief summaries of the taking of these cities [Makkedah, Libnah, Lachish, Gezer, Eglon, Hebron, Debir], much emphasis is placed on putting the populations to the sword and leaving no survivors, but there is little to suggest that the cities themselves were destroyed. (p. 153)

This statement is of course made to counter the lack of archaeology and to deny the picture of the conquest of Joshua. In so doing, the writers are quick to appeal to "flat" and "literalistic"—with no suggestion of hyperbole—wording here, since it suits their purpose.

A lengthy section discusses the archaeology of a number of sites given a significant place in the Joshua narrative (pp. 174–89). Two will be given here. First is Jericho, "often cited as a 'parade example' of how archaeology has shown the Bible to be historically unreliable" (p. 174). It is pointed out that the archaeology at Jericho does "correlate in many remarkable ways with the biblical account" (p. 174). But has not the research of Kathleen Kenyon shown something quite different? Yes, but this is apparently just a matter of dating: "The problem of Jericho has to do not so much with the material findings as with the dates assigned to these findings" (p. 174). These comments might seem strange—after all, dating is vital—but when you read a little further, all is clear: Kenyon's dating is being challenged: "A simple answer may not be apt in this case. B. Wood effectively reopened the question in 1990" (p. 175). A good number of archaeologists will be astonished to find that Wood has "effectively reopened the question," but we are assured that "Wood built an impressive case for rethinking the dating of the Jericho evidence" (p. 175). Why have professional archaeologists and others not debated this "impressive case"? If it is so "impressive," why has it been made available only in an unpublished section of a Ph.D. thesis and an article in *Biblical Archaeology Review*—hardly the professional publication one would expect.

---

[6] Josh 11:13 states that only Hazor was burned of the royal cities standing on their mounds, though the precise intent is not clear.

It is admitted that "Wood's challenge has not succeeded in gaining a large scholarly following"; nevertheless, "many observers recognize the potency of his challenge" (p. 176). Are these "many observers" the professional notice that we might expect of a significant scholarly theory? Well, hardly—the only "observers" cited are four other conservative evangelicals. From the discussion up to this point, one would expect the conclusion to be that an interesting alternative interpretation was proposed 20 years ago, gained no following, and the status quo accepted. But, no: "Further, until such time as Wood's arguments are fully aired and fairly assessed, for scholars to continue to cite Jericho as a parade example is irresponsible." As we all know, this is a proper model for scholars to follow: whenever a Ph.D. student comes up with a half-baked theory, all scholars should drop what they are doing and see that it is "fully aired and fairly assessed" as soon as it is published. But if he or she does not manage to get around to publishing it, the only responsible thing is to forget any past conclusions and wait in silence on the question until such time as it appears—assuming of course that the student's theory seems to uphold the Bible.

The next city looked as is Ai. The identification of the site is subtly doubted before the current scholarly position is summarized: an occupational gap between the Early Bronze and the twelfth century. Mr Wood has apparently not written on the question, whether in an unpublished paper or a popular magazine so is not available to use to challenge the consensus. Instead, the authors return to doubting the site identification in a much stronger way, then a number of possibilities are listed: "the site may not be correctly identified; …the archaeological finds may not be representative of the unexcavated portions of the site; the biblical accounts may not yet have been correctly read; or the biblical accounts may simply be wrong" (p. 177). So? These possibilities apply to nearly every archaeological site. These possibilities have to be weighed and the most likely situation, in the light of current knowledge, should be given. But not according to PLL: "This uncertain state of affairs, far from commending sweeping conclusions, invites caution and a withholding of judgment until more evidence comes to light" (p. 177).

Space does not allow for the discussion of other examples, but these should be sufficient for my purpose. Ultimately, what I am trying to address is the whole concept of a "biblical history of Israel." The title will no doubt resonate with a large segment of the intended evangelical readership, but few of them are likely to think through the issue further. Exactly what is a "biblical history of Israel"? In the end, I am left somewhat puzzled about what constitutes a "biblical history" except as a slogan. But as a slogan, I gather that it means to imply that the Bible is given a privileged place—sometimes even an exclusive position—as a source for Israel's history.

If so, what is the significance of this? I would compare it to writing a *"Book of Mormon* history of pre-Columbian America." What would such a history look like? The main defenders of the *BoM*'s archaeological relevance are a group of Mormons associated with the Foundation for Ancient Research and Mormon Studies (FARMS). They are quick to point out that "the Latter-day Saint Church has no official position on Book of Mormon geography" nor other identifications (Hamblin 1993); nevertheless, they are equally swift to argue that the BoM increasingly finds "support from the studies of archaeology, anthropology and history" (Ash 1998). Although FARMS does not have a single view on all the details, there is a fairly consistent core of opinions that will be summarized here.[7] Here is what a *"Book of Mormon* history of Mesoamerica" would look like in part:

First of all, we would not talk of the Olmec and the Mixe-Zoquean periods but of the Jaredite period (about 2500 to 300 B.C.E.), named from the ancient inhabitants of the continent who were called Jaredites, the descendants of Jared who sailed with his people in barges after the Tower of Babel event to the "Promised Land" (Ether 1–6). This nation eventually perished in battle (Ether 14–15). The Jaredites are widely believed by Mormon scholars to have lived during what is currently called the Preclassic or Formative Period of Mesoamerican history. One recent attempt at correlating Mesoamerican history with data from the *BoM* looks like this (Norman 1983):

Date	Standard Mesoamerican History	Book of Mormon *Narrative*
2400–2500 B.C.E.	Earliest possible antecedents of Olmec ceramics in highlands of Mexico.	Jaredites arrive in Mexico.
1450 B.C.E.	San Lorenzo built on Isthmus of Tehuántepec on large navigable river.	City of Lib built on narrow neck of land where sea divides the land.
	San Lorenzo is principal governing Olmec centre.	"Great city" of Jaredite King Lib.
	San Lorenzo is political centre for extended trade.	City of Lib is southern political centre of land northward, which is covered with people: extensive trade.
	Olmec of lowland tropics of southern Verzcruz for unknown reasons do not spread southeastward into lowland tropic of Petén.	Poisonous serpents prevented southward expansion of the Jaredites for five generations to Lib, who continues to preserve land southward for wild game.

---

[7] Most of the material cited in this section was taken from the Internet. In many cases, it appears to be items already published in print, but the original time and place of publication is not always indicated. I give as much information as is available and apologize for any ambiguities remaining.

900 B.C.E.	Massive destruction: religious monuments put away following the take-over by Nascaste-phase invaders.	Take-over by brother of Shiblon; prophets killed; great destruction and famine.
750 B.C.E.	Hiatus at San Lorenzo.	Ongoing conflict and long-term captivity of kings.
600–400 B.C.E.	Culture ties southeastward, evidenced by ceramics with Chiapa III (Escaleera) phase in Central Depression of Chiapas and Mamóm phase in Mayan lowlands.	Possible Jaredite interaction with Mulekites in land southward.
400 B.C.E.	Widespread hiatus, including at San Lorenzo.	Disintegration of Jaredite nation through war.

The final years of the Jaredites overlapped somewhat with the Nephite Period (600 B.C.E. to 400 C.E.), or what is now called the Late Preclassic Period. About the time of the Jaredite demise the family of Lehi immigrated from Jerusalem to the "Promised Land" around 600 B.C.E. (1 Nephi). These were the Nephites, named after Lehi's son who led them after Lehi's death. The descendants of Nephi were opposed by the Lamanites, who flourished from about 600 B.C.E. to the coming of the Spanish. The Lamanites were descended from two other sons of Lehi, Laman and Lemuel, though they also included some dissenter Nephites, plus some others (Alma 43.13; 47.35). The battles between the Nephites and Lamanites would take up a good portion of the history of Late Preclassic Mesoamerica, including attempts to capture the Nephite capital at Zarahemla (Sorenson 2000). The Nephites were eventually overcome by the Lamanites (Mormon 6). This final battle took place during the Protoclassic Period, about 385 C.E. The Lamanites lived on until conquered by the Spanish, for the Native Americans are descendants of the Lamanites, whose skin became dark because of their sin (Alma 3.6–10).

The "*Book of Mormon* history of Mesoamerica" would incorporate not only political events from the *BoM* but also details about society. These would include the astonishing data that the Middle and Late Preclassic society made use of horses, cattle, sheep, and goats (1 Nephi 18.25), and grew wheat and barley (Mosiah 9.9). They also forged steel, including swords of steel used as weapons, and produced silk and glass. Even elephants roamed the land during this period. On the other hand, traditional plants and animals of Central America are not referred to in the *BoM*. One might assume that such a picture would discredit the *BoM* as a historical source, but the Mormon apologists are unfazed. To them the *BoM* "is a nigh perfect genre of ancient American Literature in our hands" (Shirts 1994), just as the Bible is a nigh perfect genre of ancient Israelite historiography to maximalists.

One of the first points they make is that the *BoM* must be properly read: "If one is going to say there is no basis from archaeological investigations..., the question must first be investigated in the Book of Mormon!" (Norman 1983). "While a superficial reading of the Book of Mormon may seem to point vaguely to..., a careful reading substantiates…" (Hamblin 1993). "Nor is there a hint of any of the staff having examined the Book of Mormon in a sophisticated manner that would ensure helpful comparison with scholarly results" (Sorenson 1995). An example of proper reading is to recognize that the *BoM* "is not a continental history of the Americas or a complete history of any part of it" (Norman 1983), just as the biblical presentation is defended as not aiming to give a complete history but is only "selective and theologically oriented" (p. 192) or only "narrowly focused" (p. 272; cf. also pp. 112, 161–62, 164, 177, 272).

When it comes to specific comparison of the *BoM* picture with the results of Mesoamerican archaeology, any positive data are of course emphasized. But when the archaeological data are not supportive, this is explained away:

> The "inherent improbability" of undiscovered items mentioned in the Book of Mormon is the weakest point upon which to judge it true or false… We are reminded that lack of evidence is not negative evidence. The story of ancient American cultural history is now being written, but until the story of high civilization in Mesoamerica in particular is constructed, any negative judgments are obviously premature. (Norman 1983)

Thus, Hamblin (1993) explains at length why none of the geographical names from native American sources match those in the *BoM*, referring to such things as "the severe discontinuity of Mesoamerican toponyms between the Pre-Classic…, the Post-Classic…, and the Colonial Age" and "the fact that Mesoamerican toponyms were often translated between languages rather than transliterated phonetically." With regard to the lack of evidence for the use of steel and glass, Sorenson (1995) advises, "Caution may be recommended…because of changing knowledge." Strangely, such caution was not advised with regard to the evidence supposedly supporting the *BoM*.

What about the presence of horses and other Old World animals and plants said to be in the New World by the *BoM*? The Mormon apologists cannot quite make up their mind how they want to play that. On the one hand, it is argued that the peoples might have used names familiar to them, such as "horse," for new creatures (Sorenson 1984). This is rather strange since the *BoM* is supposed to have been put into English by divine inspiration. In any case, what animals were the people riding and were being used in pulling chariots (Alma 20.6; 3 Nephi 3.22) if not horses? On the other hand, it is argued that there is evidence of horses even in recent but pre-Spanish times, though why no mainstream Mesoamerican specialists know anything about this is unclear. One apologist (Shirts 1994) states that Mormon scholars

> noted how recent geological and archaeological finds by scientists definitely established that the horse was on this continent before the Spanish came along… He [Rasmus Michelsen] wrote how the La Brea tar pits were yielding up skeletons of mammoths, horses, sheep, goats, etc. While the ancient dating of the horse caused a problem, the other animals were clearly attested he felt.

So evidence of horses has been found, and the minor problem that it is thousands of years earlier than the "Nephite Period" can be brushed off—much as PLL (pp. 174–75) point out that the finds at Jericho "correlate in many remarkable ways with the biblical account" in Josh 6, only they just happen to be centuries too early.

The mode of reasoning used by the Mormon apologists can be illustrated by two further examples. One is the reference to elephants used by the Jaredites (Ether 9.19). Sorenson (n.d.) is quoted as follows:

> Elephants (mastodons or mammoths) have long been known in North America (including Mexico)... Now the carbon–14 method of dating provides data on the early Cochise food-gathering culture of southern Arizona, showing that the state of their development contemporaneous with elephants extends down to at least 4000 B.C. and possibly later. In the moist lands of Central America elephants and other large Pleistocene animals certainly lived later than in the drying Southwest... Since the larger part of this probably Book of Mormon area is virtually unknown to paleontologists we may feel confident that future work (by Latter-day Saint scientists?) will definitely confirm the presence of the animals credited to that area in the time of the Jaredites and Nephites.

In other words, there is no evidence for elephants in America in this period. There is only the hope that such will eventually be found. The issue is clouded by the rather indefinite (and irrelevant) statement that "camel, sloth, extinct buffalo and perhaps others lived much later in Mexico and Central America than had been supposed."

The other example to be considered here is the references to "steel swords" (1 Nephi 4.9; Ether 7.9; cf. 1 Nephi 16.18; 2 Nephi 5.14–15; 24.19; Jarom 1.8; Alma 17.37; 57.33). There are two problems: steel was not known to pre-Conquest America and swords were not among the native weapons. Again, the Mormon apologists are unapologetic:

> The translation problem haunts "steel" too. We can hardly be sure of its referent substance in the Book of Mormon... Moreover, meteroric nickel-iron has been termed "a type of steel," and this substance was well-known in Mesoamerica. Iron was used in Mesoamerica... Archaeologist Sigvald Linne found a piece of smelted iron in a tomb at Mitla, Oaxaca, while at Teotihuacan, he excavated a pottery vessel which had been used for melting a "metallic-looking" mass which contained iron and copper. Iron artifacts and minerals have appeared in numerous excavations and museum collections in Mesoamerica and are mentioned in traditions. It is not out of the question that this metal was used with some consistency before the arrival of the Spaniards. Caution may be recommended... (Sorenson 1995)

Once again a rather contradictory argument is used. First, the translation is doubted, then the translation is defended! But when one reads through all the dust thrown up, no evidence for steel has in fact been presented. Instead, "caution may be recommended" for those who would doubt the *BoM*; no caution is recommended for those defending the *BoM*, though. More recently, a Mormon-authored article referred to evidence for a steel "short sword" found in eleventh-century B.C.E. Ekron (Thomasson 2005). Unfortunately, a fellow Mormon with archaeological experience of the Ekron dig had to point out that this was a complete misinterpretation: the knife in question (not a sword) was not steel, while steel production came into Israel only about the seventh century b.c.e. (Chadwick 2006, though Chadwick himself affirmed his belief in the *BoM* statements about steel). Strangely, in the very next issue of the *Journal of Book of Mormon Studies*, another article affirming "steel in early metallurgy" in the ancient Near East and also in Mesoamerica appeared without any indication that the lesson from Chadwick's article had been learned (Sorenson 2006).

As evidence for swords it is argued that the Mayan *macuahuitl* fits the bill (Roper 1996). This weapon was apparently a club with razor-sharp obsidian blades firmly attached. It was no doubt a formidable weapon, but could one call it a "sword"? Roper quotes a number of early Spanish writers to the effect that the natives were said to fight with "swords." Since these sources are quoted in English, it would take a good deal of work to find whether the Spanish text was as clearcut, but this does not seem to be a central issue. The point is that the *BoM* description simply does not fit. These weapons were not of steel nor any metal, and they did not kill or wound by thrusting in the way that a pointed metal sword might (1 Nephi 4.9; Ether 7.9; cf. 1 Nephi 16.18; 2 Nephi 5.14–15; 24.19; Jarom 1.8; Alma 17.37; 57.33). But of course the *BoM* needs to be read in a "sophisticated" manner—which critics are unable to do.

When one sees these arguments about the limitations of archaeology, the problems with translation and interpretation, and the lengthy explanations for lack of evidence, it seems strange that, nevertheless,

> it becomes increasingly clear that the casually mundane lifestyle features mentioned in the Book of Mormon—those things which Joseph most certainly would not have known about, and those things which the critics latched upon first as evidence of fraud—now find support from the studies of archaeology, anthropology and history. (Ash 1998)

Compare this with statements from PLL (p. 192):

> We recognize that some knotty problems remain… Finally, we recognize that how we read the evidence is in some measure related to larger issues of how we see the world. All in all, we believe that such archaeological evidence as is known to us in no way invalidates the biblical testimony (provided that both text and artifact are properly read) and that at least some promising "convergencies" exist…we have found nothing in the evidence considered that would invalidate the basic biblical contours.

Make a few small changes—such as "Bible" for "*BoM*" and vice versa—and these statements could be interchangeable. PLL will of course disavow any attempt to connect the *BoM* with history, but that is precisely my point: they privilege the Bible because of their theological stance, just as Mormon apologists privilege the *BoM*. Thus, I cannot take seriously the statement of PLL:

> We do indeed offer a *biblical* history of Israel in the following pages. That is, we depend heavily upon the Bible in our presentation of the history of Israel, but not because we have "theological motivations"... (pp. 98–99)

It seems to me that their "theological motivations" are as blatant as those of the Mormon apologists.

Each section of "biblical history" has its own history of debate and its own problems, and PLL's treatment necessarily varies from section to section as it deals with these. Yet a comparison of the various sections reveals an underlying pattern that is instructive, because it is the same pattern that we find with Mormon apologists' defence of history in the *BoM*. After a discussion of what the text says, some available archaeology or inscriptional sources may be brought in. Sometimes the extrabiblical sources appear to support the biblical text (*BoM*); on the other hand, the extra-biblical information often causes problems. The approach in each case could not be more different. What happens next is that any extra-biblical data seeming to support the text are given full weight as confirming the accuracy of the Bible (*BoM*). There are no doubts, no equivocations. But when there are potential problems, several possible reactions take place, sometimes one or two but sometimes all of them:

- Readers of the text (scholars, pious lay people, non-Mormons) are chided for thinking it has the obvious meaning and told they should not read in such a "literalistic" way, that the text needs to be "taken on its own terms."
- The extra-biblical/extra-*BoM* data are said to have been misinterpreted.
- It is conceded that "some" interpret the situation so as to see a conflict, but "many others" (usually other conservative evangelicals/Mormon scholars) believe that the conflict can be reconciled.
- The extra-biblical data/Mesoamerican archaeology may indeed appear to be a problem, but we should "withhold judgment" because of what might be discovered in the future.

Some might think I am giving a caricature; unfortunately, there are many examples to illustrate my point, as already discussed above.

When PLL/Mormon apologists point out—somewhat impatiently—about how scholars have not approached the Bible/*BoM* correctly, they forget that there is another side of this coin. They look entirely at one side and ignore the other. There is a logical, scholarly counter proposal to each of those advanced by PLL/Mormon apologists:

- If the Bible/*BoM* can be proved right, it can be proved wrong.
- If the biblical/*BoM* text has not been properly understood when it shows problems and contradictions, how do we know the Bible/*BoM* has been correctly interpreted when it seems to be confirmed?
- If new discoveries might confirm the Bible/*BoM*, they might just as well disconfirm it.
- If we should withhold judgment when the extra-biblical data seem to disprove the Bible/*BoM*, we should also withhold judgment when it seems to support it.

A good example of how new discoveries might reverse an earlier interpretation that archaeology confirmed the Bible is found with regard to the supposed conquest of Joshua. As is well known, this was defended by the Albright school on the basis of the archaeology at the end of the Late Bronze. Excavations of a variety of sites seemed to suggest that many different cities were conquered and destroyed at this time; ergo, this was due to the Israelites under Joshua entering the land and taking it over. This was common opinion in North America up to about thirty years ago.[8] Now it is difficult to find a (non-conservative evangelical) scholar who would attempt to defend such a view.

There is indeed one way in which my comparison of PLL with the Mormon apologists is lacking. I believe the biblical narrative has some ancient traditions and data in it, unlike the *BoM* which I believe to be entirely the product of early nineteenth-century America.[9] PLL see their project as one "to take the biblical text seriously," but I too take the biblical text seriously, unlike the *BoM* (whose value for Mesoamerican history is, I believe, nil). Yet you can take the biblical text seriously without necessarily following it in your history or assuming it is always correct. I take some Bible texts seriously in the sense of considering them as a potential source for reconstructing the history of Israel, but critical investigation might lead me to think that the biblical account has reliable information—perhaps a little, perhaps a lot—but it might lead me to think that it has none or is too problematic to use (see my recent extensive attempt: Grabbe 2007).

In the end, *A Biblical History of Israel* seems to me an exercise in futility—indeed, it could even be considered a con. If you want to know what the biblical text says, why should you go to a paraphrase by PLL? Why not just read it for yourself? Every week, in hundreds of pulpits across the land, a "biblical" history is presented. Abraham, Isaac, and Jacob are real, historical figures; so is Adam.

---

[8] For a survey of the recent development of scholarship, see Grabbe 2000.
[9] This does not rule out a small amount of "book learning," though the Bible is one of the main sources. Unlike some (e.g. Brodie 1971) I doubt that the *BoM* was a deliberate deception, but that does not rule out the book as the subconscious product of Joseph Smith's fertile mind. See further Grabbe 2006.

The plagues of Egypt are presented as having happened at a particular place and time (though, as with PLL, a context in the real history of Egypt is absent); so did the Tower of Babel.

The reason for the long introductory chapter now seems obvious: the authors are trying to make their way of writing history look logical and respectable. But they are trying to do the impossible. Despite some statements in the introductory chapter, ultimately they are not trying to develop a new theory of historiography; on the contrary, all they want is that the biblical text be treated *differently* from any other potential historical source. Their appeal to "testimony" is simply a way to privilege the biblical account, regardless of whatever other sources are available. In spite of some of their discussion, PLL themselves do not ultimately believe that writing history is purely arbitrary. When you finally do manage to get to the actual history, it is clear that they think some events "actually happened"—certainly, in the case of the Bible, what it says happened did happen in an objective way. They are as much "positivists" as anyone they criticize.

The poverty of *A Biblical History of Israel* becomes very clear: there are no new ideas, no new approaches, no new interpretations, nothing that we did not already know. Probably for some readers this lack of imagination and innovation will be comforting. For those of us who try to be historians, it is dire.

Bibliography

[Anonymous]. 2001. Out of the Dust. *Journal of Book of Mormon Studies* 10, no. 1. Online: http://maxwellinstitute.byu.edu/publications/jbms/?vol=10&num=1&id=246.

Ash, Michael R. 1998. Archaeology "Proves" Bible Not Book of Mormon. Online: http://www.mormonfortress.com/bibarch.html.

Boyd, Kelly, ed. 1999. *Encyclopedia of Historians and Historical Writings*. 2 vols. Chicago: Fitzroy Dearborn.

Breisach, Ernst. 1994. *Historiography: Ancient, Medieval, and Modern*. 2d ed. Chicago: University of Chicago Press.

Brodie, Fawn M. 1971. *No Man Knows My History: The Life of Joseph Smith the Mormon Prophet*. 2d rev. and enl. ed. New York: Random House.

Chadwick, Jeffrey R. 2006. All that Glitters Is Not…Steel. *Journal of Book of Mormon Studies* 15, no. 1:66–67. Online: http://maxwellinstitute.byu.edu/publications/jbms/?vol=15&num=1&id=408.

Evans, Richard J. 1997. *In Defence of History*. London: Granta.

Grabbe, Lester L. 2000. Writing Israel's History at the End of the Twentieth Century. Pages 203–18 in *Congress Volume: Oslo 1998*. Edited by André Lemaire and Magne Saebø. VTSup 80. Leiden: Brill.

———. 2004. Review of I. Provan, V. P. Long, and T. Longman, *A Biblical History of Israel*. *Review of Biblical Literature*. Online: http://www.bookreviews.org/pdf/3961_3828.pdf.

———. 2006. Prophecy—Joseph Smith and the *Gestalt* of the Israelite Prophet. Pages 111–27 in *Ancient Israel: The Old Testament in Its Social Context*. Edited by Philip F. Esler. Minneapolis: Fortress.

———. 2007. *Ancient Israel: What Do We Know and How Do We Know It?* London: T&T Clark International.

Hallo, William W. 1980. Biblical History in Its Near Eastern Setting: The Contextual Approach. Pages 1–26 in *Scripture in Context: Essays on the Comparative Method.* Edited by Carl D. Evans, William W. Hallo, and John B. White. Pittsburgh Theological Monograph Series 34. Pittsburgh, Pa.: Pickwick.

———. 2005. The Kitchen Debate: A Context for the Biblical Account. *BAR* 31, no. 4 (July–August): 50–51.

Hamblin, William J. 1993. Basic Methodological Problems with the Anti-Mormon Approach to the Geography and Archaeology of the Book of Mormon. *Journal of Book of Mormon Studies* 2, no. 1:161–97. Online: http://maxwellinstitute.byu.edu/ publications/jbms/?vol=2&num=1&id=25.

Iggers, Georg G. 1975. *New Directions in European Historiography.* Middletown, Conn.: Wesleyan University Press.

———. 1997. *Historiography in the Twentieth Century: From Scientific Objectivity to the Postmodern Challenge.* Hanover, N.H.: University Press of New England.

Knauf, Ernst Axel. 1991. King Solomon's Copper Supply. Pages 167–86 in *Phoenicia and the Bible.* Edited by E. Lipiński. Studia Phoenicia 11. OLA 44. Leuven: Peeters.

Megill, Allan. 1999. Historiology/Philosophy of Historical Writing. Pages 1:539–43 in *Encyclopedia of Historians and Historical Writings.* Edited by Kelly Boyd. 2 vols. Chicago: Fitzroy Dearborn.

Norman, V. Garth. 1983. San Lorenzo as the Jaredite City of Lib. *Newsletter and Proceedings of the Society for Early Historic Archaeology* 153 (June). Online: http://ancientamerica.org.

Perks, Robert, and Alistair Thomson, eds. 1998. *The Oral History Reader.* London: Routledge.

Provan, Iain W. 2000. In the Stable with the Dwarves: Testimony, Interpretation, Faith and the History of Israel. Pages 281–319 in *Congress Volume: Oslo 1998.* Edited by André Lemaire and Magne Saebø. VTSup 80. Leiden: Brill. Repr. in pages 161–97 of *Windows Into Old Testament History: Evidence, Argument, and the Crisis of "Biblical Israel".* Edited by V. Philips Long, David W. Baker, and Gordon J. Wenham. Grand Rapids: Eerdmans, 2002.

Provan, Iain, V. Philips Long, and Tremper Longman III. 2003. *A Biblical History of Israel.* Louisville: Westminster John Knox.

Roper, Matthew. 1996. Eyewitness Descriptions of Mesoamerican Swords. *Journal of Book of Mormon Studies* 5, no. 1:150–58. Online: http://maxwellinstitute.byu.edu/publications/books/?bookid=98&chapid=1072.

Shirts, Kerry A. 1994. A Neglected Source (a letter to the editor of *The Ancient American*, June 1). Online: http://www2.ida.net/graphics/shirtail/neglecte.htm.

Sorenson, John L. 1984. Once More: The Horse. Online: http://maxwellinstitute.byu.edu/publications/books/?bookid=71&chapid=792. Repr. in pages 98–100 of *Reexploring the Book of Mormon.* Edited by John W. Welch. Salt Lake City: Desertet Book and FARMS, 1992.

———. 1995. A New Evaluation of the Smithsonian Institution "Statement Regarding the Book of Mormon." Online: http://maxwellinstitute.byu.edu/publications/transcripts/ ?id=40.

———. 2000. Last-Ditch Warfare in Ancient Mesoamerica Recalls the Book of Mormon. *Journal of Book of Mormon Studies* 9, no. 2:1–16. Online: http://maxwellinstitute. byu.edu/publications/jbms/?vol=9&num=2&id=227.

———. 2006. Out of the Dust: Steel in Early Metallurgy. *Journal of Book of Mormon Studies* 15, no. 2:108–9. Online: http://maxwellinstitute.byu.edu/publications/jbms/? vol=8&num=2&id=573.

———. n.d. Quoted in paragraph 4.6 on elephants. Online: http://www.ancientamerica.org.

Thomasson, Gordon C. 2005. Out of the Dust: Ancient Steel Sword Unearthed. *Journal of Book. Mormon Studies* 14, no. 2:64. Online: http://maxwellinstitute.byu.edu/publications/jbms/?vol=14&num=2&id=379.

"Who Is the Prophet Talking about, Himself or Someone Else?" (Acts 8:34): A Response to Lester Grabbe's Review of *A Biblical History of Israel*

Iain Provan, V. Philips Long, and Tremper Longman, III

In 2003, we published a book entitled *A Biblical History of Israel* (hereafter *BHI*). Part I of the book (pp. 3–104) constructs a detailed and extended argument in favour of viewing the biblical texts—albeit that they are texts in which art, history, and theology are interwoven in complex ways—as primary sources for the history of ancient Israel. We discuss the very nature of historical knowledge in general, and of knowledge of Israel's past in particular, arguing that testimony or storytelling is central to our access to the past (pp. 36–50). We consider at length the reasons why modern scholars have adopted a principled distrust of major sections (or even the totality) of the Old Testament testimony about Israel's past, arguing in each case that the reasons are poor ones (pp. 51–74). We give particular attention to what counts as competent reading of biblical narratives in pursuit of historical knowledge (pp. 75–97). Finally, we outline our own convictions about the proper way in which to approach the task of writing a history of Israel, integrating competent readings of biblical texts with insights gained from non-biblical texts, from archaeology, and from the social sciences (pp. 98–104). Part II of the book then offers (pp. 107–303) a telling of the history of Israel that gives expression to these convictions, while differing within its various sections (written by three different authors) as to style and emphasis. We do not after all claim that there is only one way in which to write a "biblical history of Israel" (i.e. a history in which the biblical sources are taken seriously as primary sources). We seek only to illustrate the ways in which it might, with integrity, be done.

In 2007 Professor Lester Grabbe (hereafter simply Grabbe) published a book entitled *Ancient Israel: What Do We Know and How Do We Know It?* (hereafter *AI*).[1] The first part of that book lays out his own view of how we should approach the history of Israel and indeed how we should discuss it with others (pp. 3–36). He is welcoming of the social sciences but cautious as to the manner in which social scientific studies should be appropriated—as we are. He considers archaeology to

---

[1] L. L. Grabbe, *Ancient Israel: What Do We Know and How Do We Know It?* (London: T&T Clark International, 2007).

be important, but draws attention to its nature as a highly interpretative discipline—as we do (although Grabbe puts distance between himself and us on this point, on specious grounds that we shall not here discuss for reasons of space).[2] More generally, he recognizes (as we do) the *various* ways in which subjective components influence scholarly thinking and argument. We all "gravitate towards those theories or views that we find most congenial";[3] and one of the factors here is the ideologies to which we adhere. At this point Grabbe himself confesses to a negative sensitivity in respect of what he calls "neo-fundamentalism," by which term he means to refer to conservative evangelical Christians who "often adopt a position that can be defended from a critical point of view but is the one that is closest to the biblical picture."[4] Grabbe apparently has a special distaste for this particular combination of ideology and critical scholarship, even while recognizing that all critical scholarship is combined in just such a manner with ideology. Yet he proposes that it is unscholarly to focus on the ideological motivations that allegedly inform another person's scholarship. We should, rather, evaluate the position of another "on the basis of stated arguments."[5] Even in the case of arguments and positions "that seem to arise from a fundamentalist stance with regard to the Bible" we should (as John Emerton once suggested) "reply to the specific arguments rather than what we think might lie behind them."[6] Respect for the other, it seems, is very important to Grabbe—as illustrated by his objection in *AI* to the term "pseudo-scholarship" as applied to the work of two of his British colleagues: "such *ad hominem* comments do not belong in scholarly writing or debate."[7]

What manner of review essay might the authors of *BHI* reasonably expect, then, from the author of *AI*? We might reasonably expect a review essay that engages seriously with our "stated arguments"—that replies to "the specific arguments" of our book rather than what Grabbe thinks "might lie behind them." We might reasonably expect, in fact, a marked hesitation even to *speculate* about what lies behind them, since "trying to second guess motives has become too much of a pastime in the academy."[8] After all, "we can always find reasons to say that someone takes a scholarly position because of personal or ideological motives," and "such statements have no place in scholarly argument."[9] Above all, we might reasonably expect a measured, objective response: accurate in its description, precise in its analysis and argument, and devoid of *ad hominem* attacks (especially since in inviting us to respond to his review, Grabbe actually beseeched *us* by letter to refrain from making *"ad hominem* comments").

---

[2] Ibid., 9–10.
[3] Ibid., 22.
[4] Ibid.
[5] Ibid., 23.
[6] Ibid., 24.
[7] Ibid.
[8] Ibid., 23.
[9] Ibid., 24.

The review essay that Grabbe has in fact penned sadly fails to live up to these reasonable expectations. This is true, first of all, *precisely* in terms of *ad hominem* comments. In the course of his essay, Grabbe characterizes the authors of *BHI* as the writers of "prolix, turgid, and meandering" prose;[10] as those who do not respect the biblical text and are possessed of an "artificial compulsion to deny any conflict or contradictions in the text";[11] as people lacking in integrity (and thus inclined, e.g., to construct arguments merely in the way that "suits their purpose");[12] as con-artists;[13] and as apologists for the biblical text akin to those who seek to defend the Book of Mormon as an historical source.[14] These characterizations are themselves embedded in prose which is quite often mocking in tone (as in the parenthesis "would you believe it?" on p. 219 [142, present volume]). It does not appear from this sampling of the data that Grabbe has succeeded in abiding by his own exhortations. We shall nevertheless heed the same, for we hold them to have merit; and indeed, it has been our normal practice to try to abide by such an ethic as we have entered the often volatile recent discussion about the history of ancient Israel—to try to engage the *arguments* of others seriously and courteously, avoiding both personal attacks and the return (where temptation intrudes) of like for like in this area. If others feel that we have at times infringed this rule, albeit without the intention of doing so, we gladly apologize. We do not believe that progress in knowledge of any kind is advanced by such means.

Nor is it advanced, we believe, by a lack of carefulness in describing the arguments of those that one has taken for one's opponents. Unfortunately, Grabbe's review falls prey to exactly such a lack of carefulness—and to such an extent that we ourselves often do not recognize our book in his description of it. We therefore feel obliged, lest anyone confuse the argument of the book as we have written it with Grabbe's description of this argument, to begin our response to his review with a number of denials and corrections:

(1) We do *not* regard ourselves as "maximalists" in respect of the contemporary discussion about the history of ancient Israel, that is, as those who hold "that everything in the sources that could not be proved wrong has to be accepted as historical" (Knauf, quoted by Grabbe).[15] Our own stance is that we should accept as historical exactly that amount of material in the sources that appears to *be* historical, when a number of factors bearing on the question have been weighed and reflected upon, including questions of literary convention and epistemology

---

[10] Lester Grabbe's review of our work, which appears immediately before the present response, will be referred to here as "Big Max." For a contrary opinion, see the review of *BHI* by C. E. Hauer, Jr., in *CBQ* 66 (2004): 458–60. Hauer (p. 458) states: "This rational, sober book is written in good, straightforward English."
[11] Grabbe, "Big Max," 222 [142, present volume].
[12] Ibid., 223 [145, present volume].
[13] Ibid., 231 [153, present volume].
[14] Ibid., 224–31 [147–53, present volume].
[15] Ibid., 215 n. 1 [138 n. 1, present volume].

(how do we know about the past, and what do we mean when we say that we know it?). It is a mistake, therefore, for Grabbe to begin his analysis of our book by arbitrarily applying the simplistic "maximalist/minimalist" paradigm to it.[16] *BHI* does not fit that paradigm, and Grabbe's insistence that it does leads him astray right from the start in his reading of it. He remains thereafter convinced that what we are really interested in is defending the historicity of the *biblical* text (in particular) at all costs, to the extent that he portrays all counter-examples as instances of our insincerity, not as data that should lead him to change his judgment about our project (e.g. in the case of our stated belief that Josh 10:40 is of hyperbolic character, and therefore *not* to be read as straightforwardly historical). He knows, somehow, what we are "really about"—and this leads him to exceedingly curious readings of things that we actually *say*. Yet this is the scholar who affirms that we should evaluate the position of others on the basis of stated arguments, not on the basis of what they are allegedly "really about."

(2) Contrary to the impression created by Grabbe,[17] the first chapter of *BHI* is *not* in the least confused or confusing in respect of either its argument or its vocabulary when discussing the history of historiography. Specifically, positivistic historiography is clearly defined on p. 22 of the book (see also p. 306 n. 36) in the context of a nuanced discussion of the modern scientific approach to historiography that clearly distinguishes the likes of Ranke from the likes of Comte. Chapter 2 continues the discussion, specifically referencing Dilthey and others who are to be distinguished from both Ranke and Comte on stated grounds before moving on to some general statements about the present state of affairs. It is in this last section of the argument that the lines quoted by Grabbe from p. 42 are to be found, referring to the evolution of thought as the twentieth century progressed, as a result of which historiographical work is now more often than previously understood as involving both science and art, as Grabbe himself suggests.[18] The two questions that he asks immediately following his citation of these lines (in connection with some lines cited earlier) are therefore baffling, and can only be accounted for in terms of an exceedingly casual reading of the text; for it is surely obvious that there is nothing contradictory in claiming (as we do) that a certain general state of affairs existed at the end of the nineteenth century but a somewhat different state of affairs by the end of the twentieth (at least in terms of overall trend).

(3) It is *not* true that we argue "that historians cannot be objective."[19] Again, there is a very full and nuanced discussion in the book on the history of historiography, in which the question of the appropriate *balance* of objectivity and subjectivity in human appropriation of the past is seriously pursued. In that context we do discuss qualifications that have been offered in more recent times to

---

[16] He makes the same mistaken move in *AI*, 24.
[17] Grabbe, "Big Max," 216–17 [139–40, present volume].
[18] Ibid., 217 [139, present volume].
[19] Ibid. [140, present volume].

the idea that "a purely objective reconstruction of the past" is possible, "whether in the Rankean or the positivist manner" (we are quoting here from *BHI*, 44); but we say nothing remotely similar to what Grabbe claims we say. We specifically do not believe that "history [is] just another form of fiction,"[20] nor do we misquote Hayden White in that direction. We do not, indeed, misquote Hayden White *at all.*

(4) It is *not* true that we fail in our book to explain what we mean by "testimony." We spend pp. 43–49 of *BHI* introducing the idea in some detail, and we expatiate upon it throughout pp. 51–74, making entirely clear (contra Grabbe) where archaeology fits into the argument. "If I am anywhere close to understanding what they are getting at," Grabbe tells us, "then *any* account of an event—no matter how late or how ignorant the author—has historical value."[21] But unfortunately he is *not* close to understanding what we are getting at. He is not even in the same neighbourhood. We do *not* argue that "any account of an event—no matter how late or how ignorant the author—has historical value." We argue, rather, that we cannot decide in advance *whether* an account has historical value *simply* by noting its closeness to or distance from an event. This seems to us to be an entirely reasonable line to take.

(5) We possess *no* "enthusiasm to debunk eye-witness sources," contrary to what Grabbe suggests.[22] We simply wish to give eye-witness sources their appropriate weight in historical endeavour, and to challenge some particularly simplistic views of what they can tell us, in comparison to what later sources can tell us. Contrary (again) to the impression that Grabbe creates, this involves a thoughtful *argument*, rather than simply pulling ideas out of the air.

(6) We do *not* offer in the second part of *BHI* "essentially a paraphrase of the biblical account."[23] We do offer an account of the history of Israel that takes the biblical text seriously as a major source; but we spend considerable amounts of space bringing that text into conjunction with all kinds of other historical evidence, which we discuss fully in the context of recent and older scholarship on all matters. Almost two hundred pages are devoted to the exercise; and nine hundred and ten footnotes are associated with this main body of text. To describe this enterprise as a "paraphrase of the biblical account" is to caricature, not to describe honestly.

All but the last of these denials and corrections relate to Grabbe's review of Part I of our book. Aside from its carelessness, the most disturbing aspect of this section of the review is Grabbe's almost complete lack of interest in engaging with our arguments. In the midst of his generally misleading comments about our views on subjectivity in historiography, for example, he does accurately capture something of our argument about the usefulness and limitations of archaeology. These arguments are not *engaged*, however, but dismissed in the context of a discussion

---

[20] Ibid. [ibid., present volume]
[21] Ibid., 218 [ibid., present volume].
[22] Ibid. [141, present volume].
[23] Ibid. [ibid., present volume].

of what "most historians" allegedly think about postmodernity. Then again, our discussion in *BHI* of "testimony" is a very important aspect of our overall argument. Grabbe does not engage this discussion at all, once again simply taking refuge in what he alleges that "real historians" think. Astonishingly, he thinks it odd that *we* take a lot of time "defending the concept rather than suggesting that other historians would agree."[24] The question as to whether it is in fact true (or not) that we gain access to the past mainly through testimony is simply not addressed. It seems more important to Grabbe to know whether the idea is accepted by the majority, than to know whether it is in fact true. We, on the other hand, are interested much more in what is true than in what the majority of people may or may not think about that.[25] We are therefore interested in *arguments* against the views we have expressed with respect to the doing of historiography. We are not very interested in unreasoned objections to them of the sort that Grabbe offers—and this from a scholar who holds it to be a scholarly duty to "reply to the specific arguments rather than what we think might lie behind them."[26]

This most unsatisfactory set of reflections from Grabbe on Part I of *BHI*, occupying just under 12% of his text, then quickly gives way to a discussion of one section of Part II of our book (occupying just under 41% of the review) and, bizarrely, a discussion of the Book of Mormon and historiography (occupying just under 48%). The statistics themselves provide further illustration of his lack of enthusiasm for engaging with the arguments of Part I, and his apparent preference for other modes of interaction with the book.

The example chosen for discussion from Part II is the case of the settlement of Israel in the land of Canaan.[27] Here Grabbe begins with what appear to be a series of objections to reading ancient texts seriously as literature—to paying proper attention to such realities as ancient literary convention, as we construe what the texts are saying. *BHI*'s attempts to engage in exactly this manner of serious reading in the case of the biblical texts in Joshua and Judges—to evaluate them in terms of their historiographical intent and indeed content, in line with what is known

---

[24] Ibid. [ibid., present volume].
[25] We are also interested in the best ways of ensuring that truth is arrived at—which is why we are interested in historical theory and method, irrespective of whether the majority of historians (or indeed biblical scholars) share our interest. Implicit in Grabbe's comments about the first two chapters of *BHI*, on the other hand, appears to be the view that, because "most contemporary historians are not overly concerned with historical theory" (ibid.), biblical scholars should not be concerned either. We should, it seems, just get on with the business of "doing history" much as other (real) historians are allegedly doing it—without thinking too much about our approach. Our response to such a position is a straightforward one: the real choice lies not between possession of a theory/method of historiography or not (since all historians possess such), but only between carefully reasoned, justified and personally selected theory/method, and other kinds.
[26] *AI*, 24. Precisely the same lack of engagement with Part I of *BHI* is in fact evidenced throughout Part I of *AI*, even though *BHI* directly challenges a number of the positions simply assumed by Grabbe (not argued) in the course of his presentation on historical method.
[27] Grabbe, "Big Max," 218–26 [141–46, present volume].

from extra-biblical sources that might help us[28]—are in fact portrayed by Grabbe as an attempt to "get away from the scholarly consensus that Judg 1 paints a rather different picture of the occupation of the land from that ending Joshua."[29] Once again, we encounter the "scholarly consensus." Does Grabbe change his custom on this occasion and actually *argue* for the scholarly consensus? Unfortunately not. He simply cites a very few texts from the book of Joshua and then *asserts* that

> Try as one might, one cannot get away from the overall picture of Joshua: the Israelites under Joshua's leadership came from across the Jordan and conquered the land and the indigenous peoples in what was basically a five-year campaign and then divided the country up. Those Canaanites who had not been destroyed or driven out were put into servitude. By the time of Joshua's death the work was accomplished and the promises fulfilled.[30]

This is not an *argument* over against our argument—this is merely the *reassertion* of a traditional view; and Grabbe apparently thinks that such will suffice. The "overall picture of Joshua" is, according to Grabbe, simply thus and so. Why? Because he already knows it to be thus and so. It is the tradition—the scholarly consensus. Are there not problems with such a construal of the "overall picture of Joshua"? Ah, yes: "some passages do not agree with the picture."[31] Fear not, however: for "[a]ccording to the standard scholarly understanding of the biblical books, these discrepancies present no surprises." There is the "usual explanation" to fall back upon. The "overall picture of Joshua" remains the overall picture, even although it is, at the same time, not in fact the overall picture. Not to understand this is apparently to be driven by "an artificial compulsion to deny any conflict or contradictions in the text."[32] It is difficult to know whether to be more offended than amused by these intellectual gymnastics, especially when we are urged in closing "to read the text for what it says…not in some convoluted…way."[33] By all means let us all do that. Let us all indeed read these ancient texts in terms of what they are saying, measured in terms of their ancient context; and let us be prepared to produce arguments in defence of our reading, rather than simply falling back on the tribalism of consensus among allegedly "real scholars" (which is in fact nothing else than an appeal to "those who already agree with *me*"). Let us do all this, in fact, in the context of the voluminous scholarship of the last three decades that has helped us to understand more fully the nature of Hebrew narrative and has helped those who are interested in learning this skill to avoid anachronism in our reading.

---

[28] We are interested, for example, in what is known about the nature of ancient conquest accounts in general, as articulated by scholars like K. L. Younger, Jr., *Ancient Conquest Accounts: A Study in Ancient Near Eastern and Biblical History Writing* (JSOTSup 98; Sheffield: JSOT, 1990).
[29] Grabbe, "Big Max," 221 [143, present volume].
[30] Ibid. [144, present volume].
[31] Ibid., 222 [ibid., present volume].
[32] Ibid. [ibid., present volume].
[33] Ibid. [ibid., present volume].

Chapter 4 in Part I of *BHI* would be as good a place as any to begin if help with this literature is required—a chapter whose significance in terms of how biblical texts are approached in Part II of the book Grabbe (assuming that he has read the chapter thoroughly) has certainly not understood. Finally, let us each understand that even what each of us means by "respect for the text" will be affected by our reflections on all such matters—as will our construal of the past to which the text witnesses.

Discussion of what the biblical text is "really saying" in Joshua and Judges then gives way in Grabbe's review to discussion of matters of archaeology and text.[34] We may move quickly past his curious insistence that we (the authors of *BHI*) should not be permitted to read some texts in a fairly straightforward manner, in terms of what they are saying, because in the case of other texts we claim to find such realities as hyperbole. All reading of literature inevitably involves us in such decisions about levels and types of meaning, and this includes extrabiblical ancient Near Eastern literature of the millennium in which Joshua and Judges were themselves written. This is an elementary matter, and most will require no introduction to it.

Grabbe's discussion of our treatment of Jericho and Ai follows. Once again the importance to him of established "party lines" is immediately apparent. He offers no *argument* against Bryant Wood's challenge to Kathleen Kenyon's interpretation of the Jericho findings, but wishes us simply to assume that Wood's work cannot be worthy of our attention because "professional archaeologists and others [have] not debated [it]."[35] Wood is outside the tribe—a tribe carefully defined, of course, to exclude precisely those "others" who *have* found Wood's case worthy of some attention, but who sadly turn out to be merely "other conservative evangelicals." How unfortunate; for it is obvious (is it not?) that those scholars' opinions cannot be given any more weight than Wood's. We know this in advance, without even having to read about them and consider them—even though (remember?) we should not indulge our suspicion about the ideological motivations of others but "evaluate the position on the basis of stated arguments."[36] It is a most convenient approach to the matter of knowledge—a great time-saving device, in fact. Whether it counts as serious scholarship is entirely another matter.[37] Grabbe's level of seriousness in attending to data that do not appear to fit with certain traditional scholarly opinions is even more in question in his discussion of *BHI*'s treatment of Ai; for here his articulation of "the current scholarly position" must of necessity marginalize a still greater number of dissenters or doubters than are found in the case of Jericho,

---

[34] Ibid., 222–24 [145–46, present volume].
[35] Ibid., 223 [145, present volume].
[36] *AI*, 23.
[37] It is worth noting in passing that, even apart from Wood's studies, our cautionary statements about drawing sweeping conclusions from the archaeology of Jericho find support from the likes of noted archaeologist Amihai Mazar, who writes that "the archaeological data cannot serve as decisive evidence to deny a historical nucleus in the book of Joshua concerning the conquest of this city" (*BHI*, 176).

since as *BHI* (correctly) states, "confidence in the site identifications of both Bethel and Ai has never been strong."[38] The assurance with which these alleged scholarly consensuses are pressed by Grabbe, and the vehemence with which alternative views are attacked, is especially troubling given his own response to our cautionary words about Ai, which read as follows: "the site may not be correctly identified; … the archaeological finds may not be representative of the unexcavated portions of the site; the biblical accounts may not yet have been correctly read; or the biblical accounts may simply be wrong."[39] "So?" asks Grabbe. "These possibilities apply to nearly every archaeological site."[40] Indeed so; and therefore, is not due caution justified in stating what we "know" in respect of archaeology? Is not careful consideration of different possibilities required, as we read texts and artifacts together and look for convergence or divergence among them all? Yet Grabbe is insistent that "real scholars" already know the truth in the case of Jericho and Ai. There *is* no room for doubt. To doubt is to stand outside the community of the faithful. It is not enough for Grabbe, then, that in the section of *BHI* that is under discussion here its authors at least *appear* to be behaving as scholars in the way that we handle evidence: "difficulties with the biblical picture are acknowledged," Grabbe admits, "caution in interpretation and drawing conclusions is encouraged, both biblical and extra-biblical material are discussed, and conclusions are presented as a personal view rather than a dogmatic assertion."[41] But this is not enough. In order to be *real* scholars, we must apparently also come to the "correct" conclusions. That is to say: we must come to *Grabbe's* conclusions, and those of the people of whom he approves. It is agreement on outcomes, it seems, that defines for Grabbe the fellowship of truly critical scholars—not critical thinking as such. It is end-results, not method. On this basis one is either "in" or "out"; and if it is the latter, one can (it seems) expect no serious engagement with one's work. One can expect no argument—only reminders that one is "outside." And yet this confident separating of the scholarly sheep and goats in the case of Jericho and Ai is conducted by someone who is well aware of the uncertainties surrounding the correlation of pottery assemblages, radiocarbon analysis, and absolute dates[42]—matters of direct relevance to an understanding of the case of Jericho in particular.

The transition from this confused and troubling treatment of the settlement in the land to the section of the review that touches on the Book of Mormon is by way of a brief paragraph that summarizes Grabbe's view of our entire approach.[43] Given its importance in setting up what comes next, we must at this point revert to our opening strategy of denial and correction; for the paragraph in question is, quite frankly, disgracefully misleading. In the first place, our intended readership

---

[38] *BHI*, 177.
[39] Ibid.
[40] Grabbe, "Big Max," 224 [146, present volume].
[41] Ibid., 219 [141, present volume].
[42] *AI*, 12–16.
[43] Grabbe, "Big Max," 224–26 [146–48, present volume].

is *not* evangelical, as Grabbe asserts. Our intended readership is anyone who is interested in thinking seriously about matters of history and historiography in general, and about the history of Israel in particular. We make that explicitly clear in Chapter 5 of *BHI*. We also explain, in that chapter, exactly what we mean by the phrase "biblical history of Israel": "We do indeed offer a *biblical* history of Israel… That is, we depend heavily upon the Bible in our presentation of the history of Israel…because we consider it irrational not to do so."[44] We then go on to explain *why* we consider it irrational, and what we shall and shall not be found doing in Part II of the book as a result. It is beyond understanding, therefore, that Grabbe can say that he is "somewhat puzzled about what constitutes a 'biblical history,' except as a slogan." He ought to be able to grasp the idea at least as easily as the evangelical readers of the book whom he in fact insults with his aspersions upon their lack of thoughtfulness. He ought *certainly* to understand just how indefensibly misleading his articulation of the "slogan" is: "as a slogan, I gather that it means to imply that the Bible is given a privileged place—sometimes even an exclusive position—as a source for Israel's history."[45] Consider, for example, what we actually say on *BHI*, 99–100: "we offer a biblical history of Israel that takes seriously the testimony of nonbiblical texts about Israel and about the ancient world in which ancient Israel lived. We do not take these texts *more* seriously than the biblical texts… Neither do we take them *less* seriously than the biblical texts." There is, evidently, a flat contradiction between what Grabbe says we say, and what we actually say (and indeed *do*, in the remainder of *BHI*).

The final section of Grabbe's review, and its longest, compares our *BHI* to a hypothetical "*Book of Mormon* history of pre-Columbian America." There is very little that we wish to say about this very strange piece of writing, or about the unconvincing analogy at its heart; but something must be said, lest in the dark recesses of the groves of Academe there might be some who find such an analogy plausible.

This section of the review is, first of all, injudicious in its criticism of at least some of the Mormon writing that it attacks. For example, it criticizes some who wish to use the Book of Mormon for historical purposes, for their insistence that the Book must be read properly by those interested in that project.[46] It is simply an obvious aspect of proper historical method, however, that one should strive to read properly the texts that one is dealing with. Whatever one thinks about the connection between the Book of Mormon and the American past, at least on *this* point one surely cannot fault those intent on the quest. Likewise, it is in fact *true* that "lack of evidence is not negative evidence" (Norman, quoted by Grabbe on p. 227 [149, present volume]); and the fact that a Mormon said this does not make it *less* true.

---

[44] *BHI*, 98.
[45] Grabbe, "Big Max," 224 [146, present volume].
[46] Ibid., 225–28 [147–50, present volume].

Secondly, this section of the review (like its predecessors) misrepresents *our* scholarship—precisely in its attempt to make connections between the Mormons described and ourselves, *other* than those that have to do with correct historical method. Consider the following: "PLL [Provan, Long, and Longman] will of course disavow any attempt to connect the *BoM* with history, but that is precisely my point: they privilege the Bible because of their theological stance, just as Mormon apologists privilege the *BoM*."[47] As noted above, we do not in fact privilege the Bible *at all*; we simply take it seriously as a major source for the history of Israel. In addition, we explicitly state, as Grabbe himself acknowledges, that we do this not because we have theological motivations but for other, voluminously stated reasons (throughout the entirety of Part I of *BHI*).[48] So Grabbe misstates both the facts about our attitude towards the Bible *and* also our motivations. "Some might think I am giving a caricature," he concedes;[49] indeed, some might. Caricature is in fact too gentle a word for the persistent misrepresentation of *BHI* that occurs throughout his review.

Thirdly, the analogy that Grabbe draws between the Book of Mormon and the Bible is a ridiculous one. On the one hand, we have the Book of Mormon, which so far as we know (although we are no more experts on this topic than Grabbe) is indeed "entirely the product of early nineteenth century America" and "whose value for Mesoamerican history is…nil."[50] On the other hand, we have the Bible, which *even Grabbe* acknowledges "has some ancient traditions and data in it," which is why he himself professes to "take the biblical text seriously."[51] In other words, it makes sense to read the Bible in pursuit of the history of Israel; it does not make sense to read the Book of Mormon in pursuit of the history of Mesoamerica. So what, exactly, is Grabbe's difficulty with the authors of *BHI*? It is, apparently, that we take the Bible *too* seriously for his liking, "following it" in our history and "assuming it is always correct." He, on the other hand, takes "some Bible texts seriously in the sense of considering it as a potential source for reconstructing the history of Israel," allowing "critical investigation" to suggest which texts these should be—which texts possess "reliable information" and which possess none or are "too problematic to use."[52] Once again, however, his very *description* of the matter is entirely misleading. We ourselves are thoroughly committed to "critical investigation" in the matter of the history of Israel—more so, we believe, than Grabbe, for we have an interest in critically discussing (a) crucial questions (such as what counts as a rational epistemology) that Grabbe seems intent upon ignoring, and (b) received opinions on some topics that Grabbe appears to regard as simply

---

[47] Ibid., 230 [152, present volume].
[48] For a careful and candid articulation of the common convictions—theological and otherwise—of the three authors of *BHI* and of the relationship of these convictions to the book we have written, see *BHI*, 101–4. It is our sense that scholarly understanding would be furthered if more in the guild were willing to be as biographically forthcoming.
[49] Grabbe, "Big Max," 231 [152, present volume].
[50] Ibid., 232 [153, present volume].
[51] Ibid. [ibid., present volume].
[52] Ibid. [ibid., present volume]

self-evidently true (cf. our discussion above about the settlement of Israel in Palestine). Arising out of our commitment to "critical investigation," we are certainly interested in how far our biblical texts possess "reliable information," and we spend a considerable amount of time in *BHI* discussing that issue both in general and in specific terms and developing *arguments* in respect of it. We are patently very far, therefore, from simply "assuming [the Bible] is always correct" or, for that matter, that our readings of it are always correct. As for "following it" in our history: we certainly do take the story it tells very seriously in our work, once again for stated reasons that we consider compelling. Would it not have been much better—and indeed a better indication of his "critical scholarship"—if Grabbe had spent his review engaging these reasons and arguments rather than avoiding doing so, not least by using up almost half of the review on the red herring of Mormonism? Would such engagement with the reasons and arguments not have reflected his "critical scholarship" better than the approach to our book and to ourselves that he takes instead—misrepresentation of both fact and motive, and mere dismissal of reasons and arguments where they lead to conclusions of which Grabbe disapproves?

The conclusion of Grabbe's review[53] reveals as clearly as one could wish, however, why it is that he is not in fact interested in engaging with our arguments. It is because he does not consider them to be made sincerely. We are, it seems, con-artists. The reason that we wrote the first part of *BHI* is not, it appears, that we were intent on making a serious argument about proper method in historiography, but only that we were trying to make our "way of writing history look logical and respectable." "Despite some statements in the introductory chapter" it seems that ultimately we "are not trying to develop a new theory of historiography" but that all we want "is that the biblical text be treated *differently* from any other potential historical source." Our appeal to testimony "is simply a way to privilege the biblical account, regardless of whatever other sources are available." And so it goes on. Grabbe the critical scholar is revealed as Grabbe the mind-reader, in the course of a veritable litany of appalling misrepresentations of our stated views. In a sense, resistance to this kind of "scholarship" is futile; for if Grabbe already "knows" somehow "what we are really up to," nothing that we have to say by way of objection will change his mind.

Working on the assumption, however, that at least those who *read* this current volume of collected essays are interested in what is true, and that this interest in truth extends to what we have *said* in *BHI* and what we *mean* by it, let us attempt a response. We intended Part I of *BHI* to be a serious contribution to public scholarly discourse about the discipline of the history of Israel, on its own terms and quite independently of Part II. The discussion concerning epistemology which it contains is a particularly important aspect of that contribution. No aspect of *BHI* is intended to advance the opinion that "the biblical text should be treated differently from any other potential historical source," or the opinion that it should be

---

[53] Ibid., 232–33 [153–54, present volume].

privileged "regardless of whatever other sources are available"—and indeed, no part of *BHI* in fact adopts that view, as will be obvious to anyone who reads the book. We certainly did not write Part I of the book as a way of making our way of writing history "look logical and respectable"; rather, we wrote Part II of the book out of prior convictions about what correct method looks like, as described and argued for in Part I, and in many ways as *illustrative* of this method rather than *exhaustive* in its treatment of the history of Israel as such.[54] We hoped, in writing the book in this way, to spark a wide-ranging discussion about historical method in general, and the place of the Bible in ongoing work on the history of Israel in particular; for surely, we thought, even those who do not happen to agree with the particular treatments of Israelite history in Part II will recognize the importance of fully discussing the weighty matters discussed in Part I. Surely they will understand that what is said in *any* "Part II" of a book on the history of Israel will be intrinsically connected to what is said in any "Part I"—or what is at least in the head of the person writing "Part II," whether it is written down in a "Part I" or not.

Eight years on from *BHI*'s publication date, there is some evidence that this "hope" has not been entirely ill-founded—that thoughtful reflection in respect of the matters we discuss is indeed taking place.[55] Grabbe's review unfortunately stands as evidence of a tendency in some quarters in quite a different direction. He evades, rather than engages with, our arguments; he misrepresents, rather than listens to, our words; he ridicules, rather than converses. In many ways, his essay is not a dialogue with us at all; for a dialogue has as its necessary prerequisite an appreciation of what it is that the dialogue partner is saying, and what he means by it. As we have demonstrated in this response, however, Grabbe does not come close to appreciating what we are saying and what we mean by it. In fact, he seems intent on having a dialogue with quite other partners than ourselves. Who are these? They are, we suggest, those indicated in the following revealing words:

> Every week, in hundreds of pulpits across the land, a "biblical" history is presented. Abraham, Isaac, and Jacob are real, historical figures; so is Adam. The plagues of Egypt are presented as having happened at a particular place and time…so did the Tower of Babel.[56]

---

[54] It is this fact, taken along with the different authorship of the various chapters in Part II, that results in the variation in style and content in those chapters that has sometimes been noted by reviewers. Our aim was not to write "the definitive history of Israel" (as if such a thing were possible)—not even "the definitive biblical history of Israel" (which is why the indefinite article was chosen for the title of the book). We can conceive of different kinds of histories of Israel being written, each taking the biblical text duly seriously in its endeavours and yet focusing on different areas and arriving at different conclusions to ours. Our aim was to show that a history of Israel could be written on the basis outlined in Part I of the book—not that it was the only history of Israel that could be written on that basis. We three authors chose to demonstrate that in slightly different ways in the individual chapters.

[55] It is gratifying, for example, that *BHI* appears on the student reading lists of various major universities throughout the world, suggesting that it is regarded as serious scholarly literature by many colleagues in the Academy, if not by all.

[56] Grabbe, "Big Max," 232 [153–54, present volume].

Which land is this, with its hundreds of pulpits in which such terrible things are said? We doubt if it is the England of Grabbe's current abode; it is certainly not the Canada that two of us *BHI* authors currently inhabit. Those with real, recent experience of churches in these lands will know how infrequently the Old Testament is ever preached in them at all, much less the books of Genesis or Exodus in particular. Which land does Grabbe have in mind, then? The most obvious candidate is the southern U.S.A. from which he originates—the home, certainly, of the kind of sometimes-narrow fundamentalists whom Grabbe appears to have in his sights throughout his review, and with whom he constantly confuses us *BHI* authors. It is these folks, and not we ourselves, who genuinely "privilege the Bible because of their theological stance,"[57] in matters not only of history, but also of other areas of human knowledge such as science. Grabbe knows their mindset well, because as he tells us candidly elsewhere, he was once one of their number; he is "an ex-fundamentalist."[58] The designation evidently intends to suggest that he has left behind him this unfortunate way of looking at the world. From our perspective, however, it appears not only that Grabbe is evidently confusing us with those he has "left behind" (literary pun intended), but also that he himself stands much closer still to the fundamentalist mindset than we do, for all that he is overtly opposed to it. This is so in at least two respects. First, he insists (in his discussion of Joshua and Judges) on the literal sense of the biblical text while appearing deeply uncomfortable with the idea of reading these ancient texts seriously as literature, especially if this means that we cannot simply say that they are "right" or "wrong."[59] Secondly, he looks at the world (throughout his review)

---

[57] Ibid., 230 [152, present volume].

[58] See L. L. Grabbe, "Some Recent Issues in the Study of the History of Israel," in *Understanding the History of Ancient Israel* (ed. H. G. M. Williamson; Proceedings of the British Academy 143; Oxford: Oxford University Press, 2007), 57–67 (60): "As an ex-fundamentalist I am rather sensitive to arguments by conservative evangelicals which use the trappings of scholarship but which in my opinion cloak fundamentalist motives." Ironically, in view of the treatment he metes out to us *BHI* authors in "Big Max" and elsewhere in his writing, he continues on this same page by outlining the proper scholarly course of action even in such cases: "But I think John Emerton was quite right when I once heard him say that even in such cases we should answer the actual argument and not just dismiss it because of the presumed motive. We can always find reasons to say that someone takes a scholarly position because of personal or ideological motives. 'He's just conservative. She's simply a radical. He's a Zionist. She is anti-Semitic.'" Quite so; but if this is indeed an excellent principle of scholarship, why has Grabbe chosen not follow it in practice?

[59] This obsession with "right" and "wrong" is also in evidence in *AI*, especially in Chapters 4 and 5, whose concluding sections boldly proclaim (among other things) those occasions upon which biblical data have been confirmed by research and those upon which the biblical picture has been shown to be incorrect. The apparent need to describe reality in terms of this simplistic paradigm leads to some exceedingly curious judgments. The biblical picture of the Iron IIB era is said to be "incorrect," for example, in claiming that the Aramaeans are Israel's main enemy (p. 165), when no such claim is in fact made in the biblical text—it is imputed to the biblical authors by Grabbe simply because they tell stories about the Aramaeans and not the Assyrians, and Grabbe finds this unacceptable. This strong prejudice with respect to what counts as "proper" historiography is also

in very simple terms, differentiating between "real" scholars or "real" historians and the remainder both in terms of the conclusions that they have come to about a whole array of matters and in terms of whether these beliefs are "true" or "false" from Grabbe's point of view. Grabbe's beliefs about such matters indeed apparently hold the status of self-evident truth, such that to disagree with them is by definition not to *be* a real scholar or a real historian.[60] The fundamentalist world of "real Christianity" and its basis in the literal (but somehow non-literary) truth of Scripture is thus surprisingly evoked by Grabbe, albeit in avowedly and aggressively secular form, in his review.

In sum: with whomever it is that Lester Grabbe is dialoguing in his review of *A Biblical History of Israel*, it is certainly not with us who wrote it and intended our words thus penned to be a serious guide to what we thought and meant. He must be dialoguing instead, to quote our title, with "himself or someone else." This is a pity; because we certainly welcome dialogue. We would like serious discussion of our claims about correct historical method. We would like serious discussion of our various specific ideas about how to read biblical and other texts together with non-textual artifacts in pursuit of a history of Israel. We welcome all such conversation. Perhaps this will only be possible, however, with those who have entirely eschewed fundamentalisms of all kinds, whether on the right or on the left, and are genuinely able and willing to engage with other people's arguments on their own terms, without the ghosts of convictions past haunting and subverting the enterprise. Perhaps it will only be possible with those who are prepared, while certainly belonging to "churches" and confessing their "creeds" (whether these "churches" and "creeds" are religious or secular), to adopt a charitable and open-minded attitude to the views of others and to consider, not only where they themselves may be right, but also where they may be wrong. This used to be what we thought a liberal educational and scholarly environment offered, before "critical thinking" became a theoretical tribal marker rather than a substantive reality within our corporate discourse.

---

in evidence in Grabbe's, "How Reliable Are Biblical Reports? A Response to V. Philips Long," in *Historie og konstruktion* (ed. M. Müller and T. L. Thompson; FBE 14; Copenhagen: Museum Tusculanum Press, 2005), 153–60 (154): "No historical account of Ahab could be credible if it did not include Assyria." See further Grabbe's "Are Historians of Ancient Palestine Fellow Creatures—Or Different Animals?," in *Can a "History of Israel" Be Written?* (ed. L. L. Grabbe; JSOTSup 245; ESHM 1; Sheffield: Sheffield Academic, 1997), 19–36. For a more sensible approach to the matter, see the original V. P. Long essay to which Grabbe's 2005 response represents a less than satisfactory answer in all kinds of ways: "How Reliable are Biblical Reports? Repeating Lester Grabbe's Comparative Experiment," *VT* 52 (2002): 367–84. A sound evaluation of the whole discussion is found in M. B. Moore, *Philosophy and Practice in Writing a History of Ancient Israel* (LHBOTS 435; London: T&T Clark International, 2006), 141: "Long's examination is more detailed than Grabbe's and gives more comparative examples for the reader to consider, and thus appears both more objective and more accurate."

[60] It is, rather, to display only "the trappings of scholarship" which "cloak fundamentalist motives" (Grabbe, "Some Recent Issues," 60).

Part 2

The Beginnings of Israel and the Rise of the Monarchy

Introduction to Part 2

This section mainly embraces a historical period, the time from the beginnings of settlements in the highlands of central Palestine and the Judaean hills (twelfth century BCE) to the fall of the Northern Kingdom (c. 720 BCE). Although the selection of articles covers some of the main periods and issues, it is not possible to include discussion of all the historical events of what is a time period of about five centuries. However, the Annotated Bibliography does contain a number of volumes that survey and discuss this lengthy period of time (and see also the histories of Israel in the Annotated Bibliography of Part 1).

A good place to begin is the so-called sojourn in and the exodus from Egypt. Most scholars reject the picture of the exodus found in the book of Exodus and elsewhere, though they accept that something happened, while a number of scholars question whether any such event took place in any way. Much has been written on the subject,[1] but one important indication of whether the exodus tradition is early is the geographical names in the text. This subject is especially addressed by JOHN VAN SETERS. The traditions of the settlement of Israel in the land are found primarily in the books of Joshua and Judges. ERNST AXEL KNAUF looks at both these books and extracts the probable historical data from them. There is very little that can be shown as clearly historical in these books according to KNAUF's analysis, though what little there is could be very useful. This is why most historians now rely on archaeology and insights from anthropology and sociology to try to reconstruct the origins of Israel and Judah rather than the books of Joshua and Judges.

The books of 1 and 2 Samuel are not much better, but they probably contain some information on Saul according to DIANA EDELMAN, who attempts to determine what in the tradition might be reliable. This is mainly an exercise in looking for a broad-brush picture, which is also what LESTER L. GRABBE is mainly willing to accept from 1 and 2 Samuel about Samuel, Saul, the Philistines and David. There is good reason to be sceptical of the details, he argues, but a case can be made for the existence of Saul, Samuel and David and also some of their activities as historical. The David tradition also has some credible elements, even if

---

[1] For an overview addressing most of the issues, see Grabbe (2014, with extensive primary and secondary bibliography) in the Annotated Bibliography. A volume that appeared more recently that has essays covering most aspects of the question, from a variety of points of view, is Levy–Schneider–Propp (2015).

there is much fiction there as well: so NADAV NA'AMAN and WALTER DIETRICH (as well as GRABBE) argue with a good deal of plausibility. But the picture may differ considerably from the biblical text (e.g., that David did not fight the Philistines but made a 'non-aggression' pact with them). When it comes to King Solomon and his magnificent empire, the biblical text has little credibility in the details. Yet there is evidence that Solomon existed and that his reign should be included in the development of Judah and Israel toward nationhood, as ERNST AXEL KNAUF and HERMANN MICHAEL NIEMANN show, though what they extract from the sources is rather different from the picture in 1 Kings. Similarly, ANN E. KILLEBREW finds the Jerusalem as revealed by archaeology to be rather different from that supposedly ruled over by Solomon. This does not mean that there was no 'united monarchy', as RAINER ALBERTZ wants to show, but again it was quite different from the biblical picture (this is also the conclusion of GRABBE in the article cited above).

Summary of Articles

11. JOHN VAN SETERS ('The Geography of the Exodus') examines some of the many geographical places associated with the exodus in the Bible. Noting that the work of archaeology in the past few decades has rendered much of the earlier discussion obsolete, he then goes on to look at some of the specific places, beginning with Pithom and Succoth, looking at the various suggestions of Egyptologists and biblical scholars. They show Pithom-Succoth is to be identified with Tell el-Maskhuta, a town built by Necho II about 600 BCE. Rameses-Piramesse was largely abandoned at the end of the 20st Dynasty and Tanis established as the new capital at the beginning of the 21st Dynasty. Stones, sculptures and monuments were quarried from Piramesse and taken to Tanis. In the tenth century Shoshenq I made it the temporary capital of Egypt. The name Ramesses—in the form Ramesse, rather than Piramesse—is still associated with the ruins in the sixth century BCE. Nor was the original city a fortress as the Bible states; only long afterward might people have interpreted the ruins of Piramesse as the remains of a fortress. Thus, rather than being a reference dating to the Ramesside period, as often asserted, the site Ramesses in the biblical text looks to be a late reference. As for the name Goshen, it appears in the LXX as 'Gesem of Arabia' (Gen. 45.10; 46.34). Gesem, known from late geographical texts, was the name of the 10th nome of Egypt that was created in Saite times. The *yam suf* that the Israelites crossed always designates the Red Sea in passages outside the exodus story. Yet there is evidence that the Red Sea extended north as far as Lake Timsah in antiquity. The geographical picture of Exodus 1–15 fits the Saite period (about sixth century BCE), not the Ramesside period. It was at this time that large number of foreigners, including Jews, were settled in Goshen.

12. **ERNST AXEL KNAUF** ('History in Joshua') asks, how much 'history' found its way into the present text of Joshua and also what kind of history? Accepting the historical-critical analysis of biblical literature as basically valid, he surveys the literary history of Joshua: late seventh century (first draft, end of an Exodus-Conquest-Story: Joshua 6* and 10*); 525–450 (Exodus-Conquest-Story becomes D-Composition: Joshua 6–11*); 450–400 (first Hexateuch redaction: Joshua 1–11*; 15.20–18.1*); 400–375 (second Hexateuch redaction [Joshua 13; 20–22; 24] and Joshua-Judges-Redaction [Joshua 12; 14; 18–19; 23]). There are memories of cities that were seats of rulers in the LB II and some other data. Those from the earliest through the ninth century are as follows:

1.	13th	Josh. 15.9; 18.15 ("waters of Nephtoah" = "spring-place of Mer-en-Ptah").
2.	13/12th	Josh. 17.2, 14: Manassite clan from survivors of Merneptah's Israel.
3.	a) 10th	Josh. 10.1-14* (10.12c-13c) (battle of Gibeon).
	b)	Josh. 15.63 (Jebusites still dominate Jerusalem even after David).
4.	10th/ early 9th	10th/early 9th Josh. 10.13d ('Book of Jashar/the Upright').
5.	10th/ early 9th	10th/early 9th Josh. 16.10; 17.11-13 (Canaanite cities integrated into Israel).

Quite a few other passages have historical references, but these relate to the eighth to third/second century BCE. Thus, most texts with references to datable events are post-Iron IIA. Taking all the passages—both early and late—the features from Joshua are evaluated as 'possible' or 'probable' (the difference between the two being mainly one of chronological precision). The probable/possible features tend to cluster in the pre-exilic period (which is a long one) and the Persian period, with few in the pre-state and Hellenistic periods. That is, the 'historical memory' of Joshua tends to focus equally on the pre-exilic and the Persian periods, with the pre-state little remembered and the Hellenistic coming mostly after the completion of Joshua. The oldest piece of text is quoted from the tenth century (Josh. 10.13d); larger amounts of text are preserved from the royal administrations of Israel and Judah in the ninth and eighth centuries. The fundamental expectation that the text should reflect best the time of its authors (rather than the time about which they wrote) is fulfilled in that the later features have more text and precision; however, the historicity rate of early literary strata is not necessarily higher than that of later strata. Thus, one cannot read a core narrative uncritically nor ignore possible historical information in redactional additions. Joshua has preserved elements of historical information, but the historical narrative it gives does not correspond with historical reality.

13. **ERNST AXEL KNAUF** continues his investigation in 'History in Judges'. Less than 25 percent of the book's contents derive from the tenth to ninth centuries BCE and the LB/Iron I, though almost nothing from the latter. The pre-exilic core grew by adding layers, with the 'Book of Saviours' constituting the first addition in response to the loss of the Israel's king. A Jewish adaptation, turning the anti-monarchic, anti-state attitude into pro-state propaganda, began in the Persian period. A number of passages potentially have a historical basis; of these the following could have come from the ninth century or earlier:

3.12-30:	The defeat of Eglon by the Benjaminite clan Ehud was possible during the period of weak state power, either c. 1100–875 BCE or 724–716 BCE.
3.13:	Moab's conquest of Jericho was possible once Mesha had conquered Nebo c. 850/840 BCE.
3.22-23:	This presupposes an Assyrian type of toilet, which was possible from 716 BCE onwards, with the Assyrian palaces at Samaria and Megiddo.
4–5:	The Song of Deborah was not composed before the tenth century BCE and first committed to writing in the Omride court (c. 875–850 BCE). It describes a conflict between the tribes of Zebulon and Naphtali, on the one hand, and the Sea Peoples leader Sisera, on the other. Many features of the poem are the common stock in trade of professional singers, while the prose account (ch. 4) is derived from the Song.
8.3-21:	Gideon's eastern campaign may reflect the Midianite involvement in the Rift Valley copper trade from the eleventh to ninth centuries (Low Chronology). A conflict between the clan of Abiezer and a Midianite raiding party is possible anytime during this period.
8.10:	The Israelites fought a battle with the Assyrians at Qarqar in 853 BCE.
8.13-17:	Pharaoh Shishak conducted a campaign that destroyed Penuel and Succoth, though Jeroboam I then rebuilt Penuel.
9:	Shechem was not settled between the late eleventh and the late tenth centuries (Low Chronology) but was resettled as an Israelite royal residence. The 'Abimelech/Shechem' tradition is thus unlikely to predate 1050 BCE, but it seems to describe tensions between tribe and town, perhaps David and Jerusalem or even Saul and Gibeon.

The historical memory in Judges is found in texts that are often much later than the events. In collective memory anything over 200 years old is 'distant past'; 100 to 200 years ago represent the 'past'; while things less than 100 years ago are part of the 'present'. The examples can be divided into 'probable' events (total of 11) and 'possible' events (total of 12). Of the *probable* events, 45 percent fall into the 100 years past, 27 percent into the 200 years past and another 27 percent into the 'distant past'. Of the *possible* events, 25 percent fall into the 'present' within the past 100 years, 42 percent in the 'past' up to 200 years before, while a full 33 percent were of the distant past of more than 200 years earlier. There were a number of discontinuities between 1000 and 720, which resulted in breaks in the collective memory. For example, the Omride history has no representation in Judges, and of the rich literature only the song of Deborah is preserved in the biblical text.

14. **DIANA EDELMAN** ('Saul ben Kish in History and Tradition') points out that there are factual data in the biblical text but no agreed method of determining what they are. The historian needs to use the full range of old and new literary critical methods. First comes establishing the text(s), then a close reading of the text(s). She argues, secondly, that careful observation of structuring patterns and literary devices allows a significant understanding of the intention of the original author. Comparative study of ancient Near Eastern texts can be helpful. Thirdly, the types of sources available to the original authors should be considered. Finally, the historian must consider what types of information can be derived from these sources. In the Saul tradition (1 Samuel 8–2 Samuel 1) the first major structural pattern is the ritual for installing the king. Use of this indicates lack of data: the main elements of the ritual ceremony have simply been historicized. Early source material may be found in the saying of 1 Sam. 10.11-12, 19.24, the song fragment in 1 Sam. 18.7 and 21.12, the lament over Saul and Jonathan in 2 Sam. 1.19-27, a fragment of an administrative district list in 2 Sam. 2.9, the Saulide genealogy in 1 Sam. 9.1 and 14.46, the old tradition behind 1 Sam. 9.1–10.16, passages linking Saul with Gibeon (2 Sam. 2.12–3.1, 21.1-14, and 1 Chron. 8.29-40, 9.33-44), and the alternation between Gibeah and Giba as names for the same site. Saul's career can be reconstructed, though not on the level of event. He emerged initially as a petty king of Gibeon. He expanded into surrounding Israelite territory, creating a territorial state with different levels of centralization, encompassing the Ephraimite hill country, Benjamin, the northern Samarian hills, both sides of the Jordan Valley, and part of the Transjordanian hill country. He would have found himself in competition with the Philistines and also the other states in Cis- and Transjordan, especially for markets and trade routes for local products, and died trying to expand into the Jezreel–Beth She'an corridor. Since the earliest king attested externally is Omri in the ninth century, Saul probably belongs sometime in the tenth.

15. **LESTER L. GRABBE** ('The Mighty Men of Israel: 1–2 Samuel and History') wants to ask to what extent 1 and 2 Samuel have historical data for the tenth and ninth centuries BCE. Four main historical entities are examined: the Philistines and Samuel, Saul and David. With extensive excavation in the Philistine plain in recent years, biblical data can sometimes be checked against the archaeology. The inclusion of Gath in some lists indicates knowledge from an early period. The question of architecture is more ambivalent, as is the question of whether the statement about an Achish king of Gath is an early tradition or not. However, the statements about metallurgy (1 Sam. 13.19-21) and military details seem to belong to a later period and are unhistorical for the time of Saul. The Saul tradition was evidently a problem for the narrator of Samuel. The fact that he was unable to ignore it suggests that it was too well known and too tied up with the David tradition to be suppressed, suggesting that there was a historical Saul who fought against the Philistines and established some sort of political entity (chiefdom?) in the central highlands in the tenth century BCE. David's existence is made more likely by the Tel Dan inscription (though it attests to the Davidic 'dynasty' rather than David himself). Whereas Saul is associated with the North, David is strongly identified with Judah. There is evidence that Judah historically was separate from (the other tribes of) Israel, and this is recognized in that David was first a chieftain over Judah before taking over Saul's kingdom. It is likely that David did not fight against the Philistines but maintained a truce with them throughout his reign (a truce that appears to have continued under Solomon). The most solid tradition about David is his taking over Jerusalem and making it his capital. Archaeology suggests that it would have been modest at best, which fits the context and the sort of political entity (tribal state?) set up by David. But the attempts to legitimate David's rule in the text suggests a certain struggle to achieve rule and also that the Saul and David traditions were entwined from the beginning. The tradition also recognizes that he was not the first king and that he did not build the Jerusalem temple. The figure of Samuel is most problematic, yet historically powerful religious figures are often associated with kings (e.g., in the history of England). His association with both the Saul and David traditions speaks in favour of a historical Samuel. Thus, there seems to have been three such historical individuals, with historical core traditions, who fit well into the encounters between Israelites and Philistines in the tenth century BCE.

16. **NADAV NA'AMAN** ('Sources and Composition in the History of David') begins with writing in early Israel, which he thinks was already practised in the tenth century. The reason is the use of Egyptian hieratic signs for numbers, which is found only in Hebrew inscriptions of the eighth–seventh centuries but must have been introduced earlier. He concludes that scribal activity was introduced into the Israelite court as early as Solomon and possibly even David. He then outlines several possible sources for David's activities. First is an account

of David's wars with the Aramaeans, primarily Hadadezer, king of Zobah. This figure is clearly modelled on the later Aramaean king Hazael, who ruled in the second half of the ninth century. There are several reasons for the connection, not least the fact that they both originate with Beth-Rehob. Second are David's wars with the Philistines. This account includes Gath, yet Gath had been forgotten by the later Israelite and Assyrian lists of Philistine cities. Third are David's wars with the Ammonites, Moabites and Edom. David's victory over Edom in the Valley of Salt looks very much like the victory of Amaziah over the Edomites (2 Kgs 14.7). David's cruelty against Moab seems to reflect the way Mesha treated some of the Israelites he conquered. The information about the Hazael, Moab, Edom and so on seems to have been catalogued in an Israelite chronicle, since the data appear to have been forgotten by the time of the Deuteronomist. Yet the chronicle was one of the texts used in training scribes and would thus have been familiar to the Deuteronomist, who could use the information from the chronicle to record the reign of David or, in some cases, to try to fill out the reign of David by inventing episodes. There is nothing impossible about the account of David's conquests, but whether they actually happened is a question much more difficult to answer.

17. **WALTER DIETRICH** ('David and the Philistines: Literature and History') gives a historical evaluation of David and the Philistines. He begins with a synchronic reading of the David story as a literary unity, noting that the Davidic tradition is ambivalent about the relationship between David and the Philistines. Some passages show definite conflict, but others indicate a case of cooperation. Although much could be said about the tradition history of the David story, one main source is the Deuteronomistic History which tends to pass on earlier stories. Then there is the Court History of David that was written at a later time and probably reflects later events in the history of Judah. Some of the episodes seem to be events relating to the Assyrians and Israel that are reinterpreted as events embodying the Saul–David conflict. It works to disassociate David from the Philistine defeat and death of Saul but is also the main source about conflict between David and the Philistines. Finally, there are the 'Prior Sources' that are the source of some of the individual stories about David and the Philistines. As for an overall historical evaluation, the stories of David as a bandit chief seem to have a historical core to them. The traditions relating him to Gath are very instructive, because Gath ceased to be important at a later time. These and other stories suggest that after the death of Saul, or at least after he became king, David did not fight against the Philistines but had a treaty with them. The passages alleging battles with the Philistines are few and could well be taken over from the Saulide tradition. David could then still be the ruler of a Dual Monarchy but a much more limited one, perhaps 'Dan to Beersheba', rather than 'from the River Euphrates to the border of Egypt'.

18. **ERNST AXEL KNAUF** ('King Solomon's Copper Supply') refers to the old canard of 'King Solomon's Mines', long since shown to be a fiction. Although the existence of Solomon can be accepted, the numbers in 1 Kings 5–7 (e.g., mines yielding 50 tonnes of copper; a work force of 180,000 men) are far removed from tenth-century reality. The narrative (whose final redaction was about 400 BCE) may, however, give some insights into Phoenician–Israelite relations in later centuries. Citation of court annals does not begin until Rehoboam and Jeroboam, indicating that no such annals were available for David and Solomon. No central state with an elaborate administrative hierarchy of 1 Kings 4–10 existed before Judah's experience of Assyria. The 'Solomonic empire' may have originated in Josiah's court. The pattern of Phoenician–Israelite relations as depicted in the account of Solomon existed under Omri and Ahab. Several elements in 1 Kings 6–7 relate to northern Israel rather than Judah. For example, the twelve prefects of 4.8-19 are only over the North, while Gad (1 Kgs 4.19 LXX) came under Israelite control with Ahab. This all suggests aspects of the Solomon tradition actually originated under the Omri dynasty. The story of Solomon provides an excellent condensed view of Israelite history. The historical Solomon emerges as a Palestinian prince of rather limited means, combining the kingship of Jerusalem with the chiefdom of Judah. There is no longer any need to explain 50 tonnes of copper for the temple or the molten sea weighing 35 tonnes, because these are fictions. But while copper could be imported by the Phoenicians from Cyprus, during periods when the supply broke down the works in the Wadi Arabah and Timnah provided what was needed. This was the case in the time of Solomon, while the Phoenician trade came later. Jerusalem may well have cooperated with Shoshenq in utilizing the facilities at Timnah. The historical Solomon was an Egyptian satellite, not a Phoenician dependent.

19. **HERMANN MICHAEL NIEMANN** ('The Socio-Political Shadow Cast by the Biblical Solomon') reminds us that the Annales School has shown that a historical event can be reconstructed only through a three-fold process: political history needs to be placed in the context of social history, both of which must be situated in the geomorphological-ecological environment. No epigraphic evidence for Solomon exists. Archaeologically, the 'six-chamber gates' have been assigned to Solomon, but the gates are not identical in their blueprints and not convincingly assigned to central planning. Some have assigned the six-chamber gate to Philistine development. Since the debate in *BASOR* 227-78 it is not possible to date events in the tenth and ninth centuries closer than plus or minus 50 years, meaning that an event dated to Solomon could often as easily be assigned to Ahab. The archaeological quest for Solomon's kingdom, stretching from the brook of Egypt to the Euphrates, can be called off. The biblical portrait of Solomon's time was told with theological interests in mind and includes few historical details. We should avoid any presumptions about the historical dimensions of Solomon based on the theological dimensions of the biblical

portrayal. Almost nothing from the tenth or ninth centuries can be attributed with certainty to Solomon at Megiddo, Hazor or Gezer. The keeping of royal annals does not seem to have begun until after David and Solomon. It makes sense to place Solomon in the legendary, theological pre-state of Judah/Israel, though it is possible that a historical figure of more modest dimensions might have been the basis of this picture. Two significant socio-political points appear in the Solomon account: (1) building accounts in both Jerusalem and elsewhere in the kingdom and (2) measures taken to organize and stabilize the kingdom by means of governmental functionaries and expansion northward. David had not truly expanded beyond Gibeon to the north; therefore, Solomon's functionaries were his representatives in a first attempt to establish an administrative system in the North beyond the borders of Judah, to expand beyond a chiefdom into a state. The organization described in 1 Kgs 4.7-19 could not have taken place under Solomon or indeed any Judahite king to the fall of Samaria, but it could represent the first phase of an attempted structure, either under Solomon or Ahab. The results of the investigation are that Solomon looks in outline to be a typical small oriental ruler who innovatively joined the LB city-state ruler with that of his own birth into a rural clan. David had been a rural Judaean clan chief. Solomon brought the tribal Judah into the city-state of Jerusalem. He legitimated Jerusalem by (re)constructing and expanding the city temple, building some sort of palace and fortifications (though his building outside Jerusalem is unknown, possibly in Gezer). He seems to have begun to extend influence and organization to the north, though he headed a complex chiefdom that was only beginning to move toward a state. He succeeded in integrating the urbanite Jerusalem with the rural Judahite clans but failed to bring in the northern Israelite groups. Excursus: Solomon was under the influence of Shoshenq and may even have been his vassal.

20. **ANN E. KILLEBREW** ('Biblical Jerusalem: An Archaeological Assessment') points to the controversy that had arisen because of the apparent inconsistencies between a literal reading of the biblical account of Jerusalem in the time of David and Solomon and the unimposing archaeological reality of the city in the tenth and ninth centuries. The accumulating evidence indicates that the city was prominent in two periods, the Middle Bronze and the Iron IIC, which serve as bookends when Jerusalem was a major centre; however, it was a modest settlement in the Iron I and IIA/early IIB. In more than a century of excavations, nothing has been found to match Solomon's Jerusalem as described by the Bible. A Middle Bronze wall was partially re-used in an eighth–seventh-century wall, but there is no evidence that the MB wall was used between these dates, suggesting Jerusalem was an unwalled city from the sixteenth to the mid-eighth centuries BCE. R. Reich has argued that the water systems of the Gihon Spring were not in use during the LB and Iron I-IIA. Jerusalem only became a major urban centre in the late Iron Age. Excavations to the south of the Temple Mount indicate that

the Ophel flourished only during the eighth and seventh centuries BCE. The large public structures post-date the period of the 'united monarchy'. The Broad Wall of the late eighth century and other finds support the 'maximalist' size of Jerusalem in the Iron Age IIC. Cemeteries and cave deposits and other survey data show that from the eighth to the early sixth centuries Jerusalem was a large administrative, political and residential royal city, long after David and Solomon. Jane Cahill has argued that the Stepped Stone Structure and the terrace system on which it rests were built together (contrary to Killebrew and others), but even if she is right, there is still no monumental architecture (only domestic structures) for the tenth century, which would be necessary if Jerusalem was a large administrative system. Efforts to interpret a grander tenth-century Jerusalem based on missing evidence are methodologically flawed. Accepting traditional chronology, Jerusalem in the tenth century was still a modest settlement that probably served as no more than an administrative-cultic-political centre for the surrounding villages of the Iron I and IIA. It became a major urban and cultic centre only during the eighth century.

21. **RAINER ALBERTZ** ('Secondary Sources also Deserve to Be Historically Evaluated: The Case of the United Monarchy') begins by noting the difference between primary and secondary sources and for preferring primary sources. Yet for ancient Israel few primary sources exist, apart from archaeology, yet the results of archaeology are often ambiguous. Between Merenptah and Shalmaneser III there are no real primary sources to allow control of the secondary material available. However, the traditio-historical methods allow an evaluation of the biblical texts, secondary though they may be, and thus provide some sort of control over the archaeology. With regard to the question of the 'united monarchy', there are two pieces of evidence: the Tel Dan inscription, which mentions the 'house of David', and the biblical traditions that the kingdom split after Solomon. For the latter, there are four different sources: (1) a report of the rebellion of Jeroboam (which could have come from a royal chronicle); (2) a fragment of a narrative about a failed rebellion of Jeroboam (1 Kgs 11.27-28); (3) a long historical narrative about the separation of the northern tribes from the Davidic dynasty at the beginning of Rehoboam's reign (1 Kgs 12.1*, 3b-14, 16, 18-19) which is probably no later than the time of Hezekiah; and (4) prophetic narrative on how Ahijah from Shiloh anointed Jeroboam king (1 Kgs 11.29-39*), which is probably northern in origin but nevertheless presupposes a 'united monarchy'. These sources give a different reason for the division of the kingdom than the later Deuteronomistic history. An independent source, Isa. 7.1-17 which should probably be dated about 730 BCE, also remembers a division of the monarchy. A very late text, Ezek. 37.15-22, preserves a memory of the division by prophesying a return of the unity of Israel and Judah. Therefore, there are no fewer than seven sources that confirm the 'division of the monarchy', including

some sources from the North. How can the existence of so many biblical sources for the division of the monarchy be explained if there was no such division, and how should consciousness of an overall Israelite identity have emerged if not during such a united monarchy?

Annotated Bibliography

Because only a selection of articles on the history of Israel from about 1200 to about 720 BCE could be given in this section, the bibliography here lists a number of volumes that survey the period in greater detail, especially some of the major events, but the various histories of Israel discussed and listed in Part I will help the interested reader (see especially the Annotated Bibliography there).

Becking, Bob (1992), *The Fall of Samaria: An Historical and Archaeological Study*, Studies in the History of the Ancient Near East 2 (Leiden: Brill), 51–56; ET and updating of Chapter 2 of the doctoral thesis, *De ondergang van Samaria: Historische, exegetischee en theologische opmerkingen bij II Koningen 17*, ThD (Utrecht Fakulteit de Godgeleerheit, 1985).
As the title suggests, this is the standard discussion of the last days of the Northern Kingdom and the fall of Samaria to the Assyrians. There are some discrepancies between Assyrian inscriptions about who conquered Samaria, but Becking argues that there were two conquests of Samaria, one by Shalmaneser V in 723 BCE and another by Sargon II in 720 BCE in response to a rebellion of Ilu-bi'di of Hamath. This explanation has been widely, if not universally, accepted.

Finkelstein, Israel (1988), *The Archaeology of the Israelite Settlement* (Jerusalem: Israel Exploration Society).
This is a thorough but readable archaeological presentation with regard to the settlement in the central and Judaean highlands. The various theories about the origin of Israel are examined and critiqued. A new thesis is presented: a cycle between settlement for cultivation and change to a pastoral way of life took place over the centuries in Palestine. When rainfall was abundant, most of the population lived in permanent settlements and cultivated the land. But during the periodic times of long drought conditions, much of the population reverted to a pastoral lifestyle that left few traces in the archaeology. Finkelstein argues that the Israelite settlement took place at a transition from a nomadic lifestyle to one of farming, with the settlers being mainly indigenous inhabitants (rather than outsiders) who were changing from being predominantly herders of cattle, sheep, and goats. The existence of such a long-term cycle of land use has been widely accepted, though whether this is the explanation for the Israelite settlement is more controversial.

Finkelstein, Israel, and Amihai Mazar (2007), *The Quest for the Historical Israel: Debating Archaeology and the History of Early Israel*, ed. Brian B. Schmidt, Society of Biblical Literature Archaeology and Biblical Studies 17 (Atlanta: Society of Biblical Literature).
Two major archaeologists debate what archaeology has to say about the Israelite settlement, the reigns of David and Solomon, the 'united monarchy' and the division into the two kingdoms of Israel and Judah. They have significant differences in interpretation, with Mazar tending to be more traditional (conservative) and Finkelstein more sceptical (in line with recent reconstructions of the history of Israel by biblical scholars). The editor (Brian Schmidt) gives good summaries of the main issues and differences between the two antagonists.

Finkelstein, Israel, and Nadav Na'aman (eds) (1994), *From Nomadism to Monarchy: Archaeological and Historical Aspects of Early Israel*. Jerusalem: Israel Exploration Society.
This collection of essays provides a thorough overview of the archaeology, sociology and history relating to the origins of Israel, with essays by major scholars (mostly Israeli) on different aspects of the question. Much of the archaeology up to the early 1990s is summarized.

Grabbe, Lester L. (2014), 'The Exodus and Historicity', in Thomas B. Dozeman, Craig A. Evans, and Joel N. Lohr (eds), *The Book of Exodus: Composition, Reception, and Interpretation*, VTSup 164 (Leiden: Brill), 61–87.
This is a recent detailed overview of some of the main issues associated with the question of whether the exodus took place or not. The topics examined include the geography of places, especially as listed in Exodus and Numbers, the supposed route of the exodus, the question of Semites in Egypt, the Merenptah Stela, the archaeology of the 'wilderness wanderings' and of the alleged conquest of Canaan.

Grabbe, Lester L. (ed.) (2007), *Ahab Agonistes: The Rise and Fall of the Omri Dynasty*, LHBOTS 421 = European Seminar in Historical Methodology 6 (London/New York: T&T Clark International).

Grabbe, Lester L. (ed.) (2008), *Israel in Transition: From Late Bronze II to Iron IIA (c. 1250–850 BCE)*. Volume 1, *The Archaeology*, LHBOTS 491 = European Seminar in Historical Methodology 7 (London/New York: T&T Clark International).

Grabbe, Lester L. (ed.) (2010), *Israel in Transition: From Late Bronze II to Iron IIA (c. 1250–850 BCE)*. Volume 2, *The Text*, LHBOTS 521 = European Seminar in Historical Methodology 8 (London/New York: T&T Clark International).

Grabbe, Lester L. (ed.) (2016), *The Land of Canaan in the Late Bronze Age*, LHBOTS 636 = European Seminar in Historical Methodology 10 (London and New York: Bloomsbury T&T Clark).
These collections of essays cover some of the major areas of historical research in the first part of the history of Israel. The volume on the Late Bronze Age (2016) gives background on the settlement and has extensive discussion of the settlement itself (even though this is usually dated in the Iron Age I). The volumes on the transition from the Bronze to the Iron Age (2008, 2010) have one volume devoted mainly to archaeology questions and one

volume on other topics, mostly those relating to the text. Finally, the volume on the Omri dynasty (2007) gives an extensive examination of an important period in the history of Israel and Judah. (Collections of essays covering the period after the fall of Israel are discussed in the Annotated Bibliography of Part 3.)

Levy, Thomas E., Thomas Schneider and William H. C. Propp (eds) (2015), *Israel's Exodus in Transdisciplinary Perspective: Text, Archaeology, Culture, and Geoscience*, Quantitative Methods in the Humanities and Social Sciences (Cham, Switzerland: Springer).
This is an important recent collection of essays relating to most aspects of the exodus and the issues arising from research into it. A variety of viewpoints appear, and there is no good overview evaluating the various suggestions (for this, see the essay of Grabbe above), but for a sheer up-to-date gathering of information and opinion this volume cannot be beaten.

The Geography of the Exodus

John Van Seters

The geography of the exodus story has played an important role in the discussion of the historicity and historical reconstruction of the Egyptian sojourn and liberation event as recounted in Exodus 1–15 for over a century. The reason for this is that only in the names of places in Egypt does the story give us any hope of establishing a firm connection with Egyptian historical texts and monuments. This has also involved a continuing interaction between Egyptologists and biblical scholars, often without the competence or training to fully appreciate the discussion in the other's discipline. The history of the debate has created a great confusion of issues that has thoroughly muddled the debate and left a curious residue of errors in biblical studies, still evident in biblical atlases and histories.

What has made obsolete much of the earlier discussion of the geographical names of Exodus is the archaeological activity in the last 30 years at the two sites of Tell ed-Dabʻa-Qantir and Tell el-Maskhuta in the eastern Delta of Egypt. The full impact of these excavations and their significance for re-evaluation of the older epigraphic materials has not yet been felt within the discipline of biblical studies. There is still considerable effort by both Egyptologists and biblical scholars to try to fit the exodus story into the older way of viewing things, viz. to understand the biblical scenario within the context of the 19th Dynasty of Egypt. The location of the exodus event within this period of Egyptian history is based upon two major considerations. The first is the reference to the city (or land) of Rameses (Exod. 1.11; 12.37; cf. Gen. 47.11), which is identified with Piramesse, the capital city built by Ramesses II. The second consideration is the dating of the 'conquest' of Canaan by the Israelites to the period of the late 19th or early 20th Dynasties with the exodus event preceding this by '40 years' of wilderness wanderings. In current discussion of the origins of Israel the conquest scenario may be ruled out as largely irrelevant to the discussion for the dating of the exodus. This leaves only the reference to Rameses, which is embedded within the geography of the sojourn–exodus story and must be considered within this context. It cannot be used as the sole basis for reconstructing an historical event and then eliminating elements that do not fit the reconstruction by labeling them as redactional.

Consequently, an important issue that must be faced in this discussion is literary, and this has usually been ignored. The biblical sources that make up the account of the sojourn in Egypt and the exodus in Exodus 1–15 were not contemporaneous with the events that they sought to portray. Even the earliest source, the so-called Yahwist (J), is variously dated from the tenth to the sixth centuries BCE (or even later), which by any reckoning of the date of the exodus is a long time afterwards. Furthermore, there is an increasing tendency towards the later dating of J, and it seems very likely that the geography of J's exodus account will reflect his familiarity with the Egypt of his own day rather than preserve hoary traditions of place-names from the second millennium. One cannot simply use the geography of the exodus uncritically as a way of dating the exodus. Nor can one fit the place-names into a predetermined historical period and make sense of them in that way. The possibility must be left open that the geographic background of the exodus story is Egypt in the time of the writer. Yet there has scarcely been any serious consideration of this possibility in the whole discussion about the exodus.[1] With this in mind, we will begin by reviewing the two major archaeological sites related to Pithom and Rameses (Exod. 1.11) that have been at the center of the discussion for so long.

Pithom and Succoth

In the winter of 1883, Edouard Naville conducted his excavations at Tell el-Maskhuta, the first project of the Egypt Exploration Fund.[2] Naville left no doubt about the object of his explorations in the Eastern Delta: it was to illuminate the geography of the Exodus. In this regard he considered his mission as highly successful, for he identified Tell el-Maskhuta with biblical Pithom, one of the store-cities which, according to Exod. 1.11, the Israelites built during a period of Egyptian servitude. Naville came to this conclusion by examining the monuments in the museums of Ismailia and Cairo that had been found at Tell el-Maskhuta, as well as the inscribed objects that came to light in his own excavations there. What convinced Naville of Tell el-Maskhuta's identification with Pithom was the fact that on many of these monuments the god Atum was given special honor and reference was made to his temple, Per Atum (or Pithom). It is clear from one monument, the so-called Pithom stela of Ptolemy II, that the temple of Atum gave its name to the city itself—Pithom, the Patoumos mentioned by Herodotus (2.158). At the same time, the city was also called *Tjeku* (biblical Succoth), because it was the chief city of the region of *Tjeku*. In the Greek sources of the Hellenistic and Roman periods the town was known as Heroo(n)polis, which was often shortened

---

[1] An exception is the work of D.B. Redford that will be discussed below.
[2] E.H. Naville, *The Store-City of Pithom and the Route of the Exodus* (Memoir of the Egyptian Exploration Fund, 1; London: Egypt Exploration Fund, 4th edn, 1903).

in Latin texts to Ero. Both forms were found by Naville on Latin inscriptions on the site. The large building in which Naville found monuments bearing the god's name, Atum, he identified as the temple itself. He also cleared parts of another large structure that he interpreted as a store-house. This he believed confirmed the biblical designation of 'store-city'. Finally, he traced the outlines of the large fortification walls that dominate the central portion of the site.

In spite of this rather impressive array of materials, Naville's identification of Tell el-Maskhuta with Pithom was challenged by Alan Gardiner,[3] who preferred to identify Pithom with Tell er-Retaba, about 8 miles to the west, while retaining the identity of Succoth with Tell el-Maskhuta as a separate town. Gardiner's views were popularized by T.E. Peet in *Egypt and the Old Testament* (1924), and as a consequence they became widely accepted by Old Testament scholars, including the influencial W.F. Albright. In the context of remarks on an expedition that he made to the Egyptian Delta and the Sinai in 1948, Albright states,

> A flying visit to the vast site of Tell el-Maskhuta and the smaller (but still large) site of Tell Ertabeh convinced me that Gardiner's identification of them with Sukkoth and Pithom of Exodus, respectively, is correct. The geography of the Egyptian phase of the exodus thus approaches a definite solution.[4]

Albright never says anywhere exactly what it was during this 'flying visit' that led him to such conviction, but it has become the standard view nevertheless. Yet there are Egyptologists who continue to support Naville's original identification of Tell el-Maskhuta with Pithom and Succoth.[5]

It is now generally agreed that from the time of the 19th Dynasty of Egypt onwards, the region of the Wadi Tumilat, or the eastern end of it, was known as *Tjeku*. This is to be identified almost certainly with biblical Succoth, and for convenience I will use this name henceforth. The principal god of the region was Atum of Succoth, and he may have had a temple or estate in the Wadi Tumilat called Per-Atum as early as the 19th Dynasty, but that is entirely uncertain. A text from the time of Merneptah that mentions a Per-Atum in connection with this region has called forth a lot of discussion. It is contained in a border report that states,

---

[3] A.H. Gardiner, 'The Geography of the Exodus', in *Recueil d'études égyptologiques, dédiées à la mémoire de Jean François Champollion à l'occasion du centenaire de la lettre à M. Dacier relative à l'alphabet des hiéroglyphes phonétiques, lue à l'Académie des inscriptions et belles-lettres le 27 Septembre 1822* (Bibliothèque de l'École des Hautes Études, Sciences historiques et philologiques, 234; Paris: E. Champion, 1922), pp. 203-15.

[4] W.F. Albright, 'Exploring in Sinai with the University of California African Expedition', *BASOR* 109 (1948), pp. 5-20 (15).

[5] D.B. Redford, 'Pithom', in W. Helck and W. Westendorf (eds.), *Lexicon der Ägyptologie* (Wiesbaden: Otto Harrassowitz, 1982), cols. 1054-58.

> We have finished letting the Bedouin tribes (Shasu) of Edom pass the fortress of Merneptah Hotep-hir-Maat, l.p.h. which is in Tjeku (Succoth), to the pools of Per-Atum of Merneptah Hotep-hir-Maat, which are in Tjeku, to keep them alive and to keep their cattle alive.[6]

This text is often viewed as significant, because Merneptah is frequently considered to be the pharaoh of the exodus. The text is thought to refer to two towns of the period, the fortress of Tjeku, which is identified with biblical Succoth, and Per-Atum, which would correspond to biblical Pithom. Furthermore, the fortress of Succoth would need to be situated to the east of the pools of Per-Atum, although how far east is not clear. However, it must be noted that both the fortress and the pools are said to be in Tjeku (Succoth) so that Succoth must be the name of a region and not that of a city.

Naville argued that since a large statuary group honoring Ramesses II and the god Atum of Succoth (and the god Seth) was found at Tell el-Maskhuta, as well as a large temple to Atum, it was reasonable to assume that Ramesses built Pithom at Tell el-Maskhuta.[7] For him also the towns of Pithom and Succoth were identical, based upon the occurrence of their names together in the later texts. Thus he interpreted the Merneptah text quoted above to refer to a fortress, as yet unidentified, just to the east of Pithom (= Tell el-Maskhuta). Gardiner countered this by suggesting that Tell el-Maskhuta should be regarded as the fortress of Succoth referred to in the above text and that the 'pools of Atum' lay beyond in the region of Tell el-Retaba, the actual site of Pithom.[8] He rather cavalierly dismissed all of the monumental and documentary evidence for a temple of Atum at Tell el-Maskhuta and the fact that no such temple to Atum could be identified at Tell er-Retaba. Gardiner's view was adopted by Albright and is still generally reflected in maps of the exodus route. Naville's protests against Gardiner's views were largely ignored.

A new phase in the discussion was introduced by D.B. Redford,[9] who raised two important points in the discussion of Pithom and Succoth. First, there is no evidence before the mid-first millennium BCE (the Saite period) in Egyptian records of either name being identified as *towns*. Per Atum is the name used for a number of different temples to the god Atum in various locations, but none receives the town determinative in Egyptian until the inscriptions of the late

---

[6] This rendering is based on the translation of J.A. Wilson in *ANET*, p. 259. See also R.A. Caminos, *Late-Egyptian Miscellanies* (Brown Egyptological Studies, 1; London: Oxford University Press, 1954), p. 293.
[7] E.H. Naville, 'The Geography of the Exodus', *JEA* 10 (1924), pp. 18-39, esp. pp. 32-39.
[8] A.H. Gardiner, 'The Geography of the Exodus: An Answer to Professor Naville and Others', *JEA* 10 (1924), pp. 87-96.
[9] D.B. Redford, 'Exodus I 11', *VT* 13 (1963), pp. 401-18; idem, 'An Egyptological Perspective on the Exodus Narrative', in A.F. Rainey (ed.), *Egypt, Israel, Sinai: Archaeological and Historical Relationships in the Biblical Period* (Tel Aviv: Tel Aviv University Press, 1987), pp. 137-61.

period. Similarly, Tjeku (Succoth) appears as the name of a district by the time of the Ramesside period and must be understood as a district in the Merneptah text cited above. It only receives the town determinative, signifying the name of the principle town of the region, in the late (Saite) period. This means that references to these places in the biblical record could only reflect the geography of a mid-first millennium BCE dating at the earliest. Secondly, the Merneptah text must also be understood in an entirely different way. The fortress of Tjeku can only refer to some guard post within the district of Succoth and not to the town of Succoth. The pools of Per Atum, likewise, does not refer to some body of water connected with a town of Pithom but as belonging to the temple estates of the god Atum, who was the god of the region. The temple of Atum could be situated somewhere else and the epithet 'Atum of Merneptah-Content-with-truth' strongly suggests its location in the capital of Piramesses. Thus there is no basis for finding in the two names of this text two distinct towns of Succoth and Pithom, separated from each other by several miles and therefore no basis for the positions of Gardiner and Albright.

It is true that Redford's position was challenged by W. Helck, and his article is often cited as a way of dismissing Redford's challenge.[10] Helck does accept the identity of Per Atum with Tjeku, against Gardiner, to be located at Tell el-Maskhuta. However, against Redford he argues that the lack of the town determinative with the name Tjeku (Succoth) does not necessarily mean that a town of that name did not exist in the district of Tjeku. This means that he interprets the Merneptah text differently also. He takes the temple of Atum to be in Tjeku, which he understands as a town with a fortress just to the east of it as part of the whole complex, and this town he locates at Tell el-Maskhuta as a Ramesside construction. His position that Tjeku represents a town with a temple to Atum in the 19th Dynasty rests entirely upon his acceptance of the archaeological evidence as set forth by Naville.

A new and quite decisive factor in the discussion of Pithom and Succoth is the result of the Wadi Tumilat project of the University of Toronto, directed by J.S. Holladay, Jr. The project carried out a ceramic survey of several sites in the Wadi Tumilat, including Tell er-Retaba and Tell el-Maskhuta in 1977 and 1983 and conducted five seasons of excavations at Tell el-Maskhuta in 1978, 1979, 1981, 1983 and 1985.[11] This expedition added an important critical correction to Naville's earlier work in terms of controlled stratigraphy and ceramic chronology. It also raised serious objections to the views of Gardiner and Albright about their

---

[10] W. Helck, 'Tkw und die Ramses-Stadt', *VT* 15 (1965), pp. 35-48. See Redford's own response in 'The Literary Motif of the Exposed Child', *Numen* 14 (1967), pp. 209-28 (221 n. 52).

[11] J.S. Holladay, Jr, *Cities of the Delta*. III. *Tell el-Maskhuta: Preliminary Report on the Wadi Tumilat Project, 1978–1979* (American Research Center in Egypt Reports, 6; Malibu, CA: Undena, 1982); idem, 'Maskhuta, Tell el-', in *ABD* (1992), IV, pp. 588-92; B. MacDonald, 'Excavations at Tell el-Maskhuta', *BA* 43 (1980), pp. 49-58. The writer participated as a field supervisor and associate director during the 1978 and 1981 seasons.

location of Pithom and Succoth. It is now clear from the archaeological evidence that Naville was wrong about assigning to Ramesses II the founding and building of Pithom. Naville excavated in the days before the use of ceramic chronology and dated the site solely on the basis of the inscribed objects found there. The recent excavations at Tell el-Maskhuta under Holladay make it abundantly clear that this city was built only at the end of the 7th century BCE, in the time of Pharaoh Necho II. In fact, the city was probably built in conjunction with Necho's work on the great canal that Herodotus tells us the pharaoh attempted to dig from the Nile to the Red Sea (*Histories* 2.158). Yet this revised dating of the site does not dispute the fact that Tell el-Maskhuta must be identified with Pithom, the name of the place from c. 600 BCE down to Roman times.

Naville had argued that Ramesses II was probably the founder and builder of Pithom and its store-houses, using Israelite labor, since this king's statue was found at Tell el-Maskhuta. But the ceramic evidence and dateable stratigraphy clearly exclude such a possibility. How then can we explain those Ramesside and other pre-Saite monuments found at Tell el-Maskhuta? We know from examples of other sites that fine statuary and other monuments were often transported from one place to another to adorn new palaces and temples. It seems likely that some pharaoh, perhaps Nectanebo I, adorned the temple at Tell el-Maskhuta with monuments taken from various places in the eastern Delta that bore the name of Atum of Succoth.[12] Once the canal was built and Pithom established as the religious and commercial center of the region, the whole character of the Wadi Tumilat changed. It was now the primary commercial access and trade route between Lower Egypt and the Red Sea.

Furthermore, Gardiner's identification of Pithom with Tell er-Retaba is not possible because—on the basis of the Wadi Tumilat expedition's ceramic survey of the site in 1977 and all the published materials to date—Tell er-Retaba was largely unoccupied from the Saite to Roman times, precisely the time when the monuments attest the existence of the *town* of Pithom. There were many Per-Atum temples and estates in Egypt in the Ramesside period but no indication that any gave their name to a particular town. The most important temple of Atum was the one in Heliopolis (= biblical On), and for that reason E.P. Uphill identifies it as the site of Pithom.[13] The biblical tradition, however, regards the city of On (Gen. 41.50) as quite distinct from the city of Pithom and few have followed his suggestion. It is also true that there was an important Ramesside town at Tell er-Retaba, but we do not know its name from any inscriptions on the site. Tell el-Maskhuta replaced Tell er-Retaba as the most important town of the region and the latter dwindled to a village.

---

[12] See Redford, 'Pithom', col. 1055.
[13] E.P. Uphill, 'Pithom and Raamses: Their Location and Significance', *JNES* 27 (1968), pp. 291-316; 28 (1969), pp. 15-39.

This archaeological dating of the site of Tell el-Maskhuta confirms the observations made by Redford, long before the recent excavations, about when Succoth–Pithom became a town.[14] Against Helck who depended entirely upon Naville's dating of Pithom to Ramesses II, Redford had argued that the use of the town determinative in hieroglyphic writing with either the name Succoth or Pithom after c. 600 BCE is significant for dating the founding of the town. The inscriptions also make clear that these are not two separate towns, as the maps so often suggest, but the same place. It would appear that Necho built Tell el-Maskhuta as a great frontier fortification—witness the great walls around the town—and placed a large temple there to honor the principal god of the region. The result was that the town acquired the name Pithom, because of the temple (a very common occurrence in Egypt), and also the name Succoth, because it was the major town of the region by that name.

It is now possible to suggest a somewhat different interpretation of the Merneptah texts with its mention of the 'pools of Per-Atum'. M. Bietak has recently undertaken a study of the ancient geography of the eastern Delta region.[15] He concludes that in the western part of the Wadi Tumilat there was once an ancient lake that was supplied by the overflow from the Nile (see the map, Fig. 1). It is this lake region that is referred to in the Merneptah papyrus, and the fort that the bedouin had to pass to get to the lake region may well be Tell er-Retaba, situated at the eastern end of the lake.[16] Since Tell el-Maskhuta was not occupied during the Ramesside period, there is no other candidate east of Tell er-Retaba that fits the description of this text. The text makes clear that both the pools and the fort are in the district of Succoth, but it hardly warrants identifying the fort either with a *town* of Succoth or with Per-Atum, though it is possible that there was a temple to the god Atum of Succoth at this site. Furthermore, Redford has argued that while the pools of the region of Succoth are said to belong to the estate of the god Atum, this does not mean that the temple of the god was in this region as well. He considers it much more likely that the temple of Atum of Merneptah referred to

---

[14] Redford, 'Exodus I 11', pp. 403-408.

[15] M. Bietak, *Avaris and Piramesse: Archaeological Exploration in the Eastern Nile Delta* (Mortimer Wheeler Archaeological Lecture, 1979; London: The British Academy, 1981), p. 277 (initially published in the *Proceedings of the British Academy* 65 [1979], pp. 225-96). For more detailed treatment, see his *Tell el-Dab'a II: Der Fundort im Rahmen einer archäologisch-geographischen Untersuchung über das ägyptische Ostdelta* (Österreichische Akademie der Wissenschaften, Denkschriften der Gesamtakademie, 4; Vienna: Österreichischen Akadamie der Wissenschaften, 1975).

[16] It is not possible to identify the fort in Succoth with Tell el-Maskhuta as Gardiner and Albright did, because it was not yet in existence. See also S. Herrmann (*Israel in Egypt* [SBT, 2nd series, 27; London: SCM Press, 1973], p. 26), who follows Naville in identifying Pithom with Tell el-Maskhuta in the Ramesside period. His description of the region around Tell el-Maskhuta in the 19th Dynasty as fertile could hardly be correct. Until the building of the canal it could hardly have been much more than a desert track with the fertile region lying much further to the west in the wadi.

here is that belonging to the capital Piramesse. It remains very doubtful, without further evidence, that there was a specific site or temple with the name Per-Atum in the region of Succoth in this period.[17]

Rameses–Piramesse

The identification of Rameses, the other 'store-city' mentioned in Exod. 1.11 as built by the Israelites, was a matter of controversy for several years. Most scholars accept the equation of Rameses with Piramesse, the capital of the 19th Dynasty built by Ramesses II. While many locations for Piramesse have been proposed, the excavations at Tanis (San el-Hagar), especially those conducted by Pierre Montet, seemed to put the matter to rest, because so many and so impressive were the monuments and inscriptions naming Ramesses II, his successors, and the gods of Piramesse.[18] Most biblical atlases and histories identified Tanis with Piramesse, and biblical scholars argued that since the name of the city was changed from Piramesse to Tanis with the rise of the 21st Dynasty, c. 1100 BCE, the biblical references to Rameses must preserve an old tradition from the time of the sojourn in Egypt.[19]

The presence of these monuments and the inscriptions at Tanis, however, has proven deceptive, because it is clear that they did not originate at the site.[20] They were all brought to it from elsewhere. Nowhere is the matter of careful stratigraphic evaluation more important than at Tanis. The fact is that there is no 19th and 20th Dynasty stratigraphy at Tanis. It was a new city built by the pharaohs of the 21st Dynasty. The real capital site is about 30 kilometers south in the vicinity of the modern town of Qantir. This fact seems to be well established now, since the stratified ruins of a fine palace with thousands of glazed tiles were found *in situ*, as well as other monuments. The identification of Avaris with Tell ed-Dab'a, just to the south of Qantir, through the excavations of M. Bietak further confirm this identification of the capital of the Ramessides beyond any reasonable doubt.[21]

---

[17] Redford, 'An Egyptological Perspective on the Exodus Narrative', pp. 140-42.
[18] P. Montet, 'Tanis, Avaris et Pi-Ramses', *RB* 39 (1930), pp. 5-28; *idem, Les enigmes de Tanis* (Bibliotheque historique; Paris: Payot, 1952); A.H. Gardiner, 'Tanis and Pi-Ramesse: A Retraction', *JEA* 19 (1933), pp. 122-28; H. Cazelles, 'Les localisations de l'Exode et la critique littéraire', *RB* 62 (1955), pp. 321-64. Cazelles's otherwise useful review of earlier literature on the subject is controlled entirely by his identification of Piramesse with Tanis.
[19] J. Bright, *A History of Israel* (Philadelphia: Westminster Press, 3rd edn, 1981), p. 121; also Herrmann, *Israel in Egypt*, p. 75 n. 42.
[20] See J. Van Seters, *The Hyksos: A New Investigation* (New Haven: Yale University Press, 1966), pp. 127-55; Bietak, *Avaris and Piramesse*, pp. 278-83.
[21] M. Bietak, *Avaris and Piramesse*; *idem, Avaris, the Capital of the Hyksos: Recent Excavations at Tell el-Dab'a* (Raymond and Beverly Sackler Foundation Distinguished Lecture in Egyptology, 1; London: British Museum Press, 1996). The latter has an extensive and current bibliography.

The city of Piramesse was largely abandoned at the end of the 20th Dynasty, probably because of the silting-up of the waterway on which it was located[22] and the shift of the marine traffic to a new watercourse through Tanis. It was at this time that Tanis became the new capital of the 21st Dynasty. Piramesse became a quarry for valuable stone blocks and monuments to be used at Tanis and other sites, especially Bubastis. Yet the name and remembrance of Piramesse did not entirely disappear. It appears in a list of place-names of the 21st Dynasty date, along with Tanis.[23] Under Sheshonq I (Shishak) of the 22nd Dynasty the city of Piramesse seems to have had a brief revival by a king who emulated Ramesses II's career.[24] It is no longer justified to say that the reference to Rameses in the exodus story must preserve an ancient tradition from the time of the sojourn if it was the capital of Egypt in the tenth century BCE.

How long the ruins of Piramesse continued to retain the name is a matter of some debate. What complicates the situation is the fact that monuments from the original site of Piramesse that were transplanted in both Tanis and Bubastis led to the establishment of cults to the gods of (Per) Ramesses.[25] This, in turn, may have encouraged the notion that the region from Bubastis to Tanis and eastward was known as the 'land of Rameses', as we find it used in the Joseph story (Gen. 47.11). Yet it seems unlikely to me that either Bubastis or Tanis, cities otherwise known to the biblical writers, were ever confused with Rameses. There is late testimony from the sixth century CE that the name of Ramesses was still associated with the ruins of the original Piramesse.[26] Furthermore, the shortened form of the name Rameses, with the loss of the initial element pi = per, is probably derived from the time when the cults of the gods of Piramesse flourished in the Delta cities in the first millennium BCE, because it is precisely in these texts that the name of the city has the shortened form of Ramesse (Rameses).[27]

The designation of Rameses as a 'store-city' in the exodus story, instead of the royal city, is also quite curious. The meaning of the Hebrew phrase 'arē misk^{e}nôt is not entirely certain, but judging from the reference in 1 Kgs 9.19 and its context, it suggests supply depots and fortresses on the frontier of the land. While this

---

[22] See Bietak, *Avaris and Piramesse*, pp. 271-83.
[23] A.H. Gardiner, 'The Supposed Egyptian Equivalent of the Name Goshen', *JEA* 5 (1918), pp. 218-23 (198); *idem*, 'Tanis and Pi-Ramesse: A Retraction', p. 126.
[24] D.B. Redford, *Egypt, Canaan, and Israel in Ancient Times* (Princeton: Princeton University Press, 1992), pp. 314-15.
[25] M. Bietak, *Tell el-Dab'a II*, pp. 219-21.
[26] J. Van Seters, *The Hyksos*, pp. 148-49. Redford ('Exodus I 11', p. 409) also points to a Ptolemaic inscription from Tanis with the name of Piramesse on it in the title of 'a prophet of Amun of Ramesses from Piramesse'. Whether this attests to the cult of Amun in Piramesse at that time or merely its transplant in Tanis is not clear.
[27] Redford, 'An Egyptological Perspective on the Exodus Narrative', p. 139; cf. *idem*, 'Exodus I 11', pp. 409-10.

would be quite appropriate for Pithom/Tell el-Maskhuta from the sixth century BCE onwards, it is hardly suitable as a designation for the residence of the king's palace and temples of the Ramessides, anymore than it would be for Jerusalem under Solomon. Only after the original significance of Piramesse was long forgotten could the extensive ruins of the region be interpreted as a fortress on Egypt's northeastern frontier corresponding to that of Tell el-Maskhuta in the Wadi Tumilat.

The exodus story relates that it was the Israelites who had settled down in the 'land of Rameses', also known as Goshen, that were pressed into corvée labor in order to build these two cities. Now there is a tendency to identify the Shasu bedouin who entered the Wadi Tumilat to graze their flocks, as reflected in the text of the Merneptah papyrus quoted above, as proto-Israelites and the ones who served as the labor force in Ramesses II's extensive building activities.[28] This is most unlikely, however, as W. Helck has acknowledged.[29] Egypt had many prisoners of war and their descendants, taken from the urban centers of Syria–Palestine, who were already skilled construction workers, and so it was hardly necessary to press into service those who had no such skills and training. The livestock of the bedouin, grazing on the marginal lands of the Wadi Tumilat, were a source of food supply for the frontier towns like Tell er-Retaba.

Goshen

In the Joseph story of Genesis and during the sojourn in Exodus, the Israelites live in the land of Goshen. This region is described in rather ambiguous terms as being separate from the rest of Egypt and thus a border region, but also as part of Egypt, indeed the best of the land (Gen. 46.28–34; 47.1–10). It is suitable for the grazing of livestock, but also for the cultivation of crops. The location of Goshen and its particular Egyptian identity was another subject of controversy between Naville and Gardiner, and Egyptologists have subsequently taken up positions on one side or the other. Naville identified Goshen with a region located in the eastern Delta corresponding to the 20th nome of Lower Egypt.[30] The name of the region, which occurs in a number of late geographic texts, he read as Kesem or Gesem.

---

[28] See M. Bietak, 'Comments on the "Exodus" ', in A.F. Rainey (ed.), *Egypt, Israel and Sinai: Archaeological and Historical Relationships in the Biblical Period* (Tel Aviv: Tell Aviv University Press, 1987), pp. 163-71 (168-69); also Herrmann, *Israel in Egypt*, pp. 25-26. Herrmann admits that in his interpretation of the Merneptah text the 'proto-Israelites' were being admitted into the Wadi-Tumilat peacefully in the region that he identifies with the land of Goshen long after the date of their supposed enslavement and exodus.

[29] W. Helck, 'Die Bedrohung Palästinas durch einwandernde Gruppen am Ende der 18. und am Anfang der 19. Dynastie', *VT* 18 (1968), pp. 472-80 (480 n. 1). Helck, however, still looks for a historical fit of the exodus tradition in the 19th Dynasty.

[30] E.H. Naville, *The Shrine of Saft el Henneh and the Land of Goshen (1885)* (Memoir of the Egyptian Exploration Fund, 5; London: Egyptian Exploration Fund, 1887); *idem*, 'The Geography

Its district capital was Pisoped (Saft el Henneh). The Septuagint renders the name Goshen as 'Gesem of Arabia', and Arabia was the name that Greco-Roman sources gave to the 20th nome. The Greek and Roman geographers called Pisoped 'Phakusa', which Naville argues is derived from the name of the region, Gesem. Inscribed on a shrine dedicated to the god Soped by Nechtanebo II[31] is the name of the place, given as the town of Kus, as well as the land of Kus.[32] The town of Kus or Phakusa (Kus with the article 'pha') refers to the chief city of the land of Kus (Goshen or Gesem), just as the town of Succoth is the political name for the chief city of the region of Succoth.

Gardiner, however, disputed Naville's reading of the name Gesem, because the initial hieroglyph could be read šs as well as g.[33] He associated the name with a region known as šsmt (Shesmet), the name for the mining region of the Sinai of the Old and Middle Kingdoms. However, the only point of connection between the two place names is their common association with the god Soped, Lord of the East, but that alone hardly warrants their identity. Against the identity of these two names are a number of important considerations:

1. The names of the two places are separated by at least 1000 years. There is no continuity of usage between them.
2. They represent two quite different regions, the one in the mountains of the eastern Sinai peninsula and the other in the eastern Delta, centering in a site just a few miles east of Bubastis. This is the 20th nome that does not even include the area of the 8th nome (Succoth) that is immediately adjacent to the Sinai. The fact is that the Egyptians stopped mining in the eastern Sinai many centuries before the late form of the name *gsm* appears.
3. The orthography of the two names is completely different.[34] It is true that there is one text of the 12th Dynasty that contains a possible reference to *šsm/gsm* in hieratic that is similar to the later forms and that Gardiner interprets as an alternate form of the older name, giving him his only connection between the two forms of the name. The text is variously understood by different scholars and may or may not be related to either place.[35]

---

of the Exodus', pp. 18-32. See also P. Montet, *Géographie de L'Égypte ancienne* (Paris: Imprimerie nationale, 1957), I, pp. 205-12. Montet supports Naville's position.

[31] Montet attributes this shrine to Nectanebo I.

[32] Naville, *Shrine of Saft el Henneh*, pp. 9, 12, 14-20 and pls. iv, vi. The spelling Kes (Kus) is merely a defective rendering of the name Kesem, which appears elsewhere in connection with Per-Soped.

[33] Gardiner, 'The Supposed Egyptian Equivalent of the Name Goshen'. pp. 218-23; *idem*, 'The Geography of the Exodus: An Answer to Professor Naville and Others', pp. 87-96. H. Gauthier (*Dictionnaire des noms géographiques contenus dans les textes hiéroglyphiques* [Cairo: Société royale de Géographie d'Égypte, 1925-31], V, pp. 145-46) supports the position of Gardiner.

[34] Gesem is written [hieroglyphs] and Shesmet is [hieroglyphs].

[35] See Naville, 'The Geography of the Exodus', p. 28 n. 2; also Montet, *Géographie*, pp. 207-208.

4. Finally, there is one unambiguous rendering of the name Gesem with an initial hieroglyph which must be read g or k.[36]

In my view there is no good reason to question Naville's identification of Goshen with the 20th nome of Lower Egypt.

As the name of a specific region or nome, Gesem appears in the Egyptian texts rather late. Naville's mistake was to read all of this evidence back into the Ramesside period. The region, however, probably originated as a princedom that arose in the Delta during the eighth century BCE with its capital at Pisoped. With the reunification of Egypt under the Saite rulers, it became a district or nome. The land of Goshen (Gesem) covered the western end of the Wadi Tumilat as far as Bubastis, the eastern part of the wadi being the district of Succoth with its chief city Pithom. Goshen extended north along the eastern Nile branch as far as the ruins of Piramesse. The Bible seems, in fact, to equate the 'land of Rameses' with Goshen (compare Gen. 47.6 and 11), and this is made especially clear in the LXX. The northern extent of the region may perhaps be confirmed by the fact that in later Christian times the town of Faqus rose to prominence as a bishopric and displaced Pisoped as Phaqusa—the district center of Goshen. Faqus is only 5 kilometers south of Qantir, the site of Piramesse. Within its geographic limits there was both fine agricultural land between Saft el Henneh and Qantir, and marginal grazing land in the Wadi Tumilat. The district of Goshen/Gesem would fit all the requirements of the biblical texts.[37]

The Red Sea and the Israelites' Egyptian Itinerary

The oldest source of Exodus, the Yahwist, describes the route of the exodus in the following terms (Exod. 12.37a; 13.17-18, 20):

> The people of Israel set out from Rameses towards Succoth… And moreover, a large group of bedouin left with them, along with a great number of livestock, both sheep and cattle… When Pharaoh expelled the people, God did not lead them along the route to

---

[36] Naville, 'The Geography of the Exodus', p. 29. Cf. Gardiner's rather weak rejoinder on this point in 'The Geography of the Exodus: An Answer to Professor Naville and Others', p. 94.

[37] Redford has an alternate explanation for the name of Goshen ('Perspective on the Exodus', pp. 139-40). He derives it from the Qedarites who occupied the eastern Delta in considerable numbers from the seventh century BCE onwards. The name Goshen would then be related to the dynastic name of Gasmu (Gesem) by the royal family of the Qedarites. This seems to me most unlikely. There is no evidence that the Qedarites actually controlled the Wadi Tumilat or gave their name to the region. Their base of power was the northern Sinai, and this was never known as Goshen. The Israelites have left Goshen long before they reach the region of the Sinai Peninsula. It seems to me much more likely that the biblical author would use an Egyptian name for the region within Egypt, as he did for the rest of his geographic terms.

the land of the Philistines, even though it was shorter...but God brought them around on the desert route towards the Red Sea... They set out from Succoth and encamped in Etham on the edge of the desert.[38]

On the basis of our earlier discussion of geography, these texts suggest that the people set out from the region of Qantir (Rameses) and traveled through the Wadi Tumilat to Succoth/Pithom (Tell el-Maskhuta). As the author explains, this is not the direct route towards the northeast and the coastal road to Canaan. Instead, they had to go 'around' by traveling up the Nile southwest, until they came to the mouth of the Wadi Tumilat and then turn east through the Wadi Tumilat.[39] The language of the itinerary suggests that Succoth here refers to the town of Succoth (Tell el-Maskhuta) and not just the region that stretched over the eastern half of the Wadi Tumilat. Succoth, both town and region, is outside of Goshen.

The remark about the large group of bedouin (*'ereb*) with their animals accompanying the Israelites is of interest. It adds an element of color that is very distinctive of this route. During our excavations at Tell el-Maskhuta it was common to see groups of bedouin moving through the wadi with their flocks and livestock, often in rather large numbers, some even camping temporarily at the site of our excavations.[40] There was both a supply of water from the canal and marginal grazing land. The local villagers called them '*'arab*', the same term that is used in the text above, a terms that the villagers did not apply to themselves. It was, and remains, the primary access route from the Sinai into Egypt from time immemorial. As we saw above, the region of the Wadi Tumilat from Pi-Soped (Saft el-Henneh) to Pithom in the Greco-Roman period and in the LXX was known as Arabia.

From Succoth they moved east to a place called Etham, whose identity and location is uncertain. It would appear to be at or near the sea and at the same time to mark the edge of the Sinai desert. Some have tried to associate the name Etham with the Egyptian word for fort, *ḫtm*, but the initial laryngeal *ḫ* would rule this out.[41] Redford suggests deriving the name from *ḥwt-itm*, which would be phonetically possible, and this is supported by its location in the 8th nome.[42] Yet this name, which means the temple estate of Atum, is the direct equivalent of Per-Atum and very likely refers to the same place, Pithom. This may suggest that

---

[38] Author's translation.
[39] The various routes for the exodus proposed in the biblical atlases, such as H.G. May, *Oxford Bible Atlas* (rev. by J. Day; New York: Oxford University Press, 3rd edn, 1984) whose maps are also used in the various editions of the *Oxford Annotated Bible*—NRSV or the *Oxford Study Bible*—REB version, simply ignore the basic elements of the region's geography. They draw a straight line from Qantir to Tell el Maskhuta—right through the desert sand dunes! They are entirely misleading.
[40] See Holladay, *Tell el-Maskhuta*, Pl. XLVI. It pictures a small bedouin encampment on the tell.
[41] See Redford, 'An Egyptological Perspective on the Exodus Narrative', p. 153 n. 9; G.I. Davies, *The Way of the Wilderness: A Geographical Study of the Wilderness Itineraries in the Old Testament* (SOTSMS, 5; Cambridge: Cambridge University Press, 1979), pp. 79-80.
[42] Davies, *The Way of the Wilderness*, pp. 79-80.

the author was familiar with the names Succoth and Etham and their association with the eastern Wadi Tumilat, but he understood them as two separate places with Etham (Pithom) east of Succoth. He simply used the two names as stops on his route. If Etham is Pithom, is it near the sea and on the border of the desert?

The sea is not identified in the story of the crossing itself in Exodus 14, but from the itinerary in 13.18 and 15.22 (both J) it is named as the Red Sea. Yet if the Red Sea is the Gulf of Suez, then it is too far from the direction of travel to be seriously considered. The sea directly east of Succoth/Pithom at the end of the Wadi Tumilat is Lake Timsah. One common solution to the problem of identifying the sea is to interpret the Hebrew *yam suf* as meaning 'sea of reeds', since Hebrew *suf* does mean 'reeds' in some texts (Exod. 2.3–5) and seems closely related to Egyptian *tjwf* 'papyrus'. There is, in fact, a reference in some Egyptian texts to a papyrus marsh somewhere east of Piramesse, and this has led to the suggestion of identifying the body of water along the northeastern exit in the vicinity of Lake Ballah.[43] The obvious objection to this is that this proposal would involve the rejection of the itineraries that contradict such a northern route, but to do so would also get rid of Rameses as the starting point. The fact of the matter is that *yam suf*, in all of the instances in the Hebrew Bible outside of the exodus story, clearly designates the Red Sea and its extensions in the Gulf of Aqaba and the Gulf of Suez. There are no 'reeds' in the Red Sea since the papyrus in question is a freshwater plant. A solution that proposes the same geographic term for two entirely different things does not seem to me to be acceptable.[44]

Naville proposed a different solution to the problem of the Red Sea.[45] He pointed out that studies done by a French geologist, Linant de Bellefonds, prior to the building of the Suez Canal, found evidence that the Gulf of Suez extended much further north in antiquity to include the Bitter Lakes and Lake Timsah, and in fact to reach quite close to Tell el-Maskhuta.[46] It would also explain the rather high incidence of Red Sea shells, particularly oyster shells, that were found in the recent excavations under Holladay. This would hardly be likely if the Red Sea were 80 kilometers away. In fact, the French geologists in their investigation of the Isthmus of Suez between Lake Timsah and the Gulf of Suez found many deposits of shells and other evidence of the existence of the sea in that region. As Naville points out, this geological position agrees with classical sources that gave this extension of the Red Sea north as far as lake Timsah the name Arabian

---

[43] Bietak, 'Comments on the Exodus', p. 167; *idem*, *Avaris and Piramesse*, p. 280. For a general discussion of the various proposals, see Davies, *The Way of the Wilderness*, pp. 70-74.
[44] A summary of the various views may be found in J.R. Huddlestun, 'Red Sea', *ABD* (1992), V, pp. 633-42. For an earlier review, see Cazelles, 'Les localisations', pp. 328-29, 340-43.
[45] *The Store-City of Pithom*, pp. 15-39; *idem*, 'The Geography of the Exodus', pp. 36-39.
[46] See also the review of L. de Bellefonds's work in J. Mazuel, *L'Oeuvre géographique de Linant de Bellefonds étude de géographie historique* (Cairo: Société Royale de Géographie d'Égypte, 1937), pp. 243-59.

or Heroopolitan Gulf, because it ended close to Heroopolis, the Greek name for Pithom. Herodotus, in his description of the canal built by Necho (2.158) says, 'The water [of the canal] is derived from the Nile and leaves it a little above the city of Bubastis. Flowing alongside of Patoumos (Pithom), the city of Arabia, it then enters into the Red Sea.' He elsewhere refers to the Red Sea end of the canal as the Arabian Gulf, so that it is most reasonable to interpret his description of the fresh-water canal as extending from a point near Bubastis on the west to Pithom on the east, the point at which it empties into the Red Sea.[47] Herodotus also tells of Necho's establishment of a navy in the 'Arabian Gulf', very likely in support of Red Sea and East African trade.[48] This is especially the case after the construction of the canal by Necho. Tell el-Maskhuta (Pithom) was the final terminus for the canal, and this fact would help explain its location and importance as a port and trans-shipment site, where goods coming by canal from inland could be collected and stored and then transferred to sea ships that traveled through the Red Sea and beyond. This same pattern of shipping activity in the Red Sea through the canal and the Arabian Gulf was also attested for Ptolemy II in a detailed description of his construction and expeditions in this region in the famous Pithom Stele.[49] The very close association between the main center of the region at Pithom and the point from which the sea-going expeditions set out and brought back their goods make this proximity of the Red Sea extension to Pithom obvious. In spite of some objections that have been raised against this view, none of which seem to me to be very persuasive,[50] this explanation is still the best possibility. A biblical reference to the Arabian Gulf may be seen in Isa. 11.15 with its designation of the crossing point of the sea as the 'tongue of the Egyptian sea', which is almost certainly a reference to a narrow gulf of the Red Sea.[51]

If the Red Sea was so close to Pithom/Etham and in the direct line of march by the Israelites through the Wadi Tumilat, then the event as portrayed in the J source has to do with Lake Timsah, the northern part of the Arabian Gulf. What the author has in mind is an encampment at the northwestern end of the lake in which a strong wind drove the water back so that the Israelites crossed this stretch on dry ground during the night. When the Egyptians tried to follow the next morning, they were caught by the returning waters and drowned.[52]

---

[47] See Naville's extended discussion of this text in *The Store-City of Pithom*, pp. 34-39.
[48] See A.B. Lloyd, 'Necho and the Red Sea: Some Considerations', *JEA* 63 (1977), pp. 142-55.
[49] See Naville, *The Store-City of Pithom*, pp. 18-21.
[50] See Davies, *The Way of the Wilderness*, pp. 73-74. Davies allows for the possibility of this explanation and retains the designation 'Red Sea' for *yam suf*. Nevertheless, he gives very little attention to Naville's views.
[51] Cazelles ('Les localisations', p. 343) argues that 'tongue' means 'gulf' but tries to identify the Egyptian Sea with the Mediterranean, which is unlikely.
[52] For a discussion of J's account, see J. Van Seters, *The Life of Moses: The Jahwist as Historian in Exodus-Numbers* (Louisville, KY: Westminster/John Knox Press, 1994), pp. 128-39.

The later Priestly Writer modified this account by having the Israelites turn back from Etham at the border of the wilderness and head further south to a point more centrally on the west side of the sea (Exod. 14.1-2, 9b). This was presumably to avoid the impression that the Israelites did not just go around the northern end of the lake and to enhance the miracle of the walls of water on either side as they crossed. P specifies the geography rather carefully by mention of the place-names Pihahiroth, Migdol and Baal-Zephon. It is these names, however, that have given rise to the conjectures about a northern route out of Egypt, even though they occur in the latest source. Furthermore, the remarks by P are built into the prior itinerary of J and cannot be divorced from it.

Nevertheless, northern locations have been given for Baal-Zephon either at Tell Defenne, which is not near the sea, or with Mount Casios (Ras Qasrun) on the Mediterranean coast, a route that is difficult to reconcile with the rest of P's itinerary through the desert.[53] Migdol is usually situated at Tell el-Her on the northern route several kilometers from the Mediterranean coast and a long distance from Tel Defenne or Ras Qasrun. Furthermore, the name 'Migdol' means a fortress, and it could represent any number of sites on the eastern frontier, including the eastern end of the Wadi Tumilat. What is often overlooked in the discussion is the fact that there is evidence for all three place-names being situated at the eastern end of the Wadi Tumilat, although their exact locations are not given in the texts.[54] This seems much more likely to me, since P did not contradict his earlier source by proposing an entirely different northerly route. He merely modified J's route by including a few additional geographic and narrative details.

The Geography of the Exodus Story and History

The geography of the sojourn and exodus, as it is presented in Exodus 1–15 does not provide us with any evidence of the historicity of the events in the time of the Ramessides. On the contrary, the earliest version of the story's geography, as presented by the Yahwist, presents the biblical author's understanding of the region of the Eastern Delta, which corresponds with the sixth century BCE. His portrayal of Goshen as the region in which the Israelites sojourned, his references to the town of Pithom/Succoth, and the construal of the site of Rameses as the ruins of an ancient 'store-city', all of this fits only the later period. This also agrees closely with the perceived threat on the northeastern border, expressed in Exodus 1, because from the time of the late Assyrian and the Babylonian periods onward invasions from this direction were a constant threat. As a consequence, it

---

[53] See a review of these sites in Davies, *The Way of the Wilderness*, pp. 80-82; Huddlestun, 'Red Sea', *ABD* (1992), V, pp. 639-40; Cazelles, 'Les localisations', pp. 321-64.

[54] See Redford, 'An Egyptological Perspective on the Exodus Narrative', pp. 142-44; also Davies, *The Way of the Wilderness*, p. 82; Naville, *The Store-City of Pithom*, pp. 30-31.

is precisely in the Saite period that narratives expressive of xenophobia make their appearance in Egypt and become a staple of the Egyptian self-consciousness.[55] The Goshen region also contained a large number of settlers from Asia, including Jews, and there was increasing tension between such foreign settlers and the native Egyptian population.

In the past biblical scholars have used the argument that the close fit between the traditions of the exodus, as preserved in the oldest source of the Pentateuch in Exodus 1–15, and the time of Ramesses II was a firm basis for maintaining the great antiquity of these traditions. They could in turn be used as a means by which to reconstruct the early history and religion of the people. The few place-names of Rameses, Pithom and Succoth became the key to the whole historical enterprise. However, the demise of efforts to understand early Israelite history in the context of the Middle and Late Bronze Ages should have encouraged the same caution towards the geographic details in the story of the exodus.

What I would suggest by this analysis is that all of the colorful details of the exodus story are the work of the Yahwist, including his presentation of the geography. Since there is much throughout his work that suggests a date in the exilic period, these details, especially the geography, fit this period better than any other. There is no way of dating any 'historical' exodus event. Prior to the Yahwist, there are only rather vague references to the tradition about an origin in Egypt and an exodus brought about by divine deliverance. Such notions about national origins are too common and too stereotyped to be very helpful to the modern historian. If this seems 'minimalist' to some, it is the only o#ption for the cautious historian to take. To such a cautious and dedicated historian, geographer and archaeologist, Max Miller, I am happy to offer this piece.

---

[55] See D.B. Redford, *Pharaonic King-Lists, Annals and Day-books: A Contribution to the Study of the Egyptian Sense of History* (SSEA Publication, 4; Mississauga, ON: Benben, 1986), p. 295; *idem*, 'Studies in Relations between Palestine and Egypt during the First Millennium B.C.', *JAOS* 93 (1973), pp. 3-17 (17).

History in Joshua

Ernst Axel Knauf

Is Joshua a source for the LB–Iron transition? Instead of adding to the bulk of stated opinions on this particular topic, I would like to broaden the scope somewhat and ask: How much "history" found its way into the present (Hebrew) text of Joshua, and which kind of "history"? By "history" I mean, in the context of this particular essay, every element of the past real world that can be identified by a modern, historically informed reader in the text.

I accept the principal claims of the historical-critical approach to biblical literature as basically valid: that every book of the Bible is the product of a redactional process, starting with a first draft and leading gradually to its final form; that the principal stages of this development can be distinguished in the present text (at least roughly), having left enough traces and clues in it; and that they can be (sometimes roughly) dated if there is enough text for each stratum of the tradition, and if enough of the history presupposed by it is known. In opposition to past (and some present) scholarship, I do not look for individual authors or redactors, but assume that ancient Near Eastern and biblical literary production was a communal effort, one made synchronically and diachronically, by a group of scribes in the service of palaces, temples and their attached scribal schools (of which there were not too many in Israel, and even fewer in Judah).

The chronology presupposed in this study is the Low Chronology (Iron I–IIA transition between 950 and 900; Iron IIA–IIB transition between 850 and 800). Reconstructed features are classified as *"probable"* or *"possible."* A feature termed *"possible"* is not less probable than a *"probable"* feature, as far as factuality is concerned, but its chronological window is wider than the date given here. Probabilities smaller than 0.5 will not be taken into account. Maybe "Sheshai" in Josh 15:14 serves as a monument to a Hyksos king (Redford 1967, 257)—but at least four other explanations of that name are as plausible, which leaves for Redford's proposal a probability of 0.2, or 20 percent. In addition, I will not even try to trace Joshua's "memory" beyond the LB II period (at least not in the present study).

The literary history of Joshua, as I see it, may be outlined as follows:

late 7th cent.	First draft, end of an Exodus–Conquest Story (Josh 6* and 10*)
525–450	Exodus–Conquest Story becomes D-Composition (Josh 6–11*)
450–400	First Hexateuch Redaction (Josh 1–11*; 15:20–18:1*)
400–375	Second Hexateuch Redaction (Josh 13; 20–22; 24) and the Joshua Judges Redaction (Josh 12; 14; 18–19; 23)

I will start with a list (briefly annotated) of historical features that I found reflected in Joshua.

I. The Data

0. Joshua mentions kings for several Canaanite cities. Some of these were indeed seats of rulers (not necessarily "cities" in the LB II period); some were not. This item will be excluded from the data base, but used in the discussion. In the following table, 1 = probably existed, 0 = most probably did not exist.

City	Exod–Josh*	D	1Hexa	2Hexa	Josh–Judg
Jericho	0	0	0	0	0
Ai	-	0	0	0	0
Jerusalem	1	1	1	1	1
Hebron	0	1	1	1	1
Yarmut	0	0	0	0	0
Lachish	1	1	1	1	1
Eglon	0	0	0	0	0
Makedah	-	0	0	0	0
Libna	-	0	0	0	0
Gezer	-	1	1	1	1
Debir	-	0	0	0	0
Hazor	-	1	1	1	1
Madon	-	0	0	0	0
Shimron	-	1	1	1	1
Akshaf	-	1	1	1	1
Heshbon	-	-	-	0	0
Bashan	-	-	-	0	0
Geder	-	-	-	-	0
Horma	-	-	-	-	0
Arad	-	-	-	-	0
Adullam	-	-	-	-	0

Bethel	-	-	-	-	0
Tappuah	-	-	-	-	0
Hefer	-	-	-	-	0
Afek	-	-	-	-	1
Taanach	-	-	-	-	1
Megiddo	-	-	-	-	1
Kedesh	-	-	-	-	0
Jokneam	-	-	-	-	1
Dor	-	-	-	-	1
Gilgal	-	-	-	-	0
Tirzah	-	-	-	-	0
1/1+0 ratio	2/6	7/15	7/15	7/17	12/32
	0.33	0.47	0.47	0.41	0.38

(a) There was a memory, not too vague but by no means very precise, that Canaan once was a country of city-states (*probable*). Instead of "memory" one might also think of an appropriate theoretical reconstruction by the scribes based on Canaan's survival in Phoenicia and Philistia.

(b) Hazor was the most important of these states (*possible*)—Josh 11:10d. Instead of "memory," the evidence of its large tell might have led to this insight, but it is nevertheless correct.

1. 13th century: Egyptian occupation of Canaan and Merneptah's military street (probable), *ma'yan mê-neftoax*, "Spring-place of Mer-en-Ptah," instead of "spring of the waters of Nephtoah" (Josh 15:9; 18:15) (Singer 1988; Stager 1985).

2. 13th/12th century: survivors of the Israel annihilated by Mer-en-Ptah before 1208 B.C.E. join the new tribes filling its place on Mt. Ephraim and end up as a Manassite clan (*possible*): Asriel (Josh 17:2, 14) (Lemaire 1977; Whitelam 2000; Knauf 1994).

3. 10th century: (a) battle of Gibeon (*possible*)—Josh 10:1–14* (10:12c–13c). Gibeon (major town in Iron I) and Jerusalem were rivals for the control of the southern highway between the coastal plain and Transjordan in Iron I (this geographic feature lent prominence to Benjamin under Saul). Gibeon was probably allied with Saul's Israel; Jerusalem most probably was not. So, the battle of Gibeon (the oldest source for which, though very fragmentary, was the polytheistic conjuration in Josh 10:12c–13c) probably took place during the wars between the House of Saul and the House of David, or shortly before. After Gibeon was destroyed by Shishak, it was not rebuilt by Solomon (Keel and Uehlinger 1994).

(b) When Jerusalem joined David's kingdom, its native inhabitants still dominated the life of the town (wherever the term "Jebusite" came from, and whenever it was applied to them; *probable*)—Josh 15:63 (agrees with Ezek 16:3—except for the ethnonym—and the ethnicity of the victorious party in 1 Kgs 1, and which contradicts 2 Sam 2:6–8 which is, as a text, hopelessly garbled and no base for any historical reconstruction).

4. 10th/early 9th century: "The Book of the Upright" (*possible*)—quoted Josh 10:13d. The poetic fragments in Josh 10; 2 Sam 1 and 1 Kgs 8 are polytheistic and militaristic. They reflect the culture of courts of warlords (as does Judg 5). Iconography attests to a comparative mentality in Iron I and IIA. For David's Lament I find an early-to-mid-9th-century origin most probable. As the "Book of Balaam" from Tell Deir ʿAlla shows, book production had started in 9th-century Israel (but these were, on the other hand, books quite different from those found in the Bible).[1]

5. 10th/early 9th century: the Canaanite cities like Taanach and Megiddo are integrated into the state of Israel between Solomon/Jeroboam I and Omri (*probable*)—Josh 16:10; 17:11–13. Megiddo VI (10th century) is still indigenous Canaanite, VA still largely indigenous with intrusions of an extra-muros-state.

6. 8th century (reign of Jeroboam II): (a) the status of Taanach, Megiddo, Dor, Gezer and Edrei (*probable*)—Josh 17:11; 19:37. Cities in one tribal territory are garrisoned by recruits from another, a situation which matches Megiddo IV (75% "public buildings").

(b) The fortresses of Naphtali (*probable*)—Josh 19:35–38. It was only in the 8th century that Hazor and Kinneret co-existed as fortified places (Knauf 2000).

(c) The borders of Zebulon (and perhaps Asher; *possible*)—Josh 19:10–14 (and 19:25–29*). These two border descriptions are not, like all the others, derived from Num 34:1–12, and rather precise. Dating based on 6(b)—data on Galilee seem to derive from Jeroboam's II administration (also the only one that left some Hebrew inscriptions in Galilee).

(d) The town lists of Asher, Zebulon and Issachar (*possible*)—Josh 19:15, 17–21, 25–30*. By extension of 6(b).

(e) The administrative organization of Manasseh (*possible*)—Josh 17:1–6. Instead of districts with towns, Manasseh is organized in clans and their territories (also attested by the Samaria ostraca). These and the notion of an upsurge of Israelite tribalism/"nationalism" under (Jehu and) Jeroboam II suggest the dating followed here. Alternatively, one might think of deurbanization following the Assyrian conquest (and the *pax Assyriaca*), and attribute this feature to the 7th–5th centuries.

---

[1] Knauf 1997, 2002. Work on the 9th-century date of Tell Deir ʿAlla's language is in progress; cf. preliminarily Knauf 2005.

7. 7th century: (a) the territory of Dan (*possible*)—Josh 19:40–46. Looks like the territory of Ekron after 701 B.C.E. Was it part of Manasseh's wish list after his participation in the Assyrian conquest of Egypt?

(b) The administrative organization of Judah and Benjamin in the second half of the 7th century (*probable*)—Josh 15:20–44, 48–62; 18:21–28. This describes Judah as a full-blown state (four-tier settlement hierarchy) and in the borders of, roughly, Josiah (Na'aman 1991).

(c) The first territorial concept of Eretz Israel (hereafter TCEI 1)—Josh 10:40–42. Judah in the borders of ca. 600 is presented as "the whole country," that is, the terminal of the exodus: Eretz Israel = Judah. This is an accommodation of Judean state ideology to the newly acquired Benjaminites, to whom, for reasons of historical memory, the "House-of-David" story did not sound very attractive.

(d) The town list of Simeon (*possible*)—Josh 19:1–8. An excerpt from 7(b), but probably pre-exilic: Simeon = Ishmaelites who joined Judah (Arabs later immigrating and integrating into Judah became "Kaleb," see infra).

8. 6th–early 5th centuries (525–450 B.C.E.): (a) TCEI 2 "from Dan to Beersheba" (*possible*)—Josh 11:16–23. Adding to 10:40–42, the concept of Eretz Israel is now brought in line with the territory of Israel and Judah as presupposed in Samuel–Kings. Belongs to a literary stratum which also presupposed D*, but not yet P. Dated by "sandwich" between 7(c) (prior to 597 B.C.E.) and P (later than 520 B.C.E.).

(b) "Clear forest" (*possible*)—Josh 17:14–18. After the Assyrian conquest, re-forestation in Galilee and Samaria was much more massive than in the LB period (no return to goat-herding, instead migration in search for labor). The conflict between Judah and Samaria might, however, as well be dated to the 4th century (Knauf 2003).

(c) "To hell with Bethel/Benjamin" (*possible*)—Josh 7–8 (notably 8:17; 12:16; the separation of 18:20–28 from 15:20–62). This anti-Bethel attitude was prevalent in Jerusalem from 520 to 450, but might well have lingered on into the 4th century (Knauf 2006).

9. Late 5th century: (a) TCEI 3 "Yehud and Samaria" (*probable*)—Josh 14:1–6*; 15:20–18:1. The sharp redactional cleavage between the land allotted to Judah and "Beth Joseph" and the land outside of Yehud and Samaria betrays a concept of Eretz Israel consisting of Judah and Samaria (together and in cooperation with the god of the Jewish diaspora, as illustrated by the Elephantine correspondence and the final redaction of the Torah). These are the politics and the ideology of the P group.

(b) "Make love—or covenants—not war" (*possible*)—Josh 2 and 9, showing Joshua to avoid slaughtering Canaanites under what pretext ever. The same politics as 9(a).

(c) Kaleb is Judah and is not Judah (*possible*)—Josh 14:6–15; 15:13–19. In 1 Chr 2 and 4, "Kaleb" is the genealogical anchor for Judean families of Edomite and/or Arab origin. This development seems to be prepared for by Kaleb's treatment in Josh 14–15. The mechanisms of a tribal society (which allowed families and clans to move from one tribe to another, genealogies conveniently adapted) were very much alive in the Persian period. Idumaea—from a Jerusalemite traditionalist point of view, southern Judah—was populated by Judeans, Arabs and Edomites in the 5th to 2nd centuries.

(d) "Solomon's slaves" (Ezra 2:55 par.) become temple slaves (*possible*)—Josh 9. The Gibeonite towns, probably given to Solomon by Shishak, remained royal property throughout the monarchy. After the exile, the temple claimed the palace's heritage.

10. Late 5th–early 4th centuries: (a) TCEI 4 "Nile to Sidon" (*probable*)—Josh 13 and most of the borders in Josh 15–19. A scholarly construct based on the merger of the Egyptian province of Canaan (reclaimed at least by Psammetikh and Nekho in the late 6th century, but possibly also by independent Egypt in the 4th century) with the Jordan as Israel's border (from TCEI 1), and imported into Joshua from Num 34:1–12.

(b) "Resettle Galilee (and Transjordan)" (*probable*)—Josh 18:2–19:48. Prior to the Persian period, no Judeans lived in Galilee. In the middle of the 2nd century they are there and in Transjordan, parts of which were, together with Galilee, successfully claimed by Hyrcanus and his successors. Joshua 18–19 (together with Judg 17–18) seems to indicate the beginning of Jewish (as opposed to earlier Israelite) settlement in Galilee.

(c) Temples other than "of Jerusalem" (*probable*)—Josh 22, a theologically oriented instruction relating to the construction of a temple outside of Jerusalem, a problem posed by the temples on the Gerizim (since the first half of the 5th century), as well as at Maresha (5th/4th century) and Elephantine. The "permit" granted to the Transjordanians in Josh 22 is more or less identical with the permit granted to the Jews of Elephantine in 408.

(d) Three Philistine cities (*possible*)—Josh 15:45–47. In the Persian period, only three out of five Philistine cities retained their semi-independence: Gaza, Ashkelon and Ashdod. Josh 15:45–47 obliterates its origin by naming Ashkelon "Ekron."

(e) The Prominence of Qedesh Naphtali (*possible*)—Josh 12:22; 20:7; 21:32. Qedesh was the administrative center of Upper Galilee in the late Persian and early Hellenistic periods.

11. 3rd–2nd centuries: anti-Samaritan redaction (*probable*). The only Hellenistic influence on Joshua is found in its textual history. The book is pre-Hellenistic. A town list of Ephraim was deleted in Josh 16 (but partially quoted in Josh 21), and

the venue of Josh 24 was changed from "Shiloh" (as in the LXX) to "Shechem," changing the addressees of Joshua's final speech from Judah and Samaria to Samaria only.

II. Discussion

The distribution of features from Joshua over the periods of Israel's history (separated between *probable* and *possible*) turns out as follows:

Period	Archaeological	Features (prob.)	Features (prob. + poss.)
Pre-State	LB/Ir I	2	4
Early State	Ir IIA	2	4
Independent State	Ir II B	2	5
Assyrian	Ir II C	2	4
Babylonian	Ir IIC/P	-	-
Early Persian	P I	2	7
Late Persian	P II	3	5
Hellenistic	Hell	1	1
Sum		14	30

The picture that emerges becomes clearer if the periods are merged into even larger sections:

Period	prob.	prob. and poss.
Pre-State	2	4
Pre-Exilic	6	13
Persian	5	12
Hellenistic	1	1

In the "historical memory" of Joshua, the pre-state ("Settlement and Tribe" formation) and the Hellenistic periods are only marginally presented (the latter, because the book was basically finished before that period commenced). The pre-exilic (the period on which the biblical account from Genesis to 2 Kings is written) and the Persian periods (when that account was basically written, and mostly finished) feature with nearly equal weight. The slightly higher number of pre-exilic features should come as no surprise, for:

(a) This history is much longer, four centuries as opposed to 1:5 (supposing that Joshua was finished ca. 375 B.C.E.);

(b) There are also more data on most of the 10th to 7th centuries than for each of the 6th and 5th centuries, which might be used for the correlation of Joshua's textual world with the real past world. If I knew more about the settlement history of Baal Gad and the town of Golan, I might have been able to add features for the Persian period.

The basic expectation that a literary text should reflect the time of its authors more faithfully than the time the authors write about is also fulfilled, for it is the later features which are devoted more text and more precision, as the following two examples demonstrate:

a. The Sequence of TCEIs

TCEI	Date	Texts	Ex/implicit
1	late 7th century	Josh 6*; 10*	implicit
2	6th/early 5th century	Josh 11	implicit
3	late 5th	Josh 15:20–18:1	implicit
4	late 5th/4th century	Josh 1:4; 13; 15:1–20, etc.	explicit

b. Egyptian Occupation, "Clear Forest," and "Make Peace"

Feature	Date	Number Words/ Verses/Chapters	Ratio
Egyptian occupation	13th century	3 w. (1 place name)	
clear wood	5th century	80 w. / 4vv.	13th/5th: 0.04
make peace	late 5th century	55 vv. / 2 chs.	5th/15th: 0.07

The very first table (under I 0) shows, however, that the historicity rate of earlier literary strata is not necessarily higher than that of later strata. To look for a "core narrative" and then believe everything it says is not feasible; the same can be said of the disregarding of historical information because it is found in redactional additions.

There is a clear structure as far as the genre is concerned, a feature which transports historical memory. The earliest piece of historical consciousness is contained in one place name, mentioned twice for reasons which have nothing to do with its historical content, and which was opaque to the authors of the book and to those of their readers who were (or still are) unaware of the achievements of Pharaoh Merneptah.

The oldest piece of text quoted is from the 10th century. It is poetic, and committed into writing probably at the courts of Shechem, Tirzah, Samaria or and/or Jerusalem in the 10th to early 9th century. A prose composition from that time has survived only in epigraphy (TDA) and shows convincingly that we have nothing similar (except Judg 5) in the Bible. Larger amounts of text are preserved from the royal administrations of Israel and Judah in the 8th and 9th centuries, that is, at a time when Israelite and Judaean epigraphy sets in with considerable quantity.

This is an investigation of history in Joshua, not of the book of Joshua's constructing (wrong) history which is also done in the book. It would be interesting to contrast my lists of what the authors of Joshua knew (without knowing that they knew, in most cases) with a list of LB/Iron I history which they did not know. For them it was logical that anybody crossing the Jordan from the east in order to conquer Benjamin and Judah would first come to blows with Jericho. They needed the extinct tribe of Gad to organize areas of Jewish settlement in Peraea, so they rewrote its town list, found in Num 32:34–36 (which agrees with Mesha), in Josh 13 (which does not).

III. Conclusion

A quantitative approach to the "historical memory" of the book of Joshua helps to define the order of magnitude in which one may expect the survival of correct memory in biblical literature, and the production of history (as future memory) based on the experience of the authors present. We find both aspects present in Joshua, and where there are enough data (notably on social, economic, demographic, environmental and linguistic history), these activities can be identified and distinguished from each other.

Bibliography

Keel, O., and C. Uehlinger. 1994. Jahwe und die Sonnengottheit von Jerusalem. Pages 269–306 in *Ein Gott allein? JHWH-Verehrung und biblischer Monotheismus im Kontext der israelitischen und altorientalischen Religionsgeschichte.* Edited by W. Dietrich and M. A. Klopfenstein. OBO 138. Freiburg: Universitätsverlag. Göttingen: Vandenhoeck & Ruprecht.

Knauf, E. A. 1994. *Die Umwelt des Altent Testaments.* NSK-AT 29. Stuttgart: Katholisches Bibelwerk.

Knauf, E. A. 1997. Le roi est mort, vive le roi! A Biblical Argument for the Historicity of Solomon. Pages 81–95 in *The Age of Solomon: Scholarship at the Turn of the Millennium.* Edited by Lowell K. Handy. SHCANE 11. Leiden: Brill.

Knauf, E. A. 2000. Kinneret and Naftali. Pages 219–33 in *Congress Volume, Oslo 1998.* Edited by A. Lemaire and M. Sæbø. VTSup 80. Leiden: Brill.

Knauf, E. A. 2002. The Queens' Story: Bathshebah, Maacah and Athaliah and the "Historia" of Early Kings. *lectio difficilior* 2. Online: www.lectio.unibe.ch.

Knauf, E. A. 2003. "Kinneret I" Revisited. Pages 159–69 in *Saxa Loquentur.* FS V. Fritz. Edited by C. G. den Hertog et al. AOAT 302. Münster: Ugarit.

Knauf, E. A. 2005. Deborah's Language. Judges ch. 5 in Its Hebrew and Semitic Context. Pages 167–82 in *Studia Semitica et Semitohamitica*. FS Rainer Voigt. Edited by B. Burtea, J. Tropper and H. Younansardaroud. AOAT 317. Münster: Ugarit-Verlag.

Knauf, E. A. 2006. Bethel: The Israelite Impact on Judean Language and Literature. Pages 291–349 in *Judah and the Judeans in the Persian Period*. Edited by O. Lipschits and M. Oeming. Winona Lake, Ind.: Eisenbrauns.

Lemaire, A. 1977. Le clan d'Asriel et Israël, les origines de la confédération israélite. Pages 283–86 in *Inscriptions hébraïques I. Les ostraca*. LAPO 9. Paris: Cerf.

Na'aman, N. 1991. The Kingdom of Judah under Josiah. *TA* 18:3–71.

Redford, D. B. 1967. *History and Chronology of the Eighteenth Dynasty*. Toronto: University of Toronto Press.

Singer, I. 1988. Merenptah's Campaign to Canaan. *BASOR* 269:1–10.

Stager, L. E. 1985. Merenptah, Israel and the Sea People: New Light on an Old Relief. *EI* 18:56*–64*.

Whitelam, K. W. 2000. "Israel Is Laid Waste; His Seed Is No More": What If Merneptah's Scribes Were Telling the Truth? *Biblical Interpretation* 8:8–22.

History in Judges

Ernst Axel Knauf

Introduction

In the case of Joshua, basically a product of the early Persian period (500–400 B.C.E.), ca. 50 percent of the "historical memory" contained in the book comes from this period which might be defined as the book's "present." Another 25 percent derive from the 8th through 6th centuries, considerably less from the 10th and 9th centuries, and nearly nothing from the Late Bronze–Iron transition. For Judges, the "gestation period" is somewhat more extended.[1] It starts in the late 8th or early 7th centuries with the Israelite "Book of Saviours" (Judg 3–9/12*) and does not end before the 3rd century (all dates are B.C.E.). The textual growth of Judges reminds of an onion. A pre-exilic core grew layers and layers in both directions, towards the beginning and towards the end. The "Book of Saviours" originated as a reaction to the loss of Israel's king, kingship and independence. Foreign occupation—as now experienced by the hands of the Assyrians—is nothing new, it says. A saviour will appear—and hopefully not turn into a king, for kingship has failed, and was not such a good idea, after all. In an early re-issue, now including the story of Jephthah, it ends on a very negative, nearly hopeless note: not only the kings failed, the saviours failed too, in the end. Jephthah is buried in "one of the towns of Gilead" (ויקבר בערי גלעד, Judg 12:7)—no one cares which one precisely.

So far, what was to become Judges was an Israelite book, as was the first edition of Hosea (contemporary with the "Book of Saviours," and addressing the same political situation, though proffering another solution: saviours are not really necessary, "prophetic" teacher will do). With the Persian period commences the Judaean adaptation, first by the addition of Samson. The anti-monarchic, anti-state attitude of the book is now gradually turned around to pro-state propaganda. The beginning (1:1–3:11) and the end (chs. 17–21), both produced in the course of

---

[1] Guillaume (2004) more than compensates for the absence of an up-to-date commentary; cf. further Schmid 2008, 120.

at least two redactions, were added to make the "book of Judges" fit its present context, Joshua and Samuel–Kings, in which it fills a "gap" that had not been there in the first place (in Josh 18:1 the ark reaches the location where it is found at the onset of Samuel; in Judg 1–19 the ark plays no role at all). The "book of the Saviours" became a "prophetic book" of the Hebrew Bible by means of a "prophetic redaction," one which added, among other things, the story of Gideon's "call," "Baal fight" and sacrifice (6:11–32), which was not a very original achievement, for the whole story is nothing but Elijah recycled (1 Kgs 17–19).

The possibility of a pre-exilic macro-narrative from Joshua through Kings ("DtrH") is excluded by the awkward redactional transition of Josh 23:1–Judg 3:11[2]—and by the length of the books of Joshua (656 verses) and Judges (618 verses). Only the book of Daniel (357 verses) is shorter. Had they ever formed a continuous narrative, there would never have been a sufficient reason to separate them: with 1274 verses, Joshua–Judges would still be shorter than Numbers (1288 verses), Isaiah (1291 verses), Jeremiah (1364 verses), Samuel (1506), Genesis and Kings (1534 verses) and Chronicles (1765 verses). The reason why Joshua and Judges form two separate books now is that they did so from their very beginnings.

A Brief Historical Reading

The following is a list of those sections of Judges for which a historical background comes to mind—which does not necessarily imply that the text is "based" on that particular event; the text might still be pure fantasy and any similarity between text and event a matter of pure chance. The possibility of a historical background within the known history of the 1st millennium B.C.E. does, however, diminish the probability of the text's referring to otherwise unknown events or characters of the 2nd millennium.

1. Judges 1:22–26, a text from the latest literary stratum (late 4th/3rd centuries), reads:

> The house of Joseph also went up against Bethel; and the LORD was with them. The house of Joseph sent out spies to Bethel (the name of the city was formerly Luz). When the spies saw a man coming out of the city, they said to him, "Show us the way into the city, and we will deal kindly with you." So he showed them the way into the city; and they put the city to the sword, but they let the man and all his family go. So the man went to the land of the Hittites and built a city, and named it Luz; that is its name to this day.

---

[2] Blum (1997) aptly describes the Gordian magnitude of this knot, but did not have Alexander's sword at hand to deal with it properly.

In the Samaritan tradition, the Gerizim temple is called "Bethel" and the settlement on the mount next to the temple, which flourished well into the Byzantine period, Luza. According to recent archaeological data, the temple was founded in the first half of the 5th century, that is, more or less immediately after the destruction of the Bethel sanctuary by Judaean deuteronomistic zealots.[3] The "land of the Hittites" in Persian period cuneiform texts is Syria. Without any doubt, the Gerizim is situated in (Greater) Syria, outside the borders of Yehud/Judaea.

2. Judges 3:12–30, a text of the late 8th/early 7th centuries, contains three datable features:

(a) "Ehud (a Benjaminite clan) hit, struck, beat, killed, annihilated Eglon (a town, village or clan in northern Transjordan)" (cf. Knauf 1991) is an action perfectly feasible in the Near East when central state power is (temporarily) absent or very weak (cf. Mishaqa 1988). This was the case from ca. 1100 B.C.E. (it is unlikely that the tribe of Benjamin consolidated before the end of the 12th century) to ca. 875 (the end of the civil war which marked the beginning of Omride reign) and then again 724–716 (from the capture of the last Israelite king by the Assyrians to the organization of the province of Samaria by Sargon II).[4]

(b) The concept of a Moabite occupation of Jericho[5] presupposes that the opposite side of the Jordan had become the ערבות מואב, the section of the Rift Valley belonging to Moab, which was the case following Mesha's conquest of the Rubenite town of Nebo 850/840 B.C.E., but not before.

(c) Ehud escapes from a room locked from the inside by means of Assyrian type plumbing,[6] which was not yet attested in the palaces of Samaria, but which is still visible today in the Assyrian palaces of Megiddo (III): this feature presupposes the establishment of Samaria and Megiddo as provincial capitals from 716 B.C.E. onwards.

3. Deborah, Barak and Sisera in Judg 4–5. The prose (from the late 8th/early 7th centuries) does not contain historical data other than those derived from the song, even though the song is secondarily inserted in the present literary context. The song was first committed into writing at the Omride court (875–850), and not composed before the emergence in the 10th century of "Israel" according to Judg 5, which leads geographically to the period between Eshbaal and Jeroboam

---

[3] Cf. Stern and Magen 2002; Knauf 2006. For Zech 7:2, which shows the cult of Bethel still operative in 518 B.C.E., cf. now Willi-Plein 2007, 123f.

[4] Cf., for the late 8th century, the Nimrud letter ND 2773; Mittmann 1973.

[5] Actually, Judg 3:13, "In alliance with…[Moab] went and defeated Israel; and they took possession of the city of palms," presupposes the occupation of Thamar at the southern end of the Dead Sea, which can hardly antedate the formation of the Moabite state under Mesha.

[6] Cf. my commentary *ad locum,* forthcoming in *Neue Zürcher Bibel: Kommentierte Ausgabe.* פרשדונה in 3:22 is the "canalization"; מסדרונה in 3:23 is the place in the basement where it led to; and אטר in 3:15 is not "left-handed" but "thin, nimble, flexible" (cf. אטריות, "spaghetti").

I: Saul's Israel did not yet comprise the Galilee, and by the 9th century, Gad had replaced Reuben. Except for geography, social structure, and ideology, the song does not contain more "memory" than that of a conflict between the tribes of Zebulon and Naphtali and a sea-peoples chieftain or kinglet called Sisera. All other features might be drawn from type-scenes belonging to the stock of trade goods of a professional singer of that time.[7]

4. The Gideon story Judg 6–8 contains a basic text from the late 8th/early 7th century, its "source" in 8:4–27* added secondarily (but probably very soon, if not immediately together with the "elaborated story" of Gideon's victory in 7:1–8:3, as was the case with Judg 5 in respect to Judg 4), and several later additions. Who or when and where "Gideon" was, is impossible to decide, for the name seems to be derived from a ditty[8] in which it might denote anything or nothing at all:

> Look at me, and do the same; when I come to the outskirts of the camp, do as I do. When I blow the trumpet, I and all who are with me, then you also blow the trumpets around the whole camp, and shout, "For the Lord and for Gideon!" (Judg 7:17–18)

This might be compared a ditty I was taught in the late 1950s by my maternal grandmother, to be said when a ladybird landed on one's hand:

> *Marienkäfer flieg*
> *Vater ist im Krieg*
> *Mutter ist im Pommernland*
> *Pommerland ist abgebrannt* […]
> *Marienkäfer flieg*

The text as I know it sounds incomplete, and it is to be noted that a variant circulates with *Maikäfer* instead of *Marienkäfer*. Devastating wars in Pomerania took place in 1624–48, 1672–79, 1709–14, 1757–62, and 1806. The tradition most probably traces back to the 17th or 18th century C.E.[9]

(a) "Midianite" Bedouin—Judg 6:2–6. This text, which dates from the 6th/5th century, depicts the state of affairs at Benjamin's southern border between 582 and ca. 525/450 (cf. Lam 5:9). Bedouin incursions so far west/north were previously impossible as long as Jericho, Jerusalem and the northern Shephelah were not destroyed and (largely) depopulated (cf. Blenkinsopp 2000).

(b) "Baal-fighter" Gideon—Judg 6:25–32. Dating from the 4th/3rd century(?), this text is based on "Elijah's fight against Baal," which reflects the fight of the Jerusalem monotheists against the Benjaminite traditionalists in the first half of the 5th century. The fight ended when the Samarians founded their sanctuary on

---

[7] Cf. Knauf 2005; Guillaume 2000.
[8] The term "ditty" is apt given the assonance present in the Hebrew text.
[9] Cf. for the redactional criticism of Gideon in Knauf 1988; Auld 1989.

Mt. Gerizim, which was equally monotheistic and aniconic. The god "Baal" (in the singular, without further specification) is a theological construct produced to fit that very fight. He is not the deity attested at Ugarit (where the god addressed as "Lord" bears the proper name Haddu).[10]

(c) Gideon's eastern campaign—Judg 8:3–21. This is a text from the late 8th/early 7th century telling how Midianites were involved in the Rift Valley copper trade from the 11th through the 9th centuries (Low Chronology). A conflict with the clan of Abiezer (which cannot have become a "Manassite" clan prior to the civil war under Omri) and a Midianite trading party is conceivable during the whole period. "Zalmunna" is a Taymanite name ("Salm protected"), and Tayma has now safely turned out to have belonged to the "Midianite" cultural sphere during the transition from the LB to the Iron Age.[11]

(d) A campaign which destroyed Penuel and Succoth—Judg 8:13–17. This campaign is known to have been conducted by Shishak, in the aftermath of which Jeroboam I rebuilt Penuel.[12]

(e) The battle fought by Israelites at Qarqor/Qarqar—Judg 8:10. This battle took place in 853, in which also Arabs participated (if on the Israelite side). All three traditions are predominantly anchored in the 10th/9th century, and the amount of transformation—due to the lack of detailed sources ("annals") for that period in the hands of the 7th-century scribes—is considerable.

5. Abimelech—Judg 9. The text is from the late 8th/early 7th centuries, and the final chapter of the original composition. Shechem was not settled from the late 11th through the late 10th centuries (according to the Low Chronology. In the "Rift Valley Economy," the northern Central mountains were marginal (as opposed to the Benjamin region and Galilee). Shechem did not participate in the "Canaanite revival" of the 10th century, it was resettled as an Israelite royal residence. Under these circumstances, it is most unlikely that a tradition predating ca. 1050 B.C.E. could have reached the Hebrew Bible. Würthwein regarded Judg 9 as a pure literary construct without a factual base (Würthwein 1994). As an archetypical treatise on "tribal states" and how they fail due to insurmountable tensions between tribe(s) and town(s), "Abimelech and Shechem" might well reflect "Saul and Gibeon" as well as "David and Jerusalem" (cf. Knauf 2007b).

6. Jephthah's victory—Judg 11:33. A text from the 6th century, what is described with the words "from Aroer as far as Minnith, all the way to Abel-Keramim," is the southern border of the Ammonites, from Tell ʿUmeirî to Sahâb in the east. Aroer—there is only one in Transjordan—has always been a Moabite town (cf.

---

[10] Cf. n. 3 and Davies 2007.
[11] Cf. Parr 1993; and now Hausleitner 2007; Finkelstein and Piasetzky 2008.
[12] Cf. for my interpretation of the Karnak inscription in Knauf 2000 (notably the map on p. 35); cf. Knauf 2007a.

Knauf 1992, 1998). So the aggressor came from the south; whether he was a king of Moab or the Babylonian army in 582 B.C.E., we cannot know, but the latter date is, at least, not hypothetical.

7. (a) Samson—Judg 13–16. This is a text from the 6th/5th centuries which reflects Judaean–Philistine rivalry on the village level, without any state authority interfering with Samsonite shenanigans. The presupposed political situation coincides with the supposed time of composition. Prior to David, Philistia did not have a "Judaean" neighbour, and vice versa. On the other hand, parallels to Jephthah's daughter and to Samson's pranks do not necessitate a Hellenistic date for these stories. Greeks and Hebrews share a common cultural background in the Bronze Age Levant, "Greek" themes and motives could have been imported and disseminated by the Sea People, and the penetration of the coastal region by Greek mercenaries and specialists starts in the 7th century and gains more momentum in the 5th and 4th centuries.

(b) The place-name "Mahaneh Dan"—Judg 13:25; 18:12. These are texts from the 6th through 4th century that memorize the immigration of the sea people (Danuna) in the 12th/11th century. This event was re-interpreted (at its second occurrence!) in the biblical account as a stopping point on the fictional migration of one of Israel's more fictional tribes.

8. The migration of the Danites—Judg 17–18. A text from the 4th century, this account reflects Judaean colonization of Galilee, which cannot have started later than the 4th century B.C.E. There were no Jews in Galilee prior to the 6th century, but from the late 2nd century B.C.E. onwards, there were many.

9. The Mizpah affair—Judg 19–21. This text, from the 4th/3rd century, reflects Judaean–Benjaminite rivalry between 525 and 450, which culminated in the destruction of the sanctuary of Bethel by the Returnees,[13] and the shift of provincial capital back from Mizpah to Jerusalem in 445/44. The victors are telling the defeated that it all was their fault in the first place.[14]

Conclusions

1. The 200-year span of "the past" in collective memory has re-emerged. In a story-telling community of grandparents, parents, children and grand-children, the "present" lasts ca. 100 years. (My own experience bears this out: I "know," by means of family tradition rather than books or historical documents, of events dating back as far as the beginning of the 20th century C.E.) The 100–200 years before the "present" are considered "past," though in a sense this is past is still

---

[13] Cf. Judg 1:22–26 and n. 3.
[14] Cf. Guillaume 2004, 198–226; also Amit 2006.

alive, if somewhat vaguely. (Another personal experience: my grandmother still "knew" of a relative who had been a Prussian admiral in the middle of the 18th century. While this person certainly existed, he had been, in fact, commander-in-chief of the [rather unimpressive] Prussian fleet, with the rank of captain rather than admiral.) Everything before is "distant past," another world, where donkeys see angels and talk to prophets.

2. In the table below the data offered above are summarized. "Probable" temporal distance has been marked by "x," while the siglum "?" is used to mark a "possible" distance. In the "probable" range, 5/11 features fall into the "100 years present" (45.45%), 3/11 into the "200 years past" (27.27%), and another three into the "distant past." In the "possible" range, 5/12 features belong to the "200 years past" (41.67%), 4/12 to the "distant past" (33.33%), and only 3/12 features to the "present" (25%).

Text	Date of Composition	Date of the "Event"	Less than 100 years	Less than 200 years	More than 200 years
1:22–26	325–250	500–450		x	
3:12–30: Ehud vs. Eglon	700–650	1100–875; 724–716	?	?	?
3:12–30: Arbot Moab	700–650	850–650	x		
3:12–30: Assyrian plumbing	700–650	716ff	x		
5:2–30	875–850	975–900	x		
6:2–5	500–250	582–520	?	?	?
6:11–32	325–250	500–450		x	
8:4–28: Midian and Tayma	700–650	1150–825		?	?
8:4–28: Succoth and Penuel	700–650	940–910			x
8:4–28: Karkor	700–650	854		x	
9	700–650	1000–950			x
11:33	582–500	582?	?	?	
13–16	600–450	600–450	x		
13:25; 18:12: Mahaneh Dan	600–300	1150–1050			x
17–18	400–300	400ff.	x		
19–21	400–250	500–450		?	?

Secondly, discontinuity on the level of the elites, as occurred several times in Israel between 1000 and 720, results in breaks in the historical tradition. "Popular" tradition has preserved some memory of things happening at Qarqar, Penuel and Succoth, but re-attributed these "labels" rather freely. The "silencing of Omride history" is most notable; of the rich literature which once must have existed, only the Song of Deborah survives (and, in fragments, and not from the biblical tradition, the Bileam inscription from Tell Deir ʿAlla).

Bibliography

Amit, Y. 2006. The Saul Polemic in the Persian Period. Pages 647–61 in Lipschits and Oeming, eds., 2006.

Auld, A. G. 1989. Gideon: Hacking at the Heart of the Old Testament. *VT* 39:257–67.

Blenkinsopp, J. 2000. A Case of Benign Imperial Neglect and Its Consequences. Pages 129–36 in *Virtual History and the Bible*. Edited by J. C. Exum. Biblical Interpretation 8. Leiden: Brill.

Blum, E. 1997. Der kompositionelle Knoten am Übergang von Josua zu Richter. Ein Entflechtungsvorschlag. Pages 181–212 in *Deuteronomy and Deuteronomic Literature*. Festschrift for C. H. W. Brekelmans. Edited by M. Vervenne and J. Lust. BETL 133. Leuven: Peeters.

Davies, P. R. 2007. *The Origins of Biblical Israel*. LHBOTS 485. New York: T&T Clark International.

Finkelstein, I., and E. Piasetzky. 2008. Radiocarbon and the History of Copper Production at Khirbet en-Nahas. *TA* 35:82–95.

Guillaume, P. 2000. Deborah and the Seven Tribes. *BN* 101:18–21.

Guillaume, P. 2004. *Waiting for Josiah: The Judges*. JSOTSup 385. London: T&T Clark International.

Hausleitner, A. 2007. Tema. Online: www.wibilex.de (accessed December 2007).

Knauf, E. A. 1988. Midian. Pages 34–42 in *Untersuchungen zur Geschichte Palästinas und Nordarabiens am Ende des 2. Jahrtausends v. Chr.* Abhandlungen des Deutschen Palästina-Vereins. Wiesbaden: Otto Harrassowitz.

Knauf, E. A. 1991. Eglon and Ophrah: Two Toponymic Notes on the Book of Judges. *JSOT* 51:25–44.

Knauf, E. A. 1992. Abel-Keramim. *ABD* 1:10–11.

Knauf, E. A. 1998. Aroer. Pages 1:795 in *Die Religion in Geschichte und Gegenwart*. Edited by H.-D. Betz et al. 4 vols. Tübingen: Mohr.

Knauf, E. A. 2000. Who Destroyed Megiddo VIA? *BN* 103:30–35.

Knauf, E. A. 2005. Deborah's Language. Judges ch. 5 in Its Hebrew and Semitic Context. Pages 167–82 in *Studia Semitica et Semitohamitica*. FS Rainer Voigt. Edited by B. Burtea, Josef Tropper and Helen Younansardaroud. AOAT 317. Münster: Ugarit-Verlag.

Knauf, E. A. 2006. Bethel: The Israelite Impact on Judean Language and Literature. Pages 291–349 in Lipschits and Oeming, eds., 2006.

Knauf, E. A. 2007a. Was Omride Israel a Sovereign State? Pages 100–103 in *Ahab Agonistes: The Rise and Fall of the Omri Dynasty*. Edited by L. L. Grabbe. LHBOTS 421. ESHM 6. London: T&T Clark International.

Knauf, E. A. 2007b. Jerusalem in the Tenth Century B.C.E. Pages 86–105 in *Jerusalem before Islam*. Edited by Z. Kafafi and R. Schick. BAR International Series 1699. Oxford: Archaeopress.

Lipschits, O., and M. Oeming, eds. 2006. *Judah and the Judeans in the Persian Period*. Winona Lake, Ind.: Eisenbrauns.

Mishaqa, M. 1988. *Murder, Mayhem, Pillage, and Plunder: The History of Lebanon in the 18th and 19th Centuries.* Translated by W. M. Thackston, Jr. Albany: State University of New York Press.

Mittmann, S. 1973. Das südliche Ostjordanland im Lichte eines neuassyrischen Keilschriftbriefes aus Nimrud. *ZDPV* 89:15–25.

Parr, P. J. 1993. The Early History of the Hejaz: A Response to Garth Bawden. *Arabian Archaeology and Epigraphy* 4:48–58.

Schmid, K. 2008. *Literaturgeschichte des Alten Testaments. Eine Einführung.* Darmstadt: Wissenschaftliche Buchgesellschaft.

Stern, E., and Y. Magen. 2002. Archaeological Evidence for the First Stage of the Samaritan Temple on Mount Gerizim. *IEJ* 52:49–57.

Willi-Plein, I. 2007. *Haggai, Sacharja, Maleachi.* ZBKAT 24/4. Zurich: Theologischer Verlag.

Würthwein, E. 1994. Abimelech und der Untergang Sichems—Studien zu Jdc 9. Pages 12–28 in *Studien zum Deuteronomistischen Geschichtswerk.* Berlin: de Gruyter.

Saul ben Kish in History and Tradition

Diana Edelman

What can be known about the historical Saul ben Kish, reported founder of the kingdom of Israel? Or, put differently, how much of the testimony of 1 and 2 Samuel contains accurate facts that a modern historian can use to recreate the career of this individual? What kind or level of history can be written about this person?

Using the understanding of history developed by the *Annales* School, that changes take place at different rates over time, a modern historian would ideally like to write a history on the most detailed level, that of event. For such a history, texts are essential. The existence of the corpus of biblical texts, some of which deal with Saul's career, should theoretically permit the undertaking of such an endeavor. However, the purpose and perspective of the texts and the amount of evidence they provide about the historical Saul needs to be assessed before deciding whether his career can, in fact, be recreated on the level of event.

In addition, archaeological excavations and surveys provide material cultural remains that should allow for the writing of a history on the level the *Annales* School calls conjunction, or a socioeconomic and cultural history. Such a history does not encompass the history of the person of Saul directly, but provides background about the world in which he would have operated. Data provided by material cultural remains allow the historian to present an enhanced understanding of changes that take place at the level of event by placing them within the framework of slower-paced changes at the level of conjunction.

Can a history of Saul be written at the level of event, then? This is the main question that will be considered in this essay. The central issue that will be addressed is how to sort fact from fiction in the biblical version of the reign of Saul. The good news is that there might be factual data preserved in the biblical texts. The bad news is that there is no agreed method to accomplish the task of determining what are factual data. There are no extrabiblical data available to verify the results of biblical critical analyses when it comes to the person of Saul. Since there are no independent texts against which to evaluate the biblical testimony, all argument must ultimately be based only on the biblical texts themselves.

Individuals will assess the historical reliability of 1 and 2 Samuel differently, being heavily influenced in the end by their understanding of the Bible as literature vs. history as well as by their understanding of the relationship between sacred scripture and religious belief. Clearly, the number and nature of statements that are deemed to be historically accurate information will determine what 'raw data' are ultimately linked together through chains of cause and effect by each historian to provide a meaningful creation of Saul's career. The more data that are included, the more convincing and coherent can be the proposed construction. The fewer the data, the more room there is for creative linkings of the available information. It is crucial to understand that no one can ever reconstruct and fully comprehend actual events in the past. Events take place in history, but they are always given meaning through interpretive frameworks. Given this situation, there can never be a definitive reconstruction of the past; there can only be a range of creative associations by individuals who have been influenced by their own life experiences as well as by the data they believe to be reliable and choose to link together in chains of meaning.

It is possible, but not necessarily preferable, to create a 'history by consensus', in which a majority of individuals agree that one creation of events best suits the evidence. Such a consensus cannot guarantee, however, that the creation accurately captures the actual events. Most histories are created by linking together individual data into chains of cause and effect based on logical processing; real life does not necessarily operate by the same neat, rational principles. What is plausible then, is not necessarily what actually happened. Ultimately, it is the meaning assigned to actual events rather than the events themselves that holds importance for humans and influences their lives. The attempt to establish a 'history by consensus', whose accuracy can never be verified, is a potentially dangerous goal. Such a consensus obscures the individualistic and creative nature of the historiographic enterprise, defining an unnecessary orthodoxy that discourages fresh investigations and creative imaginings and which results in a form of thought policing.

Methodological Considerations

The process by which biblical testimony can be converted to evidence for use in historical recreation will be the focus of the ensuing presentation, using the narratives involving Saul ben Kish as a case study. All claims and statements made in the biblical texts begin as testimony that may or may not provide accurate information about the subject matter they purport to describe. It is only by asking questions about the texts, questions that will vary from case to case but which address chronological and/or ideological issues, that that for which they serve as evidence can be deduced or inferred. The results of the ensuing case study on Saul will be used to answer the previous question: can his career, or aspects thereof, be recreated on the level of event?

In order to establish what will be deemed fact vs. fiction in the biblical account of the reign of Saul ben Kish, the historian needs to evaluate the biblical testimony, using the full range of old and new literary critical methods. The process should begin with textual criticism and the establishment of the critically evaluated text that will be used as the basis of testimony. In the case of 1 and 2 Samuel, the divergent readings found in the MT and the LXX provide an immediate challenge. Rather than harmonize the two traditions to produce a hypothetical text that has no known acceptance or existence within a given community, it would be better to analyze the two traditions separately and then compare the results. In this way, differences in rhetorical structure, audience, and received tradition can be taken into account and weighed accordingly in the final evaluation.

While there was an original text of the Samuel narrative, its author and date of composition are not known. LXX translations and other versions based on them provide evidence only of one or more versions of the text that existed and were used in the third–first centuries BCE. The Vaticanus ms and Old Latin mss may well contain alterations from the original LXX translation(s), given the centuries of transmission involved. Similarly, the three 4QSam manuscripts provide glimpses of one or more versions of Samuel that were used within the Qumran community in the first century CE while the MT text, dating from the ninth century CE, seems to trace back to one version that was current in ancient Palestine in the first century CE and which became normative for rabbinic Jews after the Council of Javneh ca. 90 CE. The attempt by Jewish and Christian communities to establish a canonical version of Samuel was a rather late development in the history of the book and different versions were canonized by different groups. Given the current collection of manuscripts and the long history of the book, it is impossible to recreate the original 'Ur'-text of Samuel. At most, the extant manuscripts can provide a set of texts of the book of Samuel that were used and deemed meaningful by different communities in different periods.[1]

The second step should be a close reading of the critically evaluated texts, with a focus on the patterns and literary devices that the ancient writer appears to have used to convey his message to his intended ancient audience. This step includes a host of theoretical issues and battlegrounds over which much ink has been spilled. To touch briefly upon the main ones, first is the debate over where meaning lies: in the author's intentions and words, in the interpretation by the reader or hearer, or in the text itself, which can take on a meaning independent of the one originally intended by the author. All three of these options contribute to the final reading

---

[1]   Thus, I espouse a different approach to the issue of textual reconstruction than some of the reviewers of my book. *King Saul in the Historiography of Judah* (JSOTSup, 121; Sheffield: JSOT Press, 1991); contrast the approach favored by for example S. McKenzie (*RSR* 19 [1993], p. 67), T. Mullen (*CBQ* 56 [1994], p. 101) and G. Knoppers (*JBL* 114 [1995], p. 132). Knoppers has provided a fuller discussion of the principles of textual reconstruction than the first two, indicating what some of the issues are. Unfortunately, in his comments he has failed to distinguish between the original actual audience that read the book when it was first produced and subsequent actual audiences that read the forms of the book reflected in the MT, Qumran and LXX versions. He argues that the variant forms can furnish important clues about how the original audience understood the text.

of a text. By focusing on authorial intentionality, however, the modern historian is able to map out what appear to be highly visible milestones within the text that point the way toward the writer's vision and message. Even if minor devices and patterns are missed, the delimiting of the major patterns should provide a fairly clear indication of the major points of meaning to be conveyed.

Next is the issue of 'author'. Given the long period of transmission and reinterpretation of the biblical texts within the the post-monarchic Judean, Jewish and Christian communities, can the original intention of a single author even be articulated? After all, a reader encounters a final form of the text and so is really only understanding the view of the final redactional hand that worked on it. While this is true, I would argue that the changes that have been introduced within subsequent tradition represent probably only a very small portion of the text, so that the reader sees most of the text as it was structured by its original author. In my opinion, careful attention to structuring patterns and literary devices will permit a person to understand to a significant degree the intention of the original author, regardless of whether or not one can definitively say what is primary and what is secondary in a given sentence. By the same token, by focusing on the devices that are present, a reader should be better able to decide what is likely to be part of the writer's original composition and what might be a secondary expansion.

The third main theoretical issue in a close reading is that of audience. It is particularly helpful to distinguish three main levels of audience when analyzing biblical texts: the intended ancient audience, for whom the author wrote his work; the actual ancient audience(s), who read the work and may or may not have understood the author's intended meaning; and the actual modern audience(s), of which we are a part.[2] We are separated from the writer even further than his actual ancient audience and subsequent generations of audiences by different cultural frames of reference and vastly different world-views. As a result, we need to try to understand the world-view and literary conventions that were prevalent at the time the texts were written and not superimpose our own contemporary structural and literary devices on these ancient texts. Our best recourse, which is not foolproof by any means, is to search for recurrent patterns contained within the biblical texts themselves. In addition, we need also to study comparative ancient Near Eastern texts to help with the discernment of patterns that have only been used once in the biblical texts but which were widespread regional conventions.

---

[2] For an excellent discussion of levels of audience, see P. Rabinowitz, 'Truth in Fiction: A Reexamination of Audiences', *Critical Inquiry* 4 (1977), pp. 121-41. He identifies four levels of audience: the ideal narrative audience, the imitation or narrative audience, the authorial audience, and the actual audience. While all four are valid distinctions, I think issues about the historicity of story details are adequately addressed by focusing on the authorial audience and the actual audience. However, for ancient texts like the Hebrew Bible, a further distinction between the actual ancient audience and the actual modern audience needs to be made in light of chronological and cultural distances and differences.

Finally, the issue of dating both the original writer and his intended audience should be considered. As is well known, clues for dating have to be derived from the texts themselves; so all arguments for dating can easily become circular. Let me only point out that I think that literary and structural conventions used within the biblical texts did not change appreciably from the eighth century through the end of the Persian era in the fourth century BCE. It seems that it is only with the spread of Hellenistic models and ideas that a major change is introduced into ancient Near Eastern writing conventions.[3] Thus, whether a text is dated to the late monarchic or early exilic period will probably not affect the types of patterns and devices used to structure it; it will, however, affect the message because of the different situations and life experiences of the intended audiences in each period.

The third step in converting biblical testimony to evidence should entail a consideration of the types of sources that might have been available to the authors as they constructed the biblical narratives, the likelihood and manner in which such sources might have survived to be used, and, where available, the likelihood that such sources were in fact used. The fourth and final step in the process would include a consideration of what information might have been derived from such sources. Such speculative reconstruction can only be done on the basis of prior reflection over how the narrative has been structured and what main message its author was trying to convey.

In order for a modern historian to determine the contexts or situations for which statements in biblical texts serve as evidence, an evaluative process must be undertaken. Beginning with textual criticism, the historian then needs to engage in a close reading of the critically evaluated texts, focusing on authorial intention as revealed through the use of structuring patterns and devices. In this process, he or she needs to try to read from the perspective of a member of the ancient intended audience by becoming familiar with ancient world-views and literary conventions. Next, the historian needs to consider the availability of possible sources to the biblical authors and their use of such sources to create an understanding of the past. Only after this process has been completed can the individual historian responsibly move on to the task of using creative imagining to link together data deemed relevant to the topic under investigation to provide a historical recreation of the past.

---

[3] Direct contact with Greek or Mediterranean literature by Judahites is a strong likelihood by the end of the eighth century BCE, when Greek mercenaries began to be used in Egypt and Cisjordan. Such contact may have been significantly earlier, introduced by the Sea Peoples who settled in the area at the end of the Late Bronze Age and during the early Iron Age. It is only with the spread of Hellenism, however, that such literature would likely have become a desirable norm to be emulated as part of the new dominant culture.

The Literary Saul

In my publications on Saul, I have suggested that various structuring patterns and devices were used by the original author of the narrative on the career of Saul ben Kish in 1 Samuel 8–2 Samuel 1.[4] This is not an independent narrative but a segment of a larger history of the monarchic era, composed, I believe, by the so-called Deuteronomistic historian.

The major pattern derives from the ritual ceremony for the installation of the king. It contains three elements: 1) the designation of the king-elect through anointing; 2) the testing of the candidate's worthiness to serve as Yhwh's earthly vice-regent through the successful completion of a test in the form of a military deed; and 3) the installation of the candidate as king at the completion of step 2. The elements within this pattern have been deduced from a review of both biblical and extrabiblical texts.[5] This pattern seems to have been used three times by the Deuteronomistic historian within the narrative devoted to the United Monarchy: to describe Saul's rise to power (9.1–10.16; 11.15), to explain why Jonathan would not succeed Saul on the throne (1 Sam. 13–14), and to describe David's rise to power (1 Sam. 16.13; 17; 2 Sam. 2.4; 5.1-6). In the case of Saul, the designation as king-elect through anointing occurs in Ramah in 10.1, the test by military deed in 11.1-11 in the account of Saul's rescue of Jabesh-Gilead from the Ammonites, and the final coronation as king at Gilgal in 11.14-15.

The second major pattern used to structure the account of Saul's reign is the standard regnal formula: the accession formula appears in 13.1; the account of selected deeds in 13.2–14.46; the summary of the reign in 14.47-48; and the death, burial, and succession notice in 1 Sam. 31.1–2 Sam. 5.3. The long delay between the summary of the reign and the death, burial and succession notice can be ascribed to the writer's desire to signal—on the literary level—that Saul's career as king was effectively over when David was anointed king-elect, but that he remained king in name until his death. The first two patterns have been interwoven in the present narrative.

---

[4] See especially 'Saul's Rescue of Jabesh-Gilead (1 Sam. 11.1-11): Sorting Story from History', *ZAW* 96 (1984), pp. 195-209; 'The Deuteronomist's Story of King Saul: Narrative Art or Editorial Product?', in *Pentateuchal and Deuteronomistic Studies: Papers Read at the XIIIth IOSOT Congress, Leuven 1989* (BETL, 94; ed. C. Brekelmans and J. Lust; Leuven: Leuven University Press, 1990), pp. 207-20; *King Saul in the Historiography of Judah*.

[5] The anointing and coronation elements were noted by T. Mettinger (*King and Messiah* [ConBOT, 8; Lund: Gleerup, 1975], pp. 72, 79, 86-87) and B. Halpern (*The Constitution of the Monarchy in Israel* [HSM, 24; Chico, CA: Scholars Press, 1981], pp. 51-148). Both seem to have been aware that the testing element was an integral part of the ritual, even though neither explicitly included it in the coronation pattern. I proposed it as an integral step in my article, 'Saul's Rescue of Jabesh-Gilead'. For another reconstruction of the coronation pattern, see Z. Ben Barak, 'The Coronation Ceremony in Ancient Mesopotamia', *OLP* 11 (1980), pp. 55-67.

A third structuring pattern divides Saul's career into his life 'under Yhwh's good spirit' and his life 'under Yhwh's evil spirit'. The pattern allows the writer to demonstrate that as Yhwh's anointed, who has received divine spirit, the king will remain in office and possess some form of divinely bestowed controlling spirit throughout his lifetime. The same principle is evident in the previous period of the judges, where the term of judgeship lasts the rest of a chosen individual's life; once divine spirit is bestowed, it remains until death (Judg. 2.18). The same theological understanding remains in force for the subsequent era of the kingdoms of Israel and Judah. Nevertheless, possession of the divine spirit cannot guarantee success as a leader. Disobedience of God will lead to divine rejection and the individual's inability to continue to serve his nation effectively as Yhwh's earthly vice-regent during the remainder of his term of office. The king will lose Yhwh's guiding spirit, which will result in his failure to be able to discern the divine will and act appropriately. As a consequence, his nation will suffer. A similar structuring device has been used in the account of David's career.[6]

In addition, the author appears to have used the motif of Jonathan's personal covenant with David as a major structuring device within the Saulide narrative and beyond, into the story of David's career as Saul's successor. The covenant is used first to demonstrate Jonathan's acceptance of David as Saul's divinely chosen successor, illustrating his understanding of the guilty verdict rendered against him by Yhwh in 14.42. After David kills Goliath, Jonathan makes a covenant with him, giving David his own robe, his armor, his bow, and his girdle (18.1-5). In this act, the heir-elect to the throne symbolically endows David, the secretly anointed king-elect, with the formal instruments associated with the second 'testing' stage of the three-part kingship installation pattern.

The covenant between Jonathan and David is reintroduced regularly in the narrative[7] to chronicle Jonathan's willing acceptance of David as Saul's successor and to contrast it with Saul's refusal to accept the divine plan for succession. At the same time, however, it portrays Jonathan as an astute politician who uses the covenant as a means to force concessions from David that will guarantee the future and safety of the Saulide line. By supporting David, Jonathan is depicted as hoping to have him serve as a single interloper in the Saulide dynasty and see his family maintain control of the throne in future generations.

Finally, the writer has used the contrasting word pairs $\underline{t}ô\underline{b}$ and $rā'â$ and $lē\underline{b}$ and $'ênáyim$ and the key word $yā\underline{d}$ to help focus the audience's attention on the precepts of royal power and its potential abuses through the course of the narrative.

---

[6] See R.A. Carlson, *David, the Chosen King* (Uppsala: Almqvist & Wiksell, 1964), pp. 24-25.

[7] D. Jobling has noted that the motif is developed progressively through scenes that alternately focus on Jonathan and David or Saul (18.1-5; 19.1-7; 20.1-21; 23.15b-18) and ones in which David and Saul interact (16.14–17.58; 18.16-30; 19.8-25; 21.2–23.15a [with other material]; 23.19 onward [with much other material]) (*The Sense of Biblical Narrative* [JSOTSup, 7; Sheffield: JSOT Press, 2nd edn, 1978], I, p. 15).

Potential Sources Underlying the Present Narrative

The use of a three-part pattern derived from later monarchic-era royal installation ceremonies to describe how the first king of Israel was empowered raises immediate questions about the availability of sources to the author of the Saul narrative. Had details about Saul's actual rise to power been known to the author of 1 Samuel, is it likely that the ancient audience would have expected them to be narrated within the framework of the normative coronation pattern? If so, the practice should have continued for all subsequent kings, yet it occurs again only for David. In both of these cases, the testimony suggests the lack of underlying hard evidence, which in turn led the writer to improvize by essentially 'historicizing' main elements of the ritual ceremony. According to the norm, to become a king a person must be anointed, be tested, and then be crowned, so Saul must have gone through these steps, too, but in a hypothesized past, not just in a cultic ceremony. Using this logic, it then becomes clear that if Saul is designated as king-elect in 9.16 for the purpose of delivering the people from the hands of the Philistines, his test by military deed cannot be against the group he is to fight when he becomes king, because he is not yet king. Thus, another enemy is brought in to serve as the testers—in this case, the Ammonites.

Is it possible that Saul in fact fought the Ammonites at some other point in his career, so that this story is based on actual fact, even if the writer has recontextualized it chronologically within Saul's career? The answer I would offer is 'yes'. It could be argued that the summary of Saul's career in 1 Sam. 14.47-48 is drawn from some sort of royal annal or a collection of military songs like the Book of Yashar, in which some of Saul's battles were commemorated. This cannot be proven, however, and these verses may simply represent a list of Judah's traditional enemies retrojected to the time of Saul.

The following is a list of what I consider to be materials drawn from various early sources by the Deuteronomistic historian to construct the present narrative about Saul:

1. The *māšāl* in 1 Sam. 10.11-12; 19.24, 'Is Saul also among the prophets?' Its twofold use in different contexts makes its original context and meaning uncertain.

2. The song fragment in 18.7 and 21.12, 'Saul has slain his thousands and David his ten thousands'. Taken in isolation, the statement need not indicate that Saul and David were contemporaries or successors; it could be based on legendary figures from the past, both of whom were renowned for their military prowess, with no personal connection whatsoever.

3. The lament over Saul and Jonathan in 2 Sam. 1.19-27. Whoever wrote the lament considered Saul to have been a leader of some importance, who was able to dress the 'daughters of Israel' in crimson robes covered with gold dangles or ornaments. The title *melek* is not used, and yet the portrayal of Saul seems to be on

a royal scale when compared with the stories underlying the judges, for example. Perhaps this is due to the different genres more than reality, however, so caution must be used in drawing conclusions about Saul's royal vs. non-royal status from the lament.

A careful reading of the narrative account of Saul's demise in chs. 28–31 suggests that most of the information there is a creative imagining of events based on the information in the lament. There is a noticeable overlap in vocabulary and concepts between the prose and poetic versions: the use of the verbs *ḥll*, *npl*, *bśr*, and *ṣrr*, the last in an impersonal construction; reference to the participation of royal family members alongside the army; reference to the Philistines as 'uncircumcised'; the location of the final defeat on Mt Gilboa; and the reference to Saul's sword as his primary weapon. The only information in the prose account that cannot be derived from the lament is the role of Beth She'an in the final battle. This could have been derived from an independent source or it could be the contribution of the writer's own imagination in light of the location of the final confrontation in the vicinity of Mt Gilboa. The lament can also be the source of the naming of the Philistines as Israel's prime enemies who are to be eradicated by the first king in 9.16.

4. The fragment of an administrative district list in 2 Sam. 2.9 that reflects the Saulide holdings that became Davidide. The list distinguishes between two types of holdings through the use of two idioms: *mālak 'el* and *mālak 'al*. The first is a very unusual term not attested anywhere outside the Saulide narrative. While it is true that the prepositions *'el* and *'al* sometimes substitute for one another in later texts, it is less likely that such an interchange is at work here because the resulting expression *mālak 'el* is non-idiomatic. Such an interchange tends to occur when the resulting expression can be idiomatic with either preposition. The use of the expression *mālak 'el* seems to be an attempt to distinguish more loosely affiliated regions from those under centralized control.[8] A comparison with the list of so-called Solomonic districts in 1 Kings 4 shows direct continuity over time, with territories acquired subsequently being added in as new districts.[9]

5. The Saulide genealogy in 1 Sam. 9.1 and other information that served as the basis for the family summary in 1 Sam. 14.46. The first genealogy has introduced an unnamed ancestor simply as 'a Yimnite man' and has included a female, Becorath, in order to use the literary convention of seventh-generational birth to

---

[8] For a fuller discussion of this verse, see D. Edelman, 'The "Ashurites" of Eshbaal's State (2 Sam. 2.9)', *PEQ* 117 (1985), pp. 88-89.

[9] It could also be argued that the so-called Solomonic list is earlier than the list attributed to Eshbaal and that the latter represents a loss of territory. To make this argument, however, a plausible historical situation that would account for the boundaries of Israel as delineated in 2 Sam. 2.9 would need to be set forth, as well as a cogent explanation for the difference between the *mālak 'el* and the *mālak 'al* districts.

foreshadow Saul's destiny to greatness.[10] It should be noted that the latter summary functions literarily to introduce the roster of characters for the upcoming story events except for Abinadab, who appears unannounced in 1 Sam. 31.2. He may have been introduced subsequently on the basis of the Saulide genealogy now preserved in 1 Chron. 8.33-40; 9.39-44.

6. An old tradition that underlies the current form of 1 Sam. 9.1–10.16, which told how Saul took control over a segment of Mt Ephraim. Beginning with Saul's introduction as a man destined to greatness by virtue of his position as a seventh-generation male,[11] the story goes on to reinforce Saul's character as a future hero by emphasizing his beauty and physical height as traits that set him apart from ordinary men. It then continues by having Saul search for his father's lost asses, the symbolic mount of royalty. In this task, he traverses four contiguous areas of Mt Ephraim, before learning the significance of his action, which is revealed to him in Ramah by the famous local seer, who makes him the guest of honor at a prearranged banquet. The tour through Mt Ephraim appears to function as a foreshadowing of future plot developments. The story should go on to describe how Saul becomes ruler over the area he toured. Instead, it breaks off in 10.16 and develops new themes.[12]

---

[10] For this literary convention, see J. Sasson, 'A Genealogical "Convention" in Biblical Chronology?', *ZAW* 90 (1978), pp. 171-85.

[11] It may be that the seventh-generation conventional device was an original part of the old tale, or it could be a later addition to the story by the Deuteronomistic historian, as a further means of emphasizing Saul's destiny to greatness. If it is part of the original story, then this postulated old tradition would be its source. If it is an expansion by the Dtr H, then a separate source would need to be posited for it.

[12] For the contiguous nature of the four areas, see my article, 'Saul's Journey through Mt. Ephraim and Samuel's Ramah (1 Sam. 9.4-5; 10.2-5)', *ZDPV* 104 (1988), pp. 44-58. I think the anointing scenes in 9.15-17 and 9.27–10.1 are secondary expansions of the original story, which used the banquet as a means of designating Saul as future ruler. The identification of Samuel as the seer may also be secondary, although it is noteworthy that Samuel's reported sanctuary circuit tour in 1 Sam. 7.16-17 corresponds to the same territory traversed by Saul in 9.4-5. It could be argued that the Dtr H 'created' Samuel's circuit tour based on information in this old story after he identified the unnamed seer with Samuel; the old story might have gone on to tell how Saul replaced the seer as ruler of this delineated territory, presenting irony by having the seer designate his own successor/usurper. Alternately, it is possible that the old story went on to identify the seer as Samuel, who then ended up designating the man who would take control over his own little fiefdom. In this case, the statement in 7.16-17 could be based either on this story, or on an independently preserved tradition that remembered the territory that Samuel had controlled. For other discussions of this early tradition, see for example L. Schmidt, *Menschlicher Erfolg und Jahwes Initiative: Studien zu Tradition, Interpretation und Historie in Überlieferungen von Gideon, Saul und David* (WMANT, 38; Neukirchen-Vluyn: Neukirchener Verlag, 1970), pp. 58-102; J.M. Miller, 'Saul's Rise to Power: Some Observations Concerning 1 Sam 9.1–10.16; 10.26–11.15 and 13.2–14.46', *CBQ* 36 (1974), pp. 157-74; and P.M. Arnold, *Gibeah: The Search for a Biblical City* (JSOTSup, 79; Sheffield: JSOT Press, 1990), pp. 89-93.

7. There are a number of passages that point to traditions linking Saul with Gibeon, even though there seems to have been a deliberate attempt by the so-called Deuteronomistic historian to obscure these links.[13] Whether these are historical or not remains to be seen. The main units include 2 Sam. 2.12–3.1, 2 Sam. 21.1-14, and 1 Chron. 8.29-40, 9.33-44. After Saul's death and David's coronation as king in Hebron, Abner is said to have collected the remaining Saulide heir, Eshbaal, whom he then took to Mahanaim and had crowned king. The implication of the wording and circumstances is that Eshbaal survived the slaughter at Gilboa because he was too young to fight and that Abner retrieved him from the capital to be crowned before the troops that had also escaped and had regrouped at Mahanaim (2 Sam. 2.12-13).[14] Immediately after Eshbaal's coronation, the writer narrates the episode about the ordeal by battle between Eshbaal's troops and David's troops. Although no explicit reason is given for the battle, it is portrayed to have involved a fight to control the throne of Israel. The confrontation reportedly took place at Gibeon. Since neither David nor Eshbaal was situated at Gibeon in the narrative, there is no literary motive for the arrival there of the other for the confrontation. Whether or not such an ordeal by battle ever took place, the writer is strongly implying in this narrative that he knew an older tradition that named Gibeon as the capital of Saul. Such a tradition would account for the writer's decision to situate a confrontation between representatives of the two rival kings, Eshbaal and David, at the city.[15]

---

[13] For a detailing and analysis of these passages, see esp. J. Blenkinsopp, *Gibeon and Israel* (SOTSMS, 2; Cambridge: Cambridge University Press, 1972). For an anti-Gibeonite tendency in the Deuteronomistic History, see P.J. Kearney, 'The Role of the Gibeonites in the Deuteronomic History', *CBQ* 35 (1973), pp. 1-19.

[14] This fact tends to undermine the claim in 2.10 that Eshbaal was 40 years old when he was crowned king. To the contrary, he appears to have been a pre-teen or teenager. His status as a minor tends to be corroborated by the information provided in various passages about Saul's family. Jonathan, the eldest son, is the only male child who is reported to have produced offspring before dying at Gilboa. His son Meribaal/Mephiboshet was said to have been a child young enough to have been carried and accidently dropped by his nurse when Jonathan died (2 Sam. 4.4). The other Saulide heirs that are said to have been sacrificed by the Gibeonites in 2 Sam. 21.1-14 were reportedly Saul's sons by a secondary wife or concubine and the sons of Jonathan's sister, Michal. The writer or a later editor seems to have deliberately made Eshbaal into an older man who would make a more worthy opponent of David in the struggle for the throne; he did not want it to be known that David was fighting a minor.

[15] It is possible that the old tradition does not reflect past reality, but instead is the result of an ideological dispute over which sanctuary would become the primary seat during the Persian period in Yehud. Gibeonite priests arguing for the supremacy of Gibeon might have fictitiously associated it with David's precursor Saul, in order to give it priority by associating it with an earlier founder of the state to counter the established link of the Jerusalem temple with David. If this argument is to be made, details that support it instead of the alternate view that the texts preserve a genuine association of Gibeon with Saul would need to be pointed out.

It is noteworthy that the Saulide genealogy in 1 Chron. 8.33-40 has been grafted onto one detailing the history of Gibeon (1 Chron. 8.29-40). The Chronicler makes a specific point of mentioning that in the post-exilic community, some of those who 'returned' to Gibeon, their alleged ancestral home,[16] chose to dwell in Jerusalem instead. This singling out of Gibeonites to move into Jerusalem is curious since it is not done for any other city in the genealogy. Theologically, the writer seems to be implying that Gibeon had been a rival to Jerusalem during the previous monarchic period, but that in the new era, Jerusalem would have no rival, as indicated by the voluntary association of the Gibeonites with the 'correct' sacred city. That the nature of the earlier rivalry was in part religious is suggested by the tradition in 1 Kgs 3.4 wherein Solomon offered sacrifice at Gibeon prior to the building of the temple in Jerusalem because the former had been the largest *bāmâ* sanctuary. The tradition in 2 Sam. 21.1-14 about the slaughter of members of the Saulide family in Gibeon (21.6 following the reading in Codices Vaticanus and Alexandrinus as well as Aquila and Symmachus) may also allude to the city's former status as an important cultic site.

8. The use of some sort of northern, that is, Israelite rather than Judahite source for creation of the Saulide narrative is indicated by the alternation between Gibeah and Geba as designations for the same site. As argued by P. Arnold,[17] it is likely that the two names represent dialectical variants. The Deuteronomistic historian appears to have derived the northern spelling, Gibeah, from a source and has alternated its use in the narrative with the southern spelling, Geba, so that his southern audience would know which site was being discussed.

---

[16] As noted by A. Demsky, the mention of the clans of Ner and Gedor among those who resettle at Gibeon would seem to indicate that some of those who moved into the Persian province of Yehud were indeed returning to ancestral homes. Jar handles from late monarchic Gibeon bear the names *nr'* and *gdr* ('The Genealogy of Gibeon [I Chronicles 9.35-44]: Biblical and Epigraphic Considerations', *BASOR* 202 [1971], pp. 20-23). Thus, not all the Persian population of Yehud were simply newcomers who had no former connections to the area, as suggested by T.L. Thompson, *The Early History of the Israelite People: From the Written and Archaeological Sources* (SHANE, 4; Leiden: Brill, 1992), pp. 418-23, esp. 422, and private discussion.

Alternatively, it might be argued on the basis of the evidence above that the population of Gibeon was not deported by the neo-Babylonians but remained in place through the sixth century. The results of excavations conducted at Gibeon have not been published adequately to allow a decision to be made about continuous or discontinuous occupation during the sixth century. A clear pottery sequence for the sixth century does not yet exist so even with full publication firm conclusions on this point would not be able to be made from the material remains alone. No debris associated with a general destruction by fire is reported to have been found for the Iron I or Iron II periods and jar handles stamped with the name Mozah, written in Aramaic script, provide evidence for some sort of settlement in the fifth century BCE (J. A. Pritchard, *Gibeon, Where the Sun Stood Still: The Discovery of the Biblical City* [Princeton: Princeton University Press, 1962], pp. 161, 163).

[17] So Arnold, *Gibeah*, pp. 37-38, 42.

Historical Recreation

Information drawn from these source materials provides minimal core data for the reign of Saul. Can a history of the career of Saul ben Kish be written on the basis of this scanty set of data? Yes, but not on the level of event. With so few data, however, a number of different scenarios can be postulated and chains of cause and effect drawn. In addition, motivations for territorial expansion can be postulated on the basis of archaeological and geographical data that relate to the slower changes over time associated with long duration and conjunction.

My own recreation posits that Saul emerged initially as a petty king of Gibeon. This is based on the assessment that the scattered texts that link Saul to Gibeon reflect a past reality. Although the title *melek* is not used for him in any of the early sources outlined, I would assign him this title because of his status as head of the palace state of Gibeon. It appears from the limited source material available that palace states in Cisjordan in the Late Bronze period used monarchy as the standard form of government within a social structure built on patronage. The few instances in the Amarna letters where elders are writing instead of a king could well represent extraordinary circumstances during which a king had been deposed by the Egyptians, had died creating a period of interregnum, or might have been absent from the city. Continuing a long-standing tradition, kingship would have been the rule, not the exception, at Gibeon at the end of the Iron I or beginning of the Iron II period.

From his base as king of that palace state, Saul expanded into surrounding Israelite territory, creating a territorial state with different levels of centralization. At its core, the fledgling state included the central Ephraimite hill country and Benjamin. In loose affiliation with that core were the north Samarian hills, both sides of the Jordan valley, and part of the central Transjordanian hill country. The new territorial state assumed the name of Israel (2 Sam. 1.24), a designation that was particularly associated with the population of the core districts of Mt Ephraim and Benjamin. Saul apparently had Benjaminite roots (1 Sam. 9.1, 21; 10.21), which would explain his eventual decision to adopt the name of Israel for his new state, even though he began his career among the Gibeonites.[18]

As an economic basis for his territorial state, Saul would have striven to control local trade routes and find markets for the few natural resources he would have controlled: olive oil, wine, wool, iron ore, possibly red dye, and foodstuffs and spices from oasis areas in the Jordan valley. In this quest he would have found himself in competition, particularly with the Philistines to his west in the

---

[18] If 2 Sam. 21.4-5 is set beside 2 Sam. 2.8-9, the following inference and deduction can be drawn. During the process of initial expansion, Saul may have administered the Gibeonites and the Israelites as two independent entities. At some later point in his career, however, he appears to have decided to consolidate them into a single unit, and it was the Benjaminites who prevailed over the Gibeonites. The latter were incorporated into the centralized district of Benjamin.

lowlands, but also with independent palace states in Cis- and Transjordan and other emerging fledgling territorial and palace states in both areas. He died trying to expand beyond the north Samarian hill country into the Jezreel–Beth She'an corridor. I can only use my imagination to posit why he began his career at Gibeon and the order in which certain events took place in his career that led to his control over the areas named in the administrative list in 2 Sam. 2.4. At this point I am really beyond the realm of the data.

A date for Saul cannot be firmly established on the basis of the limited information available. He was associated with Israel, so any attempt to situate him in time needs to be done in relation to other Israelite kings whose existence can be verified by extrabiblical documentation. Omri is generally recognized to be the earliest king of Israel who is mentioned outside the Bible. He is named on the Mesha stele, which is dated on palaeographic grounds usually to the first half of the ninth century BCE. Dates based on biblical quotes for lengths of reign would tend to place him in the first quarter of the ninth century: 885–874[19] or 879–869.[20] If G.W. Ahlström is correct, however, that the seal of Shema' that was found at Megiddo refers to the servant of Jeroboam I rather than Jeroboam II, as commonly assumed, then he would be the earliest king of Israel whose existence would be confirmed by extrabiblical evidence.[21] Jeroboam I is generally dated during the last third of the tenth century BCE.[22] Saul would probably precede him since the *māšāl* and song fragment relating to him cast him as a shadowy figure of the past more than as an established royal monarch in a fixed king-list. It would seem logical to place Saul sometime during the tenth century BCE.

Conclusion

More than one plausible recreation of factors that led to Saul's emergence as the first king of Israel can be made on the basis of the delineated data pool. How close to historical reality any picture comes, however, cannot be judged. Be that as it may, a scholarly consensus about the career of Saul ben Kish can perhaps be reached, in spite of our inability to determine its accuracy. But is such a consensus desirable? I do not think so. The creation of an orthodox understanding of the past will undermine the creative enterprise called historiography and will introduce a form of thought control that will eliminate individualism and freedom of expression.

---

[19] So E. Thiele, *The Mysterious Numbers of the Hebrew Kings* (Grand Rapids, MI: Academie Books, rev. edn, 1983), p. 10.
[20] So J.H. Hayes and P.K. Hooker, *A New Chronology for the Kings of Israel and its Implications for Biblical History and Literature* (Atlanta: John Knox, 1988), p. 24.
[21] G.W. Ahlström, 'The Seal of Shema', *SJOT* 7 (1993), pp. 208-15.
[22] Thiele dates his reign from 930–909 BCE (*Mysterious Numbers,* p. 10) while Hayes and Hooker date it from 927–906 bce (*New Chronology*, p. 16).

The Mighty Men of Israel:
1–2 Samuel and Historicity

Lester L. Grabbe

In my debates with my minimalist friends one of my points is that they throw out a major potential source of historical data without further consideration, namely, the biblical text. In this paper I wish to explore the question of the extent to which the biblical text of 1 and 2 Samuel passes on usable and reliable information on the 11th to 10th centuries BCE. A full treatment would of course require a book, but some indications can be given here that suggest what might and might not be useful from the text. What I wish to do is briefly look at four topics: the Philistines, and the figures of Samuel, Saul, and David. 1 Samuel begins with the story of Samuel. For my purposes, however, I shall postpone the question of the prophet Samuel to last and shall begin with the Philistines.

I. Literary Sources

No historiographical narratives occur in the ancient Near East or eastern Mediterranean as early as the 9th century BCE. What we have generally are short compositions about day-to-day business and work, the occasional short royal or public inscription, or scribal writings. Historiographical narratives similar to the Deuteronomistic History (DtrH) first occur among the Greeks, with the writings of Herodotus and others, and especially in the Hellenistic period for the ancient Near East (e.g., Berossus).[1] Thus, although it may well be that source criticism – or what some have called "textual archaeology" – will someday give us major historical insights for 1 and 2 Samuel, the lack of a present consensus makes me omit this aspect of the historical question in this paper.

---

[1] Whether there is a "Deuteronomistic History" as conceived by Noth and many since him continues to be debated, but within the literature Joshua – 2 Kings there are narratives about Israel's past. My use of DtrH implies nothing more complicated than this. For doubts about the existence of DtrH as a unified document, see E.A. KNAUF, *Does 'Deuteronomistic Historiography' (DH) Exist?*, in A. DE PURY – T. RÖMER – J.-D. MACCHI (eds.), *Israel Constructs Its History: Deuteronomistic Historiography in Recent Research* (SupplJSOT, 306), Sheffield, Sheffield Academic Press, 2000, 388-398.

Also, I do not think textual criticism makes a major difference in the historical question, even though it may help us with points on many individual passages. For example, Frank Cross argued that the extra paragraph at 1Sam 11,1-3 in 4QSam^a gave historical material. But I see no evidence that the episode encountered there is any more historical than the one in the MT.[2]

II. The Philistines[3]

The key to historicity in Samuel could well be the Philistines. We have gained a lot of information about them in recent years, primarily through archaeology. In what is clearly an unhistorical context, the Philistines first appear in Genesis where they are alleged to be active during the so-called "Patriarchal Period", which is variously dated to the early or middle second millennium BCE, when no historical Philistines existed. The Philistines were a branch of what modern scholarship calls "the Sea Peoples". They surface again in the book of Judges, especially in the story of Samson, but the main account is in the books of Samuel.

At this point, there is potential engagement between biblical text and archaeology. Israel Finkelstein, for example, has argued that the actual context for the main Philistine narrative in 1 Samuel is the 7th century BCE.[4] Others see evidence of some earlier memory there;[5] for example, the Ark Narrative is not intrinsically unbelievable overall. Unfortunately, many of the welcome archaeological finds do not impinge directly on the Bible. For example, the pebbled hearth that Aren Maeir has noted as characteristic of the Philistine area for many centuries seems to have no reflex in the biblical text.[6]

---

[2] See my criticism in L.L. GRABBE, *The Law, the Prophets, and the Rest: The State of the Bible in Pre-Maccabean Times*, in *Dead Sea Discoveries* 13 (2006) 319-338, pp. 333-334.

[3] Recent studies include A.E. KILLEBREW – G. LEHMANN (eds.), *The Philistines and Other "Sea Peoples" in Text and Archaeology* (SBL Archaeology and Biblical Studies, 15), Atlanta, GA, Society of Biblical Literature, 2013; E.D. OREN (ed.), *The Sea Peoples and Their World: A Reassessment* (University Museum Monograph, 108; University Museum Symposium Series, 11), Philadelphia, PA, University of Pennsylvania, The University Museum, 2000; E. NOORT, *Die Seevölker in Palästina* (Palaestina Antiqua, 8), Kampen, Kok Pharos, 1994.

[4] I. FINKELSTEIN, *The Philistines in the Bible: A Late-Monarchic Perspective*, in *JSOT* 27 (2002) 131-167, gives a good summary and overview of the issues, though my assessment of whether an element is early or late does not always agree with his.

[5] E.g., N. NA'AMAN, *Sources and Composition in the History of David*, in V. FRITZ – P.R. DAVIES (eds.), *The Origins of the Ancient Israelite States* (SupplJSOT, 228), Sheffield, Sheffield Academic Press, 1996, 170-186; N. NA'AMAN, *In Search of Reality behind the Account of David's Wars with Israel's Neighbours*, in *IEJ* 52 (2002) 200-224.

[6] A.M. MAEIR, *Insights on the Philistine Culture and Related Issues: An Overview of 15 Years of Work at Tell eṣ-Ṣafi/Gath*, in G. GALIL – A. GILBOA – A.M. MAEIR –D. KAHN (eds.), *The Ancient Near East in the 12th-10th Centuries BCE: Culture and History: Proceedings of the International*

1. Lists of Philistine Cities

Several lists of Philistine cities are found (Josh 11,22; 19,43; Judg 1,18; 1Sam 6,17; Jer 25,20; 2Chr 26,6). 1Sam 6,17 lists five cities that have become known as the Philistine Pentapolis: Ashdod, Gaza, Ashkelon, Gath, and Ekron. Gath was destroyed by the Aramaean king Hazael about 830 BCE and ceased to be a major Philistine site (2Kgs 2,18).[7] The biblical text seems to remember the original importance of Gath, which suggests an early memory.[8] Whether the cities were united into some sort of Pentapolis, with a council of *seranim* making decisions for it as pictured in the text (e.g., 1Sam 5,8.11), is a separate question. With Gath and Ekron both roughly the same size but also much larger than the other three cities in the Iron I and early Iron IIA,[9] would they have been content to share power and authority equally with the smaller cities? Would they not have been rivals in at least certain ways? These data do not seem to be reflected in the text in any way. As Niemann notes, "The treatment of the five Philistine main sites as a unified block was not historical: it was an element of 'theological historical writing' projected back".[10] We also have the statement in 1Sam 7,14 that the cities of Gath to Ekron were returned to Israel after the ark incident. This is clearly unhistorical in the light of archaeology: we have no evidence of Israelite/Judahite occupation in the material culture of this time. Indeed, 1Sam 17,52 evidently has Ekron in Philistine hands when David was young, not too many years afterward (Gath will be further discussed below under "David").

2. Architecture of Philistine Temples

The placement of the pillars supporting the roof in the Philistine temple in Judg 16,25-30 looks like a match to those found in archaeological excavations, where pillars placed closely side by side support the roof.[11] Yet we must qualify this positive statement with two more negative ones. First, the statement that there

---

Conference held at the University of Haifa, 2-5 May, 2010 (AOAT, 392), Münster, Ugarit-Verlag, 2012, 345-404, pp. 354-355.

[7] A.M. MAEIR – J. UZIEL, *A Tale of Two Tells: A Comparative Perspective on Tel Miqne-Ekron and Tell eṣ-Ṣâfî/Gath in Light of Recent Archaeological Research*, in S. CRAWFORD – A. BEN-TOR – J.P. DESSEL – W.G. DEVER – A. MAZAR – J. AVIRAM (eds.), *"Up to the Gates of Ekron": Essays on the Archaeology and History of the Eastern Mediterranean in Honor of Seymour Gitin*, Jerusalem, Israel Exploration Society, 2007, 29-42, pp. 31-35.

[8] Cf. NA'AMAN, *In Search of Reality* (n. 5), pp. 210-212.

[9] MAEIR – UZIEL, *A Tale of Two Tells* (n. 7).

[10] H.M. NIEMANN, *Pentapolis*, in *RGG*[4] vol. 6, p. 1087: "Den einheitlich handelnden Block der fünf Philister-Hauptorte gab es hist. so nicht, er ist Element rückprojizierter 'theol. Geschichtsschreibung'". Unfortunately, he does not provide evidence for this statement.

[11] A.M. MAEIR (ed.), *Tell es-Safi/Gath I: The 1996 – 2005 Seasons. Part 1: Text* (Ägypten und das Alte Testament, 69), Wiesbaden, Harrassowitz, 2012, pp. 29-30.

were people on the roof who could observe events on the ground floor of the temple (as if overlooking an unroofed courtyard) is not confirmed by anything so far found. Secondly, this description of a Philistine temple could be quite late, since temples existed in Philistine towns until very late (note 1Mac 10,84; 11,4).

3. Achish, King of Gath

A number of biblical passages refer to Achish, king of Gath (מלך גת: 1Sam 21,11.13; 27,2-4.11; 1Kgs 2,39). This is the only evidence for such a person; however, we have an inscription from the 7th century that reads partially as follows (in the translation of the publishers):[12]

1. The temple (which) he built, '*kyš* son of Padi, son of
2. *Ysd*, son of Ada, son of Ya'ir, ruler of Ekron,
3. for *Ptgyh* his lady. ...

Thus, in the 7th century there was an Achish (אכיש) who was ruler (שר) of Ekron. Finkelstein suggests that the author of the narrative (written in the 7th century) made use of the name of a contemporary ruler in the area of Philistia, but because Gath was already strongly in the David tradition, he made Achish a ruler of Gath.[13] This is a reasonable argument, but it seems to me that those who see Achish as a ruler of Gath in an early tradition about David also present a reasonable picture. At the moment, I see no way of demonstrating for certain whether Achish is a late introduction into the narrative or an early element in the tradition.[14]

4. Metallurgy

One passage that is often mentioned, though seldom discussed in proper depth, is 1Sam 13,19-21. The translation of the passage is quite different in modern translations from traditional ones, such as the Luther Bibel and the Authorized Version, partly because of archaeology (though the text is difficult and probably corrupt), primarily because of the finding of weights of two thirds of a shekel with the word *pym* on them, which seems to be the import of the word *pîm* in this passage:

---

[12] S. GITIN – T. DOTHAN – J. NAVEH, *A Royal Dedicatory Inscription from Ekron*, in *IEJ* 47 (1997) 1-16, p. 9.
[13] FINKELSTEIN, *The Philistines in the Bible* (n. 4), pp. 133-136.
[14] W. DIETRICH, *David and the Philistines: Literature and History*, in GALIL – GILBOA – MAEIR – KAHN (eds.), *The Ancient Near East in the 12th-10th Centuries BCE: Culture and History* (n. 6), 79-98, p. 94, argues against Finkelstein's interpretation, citing the label of Achish as *king* of Gath (1Kgs 2,39). However, the reference to the figure of Achish in the Ekron inscription as שר, which seems to me likely to be equivalent to מלך, would actually bolster Finkelstein's argument.

> No blacksmith was found in all the land of Israel, for the Philistines said, "So that the Hebrews cannot make sword or spear". Every Israelite had to go to the Philistines to repair/sharpen his ploughshare, his mattock, his axe, or his sickle [LXX; MT repeats "ploughshare"]. The price for ploughshares was one *pîm*, and the same for mattocks and a three-pronged fork and axes and to set the goads. It was the day of battle, and no sword or spear was found in the hand of anyone (from Israel) except for Saul and his son Jonathan.

Basically, this passage says that the Philistines control the working of metal, and that for repair or sharpening of farming implements Israelites had to travel to the Philistines and pay them. The passage is somewhat difficult, partly because it may be corrupt and partly because the instruments listed are not all clearly identified, though their status as metal farm tools seems obvious from the context. What is done to them by the Philistine metal workers is also not certain. Does *ltš* indicate "repair" or does it mean simply "sharpen"? To renew a ploughshare that had been blunted or even damaged by stones would probably cost two-thirds of a sheqel (the value of a *pîm*), but this would seem extremely expensive simply to sharpen a sickle. Moreover, the Israelite farmer could easily have found appropriate whet stones in the environment to use to sharpen a sickle or mattock.

In the last few years several excavations have turned up data about metal-working in the Levant at the end of the Bronze and beginning of the Iron Age. The basic situation that emerges from what is presently known is that bronze dominated metal usage until about 1000 BCE, at which point the balance shifted heavily to iron. Yet in the Late Bronze Age and the early Iron Age, both copper-based and iron-based tools and weapons were in use. Carburized steel technology had developed by the 12th century, so what had changed around 1000 BCE was one of proportions of use, not a change of technology.[15]

It was once claimed that the Hittites first monopolized iron production and that the Philistines then took that position in the Levant; however, it is now widely believed that that position has been disproved.[16] Yet quite a few commentators have still accepted the view that 1Sam 13,19-21 was basically true and showed that the Philistines controlled or limited Israelite metallurgical skills.[17] It should be noted that 1Sam 13,19-22 does not specify iron; the tools and weapons in the passage could just as well have been bronze. A recent survey by Yulia Gottlieb,

---

[15] Y. GOTTLIEB, *The Advent of the Age of Iron in the Land of Israel: A Review and Reassessment*, in *Tel Aviv* 37 (2010) 89-110, pp. 89-90.

[16] Cf. T. STECH-WHEELER – J.D. MUHLY – K.R. MAXWELL-HYSLOP – R. MADDIN, *Iron at Taanach and Early Iron Metallurgy in the Eastern Mediterranean*, in *American Journal of Archaeology* 85 (1981) 245-268.

[17] Cf. H.M. NIEMANN, *Neighbors and Foes, Rivals and Kin: Philistines, Shephleans, Judeans between Geography and Economy, History and Theology*, in KILLEBREW – LEHMANN (eds.), *The Philistines and Other "Sea Peoples"* (n. 3), 243-264 pp. 262-263; W. DIETRICH, *The Early Monarchy in Israel*, Atlanta, GA, Society of Biblical Literature, 2007, pp. 156, 213.

which takes into account a variety of earlier studies, looks at the beginnings of the use of iron in Palestine in the early Iron Age.[18] It is only in the Iron IIA (10th century), that iron begins to displace bronze as the technology to make carburized steel develops. However, she notes that our data for the Shephelah and the highlands are sparse, and her statistics are primarily reliable for the North (especially Megiddo and Beth Shean) and the South (the Negev and the Beersheba Valley). In the central highlands the stratigraphy is problematic, but in Iron I and early Iron IIA bronze seems to have prevailed for agricultural implements in sites like Khirbet Raddana, though iron is predominant at Bethel and et-Tell. Interestingly, older settled areas seem to have been more conservative and continued to prefer bronze even while newer settlements (such as in the Negev) had focused on iron.

For the Shephelah, copper-based artefacts predominate until late Iron IIA, while for the area of Philistia, the first iron tools seem to be as late as Iron IIB. Gottlieb's article was written before the important metal-working facility was found at Gath/Tel eṣ-Ṣafi.[19] Gath has provided the first physical evidence on the state of metallurgy technology in Philistia in the early Iron Age. Both bronze and iron working are attested for the early Iron IIA, once again indicating the importance of both metals at this time. But what we do not find is any indication that the Philistines controlled metal technology. As Aren Maeir notes, "one cannot speak of a Philistine monopoly on metal production in the late Iron I and early Iron IIA (the available evidence from the ancient Levant does not support this supposition)".[20] It seems to me an absurd notion that Israelites had to go to Philistia just to sharpen their farm implements, not only paying a very high price but also taking the time and trouble to travel there and back. What we find in 1Sam 13,19-22 is a statement of theology, not contemporary metal technology.

5. Military Data

We first have the question of Goliath's armour. Although there are a few who argue that it reflects Iron Age I,[21] many have followed Kurt Galling in maintaining that "the narrator … has put together the wholly singular weaponry of Goliath from diverse elements of military equipment known to him" at a rather

---

[18] GOTTLIEB, *The Advent of the Age of Iron* (n. 15).
[19] On this, see MAEIR, *Insights on the Philistine Culture* (n. 6), pp. 267-268; MAEIR (ed.), *Tell es-Safi/Gath I* (n. 11), pp. 27-28; A. ELIYAHU-BEHAR – N. YAHALOM-MACK – S. SHILSTEIN – A. ZUKERMAN – C. SHAFER-ELLIOTT – A.M. MAEIR – E. BOARETTO – I. FINKELSTEIN – S. WEINER, *Iron and Bronze Production in Iron Age IIA Philistia: New Evidence from Tell es-Safi/Gath, Israel*, in *Journal of Archaeological Science* 39 (2012) 255-267.
[20] MAEIR, *Insights on the Philistine Culture* (n. 6), p. 367.
[21] For example, I. SINGER, *The Philistines in the Bible: A Short Rejoinder to New Perspective*, in KILLEBREW – LEHMANN (eds.), *The Philistines and Other "Sea Peoples"* (n. 3), 19-27, pp. 20, 25, 27.

later time.[22] Finkelstein has argued that Goliath's armoury represents a Greek hoplite soldier of the 7th century, though he also recognizes that some parts of the description fit Assyrian equipage.[23] This last point complicates matters: is an actual soldier with his weaponry being described, or is the image of Goliath simply made up eclectically (as Galling seems to be saying)? In either case, though, a later time than the Iron I or early Iron II is being represented.

As for the Cherethites and Pelethites, Finkelstein notes that Cherethites and Pelethites do not occur among the groups of Sea Peoples.[24] He follows Albright in interpreting Pelethites as a reference to Greek peltasts (*peltastai*) or light infantry (from their *pelte* or light shield). Again, he relates them to the Greek mercenary troops widely used in the 7th century. John Van Seters has similarly argued the question at some length (see below under David).

III. Saul

King Saul was a problem for the narrator of 1–2 Samuel, which is an excellent reason for believing he was a historical personage. It seems clear that the narrator wanted to tell the story of David but had to deal with Saul as well, even though he would rather have ignored or forgotten about him. According to narrative logic, the rulership and dynasty should have begun with David. The whole story of the monarchy is of the legitimacy of the Davidic dynasty and the illegitimacy of the northern kingship. The Northern Kingdom should not have existed, and the northern kings were presented as usurpers. But how is this is to be explained, if David was also a usurper – not part of the dynasty originally chosen by God? The narrator of 1 Samuel has to present it that Saul's dynasty was not just wiped out, but that his descendants were null and void as far as kingship was concerned – a rather strange concept, if it was the king and dynasty originally chosen and anointed by Yhwh. If Saul's rulership and dynasty could be overturned, why not that of David? Yet the narrative insists on treating them quite differently.

Thus, it seems to me that the narrator was stuck with Saul and his family. The existence of Saul as the first king of Israel does not strike me as a likely fictional scenario, even if some aspects of the relationship and interaction between Saul and David could easily find their place in a work of fiction. The tradition was too firmly settled and known to the people to be given major changes, such as dropping Saul altogether. Even though there is absolutely no evidence for Saul apart from the biblical text (as far as I am aware), I firmly believe there was a historical Saul.

---

[22] K. GALLING, *Goliath und seine Rüstung*, in *Volume du Congrès Genève 1965* (SupplVT, 15), Leiden, Brill, 1966, 150-169: "Die ingesamt singuläre Waffnung Goliaths hat der Erzähler ... aus verschiedenen, ihm bekannten Ausrüstungsstücken zusammengesetzt", p. 167.
[23] FINKELSTEIN, *The Philistines in the Bible* (n. 4), pp. 145-146.
[24] *Ibid.*, pp. 148-150.

What else can we say with more or less confidence about this figure? As has long been observed, 2Sam 2,9 describes Ishbaal (or Ishbosheth) as ruling over "Gilead, the Ashurites, Jezrel, Ephraim, and Benjamin". This is reasonably the territory ascribed to Saul. It is especially important because it does not include Judah, for reasons which will be discussed below under David. Apart from some territory on the other side of the Jordan, the core of the fiefdom is the central hill country, which archaeology suggests is the centre of the Iron I settlement area. Many of Saul's activities could have been accomplished in two years (cf. 1Sam 13,1).

Much of the Saul tradition involves fighting against the Philistines. Yet he was supposed to have originally made his name by fighting the Amalekites (1Sam 15). On the surface, this appears unlikely, since the territory of the Amalekites was presumed to have been in the Negev (Num 13,29). That is a valid objection, since Saul's territory does not appear to have included Judah, much less the areas to the south of it. Diana Edelman has argued, however, that Saul attacked Amalekites who were living in the region of Samaria.[25] This is much more credible as a historical event.

It is plausible that Saul fought the Philistines, but it is more likely that Saul attacked them than the other way round. Philistines had lived happily in the coastal region for well over a century. The Shephelah acted as transition zone, and there was opportunity for Philistines to expand if they had wanted to do so, without moving into the highlands. The ones aiming to expand their territory seem to have been the Israelites. Probably, the highlanders made periodic raids into the prosperous lowlands, though that may have forced the Philistines to send troops occasionally on retaliatory incursions into the highlands. But the idea that the Philistines were wanting to expand their territory into the highlands at this time looks unlikely.

Let us note some salient points about the Saul tradition. First of all, Saul looks like a chieftain, with a court that meets under a tree (1Sam 22,6). We have two versions of how he became king: one is that he was anointed by Samuel (1Sam 9,1–10,16 [23] + 13,2–14,52), which looks like a biased account from a prophetic source that wants to make Saul subordinate to Samuel; the other – more likely to be reliable – is that he arose as a deliverer (1Sam 11,1-15).

A recent analysis of the Saul tradition by Simcha Shalom Brooks finds a historical core, though this has been filtered through the distorting lenses of Davidic court circles, prophetic circles, Deuteronomistic perspectives, and anti-monarchic views.[26] According to Shalom Brooks the population in the central highlands was already moving toward a new socio-economic situation characterized by a developing centralization. This was the background for the rise of the monarchy. Saul

---

[25] D. EDELMAN, *Saul's Battle against Amaleq (1 Sam. 15)*, in *JSOT* 35 (1986) 71-84.
[26] S. SHALOM BROOKS, *Saul and the Monarchy: A New Look* (Society for Old Testament Study Monographs), Aldershot, Hants, Ashgate, 2005.

was a successful leader, the first to develop a standing army, who had the support of the people. Saul was not only able to unite the Israelite tribes (she includes Judah, but I think this unlikely; see below under "David") but also to incorporate Canaanites and other minority groups into the emerging state. Loyalty to Saul continued after his death, creating rebellions and other problems for David; indeed, David almost wrecked the monarchy by his sabotage of Saul's rule in order to gain the throne for himself. Similarly, D. Edelman sees the historical Saul as the petty king of Gibeon with Benjaminite roots who expanded into surrounding territory to create a state called "Israel".[27] Attempts to control local trade routes and find markets brought him in conflict with the Philistines and other independent states. He died trying to expand into the Jezreel–Beth She'an corridor.

IV. David

The first thing to notice about David is that he is inextricably associated with Judah. This is important, because the relationship of Judah with Israel is one of the areas in which the data clash strongly with the surface narrative of the biblical text. It has long been known and accepted that Judah had its own national identity and was separate from and a rival of Israel from an early period.

1. David's Wars

According to the text of 2 Samuel, David continued Saul's fight with the Philistines, especially in 5,17-25 and 8,1. Yet several scholars have argued that the reality was different, and that David may not have fought with the Philistines but arranged a truce that allowed a peaceful co-existence throughout his reign.[28] There are a number of arguments in support of this. First, David's wars with the Philistines in 2Sam 5,17-25 seem only a passing episode, with little consequence; indeed, taking little space to describe. The motive for the Philistines to attack him also looks rather trumped up. Niemann notes that these campaigns (and the statement in 2Sam 5,25) fit Saul better and were probably borrowed from the Saulide tradition. Secondly, David does not defeat the Philistines (only the tacked on summary statement in 2Sam 5,25 claims this), yet the threat simply disappears from the text. Thirdly, we also have the reference to the 600 warriors from Gath, under the command of Itai, who assist David at the time of Abalom's rebellion

---

[27] D. EDELMAN, *King Saul in the Historiography of Judah* (SupplJSOT, 121), Sheffield, Sheffield Academic Press, 1991; D. EDELMAN, *Saul ben Kish in History and Tradition*, in V. FRITZ – P.R. DAVIES (eds.), *The Origins of the Ancient Israelite States* (SupplJSOT, 228), Sheffield, Sheffield Academic Press, 1996, 142-159.

[28] NIEMANN, *Neighbors and Foes, Rivals and Kin* (n. 17), pp. 259-260; DIETRICH, *David and the Philistines* (n. 14), pp. 95-98.

(2Sam 15,18-22). Fourthly, Achish king of Gath is clearly at peace with Solomon after the time of David (1Kgs 2,39-40). Finally, Judah seems to have expanded into the Shephelah in the first half of the 9th century, yet there is no evidence of conflict with Gath which would have dominated the area as a large city at this time.[29] This indicates that an earlier agreement (presumably the one made in the time of David) was still in effect.

Yet if David did not fight with the Philistines, was he seeking an essential expansion of his territory? According to 2 Samuel, David fought a variety of the surrounding peoples and expanded his territory to the north and east and south, into Moab, Ammon, Edom, and the region of Aramaean rule (2Sam 8; 10,1–11,1; 12,26-31). The extension of control into Edom and Transjordan is credible, but defeat of the Aramaeans – even placing a garrison in Damascus (2Sam 8,6) – looks contrived. Now, Nadav Na'aman has presented a compelling case that this fight against and defeat of Hadadezer of Zobah is a literary creation, based on the Aramaean king Hazael in the 9th century.[30] However, he goes on to argue that David's conquest of Moab was also a literary creation, aiming to counter the defeat of Israel by Moab under Mesha; that the defeat of Ammon was devised to compensate for the cruelty inflicted by the Ammonites on Israel as outlined in Am 1,13; and David's defeat of Edom was borrowed from Amaziah's later victory over the Edomites (2Kgs 14,7).[31] In the end, Na'aman sees in the story of David's conquests only a few historical elements, viz., the conquest of Jerusalem and the subjugation of the Philistines.[32] As we have seen above, however, it looks as if the driving of the Philistines from the central hill country is also a literary creation! This leaves us with the taking of Jerusalem, though I would argue that here we do have a genuine historical datum.

John Van Seters argues for an even later time, that the accounts of David as a mercenary leader show a dating of the narrative to the late Persian period at the earliest.[33] He points out that in the Davidic narrative David shows considerable reliance on mercenaries in his time; on the other hand, there is hardly any mention of them in the later narratives of Kings. The Saite dynasty seems to have used a variety of mercenaries, including Jews, and Greek mercenaries appear to have been stationed at Mesad Hashavyahu and Arad. This account of the Davidic monarchy fits the militaristic regimes of the late Persian period because it is only

---

[29] N. Na'aman, *Khirbet Qeiyafa in Context*, in *Ugarit-Forschung* 42 (2010) 497-526, pp. 516-517; N. Na'aman, *The Kingdom of Judah in the 9th Century BCE: Text Analysis versus Archaeological Research*, in *Tel Aviv* 40 (2013) 247-276, p. 264.
[30] Na'aman, *In Search of Reality* (n. 5), pp. 207-210.
[31] *Ibid.*, pp. 212-214.
[32] *Ibid.*, p. 215.
[33] J. Van Seters, *David the Mercenary*, in L.L. Grabbe (ed.), *Israel in Transition: From Late Bronze II to Iron IIA (c. 1250-850 BCE)*. Volume 2: *The Text* (LHB/OTS, 521 = European Seminar in Historical Methodology, 8), London – New York, T&T Clark International, 2010, 199-219.

from the 4th century onwards that Persian rulers and satraps made use of these particular Greek professional mercenaries, the Cretans and the peltasts, with their specialized skills.

Van Seters concludes that the references to mercenaries in the David Saga are so pervasive that they cannot be removed by redaction-critical methods: the narrator has freely invented a portrayal of David modelled on the monarchs of his own day. One cannot use any of it to reconstruct the Davidic monarchy of the 10th century. Van Seters makes a good case, though I am not entirely convinced by his explanation. After all, it seems that David and similar *'apiru* leaders hired themselves out as bands of mercenary soldiers, fighting for pay or for booty, which is the same thing. However, his basic point that *Greek* mercenaries were a feature of the Persian and Hellenistic periods is well taken.

2. Jerusalem

With regard to Jerusalem, the stories in Judges seem to remember a Jerusalem that came into Israelite hands only relatively late and continued to have the earlier people as a part of the population for some time afterward. What the various traditions suggest, therefore, is that there was a collective folk memory of a time when Jerusalem was not Israelite, and even that it came into Israelite hands much later than some of the surrounding territory. This is a remarkable memory, especially if we keep in mind that it would have been more convenient to believe that Jerusalem was conquered with the rest of the territory and divided up by the Israelites without any complications.

Yet the text acknowledges complications: Jerusalem is sometimes the property of Judah (Josh 15,63; cf. Judg 1,8) and sometimes within the territory of Benjamin (Josh 18,28; Judg 1,21). In both cases, it recognizes that some of the original inhabitants, the Jebusites, continued to live in the city, alongside the Judahites (Josh 15,63; Judg 1,21) or Benjaminites (Judg 1,21). In spite of this tradition, 2Sam 5,6-9 requires David to conquer the city from the Jebusites again. What sort of entity Jerusalem was is not clear. The story suggests a type of fortress, though this does not mean a large or grand settlement, as is confirmed by the image of the Jebusite king of Jerusalem who does his own physical threshing of grain at his threshing floor which occupies a central point on the ridge (2Sam 24,20-23). David's sons acted as priests at this time, possibly even before he took Jerusalem (2Sam 8,17). In any case, David made the Jebusite priest Zadok one of his two chief priests.[34]

---

[34] It was long ago recognized that Zadok was formerly a priest from the Jerusalem cult; cf. L.L. GRABBE, *Were the Pre-Maccabean High Priests "Zadokites"?*, in J.C. EXUM – H.G.M. WILLIAMSON (eds.), *Reading from Right to Left: Essays on the Hebrew Bible in Honour of David J.A. Clines* (SupplJSOT, 373), Sheffield, Sheffield Academic Press, 2003, 205-215. The other priest was probably from the traditional priestly stock, but there are textual problems. In 1Sam 22,20 and 2Sam 20,25 he is Abiathar son of Ahimelech, but in 2Sam 8,17 he is Ahimelech son of Abiathar.

3. Archaeology[35]

Archaeology, especially as it relates to the Jerusalem, is problematic: when we come to the Iron Age, the questions start to multiply. According to the text, we should find a Jebusite city for Iron I, which was then replaced in Iron IIA-B by an expanding city that functioned as an administrative centre and a capital of a considerable kingdom, under David and Solomon. Ann Killebrew refers to the two "bookends" of monumental architecture in the Middle Bronze, on one side, and in the 8th to 7th centuries BCE, on the other. She argues that the lack of other finds relating to fortification suggests that Jerusalem was unwalled and unfortified between the LB and Iron IIB (16th to mid-8th centuries BCE), and thus Jerusalem was "at best modest".[36] This of course differs from the picture of the text. Yet it is supported by a recent study by Doron Ben-Ami which argued that excavations at the Givati parking lot showed that there were no Iron IIA fortifications on the southeast ridge ("City of David" settlement); rather, "all Iron Age fortification components unearthed in Jerusalem are the outcome of one comprehensive building operation that took place at the close of the 8th century BCE".[37]

Yet we find major disputes among archaeologists over this period. Several archaeological features are contested. One of the main contentions is that we should expect monumental architecture, if the text is correct, but do we find that? Some have pointed to the Stepped Stone Structure. That does not fit what I would call "monumental architecture", but Eilat Mazar has recently argued that a building at the top of the Stepped Stone Structure dates to David's time and could be his palace.[38] This appears to be an important site and evidently the first evidence for potential monumental architecture from the time of David. Acceptance of Mazar's interpretation is by no means universal, however.

The main problem with the Stepped Stone Structure and "David's palace" is its dating. On the one hand, Jane M. Cahill dates it to the Late Bronze/Early Iron transition, arguing that both the stepped mantle and the terraces below it

---

[35] Please note that the dating of archaeology is according to the Conventional Chronology, for convenience, without implying that I reject the arguments for the Low Chronology. I discuss the several recent systems in Palestinian archaeological debate in L.L. GRABBE, *Ancient Israel: What Do We Know and How Do We Know It?*, London – New York, T&T Clark International, 2007, pp. 10-11, with the relevant secondary studies up to 2006.

[36] A.E. KILLEBREW, *Biblical Jerusalem: An Archaeological Assessment*, in A.G. VAUGHN – A.E. KILLEBREW (eds.), *Jerusalem in Bible and Archaeology: The First Temple Period* (SBL Symposium Series, 18), Atlanta, GA, Society of Biblical Literature, 2003, 329-345, p. 334.

[37] D. BEN-AMI, *Notes on the Iron IIA Settlement in Jerusalem in Light of Excavations in the Northwest of the City of David*, in *Tel Aviv* 41 (2014) 3-19.

[38] E. MAZAR, *The Palace of King David: Excavations at the Summit of the City of David: Preliminary Report of Seasons 2005-2007*, Jerusalem – New York, Shoham Academic Research and Publication, 2009; E. MAZAR, *Did I Find King David's Palace?*, in *BAR* 32/1 (2006) 16-27, 70.

were built together as a single architectural unit.³⁹ In contrast, Margreet Steiner argues from Kenyon's excavations that the Stepped Stone Structure as such was quite different in extension and construction method from the terrace system.⁴⁰ Where the terraces existed, only a mantle of stones was added, but where there were no terraces the structure was built up from bedrock. For confirmation of the dating and construction, she points to the pottery in the fill of the terraces which was Iron I, with no mix of later material. Steiner would date its construction to the tenth or early ninth century. In sum, according to Steiner the terrace and Stepped Structure Systems do not have similar boundaries, identical pottery, or the same construction techniques. Apart from considerable dispute about the Stepped Stone Structure, Eilat Mazar's claims about the "David's palace" building have been critiqued in an article by Israel Finkelstein, Ze'ev Herzog, Lily Singer-Avitz, and David Ussishkin.⁴¹ They give quite a different interpretation of the site, eventually concluding that the building is most likely late Hellenistic. Newspaper columns beginning in early March 2014 reported that the Jebusite fortress taken by David in the conquest of Jerusalem (2Sam 5,6-9) had been found near the Gihon spring.⁴² This was something of a surprise, because the lead excavator of that area, Ronny Reich, had not reported it in his recently published *Excavating the City of David*.⁴³ One might assume that it was a new excavation, made after Reich had left his post at Gihon, but this was not the case. Instead, the Middle Bronze building known as the "Spring Tower" had been identified to reporters as the fortress captured by David. The argument was that it was still in existence and being used at the beginning of Iron IIA, about 1000 BCE. We await proper archaeological reports, but according to newspaper reports Reich has not accepted this new interpretation of "the Spring Fortress".

In sum, Margreet Steiner's view is that Jerusalem of the tenth and ninth centuries was a small town occupied mainly by public buildings, not exceeding 12 hectares and approximately 2000 inhabitants.⁴⁴ It exhibits the characteristics of a

---

[39] J.M. CAHILL, *Jerusalem at the Time of the United Monarchy: The Archaeological Evidence*, in VAUGHN – KILLEBREW (eds.), *Jerusalem in Bible and Archaeology* (n. 36), 13-80, p. 42; J.M. CAHILL, *Jerusalem in David and Solomon's Time*, in *BAR* 30/6 (2004) 20-31, 62-63.

[40] M. STEINER, *The Evidence from Kenyon's Excavations in Jerusalem: A Response Essay*, in VAUGHN – KILLEBREW (eds.), *Jerusalem in Bible and Archaeology* (n. 36), 347-363, pp. 351-361; M. STEINER, *Re-dating the Terraces of Jerusalem*, in *IEJ* 44 (1994) 13-20; M. STEINER, *The Archaeology of Ancient Jerusalem*, in *CR:BS* 6 (1998) 143-168.

[41] I. FINKELSTEIN et al., *Has King David's Palace in Jerusalem Been Found?*, in *Tel Aviv* 34 (2007) 142-164.

[42] E.g., R. NGO, *Canaanite Fortress Discovered in the City of David, Biblical Archaeology Sites, News*, posted on 7 April 2014; available at http://www.biblicalarchaeology.org/daily/news/canaanite-fortress-discovered-in-the-city-of-david/ (accessed 27 June 2014).

[43] R. REICH, *Excavating the City of David: Where Jerusalem's History Began*, Jerusalem, Israel Exploration Society, 2011.

[44] M. STEINER, *Jerusalem in the Tenth and Seventh Centuries BCE: From Administrative Town to Commercial City*, in A. MAZAR (ed.), *Studies in the Archaeology of the Iron Age in Israel*

regional administrative centre or the capital of a small, newly established state, the towns of Megiddo, Hazor, Gezer, and Lachish showing similar characteristics at the same time. For the Jerusalem settlement to be little more than a village at the time of David is not a problem. This was probably all that was needed for David's state, considering its small size and complexity. It was certainly an advance on Saul's open-air court under a large tree (1Sam 22,6).

4. Relationship of Saul and David Traditions

Having argued that there is a historical core to both the Saulide and Davidide traditions, I now must ask whether there is any connection between them. The David traditions in the present narrative are in part bound up with the Saul traditions, and they need to be evaluated together. Granted, the present redacted text has the traditions heavily intertwined, but was that the case in the beginning? Can we simply see two sets of traditions, one of which described in some way the first northern king, while the other independently had the first southern king at its core? Such an interpretation is quite believable in itself and has the merit of being simple. Why must we complicate the story more than is necessary, even though the redactors certainly did?

Yet a closer examination exposes greater complexity. Note the following: There is first of all the saying, "Saul has slain his thousands, but David his tens of thousands" (1Sam 18,7; 21,12; 29,5). Not a major datum but nevertheless one worth noting, and one likely to be early according to some commentators.[45] If this is an early saying, where did it come from if the David and Saul traditions were originally separate?

Secondly, one of the major characteristics of the David tradition is the extent to which his reign is legitimated (strongly suggesting that David was a usurper[46]).

- Comes as an apprentice to Saul's court (1Sam 16,14-23).
- Performs personal duties for Saul's health (1Sam 16,14-23).
- Fights as a champion against Israel's enemies (1Sam 17).
- Marries the king's daughter (1Sam 18,17-27).
- Wins her hand by warrior-worthy deeds (1Sam 18,25-27).
- Anointed by a prophet-priest (1Sam 16,1-13).
- Even the king's son and heir recognizes David's right to rule (1Sam 18,1; 20,12-17; 23,16-18).

---

and Jordan (SupplJSOT, 331), Sheffield, Sheffield Academic Press, 2001, 280-288; M. STEINER, *Expanding Borders: The Development of Jerusalem in the Iron Age*, in T.L. THOMPSON – S.K. JAYYUSI (eds.), *Jerusalem in Ancient History and Tradition* (SupplJSOT, 381; Copenhagen International Seminar, 13), London – New York, T&T Clark International, 2003, 68-79; STEINER, *The Evidence from Kenyon's Excavations* (n. 40).

[45] E.g., Dietrich, *The Early Monarchy* (n. 17), pp. 264-265.
[46] Shalom Brooks, *Saul and the Monarchy* (n. 26), ch. 4.

Why go to all this trouble to make David's rule legitimate if he had been accepted as the first king of Judah by the tradition? This suggests that the present picture of the text (that he was not the first king but actually effected a change of dynasty) was not a secondary creation but one already there in the tradition when the text was redacted.

Thirdly, one could take the example of Michal. She could have been added to the tradition simply to give a further negative picture of Saul, since her story is ultimately a negative one in which she is rejected and childless, though remaining David's wife. But her story is more complicated and interesting than this. For example, she helps David escape from her father by a clever deception (1Sam 19,11-17). After she was married to another man, David expended some effort to get her back (2Sam 3,12-16).

Fourthly, there is also the story of Jonathan. Again, he could serve just as another reason to bolster David's legitimacy: even the heir to the throne supports David's right instead of his own. But why make him such an integral part of the story, if that were his only purpose? Not least is the question of why Jonathan did not succeed his father. There are many hazards to an heir not only growing up but acquiring the necessary military prowess and confidence of the troops meant that prime heirs did not always gain the throne. But we might have expected a different sort of story, if it was merely a literary invention to enhance David's right to the throne.

Finally, we have to ask: if the Saul tradition was simply about the first king of Israel, separate from Judah, what happened to his dynasty? We know that at a later time, kings well attested in historical sources ruled over Israel. But if the Saul tradition was completely independent of the David one, what happened to the Israelite monarchy that had begun with Saul? Did it just peter out? If so, what filled the vacuum, and how did it get started up again? It is such questions that make us turn to the David tradition and ask whether it is perhaps correct that David in some way was the successor on the throne of the inchoate state of Israel begun by Saul.

It is as if the Davidic and Solomonic traditions are *necessary* to fill the gap between Saul and the history of the two kingdoms or monarchies of Israel and Judah. If so, then the concept of the "united monarchy" is perhaps correct, after all – but only in a particular sense. That is, the first king Saul ruled over a portion of the central highlands, though apparently not Judah. The Judahite David – possibly a tribal leader of Judah or perhaps even a sort of king of Judah – took over from Saul (or Saul's son), establishing some sort of rule over both the northern highlands and the Judaean highlands.

5. Conclusions about David

What we find in 1–2 Samuel is the story of a young Judahite warrior made good. He seems to have grown up in a society that was not heavily stratified; nevertheless, there was no doubt tribal leadership, with Judahite elders and perhaps even a tribal chieftain or chieftains. Was David the heir of one of these tribal leaders? There are also some hints that his family was not so humble. After all, he was brought into Saul's court, unlikely to happen to a complete nobody. In any case, David became some sort of *'apiru* leader: surprisingly, this image appears to be agreed on by two archaeologists who otherwise take somewhat different views on the "United Monarchy".[47]

In the biblical story, David fits the image of the hero figure; there are many folkloristic elements and a variety of traditions; yet there are also traditions with some interesting twists, such as the willingness to acknowledge some of David's weaknesses, the need to legitimate David from a variety of angles – suggesting that he was not seen as legitimate by everyone – and the admission that David did not do certain things that we might have expected. One of the interesting points about the Davidic tradition is how "lumpy" it is. That is, it often disagrees with what we would expect from the biblical text as a whole. To summarize, we can note some of the points that emerge from a look at the Saul and David traditions:

- The tradition recognizes that David was not the first king.
- Saul came to the throne probably as a military leader by popular acclaim (1Sam 11,1-15), whereas the prophetic tradition that the king was subject to Samuel's choice and censure is unrealistic (1Sam 9,1–10,16.23; 13,2–14,52).
- The apparent boundaries of Saul's kingdom (2Sam 2,9) is reasonably in line with the natural and demographic resources in Cis-Jordan.
- A strong link is made between David's rise and Saul's court, but much of this looks like a deliberate attempt to legitimate David as king from a variety of angles: anointing by Samuel (1Sam 16,1-13); armour-bearer in Saul's court who plays the lyre for him personally (1Sam 16,14-23); slaying of Goliath (1Sam 17); marriage to Saul's daughter (1Sam 18,17-27).
- Contrary to expectations David does not build a temple (though a strenuous effort is made for him to do everything short of the actual building).
- Both Saul and David were mainly military leaders.
- The text itself does not suggest an extensive administrative apparatus in the case of either Saul or David.

---

[47] A. MAZAR, *The Spade and the Text: The Interaction between Archaeology and Israelite History Relating to the 10th-9th Centuries BCE*, in H.G.M. WILLIAMSON (ed.), *British Academy Conference*, Oxford, OUP for the British Academy, 2007, 143-171, pp. 164-165; I. FINKELSTEIN, *The Rise of Jerusalem and Judah: the Missing Link*, in *Levant* 33 (2001) 105-115, pp. 107-108.

The books of Samuel end at this point, but just to finish the story, Solomon – who may or may not have been David's son[48] – took over from David. He did not expand David's realm in that he was not a great military leader, but he consolidated David's conquests into Transjordan and peripheral areas. However, the truce with the Philistines seems to have been maintained, since nothing is said about them during Solomon's reign. He expanded Jerusalem, though it was still small by later standards, but, most important, he built the temple. This and other factors led later to a legend of an Oriental potentate of fantastic power, wealth, and wisdom, which we find in 1 Kgs 1–11 but which had little in the way of historical reality behind it. Apart from building the temple, Solomon's main achievement was holding together the realm he inherited from David. After Solomon's death, the rivalries, and perhaps external events such as the invasion of Shoshenq, split the kingdom. At this point, leadership passed to the northern territory which had the greater concentration of natural resources and wealth potential. After only a few decades, the rise of the Omri dynasty established the kingdom of Israel as the dominant power in the region and led to a true Israelite state. Whether Judah was its vassal, as a number have suggested, or just its junior partner, as Na'aman has recently argued, probably makes little difference.[49]

V. Samuel

Samuel seems to fill the role in the narratives about Saul and David that Merlin does in the King Arthur story. Although his activities are sometimes centre stage, his purpose is to choose and anoint the person to be king. Merlin is a sort of shaman figure, which means that he functions in both prophetic and priestly activities. Certainly, Samuel is both priest and prophet, but he is also a political leader part of his life. We do not normally expect either priest or prophet to be the king (or a similar figure), yet after the fall of the monarchy the high priest of Judah was also a political leader of the Jewish community and sometimes had prophetic functions.[50]

---

[48] E.A. KNAUF, *Le roi est mort, vive le roi! A Biblical Argument for the Historicity of Solomon*, in L.K. HANDY (ed.), *The Age of Solomon: Scholarship at the Turn of the Millennium* (Studies in the History and Culture of the Ancient Near East, 11), Leiden, Brill, 1997, 81-95, pp. 88-89, has suggested that the story of Bathsheba may not have been suppressed because there was a worse story: that Solomon was not David's!

[49] Na'aman, *The Kingdom of Judah* (n. 29), pp. 258-261.

[50] For a discussion of the Jerusalem high priest after the end of the monarchy, see especially L.L. GRABBE, *A History of the Jews and Judaism in the Second Temple Period 1: Yehud: A History of the Persian Province of Judah* (Library of Second Temple Studies, 47), London – New York, T&T Clark International, 2004, pp. 230-234.

In the present text Samuel is in many ways the linchpin that connects the Saul and David traditions. He anointed the first king but, after Saul was rejected by Yhwh, he then anointed David. Yet many literary critics have argued that the prophetic figure who first anointed Saul (1Sam 10,1) was originally an anonymous figure. This might suggest that Samuel should be better associated with David, and that he has been brought into the Saul tradition secondarily. Yet Samuel's original circuit of cities where he carried out his priestly duties were Bethel, Gilgal, Mizpah, and Ramah, all places in the North, and not everyone wants to replace the Samuel anointing Saul with an anonymous holy man. Whether Samuel should be inserted into 1Sam 9–10 (as he is now) or not, he could well have been an important shamanistic figure and king maker in the period at the beginnings of an Israelite state. He could then have been active in the rise of Saul but became disillusioned with him, at which point he would have looked around for a replacement.

One would have expected a religious figure – priest or prophet – to have been associated with the rise of the monarchy in Israel. One might think of the archbishop of Canterbury in English history. Although the archbishop was a religious figure, he had considerable power, including the power to crown the monarch. We also know that some archbishops were very political, even holding political office along with their ecclesiastical duties. The history of the English monarchy includes the activities of many of the Canterbury archbishops. From that perspective, Samuel who had both priestly and prophetic functions, as well as a community leadership role, would have been a necessary figure. In that sense, his general activities in both the Saul and David traditions are credible. However, some of the activities ascribed to Samuel are unlikely to be historical. His function as a mouthpiece for anti-monarchic speeches is one of these. Many of the passages that express hostility toward kingship for Israel (e.g., 1Sam 8) are probably late (though as so often, the matter is complicated).[51]

VI. Conclusions

This essay has attempted an all-too-brief evaluation of historicity in the books of Samuel – by "historicity" I mean both what is historical and how we might separate out in some sort of critical and systematic way the historical data that are embedded in the sea of theological and literary creation. The rapid survey could not possibly do justice to the question, but I hope it has highlighted some of the main methodological issues and also drawn attention to some individual points in the text that must be taken into account in any judgment on historicity. I would summarize my own conclusions as follows:

---

[51] Cf. W. DIETRICH, *1 Samuel*. Teilband 1: *1 Sam 1–12* (BKAT, VIII/1), Neukirchen-Vluyn, Neukirchener, 2011, pp. 42*-43*.

- The narrative about the Philistines is difficult, partly because a good deal of the new knowledge from recent excavations does not directly encounter statements in the text. There are certainly some early elements in the text, especially the recognition that Gath was an important city in the Iron I and early Iron IIA period, a rival to Ekron and even replacing it later. Yet it also seems clear that some elements in the text reflect a much later period (e.g., Israel possession of Gath and Ekron), while other elements could be early or late (e.g., the architecture of Philistine temples).
- An individual named Saul seems to have been an important figure in the origin of the Israelite polity. He fought the Philistines with some success, and set the highland clans on the course of a national state, though it began as a tribal union that Saul brought together and perhaps turned into a tribal state. This union did not originally contain Judah.
- A religious figure – a shaman-like personage, combining both cultic and prophetic elements in activities – was also probably prominent in the establishment of Saul's polity, remembered in the biblical text under the name Samuel (though whether that was his real name might be a matter of argument).
- David arose from Judah, probably from a prominent family, not the humble origins that some texts seem to suggest. In spite of not being from the Israelite area, he seems to have found a place at Saul's court where his military exploits and perhaps his intrigues made him a rival, and thus an enemy, of Saul. He left Saul's service and established himself as head of a band of mercenaries fighting for the Philistines and living by raiding, probably including some areas of Israel and even Judah. When Saul was killed, David was eventually able to unite the inchoate state of Israel with Judah under his rule, making Jerusalem his residence and capital. One of his main achievements was to make an agreement with the Philistines so that his energies were not wasted in fighting them; to what extent he expanded Saul's territory is a moot point. The hill country of Israel and Judah still seems to be the core of his kingdom. Thus, David in a sense ruled a united monarchy, but it was not the great "United Monarchy" pictured by the biblical text, especially under Solomon.
- Not a part of 1–2 Samuel, but to complete the story, Solomon succeeded David. He was possibly not even David's son, and he bore the name of the old deity of Jerusalem. His main achievement was to build a temple of Yhwh, which David had not done, but the magnificent temple, palace, city, and kingdom – and his great wisdom – are all part of a typical Oriental legend of a great potentate of fantastic achievements. His empire was greater than either Egypt or the Hittites; indeed, he controlled trade between these two entities, and even married Pharaoh's daughter, which was not normal practice at this time. The original tale seems to have spared no achievement or tale of wealth and magnificence for Solomon. However,

a later Deuteronomist, whose concern was theological, tempered the story with criticisms of Solomon's being led astray by his wealth and especially his excessive harim. What Solomon did achieve (in addition to building a temple) was to hold together David's state, which split soon after his death.

- The fact that we have no hints of a continuing dynasty of the Northern Kingdom alongside the leadership of David and Solomon is one of the reasons for assuming that the peoples of both the central and the Judaean highlands were under their domain. But the natural division between Judah and the other tribes reasserted itself after the death of Solomon, and the normal existence of two separate entities replaced the brief united rule. At this point, the natural predominance of the north prevailed, and Israel went on to gain considerable organization and power under the Omride dynasty, while Judah became a minor kingdom in Israel's shadow.

Sources and Composition in the History of David

Nadav Na'aman

1. The Introduction of Writing in the Court of Jerusalem

The date of the introduction of writing is a major problem for the evaluation of the sources regarding the history of David. The installation of the office of scribe in the courts of David and Solomon, and several lists that were possibly drawn from original documents, are usually regarded as indications of writing in the tenth-century courts of Jerusalem. Many scholars assume that the Deuteronomistic historian had before him original documents from the time of the two kings. Recently, however, some scholars have questioned this assumption. They suggest instead that (a) Jerusalem did not become the centre of a state before the eighth century BCE; and (b) that writing in the court of Jerusalem did not antedate that century. They conclude that the history of the United Monarchy was composed only on the basis of oral traditions and is devoid of historical foundations (Jamieson-Drake 1991: 138-45; Knauf 1991a: 39; 1991b: 172; Thompson 1992: 409-10; 1995; Davies 1992: 67-70; Lemche 1994: 183-89; Lemche and Thompson 1994).

No extrabiblical source mentions either David or Solomon. This is not surprising. Detailed accounts on first millennium intra-state events appear for the first time in the ninth century BCE. All Syro-Palestinian inscriptions of the tenth century refer to local affairs and shed no light on international affairs. Even if David and Solomon accomplished the deeds attributed to them in the Bible, no source would have mentioned their names. The silence of tenth-century sources neither proves nor disproves the biblical account of the United Monarchy (*contra* Garbini 1988: 16; Knauf 1991b: 171-72).

There is one exception to the local nature of tenth-century inscriptions: the topographical list of Shishak. The Egyptian king left a long list of places conquered in the course of his Asiatic campaign. An analysis of the topographical list indicates that the campaign was directed against Israel and the non-Judahite parts of the Negev, avoiding almost entirely the kingdom of Judah.

Shishak's campaign is referred to in 1 Kgs 14.25-28. The text makes it clear that it deals largely with the handing over of Solomon's golden shields to Shishak and their replacement by copper shields. Details of the Egyptian campaign are minimal and its description is schematic. What might have been the source used by the historian for the description? In my opinion, it must have been a text in which appeared a datum that in the fifth year of Rehoboam golden shields were delivered to Shishak, king of Egypt, and were replaced by copper shields. The historian logically interpreted the datum to mean that Shishak's campaign, about which he had no other source, was directed against Jerusalem and that the treasures of the palace and the temple were then delivered to Egypt. He wrote long after the conclusion of the campaign he described and was therefore entirely dependent on his sources. His interpretation of Shishak's campaign may look incomplete and even misleading, but it does not conflict with historical reality: the campaign indeed reached the area of Jerusalem and a heavy tribute was paid to Egypt on that occasion (Na'aman 1992: 79-86, with earlier literature).

The account of Shishak's campaign in the book of Kings indicates that scribal activity took place in the court of Jerusalem in the late tenth century BCE. One would naturally assume that it was not introduced by a petty king like Rehoboam, but rather by one of his ancestors, either David or Solomon. Indeed, royal scribes are mentioned in David's and Solomon's lists of high officials (2 Sam. 8.17; 20.25; 1 Kgs 4.3). This accords with some records which are included in the history of Solomon and were probably drawn from old written sources. For example:

1. The list of Solomon's high officials (1 Kgs 4.2-6).
2. The list of Solomon's twelve officers and their districts (1 Kgs 4.9-19).
3. Details of Solomon's building activity in Jerusalem and elsewhere in his kingdom (1 Kgs 9.15, 17-18).

The list of David's officers (*šālīšîm*) (2 Sam. 23.8-39) is certainly drawn from a very old document. The lists of David's wives and sons (2 Sam. 3.2-5; 5.14-16) may have been extracted from an original list. The lists of his officials (2 Sam. 8.16-18; 20.23-26) may go back to an old document, but equally might have been drawn from the list of Solomon's officials, since most of the names in the latter were sons of those mentioned in the former.

I would like to suggest an epigraphic evidence which supports the assumption that scribal activity took place in Jerusalem already in the tenth century BCE. A widespread use of hieratic numerals and signs appears in Israelite and Judean ostraca and weights of the eighth–seventh centuries BCE. They do not appear in documents of Israel's neighbours, only in texts written in the Hebrew script. Egyptian relations with the Philistine and Phoenician kingdoms were much closer in the ninth–early eighth centuries than with Israel and Judah, and it is hardly conceivable that hieratic signs would then have entered only the Hebrew script. Moreover, no definite eighth–seventh century palaeographical parallels have been found in Egypt for many hieratic signs (Lemaire and Vernus 1983), and use of the so-called 'abnormal hieratic' was waning in Egypt at that time (Goldwasser 1991: 251 n. 2). It is clear that the hieratic signs entered the Hebrew script before the ninth century BCE.

Writing in hieratic is known from southern Canaan in the late thirteenth–twelfth centuries BCE. Goldwasser (1991: 251-52) has therefore suggested that Egyptian, or Egyptian-trained, scribes, cut off from their homeland in the late twelfth century, educated local Canaanite scribes, who in their turn passed on their knowledge to the new court of Israel, probably in the age of the United Monarchy.[1]

The long gap in the use of hieratic between the twelfth and early eighth centuries is greatly narrowed by the assumption that scribes entered the court of Jerusalem in the tenth century BCE, gradually developed the Hebrew script and spread their knowledge to north Israelite centres. Canaanite centres like Gaza, Ashkelon or Gezer could have been the transmitters of the proto-Canaanite scribal tradition in the early Iron Age.[2]

We may conclude that the appearance of hieratic numerals and signs in the Hebrew script of Israel and Judah strongly supports the assumption that scribal activity was introduced in the court of Jerusalem no later than the time of Solomon, and possibly already in David's time.

It is commonly accepted today that historiography developed in Judah no earlier than the eighth century BCE and that the Deuteronomistic history was composed either in the late seventh or early sixth century BCE. The earliest Judean inscriptions are dated to the second half of the eighth century and the spread of alphabetic writing in the kingdom took place only in the seventh century. Writing in the tenth–ninth centuries BCE must have been confined to a small group of scribes in the court of Jerusalem and was mainly used for administration and for diplomatic exchange.

2. The Chronicle of Early Israelite Kings

The majority of the narratives about David's rise to power and his time on the throne are not susceptible to source analysis. These stories may be examined according to literary, ideological and theological criteria. Their use as historical sources depends mainly on the trust of a scholar in the authenticity of biblical literature, on the assumption that they rest on oral traditions and are not mere literary novels, and on the belief that they include at least some germs of truth.

---

[1] There is also a possibility that the borrowing of hieratic signs and numerals took place directly from Egypt during the tenth century BCE (Goldwasser 1991: 251 n. 2).

[2] A somewhat similar problem is involved with the migration of the script from south Canaan to south Arabia. The latest proto-Canaanite inscriptions date from the twelfth century, whereas the earliest Sabaean inscriptions are no earlier than the eighth/seventh century BCE (Knauf 1989).

There are other accounts which relate historical episodes in a way that enables us to try analysing them as historical sources. Since my subject is 'composition and redaction', rather than the history of the United Monarchy, I will concentrate on tracing the sources which could have reached the author and enabled him to describe the history of David in a fairly reliable manner. The historicity of the accounts will be discussed only sporadically and briefly.

a. David's Wars with the Arameans

David's rival in his wars with the Arameans is called 'Hadadezer *ben* Rehob king of Zobah' (2 Sam. 8.3, 12). Scholars have long recognized that *'ben* Rehob' does not refer to Hadadezer's father, but rather to his land of origin, and that he was a king of Beth-rehob and Zobah. Two biblical references (Num. 13.21; Judg. 18.28) indicate that Beth-rehob covered most of the Beqa' of Lebanon, from the area north of Dan up to Lebo-hamath. Zobah is located in the northern Beqa' and northern Anti-Lebanon region, south of the kingdom of Hamath.

Winckler (1895: 141-43; 1901: 150) was the first to note the parallel between Hadadezer's epithet and that of Ba'asa '*mār Ruḫūbi* KUR *Amanaya*' of the monolith inscription of Shalmaneser III. It is well known that the Assyrians referred to many kingdoms by eponymic or dynastic names, and that the combination *mār Ruḫūbi* should be rendered 'son of Bīt-Ruḫūbi' (Ungnad 1906). Forrer (1932a; 1932b) proposed to identify KUR Amana with the Anti-Lebanon mountain range and that the text refers to the kingdom of Zobah located there. Thus, Hadadezer and Ba'asa were natives of Beth-rehob and their kingdom encompassed the regions of Beth-rehob and Zobah/Amana.

I have recently discussed the two dedication inscriptions to Hazael from Samos and Eretria (see Bron and Lemaire 1989; Eph'al and Naveh 1989) and suggested translating them thus: 'That which Hadad gave our lord Hazael from 'Amqi in the year that our lord crossed the River' (Na'aman forthcoming). 'Amqi, Hazael's place of birth, was a name for the Beqa' of Lebanon in the second millennium BCE and was mentioned in the Amarna letters and in texts from Ḫattusha. It seems to me that 'Amqi was a geographical name for Beth-rehob, just as Amana was a geographical name for Zobah. I further suggested that Hazael was the son of Ba'asa of Beth-rehob ('Amqi), who seized Damascus and unified for the first time these two major Aramean kingdoms. According to my analysis, Hadadezer, Ba'asa and Hazael were all natives of Beth-rehob and their ancestral kingdom included two regions: Beth-rehob/'Amqi and Zobah/Amana.

It seems to me that the figure of Hadadezer, '*ben* Rehob, king of Zobah', was modelled upon the historical figure of Hazael, his most successful heir to the throne of Beth-rehob. Several distinct features are common to the two kings:

1. Both originate from Beth-rehob and their ancestral kingdom has a dual structure.
2. The area under their hegemony extended from Transjordan in the south to the Euphrates. The extent of Hadadezer's domain in the south is indicated by the dispatch of his troops to help the Ammonites against David (2 Sam. 10.6-7), and in the north by his ability to mobilize troops from 'Aram, which is beyond the River' (2 Sam. 10.16). *Ēber ha-nāhār* is identical to Assyrian *Ēbir-nāri*, which refers to the areas west of the Euphrates. Also, David conducted a surprise attack on Hadadezer when he was on his way 'to leave/erect his stela on the River' (2 Sam. 8.3; 1 Chron. 18.13). 'The River' is, of course, the Euphrates. Hazael's hegemonic power in all the areas west of the Euphrates is indicated in several inscriptions and in the Bible (Lemaire 1992: 101-106, with earlier literature; 1993).
3. Both rulers headed a coalition of vassal kings. Thus according to 2 Sam. 10.16, following the Aramean defeat at Helam all the kings who were vassals of Hadadezer became Israel's vassals (2 Sam. 10.16). The list of Hazael's vassals is indicated by the stela of Zakkur, king of Hamath and Luaʻth (see Lemaire 1993).
4. Both were able to recruit for battle an enormous number of chariots and troops.
5. Aram Damascus was under their power. As suggested above, Hazael took over Damascus and usurped its throne and was therefore called by an Assyrian scribe 'the son of nobody'. No king of Damascus is mentioned in the account of David's wars. The absence of a king is explained by the assumption that the author deliberately described Damascus as a conquered district in Hadadezer's kingdom which sent troops to support its lord after his defeat (2 Sam. 8.5-6). It was only after David's death that Damascus became the seat of its own king (2 Kgs 11.23-24).

Hazael reigned in the second half of the ninth century BCE. Details of his political and military achievements were hardly known in the time of the Deuteronomistic historian (the late seventh or early sixth century BCE). The triple designation 'Hadadezer *ben* Rehob king of Zobah' (2 Sam. 8.3, 12) is known only from the ninth century, and the elliptic form *mār* PN to designate kingdoms ('son of Bīt-PN') scarcely appears after the eighth century BCE. I therefore suggest that a 'chronicle of early Israelite kings' was composed in the eighth century BCE, when the historical achievements of Hazael were still very much alive. Details of David's wars with the Arameans must have been quite vague at that time and the author of the chronicle tried to fill in the gaps with details borrowed from the late history of Hazael's kingdom. This early chronicle must have been one of the main sources on which the Deuteronomistic historian based his work (see below).

Clearly, our source about David's wars with the Arameans is problematic. Only the name of David's major enemy, his kingdom, the names of his general (Shobach) and his allies, the location of the battlefields, and the ultimate Israelite success in battle, may date back to the time of David. Unfortunately, there can be no unqualified certainty due to the great antiquity of these historical events.

b. David's Wars with the Philistines

The point of departure for the analysis is the discrepancy between the accounts of the United Monarchy and the reality of the time of the Deuteronomistic historian. According to biblical historiography, five Philistine kingdoms, each headed by a *seren*, ruled in the pre-monarchic and early monarchic periods. They were united in a kind of confederation and fought against Israel, until David defeated them and broke their power. On the other hand, the Assyrian inscriptions and biblical prophecies (Jer. 25.20; Amos 1.7-8; Zeph. 2.4; Zech. 9.5-6) mention only four Philistine kingdoms: Gaza, Ashkelon, Ashdod and Ekron. The city of Gath, which in David's early career appears as *primus inter pares* among the five Philistine kingdoms, was a border city of Ashdod from the mid-eighth century BCE. One may ask, what could have been the source available to the historian that caused him to depict the Philistines in a way that differed from the reality of his own time?

To answer this question let me examine the words of Amos (6.2) about Gath.

> Pass over to Calneh, and see; and thence go to Hamath the great; then go down to Gath of the Philistines. Are you better than these kingdoms? Or is their territory greater than your territory?

Gath appears in the text alongside two other capital cities—Calneh and Hamath. It is evident that the text refers to the three kingdoms of Unqi/Patina, Hamath and Gath. Since Gath lost its power before the time of Tiglath-Pileser III, the prophet may have been recalling past events which were better known to his audience than to us. Scholars usually examine the available sources, namely, the Assyrian inscriptions of the second half of the eighth century BCE, and assume that the text refers to events in the time of either Tiglath-Pileser or Sargon II. They therefore attribute the verse to a later disciple or redactor of Amos (Wolff 1977: 275; Paul 1991: 201-204; Blum 1994: 32-34, with earlier literature). However, relying on these late sources is like searching under the lamppost. Despite the paucity of sources, to interpret the prophecy properly we must look for events which took place before the prophet's time.

The history of Kullani (Kinalua) between its conquest by Dayyan-Ashur in 831 BCE and Tiglath-Pileser III's campaign of 738 is unknown (Michel 1955–56: 224-27; Hawkins 1974: 81-83). But it is evident that Arpad expanded in the late ninth–early eighth century BCE and that Patina/Unqi lost its former power and parts of its territories (Elliger 1947; Ponchia 1991: 91-96; Weippert 1993: 58-59). Amos could have been referring to the destruction and decline of Kullani in the course of the struggle for the hegemony of northern Syria during that time.

The capital of the kingdom of Hamath was transferred north, to the city of Hadrach (Ḥatarikka), during the late ninth century BCE. Hadrach remained the capital of the kingdom until its conquest and annexation by Tiglath-Pileser III in 738 (Sader 1987: 216-26, with earlier literature; Ponchia 1991: 96-97). The background for the transfer of the capital and the long decline of Hamath remains unknown (but see below). We may therefore speculate that it was the (possible) destruction and decline of Hamath that is alluded to in the prophecy.

According to the account of 2 Kings (12.17), Hazael king of Aram marched to Philistia and captured the city of Gath. It seems to me that this violent conquest put an end to the status of Gath as an independent state (see Hammershaimb 1970: 97-99). Later it was taken by Ashdod and became a border town within its territory (2 Chron. 26.6; Fuchs 1994: 134, line 250; 220, line 104). One may further suggest that Hazael likewise conquered and partly destroyed Hamath, Damascus's northern neighbour, an event which led to its long decline.[3] We may conclude that the warning words of Amos could be a reference to the destruction and desolation of three Syro-Palestinian capital cities in the late ninth century BCE.

The biblical scribe who described Gath as an independent kingdom governed by its own *seren* must have recalled the city's status prior to the time of Hazael. He must therefore have lived long before the time of the Deuteronomistic historian. The source available for the historian is again the chronicle of early Israelite kings, whose author lived in the eighth century BCE, not long after the time of Hazael.

According to 2 Sam. 5.17-25 (and 1 Chron. 14.8-16) David fought two decisive battles against the Philistines. The first was launched in the valley of Rephaim, and David won by a frontal attack. The second battle apparently took place near Gibeon and David launched a surprise night attack and smote the Philistines 'from Gibeon to Gezer' (1 Chron. 14.16) (Na'aman 1994: 253-54, with earlier literature). These two victories of David are referred to by the prophetic words of Isa. 28.21: 'For the Lord will rise up as on Mount Perazim, he will be wroth as in the valley of Gibeon'. Mount Perazim refers to Baal-perazim (replacing Baal by the common noun 'mount'), where David launched his first victory (2 Sam. 5.20; 1 Chron. 14.11); and the valley of Gibeon is the location of the second battle (1 Chron. 14.13, 16). Evidently, David's victories over the Philistines were still commemorated in the time of Isaiah (the late eighth century BCE).

---

[3] It is tempting to restore in the ivory inscription from Arslan-Tash '...in the year of the [captu]re of Ha[math]' (see Puech 1981). Unfortunately, the restoration cannot be verified.

2 Sam. 8.1 summarizes David's later wars with the Philistines thus: 'After this David defeated the Philistines and subdued them and David took *meteg hā-ammâ* out of the hand of the Philistines'. The opening words ('after this') may have appeared originally after 5.25; the sequential relationship of the two episodes is self-evident. It seems to me that 2 Sam. 5.17-25 is an expanded and elaborated description of the chronicle of early Israelite kings and that the text of 8.1 is a verbatim copy of the old text. It probably mentioned the five Philistine *s⁽e⁾rānîm*, and was the source for numerous narratives about the Israelite wars with the Philistines. The early chronicle must have been the main source for the historian. He used it in different manners: sometimes he copied it verbatim, or other times he expanded and elaborated it, and in still other cases it formed the narrow core around which a whole new story was built.

c. David's Wars against Israel's Neighbours

The text of 2 Sam. 8.1 may help us to reconstruct the early form of the chronicle. It first summarizes the results of David's wars with the Philistines, and then relates that he seized *meteg hā-ammâ* from them. Various suggestions have been made to decipher this enigmatic term (see e.g., Driver 1913: 279-80; Mittmann 1983: 327-32, with earlier literature; Kobayashi 1992: 800). It seems to me that *meteg hā-ammâ* refers to a distinct booty, similar to other distinct spoils mentioned at the close of episodes which describe David's wars against Israel's neighbours. Thus, following his victory over Zobah, David took the quivers of gold carried by the servants of Hadadezer (2 Sam. 8.7); and following the conquest of Rabbah he took the crown of the god Milkom (2 Sam. 12.30) (for discussion, see Horn 1973; Barthélemy 1982: 263-64). It seems to me that the conclusion of every war with a reference to a distinct booty is an original trait of the early chronicle and was adopted by the Deuteronomistic historian. A good parallel is offered by the Mesha inscription in which the capture of important towns culminates with the taking of a distinct spoil and its dedication to the god as his preferential share in the booty (*'r'l dwdh*; the vessels of Yhwh).

What could have been the text of the chronicle which served as the main source for the long narrative of David's war with the Ammonites? Isolating the old core in chs. 10–12 is impossible, and the first part of the early chronicle's account cannot be reconstructed. Its closing part was possibly copied verbatim in 2 Sam. 12.29-30aα: 'And David gathered all the people together and went to Rabbah, and fought against it and took it. And he took the crown of Milkom from his head.'

The core of the episode of the envoy from Hamath (2 Sam. 8.9-10) should also be attributed to the early chronicle. Only a scribe who was acquainted with the realities of the tenth–eighth centuries would have described so accurately the relations of Damascus and Hamath, and the common interests of Israel and Hamath vis à vis Aram. In the time of the Deuteronomistic historian, the former kingdoms of Damascus and Hamath were split into several provinces and the ancient situation was forgotten. The name of the king of Hamath, and possibly some details about the delegation, could have been derived from an old memory of the historical event, but this cannot be established with certainty.

Did the episodes of the wars against Moab and Edom (2 Sam. 8.2, 13-14) derive from the early chronicle? The two kingdoms were well established in the early eighth century BCE. Moreover, the episode of David's victory over the Edomites in the Valley of Salt (vv. 13-14) looks like a reflection of Amaziah's victory over them in the early eighth century (2 Kgs 14.7). In my opinion, this is another example of the device of borrowing military outlines of an actual event to depict an episode of the early history of Israel. Provided that this suggestion is acceptable, then the reign of Amaziah (about 799–771) provides a *terminus post quem* for the composition of the chronicle.

The depiction of David's extreme cruelty in his war with Moab (v. 2) is a reflection of the way that the Moabites treated Israel in the time of Mesha. It looks like a literary compensation for what the Moabites had done in their wars with Israel. In the framework of the literary revenge, the author attributed to David the subjugation of Moab and the killing of a large part of its population. The text must have originated from a time in which the desire for revenge was strongly felt in Israel. In the time of the Deuteronomistic historian, on the other hand, the memory of bloody wars between Moab and Israel had already faded, and the author had no account to settle with Moab. It seems therefore that the core of the two episodes of Moab and Edom should also be attributed to the chronicle of early Israelite kings.

3. The Library of the Deuteronomistic Historian

Few texts from the time of David and Solomon could have survived and reached the Deuteronomistic historian in their original form. They were all lists originally recorded for administrative purposes. Van Seters (1983: 4, 40-51, 195-99) noted that, as far as we know, historians of the old world did not consult archives when they wrote their histories (see Momigliano 1966: 212-17). He questioned the commonly held opinion that biblical authors consulted archives and retrieved information of great antiquity from old sources. It should be noted that documents are quoted in the books of Ezra and Nehemiah for determining rights, reflecting the use of archival sources at that time (Bickerman 1946; Momigliano 1977: 31-33). However, there is no evidence of a similar use of archival documents in earlier works. So, the assumption that the Deuteronomistic historian had searched in the archives of the palace and temple for source material for his composition cannot be sustained. Some other explanation must be sought for the lists which are included in the histories of David and Solomon.

I would like to suggest that these lists, and many other documents, originated from the Jerusalemite palace or temple library, where they were used for the education and training of scribes.[4] Redford (1986: 206-28) has examined the contents of temple libraries in Egypt in the second half of the first millennium BCE and concluded that they encompassed a wide range of materials with which the fully trained scribe was supposed to be familiar (e.g., king-lists, 'annals', inventories, letters, stories, ritual literature, reference compendia, etc.). This rich source material enabled Manetho to reconstruct the ancient history of Egypt in his *Aegyptiaca*. A Babylonian temple library (or libraries), which had a rich variety of texts (e.g., Sumerian and Akkadian myths and epics, king-lists, chronicles, ritual literature, etc.), likewise enabled Berossus to write the history of the country in his *Babyloniaca* (Komoróczy 1973; Drews 1975; Burstein 1978; Kuhrt 1987: 32-48).

The contents and scope of private libraries in Assyria in the seventh century BCE were studied by Parpola (1983: 8-10). He noted that they existed in considerable numbers in this period and could be quite comprehensive, containing hundreds of tablets. He further suggests (1983: 10) that 'the libraries of specialists in a given field by no means consisted of only their professional material but could include hundreds of works outside their field of specialization. This certainly indicates the broad education and, in some cases, deep learning of the individuals in question.' It may further be noted that about one-fifth of the 30,000 tablets and fragments in the private library of Ashurbanipal (see Lieberman 1990) are non-literary texts (e.g., legal and administrative texts, letters, reports, etc.) (Parpola 1983: 6; see Oppenheim 1964: 15-24). The library also contains the so-called 'epic literature', fables, proverbs, etc. This indicates the wide range of texts that may be found in a royal library in the late Iron Age period.

The range of texts in the library of Jerusalem was certainly narrower than the rich palace and temple libraries of Mesopotamia and Egypt, but included all that was necessary for the education of scribes and for their manifold functions in the kingdom (see Lemaire 1981: 72-82, with earlier literature; for a different opinion see Haran 1993). We may assume that sign-lists, letters, judicial texts, inventories, cultic texts, literary and historical works, all of which were essential for the education and function of royal Judean scribes, were part of the Jerusalem library.

Jerusalem was the capital of Judah for four centuries, and the contents of its library must have reflected this long continuity. Old texts of an archival character were apparently used for educational purposes and copied many times, and so survived until the destruction of 587/86 BCE. Some of those texts might have been attributed—correctly or not—to prominent past figures like David and Solomon,

---

[4] Jamieson-Drake (1991: 148-49, 151) made the plausible suggestion that scribal training took place primarily if not exclusively in Jerusalem and that all professional administrators were trained exclusively in Jerusalem. For a different opinion see Lemaire 1981: 46-54; 1984: 274-81.

and been transferred with this attribution into the stream of scribal learning. The chronicle of early Israelite kings and king-lists must have been part of this educational corpus. Likewise stories, such as the pre-Deuteronomistic narratives of King Saul and David's rise to power, might have been included in this corpus. Thus, when the historian composed his work he used this corpus as his main source for writing the history of Israel, just as Manetho and Berossus were able to use temple libraries for composing their respective *Aegyptiaca* and *Babyloniaca*. The attribution of texts to particular rulers may go back to old scribal traditions; their attribution by the historian may reflect his trust in the words of his sources. This may explain why his work was accepted by the scholarly elite of Jerusalem. Since he collected all the available sources and integrated them in his work, his description of the past did not conflict with what was known to other scholars. His competence as a historian and the clear and coherent picture that he drew made his work an authoritative source for all future study of the history of Israel.

Are we free to attribute the lists of David's officers and officials, and of his wives and sons, to his time? Certainty cannot be achieved in this matter. All that can legitimately be said is that the lists of names and the toponyms mentioned therein are very old and belong to an early stage of the Judean monarchy; and furthermore, that the historian could have had textual indications which caused him to attribute these lists to the era of David.

The chronicle of early Israelite kings was the major source from which the historian extracted details for the reconstruction of the chain of events in the time of the United Monarchy. The brief descriptions of Saul's kingship (1 Sam. 14.47-48) were perhaps extracted verbatim from that source. The passage about the coronation of Ishbaʻal, the son of Saul (2 Sam. 2.8), was possibly drawn from it. The episodes of David's reign in Hebron (2 Sam. 2.1-3), his struggle with Ishbaʻal, the conquest of Jebus (2 Sam. 5.6-9), the wars with the Philistines (2 Sam. 5.17-25), and his wars with Israel's neighbours—all these could have originated in the chronicle. Also, the episodes of the uprisings against Solomon (1 Kgs 11) were possibly drawn from the same source. The Deuteronomistic historian sometimes cited the chronicle verbatim, and in other instances used it according to his literary, ideological and theological objectives. Thus, in certain episodes we are able to reconstruct the original source, whereas in others it is worked into a whole narrative and cannot be reconstructed.

This evaluation of the source material shows plainly how complicated is the task of modern historians when they try to reconstruct the history of David. I will conclude my discussion with one example: the problem of the great kingdom attributed to David in biblical historiography.

According to the biblical account, the great kingdom was short-lived and fell apart after David's death. Since we are dealing with an episode that lasted perhaps for only a few years, and since there are no contemporary documents either to support or invalidate it, a clear-cut decision cannot be achieved. Let us compare it, for example, with the successive great kingdoms established by Yaḫdunlim, by Shamshi-Addu, and by Zimrilim in northern Mesopotamia in the late nineteenth–early eighteenth century BCE. Each of these kingdoms lasted for a few years and then disappeared. We are fortunate in having rich documentation for the three kingdoms, because otherwise their memory would have fallen into oblivion. They indicate the dynamic of changes at the stage of early state formation, and one can easily add many other examples to illustrate the phenomenon of the rapid growth and decline of states at that stage. In such a fluid situation, a talented and successful leader may conquer vast areas. It was not even necessary to have a permanent urban basis for such an achievement. The historical test is whether the conqueror and his heirs were able to keep the conquered areas and establish a permanent administration.

The opinion expressed by some scholars, of the impossibility of a Davidic great kingdom administered from Jerusalem (Garbini 1983: 1-16; 1988: 21-32; Jamieson-Drake 1991: 136-45; Knauf 1991b: 170-80; Thompson 1992: 331-34, 409-12; Davies 1992: 69), is, in my opinion, too rash. There is nothing impossible about the account of David's conquests—the only problem is whether or not it really happened. Unfortunately, the sources for this episode are of such a nature that we are unable to answer the question with a definite 'yes' or 'no'.

Bibliography

Barthélemy, D. 1982. *Critique textuelle de l'Ancien Testament*. I. *Josué, Juges, Ruth, Samuel, Rois, Chroniques, Esdras, Néhémie, Esther* (OBO, 50.1; Göttingen: Vandenhoeck & Ruprecht).
Bickerman, E.J. 1946. 'The Edict of Cyrus in Ezra 1', *JBL* 65: 249-75.
Blum, E. 1994. ' "Amos" in Jerusalem. Beobachtungen zu Am 6.1-7', *Henoch* 16: 23-47.
Bron, F., and A. Lemaire. 1989. 'Les inscriptions Araméennes de Hazaël', *RA* 83: 34-44.
Burstein, M.B. 1978. *The Babyloniaca of Berossus* (Sources from the Ancient Near East, 1.5; Malibu, CA: Undena Publications).
Davies, P.R. 1992. *In Search of 'Ancient Israel'* (JSOTSup, 148; Sheffield: JSOT Press).
Drews, R. 1975. 'The Babylonian Chronicles and Berossus', *Iraq* 37: 39-55.
Driver, S.R. 1913. *Notes on the Hebrew Text and the Topography of the Books of Samuel* (Oxford: Clarendon Press).
Elliger, K. 1947. 'Sam'al und Hamat in ihrem Verhältnis zu Hattina, Unqi and Arpad', in J. Fück (ed.), *Festschrift Otto Eissfeldt zum 60. Geburtstage* (Halle: Max Niemeyer): 69-108.
Eph'al, I., and J. Naveh. 1989. 'Hazael's Booty Inscriptions', *IEJ* 39: 192-200.
Forrer, E. 1932a. 'Aram', *RLA* 1: 134.
Forrer, E. 1932b. 'Ba'asa', *RLA* 1: 328.
Fuchs, A. 1994. *Die Inschriften Sargon II. aus Khorsabad* (Göttingen: Cuvillier Verlag).
Garbini, G. 1983. 'L'impero di David', *Annali della Scuola Normale Superiore di Pisa* 13: 1-20.
Garbini, G. 1988. *History and Ideology in Ancient Israel* (London: SCM Press).
Goldwasser, O. 1991. 'An Egyptian Scribe from Lachish and the Hieratic Tradition of the Hebrew Kingdoms', *Tel Aviv* 18: 248-53.
Hammershaimb, E. 1970. *The Book of Amos: A Commentary* (Oxford: Basil Blackwell).
Haran, M. 1993. 'Archives, Libraries, and the Order of the Biblical Books', *JANES* 22: 51-61.
Hawkins, D.J. 1974. 'Assyrians and Hittites', *Iraq* 36: 67-83.
Horn, S. 1973. 'The Crown of the King of the Ammonites', *AUSS* 11: 170-80.

Jamieson-Drake, D.W. 1991. *Scribes and Schools in Monarchic Judah: A Socio-Archaeological Approach* (The Social World of Biblical Antiquity, 9; JSOTSup, 109; Sheffield: JSOT Press).

Knauf, E.A. 1989. 'The Migration of the Script and the Formation of the State in South Arabia', *Proceedings of the Seminar for Arabian Studies* 19: 79-91.

Knauf, E.A. 1991a. 'From History to Interpretation', in D.V. Edelman (ed.), *The Fabric of History: Text, Artifact and Israel's Past* (JSOTSup, 127; Sheffield: JSOT Press): 26-64.

Knauf, E.A. 1991b. 'King Solomon's Copper Supply', in E. Lipiński (ed.), *Phoenicia and the Bible* (OLA, 44; Leuven: Peeters): 167-86.

Kobayashi, Y. 1992. 'Methegh-ammah', *ABD* IV: 800.

Komoróczy, G. 1973. 'Berosos and the Mesopotamian Literature', *Acta Antiqua Academiae Scientiarum Hungaricae* 21: 125-52.

Kuhrt, A. 1987. 'Berossus' *Babyloniaka* and Seleucid Rule in Babylonia', in A. Kuhrt and S. Sherwin-White (eds.), *Hellenism in the East* (London: Gerald Duckworth): 32-56.

Lemaire, A. 1981. *Les écoles et la formation de la Bible dans l'Ancien Israël* (Fribourg and Göttingen: Universitätsverlag).

Lemaire, A. 1984. 'Sagesse et Ecoles', *VT* 34: 270-81.

Lemaire, A. 1991. 'Hazaēl de Damas, roi d'Aram', in D. Charpin and F. Joannès (eds.), *Marchands, diplomates et empereurs. Etudes sur la civilisation Mésopotamienne offertes à Paul Garelli* (Paris: Editions Recherche sur les Civilisations): 91-108.

Lemaire, A. 1993. 'Joas de Samarie, Barhadad de Damas, Zakkur de Hamat. La Syrie-Palestine vers 800 av. J.-C.', *Eretz Israel* 24: 148-57.

Lemaire, A., and P. Vernus 1983. 'L'ostracon paléo-hébreu no. 6 de Tell Qudeirat (Qadesh-Barnea)', in M. Görg (ed.), *Pontes atque Fontes. Eine Festgabe für Hellmut Brunner* (Wiesbaden: Otto Harrassowitz): 302-26.

Lemche, N.P. 1994. 'Is it Still Possible to Write a History of Israel?', *SJOT* 8: 165-90.

Lemche, N.P., and T.L. Thompson 1994. 'Did Biran Kill David? The Bible in the Light of Archaeology', *JSOT* 64: 3-22.

Lieberman, S.J. 1990. 'Canonical and Official Cuneiform Texts: Towards an Understanding of Assurbanipal's Personal Tablet Collection', in T. Abusch, J. Huehnergard and P. Steinkeller (eds.), *Lingering over Words: Studies in Ancient Near Eastern Literature in Honor of William L. Moran* (Atlanta, GA: Scholars Press): 305-36.

Michel, E. 1955–56. 'Die Assur-Texte Salmanassars III (858–824)', *WdO* 2: 137-57, 221-33.

Mittmann, S. 1983. 'Die "Handschelle" der Philister (2 Sam 8,1)', in M. Görg (ed.), *Pontes atque Fontes. Eine Festgabe für Hellmut Brunner* (Wiesbaden: Otto Harrassowitz): 327-41.

Momigliano, A. 1966. 'Historiography on Written Tradition and Historiography on Oral Tradition', *Studies in Historiography* (London: Weidenfeld and Nicolson): 211-20.

Momigliano, A. 1977. 'Eastern Elements in Post-Exilic Jewish, and Greek, Historiography', in *Studies in Ancient and Modern Historiography* (Oxford: Basil Blackwell): 25-35.

Na'aman, N. 1992. 'Israel, Edom and Egypt in the 10th Century B.C.E.', *Tel Aviv* 19: 71-93.

Na'aman, N. 1994. 'The "Conquest of Canaan" in the Book of Joshua and in History', in I. Finkelstein and N. Na'aman (eds.), *From Nomadism to Monarchy. Archaeological and Historical Aspects of Early Israel* (Jerusalem: Yad Izhak Ben-Zvi and Israel Exploration Society): 218-81.

Na'aman, N. forthcoming. 'Hazael of 'Amqi and Hadadezer of Beth-Rehob', *UF* 27.

Oppenheim, A.L. 1964. *Ancient Mesopotamia* (Chicago: University of Chicago Press).

Parpola, S. 1983. 'Assyrian Library Records', *JNES* 42: 1-29.

Paul, S.M. 1991. *Amos* (Hermeneia; Minneapolis, MN: Fortress Press).

Ponchia, S. 1991. *L'Assyria e gli stati transeufratici nella prima metà dell'VIII sec. a.C.* (Padova: Sargon srl).

Puech, E. 1981. 'L'ivoire inscrit d'Arslan-Tash et les rois des Damas', *RB* 88: 544-62.

Redford, D.B. 1986. *Pharaonic King-Lists, Annals and Day-Books* (Mississauga: Benben Publications).

Sader, H.S. 1987. *Les états Araméens de Syrie depuis leur formation jusqu'à leur transformation en provinces Assyriens* (Beirut: Orient-Institut der Deutschen Morgenländischen Gesellschaft).

Thompson, T.L. 1992. *The Early History of the Israelite People: From the Written and Archaeological Sources* (Leiden: Brill).

Thompson, T.L. 1995. ' "House of David": An Eponymic Referent to Yahweh as Godfather', *SJOT* 9: 59-74.

Ungnad, A. 1906. 'Jaua, mâr Ḫumrî', *OLZ* 9: 224-26.

Van Seters, J. 1983. *In Search of History: Historiography in the Ancient World and the Origins of Biblical History* (New Haven, CT: Yale University Press).

Weippert, M. 1993. 'Die Feldzüge Adadniraris III. nach Syrien. Voraussetzungen, Verlauf, Folgen', *ZDPV* 108: 42-67.

Winckler, H. 1895. *Geschichte Israels in Einzeldarstellungen*, I (Leipzig: Pfeiffer).

Winckler, H. 1901. 'Besprechungen zu Kittel, R. Die Bücher der Könige übers u. erklärt', *OLZ* 4: 141-52.

Wolff, H.W. 1977. *Joel and Amos* (Hermeneia; Philadelphia, PA: Fortress Press).

David and the Philistines: Literature and History

Walter Dietrich

In Biblical exegesis, one can distinguish between two methodologies of reading the text: synchronic and diachronic. The former addresses the literary or canonical setting of texts, the literary tools used to present certain themes or stories, and the literary artistry in forming the biblical text. The latter concentrates on the place of a text or of a text layer within the history of biblical literature and on its historical and ideological proximity to the issues it presents. In my examination of the relationship between David and the Philistines I use both these perspectives to analyze relevant texts in the books of Samuel, finally proposing a historical evaluation.[1]

I. Literary Analysis

The expressions פלשתי/פלשתים could be considered a leading motif in the narrative of David in the books of Samuel. It can be found in 1 Sam 16–2 Sam 24 no less than 157 times. Of those, 33 are expressed in singular, of which 32 concern

---

[1] Information on the subject of 'David and the Philistines' is found only in the Bible, hence our focus on the Bible, particularly on the books of Samuel. The relevant information in Chronicles shows dependence on the books of Samuel (In the Chronicler's narrative about David [1 Chron 11–29] the incidence of the word פלשתים is relatively low: 1 Chron 11:13,14,15,18; 12:20; 14:8,9,10,13,15,16; 12:19; 18:1,11; 20:4,5.) Secondary, or rather tertiary are two other texts from late antiquity, which celebrate David as conqueror over the Philistines or, more precisely, over Goliath: a passage in the 'Praise of the fathers' by Jesus Sirach (Sir 46:4–8), and the last passage of Psalm 151, an addition to the Psalter in the Septuagint (Ps 151:6–7). The Greek text of the two verses reads as follows: εξηλθον εις συναντησιν τω αλλοφυλω και επικατηρασατο με εν τοις ειδωλοις αυτου εγω δε σπασαμενος την παρ' αυτου μαχαιραν απεκεφαλισα αυτον και ηρα ονειδος εξ υιων ισραηλ ("I went outside to the meeting with the Philistine and he cursed me by his idols; but I pulled out the sword on his side, beheaded him and took away the disgrace from the sons of Israel"). In the Hebrew version of Ps 151 found in Qumran, only vv. 1–5 (concerning David's youth and anointing) survived intact, whereas vv. 6–7 are fragmentary.

Goliath.² The 124 occurrences in plural become more frequent in the narratives of David's rise (1 Sam 18–2 Sam 8) and in the so-called annex/appendix to the books of Samuel (2 Sam 20–24). In the so-called Succession History (2 Sam 9–20; 1 Kgs 1–2) there are only few פלשתי/פלשתים in evidence.³

The term "Philistine" appears in the stories about David mostly within certain semantic fields. The most important of these is the military one (with verbs such as 'to troop up', 'to gather', 'to march-out', 'to battle', 'to defeat', 'to take flight', etc.). Thereby the Philistines figure foremost as foes, as opponents in war. The impression of the (military) danger they pose is intensified by reference to their foreign ethnicity and religion; the adjective ערל, 'uncircumcised' and the noun ערלה are repeatedly linked to the noun פלשתי/פלשתים⁴ clearly alienating the Philistines from the covenant between Yhwh and Israel, which is sealed through circumcision.⁵

With regard to David's relationship with the Philistines, a remarkable fluctuation between conflict and cooperation can be noticed:

Conflict: In the beginning of his career, David appears as a staunch enemy of the Philistines. After beating the spearhead Goliath (1 Sam 17), he repeatedly marches out against them on Saul's orders (1 Sam 18:17–30; 19:8). An attempt to flee to Philistia from Saul's persecution fails, because hate and fear of David are too widespread there (1 Sam 21:11–16). Consequently, he seeks to establish himself in the village of Keilah, which he had saved from the Philistine grasp. But again he has to withdraw, threatened by Saul's plan to capture him there (1 Sam 23:1–13).

Cooperation: During the time of persecution by Saul, it is the Philistines who practically save David's life (1 Sam 23:27, 28; 24:2) finally granting him a hideout for a considerable length of time and even making him governor of Ziklag (1 Sam 27). As their vassal, he prepares to march on their side into the crucial battle against Saul, ultimately stopped by the Philistine commanders (1 Sam 29).

Conflict: David laments the Philistine victory on the mountains of Gilboa as a personal and political catastrophe (2 Sam 1:19–27). As king of Judah and Israel he revokes the subjection to the Philistines. When he approaches Ish-bosheth's Israel, his merits in the battle against the Philistines are

---

² The exception is 2 Sam 21:17.
³ 2 Sam 19:10 and notably 2 Sam 15:18–22; 18:2, where a troop of 600 men from the Philistine town of Gath is mentioned. Gath—the hometown of Goliath, cf. 1 Sam 17:4; 2 Sam 21:19—is encountered repeatedly in the so-called History of David's Rise (1 Sam 21:11,13; 27:2,3,4,11; 2 Sam 1:20; 4:3) and in the so-called History of the Ark (1 Sam 5:8; 6:17; 2 Sam 6:10,11).
⁴ 1 Sam 17:26, 36; 18:25, 27; 31:4; 2 Sam 1:20; 3:14.
⁵ Cf. Gen 17:9–14.

cited (2 Sam 3:14, 18).[6] After David settles in Jerusalem, the Philistines initiate two combats, both of which they lose (2 Sam 5:17–25). With the Lord giving David "rest from all his enemies around him" (2 Sam 7:1), the Philistines take the first place in the list of his defeated enemies (2 Sam 8:1, cf. 8:12).

Cooperation: According to the biblical account, David's attention to the Philistines diminished in his further reign. Only in the highly menacing crisis of the uprising of Absalom they seem an important factor. At that time, only his professional troops actually stood by David. Among them was the elite unit of the כרתי ופלתי, the "Cherethites and Pelethites" (2 Sam 15:18). It is possible that the second term refers to the Philistines,[7] but it is not certain.[8] Not in doubt, on the other hand, is the origin of a 600-men troop under the charge of a certain Ittai from the Philistine city Gath (2 Sam 15:18–22). This support is important enough to David to entrust Ittai with the command of his troops, next to Joab and Abishai, two proven Judean commanders (2 Sam 18:2).

Conflict: In the so-called annex to the books of Samuel there are two series of anecdotes, which tell of many victorious fights with the Philistines. Most of these feature David's warriors as acting subjects (2 Sam 21:16–21; 23:9–12), but obviously he himself acts as the leader in the combats (21:15, 22; 23:13–17). Here he appears again, as in the beginning, as a notable foe of the Philistines.

This fluctuation between conflict and cooperation reflects a dilemma, in which the authors of the books of Samuel found themselves. On the one hand, the Philistines were Israel's most dangerous enemy during the foundation of the state; indeed, the first king of Israel, with three of his sons (and presumably also a large number of warriors), died in a combat against them. On the other hand, it was well

---

[6] Here belongs also David's earlier diplomatic hint to the inhabitants of Jabesh-Gilead (2 Sam 2:4–7) who excelled themselves in salvaging Saul's honour, abused by the Philistines (1 Sam 31:11–13).

[7] In this case, פלתי would be an abrasion of פלשתי in favour of the assonance with כרתי; and כרתי is mostly understood as 'Cretans', well-matched with the undeniable origin of the Philistines from the Aegean region.

[8] J. Van Seters (*The Biblical Saga of King David* [Winona Lake, IN 2009], pp. 106–107) connects the two terms with Greek mercenaries: the 'Peltastes'—light-armed Hellenistic soldiers—and 'Cretan archers', both of them known from Hellenistic sources and therefore in Van Seters' eyes completely anachronistic in texts of the 10th century BCE. For a critique of his radical late dating of the Samuel traditions see my 2010 review in *RBL:* http://www.bookreviews.org/BookDetail.asp?TitleId=7252. Cf. the rejection of analogous statements of the so-called Copenhagen School by L. E. Stager, "Biblical Philistines: A Hellenistic Literary Creation?", in A. M. Maeir and P. de Miroschedji (eds.), *"I Will Speak the Riddles of Ancient Times." Festschrift Amihai Mazar, I* (Winona Lake, IN 2006), pp. 375–384.

known that David maintained close relations with that very enemy. Thus, the conclusion, that he could have been responsible together with the Philistines for the downfall of the first Israelite royal dynasty, naturally suggests itself.[9] The authors of the books of Samuel met this suspicion with great caution. One of their strategies is to present the early and the late David as a radical enemy of the Philistines, while interpreting the cooperative phases in between as caused by pure hardship: in one case, Saul's grim hostility, in another Absalom's dangerous uprising. This implies that David basically was an enemy of the Philistines, but was sometimes forced into an alliance with them.

Admittedly, this solution creates a new problem: If David had always been such an avowed enemy of the Philistines, how could they make him a vassal and even a governor of a city? One endeavour to tackle this problem can be found in the little scene in 1 Sam 21:11–16. David's first attempt to put himself under Philistine protection fails here, precisely because the Philistines know him as a foe, even quoting the popular song "Saul has killed thousands, and David his tens thousands". Being presented as such a major adversary of the Philistines—ten times more dangerous than Saul—puts David at this moment in grave danger that he can just barely dodge. Some chapters later, David's second attempt to escape to the Philistine city Gath is also carefully manoeuvred by the narrators. Against their habit, they provide a glimpse into the inner life of a character: "David said in his heart: I shall now perish one day by the hand of Saul: there is nothing better for me than to escape to the land of the Philistines; then Saul will despair of seeking me any longer within the borders of Israel, and I shall escape out of his hand" (1 Sam 27:1).[10] During his last encounter with Saul, David reveals to him the significance of his forced flight to Philistia: "they have driven me out today from my share in the heritage of Yhwh saying: 'Go serve other gods'" (1 Sam 26:19). The forced displacement signifies for David the loss not only of his own homeland, but also of the land of God.[11]

---

[9] This suspicion is explicitly raised—admittedly without mention of the Philistines—in the biblical account itself: Shim'i, a Saulide, confronts David at his moment of greatest peril saying that: "the blood of the house of Saul" is now avenged on him (2 Sam 16:8).

[10] D. Jobling ("David and the Philistines. With Methodological Reflections", in W. Dietrich [ed.], *David und Saul im Widerstreit – Diachronie und Synchronie im Wettstreit. Beiträge zur Auslegung des ersten Samuelbuches* [OBO 206, Fribourg – Göttingen, 2004], pp. 74–85, esp. 83) understands the literary character of David as an aberration from the promise given to him by several speakers in the commission of God (see 1 Sam 23:17; 25:30; 24:20). According to Jobling this is a "subterranean presence ... of an antimonarchical current" inherent in the Deuteronomistic History. This may be so when viewing the biblical account from a Deuteronomistic perspective, but this particular report is pre-Deuteronomistic, see chapter II of the present article.

[11] Behind it is the archaic, distinctly pre-monotheistic perception whereupon a god is only responsible for a certain territory and its population. Cf. on this W. Dietrich, *Theopolitik. Studien zur Theologie und Ethik des Alten Testaments* (Neukirchen-Vluyn, 2003), pp. 43–57 ("Grenzen göttlicher Macht nach dem Alten Testament").

This time, David is welcomed in Gath without any trouble (1 Sam 27:2–3)—but why?[12] Do the narrators reckon that in the meantime his shattered relationship with Saul has become known there too? Or do the 600 men he brings with him this time[13] make an impression on Achish, king of Gath? Either way, David becomes his vassal and the governor of the city of Ziklag. Henceforth, in this role he plays cat and mouse with his feudal lord. This starts with the fact, that he does not undertake raids to the east, into the region of Judah, as he leads Achish to believe, but towards the south, in the direction of the Negev (1 Sam 27:8–12)—apparently not to have a fall out with the Judeans (and Israelites).[14] There is a dramatic increase in tension before the decisive battle against Saul. The reader is taken aback when he hears how Achish reminds his vassal of his military duties regarding the upcoming battle (1 Sam 28:1). David's reaction is very diplomatic: "You shall know what your servant can do" (28:2). Does Achish really know? The reader knows that he actually does not.[15] And David does not say this time, what he has in mind to 'do'. When he and his men are mustered with the Philistine troops, the old mistrust reawakens and again, the song about the ten thousands he has slain is quoted (1 Sam 29:1–5). Achish has to send the suspicious combatant home. And again David's reaction is of remarkable ambiguity: He would really have liked to march into the battle, to "fight against the enemies of my lord, the king" (1 Sam 29:8). Of course, Achish thinks that he himself is David's "lord, the king", but David (and the reader) could just as well be thinking of Saul.[16] Had David been allowed to move north with the Philistines, he would have fought with Israel against them! Unfortunately they suspected as much and prevented it.[17]

---

[12] On this problem see J. Klein, "Davids Flucht zu den Philistern (1 Sam. XXI 11ff; XXVII–XXIX)", *VT* 55 (2005), pp. 176–184.

[13] 1 Sam 21:11–16 relates that David undertook the first attempt of crossing over to the Philistines as a single fugitive; only in 22:1–2 is it being discussed that he gathered a troop (at first of 400 men).

[14] Hither belongs also the account in 1 Sam 30:26–31, according to which David distributed plunder from a successful Amalekite campaign.

[15] R. Polzin (*Samuel and the Deuteronomist. A Literary Study of the Deuteronomic History*, Part 2, 1 Samuel [Bloomington, IN 1989], p. 217) speaks with respect to the deceived Achish "of David's growing duplicity", which gives the impression that the "story of David's rise to power is contrived as much against him as for him". P. D. Miscall on the other hand thinks that the deception of Achish is an expression of David's fear of him (*1 Samuel. A Literary Reading* [Bloomington, IN 1986], p. 166).

[16] In distinction from this, P. D. Miscall (ibid., p. 175) maintains: "we will not finally know whether David would or would not desert the Philistines and fight with Saul and Israel. Is David servant to Achish or Saul, to both, to neither?" In my opinion, the narrator leads the reader to see David as a true but hindered supporter of Israel.

[17] Jobling (op. cit. [note 10], p. 82) rejects this reading with the argument that, if David had, together with Israel, defeated the Philistines, this "would presumably have left Saul and Jonathan alive. Where could the story go then?" This question however is not of the sort of queries biblical authors are posing. To them, God would have found a way to solve this problem—had there not been the mistrust of the Philistines.

Subsequently the narrator stresses that David was as far away as possible from the battlefield. From the place of gathering near Aphek[18] he moves southwards, while the Philistines go northeast. When he reaches Ziklag (after a three day's march) and discovers that the place has been raided and plundered, he moves even further south, deep into the Negev, to retrieve the booty from the brigands, a mission successfully accomplished (1 Sam 30). On the third day after his return, a man appears in Ziklag and brings him the news of the death of Saul and Jonathan, along with the corresponding evidence (2 Sam 1:1–10). It must have taken this messenger about three days from Gilboa to Ziklag, thus the battle must have taken place in the far north, while David was in the deepest south.

II. Historical-Critical Examination

As many biblical texts, the books of Samuel should be seen as literature brought forth by tradition, not authors. This means that they are not the product of one author, like a historical novel, but grew over several stages of tradition. My present assessment is that there are three main stages or strands, which may be described as follows, from the later to the earlier:[19] (1) During the 6th and 5th centuries BCE the Deuteronomistic redaction enriched the books of Samuel with some substantial texts[20] and, by doing so, made them part of the great historiography that extended from the settlement to the exile (Deut – 2 Kgs); (2) In the late-8th century or early-7th century BCE a 'Court History of the Early Monarchy' was formed. It depicted the story from Samuel to Solomon thus comprising large parts of the present text corpus 1 Sam 1 – 1 Kgs 2 or 12 (less the Dtr texts and the annex 2 Sam 21–24); (3) The author of the 'Court History' incorporated older sources of different kinds and sizes, which each had its own history of tradition. Only a few of these sources could go back to the 10th century, and if they did, they would have been changed in the period that followed and when incorporated into the 'Court History'.

The texts about 'David and the Philistines' will now be assigned to these three narrative strands.

1. The Deuteronomistic History

The Deuteronomists obviously did not show further interest in the subject of the Philistines. The reason may be that with the Babylonian conquest of the Levant, the Philistine cities had disappeared from the political arena as independent entities. So the exilic and postexilic redactors handed down the pertinent material

---

[18] This Aphek should be looked for in the coastal plain, cf. 1 Sam 4:1.
[19] Cf. W. Dietrich, *Samuel*, I (BKAT VIII; Neukirchen-Vluyn, 2011), pp. 38*–58*.
[20] Especially 1 Sam 8; 12; 15; 2 Sam 7, are to be mentioned here.

they found in the story of David, without discernibly adding accents of their own. However, this overall picture changes when the annex 2 Sam 21–24 is assumed to have been installed by this redaction (and not subsequently).[21] The many anecdotes about battles against the Philistines in these chapters can be seen as a corrective to the abandonment of the subject matter in the later stories about David. In the annex the relations between David and the Philistines come again to the foreground, giving the impression that they ended in sharp confrontation.

2. The Court History

By contrast, in the Court History of the Early Monarchy David's relations with the Philistines gain great relevance. This comes as no surprise, since in this oeuvre 'Saul versus David', 'the Saulides versus the Davidides' and 'Israel versus Judah' are central themes that invite comparison between the sides regarding how they dealt with the Philistines. Saul emerges as a constant enemy of the Philistines throughout his career, David—only temporarily. Saul failed in the struggle, David did not.

In my opinion, this constellation suggested to the author of the Court History a transparent parallel to his own time. To realize this, one has to think of the Assyrians instead of the Philistines. In 720 BCE Samaria was conquered by the Assyrians.[22] In this, Judah played a doubtful role from the perspective of the Israelites.[23] A few years earlier, Judah became an Assyrian vassal, but unlike its northern neighbour continued to exist as such. Fugitives from the north poured into Judah, which thus became the trustee of both the Judean and the Israelite heritage.[24]

It seems that the Court History deals with these problems of the present by reflecting them into the time of the early monarchy. The position of the author is a Judean one, but he shows a great degree of openness towards the concerns of the Israelites. The whole story of Samuel and Saul (1 Sam 1–3; 7–14) takes place

---

[21] Thus T. Veijola, *Die Ewige Dynastie. David und die Entstehung seiner Dynastie nach der deuteronomistischen Darstellung* (Helsinki, 1975), pp. 124–126, who saw here DtrN at work – the last out of three formative deuteronomistic redactions.

[22] For the last years of the Kingdom of Israel and the fall of Samaria see G. Galil, *The Chronology of the Kings of Israel and Judah* (Leiden – New York – Köln, 1996), pp. 83–97, with earlier literature.

[23] In the so-called Syro-Ephraimite War (ca. 734 BCE), Judah had called the Assyrians for help against the allied Israelites and Arameans (cf. 2 Kgs 16:5–9). As the consequence, Israel was reduced to a remnant state (2 Kgs 15:29); and at the last desperate battle of remnant Israel against the Assyrians, Judah apparently played the part of passive bystander (cf. 2 Kgs 17:4–6).

[24] A specific Israelite heritage is to be discerned in the traditions about Jacob, Moses-Exodus, the settlement (a kernel of Josh 1–10), the Judges, the prophet Hosea and more. Besides this, the idea of a 12-tribe-Israel was always vivid in biblical thinking, cf. for instance Gen 29–30; Josh 13–19; 1 Chron 1–10.

in the north. Saul's struggle for the preservation of his power, the increasing deformation of his personality and the disastrous battle against the Philistines are described with much empathy. However the reader is given to understand that the north did not have a real chance under the reign of the Saulides. Its future lay in David's hands, who managed to withstand the Philistines deviously and powerfully. The hidden sense of this message would presumably have its appeal in the late-8th century or early-7th century BCE.

The author of the Court History deals with the subject matter of the Philistines in the books of Samuel mainly in two turning points: the beginning of David's ascent and the end of Saul's life. In the former he makes it plain that David (later the vassal of the Philistines) initially was a fierce enemy of the Philistines, in the latter he emphasizes that David (although a vassal of the Philistines) had nothing to do with Israel's disaster.

We start with the latter. As we noted, David comments twice on how and why he had to flee to the Philistines and how difficult this was for him: once in a speech to Saul, the other time to himself (1 Sam 26:19–20; 27:1). It is a fundamental insight of the research in redaction criticism that in narrating older traditions the editors or composers would insert their own thoughts and interpretations into direct speeches of the characters.[25] Here it is the author of the Court History, who tries to put the inconvenient fact that for some time David was a vassal of the Philistines in a David-friendly perspective.

1 Sam 29 consists almost entirely of direct speeches: the Philistines discuss whether they should trust David (1 Sam 29:3–5); and Achish explains to David the necessity of his return (1 Sam 29:6–10). Only in the narrative frame are there some short reports: the Philistine troops gather in Aphek, the Israelite troops at the fountain of Jezreel (29:1); the Philistines make a parade (29:2a), in which David and his men also take part (29:2b); finally, David heads for Ziklag (29:11a), the Philistines towards Jezreel (29:11b). If the reports about David (29:2b, 11a), as well as the long speeches (29:3–10) are left out, there remains only a brief account of the concentration and the advance of the Philistine troops (29:1, 2a, 11b). This, indeed, is probably what the author of the Court History found in his sources; everything else he added himself in order to keep David out of the battle at Gilboa.

In all likelihood, this author is also responsible for the subtle geographic scheme, by which David is kept as far away as possible from the defeat of Saul and Israel.

Thereby he arranged the (older) material so that reports from the north alternate regularly and continuously with those from the south, intensifying the impression of a great spatial distance:

---

[25] As regards the speeches of David (and Saul's) in 1 Sam 24 and 26 I have demonstrated this in an extensive analysis: W. Dietrich, "Die zweifache Verschonung Sauls durch David (I Sam 24 und I Sam 26). Zur ‚diachronen Synchronisierung' zweier Erzählungen", in W. Dietrich (ed.), *David und Saul im Widerstreit – Diachronie und Synchronie im Wettstreit. Beiträge zur Auslegung des ersten Samuelbuchs* (OBO 206; Fribourg – Göttingen, 2004), pp. 232–253.

North: The Philistines march against Israel (1 Sam *29).
South: David returns to Ziklag, pursues the Amalekites in the Negev and distributes the prey to villages in Judah (1 Sam 30).
North: The Israelites are defeated by the Philistines; Saul and his sons are killed, their corpses desecrated, but finally buried (1 Sam 31).
South: David hears of the disaster and laments bitterly (2 Sam 1).[26]

The message to the readership is crystal clear: Although David was in the service of the Philistines at that time, he had nothing to do with Israel's defeat and Saul's death.

The same careful attention apparent in his construction of the passages about David as a vassal of the Philistines, the author of the Court History devoted also to the *young* David as an enemy of the Philistines. This is most evident in 1 Sam 18. Saul, as we learn, offered David marriage with his elder daughter Merab and in return asked David to be valiant (בן חיל) and fight the "battles of Yhwh" (מלחמות יהוה; 1 Sam 18:17a).[27] Such a deal between a soldier king and a competent warrior is quite plausible. It is not stated against whom David should fight; according to the list in 1 Sam 14:47–48 it could be any of the neighbours: Moabites, Ammonites, Edomites, Arameans, Philistines, or Amalekites. But in 18:17b a closer definition of the enemy is given: "For Saul said [to himself]: Not my hand shall be against him, but the hand of the Philistines". This monologue is easily recognizable as the contribution of the Court Historian, turning a fair deal into an underhanded move: the marriage offer now looks as a mere ruse to send David to his doom.

Only a few verses earlier, it can be seen how mistrust of David awakens in Saul. When the women sang the song that honoured David more than him (1 Sam 18:7), Saul became furious and "said [to himself]: 'They have ascribed to David tens of thousands, and to me they have ascribed thousands; what more can he have but the kingdom?' So Saul eyed David from that day on" (1 Sam 18:8–9). This is another monologue verbalized by the Court Historian.

Nothing became of the marriage with Merab; it seems that Saul preferred another son-in-law (1 Sam 18:19).[28] But when his younger daughter Michal fell in

---

[26] To dissociate David from Saul's death not only geographically but also mentally, this lament (2 Sam 1:17–27) is quoted from a separate book. Moreover, the Amalekite messenger who claims to have given the mortal blow to Saul must die (2 Sam 1:13–16).

[27] I. Willi-Plein ("Michal und die Anfänge des Königtums in Israel", in I. Willi-Plein, *Sprache als Schlüssel. Gesammelte Aufsätze zum Alten Testament* [Neukirchen-Vluyn, 2002], pp. 79–96, esp. 84–85) describes the relationship to David envisioned by Saul as "Dienstehe", meaning a vassal marriage granted by the patron to a subordinate subject to tie him to himself, and not a regular marriage negotiated between two principally equal families. In such marriages the spouse as well as the common offspring would belong to the father's i.e. the patron's household.

[28] S. Bar-Efrat (*Das Erste Buch Samuel. Ein narratologisch-philologischer Kommentar* [BWANT 176; Stuttgart, 2007], p. 258) maintains that David, by his seemingly modest queries in 1 Sam 18:18, rejected the offer of the king.

love with David (18:20), his deadly thoughts immediately resurged: "Saul said [to himself]: 'Let me give her to him that she may be a snare for him and that the hand of the Philistines may be against him'" (18:21). Without this monologue revealing Saul's hidden motive the offer of marriage could be understood once more as a fair deal: David has no property (18:23), but he is a brave soldier; hence the idea of one hundred foreskins of Philistines as bride price for the king's daughter (18:25a);[29] but as soon as Saul makes this condition (18:25a), one is reminded of his motivation: "Now Saul planned to make David fall by the hand of the Philistines" (18:25b). As is well known, this plot did not work: David provided Saul with two hundred instead of one hundred foreskins[30] and became Saul's son-in-law (18:27). This seemingly conciliatory ending is followed by another glimpse into Saul's mood: having realized that Yhwh was with David, Saul began to fear David and "became David's enemy from that time forward" (18:28–29). These statements stem from the Court Historian, as does the final comment that David won many battles against the Philistines (18:30).

If one leaves out the additions by the Court Historian, the passage 1 Sam 18:17–30 yields a double tradition about David's marriage into the house of Saul: an unsuccessful attempt (Merab) and a successful one (Michal). Of this tradition—presumably available as a source text—the Historian created a story full of conflict between Saul and David, making Saul's daughters the baits and the Philistines the weapon, with which Saul intended to bring David down.[31] What is imputed to Saul here might have been imputed to David (and later, with the fall of the northern kingdom, to his successors): collaboration with Israel's enemy to bring about Israel's downfall. Keen to protect David (and Judah) from such suspicions the Court Historian returned the blame to Saul (a thinly veiled hint also to the later northern kingdom).

Also linked to the Merab-Michal-Story is the famous story of David's victory over 'the Philistine' Goliath (1 Sam 17). Here we find a motif that calls for a continuation: David, gotten unto the battlefield, hears that king Saul had set his daughter as one of the prizes for the killer of Goliath (17:25). Thus, the Merab-Michal-Story (in 18:17–27) would match the end of the Goliath-Story (in 1 Sam 18:1–5). But between them the Historian incorporated a sequence of scenes, which turn the agreement between the king and his bravest warrior into a very tense

---

[29] One is reminded of Jacob having to earn Rachel (and also Lea) with hard labour (Gen 29:15–28). Jacob works as a shepherd, David as a soldier; otherwise the cases are analogous. That both fathers-in-law expect to benefit from the effort of the sons-in-law is only natural. But that one of them harbours such deadly designs is condemnable. According to I. Willi-Plein (op. cit. [note 27]) Saul once more envisioned a "Dienstehe", but David (mis-)understood this as the offer of a regular marriage, interpreting the 200 foreskins as a bride price.

[30] Circumcision of the male foreskin was customary in all Semitic tribes and peoples, i.e. in Israel and all neighbouring countries save for the Philistines who emigrated from the Aegean.

[31] This constellation is not unlike David's disposal of the inconvenient Uriah through the Ammonites in 2 Sam 11.

relationship. First, the women's song (18:6b–7) rouses Saul's mistrust (18:8–9), which in its turn gives rises to Saul's first attempt to kill the lyre-playing David (18:10–11). When this fails, David is removed, but the result is that he achieves military success and gains support from God and the people (18:12–16). It seems that, apart from the women's song perhaps, this whole passage comes from the hand of the Court Historian.

3. Prior Sources

Some stories on the topic of 'David and the Philistines' had their origins in individual traditions. Comments on these follow the canonical order.

1 Sam 17–18: As pointed out above, the Goliath narrative is related to the Merab-Michal-story. Possibly, it came into being as a gigantic preface to the older tradition of David's marriage into the house of Saul. The Marriage tradition aroused curiosity: How could David become Saul's son-in-law? The Goliath story had the answer: because of his fairly tale victory over "the Philistine", as a prize for which the king had proclaimed marriage with his own daughter. The Goliath-material went through a long history of tradition itself: in the beginning was the victory of a certain Elhanan from Bethlehem over "Goliath, the Gittite, the shaft of whose spear was like a weaver's beam" (2 Sam 21:19). Then there was a probably especially huge and fabled "sword of Goliath" (1 Sam 21:9; 22:10). The killing of Goliath was later attributed to David: initially in the role of a young slingshot soldier, who with a masterly shot, brought about a glamorous victory over the Philistines; later in the role of a shepherd boy, who just happened to be on the battlefield and killed off the gigantic spearhead of the Philistines with a herdsman's slingshot and the warrior's own sword.[32] In this form, the story was linked to the one about Merab and Michal and incorporated into the Court History.

1 Sam 23: The story about 'David in Keilah' falls into two parts: one recounts David's effort to protect this place in the Shephela[33] against Philistine attacks (23:1–5), the other tells about his departure from Keilah threatened by Saul's approach (23:6–13). While the second half may be credited to the Court Historian, the first seems adopted from an earlier source.[34] According to this short story,

---

[32] According to my analysis ("Die Erzählungen von David und Goliat in I Sam 17", *ZAW* 108 [1996], pp. 172–191), the verses 1 Sam 17:1–9, 48b, 50, 51b–53 belong to one story, whereas all the remaining text—except later additions, particularly within 17:34–47—belongs to another story.

[33] Keilah is mostly identified as today's Khirbet Qīla in the Wādi es-Sūr, approximately 12 km northwest of Hebron. According to Josh 15:44 the place belonged to Judah, but apparently this was not the case during the period in question.

[34] T. Veijola (*David. Gesammelte Studien zu den Davidüberlieferungen des Alten Testaments* [Helsinki – Göttingen, 1990], pp. 5–42) separates the parts 1bβ, 2bβ and 5b declaring them as Deuteronomistic. This seems possible, but not necessary.

David once heard that Keilah was besieged by marauding Philistines; encouraged by two favourable oracles,[35] he advanced, defeated the Philistines, and took their cattle (23:1–5). In fact this appears like a gang war: one gang at a raid is surprised by the counter-raid of another gang. In the second half, the Court Historian steps in. He introduces the priest Abiathar (23:6), known from his previous narration (1 Sam 22:20–23). Then he brings Saul into focus—significantly with a monologue in which Saul responds to the message about David's presence in Keilah (not described as a continuous presence in the earlier source!) "Saul said [to himself]: 'God has given him into my hand; for he has shut himself in by entering a town that has gates and bars'" (21:7).[36] Saul mobilizes a big army, and David obtains again two oracles—this time through Abiathar and by use of the ephod he holds in trust.[37] The tone of David's questions this time is not that of factual issues but rather of an emotional prayer. First, he wants to know whether Saul was planning to come to Keilah, then he asks whether the inhabitants of Keilah would hand him, David, over to Saul. When both answers are affirmative, David withdraws from the city and Saul abandons the undertaking. Once more, the lessons from this doubled narrative are plain: David can handle the Philistines, but not Saul. Also: Saul fights David instead of fighting the Philistines.

1 Sam 27: David enters the service of Achish from Gath with his 600-men-troop, gets Ziklag as a fief, and stays in Philistia for one year and four months. This rather dry account in the verses 2, 3a, 6, 7 may be old; the later, David-friendly tradition would never have implicated its hero in such escapades. It honours the Court Historian that he did not suppress this splinter of tradition, although this certainly is not to say that he introduced this information without further ado. Indeed, he made a three-fold endeavour at defusing it. First he paved the way to the Achish story by placing well before it the episode of 1 Sam 21:11–16 about a first and failed attempt to cross over to Gath,[38] thus making it plain that David's

---

[35] The style gives the impression of a so-called alternative oracle, which would answer a presented question with yes or no. The technical devices would be two differently marked objects (pieces of wood, stones) one of which would jump first out of a receptacle which the priest shakes. The best known oracle of this kind was 'Urim and Tummim'. The other possibility is the so-called selective oracle which was used when a range of solutions were possible. Cf. about this Dietrich (*op. cit.* [note 19]), pp. 463–465.

[36] The military motif of the enemy self-enclosed in a fortified city is encountered again in 2 Sam 17:13—likewise a text by the Court Historian (cf. also 2 Sam 20:6, 14–15).

[37] This cult object appears repeatedly in the books of Samuel, lastly at David's dance in front of the ark (2 Sam 6:14).

[38] Ideologically, this narration is so clearly in line with the Court History that one could hardly assume an older core within it. Moreover, it consists mostly of direct speech, like 1 Sam 29, and within it—again as in 1 Sam 29:5—the women's song from 1 Sam 18:7 is quoted. This reveals a narrative horizon far beyond the single text. The motif of the faked insanity, used to rescue oneself in crisis, is known also in classical-antiquity (e.g. Odysseus, cf. D. L. Christensen, "Achish", ABD, I, pp. 55–56).

move to Gath was quite difficult and risky. Further, he interposed the remark, that David was not persecuted by Saul in Ziklag (27:4),[39] which proved the accuracy of David's thoughts, articulated by this author in 1 Sam 27:1. Finally, he provided evidence that David did not do anything against Judah (and Israel), although he made his Philistine overlord believe the contrary (27:8–12).[40]

1 Sam 29: As already indicated, only a slender basic stock of material can be isolated in this chapter, in the verses 1, 2a and 11b. Forming the opening to the account of the battle of 1 Sam 31 these verses give no consideration to David or to his whereabouts.

2 Sam 1: The addressees to the lament in 2 Sam 1:19–27 are metaphorically forbidden to spread the news about the catastrophe on Gilboa in Gath and Ashkelon so as not to bring joy to the "daughters of the Philistines" (1:20). The author—with high probability David himself—puts himself on the side of the defeated Israelites and against the Philistines. Whoever inserted the lament here—this could well be the Court Historian—graciously informed us of his source: "the (song-) book of the upright".[41]

2 Sam 5: The two episodes about battles against the Philistines in 2 Sam 5:17–21 and 5:22–25 strongly echo those about David's victory over the Philistines near Keilah (1 Sam 23:1–5, see above). This time, the Philistines advance into the plain of Rephaim (ca. 5-7km southwest of Jerusalem). Again, David obtains oracles before the battle, which announce to him his victory and once even give him tactical instructions. It is quite possible that these three stories originated in the same source. Now, attention is due to the doubled reference to the Philistines in 2 Sam 5:17a: "When the Philistines heard that David had been anointed king over Israel, all the Philistines went up in search of David". The beginning of the older narration could have been: "And the Philistines went in search of David; but David heard about it and went down to the stronghold (מצודה)" (i.e. 5:17aβb). This begs the question, to which stronghold could David have come "down" *from Jerusalem*? In 2 Sam 5:7, 9a מצודה is mentioned in connection with Zion and the city of David, but this was the highest point in the city (at that time). However, the traditions about David repeatedly refer to another מצודה: According to 1 Sam 22:1–5 it lay close to Adullam (barely 30km southwest from Jerusalem, and

---

[39] From the Court Historian originates also the mention of the two wives whom David brought along (27:3b)—a redactional allusion to 1 Sam 25:39–43. The direct speech from David to Achish in 27:5 anticipates only what is reported as a fact in 27:6; with this, David's entrustment with the kingship at Ziklag becomes the very idea of David.

[40] From a moral point of view one will find it questionable that David uses for this purpose the means of genocide.

[41] 2 Sam 1:18. This collection of songs is also mentioned in Josh 10:13 and 1 Kgs 8:13 (LXX, 3 Kgs 8:53, which reads "the book of song").

close to Keilah!); according to 1 Sam 24:23 David returned there from En-Gedi. But probably the most significant evidence is found in the annex to the books of Samuel, in 2 Sam 23:13–14. The presence of Philistines in the plain of Rephaim and in Bethlehem is counterbalanced here by the presence of David and his men in the cave of Adullam (cf. 1 Sam 22:1!) and on the מצודה, respectively. This topography is the same as in 2 Sam 5:17–25, as well as in 1 Sam 23:1–5.[42] The narration in 1 Sam 23, and probably also in 2 Sam 23 (see below), deals with a phase in which David was still the leader of a militia and not a king. Thus, 2 Sam 5:17–25 was inserted incorrectly in its present position.[43] These accounts about victorious battles with the Philistines belong to an earlier phase in David's life. It was the Court Historian who dated them to the time after the establishment of the double monarchy by inserting the little opening clause "When the Philistines heard that David had been anointed king over Israel", probably to show that David cut off his connections with the Philistines at that time.

2 Sam 15: According to 2 Sam 15:18b–22, 600 soldiers from Gath under the lead of a certain Ittai helped quell Absalom's rebellion. The passage begins and ends with concise narrative accounts (15:18b, 22b), which could be from the earlier source.[44] The intervening dialogue between David and Ittai has to be in its core from the same source, since it is the first out of three conversations David holds with important supporters at his departure from Jerusalem thus laying the foundation to his later success.[45] In our case, the verses 15:19*, 21–22a are essential: David's request that Ittai should turn back and Ittai's noble answer that he wanted to be wherever David was, for life or for death, as well as David's positive reaction

---

[42] Keilah is situated barely 3km south of Adullam!

[43] P. K. McCarter (*II Samuel* [New York, 1984], pp. 157–158) reaches a similar result, and his arguments are striking: The Philistines are said to have been "in search of David" (בקש, 5:17) which would be odd if he stayed in his new capital Jerusalem; they "spread out" their troops (5:18, 22), not a usual expression for beginning a siege; the "stronghold" cannot be Mount Zion, "because in the Bible one always goes *up*, never *down*, to the eminence of Zion". Less convincing is McCarter's idea that 5:17–25 originally was placed "between the report of David's accession to the northern throne in 5:1–3 and the description of the capture of Jerusalem in 5:6–10". It is argued above that the text tells about an earlier period of David's life.

[44] The basis of 2 Sam 15–19 constitutes quite an old narration of Absalom's turmoil, cf. W. Dietrich, "Die Fünfte Kolonne Davids beim Abschalom-Aufstand", in W. Dietrich (ed.), *Seitenblicke. Literarische und historische Studien zu Nebenfiguren im zweiten Samuelbuch* (OBO 249; Fribourg – Göttingen, 2011), pp. 91–120.

[45] Apart from the commander of the troops, Ittai, they are the priest Zadok (2 Sam 15:24–29) and the advisor Hushai (2 Sam 15:32–37). The Court Historian did not model these paragraphs from scratch, although he may have touched them up in places. The situation is different with the encounters with the Saulide Meribaal (with his trustee Ziba) and Shim'i ben Gera in 2 Sam 16:1–13. These passages the Historian modelled largely himself (possibly availing himself of another source). Cf. Veijola, *op. cit.* (note 34), pp. 58–83; F. Langlamet, "David et la maison de Saül. Les épisodes 'benjaminites' des II Sam., IX; XVI, 1–14; XIX, 17–31; I Rois II, 36–46", *RB* 86 (1979), pp. 194–213, 385–436, 481–513; *RB* 87 (1980), pp. 161–210; *RB* 88 (1981), pp. 321–333.

to this. With the addition of 15:19bβ–20, the Court Historian changes the impression considerably, suggesting that Ittai was exiled from Gath, thus excluding the possibility that the king of Gath could have sent ancillary troops to support David against Absalom.

According to the present wording, David's request that Ittai turn back appears twice: "Go back, and stay (שוב ושב) with the king [Absalom]" (15:19bα), and: "Go back, and take (שוב והשב) your kinsfolk with you" (15:20b). The intervening words may have been inserted by the Court Historian: David declares Ittai to be an exiled man who just arrived "yesterday", and should therefore not go "today" with one who knows not where his way may lead him; he should turn back and Yhwh be merciful with him.[46] This speech fits very well with the intentions of the Court Historian: If Ittai happens to be in Jerusalem involuntarily and temporarily, then neither has the ruler of Gath sent him to help the hard-pressed David, nor is he together with his troops an integral part of David's army. David himself appears a pious and modest man, entrusting himself and also the Philistine to Yhwh's care.[47] This is a demonstration of the Court Historian's way with unpleasant issues received from the older sources; he secures them against any interpretation that is adverse to David.

2 Sam 21 and 23: The passages 2 Sam 21:15–21 and 23:9–17 put together several anecdotes about fights of some of David's men with Philistine warriors which probably come from a more extensive collection of stories about wars and battles.[48]

Some details sound legendary, others seem historically plausible. Naturally, in the early days of David, there were frequent skirmishes between David's warriors and those of the Philistines in the borderland between the Philistine coastal plain and the Judean hill country.[49] The setting depicted has armed gangs

---

[46] LXX provides here a fuller text than MT, which requires as Hebrew Vorlage: יעש יהוה עמך חסד ואמת. The reduction in MT to עמך חסד ואמת may have been accidental (Homoioteleuton) or deliberate (how could David be speaking to a Philistine like that?). This is against E. Kellenberger (*häsäd wä'ämät als Ausdruck einer Glaubenserfahrung* [AThANT 69; Zürich, 1982], p. 123), who adopts the shorter version in MT and interprets it as "Go with God".

[47] Kellenberger (ibid., pp. 124–125) interprets the picture of David in the present text very beautifully. He is even able to show a chiastic structure in the present wording of David's speech to Ittai (similarly C. Conroy, *Absalom Absalom! Narrative and Language in 2 Sam 13-20* [AnBib 81; Roma, 1981], p. 144; J. P. Fokkelman, *Narrative Art and Poetry in the Books of Samuel:* vol. I, *King David* [Assen, 1981], pp. 180–182). If accurate, this interpretation goes to show the skills of the Court Historian.

[48] Possibly the short accounts of the Philistine battles in 1 Sam 23:1–5 and 2 Sam 5:17–23 belong here too, as well as some formally related anecdotes in 2 Sam 8 about battles with other neighbours. One could well imagine such a scroll (or a little collection) in the archive of the Jerusalem palace.

[49] Therefore David has to go "down" to these battles from the Judean mountains (2 Sam 21:15). The places Gath (21:20, at that time the most important Philistine city), Adullam (23:13, in the Shephelah) and Bethlehem (23:14, in the Judean hill country) are mentioned. Lachajah (23:11) and Gob (i.e. Nob: 21:16, 18, 19, in 1 Chron 20:4–8 Gezer; cf. A. S. Ehrlich, "Gob", ABD, II, p. 1041) can hardly be located.

roam a relatively sparsely populated area, subsisting on the land[50] and trying to steal or obtain zones of influence from their adversaries. In this state of rivalry the Philistines appear as the more aggressive and usually more successful party that can only be resisted with extreme boldness and bravery.

III. Historical Evaluation

When attempting to draw a historical outline of David's relationship with the Philistines, we have to rely on information from older single traditions and to examine what the Court Historian made of them.

1. David as a Bandit Chief

In 1 Sam 16–18 we have some stories which reflect the rise of David within the immediate environment of King Saul as a warrior against the Philistines. According to the biblical account, David began his career in Saul's service as a lyrist and an armour-bearer (1 Sam 16:14–23), then as a troop leader (1 Sam 18). This is not implausible, since according to another account, whose credibility we have no reason to doubt (1 Sam 14:52), the first king of Israel gathered strong, brave men to form a (small) standing army. Its primary task was the defence against the attempts of the Philistines to expand further into the hill country; Saul had considerable success, but still was defeated in the end by this overpowering enemy. If David was part of this army, he inevitably had to deal with the Philistines. That he had overpowered the giant Goliath is but a legend; his actual conqueror according to 2 Sam 21:19 was Elhanan from Bethlehem. But there is still the tradition of the two hundred Philistine foreskins for which he apparently expected to marry Saul's daughter Michal. Of course he did not necessarily have to gain these trophies single handed; if anything true is contained in the story, then under Saul David was already some kind of leader of mercenaries, probably the most capable; he would hardly have become the king's son-in-law otherwise.

The textual traces leading back to Saul's surroundings are both vague and scattered. Even so, there are many striking records about encounters with Philistines from the period that David spent as a bandit in the area of Judah.

Generally, the portrait of David as an up-and-coming military and political leader gains sharper contours. The gathering of men, mainly of his own kinship, who were "in distress […] in debt [or] discontented" (1 Sam 22:1–2), the accumulation of this irregular troop to 400—with baggage train 600—men (1 Sam 23:13; 25:13; 27:2; 30:10), the maintenance of this small—but for the circumstances

---

[50] The story of David and Nabal in 1 Sam 25 is most revealing in this regard, but also the accounts about Philistine posts and marauding troops in 1 Sam 13:3, 17–18; 14:1; 17:1; 23:27; 2 Sam 5:18, 22; 23:13.

at the time and in this place quite considerable—private army by the population through more or less voluntarily given fees (1 Sam 25) or through martial forays (1 Sam 23:1–5; 27:8–9; 30:1–20)—all seem plausible and gain further historical trustworthiness by comparison with the activities of the so-called "Hapiru". Some centuries earlier, the correspondence of Amarna by Canaanite city kings described the "Hapiru" as brave soldiers for hire, or as dangerous bandits. (The fact that Philistine warriors refer to their Israelite adversaries as "Hebrews" in 1 Sam 14, suggests some historical relationship.)

That the bandit chief, David, would sooner or later have conflicts with roaming troops and battle groups of the Philistines (or they with him) was only to be expected. The Keilah-episode in 1 Sam 23:1–5, just as the fights in 2 Sam 5:17–21 and 2 Sam 23:8–17, all lead to the same area: the borderland between the Philistine-controlled coastal plain and the hill country in which David had installed himself. Less certain is, whether David was also involved in conflicts with Saul back then. It is not impossible that Israelite troops would have marched into the politically unstable south of Palestine so as not to surrender the land to Philistine roaming troops or to gangs like David's (or the Amalekites!).[51] Some particular traditions show Saul at En-Gedi (west of the Dead Sea) or in the "desert of Maon" (southwest of Hebron[52]) when he closes in on David (1 Sam 23:24–26; 24:2), but is then distracted by invading Philistines (1 Sam 23:27).

This last piece of information catches our attention. Could it be that the habitual rivalry between David and the Philistines gave way to cooperation when they had to fight against Saul? Bandit chiefs typically with little regard for political or moral maxims, just do what seems beneficial at any given time. When conditions in the barren and embattled south became uncomfortable for David—the Philistines were too strong perhaps, Saul as well became too dangerous—he left for the west. Apparently, the Philistines offered good terms, and at the same time hoped to incorporate the vagabonding troop into their political and economic system. This arrangement benefited both parties: instead of two enemies they had only one, against whom they could unite forces. Thus the bandit chief, David, became a leader of soldiers for hire in the service of the Philistines.

2. David as a Vassal of the Philistines

That David found his overlord in the ruler of Gath, of all people, is a historically remarkable and trustworthy account. Gath was prosperous; it was in fact the

---

[51] 1 Sam 15 could contain a (small) historical core, cf. W. Dietrich, *David, Saul und die Propheten* (BWANT 122; Stuttgart, 1992²), pp. 10–12; A. Giercke-Ungermann, *Die Niederlage im Sieg. Eine synchrone und diachrone Untersuchung der Erzählung von 1 Sam 15* (EThSt 97; Würzburg, 2010), pp. 258–261. 1 Sam 30 relates that David also had to face up to these predatory nomads.

[52] The town of Maon, who gave the name to this area as well as Ziph, mentioned in the same breath (1 Sam 23:19, 24; 26:1) lay at the western edge of the Judean desert (cf. Tell Ma'in, map ref. 162.090) and in Josh 15:55 both are counted among the cities of the Judean hill country.

biggest and the leading city in Philistia—up to the end of the 9th century BCE, at which time it was levelled by Hazael, king of Aram Damascus,[53] never to regain great importance, with Ekron becoming the Philistine metropolis.[54] If—and this appears rather improbable—David's crossing-over to the Philistines were later fiction, then one would hardly have chosen Gath, of all places, as his destination.

The narrations call Achish the "king" of Gath.[55] Achish shares his name with one of his successors according to 1 Kgs 2:39, as well as with a 7th century BCE king of Ekron.[56] This, however, is of little import: Such name repetitions are not uncommon with kings (or popes). It is interesting also, that only in narratives around the 10th century and only with regard to Gath is it said that *the* Philistines had a *king*.[57] Normally in texts about this early period the leaders of the Philistine cities bear the title *seren (1 Sam 5:8,11; 6:4,12,16,18; 29:2,6,7).[58] In later times, namely in the textual witnesses of the 8th–6th centuries BCE, the four Philistine cities (without Gath!) always appear separately and have 'kings' as their individual rulers.

The location of Ziklag, the village which according to 1 Sam 27 David recieved from 'king' Achish as a fief, remains unverified down to the present day; but the context points to the southeast of Philistia.[59] Apparently it served as an outpost

---

[53] Cf. 2 Kgs 12:18. For the archaeological evidence see A. M. Maeir and C. S. Ehrlich, "Excavating Philistine Gath. Have we Found Goliath's Hometown?", *BAR* 27/6 (2001), pp. 22–31; and Maeir's article in this volume.

[54] Cf. T. Dothan, "Tel Miqne (Ekron)", NEAEHL, III (Jerusalem, 1993), pp. 1051–1059.

[55] The name is not semitic; for its possible connection to the Greek name Αγχίοσής attested in Homeric epic (Ilias 2:819), cf. D. L. Christensen, "Achish", ABD, I, pp. 55–56.

[56] On an inscription that was found in 1996 in Tell Miqne/Ekron as well as in Assyrian documents the name of Ikausu is verified, cf. I. Finkelstein and N. A. Silberman, *David und Salomo. Archäologen entschlüsseln einen Mythus* (München, 2006), p. 169. However, the assumption of these two authors that Achish of Gath in 1 Sam is in reality the 7th century BCE Achish of Ekron is rather hasty. For a detailed critique of the 'deconstructionist trend' advocated by Finkelstein see S. M. Ortiz, "Rewriting Philistine History. Recent Trends in Philistine Archaeology and Biblical Studies", in R. S. Hess, G. A. Klingbeil and P. J. Ray (eds.), *Critical Issues in Early Israelite History* (Winona Lake, IN 2008), pp. 191–204.

[57] This point is stressed by I. Shai, "The Political Organization of the Philistines", in A. M. Maeir and P. de Miroschedji (eds.), *"I Will Speak the Riddles of Ancient Times." Festschrift Amihai Mazar*, I (Winona Lake, IN 2006), pp. 347–359, esp. 349–350. Shai sums up the textual and archaeological evidence for the 10th–9th centuries BCE as follows: "even if the Philistines were not united under a single monarchy, cooperation among the five Philistine cities was the norm, and their external relations were conducted collectively" (p. 351).

[58] For the etymology of this term see Dietrich (*op. cit.* [note 19], pp. 277–278). A broader view of the phenomenon is offered by V. Wagner, "Die *srnjm* der Philister und die Ältesten Israels", *ZAR* 14 (2008), pp. 408–433.

[59] V. Fritz, "Where is David's Ziklag?", *BAR* 19 (1993), pp. 58–61, esp. 76, wanted to identify it with the layer V of Tell es-Seba. Beersheba is described in the stories about Isaac (Gen 21:22–34; 26:23–33) as Philistine, later it became a Judean town, cf. Josh 15:28; 19:2 and the formula "from Dan to Beersheba" (Judg 20:1; 1 Sam 3:20; 2 Sam 17:11; 24:2; 1 Kgs 5:5) which describes the extension of Israel and Judah as a whole.

and border station meant to protect the heartland against invasions from the Negev and at the same time to expand its own sphere of influence. As the king of the city, David practically stayed the bandit chief he was—except that now he could operate from a secure base having no longer to deal with the Philistines as an enemy. He did not have to steal provisions for his troops from the Philistines, but could provide it with their consent—allegedly not in his Judean homeland, but further south (1 Sam 27:8–9). The detailed report about a conflict with the nomadic Amalekites in 1 Sam 30:1–25 could well be historically accurate, in its core.[60] David's distribution of the spoils to Judean villages is reported (1 Sam 30:26–31), by which David sought to win them over for his own purposes.[61]

At greater conflicts, David was bound to join his overlord in the army. With good reason, the biblical tradition assumes that he was also mobilized for the decisive encounter with Saul's Israel. Certainly, the Court Historian made explicit that he was absolved. If this ideologically motivated tinge is ignored, it remains possible, in some ways even probable, that David and his men were part of the battle at Gilboa—on the Philistine side. To be sure, this is a possibility rather than a fact sustained by positive evidence.

It also has to remain open, to what extent the Philistines, and especially the king of Gath, were informed about David's switch-over from Ziklag to Hebron and his proclamation there to be king of Judah (cf. 2 Sam 2:1–4a), or if they were even involved in these processes. From a vassal king of a city David became the ruler of a rather considerable territory.[62] The Philistines could have been quite in agreement with that. At least nominally, David was still their vassal: apparently, he did not give up his dominion over Ziklag, for it says explicitly that the city has belonged to the Judean kings "to this day" (1 Sam 27:6).[63] Thus the Philistines could see the strengthening of David as a counterbalance to their strongest adversary, hoping to use it as an effective spearhead against Israel. As a matter

---

[60] The following texts deal with conflicts between Israel and this tribe of nomads: Ex 17:8–16; Num 14:39–45; Judg 6:3,33; 7:12; 1 Sam 15; 30. The assumption of H. A. Tanner (*Amalek, der Feind Israels und der Feind Jahwes. Eine Studie zu den Amalektexten im Alten Testament* [Zürich, 2005]) that all these texts belong to a later, Dtr layer is probably not accurate.

[61] According to Finkelstein and Silberman (*op. cit.* [note 56]), this list of places is replete with anachronisms in view of which it is attributed to the time of Josiah. But what is the import of Bethel, Aroer and Ramat-Negev being "zur Zeit Josias besonders bekannt" (especially well known in the time of Josiah)? It seems to weigh more that Jattir was not "even inhabited before the 7th century"; but this would require the—sometimes supposed, but hardly proved—identification with Chirbet 'Attir (not: 'Attir!; cf. J. L. Peterson, "Jattir", ABD, III, pp. 649–650). A. A. Fischer ("Beutezug und Segensgabe. Zur Redaktionsgeschichte der Liste in I Sam 30, 26–31", *VT* 53 [2003], pp. 48–64) also doubts the historical reliability of the mentioned place list.

[62] It seems we are looking here at the founding of 'Judah' as a political entity, with David forming a unity out of the different settling tribes (namely Kalibbites, Kenites and Jerachmeelites, cf. 1 Sam 25:3; 27:10).

[63] The time of the Court Historian must be meant, namely the late-8th century possibly early-7th century BCE.

of fact, David's troops can be seen involved in skirmishes with Israelite troops (2 Sam 2:8–32) soon afterwards. Of note, the battles are located near Gibeon (2 Sam 2:12–17), not in the middle or even in the south of Judah, but on or beyond its northern border. This can very well be understood as an attempt to destabilize the Saulide rule, a move that would have certainly met with Philistine approval.

3. David as King of Judah and Israel

According to the biblical account, David radically changed his attitude towards the Philistines after Saul's death or, at the latest, after his own accession to the throne in Israel. As noted, in his lament on Saul and Jonathan, he already distances himself distinctly from the victorious Philistines (2 Sam 1:20). Abner, the Israelite (and Saulide!) commander-in-chief, having submitted to David, advocates for him with his compatriots, citing Yhwh's promise: "Through the hand of my servant David I will save[64] my people Israel from the hand of the Philistines" (2 Sam 3:18).[65] As soon as David becomes king over Israel, the Philistines react with repeated attacks against his new residence Jerusalem, but they are defeated (2 Sam 5:17–25). Finally the Philistines head the list of David's wars and victories: "David attacked the Philistines and subdued them; and David took the metheg-ammah out of the hand of the Philistines" (2 Sam 8:1).[66]

This picture of animosity between King David and the Philistines is due to the Court Historian who arranged his sources and commented on them accordingly.

The negative statement about the Philistines in 2 Sam 1:20 is on one hand traceable to the genre (honouring the dead requires blaming those responsible for

---

[64] *Textus emendatus*, see BHS.
[65] Admittedly, nothing was said before of such a divine promise concerning David. It was rather Saul who was the subject of such promise (1 Sam 9:16a)—with a phrase formulated by the Court Historian (cf. Dietrich, *op. cit.* [see note 19], pp. 402–405). The relation between the two writings is not one of dissent, rather of a subtle interaction: The promise in 1 Sam 9:16a was accomplished (1 Sam 13–14), but only partially; with Saul's defeat on Gilboa it became obsolete, so that it could be given from the Saulide Abner to David in 2 Sam 3:18. The final phrase "…and from the hand of all of his enemies" serves as a revision of Saul's lifetime and the preparation for 2 Sam 8.
[66] The meaning of the expression is not conclusively clarified. מתג is a 'bridle', the piece of metal which lies in a horse's mouth, used to lead it. אמה could be 'ell' or 'channel' (HALOT, s.v.). Thus one may translate quite helplessly 'big bridle' or the like, taking it as a metaphor for the foreign domination that David shook off. Alternatively, מתג stands for an unknown object very important to the Philistines, or for the city of Gath, following the Chronicler (1 Chron 18:1) who obviously read מתג as מגת ("from Gath"), thus the phrase may refer to "Gath and its affiliated cities". Another option accepts "Gath", but takes also אמה as a place name: "from Gath to Amma". Very attractive is the proposal of B. Halpern (*David's Secret Demons: Messiah, Murderer, Traitor, King* [Grand Rapids, MI – Cambridge, 2001], pp. 320–321) that *meteg* is "a corruption of the term *ptg*-, which appears as a name or title of the goddess of Ekron in an inscription of the early 7th century", so that מתג/*פתג "may well be the icon" (or one of several icons), which David captured from the Philistines according to 2 Sam 5:21.

the killing); on the other hand it is politically motivated (David restages himself as a defender of Israel). Abner's words in 2 Sam 3:18 originate from the Court Historian himself. It is that same historian who installed probably historically inaccurately both battle accounts in 2 Sam 5:17–25 in their current place. The note on the Philistines in 2 Sam 8:1 is at once very general and very mysterious;[67] above all, it lacks any genuine chronological data[68] so that the implied animosities with the Philistines (like those in 2 Sam 5:17–25) could have happened much earlier.

The older sources bring to mind a scenario different from the one that the Bible (namely, the Court Historian) draws of the relationship between David and the Philistines: the Philistines, content to see the rule over Judah and Israel in the hands of an ally (or still a vassal?), abandon their military activities in the hill country. David, on his part, makes no attempt to expand his rule into the coastal plain. Altogether, a picture of a peaceful coexistence emerges, in which at least economically, possibly also politically and militarily, the littoral states hold the upper hand.

If David conducted himself in a defensive way towards the west, he followed an aggressive strategy towards the east as specified by the detailed accounts about military conflicts with the people east of the Jordan.[69] The Philistines would be satisfied with the forces of the United Monarchy bound in the east, since in these circumstances these forces would not turn west. Moreover, the second most important trade route next to the Via Maris, the so-called King's Highway from the Gulf of Aqaba to Damascus, could also be controlled in this way, as of course also the east-west routes from the coastal cities to Arabia.

The presence of Philistines, especially Gathites, in and around Jerusalem is a strong hint to the relationships between David and the Philistines being marked by cooperation rather than by confrontation. According to an unpretentious and therefore unsuspicious note in the narration about the transfer of the ark to Jerusalem, this holy device was given for three months to a Gathite named Obed-Edom for safe-keeping following an unpleasant incident, whereupon he experienced Yhwh's blessing (2 Sam 6:10–12). Even more significant is the already discussed account of the 600 Gathites under Ittai's charge, who supported David in his battle against Absalom (2 Sam 15:18–22). If Ittai was not expatriated from Gath, as the present text has it, but rather was sent to support David, the resulting picture would be

---

[67] How much more vivid and detailed are the short accounts that follow in 2 Sam 8 and even more so the account of the war with the Ammonites 2 Sam 10:1–19; 12:26–31.

[68] The preliminary sentence "And it happened after this" assigns, strictly speaking, every following report of victory to the time past 2 Sam 5–7.

[69] Cf. 2 Sam 8:2–14; 11:1; 12:26–31. Compared with these, the account of the Ammonite and Aramean war in 2 Sam 10 is a younger literary component and should be evaluated with care. Still there is some exaggeration also in the claim of 2 Sam 8:6 that Aram-Damascus was permanently conquered.

more round shaped: Absalom's rebellion supported mainly by (northern-)Israel,[70] gets the Philistines worried about a foul reprise from a possibly victorious Absalom. He could follow in Saul's footsteps, reinforced even by Judah. Thereby, an almost eerie analogy suggests itself: In the past, David (perhaps) helped the Philistines to crush Saul; now they (most likely) helped David to crush Absalom.

It is no easy task to correlate this supposed relationship between King David and the Philistines with the recent archaeological discoveries at Khirbet Qeiyafa, situated 12km east of Gath/Tell eṣ-Ṣafi in the valley of Elah, on the border between the hill country and the coastal plain. The location is encircled by a wall of 700m in length, and has been populated mainly in two periods: in the Hellenistic era and in the Iron Age IIA. This early occupation lasted only a few years; thereafter the site was destroyed. The excavator, Y. Garfinkel,[71] interprets the Iron Age remains as a 'city'—possibly the term 'military outpost' would be more suitable—founded by the kingdom of Judah, practically by King David. Radiocarbon measurements[72] and the pottery analysis[73] make the assumed foundation time in the early-10th century fairly certain. It remains less clear whether Khirbet Qeiyafa was actually a Judean site or a Philistine one. The faunal assemblage[74] as well as a newly unearthed sanctuary with ingredients of an uniconic cult[75] point to the first possibility.[76] These arguments would be strengthened by G. Galil's reading of the famous Qeiyafa ostracon, if it is correct.[77] On the other hand, the fact that fine pieces of typically Philistine pottery were found in buildings from

---

[70] So A. Alt, "Die Staatenbildung der Israeliten in Palästina", in A. Alt, *Kleine Schriften zur Geschichte des Volkes Israel*, II (München, 1964³), pp. 57–58. H. Bardtke in contrast reckons with a strong participation of Judah in the rebellion ("Erwägungen zur Rolle Judas im Aufstand Absaloms", in H. Gese and H. P. Rüger (eds.), *Wort und Geschichte. Festschrift Karl Elliger* [AOAT 18; Münster, 1973], pp. 1–8). F. Crüsemann postulates a cooperation between the Israelite and the Judean militia (*Der Widerstand gegen das Königtum. Die antiköniglichen Texte des Alten Testaments und der Kampf um den frühen israelitischen Staat* [WMANT 49; Neukirchen-Vluyn, 1978], pp. 96–98).

[71] Y. Garfinkel and S. Ganor, *Khirbet Qeiyafa. Vol. I, Excavation Report 2007–2008* (Jerusalem, 2009).

[72] The calibration shows a time span between 1050 and 975 BCE.

[73] Cf. the solid presentation in Garfinkel and Ganor, *op. cit.* (note 71), pp. 119–149.

[74] Garfinkel and Ganor, ibid., p. 205: "The Iron Age assemblage for the site is dominated by cattle and sheep/goat bones"; p. 204: "No pig bones were found in the Iron Age stratum".

[75] So Garfinkel in a lecture held in Bern in September 2010.

[76] See also Garfinkel's article in this volume.

[77] See G. Galil, "The Hebrew Inscription from Khirbet Qeiyafa/Netaʿim: Script, Language, Literature and History", *UF* 41 (2009) [2010], pp. 193–242. Different analyses of the inscription are to be found in Garfinkel and Ganor, *op. cit.* (note 71), pp. 243–270. Galil's reading is now accepted by other scholars including B. Becking and P. Sanders ("De inscriptie uit Khirbet Qeiyafa: Een vroege vorm van sociaal besef in oud Israel?", *NTT* 64 [2010], pp. 238–252), R. Achenbach ("The Protection of *Personae miserae* in Ancient Israelite Law and Wisdom and in the Ostracon from Khirbet Qeiyafa", *Semitica* [forthcoming]), and more.

the Iron Age IIA[78] speaks for the second possibility.[79] But supposing it was David who erected Khirbet Qeiyafa as a border post against Philistia, and it was the Philistines who destroyed this post:[80] how does this fit into our picture of David's rather close connections with the Philistines after his coronation in Jerusalem? In my opinion, such a relationship would not necessarily exclude attempts by one side to mark its sovereignty, nor would it counter possible attacks from the other side to remove such markers of sovereignty.[81] The destruction of Khirbet Qeiyafa by the Philistines may have been a strong warning to David not to overburden the mutual relationship and not to disclaim the hierarchy between the king of Gath and the king of Jerusalem.

The above drawn picture of 'David and the Philistines',[82] differs significantly from the one drawn in the Bible (that is mostly by the Court Historian). David's power, at any rate his power over the Philistines, appears diminished, but not at all minimized. For David (and later Solomon) would still be the ruler of a Dual-Monarchy which albeit not from "the river [Euphrates] to[83] the land of the Philistines, even to the border of Egypt" (1 Kgs 5:1), stretches from "Dan to Beer-sheba" (2 Sam 24:15; 1 Kgs 5:5).

---

[78] According to the excavators (see Garfinkel and Ganor, *op. cit.* [note 71], pp. 151–158) they represent the missing link between the 'Philistine Bichrome' pottery of the late 11th century and the 'Late Philistine Decorated Ware' of the 9th and 8th centuries BCE.

[79] As J. Uziel states, pottery "is probably the most distinctive feature of the assemblage" ("The Development Process of Philistine Material Culture: Assimilation, Acculturation and Everything in between", *Levant* 39 [2007], p. 168).

[80] As suggested by Galil, *op. cit.* (note 77).

[81] The coastal cities had a strong interest in controlling the economy and the markets in their hilly hinterland. A. Shalit ("Settlement Patterns of Philistine City-States", in A. Fantalkin and A. Yasur-Landau [eds.], *Bene Israel. Studies in the Archaeology of Israel and the Levant during the Bronze and Iron Ages, Festschrift Israel Finkelstein* [Leiden, 2008], pp. 135–164) demonstrates convincingly the lack of a greater number of rural settlements in the immediate environment of the Philistine cities over the centuries, which made the inhabitants dependent on other sources of supply for their food.

[82] It is in some findings similar to that of the popular article of H.-M. Niemann, "David gegen Goliath. Waren Philister und Israeliten Erzfeinde?", *WUB* 49 (2008), pp. 34–39.

[83] *Textus emendatus*, see BHS.

King Solomon's Copper Supply*

Ernst Axel Knauf

Introduction

Why have "King Solomon's Copper Mines", so far, escaped discovery? Could it be that they have been looked for in the wrong region? Or did they never exist? Are we dealing with a mirage produced by various layers of narrative tradition,— whose most recent stages are represented by current historiography,—which lack any foundation in historical reality? I suggest that both suspicions can be validated to a certain degree. I also suggest that the relations between Phoenicia and Solomon's Israel as depicted in the Bible are a narrative construct which does not portray the social, political and economic reality of the tenth century B.C. correctly. This can be demonstrated by a re-evaluation of Palestine's copper supply. As a narrative construct, the stories about King Solomon and Tyre do, however, allow some basic insights into the nature of the Phoenician-Israelite relationship during the time in which these stories were shaped and reworked, *i.e.* the ninth through fifth centuries B.C. Writing about King Solomon today puts one easily in the position of the man who escaped the lion and encountered the bear, and escaped the bear and was bitten by the snake. Those who maintain that Solomon is pure literary fiction without any foundation in historical facts—as one of my colleagues at Heidelberg does[1]—will charge me with romanticism and conservatism, because I still think that the king existed. Those who are inclined to credit Solomon with approximately the amount of power and glory with which he is characterized in the first eleven chapters of the Books of Kings may like to call me a nihilistic radical, because I cannot share their views either. There can, however, be no doubt that the stories about King Solomon will always play an important role in any discussion of the relationship between Phoenicia and the Bible.

---

* I am grateful to the participants of the Louvain colloquium for their criticism and their suggestions which undoubtedly improved this paper, even if I was unable to change my conclusions. It was in the house of T.L. Thompson in Milwaukee where the unpublished dissertations of D.W. Jamieson-Drake (*infra*, n. 19) and Handy (*infra*, n. 66) came to my attention.

[1] B.J. Diebner is preparing a study which will argue towards this end. Cf. *for a* competent presentation of the traditional view, A. LEMAIRE, *The United Monarchy, Saul, David and Solomon*, in H. Shanks (ed.), *Ancient Israel. A Short History from Abraham to the Roman Destruction of the Temple*, Washington D.C. 1988, p. 85-108.

A Political and Economic Evaluation of the Biblical Solomon

According to the biblical account, Phoenician-Israelite relations were never as intense as they were in the days of Solomon. The courts of Jerusalem and Tyre exchanged messengers and entered a treaty (1 Kgs 5).[2] Phoenicia supplied Solomon with cedar wood (5:20.22-24), gold (9:11.14) and skilled labor (7:13-14) for his ambitious building projects. Solomon gave in return basic subsistence goods—oil and wheat (5:25)—as an annual tribute, unskilled labor (5:28), and territory (9:10-14).[3] The trade pattern as depicted—luxury goods in exchange for subsistence goods—is a familiar one. It is typical for the exchange between first world countries and third world countries, between developed and developing nations.[4] It is also typical for secondary States in their ascendancy: the new ruler allows the advanced civilization to exploit the economic potential of his realm, and receives prestige goods in return—that is, power,[5] though, in more recent history, power is usually conferred to client States without such a deviation into the symbolic sphere. Evaluated from the point of view of core-periphery relationships, Solomon's Israel was a commercial dependent of Tyre.[6] Typically, the colony was used by the leading power for further explorations and exploitations in even more uncivilized regions: Solomon supplied the harbor and the ships, and Tyre the sailors and captains, no doubt, and Tyrian trade commenced to conquer the Red Sea (9:26-28).[7]

---

[2]   According to the Septuagint (3 Kgdms 5:1; MT: 1 Kgs 5:15), Solomon became a vassal of Hiram; cf. J.K. KUAN, *Third Kingdoms 5.1 and Israelite-Tyrian Relations during the Reign of Solomon*, in *JSOT* 46 (1990). p. 31-46. In a number of cases, the Septuagint of 1 Kgs 3-11 contains readings older than, and superior to, the present Hebrew text (see *infra*, n. 64). The problem of whether 3 Kgdms 5:1 originally referred to Solomon (or to another Israelite king) will be discussed *infra* (with n. 45 and 46).

[3]   As E. Lipiński has argued (this volume, p. 153-166). Solomon gave Hiram territory which had always been Phoenician. It is likely, therefore, that this "transfer" is a midrashic elaboration on Jos. 19:23-31 which explains why territory allotted to one of the Israelite tribes never was part of Israel, at least at no time within recorded history. 1 Kgs 9:10-14 would then date to the post-exilic period (cf. for the redactional history of Jos. 13-19: M. WÜST, *Untersuchungen zu den siedlungsgeographischen Texten des Alten Testaments. I: Ostjordanland* [BTAVO B 9], Wiesbaden 1975), and has no historical implications.

[4]   Cf. I. WALLERSTEIN, *The Capitalist World-Economy*, Cambridge 1979, especially *Chap. 1. The Inequalities of Core and Periphery.*

[5]   Cf. for this structure, exemplified by Palestine in the Early Bronze Age, C.S. STEELE, *Early Bronze Age Socio-Political Organization in Southwestern Jordan*, in *ZDPV* 106 (1990), in press.

[6]   Cf. for Solomon's dependency on Phoenicia already H. DONNER, *The Interdependence of Internal Affairs and Foreign Policy during the Davidic-Solomonic Period (with Special Regard to the Phoenician Coast)*, in T. ISHIDA (ed.), *Studies in the Period of David and Solomon*, Tokyo 1982, p. 205-214; ID., *Geschichte des Volkes Israel und seiner Nachbarn in Grundzügen. Teil I: Von den Anfängen bis zur Staatenbildungszeit*, Göttingen 1984, p. 217-219.

[7]   Cf. A. LEMAIRE, *Les Phéniciens et le commerce entre la Mer Rouge et la Mer Méditerranée*, in E. LIPIŃSKI (ed.), *Studia Phoenicia V. Phoenicia and the East Mediterranean in the First Millennium B.C.* (OLA 22), Leuven 1987, p. 49-60.

Se non è vero, è ben trovato. Even if this account should not prove true on the level of events, even if nothing like this should have happened in the tenth century B.C., it may still be valid on the level of structures and conjunctures, that aspect of history that Fernand Braudel, foremost among others, has taught us to analyze, and appreciate. Throughout recorded history, *i.e.* from the middle of the third millennium B.C. to the present, the hill-country of Palestine—comprising, among other cultures, ancient Israel—has been the agricultural *hinterland* of the coastal cities, which were Phoenician or Philistine in the Iron Age.[8] Judah and the land of Israel traded with you; wheat and resins and wax, honey, oil and balsam they delivered to you", remarks Ezek. 27:17. The verse forms part of Tyrian trade statistics from the late seventh or early sixth century B.C., and is corroborated by an Israelite seal of the seventh century dedicated to the Astarte of Sidon.[9] In Ezek. 27:12-24, no other trade partner's deliveries are as basic, or as poor.

But did this structure, this dependency, apply to the tenth century B.C. to the same degree as it applies to the Late Bronze Age and the Iron II period? Given that the Mediterranean economic system seems not to have fully recovered from its first breakdown *ca.* 1200 B.C. before the ninth century,[10] some doubts are called for. These doubts can be substantiated by resuscitating the nearly forgotten problem of King Solomon's copper supply. This does not suggest by any means that the search for "King Solomon's mines" be renewed. These have expired for good.[11] Such mines need not have existed at all, because Solomon cannot possibly have embellished the temple with all the metal implements accounted for in 1 Kgs 7. They amount to *ca* 50 tons of copper: an incredible amount given that an Egyptian mining expedition to Timna retrieved between one half and 5 tons of copper.[12]

---

[8] Cf. E.A. KNAUF, *Vallée et montagne, cité et tribu; éléments d'une histoire palestinienne de cinq millénaires*, in *Mémoire de Soie. Costumes et parures de Palestine et de Jordanie. Catalogue de la collection Widad Kamel Kawar, présentée à l'Institut du Monde Arabe*, Paris 1988, p. 26-35, 402-403; ID., *O Gott, ein Tau vom Himmel giess: Kanaunäische Mythologie im Kirchenlied*, in *Biblische Notizen* 50 (1989), p. 34-45, here p. 37-38; ID. and C.H. BROOKER, review of JOSHUA PRAWER, *Crusader Institutions* (1980), in *ZDPV* 104 (1988), p. 184-188, here p. 187-188.

[9] Cf. for that seal which, like most Israelite seals from the seventh and sixth centuries B.C., is usually misclassified as "Ammonite", E.A. KNAUF, *War Biblisch-Hebräisch eine Sprache? Empirische Gesichtspunkte zur Annäherung an die Sprache der althebräischen Literatur*, in *ZAH* 3 (1990), p. 11-23, here p. 23; U. HÜBNER and E.A. KNAUF, review of W.E. AUFRECHT, *A Corpus of Ammonite Inscriptions* (Ancient Near Eastern Texts and Studies 4) (1989), forthcoming in *ZDPV*. Ezek. 27:12-24 is posterior to the fall of Samaria, 722 B.C., and predates the fall of Edom, 552 B.C.; cf. E.A. KNAUF, *Supplementa Ismaelitica 13. Edom und Arabien*, in *Biblische Notizen* 45 (1988), p. 62-81, here p. 73-74.

[10] Cf. A.B. KNAPP, *The History and Culture of Ancient Western Asia and Egypt*, Chicago 1988, p. 219-222, 244-245; E.A. KNAUF, *The Migration of the Script, and the Formation of the State in South Arabia*, in *Proceedings of the Seminar for Arabian Studies* 19 (1989), p. 79-91.

[11] Cf. J.D. MUHLY, *Timna and King Solomon*, in *BiOr* 41 (1984), p. 275-292.

[12] Cf. G. MANSFELD, review of H.G. CONRAD-B. ROTHENBERG, *Antikes Kupfer im Timna-Tal: 4000 Jahre Bergbau und Verhüttung in der Arabah* (Bochum 1980), in *ZDPV* 99 (1983), p. 219-224, here p. 221-222; J.D. Muhly, *art. cit.* (n. 11), p. 280-281.

The volume of metal employed in 1 Kgs 7 was so exuberant for ancient Palestine that the author shied from calculating it (7:47)—the same author who had no qualms in crediting Solomon with a work force of 180,000 men (1 Kgs 5:27-29), which exceeds the number of able-bodied males that can be calculated for the whole of Palestine, including the Philistines, in the tenth century B.C.[13] The numbers in 1 Kgs 5-7 are so far removed from the reality of the tenth century, and are so close to the exaggerated numbers common in the Priestly source and Chronicles, that serious doubts arise whether the author or authors of the Solomon story had at their disposal any documentary material concerning that king. This problem will be discussed in the following section. There can be no doubt, however, that the Solomonic State economy needed some copper if there indeed had been such a State, and this question can be meaningfully investigated.

Towards a Literary History of the Biblical Solomon

It is inevitable now to discuss the biblical narrative, its origin, and its reliability, in some detail. The modern historian cannot take any ancient literary source at face value, because ancient historiographers generally do not report what had happened but rather what they supposed should have happened—even in cases where they could have known better.[14] Once the necessity of historical criticism, the necessity of a critical evaluation of the sources is acknowledged, historians have basically two choices. They may opt for a maximalist approach which implies that everything in the sources that could not be proved wrong has to be accepted as historical; or for a minimalist approach which means that everything which is not corroborated by evidence contemporary with the events to be reconstructed is dismissed. As it is a minority of historians who follow the minimalist approach, which is adopted in this essay, its methodological presuppositions may briefly be outlined.[15]

---

[13] Cf. already E. WÜRTHWEIN, *Das Erste Buch der Könige, Kapitel 1-16* (ATD 11,1), Göttingen 1977, p. 56: an estimated population of 1 million people cannot provide 150,000-180,000 corvée workers. But the initial estimate is far too high, cf. now I. Finkelstein, *The Emergence of the Monarchy in Israel. The Environmental and Socio-Economic Aspects*, in *JSOT* 44 (1989), p. 43-74, here p. 59.

[14] Cf. H.J. NISSEN, *Grundzüge einer Geschichte der Frühzeit des Vorderen Orients*, Darmstadt 1983, p. 4-5; N.P. LEMCHE, *On the Problem of Studying Israelite History*, in *Biblische Notizen* 24 (1984), p. 94-124; E.A. KNAUF, review of H.M. Niemann, *Die Daniten. Studien zur Geschichte eines altisraelitischen Stammes* (1985), in *ZDPV* 101 (1985), p. 183-187, here p. 184; ID., *Midian, Untersuchungen zur Geschichte Palästinas und Nordarabiens am Ende des 2. Jahrtausends v. Chr.* (ADPV), Wiesbaden 1988, p. 41-42, 147-149, 170.

[15] The practical justification of supplementing the various maximalist reconstructions of Solomon by a minimalist approach lies in the spectre defined by those two extremes. "Current historical knowledge" may be equated with that spectre rather than with one of its points. I should point

The historical books of the Hebrew Bible are a primary source for the period of their final redaction only. The final redaction of 1-2 Kgs can be dated to *ca* 400 B.C. on linguistic grounds.[16] A margin of plus or minus one hundred years does not bring the text significantly closer to the tenth century B.C. 1 Kgs 1-11 is a secondary source for the tenth century B.C. insofar, as the text contains contemporary documents. As such documents are hypothetical reconstructions, they cannot compete with primary historical documentation from the tenth century such as exists, provided, *e.g.*, by archaeology and Shoshenq's list. If material in 1 Kgs 1-11 can be shown to pre-date the final redaction, the lowest possible date for that material is the most likely date, given that memories, historical traditions, and books evaporate in the course of time, very much like carbon-14 molecules.[17] As history is not an entity outside of our minds which can be explored to its full width, length and depth—the past is irretrievably gone! —, but rather a hypothetical reconstruction, *i.e.* a creation of the historian, the minimalist approach is nothing but an application of Occam's razor: *entia non sunt multiplicanda praeter necessitatem*.[18] The question cannot be "Is it possible that event E mentioned in source S did happen?", as many traditional historians still ask. In a field of unlimited possibilities the question can only be "What can we responsibly assume to have happened in the area A, at the time T, on the basis of the complete primary documentation that is available concerning A and T?".

It is common practice to conclude from the biblical account that Solomon was the head of a State with a vast administrative network. It is then assumed that Solomon's administration produced annals, and that the biblical account is basically trustworthy because it is based on documents which originated at Solomon's court. The argument appears circular. It can be refuted from both perspectives: archaeology provides sufficient evidence to conclude that Jerusalem did not become the center of a State prior to the end of the eighth century B.C.,[19]

---

out that I respect the maximalist endeavor as a possible (though not recommendable) *scholarly* approach, as opposed to blatant fundamentalism as the minimalist attitude is opposed to historical agnosticism.

[16] Cf. E.A. KNAUF, *War Biblisch-Hebräisch* (*art. cit.*, n. 9), p. 20-22. A comparison of the Hebrew text of Kings with the Greek suggests a further minor redaction, characterized by deleting "offensive" passages without changing the overall appearance of the text, which may have been conducted in the second or even first centuries B.C., cf. n. 2 and 64.

[17] Traditions, of course, grow constantly in detail and content. This growth, however, diminishes the tradition's historicity proportionally to its growth: a small group of anonymous magi became, in the course of the centuries, three kings, who were finally given names. Cf. also L.L. GRABBE, *Josephus and the Reconstruction of the Judaean Reconstruction*, in *JBL* 106 (1987), p. 231-246, here p. 237 with n. 28, and p. 245; E.A. Knauf, *Midian* (*op. cit.*, n. 14), p. 147.

[18] I have discussed the methodology of historical criticism in more detail in *From History to Interpretation* forthcoming in D. EDELMAN (ed.), *Archaeology, History, and the Bible*.

[19] Cf. D.W. JAMIESON-DRAKE, *Scribes and Schools in Monarchic Judah: A Socio-Archeological Approach*, Ph.D. Duke University 1988 (UMI 882201), p. 203-216. To conclude from settlement

and biblical historiography strongly suggests that either there were no annalistic records for David and Solomon or, if there had been, they were lost before the authors of Samuel-Kings commenced to work.[20]

From Jeroboam and Rehoboam down to the last kings of Judah, the present Books of Kings give detailed figures about each king's rule. There can be no doubt that these figures derive either from an annalistic source, or from a source based on an annalistic source, such as the "Chronicles of the kings of Israel (or Judah)" which are frequently mentioned. The basic reliability of the biblical chronology from Jeroboam and Rehoboam through Zedekiah—minor problems discounted—is corroborated by synchronisms with Assyrian and Egyptian chronology starting in the middle of the ninth century B.C. In the cases of Solomon and David, only the round—and suspicious—figure of a rule of "40 years" is provided (2 Kgs 2:11; 11:42). This is an indication that no records survived from these two rulers' courts—if there ever had been such records. In a similar manner, Mesha of Moab attributes "40 years" to the Omrides' suppression of Moab. This figure is irreconcilable with Omride chronology,[21] but Mesha' may not have been

---

size and distribution and social stratification that Judah could not have become a State before the end of the eighth century B.C. does, of course, presuppose a general definition of "State"—something that is missing from almost all traditional histories of Israel. But even a traditional archaeologist who links tenth century Hazor and Megiddo with Solomon (a link that simply cannot be provided by archaeology, apart from the still unsettled stratigraphic problems at both sites) cannot fail to observe the discrepancy that exists between Solomon's realm as depicted in 1 Kgs 1-11 and Palestine in the tenth century, cf. J.B. PRITCHARD, *The Age of Solomon*, in J.B. Pritchard (ed.), *Solomon & Sheba*, London 1974, p. 17-39, here p. 35-36; H. WEIPPERT, *Palästina in vorhellenistischer Zeit* (Handbuch der Archäologie: Vorderasien II 1), München 1988, p. 426, 492, 510. Note that the "fortresses" attributed to Solomon *ibid.*, p. 480-484, are neither fortresses, nor do they derive from the tenth century B.C.; cf. I. FINKELSTEIN, *The Iron Age "Fortresses" of the Negev Highlands: Sedentarization of the Nomads*, in *Tel Aviv* 11 (1984), p. 189-209; E.A. KNAUF, review of R. COHEN-G. SCHMITT, *Drei Studien zur Archäologie und Topographie Alt-Israels* (1980), in *ZDPV* 102 (1986), p. 175-176, here p. 175.

[20] One cannot rule out the possibility that annalistic records set in during the reign of Solomon: an assumption that would facilitate the use of some notes scattered through the present account which invite the historians' credulity (as, *e.g.*, 1 Kgs 9:16-18 and, perhaps, 7:46). In this case, however, it remains difficult to understand why by the time annal keeping set in, Solomon's regnal year was not precisely remembered. There can be little doubt that Canaanite Jerusalem prior to David's conquest kept annals like Byblos at the time of Unamun's visit. It seems, however, that such annals were either destroyed or discontinued when David, and later Solomon, took over the city, an observation that—among others—gives rise to the suspicion that Solomon's access to power was even more violent (and anti-Davidic?) as 1 Kgs 1-2 betrays (cf. also n. 61). The precise descriptions—and dates—in chapters 6-7 do not require an annalistic source; otherwise, such a source must also be postulated for Exod. 25-31:11; 35:4-40:33. The dates in 1 Kgs 6:1, 37-38 seem to operate on the same level as Exod. 40:17: the regnal years are calculated to match the year 480 *post Exodum* (twelve generations!), and the conclusion of the temple after seven years makes it an image of the world that was created in seven days.

[21] Cf. for previous—and generally unsuccessful—attempts to deal with the chronological problem provided by line 8 of the Mesha' inscription: "He (sc. Omri) dwelt in it (sc. Madeba) in his days

able to know that. Mesha''s inscription contains two excerpts from his royal annals;[22] given that obviously there was no record where he could have looked up the date of Omri's conquest of Ataroth, Moabite annal writing can be assumed to have commenced under Mesha', whose activities as recorded in his inscription characterize him in any case as the founder of the Moabite State.[23] For what had happened before his time, the round figure of "40 years" indicates that it was a long time of unknown extent, but of human, not mythical measure. Analogously, it must then be argued that Israelite and/or Judaean annals' production began under Jeroboam or Rehoboam.[24]

That there was no entry for Solomon in the "Chronicles of the kings of (Israel and) Judah", which otherwise provide us with a generally working chronology for the late ninth through sixth centuries B.C.,—nor was there one for David, the half-legendary founder of the dynasty,[25]—is corroborated by 1 Kgs 11:41 which refers rather to a "Chronicle of Solomon". I suggest that the bulk of the material contained in 1 Kgs 3-11 is drawn from this literary work which was probably composed during the reign of Josiah. It depicts Solomon as the king that Josiah intended to be.[26] Josiah's politics were basically an ill-fated attempt at imperialism,

---

and half the days of his son(s)—40 years" J.A. DEARMAN, *Historical Reconstruction and the Mesha Inscription*, in J.A. DEARMAN (ed.), *Studies in the Mesha Inscription and Moab* (Archaeological and Biblical Studies 2), Atlanta 1989, p. 155-210, here p. 164-167.

[22] Cf. for the Mesha' inscription's lines 10-21 E.A. KNAUF, review of K.A.D. SMELIK, *Historische Dokumente aus dem Alten Israel* (1987), in *ZDPV* 104 (1988), p. 174-176, here p. 175.

[23] Cf. J.A. DEARMAN, *Historical Reconstruction* (*art. cit.*, n. 21), p. 167-170; M. WEIPPERT, *The Relations of the States East of the Jordan with the Mesopotamian Powers during the First Millennium BC*, in *Studies in the History and Archaeology of Jordan* 3 (1987), p. 97-105; E.A. KNAUF, *Migration of the Script* (*art. cit.*, n. 10), p. 82-83.

[24] Accordingly, there is no absolute chronology for the Israelite/Judaean rulers prior to the first year of Rehoboam/Jeroboam (926/5 B.C.). Roughly, one may assign to Saul the first quarter of the tenth century B.C., to David its second quarter, and to Solomon the third quarter. Solomon's adherence to Saulide traditions (1 Kgs 3:4-4:1, see *infra* n. 49) indicates that there were hardly forty years that separated Saul's death from Solomon's accession.

[25] As I hope to discuss in another context, all reliable traditions about David derive from Hebron. His rule over Jerusalem may not have been more successful than Abimelech's kingship over Shechem.

[26] The fifth century may have contributed the wisdom complex, *i.e.* 1 Kgs 5:9-14 together with the Queen of Sheba, 1 Kgs 10:1-13 (with even later additions in 10:14-29). These texts reflect the internationalism of the Persian period, an internationalism both of trade relationships and intellectual life, which was building up since the end of the eighth century B.C.—as does the trade network depicted in 10:22-29 (cf. *infra*, n. 50). Cf. for 1 Kgs 5:9-14 E.A. KNAUF, *Ismael. Untersuchungen zur Geschichte Palästinas und Nordarabiens im 1. Jahrtausend v. Chr.* (ADPV), 2nd ed., Wiesbaden 1989, p. 148, and for the "Queen of Sheba", a story that betrays a significant distance from the historical reality of the eighth century B.C., when Sabaean-Judaean contacts were first established, cf. E.A. KNAUF, *Midian* (*op. cit.*, n. 14), p. 29-31; ID., *Migration of the Script* (*art. cit.*, n. 10), p. 85-86. It goes without saying that characteristically "deuteronomistic" passages such as 11:1-13 are also post-Josianic. For the excursus on Aramaean history (11:14-25)—cf. A. LEMAIRE, *Hadad l'Edomite ou Hadad l'Araméen?*, in *Biblische Notizen* 43 (1988), p. 14-18. This may be drawn from

ill-fated, because a poor and marginal country like Palestine could not sustain such a political program for long. Josiah's politics, and the concept of a Davidic-Solomonic "Empire", which could hardly have emerged before that period as well, are only conceivable as a national reaction to the experience of Assyrian imperialism, or as an attempt to emulate the waning masters of yesteryear.[27] There was no central State with the elaborate administrative hierarchy depicted by 1 Kgs 5:30; 9:23 in the tenth century B.C.[28] Nor was there room for 4,000 chariots and 12,000 cavalry.[29] The figures in 1 Kgs 4-10 are only conceivable when one considers Judah's experience with the Assyrian army—and Assyrian corvée,[30] which 9:22 tries to emulate in blatant contradiction to 5:27.[31] The concept of a rule "from the Euphrates to the border of Egypt" (1 Kgs 5:1.4), reminiscent as the formula is of the Persian province of Transeuphratesia, can be traced back to the last decades of the seventh century, when such a rule was a reality for a short time.[32]

Aramaean sources and actually pertain to the tenth century B.C., although its inclusion in its present context presupposes 11:1-13. On the other hand, a case for the Josianic origin of 1 Kgs 3:16-28 can be made, although the story is indisputably legendary, cf. H. and M. Weippert, *Zwei Frauen vor dem Königsgericht*, in B. BECKING et al. (ed.), *Door het oog van de profeten: Exegetische studies aangeboden aan prof. dr. C. van Leeuwen*, Utrecht 1989, p. 133-160; M. WEIPPERT, *Die Petition eines Erntearbeiters aus Meṣad Ḥāšavyāhū und die Syntax althebräischer erzählender Prosa*, in E. BLUM et al. (ed.), *Die Hebräische Bibel und ihre zweifache Nachgeschichte* (Festschrift R. Rendtorff), Neukirchen-Vluyn 1990, p. 449-466.

[27] Cf. J.M. MILLER-J.H. Hayes, *A History of Ancient Israel and Judah*, Philadelphia 1986, p. 103-105, 138-139; R.B. COOTE-K.W. WHITELAM, *The Emergence of Early Israel in Historical Perspective*, Sheffield 1987, p. 172-173.

[28] Cf. *supra*, n. 19.

[29] Cavalry does not appear in the Assyrian army prior to Ashurnasirpal II (883-859 B.C.), and could have spread to Palestine only later: cf. B. HROUDA, *Die Kulturgeschichte des assyrischen Flachbildes*, Bonn 1965, p. 100. Ahab, who rules over a larger population and commanded a higher income than any Palestinian ruler of the tenth century B.C. could have done, sent no more than 2000 chariots into the battle of Qarqar. Given the precarious situation, this was presumably all he could muster. 1 Kgs 10:26, which reduces Solomon's chariotry to 1400, reads like an attempt to reconcile the tradition with the rather limited reality of Palestine through the ages (a similar vein is betrayed by 7:47).

[30] In 673 B.C., Judaeans were among the contingents from Assyria's western vassals which were summoned to expand the armory of Niniveh (Ash. Nin. A V 40-VI 1). The text was most recently treated by S. TIMM, *Moab zwischen den Mächten. Studien zu historischen Denkmälern und Texten* (ÄAT 17), Wiesbaden 1989, p. 360-366.

[31] 1 Kgs 9:20-22 reads like a midrash on 5:27-28 which aims at a reconciliation of the Josianic Solomon in 5:15-32 with Deut. 17:14-20.

[32] Assyrian, and later Egyptian rule "from the brook of Egypt to the Euphrates" is foreshadowed by the activities of the Damascene Hazā'el at the end of the ninth century B.C.; cf. F. BRON-A. LEMAIRE, *Les inscriptions araméennes de Hazaël*, in *RA* 83 (1989), p. 35-44, here p. 43, and also I. EPH'AL-J. NAVEH, *Hazael's Booty Inscriptions*, in *IEJ* 39 (1989), p. 192-200. Hazael's supremacy cannot, however, have been comparable to the strict suzerainty introduced by Assyria from 738 B.C. onwards. The range of Hazael's military activities does, of course, from a momentum in the growth

The reality was, however, that of an Egyptian Empire (2 Kgs 24:7), not an Israelite kingdom, and Josiah was *de facto*—and probably also *de jure*—an Egyptian vassal.[33] As an Egyptian vassal, Josiah appears to have aspired to acquire that part of his suzerain's realm which is described as "Solomon's Empire" in 1 Kgs 5:1. Such a program, and the attempt to implement it, may explain Josiah's violent death in 609 B.C., whereas the death he met—execution without a battle (2 Kgs 23:29)—reflects his true political status in relation to Egypt.[34] On the basis of these observations it can be suggested that the "Chronicle of Solomon", which the compiler of the Solomon-story in the Books of Kings used, originated at Josiah's court.

A relatively late origin for the basic account on Solomon also agrees with the redactional history of 1-2 Kgs as reconstructed by Helga Weippert.[35] Weippert was able to distinguish three stages. The first redaction covers only the rulers from Josaphat through Hosea; it was probably composed by a northern refugee in the time of Hezekiah. The second stage covers the kings from Rehoboam/Jeroboam down to Josiah, and must have been concluded shortly after Josiah's death.[36] In the third stage, the last four canonical kings of Judah were added.[37] It is not necessary to discuss at this point whether the stories of (David and) Solomon were added at the third or—more likely—at even a later stage, but they definitely were not included prior to the Exile.

It is the beginning of this redactional process that warrants further consideration in connection with the literary history of Solomon. There is a considerable discrepancy at the beginning of the first redactor's work. Why should an Israelite start his history with the Judaean king Josaphat and leave a blank for Josaphat's Israelite contemporaries? If, however, he had actually started with Josaphat's contemporaries, the sons of Omri, his history would make perfect sense as an

---

of supra-national structures in the Near East which was finally to lead, via the Assyrian, Neobabylonian, Persian and Diadoche empires, to the unity of the Roman world. Whereas the ninth century B.C. saw the ancient world on the road to its final culmination, the tenth century did not yet.

[33] Cf. J.M. MILLER-J.H. HAYES, *A History* (*op. cit.*, n. 27), p. 383-402.

[34] The "Deuteronomistic Historians" (*i.e.*, the editors of the pre-priestly part of Genesis through 2. Kings) convey by their work a specific reaction to Josiah's failed imperialism which is diametrically opposed to the reaction of Jeremiah (and his editors) to the same problem, cf. R. ALBERTZ, *Die Intentionen und die Träger des Deuteronomistischen Geschichtswerks*, in R. ALBERTZ et al. (ed.), *Schöpfung und Befreiung. Für Claus Westermann zum 80. Geburtstag*, Stuttgart 1989, p. 37-53, and for the psychopolitical mechanisms involved, A. and M. MITSCHERLICH, *Die Unfähigkeit zu trauern. Grundlagen kollektiven Verhaltens*, München 1967.

[35] Cf. H. WEIPPERT, *Die "deuteronomistischen" Beurteilungen der Könige von Israel und Juda und das Problem der Redaktion der Königsbücher*, in *Biblica* 53 (1972), p. 301-339.

[36] Josiah's failure could explain why his program—Solomon—was disregarded by the second redaction which supposedly took place immediately after his death.

[37] The canonical Judaean king list disregards the last king of Judah, Gedaliah (586-582), because he was not of Davidic descent; cf. J.M. MILLER-J.H. HAYES, *A History* (*op. cit.*, n. 27), p. 421-426.

Israelite history.[38] The Assyrians saw in Omri the actual founder of the Israelite State, calling it *Bīt Ḫumrī*, and the epigrapher and historian can only agree with them. It is with Omri and his successors that we find the material appurtenances of a State: imperial architecture and administrative documents.[39] The first redactor's history—or historical source—supports this view. At the same time, it is obvious why it had to be cut out within the conceptual framework of the present 1-2 Kgs. It can be suggested that some material covering the dynasty of Omri was not completely lost, but had rather been conferred on the biblical Solomon. Accepting Miller-Hayes' theory of only one king Joram/Jehoram who ruled over both Israel and Judah,[40] there had been a "united kingdom" at the beginning of that history, extending from Dan to Beersheba, although its center was not Jerusalem.[41] Under Omri and his successors, the pattern of Phoenician-Israelite relations as depicted in the account of Solomon did undoubtedly exist. Phoenician luxuries enhanced the glamour of the Israelite court, which, undoubtedly, had to be paid for with primary subsistence goods in return. Phoenician-Israelite trade cooperatives operated south of Judah from the middle of the ninth to the middle of the eighth century, as shown by the finds from Kuntillet 'Ajrūd.[42] Israel and, presumably, the Phoenicians too were active on the Red Sea, where a Judaean attempt to circumvent their monopoly failed (1 Kgs 22:48-49).[43]

Either the Phoenician-Israelite relationships at the time of Solomon were as they are depicted in the Bible,—in which case they came 100 years too early, led nowhere, and left no further trace in history beyond the literary account,—or the Phoenician section in the story of Solomon is a projection of relationships that had existed indeed, but 100 years after Solomon, when they are well attested by the epigraphical and archaeological record. Methodologically, the second option recommends itself.

---

[38] The Judaean claim—advanced after 722 B.C.—to represent the true Israel has decisively obscured the fact that Israel and Judah were, up to this point in history, two different and independent states and societies with quite different languages (see *supra*, n. 16) and even religions (see *infra*, n. 66: while Asherah was Yahweh's spouse in Judah, it was 'Anat in Israel).

[39] The Assyrian recognition of Omri's achievement is corroborated by the material culture remains: with Omri, imperial architecture and a conspicuous consumption of luxury goods set in. That Omri's historical significance is obscured by his treatment in Kings has already been pointed out by S. TIMM, *Die Dynastie Omri. Quellen und Untersuchungen zur Geschichte Israels im 9. Jh.* (FRLANT 124), Göttingen 1982.

[40] Cf. J.M. MILLER-J.H. HAYES, *A History* (op. cit., n. 27), p. 280-284.

[41] Although David's and Solomon's rule over Israel (and not just Judah) could well be another projection of Judaean aspirations after 722 B.C., the conflicts between David and Eshbaal, David and the northern "insurgents", and Solomon's incubation at Gibeon indicate that both contended for Saul's inheritance—rather unsuccessfully, as one may conclude from Shoshenq's list of conquests (see *infra*, n. 60).

[42] Cf. A. LEMAIRE, *Commerce* (art. cit., n. 7), p. 52; H. WEIPPERT, *Archäologie* (op. cit., n. 19), p. 618, 671-672.

[43] Cf. J.M. MILLER-J.H. HAYES, *A History* (op. cit., n. 27), p. 279-280.

There are other indications that part of what now is told about Solomon had originally been part of the first redactor's or his source's treatment of the Dynasty of Omri. A linguistic observation indicates that at least parts of the building accounts in 1 Kgs 6-7 are of northern, Israelite, and hence not Jerusalemite, origin. In the account of the temple-building, which is a restoration report rather than a building report,[44] *qōf* appears once for etymological *ḍād, viz.* in *ql'ym* (6:34), otherwise *ṣl'ym*. This is a northern, Israelite, linguistic trait.[45] The list of the so-called "twelve districts" covers Israelite territory only to the exclusion of Judah (1 Kgs 4:8-19). Its mention of Gad in 4:19 (according to the LXX) viewed in the light of Meshaʻ's inscription, who points out that Gad had never been Israelite except for a hostile invasion by Omri,[46] makes an Omride date for this list very likely.

Given all the material in 1 Kgs 1-11 that recognizably refers to structures and events post-900 B.C., what remains from the biblical account for the historical Solomon? Possibly the "Court History" ending in 1 Kgs 1-2, composed around 700 B.C.,[47] which may have drawn on local traditions of Jerusalem and memories of Jerusalemite families. Possibly the story of Solomon's incubation and divine designation to the kingship at Gibeon (1 Kgs 3:4-5.15; 4:1),[48] which serves as the

---

[44] As K. Ruprecht has convincingly argued, the architectural details presented by 1 Kgs 6-7 do not make Solomon the builder, but rather the restorer of a temple; cf. K. RUPRECHT, *Der Tempel von Jerusalem: Gründung Salomos oder jebusitisches Erbe?* (BZAW 144), Berlin 1976. The redactional-critical and linguistic observations presented here cast further doubt on who originally built and/or restored what, when, and at which location.

[45] Cf. for Israelite <q> representing Proto-Semitic /ẓ/ (the voiced lateral fricative which is preserved in Modern South Arabic, and became /ḍ/ in Arabic), E.A. KNAUF, *War Biblisch-Hebräisch* (*art. cit.*, n. 9), p. 16-19. An Israelite *Vorlage* of a Judaean text can, of course, only be detected whenever the Judaean redactors overlooked—or misinterpreted—an "Israelitism". Except for the fact that an Israelite source was used in 1 Kgs 6, the linguistic observation does not help to deliminate clearly which parts of the chapter were drawn from that source, and to whose building activities it originally referred.—In 5:32, one may read *wa-hagbīl-ām* instead of *wĕ-hag-giblīm* and think of rusticated ashlars as are known from, *e.g.*, Samaria, but not from tenth century Jerusalem (H. Weippert, *Archäologie* [*op. cit.*, n. 19], p. 461, pace E.-M. LAPERROUSAZ, *Après le "temple du Salomon" la Bamah de Tel Dan*, in *Syria* 51 [1982], p. 223-237).

[46] Whenever there was a Moabite claim to territories which Omri had brought under Israelite control, Meshaʻ carefully stated his case: "The people of Gad had lived in the country of Ataroth since time immemorial. Then came the king of Israel and fortified Ataroth for himself" (lines 10-11). There can be little doubt that Meshaʻ of Dibon himself stemmed from the tribe of Gad, cf. Numb. 33:45-46 (E. A. KNAUF, *Midian* [*op. cit.*, n. 14], p. 162). It is nowhere stated that the inhabitants of the Israelite fortress-city of ʻAṭarōth, whom Meshaʻ slaughtered, were Gadites—thus J.A. DEARMAN, *Historical Reconstruction* (*art. cit.*, n. 21), p. 190, n. 143. Meshaʻ represents an indigenous tradition that saw Gad as part of Moab, not Israel.

[47] Cf. for the date of the "Succession Narrative" O. KAISER, *Beobachtungen zur sogenannten Thronfolgeerzählung Davids*, in *ET* 64 (1988), p. 5-20.

[48] Cf. for the connection between 3:15 and 4:1, and the political purpose of the pre-deuteronomistic account, E. WÜRTHWEIN, *Könige* (*op. cit.*, n. 13), p. 30-35.

legitimation of King Solomon from an Israelite perspective as much as 1 Kgs 1-2 legitimates him from a Jerusalemite point of view.[49] Possibly, scattered pieces of poetry (1 Kgs 8:12-13; 10:28), whose relation to the historical Solomon has to be argued on internal grounds, as their attribution to that king in the present redactional compilation is worthless.[50] Possibly also, scattered notes on his activities which may have been preserved in the memory of Jerusalem and Judah (1 Kgs 9:16-18), whose accuracy can be checked against external evidence.

The story of Solomon as it stands forms in essence the overture for the opera which unfolds through 1-2 Kgs. Like an overture, it presents the main motifs of the following drama, and was, as is usually the case with overtures, composed after the opera was basically completed. It is a comprehensive account of what, in the mind of its final redactors, the State of Israel was supposed to be, and incorporates the experience of 500 years of hopes and history. As an account of tenth century history, it is aberrant. As a condensed view of Israelite history throughout the reign of her kings, and the role of Phoenicia throughout that period, it is rather excellent.

An Historical Reconstruction of King Solomon

The Biblical Solomon is a narrative construct. In order to evaluate the historical information that the narrative still may contain, it is necessary to turn to the primary evidence.

The Late Bronze and Iron Ages are not the first, nor the last period in which the demise and resurgence of statehood in Palestine can be observed.[51] In every case, statehood spreads from west to east and from north to south, following the patterns of rainfall—indispensable for agricultural surplus production—and international trade. Phoenician economic expansion led, in the first half of the ninth century, to secondary State formation in Israel which, in turn, led to secondary States in Moab

---

[49] Cf. for Gibeon as Saul's capital, comparable to Abimelech's Shechem, David's Hebron, and Solomon's Jerusalem, J. BLENKINSOPP, *Gibeon and Israel*, Cambridge 1972, p. 86; D. EDELMAN, *Saul's Rescue of Jabesh-Gilead. Sorting Story from History*, in ZAW 96 (1984), p. 195-209, here p. 204.

[50] The authenticity of 1 Kgs 8:12-13 is strongly supported by its heterodox character within the present canonical text (see *infra*, n. 65). The fragment provides necessary—and sufficient—historic background for the historical tradition of Solomon the temple builder. On the other hand, there is nothing in 10:28 that links its content more closely with the tenth century B.C. rather than Ezek. 27:12-25. Cf. for the poetic nature of 10:28, and its limited historical value, D.R. SCHLEY, *1 Kings 10:26-29: A Reconsideration*, in *JBL* 106 (1987), p. 595-601.

[51] Cf. for a macro-historical approach to the history of Palestine, 3000 B.C. through 1948 A.D., which connects the ups and downs of Palestinian cultural and political history to the rise and fall of world economic systems, R.B. COOTE-K.W. WHITELAM, *Early Israel* (*op. cit.*, n. 27); E.A. KNAUF, *Vallée et montagne* (*art. cit.*, n. 8); Id., *Edom* (*art. cit.*, n. 9), p. 62-81.

in the second half of the ninth century.⁵² Well into the eighth century, Judah was a chiefdom in the shadow of, if not the direct dependency on, Israel.⁵³ Macro-historical considerations like these do not, of course, imply that David and Solomon did not exist. They do, however, constitute a framework of conditions and a scale for their possible existence.⁵⁴ David's and Solomon's exercise of power may be evaluated in the line of Gideon, Abimelech, and Ẓāhir al-'Umar,⁵⁵ and was rather different from the rule of an Omri, Hezekiah, or Herodes.

The archaeological record for Palestine in the tenth century shows a rather poor country with incipient, but decentralized, urbanism. If there is anything like an economic and cultural core area, it is Philistia—and for the region north of the Jezreel valley, Phoenicia.⁵⁶ It is impossible to tell from the archaeological record whether Hazor in the tenth century was the center of an independent principality, or was rather a local stronghold of a power outside its own territory, as public buildings cover less than 10% of the walled-in area. It is impossible not to see that Megiddo around 800 B.C., and Lakish around 700 B.C., were outposts of a central State, public buildings consuming up to 50% of the built-in area.

The most important piece of documentary evidence for late tenth century Palestine is Shoshenq's list of conquered cities.⁵⁷ Nor does chronology leave much

---

⁵² Cf. for secondary state formation in general, B.J. PRICE, *Secondary State Formation: An Explanatory Model*, in R. COHEN and E.R. SERVICE (ed.), *The Origins of State: The Anthropology of Political Evolution*. Philadelphia 1978, p. 161-186; and for Palestine and Arabia in the first millennium B.C., E.A. KNAUF, *Migration of the Script* (*art. cit.*, n. 10).

⁵³ Cf. for Judah as a vassal state of Israel in the period of Omri, and of Damascus in the following decades, J.M. MILLER-J.H. HAYES, *A History* (*op. cit.*, n. 27), p. 275-307. In Judah, political dependency on a higher developed nation enhanced rather than impeded State-formation, as was the case with Moab under the Omride dynasty, and the Transjordanian States in general under Assyrian rule, cf. M. WEIPPERT, *Relations* (*art. cit.*, n. 23); E.A. KNAUF, *Edom* (*art. cit.*, n. 9), p. 70-75.

⁵⁴ It is not necessary to deny that David and Solomon could have exercised some form of supremacy over Ammon, Moab and what existed of Edom in the tenth century B.C. (cf. E.A. KNAUF, *Edom* [*art. cit.*, n. 9], p. 68-70) in order to maintain that they were heads of a complex chiefdom rather than heads of States. At the beginning of the eighteenth century A.D., Jan Wellem ruled over the Palatinate, the dutchy of Cleve and the county of Berg, but that did not put him on an equal footing with the Roi Soleil.

⁵⁵ It is by the fortunes of literary and redactional history, not by any significant historical differences between them, that Abimelech ended up as a "judge" whereas Saul, David and Solomon became known as "kings". Cf. for Hebrew *šōpēṭ* "chief, ruler" W. RICHTER, *Zu den "Richtern Israels"*, in *ZAW* 77 (1965), p. 40-71; J.W. ROGERSON, *Was Early Israel a Segmentary Society?*, in *JSOT* 36 (1986), p. 17-26. Hebrew *melek*, Assyrian *šarru* do not always signify more than a tribal chief; cf. Jer. 25:20; 24 and E.A. KNAUF, *Ismael* (*op. cit.*, n. 26), p. 101.

⁵⁶ Cf. for the contrast between the tenth century and the ninth century H. WEIPPERT, *Archäologie* (*op. cit.*, n. 19), p. 510-530, and for a general resemblance of the tenth-century hill-country culture to the (proto-urban) Early Bronze Age *ibid.*, p. 417.

⁵⁷ Like most Egyptian topographical lists, the Shoshenq list needs re-publication; cf. preliminarily A. JIRKU, *Die ägyptischen Listen palästinischer und syrischer Ortsnamen in Umschrift und mit historisch-archäologischem Kommentar herausgegeben*, Leipzig 1937, p. 47-50, No. XXV;

doubt that he was a contemporary of Solomon.[58] He is the most likely candidate for the conqueror of Gezer, and Solomon's Egyptian father-in-law (1 Kgs 9:16-17), provided that this Egyptian marriage is based on a fact and not just another phantasy of the seventh century B.C. in historical disguise.[59] Shoshenq's list which excludes Jerusalem and its immediate vicinity from conquered Palestine is the most authentic document for the existence—and extension—of Solomon's principality that exists. Concomitantly, the list shows that any exercise of power by Solomon over an area extending the limits of 1 Kgs 9:17-18 was a claim rather than a reality, if even a claim.[60]

J. SIMONS, *Handbook for the Study of Egyptian Topographical Lists Relating to Western Asia*, Leiden 1937, p. 178-186, No. XXXIV; M. NOTH, *Die Wege der Pharaonenheere in Palästina und Syrien. Untersuchungen zu den hieroglyphischen Listen palästinischer und syrischer Städte, IV. Die Schoschenkliste*, in ZDPV 61 (1938), p. 277-304 = *Aufsätze zur biblischen Landes- und Altertumskunde* II, Neukirchen-Vluyn 1971, p. 73-93; B. MAZAR, *Pharaoh Shishak's Campaign to the Land of Israel*, in *The Early Biblical Period* (ed. S. Ahituv and B.A. Levine), Jerusalem 1986, p. 139-150.

[58] If Rehoboam ascended the throne in 926/5 B.C., there can be little doubt that Shoshenq cannot have campaigned in Palestine in Rehoboam's fifth year, as 1 Kgs 14:25 has it. Shoshenq most probably ruled from 945-924 B.C., cf. M.L. BIERBRIER, *Scheschonq*, in *Lexikon der Ägyptologie* V, Wiesbaden 1984, p. 585. The chronological problem has recently been presented, and quite clearly, by G. GARBINI, *History and Ideology in Ancient Israel*, New York 1988, p. 29-30.

[59] It is more than unlikely that Siamun (ca. 980-960 B.C.) was a conqueror of Gezer, and Solomon's Egyptian father-in-law. As a ruler of the XXI dynasty, he was committed to the concepts and ideals of the Ramesside period, and Garbini's objections against the possibility of Solomon's Egyptian marriage (*History and Ideology*, p. 27-28) would fully apply (they are not necessarily appropriate to Shoqhenq's mentality, who was a Lybian barbarian to begin with). Gezer appears as No. 12 in Shoqhenq's list, whereas Siamun's "Philistaean victory" relief may well be a re-used artefact deriving from the XXth dynasty and could hardly refer to the Canaanite city of Gezer anyway, *pace* J. VON BECKERATH, *Siamun*, in *Lexikon der Ägyptologie* V, Wiesbaden 1984, p. 921.

[60] If Jerusalem would have paid tribute to Shoqhenq as 1 Kgs 14:26 has it, Jerusalem would certainly have been included in the Pharaonic list of cities subdued. 1 Kgs 14:25-28 is by no means an excerpt from Rehoboam's annals, but rather a literary construct to remove treasures from Jerusalem which had not been there in the first place. All one can state within a reasonable margin of probability is that 1 Kgs 9:16 agrees with Shoshenq's list. It appears that the Egyptian marriage—which, as a diplomatic marriage, made Solomon as much of an Egyptian dependent as their Phoenician marriages made the Omrides Phoenician vassals—was concluded during or after Shoshenq's campaign. Whether Shoshenq decided that Jerusalem and its environs were too strong to be attacked, or Solomon decided that peace with the Pharaoh was preferable to war, we cannot say. The area between Hebron and Jerusalem that was left out by the Egyptian armies defines in any case the limits of Solomon's effective rule. The further relations between Shoshenq, Solomon and Jeroboam are open to speculations. According to the imperialistic device of *divide et impera*, it is not inconceivable that Shoshenq supported both Jeroboam and Solomon, and that he conducted his campaign partially on behalf of his allies. It is equally possible that Jeroboam's rule at Shechem—another area not invaded by Shoshenq—commenced during Solomon's lifetime. In this case, the "fifth year" of 1 Kgs 14:25 could originally have referred to Jeroboam, as 14:25-26 possibly reflects an Israelite tradition about Shoshenq, while 9:16 refers to his campaign from a Judaean point of view.

The historical Solomon, then, emerges as a Palestinian prince of rather limited means, combining the kingship of Jerusalem with the chiefdom of Judah, at least its northern part.[61] He was a son of David and fathered his successor Rehoboam with an Ammonite princess (1 Kgs 14:21). His ascendancy to the throne of Jerusalem was not peaceful; he gained power by a *coup d'état* which eliminated the Davidic, Judaean elite in favor of a new Jerusalemite elite (1 Kgs 1-2). One may even speculate that Solomon eliminated more of David himself than the present account written *ca.* 200 years after the events, at a time when the concept of Davidic legitimacy for the rule over Jerusalem was well established, can admit. Like David, he claimed the "kingdom", *i.e.* chiefdom of Israel in the footsteps of Saul (1 Kgs 3:4-4:1).[62]

Solomon did not build the temple of Jerusalem or any other temple that is presently known,[63] but he introduced the Israelite and Judaean tribal god Yahweh into the main temple of Canaanite Jerusalem, where Yahweh joined El (*'El qōnē 'arṣ, 'Elyōn*) and Asherah as a lesser god. Solomon's inaugural incantation is only incompletely transmitted in the Hebrew Bible (1 Kgs 8:12-13) and slightly less incompletely in the Septuagint (3 Kgdms 8:53a):

> "...placed the sun in the sky,
> But Yahweh had decided to dwell in the dark of the rain-cloud.
> I, however, verily built a house for you to be prince,
> A place for your eternal abode,
> as is written in the 'Book of the Upright'[64]".

This is a proud declaration of the domestication of an unruly tribal god by the ruler of a Canaanite city, fully in line with Solomon's politics as exhibited by 1 Kgs 1-2. Furthermore, it is a polytheistic text, a fact that explains the text's mutilation in the course of its tradition. Within the context of pre-Exilic Jerusalemite theology, the god who put the sun in his place could only have been *'El*,

---

[61] According to the Shoshenq list, Solomon's realm no longer comprised the primary power base of David, the southern part of the Judaean hills and the northern Negeb (cf. 1 Sam. 25; 27:6-12; 30). Ziqlag, as V. Fritz has convincingly argued in an as yet unpublished lecture at the 1988 meeting of the "Deutsche Verein zur Erforschung Palästinas", can be identified with Tell es-Seba' (Tel Bē'ērsheva').

[62] See *supra*, n. 48 and 49.

[63] For the fact that Solomon could not have built the temple, see *supra*, n. 44 and 45.

[64] The source-reference is only preserved in the Septuagint, whose "Book of Songs" can easily be corrected to "The Book of the Upright" (cf. Jos. 10:13; 2 Sam. 1:18): **yšr → š(y)r(y)m*. Judging from its surviving fragments, the "Book of the Upright" contained collections of songs typical for a tribal warrior aristocracy, the court of a tribal chieftain, or a war lord. Thus, it represents the kind of "literature" (regardless of whether it then existed in a written form, or only orally) which can be expected for Palestine in the tenth century B.C. Yahweh is in 1 Kgs 8:12-13 still the storm- and weather-god of his beginnings (cf. Judg. 5:4-5, 20-21), and far removed from the universal god that he became in the Persian period.

'Elyōn or 'El qōnē 'arṣ, all of which are attested for the pantheon of Jerusalem; 'El, qōnē 'arṣ is in Jerusalem still epigraphically attested for the seventh century B.C.[65] Thus, Solomon laid the foundation for Yahweh's becoming one of El's sons (Deut. 32:8-9)[66] and, later, for himself becoming the founder of the temple of that Yahweh who had absorbed, and eliminated, El and the other gods and could not conceivably ever have moved into a pre-existing pagan building primarily dedicated to somebody else. Because the historic Solomon never built a temple, he did not need Phoenician craftsmen and expertise for that purpose, and as the temple of Jerusalem that Solomon took over had never been anything but an average Canaanite sanctuary in nature and, presumably, architecture, he did not need Phoenician design to make the temple of Jerusalem look as Canaanite as it appears in all extant descriptions.

King Solomon's Copper Supply

What, then, had the historical Solomon to do with Phoenicia? Nothing, as can be finally demonstrated by further reflecting on his copper supply. There is no need anymore to explain where he got his 50 tons of copper from, for these 50 tons are as fictitious as his 180,000 corvée workers. Although there is the note that Solomon had his various copper utensils cast in the middle Jordan valley, between Zarethan and Succoth (1 Kgs 7:46), it is not necessary to consider how he brought the molten sea, weighing approximately 35 tons, from the wrong side of the Jordan up to Jerusalem using tenth century means of transport and tenth century B.C. roads. The note on Succoth and Zarethan is remarkable because there had been some metal-casting at Succoth (Tell Deir 'Allā) indeed, by transient laborers, who came to the site seasonally for their metal-working.[67] For this twelfth-century cottage industry, it is easily conceivable why they came to Succoth: in spring,

---

[65] Cf. for 'El, 'Elyōn and 'El qōnē 'arṣ at Jerusalem Gen. 14:19 and H. GESE, *Die Religionen Allsyriens*, in H. GESE-M. HÖFNER-K. RUDOLPH, *Die Religionen Altsyriens, Altarabiens und der Mandäer* (RM 10/2), Stuttgart 1970, p. 1-232, here p. 113-115, and for the [']*qn'rṣ*-ostracon from Jerusalem E.A. KNAUF, *Yahweh*, in *VT* 34 (1984). p. 467-472, here p. 470, n. 11. The interpretation of *qn'rṣ* that is advanced by, *e.g.*, J.H. TIGAY, *You Shall Have No Other Gods. Israelite Religion in the Light of Hebrew Inscriptions* (Harvard Semitic Studies 31), Atlanta 1986, p. 24 with n. 17, is untenable on orthographic grounds (*qn'rṣ ≠ qnh 'rṣ*).

[66] Cf. for the pre-exilic Judaean pantheon, as referred to by Deut. 32:8-9, and the role of Asherah in Judah (as opposed to 'Anat in Israel) M. WEIPPERT, *Synkretismus und Monotheismus. Religionsinterne Konflikthewältigung im Alten Israel*, in J. ASSMANN (ed.), *Kultur und Konflikt* (Ringvorlesung Heidelberg 1987/88), in press. According to L.K. HANDY, *A Realignment in Heaven: An Investigation into the Ideology of the Josianic Reform*, Ph.D. diss. Chicago, August 1987, Josiah made Yahweh not the only god, but the supreme god of Jerusalem—something Yahweh had not been previously.

[67] Cf. for the identification of Tell Deir 'Allā with Succoth E.A. KNAUF, *Midian* (*op. cit.*, n. 14), p. 40, n. 200. The latest summary of the site's archaeological record provided by the excavator,

one can encounter very strong and dependable eastern winds at the mouth of the Zerqa river, which could have been made use of to facilitate the labor of those working the bellows.[68] But such a consideration only applies to a cottage industry, whose operators have plenty of time, but relatively little manpower. A real king, of course, has the personnel to have his metal casting done for him in his palaces' workshops.[69] If 1 Kgs 7:46 is not another anachronistic note from, *e.g.*, the Persian period, when pre-State economic structures re-emerged in some marginal areas of Palestine, it can serve as another attestation of the relative simplicity, and poverty, of Solomon's realm.

One of the major factors contributing to Phoenicia's central role in the ancient Near Eastern trade network was that it functioned as a conduit for the copper from Cyprus into the Syrian and Palestinian market. But there were periods when, due to trouble in the Mediterranean—or with Phoenicia—the Cyprus copper supply broke down. In these periods, especially the twelfth and eleventh centuries and the seventh century B.C., the Palestinian copper market turned to the ore deposits in Wadi Arabah, with all of their inherent logistic difficulties. One had to get there, one had to sustain one's work-force when there, and one had to get back from there with the copper. Nevertheless, whenever the Cypro-Phoenician copper supply failed, the mines and smelting places in the Wadi Arabah flourished.[70] If Solomon's copper came from Phoenicia, it would have made even less sense to first bring it down to Succoth and then back to Jerusalem again. When the non-sedentary metal workers visited Succoth in the twelfth century, of course, no copper came from Phoenicia, and refining copper from the Arabah in the Jordan valley did make sense.

The latest Iron Age copper mining and melting activities at Timna can be attributed, with good reasons, to Shoshenq.[71] There is no need to assume that he sent a mining detachment south while he went with his army north. His interest and engagement in Palestine were presumably longer standing. There is no proof that Solomon, his contemporary, vassal and/or ally, cooperated with Shoshenq

---

whose resistance to the identification with Succoth is waning, is H.J. FRANKEN, *Deir 'Allā*, in B. Hennessy-D. Homès-Fredericq (ed.), *Archaeology of Jordan II. Field Reports* (Akkadica, Suppl. VII-VIII), Leuven 1989, p. 201-205.

[68] In spring 1983, the wind was too strong on top of Tell Deir 'Allā for my daughters (then 5 and 4 years old) to stand upright. Because of that geographic-climatologic conditon, the excavators lost numerous days when work was made impossible by the eastern winds.

[69] Cf. for a typical palace workshop B. FRISCH-G. MANSFELD-W.-R. THIELE, *Kamid el-Loz 6. Die Werkstätten der spätbronzezeitlichen Paläste* (SBA 33), Bonn 1985.

[70] Cf. E.A. KNAUF-C.J. LENZEN, *Edomite Copper Industry*, in *Studies in the History and Archaeology of Jordan* 3 (1987), p. 83-88, and for the scarcity of copper during the twelfth through tenth centuries B.C. in those regions of Palestine where Phoenician trade would have provided it, H. WEIPPERT, *Archäologie* (*op. cit.*, n. 19), p. 392.

[71] If Timna' stratum I can be linked to the XXII Egyptian dynasty, then it can also be linked on firm historical grounds to the beginning of that dynasty, i.e. the second half of the tenth century B.C. (*pace* J.D. MUHLY, *art. cit.* [n. 11]. p. 283).

during the last phase of the Timna mining operations; it is nevertheless likely that somebody from Palestine did, and Shoshenq's list hardly leaves another candidate for local support other than the principality of Jerusalem. In any case: the last visit to the Wadi Arabah copper deposits in the Early Iron Age, which occurred during the reign of Solomon, does indicate that the "Phoenician trading Empire"—or any other trading Empire—had not yet been fully developed by the second half of the tenth century B.C., and that the Mediterranean world had not yet fully recovered from the breakdown of its first world economic system around 1200 B.C. In the economic world of the tenth century, there was no place yet for the Phoenician "multi-national concerns", nor for Phoenician investments in "developing countries"; there was no place for a King Solomon as he is depicted in the Bible, nor for the queen of Sheba, who made history in spite of her lacking historicity.[72]

The historical Solomon was an Egyptian satellite, not a Phoenician dependent. In the Biblical literature, King Solomon represents the overture of a new chapter in history. In the historical record, he may well be regarded as the last convulsion of the dying world of the Late Bronze and Early Iron Age.

---

[72] As is the case with Solomon, the "historical core" of the Queen-of-Sheba episode (provided by Judaean-Arabian relations from the eighth through fifth centuries B.C.) is far outweighed by the history that the episode created. In Ethiopia's last imperial constitution of 1955, article 2 stated that "the Imperial dignity shall remain perpetually attached to the line of Haile Selassie I., ... whose line descends without interruption from the dynasty of Menelik I, son of the Queen of Ethiopia, the Queen of Sheba, and King Solomon of Jerusalem". Cf. E. ULLENDORFF, *The Queen of Sheba in Ethiopian Tradition*, in J.B. PRITCHARD (ed.), *Solomon & Sheba*, London 1974. p. 104-114, here p. 105.

The Socio-Political Shadow Cast by the Biblical Solomon*

Hermann Michael Niemann

(Translated by Michael Johnson)

For all sceptics, minimalists and nihilists the point must be stressed: the existence of the biblical Solomon is a fact! The same cannot, with absolute certainty, be said of the historical Solomon.

1. First Thoughts and Methods

To establish something concerning the socio-political situation in the Solomonic epoch[1] is not easy, because there is not one single non-biblical witness to the historical Solomon which can be compared with the biblical data. So it seems that everything concerning the socio-political situation of a character, who himself cannot be historically proven, is destined from the very beginning to have, at the best, the "reality" of a shadow. Although the author considers himself, methodologically, to be near the minimalists' (not the nihilists') camp, he does not think it necessary to end the essay at this point. The reason is that, contrary to the usual approach, here the historical accuracy of the biblical account of Solomon, either prescribed or deducted, is not a prerequisite. We begin by contemplating the

---

*   This essay is gratefully dedicated to my colleague Winfried Thiel (Bochum University, Germany). He is a noble example of the fact that diametrically opposed scientific opinions do not inherently have negative implications for personal friendships. My former student, Michael Johnson, has taken care of the translation into English and my friend, Axel Knauf, discussed with me an early draft of this paper, for which I owe Axel and Michael my thanks. [Editor's note: this chapter has been edited to conform to the requirements of the volume.]

[1]   What does "socio-political" mean? "Politics/social politics" deal with concepts and measures concerning the organisation of a community. This must not refer to a community which has developed into a "state." The more organised the community is, the more differentiated is the ruling group ("tertiary sector") as well as their tools and activities; in modern terms these would include the executive and legislative. Important factors include: prestige goods, prestige activities, the organisation of rule and the ruling class and attempts to attain a generally accepted ideological/religious basis. For terminology ("chiefdom," "state," "tertiary sector," and others) see below n. 87.

socio-political situation in the "Solomon-epoch" using an ecological framework and non-biblical sources (epigraphic and archaeological). Of course it is not possible to work totally free of presuppositions. We have to limit ourselves chronologically in that Solomon is assumed to be a personage at the transition from the Iron Age I (*ca.* 1250-950 BCE) to the Iron Age IIA (*ca.* 1050-850 BCE) and a contemporary of Sheshonq (950/45-929/24 BCE). As far as it is possible to draw an outline of the "Solomonic epoch," this outline should provide the framework for possible behavioral patterns of a personage such as Solomon. These patterns should be checked against the historical facts about a comparable contemporary. Finally the historical framework result thus attained can be compared to the biblical texts concerning Solomon.

A sketch of this brevity does not allow space to deal with all the questions that arise in a detailed manner.[2] It is achievement enough to separate the certain from the uncertain and the non-ascertainable.

2. Background and Sources

A. Background: The Three-Stepped Stage of Solomon's Appearance

Ever since the pioneering work of Karl Lamprecht in Germany and the Annales-School in France,[3] no historical analysis can avoid the fact that a responsible portrayal of a historical personage or event can only be reconstructed on the basis

---

[2] For Solomon in general, cf. recently J. M. Miller and J. H. Hayes, *A History of Ancient Israel and Judah* (Philadelphia: Westminster, 1986) 189-217; E. A. Knauf, "King Solomon's Copper Supply," *Phoenicia and the Bible: Proceedings of the Conference held at the University of Leuven on the 15th and 16th March 1990* (OLA 44; Phoenicia 11; Leuven: Peeters, 1991) 167-86; J. A. Soggin, *Einführung in die Geschichte Israels und Judas von den Ursprüngen bis zum Aufstand Bar Kochbas* (Darmstadt: Wiss. Buchgesellschaft, 1991) 62-75; G. W. Ahlström, *The History of Ancient Palestine from the Paleolithic Period to Alexander's Conquest* (JSOTSup 146; Sheffield: Sheffield Academic, 1993) 498-542; H. M. Niemann, *Herrschaft, Königtum und Staat: Skizzen zur soziokulturellen Entwicklung im monarchischen Israel* (FAT 6; Tübingen: Mohr, 1993) 17-41, 96-104, 151, 169-73, 192-205, 246-51; P. Särkiö, *Die Weisheit und Macht Salomos in der israelitischen Historiographie* (SESJ 60; Helsinki: Finnish Exegetical Society; Göttingen: Vandenhoeck & Ruprecht, 1994); and H. Donner, *Geschichte des Volkes Israel und seiner Nachbarn in Grundzügen* (ATD Erg. 4.1; Göttingen: Vandenhoeck & Ruprecht, 1995) 242-57.

[3] K. Lamprecht, *Alternative zu Ranke: Schriften zur Geschichtstheorie* (RUB 1256; Leipzig: Reclam, 1988); F. Braudel, *The Mediterranean and the Mediterranean World in the Age of Philip II* (London: Fontana, 1972); for the ANNALES School and their principles and the texts upon which they are based, see M. Middell and S. Sammler, eds., *Alles Gewordene hat Geschichte: Die Schule der ANNALES in ihren Texten 1929-1992* (Leipzig: Reclam, 1994); as for their consequences for archaeologists, see A. Sherratt, "What Can Archaeologists Learn from Annalistes?" *Archaeology, Annales, and Ethnohistory* (ed. A. B. Knapp; Cambridge: Cambridge University, 1992) 135-42; for important anthropological approaches for archaeologists, see L. Binford, "Archaeology as Anthropology," *American Antiquity* 28 (1962) 217-25; I. Hodder, *Symbolic and Structural Archaeology*

of a threefold stepped stage. The constantly changing *political history* must be placed in the context of the longer term *social history*. Both of these must then be seen in light of the very slowly changing *geomorphological-ecological environment*. Additionally, more weight and more explanation than hitherto must given to *behavioral patterns and structures instead of (only) events and personages.*[4]

1) ***Geomorphologic/environmental factors to consider***
– Syria-Palestine as a land-bridge between Mesopotamia and Egypt.
– Palestine as a narrow north-south oriented area between the Mediterranean and the Syrian-Arabian desert.
– Of importance within Palestine is the east-west division into coastal strip, transitional area, highlands, Jordan Valley and the Transjordan plateau. Prosperity and cultural development are dependent on the rain and wind, which are oriented from the NW to the SE in Palestine. This means that the coastal region in comparison with the highlands, the north(west) with the south(east), Phoenicia/Philistia with Israelite/Judean mountainous country, and the northern kingdom of Israel, rather differentiated in comparison with the smaller, more isolated and more isolationist southern kingdom of Judah, all had advantages in relation to prosperity and development. These natural advantages favoring the north and west could be limited by geopolitical and trade related politics. In times of crisis the secluded position and relative uniformity of the Judean highlands seemed an advantage,

---

(Cambridge: Cambridge University, 1982); *idem*, *Reading the Past* (Cambridge: Cambridge University, 1991); and *idem*, ed., *Theory and Practice in Archaeology* (London: Routledge, 1992). See also an overview by C. Renfrew and P. Bahn, *Archaeology: Theories and Practice* (New York: Thames & Hudson, 1993).

[4] Under the same, or only slowly changing, geomorphologic environmental conditions, social processes and action run their course over decades, centuries, even millennia with, in principle, very little change, unless they are affected by a strong impulse for change from without (disturbance, interruption). For ethnological literature as case studies, see n. 98. In the interest of completing the picture and drawing connections concerning the interrelatedness of movements lasting over centuries and millennia (*longue durée*) detailing and quantifying examinations are indispensible; see for example the studies of survey-archaeology, M. Kochavi, ed., *Judaea, Samaria and the Golan: Archaeology Survey 1967-1968* (Jerusalem: Carta, 1972) and more recently A. Ofer, "'All the Hill Country of Judah': From a Settlement Fringe to a Prosperous Monarchy," *From Nomadism to Monarchy: Archaeology and Historical Aspects of Early Israel* (eds. I. Finkelstein and N. Na'aman; Jerusalem: Yad Izhak Ben-Zvi, 1994); for the socio-economic and social structures of Ottoman Palestine, see W. D. Hütteroth and K. Abdulfattah, *Historical Geography of Palestine, Transjordan and Southern Syria in the Late 16th Century* (Erlanger Geographische Arbeiten 5; Erlangen: Fränkische Geographische Gesellschaft, 1977); W. D. Hütteroth, *Palästina und Transjordanien im 16. Jahrhundert: Wirtschaftsstruktur ländlicher Siedlungen nach osmanischen Steuerregistern* (BTAVO B33; Wiesbaden: Harrassowitz, 1992); A. Cohen, *Palestine in the 18th Century: Patterns of Government and Administration* (Jerusalem: Magnes, 1973); as well as detailed economic studies such as C. Zaccagnini, "The Price of the Fields at Nuzi," *JESHO* 22 (1979) 1-31; and M. Liverani, "Reconstructing the Rural Landscape of the Ancient Near East." *JESHO* 39 (1996) 1-41.

whereas the land along the coast and the Northern Kingdom with the international routes seemed to be at a disadvantage. It is interesting to look through the history of Syria-Palestine to see when people from the east and south looked to the west and north for prosperity and development so as to consider when and why colonisation occurred in the opposite direction.

– The frontier between Judah and Israel is the mountainous "saddle" running from east to west in which Jerusalem and Benjamin lie. This "saddle" is an area of climatic transition. South of it the rainfall decreases overproportionally toward the southern desert border.[5]

– The characteristics of the Palestinian landscape: the highland, the plains, the small mountain valleys, each separated from the other, the steppe and the desert with its borders, must all be considered along with their hierarchy of settlements, their impact on cultural, economic and socio-political lifestyle and history of the inhabitants.[6]

2) *Social and economic facts to consider*

The data presented above explain the much more modest and slow economic and cultural development of Judah in comparison with Israel.

– On the basis of the geomorphologic background, the following factors are important for social economic history: The area north of Jerusalem (the Northern Kingdom) is geomorphologically subdivided into the Ephraimite-Samarian highland, the plain of Jezreel and the Galilean highland which itself is further subdivided. The Judean highland with the southern steppe does not show such strong divisions. Due to these small mountain valleys, each being separated from the other, both socio-economic and socio-political differentiation can be seen in the populations of Judah and Israel. The stark contrasts in the landscapes bring with them not only political differentiation among the inhabitants, but also advantageous large economic differentiation and therefore less vulnerability in times of crisis.[7] The emergence of central places ("cities") of various rank with

---

[5] The main area of the northern kingdom of Israel, between north Galilee and Jerusalem, receiving an average annual rainfall varying from over 900 mm to 550 mm, is much more fertile than the southern area extending from Jerusalem south to the desert border near Beersheba. This southern area is only a third of the size of the north and the precipitation falls drastically from 550 mm to only 200-150 mm; O. Keel, M. Küchler and C. Uchlinger, *Orte und Landschaften der Bibel, Band 1* (Zürich: Benziger; Göttingen: Vandenhoeck & Ruprecht, 1984) 46.

[6] Niemann, *Stadt, Land und Herrschaft: Skizzen und Materialien zur Sozialgeschichte im monarchischen Israel* (Habilitationsschrift; Rostock: Theologische Fakultät der Universität, 1990); and G. Lehmann, *Biblische Landeskunde oder kultur- und sozialgeographische Raumanalyse? Ein Forschungsbericht über aktuelle Entwicklungstendenzen in der historischen Geographie von Palästina* (forthcoming).

[7] D. C. Hopkins, "The Dynamics of Agriculture in Monarchical Israel," *SBL 1983 Seminar Papers 22* (Chico, Calif.: Scholars, 1983) 177-202; idem, *The Highlands of Canaan: Agricultural Life in the Early Iron Age* (SWBA 3; Decatur, Ga.: Almond, 1985); idem, "Life on the Land," *BA* 50 (1987) 178-91; B. Rosen, "Subsistence Economy in Iron Age I," *From Nomadism to*

their potential for innovation, is based on the existence and development of differentiated economic units.[8]

– The following are important for the long-term cultural rather than the short-term political history: As is true of the Early and Middle Bronze Ages, a formation period, a main period and a period of decline can, for the most part, be seen and differentiated in the Iron Age as well.

The *political history*, on the basis of the two points mentioned above, requires most detailed information for its presentation. In attempting to shed light on the socio-political situation of the Solomon-epoch, the larger picture of the entire Middle East must be taken into account. All of these factors cannot be dealt with here *in extenso*.

B. Sources

1) *Epigraphical Sources from Within and from Outside Israel and Judah*

At this time not one documented piece of extrabiblical evidence exists from the Israelite-Judean context or from cultures or societies near or far in time or place for the historical existence of Solomon. This has to be stressed. This observation contrasts sharply with the biblical portrayal (upon which the historical depiction of Solomon has usually been based) of him as an outstanding ruler of a "mighty kingdom."

With what we know today about the political and cultural situation and the stage of the social development of the region and time in which the biblical narrative of Solomon takes place, an abundance of written records should not be expected. At the transition from the Bronze Age to the Iron Age and for some time following, a general state of upheaval ruled![9] That can be interpreted to mean that in a low state of development the lack of primary sources is normal, so this fact can be used neither as positive proof in favour of Solomon's existence nor against his

---

Monarchy: Archaeology and Historical Aspects of Early Israel (eds. I. Finkelstein and N. Na'aman: Jerusalem: Yad Izhak Ben-Zvi, 1994) 339-51. For important developing tendencies in cultural and sociogeographical analyses of Syria-Palestine, see Lehmann, *Biblische Landeskunde*.

[8] Niemann, *Stadt. Land und Herrschaft*, 1-62; for a comprehensive definition of the "city" phenomenon, with special consideration of Iron Age Palestine, see *idem*, "Das Ende des Volkes der Perizziter: Über soziale Wandlungen Israels im Spiegel einer Begriffsgruppe," *ZAW* 105 (1993) 233-57, especially n. 4.

[9] N. K. Sandars, *The Sea Peoples* (Ancient Peoples and Places; London: Thames & Hudson, 1978); L. Marfoe, "The Integrative Transforamtion: Patterns of Sociopolitical Organization in Southern Syria," *BASOR* 234 (1979) 1-42; W. H. Stiebing, "The Mycenean Age," *BA* 43 (1980) 7-21; D. N. Freedman and D. F. Graf, eds., *Palestine in Transition* (SWBA 2; Sheffield: Sheffield Academic, 1983); L. E. Stager, "The Archaeology of the Family in Ancient Israel," *BASOR* 260 (1985) 1-35; N. P. Lemche, *Early Israel: Anthropological and Historical Studies on the Israelite Society Before the Monarchy* (VTSup 37; Leiden: E. J. Brill, 1985); R. B. Coote and K. W. Whitelam, *The Emergence of Israel in Historical Perspective* (SWBA 5; Sheffield: Sheffield Academic, 1987); M. Liverani, "The Collapse of the Near Eastern Regional System at the End of

historicity. However, the total absence of a single source mentioning Solomon "the Great" from within or outside the region of Canaan is suspicious. As far as it is characteristic that not until after a hundred years of excavation in 1993 the first extrabiblical source (from Iron Age IIB) mentioning the *"House* of David" was found.[10] So, too, it is characteristic that not one non-biblical text concerning Solomon has been found. This sheds light on the low state of development at that time and on the modest cultural situation.

---

the Bronze Age: The Case of Syria," *Centre and Periphery in the Ancient World* (eds. M. Rowlands, M. Larsen and K. Kristiansen; Cambridge: Cambridge University, 1987) 66-73; H. Weippert, *Palästina in vorhellenistischer Zeit* (Handbuch der Archäologie. Vorderasien 2.1; Munich: Beck, 1988) 340-417; I. Finkelstein, *The Archaeology of the Israelite Settlement* (Jerusalem: IES, 1988); and *idem*, "The Emergence of the Monarchy in Israel: The Environmental and Socio-Economic Aspects," *JSOT* 44 (1989) 43-74; A. Leonard, Jr., "The Late Bronze Age: Archaeological Sources for the History of Palestine," *BA* 52 (1989) 4-39; G. London, "A Comparison of Two Contemporaneous Lifestyles of the Late Second Millennium B.C.," *BASOR* 273 (1989) 37-55; S. Timm, *Moab zwischen den Mächten* (ÄAT 17; Wiesbaden: O. Harassowitz, 1989); A. Mazar, *Archaeology of the Land of the Bible, 10,000-586 B.C.E.* (ABRL; New York: Doubleday, 1990); *idem*, "The Iron Age I," *The Archaeology of Ancient Israel* (ed. A. Ben-Tor; New Haven, Conn.: Yale University, 1992) 258-301; U. Hübner, *Die Ammoniter: Untersuchungen zur Geschichte, Kultur und Religion eines transjordanischen Volkes im 1. Jahrtausend v. Chr.* (ADPV 16; Wiesbaden: Harrassowitz, 1992); P. Bienkowski, ed., *Early Edom and Moab: The Beginning of the Iron Age in Southern Jordan* (SAM 7; Sheffield: Sheffield Academic, 1992); R. Drews, *The End of the Bronze Age: Changes in Warfare and the Catastrophe ca. 1200 B.C.* (Princeton, NJ: Princeton University, 1993); E. Noort, *Die Seevölker in Palästina* (Palaestina Antiqua 8; Kampen: Kok Pharos, 1994); I. Finkelstein and N. Na'aman, eds., *From Nomadism to Monarchy: Archaeological and Historical Aspects of Early Israel* (Jerusalem: Biblical Archaeology Society, 1994); K. W. Whitelam, "The Identity of Early Israel: The Realignment and Transformation of Late Bronze-Iron Age Palestine," *JSOT* 63 (1994) 57-87; S. Bunimovitz, "The Problem of Human Resources in Late Bronze Age Palestine and Its Socioeconomic Implications," *UF* 26 (1994) 1-20; *idem*, "On the Edge of Empires: Late Bronze Age (1500-1200 BCE)," *The Archaeology of Society in the Holy Land* (ed. T. E. Levy; London: Leicester University, 1995) 320-31; I. Finkelstein, "The Date of the Settlement of the Philistines in Canaan," *Tel Aviv* 22 (1995) 213-39; *idem*, "The Great Transformation: The 'Conquest' of the Highlands Frontiers and the Rise of the Territorial States," *The Archaeology of Society in the Holy Land* (ed. T. E. Levy; London: Leicester University, 1995) 349-65: *idem*, "The Archaeology of the United Monarchy: An Alternative View," *Levant* 28 (1996) 177-87; L. E. Stager, "The Impact of the Sea Peoples in Canaan (1185-1050 BCE)," *The Archaeology of Society in the Holy Land* (ed. T. E. Levy; London: Leicester University, 1995) 332-48; K. Bartl, "Das Ende der Spätbronzezeit und das 'Dunkle Zeitalter,'" *Zwischen Euphrat und Indus: Aktuelle Forschungsprobleme in der Vorderasiatischen Archäologie* (Hildesheim: G. Olms, 1995) 175-92; Ø. S. LaBianca and R. W. Younker, "The Kingdoms of Ammon, Moab and Edom: The Archaeology of Society in Late Bronze Age Transjordan (ca. 1400-55 BCE)," *The Archaeology of Society in the Holy Land* (ed. T. E. Levy; London: Leicester University, 1995) 399-415; N. P. Lemche, *Die Vorgeschichte Israels* (BibEnz 1; Stuttgart: Kohlhammer, 1996).

[10] *Editio Princeps*: A. Biran and J. Naveh, "An Aramaic Stela Fragment from Tel Dan," *IEJ* 43 (1993) 81-98; *idem*, "The Tel Dan Inscription: A New Fragment," *IEJ* 45 (1995) 1-18; bibliography concerning the discussion, H. P. Müller, "Die aramäische Inschrift von Tel Dan," *ZAH* 8 (1995) 121-39.

As far as it is correct to speak of statehood in Israel beginning with Omri and in Judah with Uzziah, then Solomon is to be placed in the pre-state period.[11] In light of the obviously idealized and typical portrayal of Solomon, which possibly reflects Hezekiah and/or Josiah, Solomon perhaps is found in an idealized Judean/Israelite dawn of history.

2) *Archaeology*

Despite the remaining uncertainties, today a picture can be drawn of the cultural development in the Palestinian coastal plain as well as in the central highlands during the Iron Age I and the beginning of the Iron Age II. According to this picture Late Bronze Age settlements of the coastal plain survived the disturbances, some of them on a reduced scale. In the central highlands, the number of settlements increased, varying from region to region. However, not all of these new settlements survived.[12]

It seems that in the Iron Age IB there was a cultural innovative expansion from the coastal plain towards the highlands.[13] Traditionally, based on biblical texts, a steep ascent of the highland area, associated with the "mighty kingdoms" or "empires" of David and Solomon, has been assumed during the Iron Age IIA.[14] Monumental architectural works of the Iron Age have also been attributed, by using biblical texts, to David and Solomon.[15]

---

[11] See Niemann, *Herrschaft*; D. W. Jamieson-Drake, *Scribes and Schools in Monarchic Judah: A Socio-Archaeological Approach* (SWBA 9: Sheffield: Sheffield Academic, 1991); E. A. Knauf, "King Solomon's Copper Supply"; and *idem*, "The Archaeology of Literature and the Reality of Fictitious Heroes," forthcoming.

[12] The varying degrees of intensity and duration of the new settlements in different regions are to be taken into consideration: Kochavi, ed., *Judaea, Samaria and the Golan*; Stager, "Archaeology"; Finkelstein, *Archaeology of the Israelite*; Mazar, *Iron Age I*; Finkelstein and Na'aman, eds., *From Nomadism*.

[13] Noort, *Seevölker*, and n. 20. See also my comments (p. 255) concerning the structural changes caused by the geographic-climatic gradient from the northwest to the south-west.

[14] These or similar terms and ideas related in such exaggerated and misleading dimensions can be found in research literature all over, right up to the present; see, for example, N. P. Lemche, *Ancient Israel: A New History of Israelite Society* (Biblical Seminar 5; Sheffield: Sheffield Academic, 1988) 125, 130, 137ff; M. J. Mulder, "Solomon's Temple and YHWH's Exclusivity," *New Avenues in the Study of the OT: A Collection of OT Studies* (ed. A. S. van der Woude; OTS 25; Leiden: E. J. Brill, 1989) 49-62; Soggin, *Einführung*, pp. 42ff, 62ff; W. E. Rast, *Through the Ages in Palestinian Archaeology* (Philadelphia: Trinity, 1992) 129; Ahlström, *History of Ancient Palestine*, p. 480; A. R. Millard, "Texts and Archaeology: Weighing the Evidence: The Case for King Solomon," *PEQ* 123 (1991) 19-27; *idem*, "King Solomon's Shields," *Scripture and Other Artifacts: Essays on the Bible and Archaeology in Honor of Philip J. King* (eds. M. D. Coogan, J. C. Exum and L. E. Stager: Louisville: Westminster/John Knox, 1994) 286-95; and Donner, *Geschichte des Volkes Israel*, pp. 220ff.

[15] See for example, Y. Yadin, *Hazor* (Schweich Lectures 1970; London: Oxford University, 1972) 147ff; Y. Aharoni, "The Building Activities of David and Solomon," *IEJ* 24 (1974) 13-16; W. G. Dever, "Monumental Architecture in Ancient Israel in the Period of the United Monarchy," *Studies*

The example of the 6-chamber-gates. Because no existing finds can be archaeologically traced directly to Solomon, the stately 6-chamber-gate is often given as a concrete illustration of the biblical portrayal of Solomon's kingdom as portrayed in 1 Kgs 9:15, 17-19. Examples of this type of gate from the Iron Age have been found at Hazor X, Megiddo IVB, Gezer 6, Lachish IV-III, Asdod 9, Tel Ira (*Ḥirbet Ġarra*) and possibly Timna.[16] Their distribution across Palestine fits into the traditional picture of the outstandingly great kingdom of Solomon, who is said to have carried out building projects throughout the land.[17] Further, the argument that the gates are identical in their blueprint and must therefore be the product of central planning in the capital of Solomon's "empire" is not convincing. The gates are not so precisely alike as to be necessarily the product of one builder or one architect.[18] The idea of central planning is dependent on the thesis of a centrally controlled "mighty kingdom," which at this time seems ever more unlikely. The gates can be neither dated to the epoch of Solomon nor be attributed to Solomon, whose rule cannot be dated; the sole clue is 1 Kgs 9:15, 17-19. Such a claim would require proof of Solomon's local control of one of the gate sites or proof of his centralised authority.[19] Is there another plausible explanation for the existence of this element in the Iron Age architecture of Palestine? E. Noort demonstrates that it is unacceptable historically and archaeologically to suddenly in 1200 BCE speak of a homogenous Philistine people living on the coastal plain who subjected the previous inhabitants. The people the Bible lumped together as "Philistines" consisted both of natives from Canaan and "sea peoples" settlers including *plst*. One element of the new Philistocanaanite coastal culture was the so-called submyceenean *monochrome ceramic* (belonging to Myc IIIC 1b) and the so-called *bichrome Philistine ceramic*. However, they developed not only this

---

in the Period of David and Solomon and Other Essays (ed. T. Ishida; Tokyo: Yamakawa-Shuppansha, 1982); B. S. J. Isserlin, "Israelite Architectural Planning and the Question of the Level of Secular Learning in Ancient Israel," *VT* 34 (1984) 169-78. Critical of this with reference to the history of research, Finkelstein, "Archaeology of the United Monarchy," pp. 178f.

[16] D. Ussishkin, "Notes on Megiddo, Gezer, Ashdod, and Tel Batash in the Tenth to Ninth Centuries B.C." *BASOR* 277-278 (1990) 82-88; G. L. Kelm and A. Mazar, *Timnah: A Biblical City in Sorek Valley* (Winona Lake, Ind.: Eisenbrauns, 1995) 109f, 122-27.

[17] A critical question can be raised against this interpretation: Why would Solomon have built a 6-chamber-gate in the Philistocanaanite Ashdod and possibly Timna? And who built the gate at Tel Ira (*Ḥirbet Ġarra*) in the 7th century BCE?

[18] Contra Isserlin, "Israelite Architectural Planning," in agreement with Herzog, "Settlement and Fortification Planning in the Iron Age," *The Architecture of Ancient Israel: From Prehistoric to the Persian Periods* (eds. A. Kempinski and R. Reich; Jerusalem: Israel Exploration Society, 1992) 272-74; *idem, Das Stadttor in Israel und in den Nachbarländern* (Mainz: Zabern, 1986) 89-128; see also D. Milson, "On the Design of the City Gates at Lachish and Ashdod," *Jahrbuch des Deutschen Evangelischen Instituts für Altertumswissenschaft des Heiligen Landes* 2 (1990) 15-21.

[19] I still consider it convincing that Judah was socio-politically a chiefdom in the 10th century BCE; contra C. Schäfer-Lichtenberger, "Sociological and Biblical Views of the Early State," *The Origins of the Israelite States* (eds. V. Fritz and P. R. Davies; JSOTSup 228; Sheffield: Sheffield Academic, 1996) 78-105.

ceramic, which spread through the highlands, but also, according to Noort, the 6-chamber-gate.[20] This is a design originating in the coastal plain, an area more innovative than the highlands. Philistocanaanite craftsmen could be responsible for the various 6-chamber-gates in the highland as well as in their homeland (Ashdod, Timna?).[21] For whom these were built is another question; on the coastal plain, for the Philistocanaanites themselves, in the highlands for local or regional rulers. Whoever looks critically at the allocation of monumental building projects to the Solomon-epoch has even more reason for scepticism when Jerusalem in the early Iron Age (IB-IIA) is considered. There are no architectural finds for this time except for single remains of walls and supporting works.[22] That does not have to mean the biblical reports of Solomon's palace and temple construction are pure fantasy; however, it is important to remember the modest dimensions of Jerusalem in the early Iron Age.[23] The dimensions of Solomon's temple and palace were likewise modest.[24] The main problem lies in the discrepancy between the presentation of Solomon's glorious rule in the biblical-theological report and the very modest archaeological evidence. The biblical-theological presentation arouses false expectations for the true historical dimensions of Solomon's building projects. One should also be careful when considering the dimensions of Solomon's "mighty kingdom," in light of the very modest size of Jerusalem and

---

[20] Noort, *Seevölker*; for architectural impulses from the coastal plain in the inland areas recorded prior to Noort, see H. Weippert, *Palästina*, pp. 440-41; Niemann, *Herrschaft*, pp. 97-98.

[21] A single specialised "house of builders" or two? That could explain the relative similarity in the planning despite the differences.

[22] Y. Shiloh, *Excavations at the City of David I: 1978-1982* (Qedem 19; Jerusalem: Hebrew University of Jerusalem, 1984) 26f; idem, "Jerusalem," *The New Encyclopedia of Archaeological Excavations in the Holy Land* (ed. E. Stern; New York: Simon & Schuster, 1993) 702ff; Mazar, *Archaeology*, pp. 347-80; H. Weippert, *Palästina*, pp. 449f. That the few stone remains, dated by Shiloh to the 10th century, possibly belong to the 13th-11th centuries BCE is argued in the new analysis by J. M. Cahill and D. Tarler, "Excavations Directed by Y. Shiloh at the City of David, 1978-1985," *Ancient Jerusalem Revealed* (ed. H. Geva; Jerusalem: Israel Exploration Society, 1994) 34-36. But also see M. L. Steiner, "Redating the Terraces of Jerusalem," *IEJ* 44 (1994) 13-20, who distinguishes between older terraces (13-12th century) and the "stepped stone structure" as an addition from the 10th century, as Shiloh did.

[23] The south-east hill has a length of *ca.* 400 m. and width of *ca.* 60-80 m. Additionally, there is the expansion beyond the cleft to the north of the Ophel with the assumed new palace building and its temple annex, both of which belong to the modern temple mount.

[24] H. Weippert, *Palästina*, pp. 460ff; idem, "Der Ausschließlichkeitsanspruch des salomonischen Tempels," *Spuren eines Weges: Freundesgabe für Bernd Janowski zum fünfzigsten Geburtstag am 30. April 1993* (eds. T. Podella and P. Riede; Unpublished manuscript on file, Wissenschaftlich-Theologisches Seminar, Universität Heidelberg, 1993) 265ff; A. Mazar, *Archaeology*, pp. 375ff. For temples see overview by idem, "Temples of the Middle and Late Bronze Ages and the Iron Ages," *The Architecture of Ancient Israel: From Prehistoric to the Persian Periods* (eds. A. Kempinski and R. Reich; Jerusalem: Israel Exploration Society, 1992) 161-87; for palaces, R. Reich, "Palaces and Residences in the Iron Age," *The Architecture of Ancient Israel: From Prehistoric to the Persian Periods* (eds. A. Kempinski and R. Reich; Jerusalem: Israel Explorarion Society, 1992) 202-22.

its surrounding communities (as well as the area south to Hebron and the sparse population there) between 1200 and 900/850 BCE. This was a rather remote place and region in no way lying at the intersection of major crossroads.[25]

In general, it has become clearer recently that archaeological finds cannot be dated according to biblical records. At the very latest, since the debate in *BASOR* 277-78, it has no longer been possible to date archaeological finds from the 10th or 9th century BCE more exactly than ± 50 years.[26] That means that archaeological finds cannot be convincingly attributed to a specific ruler of Israel/Judah. For example, whether a find tentatively dated around 900 actually is to be ascribed to Solomon (*ca.* 940 BCE) or to Ahab (*ca.* 860 BCE) cannot at this time be determined with desirable certainty. G. J. Wightman's suggestion of lowering the archaeological dating has already been corrected in *BASOR* 277-78 and by R. Tappy, while the new approach by I. Finkelstein places the discussion on a promising basis even in the case of socio-political thought concerning Solomon.[27]

Because the monumental building projects in Megiddo and Hazor have been dated less according to archaeological arguments than to the biblical records of 1 Kgs 9:15, 17-19, Finkelstein has looked for an independent basis for dating archaeological finds. He determined that the Philistocanaanite bichrome ware existed until the middle of the 10th century BCE so that following strata without this ware must be dated after the middle of the 10th century BCE. The consequences are: Beer-sheva V is 9th century, Arad XII (destroyed by Sheshonq) is 10th, Arad IX is 9th. Megiddo VIA, dated to mid-10th century and possibly destroyed by Sheshonq, contains the last of the degenerated Philistine ceramic. Then Megiddo VB must be *ca.* 900 and VA-IVB (with the palaces 6000+1723) in the 9th century. Stratum IVA (6-chamber-gate, water facility and "pillar houses") belongs to the end of the 9th/first half of the 8th century BCE. The one-phase compound of Jezreel (*Ḥirbet Zerʿîn*) contains ceramic from the middle of the 9th century comparable to Megiddo VA-IVB. Further, Finkelstein's method solves the "gap" problem. In the past many excavators noticed a "gap" in the 9th century at

---

[25] A. Mazar, "Jerusalem and Its Vicinity in Iron Age I," *From Nomadism to Monarchy: Archaeology and Historical Aspects of Early Israel* (eds. I. Finkelstein and N. Na'aman; Jerusalem: Yad Izhak Ben-Zvi, 1994) 70-91; Ofer, "All the Hill," pp. 92-121; A. Alt, "Jerusalems Aufstieg," *Kleine Schriften zur Geschichte des Volkes Israel III* (Munich: Beck, 1968) 243-57; H. Weippert, *Palästina*, p. 451.

[26] G. J. Wightman, "The Myth of Solomon," *BASOR* 277-278 (1990) 5-22; J. S. Holladay, Jr., "Red Slip, Burnish, and the Solomonic Gateway at Gezer," *BASOR* 277-278 (1990) 23-70; Ussishkin, "Notes on Megiddo," pp. 71-91; L. E. Stager, "Shemer's Estate," *BASOR* 277-278 (1990) 93-107; I. Finkelstein, "On Archaeological Methods and Historical Considerations: Iron Age II Gezer and Samaria," *BASOR* 277-278 (1990) 109-19; W. G. Dover, "Of Myths and Methods," *BASOR* 277-278 (1990) 121-30.

[27] R. E. Tappy, *The Archaeology of Israelite Samaria, 1: Early Iron Age through the Ninth Century BCE* (HSS 44; Atlanta: Scholars, 1992); Finkelstein, "Archaeology of the United Monarchy," pp. 177-87; and *idem*, "Date of the Settlement," pp. 213-39.

many sites. For example, Megiddo IVA (Ahab *and all following kings*) is supposed to be followed directly by the Assyrian Megiddo (III)! Archaeologically speaking, where is the cultural and economic "golden age" of the first half of the 8th century? Finkelstein's solution is very convincing here! Yet another consequence is the dating of Gezer strata. Here bichrome ware appears last in Stratum XI; Strata X-IX were destroyed by the Egyptians in the second half of the 10th century and Stratum VIII, with its 6-chamber-gate, belongs in the 9th century BCE.

It is especially important in Finkelstein's results that Iron Age I stretches into the 10th century and that the 11th and 10th centuries are more closely related to each other in the highlands than previously thought. The 10th century belongs more to Iron Age I than to Iron Age II. A cultural impetus or cultural turning point upwards began in the north during the 9th century, not in the south during the 10th century. Through the lowering of the dates, the difficult problem concerning the missing finds of the 9th century in many places has been solved. The cultural development in Iron Age I and IIA would no longer have to make unexplainable leaps forward, but could orderly unfold from its modest beginnings. The "gaps" in so many finds from the 9th century would no longer exist. Works previously attributed to Solomon without any archaeological evidence belong in the 9th century. Not only through literary criticism, but also on the basis of archaeological finds, Solomon can now be reckoned to Judean pre-state history. The problematic dissonance between the absence of historical knowledge concerning Solomon and the supposedly huge archaeological finds is now past. It is this archaeologically based result of Finkelstein which corresponds to the expected cultural development and critical biblical exegesis.[28]

Finkelstein also calls attention to a significant population difference from the west to the east and from north to south, which can be calculated using the amount of building space (built-up area) in communities with bichrome ceramics in the 10th century BCE.

From West to East:
Philistine south of Jarkon
  including Shefela   160ha × 200 persons/ha =   32000 persons
  Central highlands   220ha × 200 persons/ha =   44000 persons

From North to South (central highlands)
  from the Plain of Jezreel
  to Jerusalem   210ha   42000 persons
  Judah   11ha   2200 persons[29]

---

[28] Jamieson-Drake, *Scribes and Schools*; Niemann, *Herrschaft*.
[29] More extensive information in Ofer, "All the Hill."

When the cultural developments as presented by archaeological research are considered it is clear that the time between the "cave period" and the "village culture" of Iron Age IA and the further development to Iron Age IIB-C (i.e., Iron Age IB-IIA) is the *beginning* and not, as presented in the biblical-literary tradition and research based upon it, the *cultural golden age* of Israel/Judean history! It is a point of departure that belongs to the pre-state history of Israel/Judah. If that is the case, it is possible to suggest a corridor in time in which the Solomon-epoch is to be surmised. Within the cultural evolution, this epoch belongs to the Iron Age *formative period*, not to the later differentiated main Iron Age II. As a biblical clue, it fits that the age of Solomon shouldn't lie far from that of Sheshonq. I therefore see the time frame of the Solomon-epoch running from *ca.* 970-900 BCE.

Archaeologically this time frame does not offer any concrete evidence for Solomon, except the recognition that during the presumed reign of Solomon Judah and Jerusalem were, culturally speaking, very modest. Solomon is truly far from the level of development found at the time of the Omrides or even Uzziah and Jeroboam II. The archaeological quest for the golden "mighty kingdom" of Solomon, which stretched from Egypt's brook to the Euphrates and from Saba to Lebanon, can be called off.[30] Still, the stage for the presumed reign of Solomon is not empty and some historical structures and the general background for the biblical Solomon can be pieced together.

3) *Ethnographic Comparison*[31]

Ḍâhir b. ʿUmar, as the youngest (!) son, followed his father as high sheikh of Galilee, with authority from the Sublime Porte and regional representative in Sidon. At that time the Ottoman Empire was in crisis and in order to keep control it turned to native forces. During the first half of the 18th century CE, Ḍâhir put together an armed troop and extended his control from his ancestral seat of Tiberias all the way to the Mediterranean. He gained economic profit by working together with foreign traders. With his increasing political clout, he stood above

---

[30] J. Van Seters, *In Search of History: Historiography in the Ancient World and the Origins of Biblical History* (New Haven, Conn.: Yale University, 1983) 307ff; J. D. Muhly, "Timna and King Solomon," *BO* 41 (1984) 275-92; E. Würthwein, *Die Bücher der Könige: 1. Könige 1-16* (ATD 11.1; Göttingen: Vandenhocck & Ruprecht, 1985); G. Garbini, *History and Ideology in Ancient Israel* (New York: Crossroad, 1988) 1ff, 27ff; J. B. Pritchard, "The Age of Solomon," *Solomon and Sheba* (ed. J. B. Pritchard; London: Phaidon, 1974) 17-39; Knauf, "King Solomon's Copper Supply"; J. M. Miller, "Solomon: International Potentate or Local King?" *PEQ* 123 (1991) 28-31; Niemann, *Herrschaft*; M. M. Gelinas, "United Monarchy—Divided Monarchy: Fact or Fiction?" *The Pitcher Is Broken: Memorial Essays for G. W. Ahlström* (eds. S.W. Holloway and L. K. Handy; JSOTSup 190: Sheffield, Sheffield Academic, 1995) 227-37; G. Auld, "Re-Reading Samuel (historically): 'Etwas mehr Nichtwissen,'" *The Origins of the Israelite States* (eds. V. Fritz and P. R. Davies; JSOTSup 228; Sheffield: Sheffield Academic, 1996) 167-68.
[31] Cohen, *Palestine in the 18th Century*; the following essay excerpts should be read keeping the biblical stories of David and Solomon constantly in mind!

his Ottoman "superior" in Sidon. He fortified his hometown of Tiberias; enlarged the port of Acco, established law and order in the city and made it his capital. In time Ḍâhir also took on regional politics, taking Sidon in 1771 and in 1772 Ramle, Gaza, Jaffa, and almost capturing Jerusalem. He always tried to induce the Ottoman authority (mostly belatedly) to legitimate his actions. Only after lengthy hesitation, as his independence became too great, did the Ottoman Empire intervene. His capital Acco, as well as other coastal cities, was taken by the Ottoman fleet and Ḍâhir was killed in Acco in 1775.

Politically Ḍâhir dextrously maneuvered among Sublime Porte, his own governor in Sidon and the governors in Damascus. It was a period structurally comparable to the time of El-Amarna: a non-present ruling power from abroad let the reins slip in Palestine. Like the kings of the city-states in the Late Bronze Age, the Ottoman dignitaries barely felt safe enough to leave their bases. In this type of situation a merely formal ruling power uses the services of a local chief. Also typically, with growing power and independence, the chief shows the rulers less respect while his own ambitions rise.

The instruments and methods used by Ḍâhir for gaining and executing power are important. As long as they remained loyal to him, he left local and regional rulers in peace. For safety's sake he arranged marriages between his family and local rulers. He posted sons and close relatives at strategically important points. Sometimes his sons rebelled and both singly and in various combinations fought against their father. At one point, with the help of Bedouin, three of his sons held the stronghold at Tiberias. Once Ḍâhir captured a son and thereby kept the rebel in Egypt in check. The sons even sought help from their father's arch rival in Damascus; however, when Ḍâhir was threatened from abroad, all his sons fought on his side.

Ḍâhir is a perfect example of how a member of a Bedouin clan can step by step take control of a region and its population. He enjoyed the support of the Bedouin tribe *Banū Ṣaḥr* for a long time, but this changed as it became clear that Ḍâhir was establishing a strict central authority and they deserted him, joining forces with his opponents. The Ḍâhir epoch shows that even in the Ottomon Empire the north was economically and politically more important than the south and that the west (the coast) more than the east, from whence Ḍâhir led his campaigns as David and Solomon had from the south.

Ḍâhir had roots in the region, paid attention to legitimisation (at least *pro forma*), maintained permanently armed troops and constantly enlarged his urban-based central control. He made up for his lack of authority in certain places through military and economic strength as well as through the dispersal of trusted representatives. His rise to power happened at a time of weak central control!

As a member of a nomadic people, Ḍâhir was accepted by the settled inhabitants of Galilee because he offered security and stability in return for loyalty. As ruler he first relied on independence-oriented relatives (Bedouin). To free himself of their sensitivities regarding independence, he expanded his central control.

The Galilean farmers had to pay 1/6 to 1/4 of their income as tax. At the end of his reign it was half! A state and a ruler are expensive! The consequence of this economic pressure was that at the end of his reign many farmers had fled his territory.[32]

Whoever is familiar with the biblical stories of David and Solomon does not need the many structural parallels pointed out. This is how it *could* have been in the time of David and Solomon. This is perhaps how it often was in Palestine and similar societies under similar conditions. The biblical portrayal of David and Solomon is, at least in part, structural,[33] but that does not necessarily mean that it is totally non-historical.[34] The structural character of the text makes giving it an exact and exclusive date in the Iron Age IB-IIA difficult. However, with the help of the information concerning Ḍâhir b. ʿUmar and by comparing the typical structures which go beyond individuals and single epochs, it is easier to recognise the stories of David and Solomon as stories or to recognise the structures as such. The contemporary religious-ideological tendency of Solomon can be better understood and picked out from historical background. That is an achievement because this makes it possible to notice structural differences in the future analysis. Historical, nonstructural contemporary information might be hidden behind such differences. This might not only reflect information concerning the age in which the Solomon stories were composed, but also perhaps even information from the Solomonic Age itself.

4) *Biblical Evidence: A Critical Review*

Traditionally Solomon stands at a turning point in the history of Israel.[35] For an accurate portrayal of the Solomonic epoch it is important to have as deep as possible an understanding of the time which led to it.

---

[32] For structurally related events at the end of the Late Bronze Age, see Bunimovitz, "Problem;" and *idem*, "On the Edge."

[33] Therein lies an applicable element in C. Schäfer-Lichtenberger's general thesis, *Josua und Salomo: Eine Studie zur Autorität und Legitimität des Nachfolgers im Alten Testament* (VTSup 58; Leiden: E. J. Brill, 1995); but also see the criticism of T. Veijola, Review of C. Schäfer-Lichtenberger: *Josua und Salomo* (VTSup 58; Leiden: E. J. Brill, 1995) in *TLZ* 121 (1996) 27-29. The biblical-theological portrayal of David and Solomon was intended to be both exemplary and didactic; see the structures "representative building construction," "wealth" and "wisdom of the ruler," "the just king," and others.

[34] On the other hand, when it seems probable that an event occured as portrayed in the biblical text, that does not mean that it, in fact, so happened. The sentence *Potest ergo est* is worthless as scientific proof; Donner, *Geschichte des Volkes Israel*, pp. 30-31.

[35] "Break" in the sense of "the breaking apart of David's empire," the collapse of the "double monarchy," or the "personal union," that is, "break" in the sense of a rapid decline. This assumes, or suggests, that the "kingdom" had stood at a political and cultural high point. It will be shown that Solomon was *more likely at the beginning of a planned ascent*, which, however, broke from the plan after his death.

The Bible portrays Saul's reign as a first socio-political stage of development after which follows a hard fall for religious reasons. Behind the biblical-theological portrayal there are historical reasons to assume that Saul fit into a Late Bronze Age pattern for rulers.[36] He was more successful and talented than shown in the biblical portrayal, which is not historically, but theologically directed. In some ways he was even more successful and innovative than David.[37] He designed and introduced measures for the ruling structure from which both David and Solomon greatly profited.[38]

---

[36] For Saul: K.-D. Schunck, *Benjamin: Untersuchungen zur Entstehung und Geschichte eines israelitischen Stammes* (BZAW 86; Berlin: de Gruyter, 1963); idem, "König Saul-Etappen seines Weges zum Aufbau eines israelitischen Staates," *BZ* 36 (1992) 195-206; J. Blenkinsopp, *Gibeon and Israel* (Cambridge: Cambridge University, 1972); idem, "Did Saul Make Gibeon His Capital?" *VT* 24 (1974) 1-7; Miller and Hayes, *History*, pp. 120-49; E. A. Knauf, "Das zehnte Jahrhundert: Ein Kapitel Vorgeschichte Israels," *Heidel-Berger Apokryphen: Eine vorzeitige Nikolausgabe zum 50. Geburtstag von Prof. Dr. K. Berger* (Unpublished manuscript on file, Wissenschaftlich-Theologisches Seminar, Universität Heidelberg, 1990) 156-61; N. Na'aman, "The Kingdom of Ishbaal," *BN* 54 (1990) 33-37; Ahlström, *History of Ancient Palestine*, pp. 423-54; Niemann, *Herrschaft*, pp. 3-8, 192-93; D. V. Edelman, "Saul's Rescue of Jabesh-Gilead (1 Sam 11,1-11)," *ZAW* 96 (1984) 195-209; idem, "The 'Ashurites' of Eshbaal's State (2 Sam 2,9)," *PEQ* 117 (1985) 88-91; idem, "Saul," *ABD* 5.989-99; idem, "Saul ben Kish in History and Tradition," *The Origins of the Ancient Israelite States* (eds. V. Fritz and P. R. Davies; JSOTSup 228; Sheffield: Sheffield Academic, 1996) 142-59. See below nn. 37-38, 57.

[37] See the map in Edelman, "Saul," p. 997. The area in which Saul held influence (2 Sam 2:9) was economically and politically much more important than Judah; see for Judah the detailed archaeological survey study by Ofer, "All the Hill," pp 92-121, and his demographic conclusions. Both Saul and Solomon were more successful than David in the dynastic continuation of their regimes (Saul only short term), whereas in this David suffered his worst defeat. On the other hand, David, as a leader of mercenaries, had a more difficult starting point than either Saul or Solomon; he had first to build a support base (1 Sam 21ff) and in so doing, establish himself. Saul and Solomon both established themselves using a different, but in both cases, preexisting and merely expanded tribal or urban power base.

[38] The most important factors are: 1. *Securing a functionally important central city for an urban-supported territorial rule* in the Late Bronze Age model (e.g. Lab'ayu: EA 237; 244-46; 249-50; 252-53; 255; 263; 280; 287; 289); for *Saul*: from Zela (2 Sam 21:14) to Gibea after his victory (1 Sam 13-14) and then to Gibeon (see Schunck, Blenkinsopp, Knauf, Niemann, and Edelman, in n. 36); for *David*: Hebron and then Jerusalem. 2. *Possessing a traditional and integrated shrine*, for *Saul*: the Great High Place (הבמה הגדלה) near Gibeon (see also n. 57); for *David and Solomon*: Gibeon and Jerusalem. 3. *An ever-ready military corps*: for *Saul*: see 1 Sam 14:50-52; 17:55: for *David*: see 1 Sam 22:1-2; 1 Sam 27 and 2 Sam 23:8-39. 4. *Establishment through fighting against the Philistocanaanites*, who represented the greatest threat to Israel and Judah on the western flank: for *Saul*: see 1 Sam 13-14 with limited, but successful, measures, which seem to have been a signal for further campaigns in the mountains of Ephraim, but which also provoked a response by the Philistocanaanites (1 Sam 29 and 31). For *David*: see also local and regional limited skirmishes and duels: 1 Sam 23:1-5: 2 Sam 5:17-25; 21:15-22; 23:9-10, 11-12 and 13-17. Nothing points to a great battle or victory by the Philistocanaanites over David or by David over the Philistines. Maybe the Philistocanaanites finally gave up (because of the constant skirmishes?) their attempts at colonising

The biblical portrayal of David's and Solomon's time was told with theological interests in mind. So it includes few historical details. The lack of historical interest in and the lack of historical information concerning David and Solomon is contrasted with the previous texts dealing with Saul and the later texts telling of Rehoboam, Jeroboam I and their followers where we find more historical information. This is made clsear by the fact that, as opposed to their predecessor[39] and successors,[40] especially for the reign of the two greatest (?) kings, David and Solomon, no specific dates are given (or perhaps even known)!

Whoever tries to analyse Solomon using the *biblical-theological* portrayal as the basis of a *historical* analysis without considering the *theological* motives lying behind this tradition, brings the same tendency to the historical analysis as the biblical authors had toward idealised dimensions of the protagonist. The picture of the temple-founding and God-fearing wise ruler arrived at through precisely such flawed analysis has, in the past, led to false interpretations and disappointment when comparing literary results with archaeological research. Its influence has also sometimes led to misreading the archaeological finds themselves.[41] It is very important for a proper analysis to avoid any presumptions concerning the *historical dimensions* of Solomon based on the *theological dimensions* of the biblical portrayal.

The biblical Solomon complex consists of:

Story concerning coming to the throne and the beginning of Solomon's reign	1 Kgs 1-2

---

the highlands. Normal relations then developed (2 Sam 8:18; 15:18; 1 Kgs 2:39-40). The summary of the successful defence against the Philistocanaanites in 2 Sam 5:25 ("from Gibeon to Gezer") of course, does not geographically fit in the context of David's battles south-west of Jerusalem (2 Sam 5:17-25), but does describe the geographical area from which Saul, in defence of his residence Gibeon, might have driven the Philistines back to their starting point (Gezer). It seems that this success, for which Saul was remembered, was later credited to his more lucky Judean competitor David.

[39] For a long time Saul was, unjustly, assumed to have ruled for only two years: an "Episode," classically, M. Noth, *Geschichte Israels* (Göttingen: Vandenhoeck & Ruprecht, 1966) 163. See against that Schunck, *Benjamin*, pp. 108-24; and Edelman, "Saul," pp. 992-93. One can reckon with more than one decade: 12 or 22 (or 32?) years.

[40] According to 1 Kgs 11:41, annals were begun by Rehoboam, which is in line with the synchronisms from the reigns of Rehoboam and Jeroboam I (see 1 Kgs 14:19-20,29). The keeping of annals begins, traditionally, with the situation of the predecessor, in this case, Solomon. The annals from the time of Rehoboam may, as portrayed in 1 Kgs 11:40f, contain some information concerning the time of Solomon, but they cannot even exactly say when Solomon's reign began (much less that of David) giving just round "40 years" (1 Kgs 11:42 and 2 Sam 2:11, 5:4-5); Ahlström, *History of Ancient Palestine*, pp. 500-501. Knauf, "King Solomon's Copper Supply," pp. 174-76, conjectures with good reason that 1 Kgs 11:41 is from the time of Josiah.

[41] See discussion of 6-chamber-gates above; also history of research in Finkelstein, "Archaeology of the United Monarchy," pp. 178-79.

Exemplary deeds, prestige and large numbers:
Fame, piety and righteousness	1 Kgs 3
Clever and organised ruler	1 Kgs 4
Prestige, wealth, wisdom and trade policy	1 Kgs 5[42]
Wisdom, prestige and trade in prestige goods	1 Kgs 10[43]

This is a characteristic structured way of acting in the framework of the 1st millennium BCE.

Critical theological conclusion
Foreign women and idolatry	1 Kgs 11:1-8
Consequences and threats	1 Kgs 11:9-13
"Trio of 'Bad guy' characters"	1 Kgs 11:14-28[44]
The successors	1 Kgs 11:29-43[45]

---

[42] Despite all the theological-ideological changes and expansions, 1 Kgs 5:15-32 still allows an insight into the relationships of strength and power: The Phoenician-Tyrian coastal trading power ("first world") supplied the developing lands ("third world": Judean highlands, that is the Philistine/Phoenician backlands) with luxury/prestige goods *in limited quantity* and craftsmen too. The developing land of Judah not only had to supply labourers, but also, as is typical, agricultural and similar raw materials *in almost unlimited quantities*; see also Knauf, "King Solomon's Copper Supply"; and J. K. Kuan, "Third Kingdoms 5.1 and Israelite-Tyrian Relations During the Reign of Solomon," *JSOT* 46 (1990) 31-46. As to prestige and its trade; see n. 43.

[43] Prestige goods and the trade in them is, to a large extent, a *socio-political* factor of rule. *Socio-economically* they carry less weight. That being the case, prestige goods and their trade do belong here (see n. 46). As to the term and to the individual items of prestige, prestige goods and the trade in prestige goods, see S. Morenz, *Prestige-Wirtschaft im Alten Ägypten* (SBAW 4; Munich: Beck, 1969), for Egypt; as well as M. H. Fried, *The Evolution of Political Society: An Essay in Political Anthropology* (New York: Random, 1967) 32f, 73ff, 106ff, 115, 118, 131ff; U. Rüterswörden, *Die Beamten der israelitischen Königszeit* (BWANT 117; Stuttgart: Kohlhammer, 1985) 113f; B. Streck, ed., *Wörterbuch der Ethnologie* (Dumont Taschenbücher 194; Köln: Dumont, 1987) 164-67; S. Breuer, *Der archaische Staat: Zur Soziologie charismatischer Herrschaft* (Berlin: Reimer, 1990) 42, 45ff, 52, 58, 63ff; Kuan, "Third Kingdoms"; A. and S. Sherratt, "From Luxuries to Commodities: The Nature of Mediterranean Bronze Age Trading Systems," *Bronze Age Trade in the Mediterranean: Papers Presented at the Conference Held at Rewley House, Oxford, in December 1989* (Studies in Mediterranean Archaeology 90; Jonsered: P. Alström, 1991) 351-86; Niemann, *Herrschaft*, p. 53, n. 221; N. Crüsemann, B. Feller and M. Heinz, "Prestigegüter und Politik: Aspekte internationaler Politik im 2. Jt. v. Chr.," *Zwischen Euphrat und Indus: Aktuelle Forschungsprobleme in der Vorderasiatischen Archäologie* (eds. K. Bartl and others; Hildesheim: G. Olms, 1995) 175-92; Bartl, "Ende der Spätbronzezeit," p. 203 (exchanging prestige goods). The existence of prestige goods such as "golden shields" in other regions and times says nothing about Solomon; contrary to Millard, "King Solomon's Shields."

[44] See the convincing analysis by D. V. Edelman, "Solomon's Adversaries Hadad, Rezon and Jeroboam: A Trio of 'Bad Guy' Characters Illustrating the Theology of Immediate Retribution," *The Pitcher Is Broken: Memorial Essays for Gösta W. Ahlström* (eds. S. W. Holloway and L. K. Handy; JSOTSup 190; Sheffield: Sheffield Academic, 1995) 227-37, "sorting story from history."

[45] See H. Weippert, "Die Ätiologie des Nordreiches und seines Königshauses (I Reg 11,29-40)," *ZAW* 95 (1983) 344-75.

As a central point and not to be overlooked with formal and technical content:

Building of the Temple	1 Kgs 6
Building of the Palace	1 Kgs 7:1-12
Temple ornaments and dedication	1 Kgs 7:13-8:66
Promises and threats	1 Kgs 9:1-9

Standing out from the typical structures and generalised and idealised blocks and therefore worth considering in light of the contemporary socio-political situation:

Concrete historical (?) details	1 Kgs 9:10-28
The area of Kabul	1 Kgs 9:10-14
Forced labour used in *building projects*	1 Kgs 9:15
How Gezer came under Solomon's rule	1 Kgs 9:16, 17a
Further *building projects*	1 Kgs 9:17b-19
Forced labour	1 Kgs 9:20-22
Leading functionaries	1 Kgs 9:23
Pharaoh's daughter, Millo	1 Kgs 9:24
Offerings upon completion of Temple	1 Kgs 9:25
Fleet of Hiram/Solomon, gold from Ophir	1 Kgs 9:26-28[46]

The exemplary generalising style of 1 Kgs 3-5 and 10 on the one hand arouses historical sceptisim, but on the other hand draws attention to the obvious theological intentions. Likewise, 1 Kgs 6:1-9:9 does nothing to further the understanding of Solomon's historical situation.

Recently several scholars have emphasised the Solomon tradition as ideological, legitimising, theological and of limited worth as historical evidence.[47] With this came the problem of dating archaeological structures and strata as no longer certain. In fact, almost nothing from the 9th or 10th centuries BCE can be attributed with certainty to Solomon (or to any single ruler) at Megiddo, Hazor or Gezer.[48]

---

[46] Provisionally critical D. G. Schley, Jr., "1 Kings 10:26-29: A Reconsideration," *JBL* 106 (1987) 595-601; Niemann, *Herrschaft*, pp. 25, 169-73. Just as the legendary depiction of the "wisdom of the ruler" following this text in 1 Kgs 10:1-13 is to be understood as a "structure," so too is the further depiction of fairy tale-like riches and trade in prestige goods in 1 Kgs 10:14-29 structural in nature. If I am correct, it is not possible to concretely limit even one single fact from this text in place and time to the Solomonic epoch.

[47] In principle, Van Seters, *In Search of History*, pp. 307ff; Gelinas, "United Monarchy;" Auld, "Re-Reading Samuel," pp. 167-68; more concretely, Garbini, *History and Ideology*, pp. 1ff, 27ff; Knauf, "King Solomon's Copper Supply;" Miller, "Solomon"; Würthwein, *Bücher der Könige*; Soggin, *Einführung*, pp. 62-75; and for 1 Kgs 10:1-13, Pritchard, "Age of Solomon," pp. 17-39.

[48] See above, pp. 262-64 [320–22, present volume], with nn. 26, 28, 30.

That Solomon should be reckoned to the legendary pre-state history of Israel/ Judah is not only based on the lack of dates for his reign.[49] Evidently the keeping of royal annals did not begin under the alleged two greatest kings, but under their less important successors. How does that fit in with the precise enumeration of the literally fairy-tale-like representation of the building projects, great deeds and other data concerning Solomon? One need only observe the size of the Temple and the palace in Jerusalem in the 10th century BCE to bring the correct dimensions into focus![50]

It makes sense to place Solomon in the legendary, theologic pre-state of Judah/ Israel because the biblical description of Solomon corresponds to the idealisation and perfectness of protagonists in stories concerned with the origin and legitimisation of a constituency. In addition, the introduced verses critical of Solomon can easily be picked out. Thus, I consider the biblical Solomon to be part of the legendary pre(-state) history of Israel. It is possible that a historical figure, of different, more modest dimensions, was the basis of this picture. We have to concentrate on points of departure for socio-political elements behind the biblical Solomon.

I see two groups of structural socio-political factors in the Solomon stories: 1) Building projects as a provision for religious/ideological and representative prestige to legitimate the reign alongside with political marriage and trade to support royal authority. This includes: A) Building projects in Jerusalem and B) Building projects outside Jerusalem, political marriage and trade. 2) Measures taken to expand, organise and stabilise the kingdom. This includes: C) Government functionaries and D) Attempt to expand northward in 1 Kgs 4:7-19.

A) *Building projects in Jerusalem, especially the Temple and Palace.* Only as a subordinate clause does the biblical tradition of 2 Sam 6:17 mention that David placed the Ark of YHWH in a tent. That chapter is interested in other things. The fact that the holy object *from the north* was brought *to Jerusalem* is more important. In his moving prayer of dedication for the Temple (1 Kgs 8:17-21), Solomon states something apparently newly known: David played with the idea of building a YHWH Temple in Jerusalem, but YHWH had turned down the offer, honouring David's good intentions, but giving no concrete reasons why. "Your son, who shall be born to you shall build the house for me" (8:19). Naturally, one can speculate about the reasons why there are no temple building reports

---

[49] "If 'history' is distinguished from 'pre-history' by the availability of contemporary written narrative source material both David and Solomon still belong to Israel's pre-history"; Knauf, "Archaeology." See Auld, "Re-Reading Samuel," p. 167; however, H. J. Nissen, "History Before Writing" (unpublished paper, Mario Liverani Seminar om Oldtidshistorie, Copenhagen, November 17, 1995).

[50] H. Weippert, *Palästina*, pp. 452, 457-76; *idem*, "Ausschließlichkeitsanspruch," pp. 265ff; Mazar, *Archaeology*, pp. 375ff; above, nn. 22-24.

from David.⁵¹ That an old, Middle and Late Bronze Age city like Jerusalem did not have any city temple, albeit a modest one, is out of the question. H. Donner recognised an "anti-aetiology" behind 2 Sam 24: the story claims that a temple and even a place for a temple existed for the first time under David.⁵² The historical-religious probability of *stabilitas loci* should be sorted out; no temple to a god besides YHWH existed in Jerusalem before David. The creator of this story seems to have seen reason enough to fight against the opposing tradition. For this reason K. Rupprecht's argument makes sense, that Solomon did not build a *new* temple in Jerusalem, but rather *modified or expanded* an older one, while E. A. Knauf saw artisans at work on the temple during Solomon's reign as probable.⁵³

If Solomon is justifiably connected with a modification or expansion of the Jerusalem temple, that lies in the interest of the ideological line of deuteronomistic theology.⁵⁴ Solomon deals with this historically plausible measure exactly as is required in the obligatory canon of an ancient oriental (city) ruler. However, if Solomon acted so, why hadn't David before him? Are there different legitimising traditions between David and Solomon? It has been assumed that Solomon, with his Jerusalem city mother (as opposed to the Judean rural David) triumphed in conflict for succession because of support from the Jerusalem city party at the expense of the Judean rural party and the traditional Davidic clan.⁵⁵ If true, this turn in lineal descent would have been a sore spot with later listeners from the house of David and the people of Judah. It is striking that in 1 Kgs 8-9 the fact (?) that Solomon was David's son is conspicuously repeated.⁵⁶ Was there justifiable doubt? We see in the Solomon tradition that, even after

---

⁵¹ Even the biblical authors had been doing this. 1 Kgs 5:17: no time because of the enemies; 1 Chr 17: YHWH was not interested in a temple at that time, but at a later time David's descendants should build a temple. Every author has his ideas, but no one knows exactly why. However, in 2 Sam 12:20 we find a reference to the old pre-Davidic and pre-Solomonic city temple in Jerusalem.

⁵² H. Donner, "Der Felsen und der Tempel," *ZDPV* 93 (1977) 5-6.

⁵³ K. Rupprecht, "Nachrichten von Erweiterung und Renovierung des Tempels in 1. Könige 6," *ZDPV* 88 (1972) 38-52; *idem, Der Tempel von Jerusalem: Gründung Salomos oder jebusitisches Erbe?* (BZAW 144; Berlin: de Gruyter, 1977); and Knauf, "King Solomon's Copper Supply."

⁵⁴ See also 1 Kgs 8:12-13 in the Septuagint; and *ibid.*, pp. 183-84; *idem*, "Le roi est mort, vive le roi! A Biblical Argument for the Historicity of Solomon," pp. 81-95 [this volume]; O. Keel, "Fern von Jerusalem: Frühe Jerusalemer Kulttradition und ihre Träger und Trägerinnen," *Zion: Ort der Begegnung: Festschrift L. Klein zur Vollendung des 65. Geburtstags* (eds. F. Hahn, F. L. Hossfeld, H. Jorissen and A. Neuwirth; BBB 90; Bodenheim: Athenäum, 1993) 486ff; and *idem*, "Zur Theologie in Europa: Eine Kurzbiographie der Frühzeit des Gottes Israels im Ausgang von Ausgrabungsbefunden im Syro-Palästinensischen Raum," *ET Bulletin* 5 (1994) 168.

⁵⁵ E. Würthwein, *Die Erzählung von der Thronfolge Davids-theologische oder politische Geschichtsschreibung?* (Zürich: Theologischer, 1974); *idem, Bücher der Könige*, pp. 1-28, 146-49; T. Veijola, "Salomo—der Erstgeborene Bathsebas," *Studies in the Historical Books of the Old Testament* (ed. J. A. Emerton; VTSup 30; Leiden: E. J. Brill, 1979) 230-50; Keel, "Fern von Jerusalem," pp. 470ff; *idem*, "Theologie," p. 166; Knauf, "Le roi est mort."

⁵⁶ 1 Kgs 8:15, 17, 18, 20, 24-26; 9:4-5; see 8:19: "Your son who issues from your loins (חלציך)" (or "who shall be born to you") which means that even the thought of adoption is preventively ruled out! See n. 100.

David, Gibeon played an important role for Solomon up to the building of the palace and Temple in Jerusalem. Until this point the sacred precinct of Gibeon seemed to play a decisive role for him. Did the urban ruler of Jerusalem use this to attach himself to or even bypass the rural Judean David? With this he connected himself as a city ruler to the city of Gibeon, to the YHWH cult in Gibeon, to Gibeon as Saul's capital,[57] even to the kingdom of Saul and to Saul himself, who had been the most successful ruler north of Jerusalem! Whereas David had taken advantage of some clever and innovative manoeuvres of the often underestimated Saul, Solomon connected himself even more consistently to Saul, although being not always successful and smart enough concerning northern sensitivities.[58]

If these suppositions lead in the right direction, Solomon continued David's attempt to socio-politically integrate the northern groups by means of religion, bringing Gibeon's tradition of a *sacred precinct* to the *temple building* in *Jerusalem* as David had brought the *sacred object* (Ark) of Shiloh to the *temple of Jerusalem*. David had taken on what Saul recognised: to be a successful territorial ruler, one must have an integrated shrine! The expansion of the temple and the integration of two sacred traditions as stabilising and religious legitimising factors for a ruling city is a socio-political measure of the first degree. The northern *tribal sacred object* (Ark of Shiloh) and the *city of Gibeon's sacred place tradition* (הבמה הגדלה near Gibeon) were combined with the *city temple* of Jerusalem. The northern tribal deity YHWH and YHWH as the dynastic-god of David were integrated in Jerusalem.[59]

---

[57] For the connection of Saul to Gibeon, see first Schunck, *Benjamin*, pp. 114f, 131ff; then Blenkinsopp, *Gibeon and Israel*, and *idem*, "Did Saul"; and finally, Niemann, *Herrschaft*, pp. 4-5: Edelman, "Saul," and *idem*, "Saul ben Kish," pp. 154-59. Also nn. 36, 38 above. It is important to note Saul's far-sighted efforts at establishing legitimising contacts with important shrines: first with Shiloh and with the Eli priesthood (1 Sam 1; 1 Sam 14:3), which continued in Nob but were later destroyed by the struggle between David and Saul (1 Sam 22) and also with the "Great High Place" near Gibeon (as well as with Zadok, the Gibeonite priest; 1 Chr 16:39). The relationships came about after Saul moved from Zela (2 Sam 21:14) to Gibea (after liberating the city from the Philistocanaanite post; 1 Sam 13-14) and then in more important urban Gibeon as his residence.

[58] For structural and factual similarities between Saul and Solomon on the one hand, and differences between both of them and David, see nn. 37-38.

[59] See among others, J. Jeremias, *Das Königtum Gottes in den Psalmen* (FRLANT 141; Göttingen: Vandenhoeck & Ruprecht, 1987) 167-82; H. Niehr, *Der höchste Gott: Alttestamentlicher JHWH-Glaube im Kontext syrisch-kanaanäischer Religion des 1. Jahrtausends v. Chr.* (BZAW 190; Berlin: de Gruyter, 1990); B. Janowski, "Keruben und Zion: Thesen zur Entstehung der Zionstradition," *Ernten was man sät: Festschrift für Klaus Koch zu seinem 65. Geburtstag* (eds. D. R. Daniels and others; Neukirchen: Neukirchener, 1991) 231-64; Niemann, *Herrschaft*, pp. 203-205. For integrating achievements of Solomon, see O. Keel, "Fern von Jerusalem"; and *idem*, "Theologie," pp. 165ff, especially 168-69. In light of the cultural history, Solomon's achievements in the area of integration are, in respect to the shrine and temple traditions a "fall back," that is, Solomon joined the old *urban temple* tradition of the (Late) Bronze Age with the just emerging rural home-shrine or open-air-shrine tendency outside of cities (epoch of Saul and David); H. Weippert, "Ausschließlichkeitsanspruch," pp. 272-80.

The building of a palace in Jerusalem means a representative symbol of rule.[60] But archaeologically nothing can be proved. According to the biblical report, the palace was comprised of several buildings.[61] That is possible, but what dimensions did the Jerusalem complex have at the time of Solomon? Does the description of the many palace buildings have its origin in the time of Solomon or is it textually a later work (developed over decades or centuries)? Were all these buildings erected simultaneously and all during the reign of Solomon? Many questions, but few substantiated explanations![62]

B) *Further Measures taken for Prestige* (Building Projects outside of Jerusalem, Political Marriage, Trade). Royal building outside of the capital is also socio-politically relevant. It documents royal protection as well as having a representative function. A fortified and recognized border hints at a phase of sociological development with the state emerging. This phase overlaps that of the chiefdom.[63] 1 Kgs 9:15-19 tells of Solomon's building projects outside of Jerusalem.

One has to assume that the narrator wants to express something meaningful when he reports that Solomon built both in *Hazor* and *Megiddo* (1 Kgs 9:15); utilising these places as border fortifications is too punctual.[64] Both are functional places and traditional centres of operation. Hazor plainly represents the centre of operations in the north and guarantees safety in the direction of Aram and Damascus.[65] Megiddo rules the Plain of Jezreel, holds a key position between Galilee and the northern central Palestinian highlands and controls one of the most crucial north-south passes from the coastal plain to the north (Phoenicia) and/or northeast (Syria). Whoever reports that a ruler controls the area is saying that the ruler understands strategy, shows the flag and either defends, raises or announces a claim. But how can we be sure that the historical reality of Solomon's time is behind this theoretical recognition of the importance of both locations and the reason why the author mentions them? Archaeology seems to say the opposite.

With Gezer (1 Kgs 9:16) comes another peculiarity, although the only witness is the Bible: the addition of the key phrase concerning Pharaoh's daughter (see also 1 Kgs 3:1; 9:24) is increasingly mistrusted. Notwithstanding, a seed of truth

---

[60] K. W. Whitelam, "The Symbols of Power," *BA* 41 (1986) 166-73; Niemann, *Herrschaft*, pp. 91-96.

[61] 1 Kgs 7:1-11; H. Weippert, *Palästina*, pp. 474-76; A. Mazar, *Archaeology*, pp. 378-80.

[62] As to the city wall and "Millo," they need not be discussed here, see H. Weippert. *Palästina*, pp. 457-61. Such defensive construction can be rated as part of a ruler's social prestige and therefore of social-politics. However, up to this point there are no archaeological clues; most recently, J. M. Cahill and D. Tarler, "Excavations Directed by Y. Shiloh at the City of David, 1978-1985," *Ancient Jerusalem Revealed* (ed. H. Geva; Jerusalem: Israel Exploration Society, 1994) 31-36.

[63] Fried, *Evolution of Political Society*, p. 175; E. R. Service, *Ursprünge des Staates und der Zivilisation: Der Prozeß der kulturellen Evolution* (Frankfurt am Main: Suhrkamp, 1977) 99.

[64] Not necessarily "new" construction, but rather large or small scale "expansions" or "reconstruction" of existing buildings, that is, changed to fit him and his purposes, Niemann, *Herrschaft*, p. 142, map 2.

[65] Even Joshua 11:10 knew of its country-wide leading function.

is not to be ruled out [see excursus]. Gezer's location is not as geopolitically strategic as Hazor or Megiddo, but it is important as a stronghold in the middle of the southern half of the coastal plain, between Egypt's brook and the Carmel/ Acco. From the east the city does have value for exhibiting influence on the coastal plain to the north and south. From the west it is strategically valuable in exercising influence in the highlands. Gezer lies exactly between the Judean highlands in the south and the middle Palestinian mountains in the north, facilitating the ascent into the mountains from west to east. A strong power in Gezer can be uncomfortable for a ruler in Jerusalem, but he can guard himself against Gezer by placing Judean forces at Baalat/Kirjat-Jearim north-west of Jerusalem at the upper mountain's edge and additionally Lower-Bethoron at the lower mountain's edge,[66] between himself and Gezer. Best of all is when he controls Gezer himself.

Lower Bethoron, Baalath and Tamar appear in 1 Kgs 9:17b-18; while the function of the first two cities has been mentioned, that of Tamar is difficult to state since there is not even a decisive identification.[67] That this was a single remote place serving as a border point or stronghold is unlikely. Assumably it had the function of showing the ruler's presence in and claim to the south. Archaeology does not offer help in the interpretation of these places.

In verse 19 no further cities are mentioned, rather, Solomon's functional locations named in verses 15-18 are meant.[68] The biblical author now describes his ideas concerning the function of these cities as had been handed down in the traditionally glorious and phenomenal portrayal of Solomon. This summarising sentence, sprung from the idealised picture of the king, doesn't provide any new details. "Lebanon" could be erroneous (LXX didn't yet know *lbnwn*) being an addition *ad maiorem regis gloriam*, but understandable in light of 1 Kgs 5:1, 4; it does not fit into the geographic framework at all.[69]

The section of verses 20-22 is purely ideological. Various "peoples," some of whom never existed,[70] serve here as the compulsory labourers. Verse 22 rejects the idea that Solomon had forced Israelites into compulsory labour, thus removing shame from both him and the Israelites, despite the detailed and realistic reasons given for the "discharge" of the northern groups during their negotiations with Solomon's successor (1 Kgs 12). If what verse 22 states were historic there would have been no reason for the northerners to complain to Rehoboam and distance themselves from the House of David after Solomon's death.

---

[66] For both places, Niemann, *Herrschaft*, pp. 20-22, 97-102, 106, 118-19, 143, 146, 151; for Baala(t) in particular, pp. 192-93.

[67] Rather to be identified with ʿĒn el-ʾArûṣ = ʿĒn Tamar; ibid., p. 97 n. 434; less likely with ʿĒn Ḥaṣb, most recently, Cohen-Yisrael, "Iron Age Fortresses."

[68] Würthwein, *Bücher der Könige*, pp. 109, 112; Niemann, *Herrschaft*, pp. 99-102.

[69] Würthwein, *Bücher der Könige*, p. 112; G. H. Jones, *1 and 2 Kings* (NCB; Grand Rapids: Eerdmans; London: Marshall, Morgan & Scott 1994) 217.

[70] Niemann, "Ende des Volkes."

In summary, buildings of unknown art and size are claimed literarily in the biblical texts in all of the locations, but cannot be verified through archaeology. The historical content is not clear and our knowledge of cultural development in the 10th century BCE seems to advise scepticism. Only in Gezer is there a scenario open to discussion; maybe Solomon's possessing the city is more than an ideological claim. Hazor and Megiddo are traditional central cities, but without any recognisable (historical) connection with Judah and Jerusalem or David and Solomon. The naming of them could have functional and structural (ideological and legitimising) meaning.[71] In any case, neither city can be seen as part of a chain of cities created by Solomon for the border security of a "state."[72] At the most they represent a first isolated attempt at royal presence.

Trade in the Solomonic epoch is not the issue here. Solomon's alleged middle-man trade in war-chariots and horses (1 Kgs 10:28-29) can be set aside as this mode of Solomonic trade is most likely neither historic nor provable.[73] However, we hear in the Bible (typical for a "Third-world-country") of the import of luxury goods, prestige goods and craftsmen on the one hand and the export of raw materials (e.g., foodstuff) on the other hand (1 Kgs 5:20ff; 9:26-28; 10:14ff). Luxury goods and prestige goods are means of legitimising rule, so the biblical contention of Solomonic trade in such items must be dealt with here. Whoever wants to depict Solomon in a theological idealising manner as a world famous, wise, immeasurably rich king has to say from whence this wealth in the poor Israelite-Judean highlands at the end of a cultural depression comes. Maybe historically the biblical writers are referring to the (friendly) relations (below in the excursus suspected as vassalage) of Solomon to Tyre as a starting point. An archaeological point of departure cannot be *Tell el-Ḫlēfe* (=Elat) as previously thought since it came into existence in the 8th century as the successor settlement of Ezion Geber.[74] Rothenberg reported settlement remains and ceramics from Iron Age I-II;[75] if this date is correct, maybe we can see in this fact an historical point behind the biblically reported trade and fleet cooperation between Hiram and Solomon. Taking the

---

[71] For this functionally typical structural language and manner of portrayal, in which successful kings constructed important buildings, organised armies and were victorious in wars, see P. Welten, *Geschichte und Geschichtsdarstellung in den Chronikbüchern* (WMANT 42; Neukirchen-Vluyn: Neukirchener, 1973); and Whitelam, "Symbols of Power," pp. 166-73.

[72] Until recently I, too, thought too optimistically; Niemann, *Herrschaft*, p. 101.

[73] Würthwein, *Bücher der Könige*, pp. 128-29; Schley, "1 Kings 10:16-29," pp. 595-601; Garbini, *History and Ideology*, p. 31; Knauf, "King Solomon's Copper Supply," pp. 178-79; Niemann, *Herrschaft*, p. 172.

[74] Probably *Ǧezīret Farʿūn*, Niemann, *Herrschaft*, pp. 169-71 with bibliography.

[75] B. Rothenberg, *Timna: Das Tal der biblischen Kupferminen* (Bergisch-Gladbach: Lübbe, 1973) 201-207; M. Weippert, "Edom: Studien und Materialien zur Geschichte der Edomiter auf Grund schriftlicher und archäologischer Quellen" (Unpublished dissertation, Universität Tübingen, 1971) 433; O. Keel and M. Küchler, *Orte und Landschaften der Bibel, Band 2* (Zürich: Benziger; Göttingen: Vandenhoeck & Ruprecht, 1982) 290.

historicity for granted, the Phoenicians were the dominating part of this cooperation. Solomon as a vassal or subordinate of Tyre may have rendered assistance and partook (adequately?) in the trade profits. This may be a possible scenario, yet it is unproven. The "efficiency" of Solomon's acquired prestige-goods and wealth for legitimising his rule was of such "amount" that it did not prevent the collapse of Solomon's rule after his death.

C) *Government Functionaries.* The existence of full-time functionaries ("tertiary sector") in the service of the government organisation serves as an important characteristic when determining the degree of socio-political development in a given society. During the reign of Saul and David a "tertiary sector" is almost totally missing. Therefore, I have to refer to this time as a "chiefdom," and not yet a "state."

Saul relied almost exclusively on family members to serve as royal functionaries and David made only minimal changes; the vast majority of his dignitaries came from the "House of David," in other words, from his clan.[76] Only twice did their socio-political functions extend beyond the royal court.[77] David did introduce an important new dimension: based on common interests, he made and nursed relationships with local and regional elite in areas of interest to him.[78] The Solomonic epoch left a divided impression on the socio-political aspects of the governmental organisation (1 Kgs 4):[79] on the one hand, there appears to have been little development in comparison to David concerning the functionaries in Solomon's immediate residential situation, as well as their number and range of tasks given to them, aside from the fact that "civilian" in contrast to "military" functionaries did increase under Solomon. On the other hand, there are two areas in which administrative and therefore socio-political development can be seen: forced labour (1 Kgs 4:6; 5:20-32; 9:15-23; 11:28) and Solomon's 12 נצבים (1 Kgs 4:7-19).

Forced labour is a socio-economic factor with possible socio-political consequences. In fact, it is very likely that forced labour did exist at the time of Solomon, because without it the refusal of the northern groups to pass on their allegiance to Rehoboam (1 Kgs 12) would be unexplainable. Because the product of this forced labour (above all Solomon's building projects) is not clear, the amount of forced labour actually used cannot be properly calculated and, hence, I decline to make any speculation.

---

[76] Niemann, *Herrschaft*, pp. 3-17.

[77] Joab led the *ad hoc* summoned conscription and Ado(ni)ram is responsible for the forced labour (2 Sam 20:24). The existence and the extent of forced labour at the time of David is controversial; *ibid.*, pp. 11-12.

[78] 2 Sam 15-19, where the Absalom revolt makes clear how important good (or bad) relations with the local and regional elite were for David. See especially also 2 Sam 19; 2 Sam 20:1-22, and for the interpretation, *ibid.*, pp. 14-17.

[79] See provisionally summarised, *ibid.*, pp. 17-41.

D) *Attempt at Northern Expansion.* Within the Solomon tradition, with its idealisations, we come upon a section (1 Kgs 4:7-19) which gives the impression of a sober administrative document. This list has long been the basis of a strong argument claiming that Solomon was historically the far-sighted ruler portrayed in the theological and idealising description, who had his sphere of interest outside of Judah under effective control using an all-encompassing administrative system with "governors" at the top of administrative departments.[80] When it is normally presumed that David (and Solomon) controlled the entire northern region (even had influence from the Brook of Egypt to the Euphrates), then it is not amazing to hear of the hypothetical system of administrative organisation mentioned in 1 Kgs 4:7-19. However, in light of the rather modest archaeological finds in the main functional Palestinian cities of the 10th century BCE, one must be amazed by these reports of a thoroughly organised provincial and administrative system. One has to wonder, how did the House of David come to have such complete organisational control over the north as is seemingly the case in 1 Kgs 4:7-19, by W. Thiel's interpretation.[81] And why did this alleged highly differenciated administrative system break down so quickly (1 Kgs 12)? A short look at the biblical tradition of David holds some surprises.

David's campaigns that can claim historical probability were confined to a limited radius in the area around Gibeon in the north to the Negev in the south.[82] In the west one can only say David succeeded in defending the highlands against the Philistocanaanites (from Gibeon to Gezer, 2 Sam 5:25). Limited conflicts east of the Jordan are credible.[83] David and his people were conspicuously often to be found near Saul's urban base Gibeon (2 Sam 2:12-17, 18-32; 2 Sam 5:25). Even in the crisis between David and the Benjaminites, Gibeon played an important role (2 Sam 20:1-22). The pursuit of his enemies went non-stop from Gibeon to the northern border, because David enjoyed only sporadic or no influence up to the northern border/Abel Beth-Maacha. David never truly expanded beyond Gibeon to the north! However, David valued good relations with the elite in the north, which seemed to be necessary, but also proved helpful in time of crisis (2 Sam 9; 17:27-29). It seems that his authority wasn't so unlimited as to make

---

[80] The classical/traditional *Opinio communis* was last represented by V. Fritz, "Die Verwaltungsgebiete Salomos nach 1 Kön 4,7-19," *Meilenstein: Festgabe für H. Donner* (eds. M. Weippert and S. Timm: ÄAT 30; Wiesbaden: Harrassowitz, 1995) 19-26: and *idem*, "Monarchy and Re-urbanisation: A New Look at Solomon's Kingdom," *The Origins of the Ancient Israelite States* (eds. V. Fritz and P. R. Davies; JSOTSup 228: Sheffield: Sheffield Academic, 1996) 187-95.

[81] W. Thiel, "Soziale Auswirkungen der Herrschaft Salomos," *Charisma und Institution* (ed. T. Rendtorff; Gütersloh: Mohn, 1985) 297-314.

[82] 1 Sam 22:1-5; 25:2-43; 27:4-12; 30; 2 Sam 2:1-4, 12-17; 5:17-25 (?); 8:1-2; 10:1-14 (?); 12:26-31; 22:15-22; 23:8-39.

[83] With cities of origin (almost entirely Judah and Benjamin), P. K. McCarter, *II Samuel* (AB 9: Garden City, NY: Doubleday, 1984) 529, map, and the radius of activity of David's most important soldiers, 2 Sam 23:8-39 offers a realistic picture of David's military sphere of operation as opposed to the later theologically determined amplification of far beyond Syria or to the Euphrates.

it possible for him to give orders everywhere. The often underestimated Saul seems to have been active in at least as expansive an area (2 Sam 2:9) as the often overestimated David! It is worth noticing that David had to fight against his own family and his clan Judah to overcome his worst crisis.[84] The biblical record is correct in that the only basis for David's rule in the north was the voluntary and retractable support for his authority given by the northern groups. He did not lead any military campaigns in the north. The degree to which David or Solomon actually "ruled" in the north, and especially in Syria, must therefore be much more cautiously estimated. This also helps explain 1 Kgs 4:7ff. If the differentiated administrative network, as suggested in and assumed by research literature, the socio-political influence and the supposed degree of organisation of David's and Solomon's reign were all exaggerated, how then should 1 Kgs 4:7ff be interpreted, if *not* as the reflex of an intensive administrative organisation?

I have already given details as to proposed new interpretations of the personnel and the geographic aspects of the so-called "list of Solomon's governors."[85] My point of departure entailed a fresh look at the structure (abnormal for a "provincial administrative system"), the personnel and the geographic information concerning Solomon's 12 representatives. A community, location or region is listed after the name of each person in 1 Kgs 4:7-19. The first (or only) location has been accepted as the "residence," in the sense of an administrative centre for the respective "province." However, if the unproved presumption of a pre-existing administrative system is questionable, then I suggest that the first (or only) location describes the family city, or the current place of residence, whereas each regional name represents the native region of the respective representative of Solomon. Also supporting this argument is the fact that two of the communities previously interpreted as provicial *capital* cities, were in reality very small, unimportant and unidentifiable (Makaz, v. 9, Arubbot, v. 10). If Solomon was just *beginning* to put together a corps of representatives for his plans and goals it is understandable that he would not immediately have found persons from the local and regional elite as representatives everywhere or be able immediately to establish his relatives or courtiers everywhere. This explains the uneven distribution of locations and representatives and the uneven size of the regions. These were in no way provinces with exactly defined borderlines. The names of further communities and landscapes might have been added whenever the hometown of the respective representative was little known or traditionally important cities were in his area. The detailed analysis leads to the following conclusion:

The persons mentioned in 1 Kgs 4:7-19 are selected relatives or courtiers of Solomon and the king's allies from the local and regional elite. They are Solomon's representatives spread out in the non-Judean northern areas. Because Solomon's presumed provincial administration, great building projects, and so

---

[84] 2 Sam 15:1-19:16; the parallels with the family of Ḍâhir are evident.
[85] Niemann, *Herrschaft*, pp. 27-41, 246-51.

forth, cannot be assumed to have existed, the above mentioned should not be seen as established functionaries who hold on to and expand Solomon's already existing stable dominion. It would be more accurate, and in better agreement with the archaeological evidence, to say that they are there to help transfer the authority and sovereignty, which had been offered to David on a voluntary basis (2 Sam 2:4; 3:12-13; 5:1-3; 16:7-8), to his successor, Solomon. It is no coincidence that the Bible does not report any voluntary pledges of allegiance by the northerners to Solomon as to David. There was obviously no parallel action. Solomon tried to make up for this through the careful construction of a network of representatives for his expansive plans and aims. Therefore 1 Kgs 4:7-19 does not document an existing administrative system, but rather the careful *first attempt* at building such a system.

Whereas Saul relied almost exclusively on his clan for the closest advisors in his dominion, the (relatively small) circle of leaders around David showed a limited, but nonetheless observable extension beyond his family.[86] The tendency shown in the list of Solomon's functionaries represents the evolution of this process, in that he installed as "representatives" (נצבים), alongside members of his family and courtiers, increasingly trustworthy men from the local and regional elite in the non-Judean north. The way he acted in regards to this socio-political question was guided throughout by one basic intention: Solomon distributed his representatives according to their reliable allegiance to him and according to the economic, trade politics and strategic importance of the area. His relatives and sons of his courtiers were stationed at especially important economic and strategic points. As people with their roots in the local and/or regional elite, the other officials could best make use of their own authority for royal purposes. As a matter of practicability, a complete uninterrupted network of officials had to be achieved as best as possible, but the availability of qualified candidates sometimes limited this, so that some geographically problematic "provinces" came into being (vv. 10, 12 and 13 in connection with vv. 14 and 19). That one of Solomon's court functionaries in Jerusalem, Asarja b. Nathan (1 Kgs 4:5), played a co-ordinating role, shows that the נצבים were not in Jerusalem, but represented the king's interests in their home regions. That supports the idea of honorary posts, not fully institutionalised professional functionaries. As for the two relatives of courtiers listed as "representatives," here one can speak of institutional functionaries and the same goes for Solomon's sons-in-law. That means that at this time his reign *began* to partially develop from the status of a chiefdom into that of a state. For one of the distinguishing factors of a "state" is the presence of professional functionaries (tertiary sector).[87] What did the representatives do to stabilise royal influence and

---

[86] See above, pp. 279-80 [335, present volume], with nn. 77-79, and text discussion there.
[87] For details concerning the terms *chiefdom, state, tertiary sector* see Niemann, *Herrschaft*, p. 7 n. 34; pp. 34-35. For now, a brief differentiation might suffice: In a chiefdom, the power is personalised and concentrated, whereas in a state it is institutionalised and organised by the elite and functionaries. A chiefdom is characterised by a society organised into two classes: "the chief and his

how did they serve a representative function for Solomon's interests? 1 Kgs 4:7 and 5:7f mention that they provided food for the court as well as for the horses of Solomon's army. The rotational system of supply, each of the 12 men being responsible for one month, was mechanically thought up and does not take into account the reality of the agricultural calendar. In contrast one need only look at the differences in the size and economic capabilites of the various regions. Furthermore, what is the use of the harvests from the Judean-Davidean royal property, from which one would expect the court to be provided? Traditionally, it has been thought probable that the נצבים were held responsible for helping supply the fortifications (1 Kgs 9:15, 17-19) in their areas. One notices, however, that not one of the fortified towns in the north (Hazor) or the west (Megiddo, Gezer, Lower Bethoron) was listed as the residence of נצבים, which would be expected from an administrative-organisational or military-strategic point of view or when considering the assumed job as provider and supplier. That again speaks both for the above mentioned interpretation of the first named communities in verses 9, 10, 13 and 14 as their hometown and not the "provincial capital." There is also no evidence that they had military enforcement power (troops).[88] In light of falling income from tributes in the second half of Solomon's reign and after the construction of his Temple and palace as well as fortifications and other building projects of unknown size outside Jerusalem, one could expect to see a scale of financial planning and organisation (tax collection) with the implementation of the נצבים (1 Kgs 11:14ff in connection with 2 Sam 8:6). The abandonment of claims against

---

personal clientele" and the "underclass." A state, on the other hand, has three classes: the ruler along with the ruling apparatus, an upper-class and an underclass. It is important to note that the ruling apparatus ("tertiary sector") is, for the most part, recruited from the upper-class and therefore tends to be a functional and institutional class of full- and part-time dignitaries between the ruler and the underclass/people. It is also characteristic of a chiefdom that the chief must constantly prove his authority. Horizontal forms or ranking systems exist equally alongside the vertical structures. Through further development of the vertical and hierarchic structures (stratification) of the society, the chiefdom gives rise to the state. A state, as opposed to a chiefdom, tends to constantly lay increasing claim to a monopoly of power, and tends to build an enforcement body. Power and rank are distinctly institutionalised. Fried, *Evolution*; Service, *Ursprünge des Staates*; B. Price, "Secondary State Formation: An Explanatory Model," *Origins of the State: The Anthropology of Political Evolution* (eds. R. Cohen and E. R. Service; Philadelphia: ISHI, 1978) 161-86; T. K. Earle, "Chiefdoms in Archaeological and Ethnohistorical Perspective," *Annual Review of Anthropology* 16 (1987) 279-308; Breuer, *Der archaische Staat*; Y. Portugali, "Theoretical Speculations on the Transition from Nomadism to Monarchy," *From Nomadism to Monarchy: Archaeology and Historical Aspects of Early Israel* (eds. I. Finkelstein and N. Na'aman; Jerusalem: Yad Izhak Ben-Zvi, 1994) 203-18; Renfrew and Bahn, *Archaeology*, pp. 153-94.

[88] The voluntary transfer of authority over the northern groups to David (2 Sam 5:1-3) corresponds, realistically and factually, to a denoucement, without the need of a battle for independence, of further recognition of the Davidic authority in 1 Kgs 12. Although this report is surely Judean tendentious, it shows that not one of the (according to the traditional view) powerful "provincial capitals" and their "governors" and "garrisons" (1 Kgs 4:9ff) stood up to fight for Solomon's successor. They were simply not "provincial capitals," there were no garrisons.

the Phoenicians in Tyre to the rich "Land of Kabul" (1 Kgs 9:10-14)[89] might be a second sign of financial and liquidity problems along with lack of Solomon's political influence in the north.[90] However, nothing is known of tax collection during Solomon's reign. The existence of tax collection at all has become rather improbable in light of U. Rüterswörden's reasoning.[91]

In my view, the people in 1 Kgs 4:7-19 are to be seen as "delegates" or "representatives" who were trusted by the king and who had authority either through their personal relations with the ruler, or through their position as members of the local or regional elite, in which case they were to use this authority to better integrate the (north) Israelite groups and regions into the Judean-Davidic territory. An administrative-organisational planning intention[92] *could* have been coupled with this command stabilising function, for which the representatives should have prepared the way. All together, this formed a cautious, loose, wide-meshed, sociopolitical *attempt* at organisation. Later in northern Israel, the after-effects of this attempt are nowhere to be seen.[93] Indeed, this attempt could only be successful as long as the population voluntarily co-operated with the representatives. And that

---

[89] Even if the most accepted (and in my opinion most probable) identification of Kabul with Ḥurbat Rōš Zayit (*Râs ez-Zētūn*; 10 km = 6 mi. east of Acco) is inaccurate, the biblical "Land of Kabul" must lie in the Plain of Acco, which was surely in the Phoenician-Tyrian sphere of influence; R. Frankel, "Upper Galilee in the Late Bronze-Iron I Transition," *From Nomadism to Monarchy: Archaeology and Historical Aspects of Early Israel* (eds. I. Finkelstein and N. Na'aman; Jerusalem: Yad Izhak Ben-Zvi, 1994) 18-34; Z. Gal, "Iron I in Lower Galilee and the Margins of the Jezreel Valley," *From Nomadism to Monarchy: Archaeology and Historical Aspects of Early Israel* (eds. I. Finkelstein and N. Na'aman; Jerusalem: Yad Izhak Ben-Zvi, 1994) 35-46. As to the situation of the Plain of Acco, which, because of its economic and geographic importance, must have been of interest to Solomon; see the thorough archaeological and cultural-historical analysis by G. Lehmann, "Zur Siedlungsgeschichte des Hinterlandes von Akko in der Eisenzeit," forthcoming. As to possible relations between the populations of the Ephraim mountains and the area north of the Plain of Acco; see D. V. Edelman, "The 'Ashurites' of Eshbaal's State"; *idem*, "Asher," *ABD* 1.482-83; and *idem*, "Ashurites," *ABD* 1.494. I suspect that Tyrian pressure on Solomon to renounce any claim as ruler of the plain, lies behind 1 Kgs 9:10-14. Such ambitions on Solomon's part may have been inspired by the relations between the populations of western Ephraim and the western Galilaean Asser region. That the (later) ideal king Solomon gave in to this pressure, or was forced to give in to it, was later theologically qualified through the assertion that the area was worthless anyway.

[90] 1 Kgs 5:1 LXX; Kuan, "Third Kingdoms 5.1"; and excursus at the end of this chapter.

[91] Rüterswörden, *Beamten*, pp. 127ff, is correct in his assertion against the whole of previous research, which has not produced a justified counter-argument; see for example, J. Gray, *I and II Kings: A Commentary* (OTL; London: SCM, 1980) 130f, 135f; N. Na'aman, "The District System in the Time of the United Monarchy (1 Kings 4:7-19)," *Borders and Districts in Biblical Historiography* (Jerusalem Biblical Studies 4; Jerusalem: Simor, 1984) 167ff; G. W. Ahlström, *History of Ancient Palestine*, pp. 476, 478, 489, 508 and passim.

[92] A much later realisation of a Judean division, might lie behind Josh 15:21-44, 48-62; Niemann, *Herrschaft*, pp. 251ff. When put together with Josh 13-14; 15:1-20; 16-19; a theological ideal division is depicted. The unrealistic ideal helped to preserve the integrated historical report.

[93] Against Na'aman, "District System" pp. 194-201; T. N. D. Mettinger, *Solomonic State Officials* (ConBOT 5; Lund: CWK Gleerup, 1971) 124, whose arguments are not convincing.

could be assumed only as long as the requirements made by the king remained tolerable and understandable. That the delegates never came far with this attempt at stabilising the sovereignty in Solomon's interests, can be seen in the rapid retreat of the northern groups from the House of David after Solomon's death.

It can be recognised that through the installation of relatives and courtiers as well as trusted men from the local and regional elite of Israel as stabilising representatives of his claim to sovereignty, Solomon strove towards the better political-ideological and perhaps economic integration of the area north of Jerusalem. That marks the socio-political transition phase, from an organisation based on the ruler's family and courtiers to one taking in the local and regional elite, even if these elite cannot be described as truly professional functionaries ("tertiary sector"). From a cultural sociological point of view, Solomon's reign therefore represents the beginning of the change from a chiefdom to a state. This is only true of the north; corresponding evidence for such a socio-political organisation is not existent for the south (Judah) and the Philistocanaanite coastal area ruled, according to the leading research, by David and Solomon.

Is it possible to fit Solomon's suggested presumably socio-political attempt at organisation in the north into a more comprehensive picture of the Solomon epoch and the general Middle Eastern history? If Solomon truly was a vassal to or under the influence of Sheshonq as suspected below [excursus], is it then impossible that he tentatively expanded northwards tolerated by, supported by, or perhaps even in the interest of, Sheshonq? Maybe he was a kind of viceroy or governor to Pharaoh, rewarded with and authorised by the handing over of the Libyan aristocratic princess or "court-lady" and the city of Gezer as a foothold and instrument of power in the direction of the north. As a ruler of Jerusalem who watched over the north, could he not also, in the interest of Pharaoh, keep an eye on the coastal inhabitants, the Philistocanaanites?

However, is it believable, in light of the lack of sources from the tenth century, that an "administrative organisational document" (1 Kgs 4:7-19) would have been preserved in its original form until after the fall of Judah and Jerusalem?[94] Perhaps the question is not correctly stated. In no way does it have to be an administrative document in its original condition. The unique distribution of names, places and regions, as well as the unbalanced personnel and geographic details do not fit the description of a completed departmental system of government. For that, a more balanced and polished system would be needed (compare Josh 13-19). From the time of Rehoboam up to the fall of the Northern Kingdom,

---

[94] The question has most recently been raised and denied by P. S. Ash, "Solomon's? District? List," *JSOT* 67 (1995) 67-86. He reckons with oral information brought to Judah after the fall of the northern kingdom, "selected, abbreviated and garbled," with which the tradents in the south wanted to legitimise their claims. That is a possible scenario. However, Ash's attempt does not fully explain the specific structure of the information brought from the north. My own suggestion was obviously unknown to Ash; Niemann, *Herrschaft*, pp. 27-41, 246-51.

there was no time any real chance of Judah organising the north in the manner implied in 1 Kgs 4. Therefore, the text, that is the intentions and structures behind it, truly does belong to the time before Rehoboam and Jeroboam I, or it represents a plan for northern expansion after the fall of the Northern Kingdom.[95] The personal names listed in the text and the make-up of the geographical and local names' structure in 1 Kgs 4:7-19 need not necessarily be of the same mould. It would have been no problem for an informed author to put together the geographic structure for the covered socio-political diagram of the area as a "desktop project" and decide upon the points of interest based on his own knowledge, sometimes detailed and sometimes vague. Within this framework, a third possibility for the origin of the text, or at least its structure, can be seen: It could be the socio-political structure of important regions and places in the Northern Kingdom according to the knowledge and the intentions of an author from the north.[96] An author from Judah could also be behind this scheme.[97] Once such a geographic portrayal scheme was devised, it could have been filled in at various times with various people's names and fit into various text-complexes and chronological situations (i.e., for legitimasing purposes). With the precondition that 1 Kgs 4:7-19 was not first composed during the reign of Omri or later and then retroactively placed in the time of Solomon (which cannot be ruled out), the text and its structure make sense using the suggested interpretation as a cautious probing, a punctual attempt to gain influence with the help of the local and regional elite within the framework of the cultural and socio-political situation during the Solomon epoch. Together with the comprehensive regional historical and archaeological evidence, the text fits the natural ruling-structure element of a socio-political phase of formation, which began to develop again

---

[95] Was the sphere of retroactively legitimised influence in the north ascribed to Solomon on such a scale as Hezekiah and Josiah planned to achieve? See Knauf, "King Solomon's Copper Supply," pp. 174-76. Another argument put forward by Knauf, *ibid.*, pp. 178-79, fits into this consideration: if in 1 Kgs 4:19 according to LXXRD "Gad" instead of "Gilead" (MT) is correct (which I consider at this time less likely, Niemann, *Herrschaft*, pp. 30-31, n. 120), then it can be argued that the names in the list (e.g., "Gad" in v. 19) could at least in part have their roots in the time of Omri because, according to the Mesha-Inscription (ll. 10-11) Gad was not Israelite before Omri's invasion, but rather only through the Israelite occupation. However, in contradiction to Knauf's suggestion, the other possibility must be considered, that the old Gilead area, which in the Omridic and post-Omridic time was expanded to the south, then included Gad (1 Sam 13:7). Maybe this expansion southwards to Gad led to the change from "Gilead" to "Gad" in the LXX text (likewise the unnecessary and geographically improbable addition of "Gad" next to the realistic "Gilead" in 1 Sam 13:7). As a consequence of the change from "Gilead" to "Gad" in 3 Kgs 4:18 LXX, the remark "(in) the land of Sihon [from Heshbon, not far from Gad], the king of the Amorites and the king Og from Bashan" fit Gad. "Gilead" would then be the older name in v. 19 MT and the *lectio difficilior* (see Ash, "Solomons?" p. 75 n. 37; p. 78).

[96] Knauf, "King Solomon's Copper Supply," p. 178 (Omride time). It is possible that this knowledge came to Judah during the reign of Atalja.

[97] Ash, "Solomon's?" pp. 84-85, is thinking, in general, of the time following the fall of the Northern Kingdom.

upwards after a "depression" (Iron Age IA). If 1 Kgs 4:7-19 represents an *attempt* at the stabilisation and expansion of Solomon's power, it sketches the *beginnings and not an already existing system*. It is possible that names now present in the list do not all stem from the Solomon-epoch. The structure could have been filled later with new material and names in comparable situations (Omridian Age?). In any case, whether the basic structure is Solomonian or Omridian, it is still true that it represents a cautious, wide-meshed first phase. It does not document a completed stable and efficient socio-political administrative structure. Such a structure would look different.

3. Result: The Socio-Political Shadow Cast by the Biblical Solomon

We can now sketch a shadowy outline of the socio-political situation of the Solomonic epoch. In light of the cultural situation in the central Palestinian highlands during the transition from Iron Age I to II, the non-existence of epigraphical witness to the presumed Solomon epoch is understandable. That fact sheds light on the modest cultural and socio-political situation. Archaeological results further illustrate this. Currently, it is not possible to place finds from the presumed Solomon epoch (traditionally within the last two-thirds of the 10th century) with any degree of certainty within Solomon's reign. It is, however, possible to create a rough sketch of the situation in which Solomon presumably belongs based on the known geomorphologic-environmental facts, the cultural development of Syria-Palestine and the archaeological research. The outline thus achieved could then, to some extent, be filled in by comparing regional as well as typical living conditions and behavioral structures from ethnological research. This is acceptable because the Palestinian ecology remained the same and the economic patterns and structures changed so little between the Late Bronze Age and the Ottoman Empire, that indeed such comparisons are worthwhile.[98] In light of such ethnological comparisons the critically analysed biblical evidence, differentiated between "story" and "history," can then be more fully appreciated.

---

[98] For good socio-structural comparative material, see among others, H. Kopp, *Al-Qāsim: Wirtschafts- und sozialgeographische Strukturen und Entwicklungsprozesse in einem Dorf des jemenitischen Hochlandes* (BTAVO B31; Wiesbaden: Reichert, 1977); W. Dostal, "The Shihūh of Northern Oman: A Contribution to Cultural Ecology," *Geographical Journal* 138 (1972) 1-7; *idem*, "Sozio-ökonomische Aspekte der Stammesdemokratie in Nordost-Jemen," *Sociologus* 24 (1974) 1-15; and *idem, Egalität und Klassengesellschaft in Südarabien: Anthropologische Untersuchungen zur sozialen Evolution* (Wiener Beiträger zur Kulturgeschichte und Linguistik 20; Vienna: Ferdinand Berger & Söhne, 1985) (South Arabia); see also the detailed report of scholarly investigations by Lemche, *Early Israel*, pp. 95-201; C. Kramer, ed., *Ethnoarchaeology: Implications of Ethnography for Archaeology* (New York: Columbia University, 1979); C. Kramer, *Village Ethnoarchaeology: Rural Iran in Archaeological Perspective* (Studies in Archaeology; New York: Academic, 1982);

When one looks at the socio-political structural elements of his time and reign, Solomon is recognisable, in rough outlines at least, as a typical oriental (small) ruler. He stands in the tradition and the evolutionary line of both Saul and David. Apart from the theological and critical make-over, Saul innovatively joined his two traditional roots: that of a Late Bronze Age city-state ruler and that of his own birth into a rural clan. Without giving up his clan base, he strove towards a territorial domination with an urban centre (Gibeon). His territory may have reached as far as the Plain of Acco. If this territorial claim was truly made by Saul, passed on to David and then to Solomon, it must have been given up at the latest by Solomon (1 Kgs 9:10-14). Although Saul held success and finally defeat at the hands of the Philistocanaanites of the coastal plain in balance, his differentiated and loose regional sovereignty was (even if it only lasted a single decade, with a size not achieved since the rule of Laba'yu in the Late Bronze Age) as large, if not larger (and in any case economically more potent) than David's Judean homeland.

David was a rural Judean clan *chief*. The power relationships among the elite and the fighting between rural and urban parties upon his death imply this; but he too clearly recognised the value of an urban base. He also realised that every city isn't the same and that Hebron was of lesser functional geographic value than Jerusalem. Jerusalem held many advantages for his reign. David combined this insight with his traditionally tribal oriented organisation. It seems that David formed the tribe of Judah from two parts (1 Sam 21ff): Core-Judah from Bethlehem to Hebron, and various southern groups. Subsequently, he tried to integrate the *city-state* Jerusalem into his *tribal* rule. However, in his *coup d'état*, Solomon ended up doing the opposite. He brought the tribal Judah into the city-state of Jerusalem. But this remained an issue of contention. The tribal Judean elite occasionally made a play for power in Jerusalem (2 Kgs 11; 14:19ff; 21:24). As Knauf recently pointed out (in this volume), Micah 5:1-4 depicts the voice of rural Judah opposed to the possibly non-Judean urban dynasty in Jerusalem at the end of the 8th century BCE. In addition to moving the centre of power from Hebron to Jerusalem, with its long-term consequences, David's main achievement was the continuation of what Saul had only been able to temporarily accomplish: defending the highlands against the Philistocanaanites and expelling them from the area "from Gibeon to Gezer" (2 Sam 5:25). He was not active beyond the region of Benjamin to the north: he was satisfied with the role of recognised protector of the groups north of Jerusalem. This had nothing to do with modesty, but rather the authority was given to a person according to his actual achievements. In any case, it wasn't little that he so attained: a sphere of *influence* of this size was unknown in

---

for Palestine see Cohen, *Palestine*; and E. A. Knauf, "Berg und Tal, Staat und Stamm-Grundzüge der Geschichte Palästinas in den letzten fünftausend Jahren," *Pracht und Geheimnis: Kleidung und Schmuck aus Palästina und Jordanien* (eds. G. Völger and others; Köln: Rautenstrauch-Joest-Museum der Stadt Köln, 1987) 26-35.

the preceding age. To his power base, Judah, David added Saul's political inheritance, those areas that transferred authority and duties to him. Peace outside his dominion spared him having to prove his ability as a powerful protector to hold all of Palestine from Dan to Beer-sheba and Tamar. Small campaigns in middle and south Transjordan remained regionally limited. David seemed less far-sighted, despite moving the northern Israelite Ark to Jerusalem, when it came to creating an integrated societal and religious symbolism for his entire dominion.[99] In regards to setting up such a basic symbolism, it looks as if Saul before him (Gibeon) and Solomon after him achieved more.

David's successor (son?[100]) Solomon worked at precisely this deficit. As an urbanite, more specifically a Jerusalemite, he enjoyed inherent advantages over David.[101] When it came to religion, Solomon attached himself to Saul's politics (Gibeon) and continued the religious integration of the north (Shiloh, the Ark) and the urban-Gibeonite tradition with the Jerusalemite tradition. It certainly seems that Solomon, even more than Saul, fits into the tradition of the Late Bronze Age Canaanite city-state ruler. He connected the rulal protoisraelite (Saul) and the rural Judean (David) with urban Jerusalemite traditions. Solomon was, more than David, the one who brought the north, south, and Jerusalem together to the future importance of Jerusalem.[102]

His socio-political goal was a complex, urban-based territorial rule. The duties and instruments traditionally needed for such complex sovereignty placed burdens on the population which surpassed the possibilities of David's economically modest clan area or Solomon's Jerusalem. Thus Solomon's attempts were to no avail, though the dimensions were measurably more modest than later idealisingly portrayed. The burden was enough to provoke the north to revoke the voluntary loyalty[103] they had given, not him, but David. The following concrete socio-political measures were taken:

---

[99] Keel, "Theologie," p. 166. Does David show his rural Judean roots here, tending less towards urban supported territorial rule than the (more) urban oriented Saul and Solomon?

[100] Was Solomon David's son? In an excellent study Veijola, "Salomo," pp. 230-50, raised the possibility that he was more likely Uriah's son. The consequence that after David no other Davidic even sat on David's throne would have been so explosive for later Judean listeners or readers that the existing biblical report of David's scandalous adultary was the less embarrassing of the two and was used to cover the more serious scandal. See also Knauf, "Biblical Argument."

[101] Keel, "Theologie," pp. 167ff.

[102] Against Alt, "Jerusalem," pp. 253ff, in agreement with Keel, "Fern von Jerusalem"; and *idem*, "Theologie."

[103] Herein possibly lies the key to understanding the *seemingly* incomprehensibly stupid actions on the part of Rehoboam when dealing with the northern groups (1 Kgs 12). I assume that he did not, as is theologically portrayed, place such hard and provoking demands out of youthful wantonness or on poor advice. As son of the (non-Judean, non-tribal) Jerusalemite Solomon, he saw the obvious need for forced labour, and insisted on the normal Late Bronze Age ruler's right of disposal over his subjects; see below n. 114. What one can accuse him of is a lack of sensitivity towards the northern groups, who were as tribal non-urbanites sociologically distanced from him.

1. The intensification of the legitimising role of Jerusalem through the reconstruction and expansion of the city temple, itself reclaimed as the temple of YHWH connected to both David and Israel; thereby supporting Jerusalem's claim to Judah *and* the northern groups.

2. The representative building of the palace and fortifications in Jerusalem of unknown dimensions.

The socio-political legitimising elements of rule mentioned above cannot be archaeologically proven. Their assumed existence is based solely on biblical reports. Through the general knowledge of the cultural development in Palestine and comparable ethnographic structures, it can be said that they might have existed.

3. If and what Solomon did, in fulfillment of the ancient oriental ruler's duty, in terms of buildings and fortifications outside of Jerusalem is unknown. Despite claims to the contrary, in the six places mentioned in 1 Kgs 9:15, 17-19 nothing can, at this time, be archaeologically traced without a doubt to the Solomon epoch, much less to Solomon himself. If and in what measure Solomon even had influence in Hazor and Megiddo is not known to us. If in both locations archaeological caution is called for the possibility of Solomon having had influence in Gezer is greater. In the case of Lower Bethoron one can only, in general, point to the strategic (and in the case of Baalat, religious) value of the cities as seen from Jerusalem looking northwest toward the coastal plain and, in the case of Tamar, to the value as a foothold and an outermost point of influence in the south-east. A chain of fortresses for defending the border of the Solomonic territory and as such a characteristic of a state-typical border-guarding cannot be seen in these scattered points around Solomon's claimed sphere of influence.

4. If Solomon's marriage to a Libyan-Egyptian princess (or "court-lady") has a historical basis it could be connected with Sheshonq's campaign into Palestine, an Egyptian occupation of Gezer and a transfer of the city to Solomon. That could hint at a vassal relationship giving Solomon the role of an Egyptian viceroy or governor in the direction of the Philistocanaanite coast on the one side and the central Palestinian highland north of Jerusalem on the other. At the same time this Egyptian-Solomonic vassal-relationship might hint at an Egyptian attempt to counterbalance the Phoenician-Tyrian influence on Solomon. The absence of Jerusalem in the Sheshonq list could be thus explained: There already existed such a relationship, or, more likely, a dependent relationship might have been achieved during the Sheshonq campaign. This scenario is neither archaeologically nor Egyptologically certain.

5. Either in connection with the suspected Egyptian supported vassal role "from Dan to Tamar," or as an independent strategy without Egyptian initiative, Solomon might have begun to gain a foothold in the north. He tried to stabilise his influence and authority through the establishment of members of the northern local and regional elite who gained his confidence, as well as relatives and courtiers.

This cautious attempt and the failure of similar actions in Judah as well as the Philistocanaanite coastal plain, sheds an interesting light on the socio-politically loose, little structured organisation of Solomon's rule, which was still a *complex chiefdom* at the very most, only just beginning to head towards a state.

Likewise, there exists no epigraphical or archaeological evidence for this socio-political action. It is understandable in light of the general cultural tendency of this epoch not proven but deducted from the interpretation of biblical texts. This interpretation of 1 Kgs 4:7-19 lies consequentially within the tendency towards the development of personnel as socio-political instruments of rule by Saul over David to Solomon.

The presumed socio-cultural scenario is further emphasised through the ethnological comparison with Ḍâhir b. ʿUmar. This makes the pattern of action, which can be seen in the biblical record of David and Solomon structurally believable and historically possible. The comparison does not, however, fix the biblical portrayal of Solomon in the 10th century and therefore cannot be used as evidence to prove historically the 10th century's existence of Solomon as well as his biblical portrayal.

All told, one can say that some of the socio-political beginnings of the ruling organisation and legitimisation in Judah/Israel probably are rooted in the presumed Solomon epoch. Most important among these was the functional strengthening of Jerusalem's role, especially the religious components. This was also the factor with the most lasting consequences, especially because the second measure worth mentioning, the attempt to structurally integrate the northern groups' region through Solomon's "delegates," (if this measure even belongs only in the time of Solomon and not also/only in the time of the Omridic dynasty) failed to achieve its desired effect. The intention behind this measure (stronger governing integration) and the burden of unknown degree, which Solomon's royal building and representative projects caused, hindered each other. So the northern groups ended by withdrawing their loyalty to the House of David precisely because of the burdens caused by prestige measures, which were supposed to stabilise Solomon's reign.

It is especially important to emphasise that, contrary to the previous leading interpretation, the assumed socio-political measures behind 1 Kgs 4:7-19 represent a beginning, a first attempt at socio-political organisation. During Solomon's reign the time was not necessarily unfavorable for a strict socio-political unification of Palestine, because Syria, Mesopotamia and Egypt had little or no imperial expansive tendencies. But such a unification is a difficult task in a geomorphologically differentiated mountainous territory and among a population traditionally living in small groups. The situation was not such that the traditional groups with their regional composition and basis urgently needed strong central rule to guarantee their own survival. After David, a Judean tribesman, had succeeded in transforming the northern Judeans and the groups in the south of Hebron from a regional tribal power (Judah) to an urban-based power (Judah and Jerusalem), the main achievement of Solomon, an urbanite (from Jerusalem), was *attempting* to form a territorial reign combining Judah and Israel around his urban centre of Jerusalem. To do this Solomon first had to repress the Davidic/rural Judean element within his city-state Jerusalem. As soon as he had secured his position, he integrated the fresh Judean tribal powers so firmly into his Jerusalemite rule, that Judah steadfastly remained loyal to the "House of David." However, the feat of integrating the differentiated and separating (centrifugally) forces of the northern Israelite groups as a third party to the urban Jerusalemite and rural Judean basis proved to be too great in the given historical situation.[104] So Solomon's assumed attempt at socio-political organisation in the north, if indeed the structures, names, places and regions, handed down in 1 Kgs 4:7-19 truly belong to the Solomonic epoch, proved to be from a culturally evolutionary point of view merely a first short trial without direct lasting results. The total absence of a corresponding attempt in Judah points in the same direction. The socio-political summit, upon which Solomon today appears to stand according to the contextual portrayal, proves to be ideological and theological, not historical.

Excursus

Solomon, Rehoboam and "the Egyptian (Dynastic) Connection"

The following factors are in need of co-ordinated interpretation:

1. An unnamed pharaoh moves on Gezer, occupies it and gives it to "his daughter," who becomes Solomon's wife. The time frame of Solomon's reign is not clear. We can only assume it is to be placed before that of Rehoboam, whose enthronement can be dated by means of synchronisms around 926/5 BCE.[105] But the identity of the pharaoh who conquered Gezer remains a mystery (Siamun? Psusennes II? Sheshonq?).

2. "In the fifth year of King Rehoboam" Sheshonq moved on Palestine (1 Kgs 14:25).

---

[104] The prospect of a loosely organised structural union of Judah with the northern groups on a culturally further developed niveau and under favorable foreign-political conditions, existed first during the time of Ahab, then even more so at the time of Jeroboam II and Uzziah. However, Judah and the Northern Kingdom soon fell into the maelstrom of the rising Assyrian empire. The perspective of profitable co-operation awakened during the Omride time and during the late Nimsidic time (Jeroboam II), was, if not Hezekiah, then under Josiah again intensively strived towards. The latter planned for the integration of the "lost" northern area. This Greater Israel was projected into a time before the numerous hostile relations between Judah and Israel: into the time of the ideal ancestors David and Solomon.

[105] J. H. Hayes and P. K. Hooker, *A New Chronology for the Kings of Israel and Judah and Its Implications for the Biblical History and Literature* (Atlanta: John Knox, 1988) 16ff.

3. The so-called List of Sheshonq[106] dates from his 21st year (929 or 924 BCE).[107] That means that the described military campaign took place before either 929 or 924 BCE. How long before is not at all clear.

4. The list does not mention Jerusalem: accident or intended? If on purpose, why? Interpretation: The fact that the list dates from the end of Sheshonq's reign could imply that it summarises the achievements of his rule; it may represent the combined results of several campaigns.[108] The campaign(s) took place before 929/924 BCE, but how long before is uncertain. It is therefore likely that Sheshonq's Palestinian campaign(s) took place *before* Rehoboam's reign (from 926/5) during the time of Solomon. The fact that Sheshonq and Solomon were contemporaries is further supported by 1 Kgs 11:40. Taking into account the vagueness of the dates, in Rehoboam's fifth year (1 Kgs 14:25 = 922/921), Sheshonq was probably no longer living. Is it possible that the original biblical document contained "the fifth year of king Solomon" or "Jeroboam"[109] or "the fifth year of Sheshonq"? There are no facts which help answer this question. We are limited to proposing scenarios which appear reasonable in light of our knowledge of the tendencies in the biblical texts and within the framework of the historical situation. To do the opposite, to reconstruct the historical facts based on the biblical-theological picture, is not an option for a scientific-critical portrayal. Which means that one should distance oneself from vague or unknown dates. The interesting fact that Jerusalem is not explicitly mentioned in the Sheshonq list cannot be fully weighed as an *argumentum e silentio*. Because the missing fragments are so large it is possible that Jerusalem was not touched, but it is also possible simply that the name has not survived.[110]

---

[106] Editions and interpretations of the Sheshonq list: J. Simons, *Handbook for the Study of Egyptian Topographical Lists Relating to Western Asia* (Leiden: E. J. Brill, 1937) 178-86, no. XXXIV; A. Jirku, *Die ägyptischen Listen palästinischer und syrischer Ortsnamen in Umschrift und mit historisch-archäologischem Kommentar herausgegeben* (Aalen: Scientia, 1967) 47-50; M. Noth, "Die Wege der Pharaonenheere in Palästina und Syrien: Untersuchungen zu den hieroglyphischen Listen palästinischer und syrischer Städte, IV: Die Schoschenkliste," *ZDPV* 61 (1938) 277-304 (= idem, *Aufsätze zur Biblischen Landes- und Altertumskunde II* (Neukirchen-Vluyn: Neukirchener, 1971) 73-93; B. Mazar, "Pharao Shishak's Campaign to the Land of Israel," *The Early Biblical Period* (eds. S. Ahituv and B. A. Levine; Jerusalem: Israel Exploration Society, 1986) 139-50; G. W. Ahlström, "Pharaoh Shoshenq's Campaign to Palestine," *History and Traditions of Early Israel: Studies Presented to Eduard Nielsen, May 8th 1993* (eds. A. Lemaire and B. Otzen; VTSup 50; Leiden: E. J. Brill, 1993) 1-16; Soggin, *Einführung*, pp. 135-37.

[107] E. Hornung, *Grundzüge der ägyptischen Geschichte* (Darmstadt: Wiss. Buchgesellschaft, 1992) 117; M. L. Bierbrier, "Scheschonq," *LÄ*, p. 585 (Sheshonq I, 945-924 BCE); Garbini, *History and Ideology*, pp. 29f (950-929 BCE).

[108] According to Ahlström, "Pharoah Shoshenq," Sheshonq's list consists of combined reports from various parts of the armies under Pharaoh's control.

[109] Knauf, "King Solomon's Copper Supply," p. 182.

[110] In this regard, *ibid.*, pp. 181-82; Ahlström, "Pharoah Shoshenq," pp. 15f. Knauf, "Biblical Argument," recently gave reasons why Jerusalem and Judah, as well as Shechem and its vicinity were intentionally not mentioned in the list.

Since the old argument does not bring us any further, a new way of looking at the problem is desirable. For this it must be clearly stated that the Egyptian king mentioned in 1 Kgs 9:16 might well have been Solomon's contemporary Sheshonq. If Sheshonq did, in fact, occupy the city and thereby (partially) destroy it, it would make sense, despite possible damage, to give it to a local or regional ruler of the hinterland/inland presiding near the important coastal plain as a vassal responsibility, in line with traditional Egyptian colonial practices. The ruler of Jerusalem would be one possibility for such a position. This makes even more sense in light of the fact that the region of Canaan, traditionally claimed by Egypt, had also become of political-economic interest for the aspiring Phoenician coastal power Tyre. 1 Kgs 5:1 LXX clearly supports this idea.[111] It may be that Egyptian diplomacy also used a marriage connection with the ruler of Jerusalem to further limit or end Tyrian influence. That Egyptian princesses were not generally given in marriage abroad may be true,[112] but the "princess" need not necessarily have been a very high ranking member of the royal court (at least from the Egyptian point of view!). This would naturally have been seen differently in Jerusalem and taken advantage of for propaganda purposes. Additionally, Sheshonq was not a classic Egyptian or traditional Pharaoh, but an assimilated Libyan.[113] So it may be that in the Bubastidic times the ends occasionally justified the non-traditional means. For *Solomon*, Egypt's condescension to such an atypical "dynastic" marriage might have been worth an impressive gift (=tribute in the form of golden shields, 1 Kgs 14:25-26).[114] However, in later portrayals this temple tribute must have appeared a sacrilege or weakness, which could not be attributed to the Temple builder, but better to Rehoboam, he who gambled away the chance to unite Judah and Israel in his time.

The archaeological finds in Gezer do not bring any clarity to the picture.[115] If, according to Finkelstein, bichrome ware last appears in stratum XI and stratum

---

[111] Kuan, "Third Kingdoms 5.1."

[112] Considerations and bibliographical references *pro et contra* in Soggin, *Einführung*, pp. 40, 70-71; Garbini, *History and Ideology*, pp. 27ff; Knauf, "King Solomon's Copper Supply," pp. 181-82.

[113] E. Otto, *Ägypten: Der Weg des Pharaonenreiches* (Stuttgart: Kohlhammer, 1955) 218-26; Knauf, "King Solomon's Copper Supply," p. 182 n. 59.

[114] W. L. Moran, *The Amarna Letters* (Baltimore: Johns Hopkins, 1992) 366; EA 369; where the Pharaoh demanded both beautiful women and gold from Milkilu of Gezer(!): parallels pointed out to me by E. A. Knauf. We do not know anything about other dynastic marriages of Solomon besides the case of the Egyptian princess. Marriages with daughters of princes or petty rulers around Judah (and Israel) may be plausible (1 Kgs 11:1-8). Yet, not even in the case of Rehoboam's mother, Naama the Ammonite (1 Kgs 14:21, 31) can we be sure that she was of royal birth: against Hübner, *Die Ammoniter*, p. 181. David and Solomon knew of the principal importance of close relations to the local and regional elite. In any case it was not necessary for a diplomatic marriage to be of *royal* origin.

[115] Niemann, *Herrschaft*, p. 97 n. 431 with bibliography; W. G. Dever, "Gezer," *The New Encyclopedia of Archaeological Excavations in the Holy Land* (ed. E. Stern; New York: Simon & Schuster, 1993) 502-05.

X-IX was destroyed by the Egyptians (2nd half of 10th century), as most accept, then stratum VIII already belongs in the 9th century, which further means that this stratum including the 6-chamber-gate cannot possibly be connected with Solomon.[116] In light of the sparse excavation in Gezer to date, there might still be much left to discover. But for the time being, archaeology does not offer an answer to the questions as to whether Solomon truly built anything in Gezer, and if so what. That he did order some construction remains possible.

If the assumed vassal relationship of Solomon to Egypt (1 Kgs 9:16) as well as the vassal and economically dependent relationship with Tyre (1 Kgs 5:1 LXX and 1 Kgs 5:15ff; 9:10-14) are at least in tendency true, then in the eyes of later Jerusalem-centered thought, these relationships could easily have been mutated into a new constellation in which both powers, Egypt and Tyre, zealously endeavoured to maintain friendly relations with the ruler of Jerusalem through both trade and marriage. From the Jerusalemite point of view, the interests of wisdom-oriented intellectual (1 Kgs 10:1-13), military (trade in arms), and economic (1 Kgs 10:14-29) worlds seemed to come together.[117]

Of course, this cannot be historically proved, but as a possible scenario it is based on historical facts. It integrates biblical tendential theological interpretation, which is, in a theological way, understandably rationed out to the ideal king Solomon (positive: connections to the Egyptian court) and to his imperfect successor (negative: payment of the "golden shields" tribute to Egypt).

---

[116] Contra *ibid.*; Finkelstein, "Archaeology of the United Monarchy," p. 183.
[117] When Solomon is credited with making Jerusalem a world centre of importance and riches, this may represent a possibly dangerous oversimplification of itself and a deceiving hopefulness at the time of Hezekiah (2 Kgs 20:12-13), with even more dangerous consequences during the time of Josiah; see also Knauf, "King Solomon's Copper Supply," pp. 174-76.

Biblical Jerusalem:
An Archaeological Assessment

Ann E. Killebrew

Jerusalem, as both a spiritual concept and physical reality, has long been the focus of the biblical authors, the theme of theological treatises and interpretations, and the topic of countless scholarly speculations. It is the most extensively excavated ancient site in biblical Israel, a fact that is due in no small measure to its spiritual centrality for the three major monotheistic religions, its contested past, and modern-day concerns of "ownership." For these reasons Andrew G. Vaughn and I selected Jerusalem as the centerpiece of a cross-disciplinary dialogue between biblical scholars, historians, Assyriologists, Egyptologists, and archaeologists within the framework of the Society of Biblical Literature Consultation on "Jerusalem in Bible and Archaeology" held during the Society for Biblical Literature Annual Meetings from 1998 to 2001.

As an archaeologist and a long-time resident of Jerusalem, I deemed any attempt to interpret Jerusalem's past as a foolhardy exercise that was limited by inescapable cultural and personal preconceptions, ideological biases, and circular academic arguments. Though I retain my skepticism regarding the objectivity of archaeology—mute stones do not speak; rather, we translate their words and then interpret them—we should nevertheless attempt the daunting task of reconstructing Bronze and Iron Age Jerusalem based on interdisciplinary dialogue and open debate.

During the past decade in particular, the topic of Jerusalem has provoked especially acrimonious and polemical debates, even as the archaeological evidence, or lack thereof, is being published in increasingly frequent final excavation reports. The focus of the controversy has been the apparent inconsistencies between a literal reading of the biblical account of Jerusalem describing the reigns of David and Solomon and the unimposing archaeological reality of the city during the tenth and ninth centuries B.C.E. Thus, it was with some surprise that with each passing year of our consultation, and during the course of the compilation of this volume, I became increasingly more optimistic that some consensus can be reached regarding Jerusalem's past based on the combined efforts of archaeologists, historians, and biblical scholars, while simultaneously recognizing the personal and professional biases we all bring to the discussion. As this volume demonstrates, archaeology has much to add to this discussion.

In spite of Jerusalem's difficult archaeological record, which has been the topic of many articles and books as summarized in several essays in this volume,[1] I see a coherent image of ancient Jerusalem slowly emerging from the remnants and ruins of ancient Jerusalem, especially from excavations conducted during the past four decades. In addition, numerous well-documented final excavation reports and publications have recently appeared that add significantly to the evidence, with many more primary reports in various stages of preparation.[2] The focus of my

---

[1] In particular, see the essay by Cahill for a summary of the history of research on Jerusalem as it relates to the united monarchy. See the essays by Geva and Schniedewind for a summary of the history of research as it relates to the end of the Judahite monarchy.

[2] The most relevant and archaeologically well-documented field reports include the excavations on the southeastern hill ("City of David") by Kathleen M. Kenyon (1961–67), excavations in the Jewish Quarter by Nahman Avigad (1969–1982), Benjamin Mazar's (1968–77) and Eilat Mazar's (1986–87) Southern Wall (Ophel) excavations to the south of the Temple Mount, Yigal Shiloh's excavations in the City of David (1978–85), excavations of several Iron II cemeteries at several locales in East Jerusalem, and most recently Ronny Reich's and Eli Shukron's (1995–present) excavations at the base of the eastern slope of the City of David and around the Gihon Spring. The most significant final excavation reports that present relevant primary data for this discussion include the following publications: City of David (Kenyon's final excavation reports): A. Douglas Tushingham, *Excavations in Jerusalem, 1961–1967, vol. I* (Toronto: Royal Ontario Museum, 1985); Hendricus J. Franken and Margreet L. Steiner, *Excavations by Kathleen M. Kenyon in Jerusalem 1961–1967, vol. II, The Iron Age Extramural Quarter on the South-East Hill* (Oxford: Oxford University Press, 1990); Margreet L. Steiner, *Excavations by Kathleen M. Kenyon in Jerusalem 1961–1967, vol. III, The Settlement in the Bronze and Iron Ages* (Copenhagen International Seminar 9; New York: Sheffield Academic Press, 2001); Itzhak Eshel and Kay Prag, eds., *Excavations by Kathleen M. Kenyon in Jerusalem 1961–1967, vol. IV, The Iron Age Cave Deposits on the South-East Hill and Isolated Burials and Cemeteries Elsewhere* (Oxford: Oxford University Press, 1995); City of David (Shiloh's final excavation reports): Yigal Shiloh, *Excavations at the City of David I, 1978–1982: Interim Report of the First Five Seasons* (Qedem 19; Jerusalem: Institute of Archaeology, Hebrew University of Jerusalem, 1984); Donald T. Ariel, *Excavations at the City of David 1978–1985 Directed by Yigal Shiloh, vol. II, Imported Stamped Amphora Handles, Coins, Worked Bone and Ivory, and Glass* (Qedem 30; Jerusalem: Institute of Archaeology, Hebrew University of Jerusalem, 1990); Alon De Groot and Donald T. Ariel, *Excavations at the City of David 1978–1985 Directed by Yigal Shiloh, vol. III, Stratigraphical, Environmental, and Other Reports* (Qedem 33; Jerusalem: Institute of Archaeology, Hebrew University of Jerusalem, 1992); Donald T. Ariel and Alon De Groot, eds., *Excavations at the City of David 1978–1985 Directed by Yigal Shiloh, vol. IV, Various Reports* (Qedem 35; Jerusalem: Institute of Archaeology, Hebrew University of Jerusalem, 1994); Donald T. Ariel, ed., *Excavations at the City of David Directed by Yigal Shiloh, vol. V, Extramural Areas* (Qedem 40; Jerusalem: Institute of Archaeology, Hebrew University of Jerusalem, 2000); Donald T. Ariel et al., *Excavations at the City of David 1978–1985 Directed by Yigal Shiloh, vol. VI, Inscriptions* (ed. D. T. Ariel; Qedem 41; Jerusalem: Institute of Archaeology, Hebrew University of Jerusalem, 2000); City of David (Gihon Spring and Lower Southeastern Hill [only preliminary reports]): Ronny Reich and Eli Shukron, "The Excavations at the Gihon Spring and Warren's Shaft System in the City of David," in *Ancient Jerusalem Revealed* (ed. H. Geva; Jerusalem: Israel Exploration Society, 2000), 327–39; Jewish Quarter (Avigad's final excavation reports): Hillel Geva, ed., *Jewish Quarter Excavations in the Old City of Jerusalem Conducted by Nahman Avigad, 1969–1982, vol. I, Architecture and Stratigraphy: Areas A, W and X–2, Final Report* (Jerusalem: Israel Exploration Society, 2000). Southern Wall (Mazars' first final excavation report of the

archaeological audit is the material culture evidence presented in these primary reports, with an emphasis on what has actually been uncovered rather than on speculations regarding what may have (or should have) existed in antiquity.[3] While there are many details that are unknown or remains that are no longer preserved, a fairly clear outline of Bronze and Iron Age (ca. 3000–586 B.C.E.) Jerusalem is emerging.

The accumulative archaeological evidence categorically indicates that the ancient city was prominent during two periods—the Middle Bronze Age II (ca. 1800–1550 B.C.E.) and the Iron Age IIC (late eighth–seventh centuries B.C.E.). During the intervening periods (the Late Bronze and the Iron Age I and IIA/early IIB periods),[4] Jerusalem was a far more modest settlement.[5] The most contested period of time, both archaeologically and biblically, relates to our understanding of Jerusalem during the tenth century, specifically the reigns of David and Solomon. Thus far no physical remains have been found in over a century of excavations

---

"Millo"): Eilat Mazar and Benjamin Mazar, *Excavations in the South of the Temple Mount: The Ophel of Biblical Jerusalem* (Qedem 29; Jerusalem: Institute of Archaeology, Hebrew University of Jerusalem, 1989); Iron II Cemeteries: Gabriel Barkay, "Northern and Western Jerusalem in the End of the Iron Age" [Hebrew] (Ph.D. diss., Tel Aviv University, 1985); and an updated summary of his dissertation in idem, "The Necropoli of Jerusalem in the First Temple Period" [Hebrew], in *The History of Jerusalem: The Biblical Period* (ed. S. Ahituv and A. Mazar; Jerusalem: Yad Izhak Ben-Zvi, 2000), 233–70; David Ussishkin, *The Village of Silwan: The Necropolis from the Period of the Judean Kingdom* (Jerusalem: Israel Exploration Society, 1993); Ronny Reich, "The Ancient Burial Ground in the Mamilla Neighbourhood, Jerusalem," in *Ancient Jerusalem Revealed: Expanded Edition 2000* (ed. H. Geva; Jerusalem: Israel Exploration Society, 2000), 111–18. For a summary of archaeological research and relevant publications through 1993, see Hillel Geva, "History of Archaeological Research in Jerusalem," *NEAEHL* 2:801–4 and Cahill's essay in this volume.

[3] Although I am focusing on what has been found, it is necessary to note that Mount Moriah (encased in the Temple Mount podium or the Muslim Haram esh-Sharif) has not been excavated due to obvious political and religious considerations. Thus, one of the potentially most promising areas for the exploration of ancient Jerusalem has not and will not be excavated in the foreseeable future. It cannot be ruled out that there may, though not necessarily, be archaeological remains from the Bronze and Iron Ages underneath the present Islamic structures. See Ussishkin's essay in this volume for a discussion of various suggestions regarding a preexilic occupation on the Temple Mount. See also Ernst Axel Knauf's proposal in "Jerusalem in the Late Bronze and Early Iron Ages: A Proposal," *TA* 27 (2000): 75–90.

[4] There are several variations on the absolute dating for the Bronze and Iron Ages. I follow Amihai Mazar's suggested chronology and dating for these periods of time: Middle Bronze IIA (2000–1800/1750 B.C.E.), Middle Bronze IIB–C (1800/1750–1550 B.C.E.), Late Bronze I (1550–1400 B.C.E.), Late Bronze IIA–B (1400–1200 B.C.E.), Iron IA–B (1200–1000 B.C.E.), Iron IIA (1000–925 B.C.E.), Iron IIB (925–720 B.C.E.), and Iron IIC (720–586). See Amihai Mazar, *Archaeology of the Land of the Bible 10,000–586 B.C.E.* (ABRL; New York: Doubleday, 1990), 30.

[5] This general conclusion is valid whether one accepts the conventional chronology for dating tenth-century archaeological strata or whether one follows a new "low chronology" for dating these strata. See the essays by Finkelstein and Ussishkin in this volume for a summary of this chronological debate.

that come near to matching the biblical magnificence of the Solomon's Jerusalem that served as the capital of a "united monarchy." The core of the debate is not over whether David and Solomon existed but rather over the character of Jerusalem during their reigns: Was it an urban administrative city that could have served as the capital of a united monarchy? Was it an unfortified village? Or was it an unimpressive settlement that served as a regional administrative and/or religious center with some commercial and cultic functions? In this assessment, I discuss the scant archaeological evidence that points to a modest settlement during the fourteenth–ninth centuries B.C.E. Depending on the dating of the infamous "stepped stone structure," Jerusalem either (1) served as a regional administrative hub with some evidence of public structures or (2) was a provincial center that consisted mainly of domestic structures.

Archaeological Consensus: Middle Bronze IIB (ca. 1800–1550 B.C.E.) and Iron IIC (ca. 720–586 B.C.E.)— An Urban Fortified Jerusalem

The Middle Bronze IIB and Iron IIC periods are similar to two bookends: they represent a period of time when Jerusalem was clearly an urban and fortified major center of the region. There is an increasing consensus regarding the eighteenth to mid-sixteenth centuries B.C.E. and the eighth to seventh centuries B.C.E. based on the monumental and public structures that have been excavated in Jerusalem. The most important sources of information regarding Middle Bronze Age Jerusalem are Kathleen Kenyon's 1961–67 excavations on the southeastern slope of Silwan village (City of David), Yigal Shiloh's 1978–85 excavations in the City of David, and Ronny Reich's and Eli Shukron's recent work at the Gihon Spring at the foot of the eastern slope of the City of David.[6]

The only final excavation report of the Middle Bronze Age remains in the City of David thus far published is Margreet Steiner's recent volume presenting the results of Kenyon's excavations.[7] Most noteworthy for our discussion is the detailed description of the Middle Bronze IIB fortifications that Kenyon uncovered. The published results provide clear archaeological evidence that this wall was constructed during the second half of the Middle Bronze Age (either at the end of the Middle Bronze IIA or early IIB, ca. 1800 B.C.E.) as a city fortification.[8] A second, later but much broader city wall dating to the eighth–seventh centuries B.C.E. was constructed partially over and occasionally reutilized sections of this

---

[6] For a detailed summary and analysis of the results of these excavations, see Cahill in this volume.
[7] Steiner, *Excavations in Jerusalem III*, 10–23.
[8] Ibid., 10–12.

Middle Bronze Age wall as its foundations.[9] Both Kenyon's and later Shiloh's excavations revealed that there were clearly two city walls: an earlier Middle Bronze IIB wall and a second but separate Iron IIC wall that reused parts of the Middle Bronze Age wall fortifications. Although in her preliminary reports Kenyon suggests that the city wall remained in use from the "Canaanite-Jebusite" periods and the "greater part of the Jewish Monarchy," she clearly states that there is no archaeological proof for a continued use of this wall following the end of the Middle Bronze Age until the eighth/seventh centuries B.C.E.[10] In agreement with Kenyon, Shiloh also "assumes" in his preliminary report that this wall remained in use from the end of the Middle Bronze Age until it was rebuilt in the late eighth century B.C.E. However, Shiloh notes that there is no archaeological evidence for this assumption and supports it with the statement: "The fact that no other line of fortifications, of any period, was found in the sectional trenches outside and below the existing line, in Areas B, D1 and E2, bolsters this conclusion."[11] Unfortunately this finding would bolster the conclusion that ancient Jerusalem was unwalled and lacked fortifications during the Late Bronze through Iron IIB periods.

In the final excavation report of Kenyon's excavations, and departing from the views of Kenyon and Shiloh, Steiner presents archaeological evidence that the wall went out of use at the end of the Middle Bronze Age and was not in use during the subsequent Late Bronze, Iron I, and Iron IIA/B periods.[12] Not until the late eighth–seventh centuries B.C.E. are there signs of reoccupation to the east (i.e., outside) the Middle Bronze Age city wall. Based on the complete lack of any archaeological or stratigraphic evidence for the continued use of the Middle Bronze Age city wall until the end of the Iron Age, one must reject suggestions that this wall remained in use during the Late Bronze through Iron IIA–B periods. Since no other suitable wall has thus far been uncovered, the only possible conclusion is that ancient Jerusalem from roughly the sixteenth to mid-eighth centuries B.C.E. lacked a city fortification wall. Attempts to explain this absence of archaeological evidence for the continued use of this wall from the fifteenth–late eighth centuries as a result of "erosion" are methodologically unacceptable and lack any proof. The paucity of even sherds dating from the sixteenth–ninth centuries B.C.E. in the fills and slope wash of the eastern slope provides an additional indication that settlement in the City of David was at best modest during the Late Bronze through Iron IIB periods. In particular, I reject suggestions that Jerusalem was fortified in the Late Bronze Age. All evidence indicates that Jerusalem was small and certainly unfortified,

---

[9] See Yigal Shiloh, *Excavations at the City of David I*, 12, 26.
[10] Kathleen M. Kenyon, "Excavations in Jerusalem, 1962," *PEQ* 94 (1963) 9–10; and see Cahill in this volume.
[11] Shiloh, *Excavations at the City of David I*, 35 n. 132; see also p. 28.
[12] For a description of the stratigraphic sequence of layers related to Wall 3, see Steiner, *Excavations in Jerusalem III*, 10–12; regarding the lack of evidence for any fortifications during the Late Bronze Age, see ibid., 39.

matching the general trend of unfortified cities throughout Canaan in the Late Bronze Age. Jerusalem of the Amarna period is hardly likely to have been the exception to this archaeological phenomenon.

Further evidence for a fortified Middle Bronze II settlement includes the recent discovery by Ronny Reich and Eli Shukron of two monumental towers dated to the Middle Bronze IIB period. These towers formed part of a public water system connected to a tunnel that led to the Pool Tower and Spring Tower protecting the Gihon Spring. Their excavations have also revealed that Channel II and Tunnel III are part of this monumental public water system, together with remnants of additional structures dating to this period. Reich and Shukron have convincingly shown that the shaft of "Warren's Shaft" never served as a water system. No less important is their discovery that the tunnel intersecting Warren's Shaft was constructed in two phases: the earlier phase dating to the Middle Bronze IIB and the later recutting of the tunnel dating to the eighth–seventh centuries B.C.E.[13] There is no archaeological evidence that the water system remained in use during the Late Bronze through Iron IIA/B periods, especially if the settlements during this six-hundred-year span were unfortified.[14] The recent excavations in the Gihon Spring area provide indisputable support for Jerusalem's importance as a fortified center during the Middle Bronze IIB period.

The late eighth and seventh centuries B.C.E. form the second bookend of preexilic Jerusalem. There is abundant evidence indicating Jerusalem's significance as a major urban center during the late Iron Age. Nearly all excavators working in the City of David, the Ophel, and the Jewish Quarter have uncovered significant remains from the late eighth and seventh centuries. Kenyon's[15] and Shiloh's[16] excavations revealed that the eastern slope of the City of David served as a residential quarter of mixed neighborhoods of affluent and poorer families during the later eighth and seventh centuries B.C.E.

---

[13] Ronny Reich and Eli Shukron, "Light at the End of the Tunnel," *BAR* 25/1 (1999): 22–33, 72; idem, "Excavations at the Gihon Spring," 327–39; idem, "Jerusalem, City of David," *Hadashot Arkheologiyot* 112 (2000): 82*–83*, figs. 150 and 151; idem, "New Excavations on the Eastern Slope of the City of David" [Hebrew], *Qad* 34/2 (122) (2001): 78–87; idem, "Jerusalem, City of David," *Hadashot Arkheologiyot* 114 (2002): 77*–78*, fig. 118; see also the essay by Cahill in this volume.

[14] In fact, based on the lack of sherds from the Late Bronze through Iron IIB periods, Reich proposes that the Gihon Spring and water systems were not used during the sixteenth–ninth centuries B.C.E. Reich, oral communication (1 January 2003).

[15] Steiner, *Excavations in Jerusalem III*, 54–111.

[16] For a summary of Shiloh's excavation results, see Shiloh, *Excavations at the City of David I*, 28–29. Only the final excavation report from Area D has been published thus far. See Donald T. Ariel et al., "Area D1: Stratigraphic Report," in Ariel, *Excavations at the City of David V*, 33–72; and Donald T. Ariel and Alon De Groot, "The Iron Age Extramural Occupation at the City of David and Additional Observations on the Siloam Channel," in Ariel, *Excavations at the City of David V*, 155–64.

Equally significant are the recent excavations by Reich and Shukron on the eastern slopes of the City of David, where they have uncovered additional sections of the so-called "extramural" residential quarter that are in fact enclosed by several previously unknown eighth–seventh century outer fortification walls (most notably Wall 502). These walls run parallel and down slope from the well-known Iron IIC city wall measuring approximately 5 m wide, the latter uncovered by several Jerusalem excavators, including Kenyon (Wall 1),[17] Shiloh (Wall 219),[18] as well as Reich and Shukron (Wall 501).[19] The recently discovered walls to the east of the main city wall indicate additional expansions of late Iron II Jerusalem.[20]

Excavations to the south of the Temple Mount in the Ophel area have not revealed any evidence that the area was settled earlier than the ninth century B.C.E. Further, the evidence from the excavations suggests that the biblical Ophel flourished only during the eighth and seventh centuries B.C.E. Charles Warren's 1867 excavations in the Ophel south of Mount Moriah revealed two towers, referred to as Towers A and B. Renewed excavations in this area by Benjamin Mazar (1976) and later by Eilat Mazar (1986–87) uncovered two additional monumental public buildings, designated as Buildings C (a possible gate) and D. Together these structures form a fortified complex that dates to the eighth–early sixth centuries B.C.E., the Babylonians destroying it in 586 B.C.E. Eilat Mazar has suggested that this complex may have been constructed as early as the ninth century, based on the discovery of a complete "black juglet" nestled in the foundation stones of Building D. She posits that the juglet was placed as a foundation deposit, but her suggestion is impossible to prove (or disprove). It should be pointed out that this juglet indicates a terminus post quem date (ninth century or later) for the construction of the gate and not necessarily its use. Thus, following the archaeological record in other areas of biblical Jerusalem, these large public structures postdate the period of the united monarchy and were in use during the peak of Jerusalem's biblical history: the eighth–seventh centuries B.C.E.

Evidence for a greatly expanded Jerusalem, outside the boundaries of the City of David and Ophel, is presented in volume I of the Jewish Quarter excavations. The results of these excavations prove conclusively that Jerusalem served as the major center of the southern kingdom of Judah. The highlights of Nahman Avigad's excavations include (in addition to residential structures) the discovery of the Iron IIC western fortification system that comprises a monumental city wall dating to the late eighth century (referred to as the "Broad Wall") together with an

---

[17] Franken and Steiner, *Excavations in Jerusalem II*, 50–56; Steiner, *Excavations in Jerusalem III*, 89–91.

[18] Shiloh, *Excavations at the City of David I*, 10, 12–13, 28.

[19] See the essay by Ronny Reich and Eli Shukron in this volume for a discussion of the "extramural" residential quarter and its relationship to a second outer-wall fortification.

[20] Reich and Shukron, "Jerusalem, City of David," 112:82*–83*; idem, "New Excavations on the Eastern Slope," 85–87; and Reich, oral communication (1 January 2003).

impressive tower. The "maximalist" proposal regarding the size of Jerusalem has been proven correct by the unambiguous archaeological evidence uncovered in the Jewish Quarter.[21] Today a consensus is emerging regarding both the archaeological evidence for Jerusalem of the Iron IIC and its close correspondence to the biblical account's view of the centrality of Jerusalem during the period following the Assyrian destruction of Samaria and the northern kingdom of Israel.

A second reliable indicator of Jerusalem's importance and impressive size is observable in the late eighth- and seventh-century cemeteries and cave deposits. Many of the burials are rock-cut tombs remarkable for their monumental size and impressive decorative features. These cemeteries again indicate the increased prosperity and wealth of Jerusalem during the late Iron II period. Gabriel Barkay has suggested that the numerous cemeteries as well as their location can be used as indicators of Jerusalem's boundaries and the existence of extramural settlements during the Iron IIC period.[22] This view, termed by Barkay as the "super-maximalist" theory, posits that Jerusalem's eighth- and seventh-century boundaries extended to the north and west, beyond the City of David, Ophel, and western hill.[23] Recently published surveys in the vicinity surrounding Jerusalem confirm the dense population of late Iron II Jerusalem and the existence of numerous small settlements that include tells, fortified sites, villages, structures, agricultural installations, towers, and concentrations of sherds.[24] This provides further evidence for the centrality and significance of Jerusalem during the Iron IIC period.

In summary, archaeological discoveries of the last four decades have transformed our understanding of Jerusalem and clearly supported maximalist views regarding its size and significance during the eighth–early sixth centuries B.C.E. The undeniable physical remains provide proof that Jerusalem served as a large administrative, political, and residential center with a well-developed environs. Further, it may well have been the most important and impressive center in Judah. Based on excavations conducted to date, the Ophel (and perhaps the unexcavated Mount Moriah/Temple Mount) functioned as the administrative-religious-public area of the city, with the City of David and the western hill serving as the residential quarters of the city. The entire city was enclosed by impressive city fortification systems (walls, towers, gates). This royal city of

---

[21] See Hillel Geva's detailed discussion of the Jewish Quarter excavations in this volume and the first final report of Avigad's excavations, Geva, *Jewish Quarter Excavations I*. For a summary of the "maximalist" and "minimalist" views of eighth- and seventh-century B.C.E. Jerusalem, see Andrew G. Vaughn, *Theology, History, and Archaeology in the Chronicler's Account of Hezekiah* (SBLABS 4; Atlanta: Scholars Press), 59–71.

[22] For a summary of the various Iron II cemeteries, see Barkay, "Necropoli of Jerusalem," 233–70. For Iron II cave deposits excavated by Kenyon, see also Kay Prag, "Summary of the Report on Caves I, II and III and Deposit IV," in Eshel and Prag, *Excavations in Jerusalem IV*, 209–20.

[23] Vaughn, *Theology, History, and Archaeology*, 69–70.

[24] For a recent summary of the results of these surveys, see, e.g., Nurit Feig, "The Environs of Jerusalem in the Iron II" [Hebrew], in Ahituv and Mazar, *History of Jerusalem*, 387–410.

Hezekiah and Josiah, the capital of the kingdom of Judah, does indeed match in glory the earthly Jerusalem described in the biblical accounts. However, the archaeological remains undeniably reveal that the correspondence of earthly Jerusalem to the biblical description of Jerusalem does not occur until the late eighth century.

Archaeological Controversy: Late Bronze–Iron IIB (ca. 1550–720 B.C.E.)— A Fortified Urban City or Modest Regional Center?

Unlike the impressive and unambiguous archaeological evidence for Jerusalem in the Middle Bronze IIB and Iron IIC periods, the excavated record for Jerusalem during the Late Bronze through Iron IIB periods is scant and fraught with controversy. Our most important source of information regarding Jerusalem during the Late Bronze II period is several Amarna letters documenting correspondence between the Egyptian pharaoh and Abdi-heba, the local ruler of Jerusalem.[25] Although Steiner has suggested that there was no settlement on the southeastern hill (i.e., City of David) during the Late Bronze Age,[26] Cahill has argued convincingly that Jerusalem was indeed inhabited, based on numerous Late Bronze II sherds found in the terracing system of the City of David's eastern slope that she dates to the fourteenth and thirteenth centuries B.C.E. as well as on fragmentary architectural remains uncovered by the Shiloh expedition.[27]

Although much ink has been spilled regarding the reference to Jerusalem in the fourteenth-century Amarna letters, there is little doubt that Jerusalem was occupied during the Late Bronze Age, though on a significantly smaller scale than its Middle Bronze II predecessor. As discussed above, and contrary to the opinion of Kenyon, Shiloh, and Cahill,[28] I would challenge the hypothesis that the Middle Bronze Age city wall remained in use during the Late Bronze Age and early Iron Age. This highly speculative view that early second-millennium

---

[25] William L. Moran, *The Amarna Letters* (Baltimore: Johns Hopkins University Press, 1992), 325–34 (EA 285–290).

[26] Steiner, *Excavations in Jerusalem III*, 24. Steiner dates the Late Bronze Age sherds to the very end of the thirteenth century B.C.E., concluding that there is no evidence for settlement during the fourteenth and through most of the thirteenth centuries B.C.E. Regarding Jerusalem's mention in the Amarna letters, she suggests that either Urusalim should not be identified with Jerusalem or that Jerusalem was a royal estate and Abdi-heba was the manager of this small stronghold, perhaps located near the Gihon Spring (ibid., 40–41; however, see below and note 29 regarding the absence of evidence near the spring).

[27] See Cahill's detailed description in this volume.

[28] See Cahill in this volume regarding the hypothesis that the Middle Bronze Age city wall remained in use through the Iron IIB period.

fortifications were reused is unsupported archaeologically, a fact that is admitted by all. Reich has even gone so far as to suggest that the water systems of the Gihon Spring were not in use during the Late Bronze and Iron I–IIA periods due to the lack of any evidence, even sherds, in this area.[29]

The physical evidence of fragmentary walls found on the upper slopes of the City of David excavations and the numerous Late Bronze Age sherds recovered mainly from the fills of the terracing system below the mantle of the stepped stone structure point to the existence of a small, unfortified settlement during the fourteenth–thirteenth centuries B.C.E. This interpretation fits well into the general pattern of Late Bronze Age Canaan under Egyptian domination, when the central hill country region was underdeveloped, sparsely populated, and subject to Apiru raids.[30]

The controversies swirling around Jerusalem intensify as we examine the contested evidence attributed to the twelfth–ninth centuries B.C.E. Due to the lack of contemporary textual evidence for any site in the region until the ninth century B.C.E., Jerusalem is not alone in the chronological crisis facing archaeologists during the past decade.[31] The key element to our understanding of Iron I–IIA Jerusalem is the interpretation and dating of the stepped stone structure. For the purposes of my discussion and to avoid confusion, I will use the conventional chronology for the twelfth to ninth centuries B.C.E., though I recognize the serious and valid chronological challenge to the traditional interpretation and dating of Iron I–Iron IIA layers at sites throughout the Levant.[32]

Interpretations of Jerusalem during the tenth/ninth centuries B.C.E. based on archaeological evidence can be divided into two approaches: (1) Jerusalem was a fortified urban center and could have served as the capital of the united monarchy under David and Solomon, consisting of (a) mainly public structures (Kenyon and Shiloh) or (b) both domestic and as yet undiscovered

---

[29] Reich, oral communication (1 January 2003).

[30] Most of the letters from Abdi-heba mention the threat of the Apiru; see, e.g., Moran, *Amarna Letters*, EA 286–290.

[31] Regarding the lower chronology, see, e.g., Israel Finkelstein, "The Archaeology of the United Monarchy: An Alternative View," *Levant* 28 (1996): 177–87; idem, "Bible Archaeology or Archaeology of Palestine in the Iron Age? A Rejoinder," *Levant* 30 (1998): 167–74; Israel Finkelstein and Neil A. Silberman, *The Bible Unearthed: Archaeology's New Vision of Ancient Israel and the Origin of Its Sacred Texts* (New York: Free Press, 2001), 123–48; and Finkelstein's essay in this volume. Regarding the conventional chronology and replies to Finkelstein, see, e.g., Amihai Mazar, "Iron Age Chronology: A Reply to I. Finkelstein," *Levant* 29 (1997): 157–67; William G. Dever, "Save Us from Postmodern Malarkey," *BAR* 26/2 (2000): 28–35; idem, *What Did the Biblical Writers Know and When Did They Know It? What Archaeology Can Tell Us about the Reality of Ancient Israel* (Grand Rapids: Eerdmans, 2001), 124–57.

[32] Preliminary radiocarbon C-14 dates tend to support the lower chronology (see, e.g., Ayelet Gilboa and Ilan Sharon, "Early Iron Age Radiometric Dates from Tel Dor: Preliminary Implications for Phoenicia, and Beyond," *Radiocarbon* 43 [2000]: 1343–51); however, the jury is still out regarding which chronological scenario is correct.

public structures (Cahill);[33] (2) Jerusalem was a more modest fortified citadel or unfortified center that might have served as a regional administrative and commercial hub (Steiner, Lehmann, Finkelstein, and Ussishkin, either in the tenth or ninth centuries B.C.E.).[34]

The centerpiece of the tenth-century discussion rests on the dating and interpretation of the stepped stone structure. The majority of excavators of the City of David have dated the stepped stone structure to the tenth (or tenth/ninth centuries) B.C.E. These include Kenyon, Shiloh, and Steiner. Recent reinterpretations by archaeologists who have not personally excavated in Jerusalem (Lehmann and Finkelstein) have suggested a ninth-century B.C.E. date.[35]

The only detailed documentation and publication of primary data that presents evidence for a tenth-century B.C.E. date for the stepped stone rampart appears in Steiner's recent final report of Kenyon's excavations.[36] She provides convincing evidence for Kenyon's initial dating of the stepped stone structure as well as for the claim that the stepped stone structure is later in date and structurally distinct from the twelfth-century terracing system below the large boulders of the rampart. Steiner concludes that the terraces were built during the twelfth century[37] and suggests a tenth/ninth century or later date for the construction of the rampart's mantle.[38]

The dating of this monumental rampart to the tenth century still forms the centerpiece of nearly every discussion of Solomon's Jerusalem. Views diverge regarding the existence of city fortifications. Kenyon and Shiloh propose that the Middle Bronze IIB city wall remained in use through the ninth century, making Jerusalem a fortified city. Steiner's analysis of Kenyon's excavations reaches somewhat different conclusions. She accepts Kenyon's dating of the stepped stone structure to the tenth/ninth century, but she also recognizes that there is no proof of a larger fortified Jerusalem. In her view, the city was apparently confined mainly to the ridge of the City of David and consisted mainly of a fortified citadel and presumably several public structures that have yet to be found. In Steiner's view, no evidence has yet been uncovered for domestic structures in tenth-century Jerusalem. She concludes that Jerusalem was little more than a regional administrative center.[39] However, I would point out that, when compared to archaeological evidence at other so-called "royal cities" built by Solomon (Gezer, Megiddo, and Hazor) traditionally dated to the tenth century, the excavated physical reality of Jerusalem is modest.

---

[33] See Cahill's detailed description and discussion in this volume.
[34] See Steiner, *Excavations in Jerusalem III*, 42–53 and 113–16; see Lehmann's, Finkelstein's, and Ussishkin's articles in this volume.
[35] See note 34 for references.
[36] Steiner, *Excavations in Jerusalem III*, 42–53.
[37] Ibid., 36–37.
[38] Ibid., 51–53.
[39] Ibid., 42–53.

In contrast, several scholars, most recently Cahill, have dated the stepped stone structure to the twelfth century B.C.E., or the "Jebusite" period. The archaeological evidence for this theory is presented for the first time in Cahill's essay in this volume. The stepped stone structure would be roughly contemporary with the site of Giloh, located southwest of Jerusalem not far from the City of David. In Cahill's well-documented presentation of several key loci, she argues that the stepped stone structure and the terracing system below the stone mantle were constructed simultaneously in the twelfth century, with the terracing system providing the necessary structural support for the mantle. It is noteworthy that Shiloh, in his preliminary report, clearly states that in one area it appears that the mantle and terracing system were bonded together while in another section the two elements appear to have been constructed separately,[40] thus also supporting Steiner's stratigraphic interpretation of the stepped stone structure. Contra Shiloh and Steiner, Cahill claims that this rampart went out of use in the tenth century with the construction of four-room houses that cut into its mantle. The earliest floors of these houses contained tenth-century pottery.[41] Other fragmentary remains of domestic structures were found during the Shiloh expedition, evidence that Cahill uses to propose a larger settlement, though one remarkable for its lack of public structures that would be necessary for Jerusalem's function as the center—administrative or otherwise—for the united monarchy under David and/or Solomon.[42]

Less convincing and lacking any archaeological support are suggestions proposed by Cahill and several scholars (as noted above) for the reuse of the Middle Bronze Age fortification system in the Late Bronze Age through the Iron Ages, including the tenth century. Though an attractive suggestion because it would lend support to the biblical description of Solomon's Jerusalem, it is purely speculative and lacks any archaeological evidence, such as structures or floors that can be demonstrated to relate stratigraphically to this wall's use past the Middle Bronze Age.

If one accepts Cahill's evidence that the stepped stone structure was constructed in the twelfth century, Iron I Jerusalem appears to have consisted of a small, fortified citadel that may have served as a tribal center for the immediate region. However, as pointed out by Lehmann,[43] lack of any evidence of settlement or even the appearance of any architectural remains beyond the City of David rules out any suggestion that Jerusalem was a major urban center. Cahill's comparisons to the very large, highly urbanized, and socially stratified cities, complete with industrial areas and public buildings, of the Philistine and coastal

---

[40] Shiloh, *Excavations at the City of David I*, 17.
[41] See Cahill's article in this volume.
[42] Ibid.
[43] See Lehmann's essay in this volume.

plain are untenable. Following Cahill's description of the actual archaeological evidence for the traditional tenth century, we are left with remnants of domestic structures—with no evidence for any public or monumental buildings thus far discovered. Apologetics for what may have existed, or what has not been found even after over a century of intense archaeological exploration, is inadequate to explain the obvious contradiction between the idealized biblical descriptions of Solomonic Jerusalem and what actually existed. Although some of the most significant structures theoretically could have existed on the archaeologically inaccessible Temple Mount/Haram esh-Sharif compound, the missing strata dating to periods predating the late eighth–seventh centuries B.C.E. in the area north of the City of David (the Southern Wall or "Ophel" excavations) seem to reinforce the existing picture that Jerusalem was a relatively minor settlement in the tenth/ninth centuries B.C.E., confined to the crest of the City of David.[44]

Summarizing the available archaeological evidence and its possible interpretations (if one accepts the attribution of the stepped stone structure to the tenth century, as proposed by Kenyon, Shiloh, and Steiner), we are still left with a modest tenth- (or ninth-)century Jerusalem whose size was limited and consisted mainly of a fortified citadel that likely served as a rather limited regional center. If we accept Cahill's interpretation and the actual archaeological evidence, we are left with an even less impressive settlement or village, consisting of domestic structures and no remnants of any public or monumental buildings or fortifications. Could such a modest Jerusalem have served as a capital for the entire kingdom?[45] Moving the dates approximately a century later, as suggested by Finkelstein and others, still does not change the general conclusions regarding Jerusalem during the twelfth–ninth centuries B.C.E.; that is, the settlement was modest in size, thus far lacking in any monumental structures, with the exception of the chronologically contested stepped stone structure, rivaling those in other Iron IIA centers.[46] Additional support for the regional role

---

[44] The lack of evidence for any fortification system, with the exception of two fragmentary walls at the crest of the City of David that Kenyon postulated may belong to a casemate city wall (a possible proposal that needs to be investigated further), together with an out-of-situ fragmentary Proto-Aeolic capital and a few scattered ashlar blocks, only further reinforces the view that Jerusalem was neither a large urban capital of a united monarchy nor a village but rather an administrative center that served the immediate region. See Steiner, *Excavations in Jerusalem III*, 48–50, 113.

[45] See Andrew G. Vaughn's essay in this volume for a positive reply to this question in spite of the paucity of archaeological evidence.

[46] Geva has also recently published similar conclusions in an article that summarizes new discoveries in Jerusalem at the present time; see Hillel Geva, "Innovations in Archaeological Research in Jerusalem during the 1990s" [Hebrew], *Qad* 34/2 (122) (2001): 70–77, esp. 72–73. Please note that Cahill and Steiner (in this volume) do not agree with my conclusions regarding Jerusalem's relatively minor role as a regional administrative/cultic/political center. Steiner proposes that Jerusalem was a principal settlement that served as a major regional center of the "state" of Judah, while Cahill prefers to see Jerusalem as a fortified, urban city that was indeed the capital of the united monarchy of the tenth century B.C.E.

of Jerusalem within the framework of a relatively underdeveloped hinterland during this period is evident from recent archaeological surveys conducted in the vicinity of Jerusalem.[47]

Conclusions

In spite of our inabilities to free ourselves of modern preconceptions, the archaeological evidence—or the lack of evidence—does provide us with a physical reality and starting point for our reconstruction of a material preexilic Jerusalem that needs to be fully acknowledged. During periods when Jerusalem served as a significant urban center in the Middle Bronze and Iron IIC periods, abundant archaeological evidence has been excavated and recovered. The contrary must also be acknowledged that during ebbs in Jerusalem's (or the region's) centrality, the archaeological evidence is scant or nonexistent. The physical remains for the Late Bronze through Iron IIA/B periods do in fact indicate with some certainty a material reality that cannot be ignored. However, we do need to recognize that Jerusalem's significance declined, together with a broader regional contraction, during these periods.

The most emotionally contested segment of Jerusalem's past revolve around the attempts to match the physical record with biblical descriptions of David's and Solomon's kingdoms. Although doubtlessly based on a historical kernel, these accounts were aggrandized over time until finally evolving into their final form as presented in the historical books of the Bible. Our attempts to interpret (and manipulate) the scant archaeological record, in spite of extensive excavations, to fit biblical descriptions of the tenth century are increasingly problematic in light of the lack of evidence for Jerusalem as a city with monumental structures and as the central administrative and cultic hub for all of the twelve tribes under a united leadership as described by biblical authors. This dovetails well with most critical analysis of the dating of the redaction and authorship of the Deuteronomistic History to the eighth or seventh centuries B.C.E. Although most mainstream scholars will admit that the histories of tenth- and ninth-century Israelite kings are based on earlier documents, the compilation of these records into a text that resembles our Bible today first occurred during the reign of Hezekiah or later.[48]

Today there is a consensus by most that David and Solomon are in all probability historical figures and that Jerusalem was settled in the tenth century B.C.E., but the physical reality of Jerusalem (no matter which chronology is followed)

---

[47] See Lehmann's article in this volume for a detailed discussion of the survey data.
[48] For a detailed discussion and bibliography relevant to these points, see William Schniedewind's essay in this volume. For alternative solutions, see also J. J. M. Roberts's and Richard E. Friedman's essays in this volume.

is far from the city described by the Bible. Heroic efforts to interpret a grander tenth-century Jerusalem based on missing evidence are methodologically flawed and at best misleading, especially to nonarchaeologists. The highly idealized and romantic notions of a glorious Jerusalem as a historically accurate description of a tenth-century reality must be carefully examined in light of what remains rather than what might have been.[49]

Whether we accept the traditional chronology or the low chronology, Jerusalem during the tenth century was a modest settlement that probably served as no more than an administrative-cultic-political center for the surrounding villages of the Iron I and IIA. In light of surveys and excavations, it is difficult to conceive that Jerusalem was the major capital city of a unified southern and northern confederation of tribes. There can be no doubt that Jerusalem was inhabited, but it was hardly the glorious city described in the Bible. Based on the actual physical evidence and critical analysis of the Deuteronomistic History, we are left with the unavoidable conclusion that spiritually, politically, and physically Jerusalem became a major urban and cultic center only during the eighth century, most likely in part due to political policies of the Assyrian Empire and the northern kingdom's fate at the hands of the Assyrians. The archaeological evidence is indisputable and complements what many scholars have already proposed regarding Jerusalem's actual role in biblical Israel. This should not detract from biblical and modern concepts of an idealized Jerusalem that symbolically or otherwise served as a religious and spiritual center throughout the ages until our present times. Having said this, we must all leave open the possibility that the future could bring new revelations and exciting discoveries that will only add to the lively debate surrounding the spiritual and material worlds of Jerusalem. In the meantime, during our cross-disciplinary discussions we need to keep in mind what exists and is probable rather than what has not been discovered and is desirable based on our modern conceptions of what biblical Jerusalem should be.

---

[49] See Neil A. Silberman's essay in this volume, which questions our ability ever to approach an "objective" interpretation of what existed in the past, and Vaughn's article, which encourages a more positive view of our ability in our attempts to reach a historical reconstruction.

Secondary Sources Also Deserve to Be Historically Evaluated: The Case of the United Monarchy

Rainer Albertz

In his recent book, *Ancient Israel: What Do We Know and How Do We Know It?* (2007), Lester Grabbe, to whom I wish to convey my warmest greetings with this essay, has drawn a fascinating outline of how a reconstruction of Israel's history from the twelfth to sixth centuries B.C.E., one that fully meets the requirements of strict historical standards, could work. Remembering the heated debate between so-called minimalists and maximalists of recent decades, I very much appreciate this attempt; it is an important step forward. I would also like to take the opportunity to thank Lester Grabbe for his constant efforts in bringing both "parties" into a critical dialogue on the panel of the European Seminar in Historical Methodology (ESHM), and his friendly invitation to me to participate. I consider the ESHM to be an important venture, forcing all of us to reconsider the material basis and methodical approach of our historical reconstructions. I hope he will enjoy the present contribution to those discussions.

Remaining Methodological Questions

Grabbe (2007, 3–36) has greatly clarified, probably more than any other historian of ancient Israel, the methodological questions of historiography. I will mention here only the question of the status of sources. Like many others, Grabbe distinguishes fundamentally between primary and secondary sources:

> Primary sources are those contemporary (or nearly so) with the events they describe and usually have some other direct connection (eyewitness report, compilation from eyewitness reports or other good sources, proximity to the events or those involved in the events). Secondary sources are those further removed in time and space from the original events. (Grabbe 2007, 220)

He rightly concludes: "Preference should be given to primary sources...this means archaeology and inscriptions" (2007, 35). As long as suitable sources of this first category are available, I think no one would argue against that general rule. According to Grabbe, the texts of the Hebrew Bible generally belong to the second category:

> The biblical text is almost always a secondary source, written and edited long after the events ostensibly described. In some cases, the text may depend on earlier sources, but these sources were edited and adapted; in any case the source has to be dug out from the present context. (2007, 35)

Grabbe does not wish to attack or vilify the Hebrew Bible by categorizing the biblical texts in such a way (2007, 219). Rather, he opposes a "dogmatic scepticism that continually looks for a way to reject or denigrate the biblical text" (2007, 23), an attitude that Barstad (1998) has called "bibliophobia." In contrast to a strict minimalist view, Grabbe demands:

> The biblical text should always be considered: it is one of the sources for the history of ancient Israel and needs to be treated like any other source, being neither privileged nor rejected a priori, but handled straightforwardly and critically. (2007, 224)

According to Grabbe, "we cannot say that the biblical text is reliable or unreliable, because it all depends on which episode or text one has in mind" (2007, 219). From this insight he derives the methodical demand: "secondary sources normally need some sort of confirmation" (2007, 220). Thus, compared with some radical minimalist positions, Grabbe's methodical approach seems well-balanced and fair.

Yet some serious material and methodological questions remain. First, we must recognize that our primary sources for the pre-exilic history of ancient Israel, despite their theoretical importance, are very limited. This is especially true of the epigraphic material: unfortunately, we have not a single monumental inscription or written document from monarchic archives of Israel and Judah that would allow us to reconstruct the political history of these states. The reasons for this strange situation are not totally clear. On the one hand, they may have to do with the frequency of warfare in that area, which could have damaged many of the potential written or inscribed sources. On the other hand, official documents were mostly written on papyrus in Palestine, a medium that is rarely preserved, given the wet climate. The only two—fragmentary—monumental inscriptions from Palestine that we have come from neighbouring states, the Mesha stele from a king of Moab, and the Tel Dan stele, probably from a king of Aram (Damascus). Together with several Assyrian, and a few Babylonian, royal inscriptions and chronicles concerning events in Palestine, these are the only epigraphic sources enabling us to control the historical data supplied by the biblical texts; unfortunately, however, these potential sources are restricted to the period from middle of the ninth to the sixth century.

The other kind of primary source, the results of archaeological excavations including stratigraphy, architecture, pottery and other small finds, together with demographic calculations derived from surveys, comprises a huge amount of data, more than from any other place in the ancient Near East. Yet historical conclusions—especially conclusions based on an absence of evidence—are often ambiguous. While Grabbe earlier stressed the significance of "textual material, which provides much of the interpretative framework," stating that "without textual data, the archaeology is much less helpful" (2000, 217), he now grants the archaeological data the highest status of objectivity, because they "actually existed in real life," while "a text always contains human invention, and it is always possible that a text is entirely fantasy" (2007, 10).[1] But if we note the very different interpretations of archaeological results relating to the twelfth to tenth centuries, reported by Grabbe in detail, his earlier opinion seems equally to be justified. Important as such results may be for developments of the *longue* and *moyen durée*, without the interpretative framework of epigraphic material they do not provide the exact historical data necessary for reconstructing the *histoire événementelle*, the political history of Israel and Judah. Thus, for the whole period of about 350 years from the stele of Merneptah (1209/8 B.C.E.), which mentions Israel for the first time, to the Kurkh Monolith of Shalmaneser III (853 B.C.E.), which mentions King Ahab in the battle of Qarqar, we do not have the primary sources that we need in order to control the reliability of the secondary sources in the Bible. Since the biblical texts concerning this earlier period cannot be evaluated by external primary sources, Grabbe, in accordance with his methodological demands, concludes that they cannot be used for historical reconstruction. The outcome of this procedure is demonstrated in his book: despite the many possible suggestions about the early history of ancient Israel that Grabbe discusses in detail, no reliable historical reconstruction from the twelfth to tenth centuries B.C.E. is possible.

Can we really be satisfied with such a negative result, which depends merely on a fortuitous lack of all epigraphic inscriptions? As long as this situation is not altered by new findings, should we not make use of the possibilities provided by the Hebrew Bible?

---

[1] Thus, Grabbe is now ready to concede archaeology has paramount importance for his historiography: "The importance of archaeology cannot…be overestimated" (2007, 6); "The proper attention to archaeology is vital for any history of ancient Israel, and it is my intention to try to give it the prominence it deserves" (2007, 10).

Grabbe sometimes relativizes his strict division between primary and secondary sources, as, for example, when he concedes:

> Primary sources are not always trustworthy, and secondary sources may sometimes contain reliable information, and no two sources agree entirely. Thus, the historian has to make a critical investigation of all data, whatever the source. (2007, 220)

I appreciate this statement: it implies that the texts of the Hebrew Bible, despite being classified as "secondary sources," should be historically evaluated. Some may contain reliable historical information, some less, and some none. But, unfortunately, Grabbe is not really interested in developing internal criteria for distinguishing those biblical texts that may contain reliable historical information from those in which no clear external evidence is available. He reckons with the possibility that a biblical text may depend on earlier sources that might be retrieved (2007, 35), but does not offer much by way of examples. The results of literary historical exegesis seem too uncertain to him:

> The complicated history of the biblical text has been partially worked out in the past two centuries, but there is still much unknown and much on which there is disagreement. (2007, 220)

Thus in most cases he prefers to deal with the biblical text (often taken in the singular!) as if all passages stand on the same level. But can that be the solution? The disagreement about the dating and interpretation of biblical texts is no worse than about the interpretation of archaeological data. In the realm of history we can never be absolutely sure. Nevertheless, there are some literary-historical criteria that provide us with a rough guideline for the historical evaluation of biblical texts. First of all, the uniformity or non-uniformity of a given text has to be proven by literary criticism and its units have to be dated: texts that lie closer to the events are normally more reliable. Form-critical classifications are also important: reports often contain more reliable information than narratives, narratives more than sagas and legends, and prophetic accusations more than prophetic announcements. In any case, all texts have to be interpreted against their *Tendenz* or ideology, which also has to be evaluated first. Of course, identical or similar information given by more than one independent biblical source has a higher degree of historical probability. This means that the same literary tools used for the historical interpretation of the epigraphic material are valid for evaluating the degree of historicity of a biblical text. Because of the longer editorial history of the latter, however—which Grabbe rightly notes—the historical evaluation of biblical texts is more complex and must be handled very carefully.

Grabbe has demonstrated in great detail that there is no reason for mistrusting the historicity of biblical texts in general: he has shown that in many of those cases where we have external evidence from epigraphic sources, the information in biblical texts can be confirmed or brought into a meaningful correlation with such data (2007, 144–49, 163–64, 200, 209–10, 224–25). In other cases where they deviate, the discrepancy often can be explained by the specific ideological interest of the biblical author. The importance of form-critical categories can be demonstrated in the case of Sennacherib's invasion of Judah in 701: the report of this event in 2 Kgs 18:13–16 perfectly accords with Sennacherib's inscription (see Grabbe 2007, 200), while the Isaiah–Hezekiah legend (18:17–19:10, 32*, 36*) disagrees with both, despite including some historical details (but in an inaccurate way). For Sennacherib never besieged Jerusalem, but withdrew from Lachish after Hezekiah paid him a huge tribute.[2] In any event, the Deuteronomistic author concealed Sennacherib's devastation of the Shephelah and the deportation of many of its inhabitants, presumably because he wanted to give a positive judgement on Hezekiah for ideological reasons. So, while it can be legitimately argued that without the Assyrian inscriptions and the archaeological evidence we would not see the overall extent of the catastrophe, nevertheless a sound literary-historical evaluation of the biblical accounts, giving the report priority over the legend, would not deliver entirely misleading results. I ask, therefore: Should we not similarly scrutinize the biblical texts for that period between the twelfth and the tenth centuries when no other written sources are available (especially for the tenth century B.C.E.)?

The Case of the "United Monarchy"

The archaeological results concerning Jerusalem in the tenth and early ninth centuries (Iron IIA) are unfortunately very ambiguous, and Grabbe (2007, 71–73) describes in detail the dispute between archaeologists. On one side (Ussishkin 2003; Finkelstein 2003; Steiner 2003; Lehmann 2003; Herzog and Singer-Avitz 2004), Jerusalem was only a minor settlement, a village or possibly a citadel. On the other side (Cahill 2003; Mazar 2007), it was a substantial city, the capital of an emerging state. The uncertainty has to do not only with the heavy destruction Jerusalem suffered during its long history and the severe restrictions to which all excavations in the Old City are subjected under the complicated political and religious regime, but also with the fact that archaeology has not so far found clear answers to substantial material questions. Were the impressive fortifications of the Middle Bronze (IIB) reused in later LB and Iron IIA–B periods, or was Jerusalem an unfortified settlement until the eighth century? What was the date and the purpose of the so-called stepped structure on the south-eastern slope? Was it already built in the tenth century or later? Did it served as a foundation

---

[2] The expression URU.ḪAL-ṢU.MEŠ in Sennacherib's inscription does not denote "ramps," as is often suggested (*ANET* 288: "earthwork"), but "forts" which the Assyrian king had built in order to control the access to Jerusalem. So argues, rightly, Mayer (1995, 355–63).

of a monumental building such as a palace, or not? Depending on the answers to these and similar questions, very different reconstructions of the history of the tenth century can be supported.

Weighing up these two alternative reconstructions, Grabbe tends to follow the minimal position. He does not wish to deny that Saul, David and Solomon really existed, but would severely reduce the portrait of a great and renowned Davidic empire drawn by the Hebrew Bible:

> Perhaps a city-state, much like the city-states of Shechem under Lab'aya or of Jerusalem under 'Abdi-Ḫeba, would be feasible… It seems unlikely that David controlled anything beyond a limited territory centred on the southern hill country and Jerusalem. (2007, 121)

Moreover, following Finkelstein and Silberman (2001, 121–45; cf. Finkelstein 2003, 79) and others, Grabbe feels obliged to deny the existence of a "united monarchy" for more general reasons.[3] In his view, the ecological conditions and the economic and demographic development of northern Israel and the southern hill country were so different (2007, 70–71) that a unification of Judah and Israel in one territorial state under David "would have been an unusual development" (2007, 121)—perhaps not impossible, but rather unlikely. According to him, it is much more likely that the first Israelite state would have been established in the ecologically privileged northern area, where the Omride kingdom emerged. Thus he states:

> The first kingdom for which we have solid evidence is the northern kingdom, the state founded by Omri. This fits what we would expect from the *longue durée*; if there was an earlier state, we have no direct information on it except perhaps some memory in the biblical text. This does not mean that nothing existed before Omri in either the north or the south, but what was there was probably not a state as such. (2007, 222–23)

As plausible as this historical reconstruction may be, our limited external sources mean that the problem remains "what to do with the biblical traditions about the rise of the Israelite kingship," as Grabbe puts it (2007, 121). He tries to explain why their authors came to the idea of a "united monarchy": the territory controlled by David "might have overlapped with territory earlier controlled by Saul, which would lead to some of the biblical traditions that made David the usurper and successor of Saul" (2007, 121). But is this a sufficient explanation? There are not just "some traditions," but dozens of texts between 1 Sam 10 and 2 Sam 21 which without exception describe the complicated start of Israel's monarchic history in this way.

---

[3] The main archaeological argument for a "united monarchy," the similar six-chambered gates in Gezer, Megiddo and Hazor (cf. Mazar 2007, 130–31), is no longer mentioned by Grabbe. This feature has probably lost plausibility for him, since their traditional dating in the tenth century was questioned (cf. Finkelstein 2007, 111–13) in the controversy about the low chronology.

There is no space here to discuss all the biblical texts concerning the "united monarchy." I would mention just two pieces of evidence which seem not to be taken sufficiently into consideration by Grabbe. The first is the external evidence of the Tel Dan inscription, which—astonishing enough—Grabbe does not use for his reconstruction of early monarchic history.[4] In line 9 of the inscription occurs the expression *bytdwd*, which in the political context of the inscription can only be rendered "house of David." The element *beit* in this expression can have two meanings, "family/dynasty [of David]" and "state [of David]," just as we find with the expression *bît ḥumri*, "house of Omri," in the Assyrian inscriptions (Weippert 1978), one of the terms denoting the northern kingdom.[5] Thus the Aramaean ruler of the ninth century (probably Hazael) regarded David as the founder of a dynasty and a founder of a state. This evidence not only calls into question all suggestions that Judah did not became a state before the eighth century,[6] but also shows that the political organization founded by David belonged to the same category as the Omride kingdom, even if it probably represented a less developed form of it.[7] The Tel Dan inscription does not, of course, refer to the "united monarchy," only the kingdom of Judah, but it does not exclude the possibility, since the extent of the "house of David" may have varied.

The second issue I will mention is the biblical traditions about the division of the monarchy, which seem to me overlooked in the present discussion. Relating the end of the Solomonic empire and the foundation of a separate northern kingdom makes sense only if a "united kingdom" had existed. The bulk of the traditions is collected and commented on by the Deuteronomistic historian in 1 Kgs 11–12, and a literary-critical analysis can distinguish four different sources, each with different degrees of historicity:

1. *A report of the rebellion of Jeroboam ben Nebat, an Ephraimite from Zeredah, against King Solomon.* First the rebellion failed; Solomon sought to kill Jeroboam. He had to flee to Egypt, but after Solomon's death he

---

[4] See his very restricted reconstruction and cautious interpretation (2007, 129–30). For a more extensive reconstruction and historical interpretation, see Kottsieper 1998.

[5] Also in the Hebrew Bible the term בית can denote a nation or a state: 2 Sam 2:4; 12:8; 16:3; 1 Kgs 12:21; 20:31; Isa 8:14; Jer 2:26; 5:11; Hos 1:4; 5:12, 14 etc.

[6] This view is also questioned by the discovery of 170 clay bullae from the ninth century by near the Gihon spring, on which see Reich, Shukron and Lernau 2007, 156–57. Together with a large quantity of fish bones in the same area, these bullae verify that Jerusalem was a commercial and administrative centre in the late ninth century at least. The suggestion that this centre emerged only under the influence of the northern state, whose ally Judah was during the Omride period (Grabbe 2007, 127), is possible, but in no way necessary, and depends on the view that Judah was still much less developed than Israel.

[7] Using the categories of Claessen and Skalník (1978)—namely, of an "inchoate early state" in contrast to a "typical early state." I have argued (Albertz 2007, 358–59) that the Omride state should be categorized as a "transitional early state" on the way to a "mature state," a stage reached in the eighth and seventh centuries.

came back to Israel and was crowned as the first king of the northern kingdom (1 Kgs 11:26, 40; 12:2,[8] 20a[9]). This short report could have come from the "Chronicle of the kings of Judah and Israel." From its *Gattung* and its possible origin, it claims a high degree of historicity.[10]

2. *The fragment of a narrative about Jeroboam's failed rebellion (1 Kgs 11:27–28)*. Its summary, probably given by the Deuteronomistic historian (v. 27), confirms that Jeroboam raised his hand against King Solomon when the latter was building the Millo. The narrative relates that Solomon had promoted Jeroboam because of his achievements and put him in charge of the labour-gangs of the tribal district of Joseph (v. 28). Unfortunately, the rest of the story is broken off, giving way to the Ahijah story. Although a narrative, the text accords with the report mentioned above. Its contention that the king himself fostered his later enemy runs against a tendency to glorify Solomon and so seems to be trustworthy.

3. *A long historical narrative about the separation of the northern tribes from the Davidic dynasty at the beginning of the reign of Rehoboam (1 Kgs 12:1*, 3b–14, 16, 18–19)*.[11] The negotiations between the northern tribes and Rehoboam concerning the burdens of corvée, in which Jeroboam was originally not included (cf. v. 20), are stylized in a didactic manner and probably did not happen in this way. But the fact that the main reason for the division of the monarchy was a social conflict about compulsory labour accords with the fragmented narrative (11:27–28) and seems to be trustworthy. This is confirmed by the detail of the murder of Adoram, the commander in charge of the labour (v. 18). Since v. 19 characterizes the separation of the northern tribes as a sinful rebellion (פשע) against the Davidic dynasty, the narrative is of Judean origin. As the aetiological motive ("until the present day") at the end shows, it presupposes an interval from the events reported; yet its self-critical intention implies that the

---

[8] That the verse does not really fit the narrative of 1 Kgs 12:1–19 is shown by the fact that it is missing here in the LXX; it comes at the end of ch. 11. In the MT its final clause is aligned to the context. As the deviating text of 2 Chr 10:2 and the LXX and Vulgate show, the verse should run: As Jeroboam ben Nebat heard (that), while he was still in Egypt, where he had fled from Solomon, he *came back from Egypt*. Originally the message heard by Jeroboam was not the assembly in Shechem but the death of Solomon (11:40, now explicitly reported by the Dtr's final clause, v. 43; see the LXX). Furthermore, his return did not originally lead him to the assembly, where he was only secondarily included by DtrH (12:3a, 12, 20*), but somewhere else (according to the LXX in 11:43: "straight to his town in the land of Samaria on the mountain of Ephraim"), from where he had to be called (12:20).

[9] Only the words "in the assembly" are a Dtr addition. Whether v. 20b originally belonged to the report is not certain. In any case, it is a doublet to the end of the narrative in v. 19.

[10] For more details, see Albertz 1994, 138–43.

[11] Verse 2 originally belonged to the report: vv. 3a, 15 are Dtr additions. Verse 17 is a different interpolation reminiscent of 1 Chr 11:16–17.

problem of the division of monarchy was still present. Thus, it should be assigned to not later than the time of Hezekiah and can claim a kernel of historicity for itself.

4. *The prophetic narrative on how Ahijah from Shiloh anointed Jeroboam king (1 Kgs 11:29–39*).* The narrative has been heavily reworked by the Deuteronomists (vv. 32–36, 38a, 39); but the underlying plot containing Ahijah's symbolic act of tearing his new cloak in twelve pieces and offering Jeroboam ten of them already presupposes the existence of a "united monarchy." As a prophetic legend, however, its degree of historicity is rather low.

It probably originated as a legitimating story about the beginning of the northern monarchy. Nevertheless, as such it confirms that the "united monarchy" was a concept not only promoted in Judah, but also acknowledged in a foundation story within the northern kingdom.

In contrast to his sources the Deuteronomistic historian presented his own view of the "division of the monarchy." According to him, the main reason for this division was the later apostasy of Solomon, who has been seduced by his foreign wives (1 Kgs 11:1–13; generalized in 12:33). In his view the Judean state survived only because of the divine election of David, which remained valid (11:13). Such a difficult theological construction would have been superfluous had a considerable loss of power for the Davidides not taken place. Thus, even the Deuteronomistic historian, probably in the exilic period, in some way attests the division of the united monarchy.

The critical modern historian may nevertheless raise the objection that the sources intertwined in 1 Kgs 11–12 are not really independent of each other. Apart from the Ahijah legend they could perhaps have come from a similar Judean milieu. There is, however, an independent source which has nothing to do with Deuteronomistic History and its possible sources. It consists in a prophetic oracle in the book of Isaiah:

> Yhwh will bring on you [and your people] and the house of your father a time, the like of which has not been come since the time that Ephraim deviated from Judah [the king of Assur]. (Isa 7:17)[12]

This verse constitutes the final oracle of judgment uttered by Isaiah against Ahab in his activity during the Syro-Ephraimite war (Isa 7:1–17). It is generally acknowledged that the verse belongs to the earliest layer of the book, often called the *Denkschrift* (Isa 6:1–8:19*), which was probably written shortly after the events of 734–32 B.C.E.[13] I have pointed out above that prophetic announcements

---

[12] The passages set in brackets are probably, as their syntactical isolation shows, generalizing and explaining glosses.
[13] Cf. Blum 1996/97, 552–57. According to Blum, this *Denkschrift* acquired its final form (including ch. 6) in the second stage of Isaiah's "testament," written at the end of the prophet's life

are obviously not reliable historical sources, because they can turn out to be wrong. Yet, in our case the reference to the division of the monarchy is a memory used as a comparison for the future. Indeed, the rather surprising comparison with its unusual terminology[14] probably provides the verse with a high degree of historicity. Thus, this prophetic source confirms that even more than two centuries after the event the separation of the northern tribes from the Davidic kings was remembered as a traumatic experience. It was seen as the worst catastrophe that had ever happened in the history of Judah so far. According to this source, the "division of the monarchy" was strongly anchored in the historical memory of Judah in the eighth century; thus it seems very improbable that this event should have been an invention.

There is a second prophetic reference to the united monarchy in a salvation oracle of the book of Ezekiel, probably coming from the late exilic period. According to Ezek 37:15–22, Judah and Israel will be reunited under one king in the future. If v. 22 proposes that Judah and Israel should no longer be two separate nations and should never again split into two kingdoms, the memory of the former division is still present. The use of the verb חצה ("divide"), uncommon in this context, shows that this prophetic announcement depends neither on Isaiah nor the Deuteronomistic historian. This late text reveals that it is impossible to regard the "united monarchy" as merely a projection of an exilic hope into the past. On the contrary, the exilic hope tries to overcome the unhappy experience of a political division that occurred in the past.

Conclusion

A more detailed investigation of the biblical texts reveals that there are no fewer than seven different sources that confirm the "division of the monarchy." At least three of these are independent of each other (the Deuteronomistic historian; Isa 7:17 and Ezek 37:22), and at least two of them, according to their features and content, are furnished with a high degree of reliability (1 Kgs 11:26, 40; 12:2*, 20a; Isa 7:17), while at least three come from the monarchic period (1 Kgs 11:26, 40; 12:2*, 20a; 12:1–19*; Isa 7:17). Naturally, the withdrawal of the northern tribes was remembered more in Judah, because it included here a considerable loss of power (six sources). Yet it was also preserved in the tradition of the northern kingdom (1 Kgs 11:29–39*). Although different in shape and content, each of

---

shortly after 701 B.C.E. Liss (2003, 72–92) wants to date Isa 7:1–17 in the time of Josiah, while Becker (1997, 21–60) has even pleaded for post-Dtr dating. Nevertheless, Blum is right to argue that Isa 6–8* contains a vivid dispute with Isaiah's pupils, which cannot have taken place long after the death of the prophet. For the complex structure of the unit, cf. Steck 1982a, 1982b.

[14] In contrast to the pejorative terminology in 1 Kgs 12:19 (פשע ב, "sinned or rebelled against"), the expression used by Isaiah (סור מעל, "deviate from, separate from") lacks any negative assessment.

the sources corroborates the others; there is no single source that draws a totally different picture.[15] Assessed with the usual historical criteria, this result should be sufficient to establish the historicity of the division of the monarchy. Therefore, there is also good reason to postulate the existence of the united monarchy, whatever its shape and extent.[16]

I think Grabbe is right in pointing out that we should expect the emergence of statehood first in the more developed areas in the north. However, in accordance with the biblical tradition I think that this happened already with the arrival of Saul (1 Sam 9–11). Generally speaking, there is no fundamental doubt that a strong character like David could have been able to turn the normal development in a different direction: after having become the king of Judah he actually usurped the throne of Saul in a bloody civil war and united the three dominions of Judah, Israel and Jerusalem under his rule (2 Sam 2–5). The united monarchy was precarious from its beginnings, as reflected in the stories of the Absalom and Sheba rebellions (2 Sam 16:5–14; 19:9b–41; 19:42–20:22). Nevertheless, it strengthened, or even created, an overall Israelite identity that embraced the north and the south (2 Sam 13:12, 15–19). In spite of the division of the monarchy after Solomon's death, some kind of overall Israelite identity must have survived. This is because it is presupposed by the prophets of the eighth century (cf. Isa 5:7; 8:14; 9:7–20) and it is the prerequisite of the assumptions that thousands of refugees from the north fled to Judah when the Assyrians conquered Samaria (722–720 B.C.E.). It therefore makes sense to assume that the first history of the early monarchy from Saul to Solomon (1 Sam 10–2 Kgs 2*) was composed in the time of Hezekiah (Dietrich 2002, 259–73; Albertz 2009), when a compromise between the competing historical traditions of the inhabitants of Judah and the refugees from the north had to be found.

From these insights I would like to outline the following methodical demands: anyone who denies the historicity of the united monarchy for any reason should be obliged to answer two questions. First, how can the existence of so many biblical sources for the division of the monarchy be explained if a united monarchy had never existed? Second, if not during the united monarchy, when should the consciousness of an overall Israelite identity have emerged—a consciousness already testified in the eighth century B.C.E.?[17]

---

[15] This is also true for the shape of the tradition given by Chronicles (1 Chr 10:1–12:4; 13:4–12). This source is here intentionally excluded, because it clearly depends on DtrH and is much later. Its slightly different view of the event is not derived from older traditions, but depends on its dispute with the Samarians of the fourth century B.C.E. See Bae 2005, 67–77.

[16] For me, it is important to see that Na'aman (2006, 14–15), although reducing the biblical picture of David's and Solomon's rule considerably, does not deny the existence of a united monarchy.

[17] Finkelstein and Silberman (2001, 275–88) regard Josiah's reform as the period that gave birth to such an identity, but that would be rather too late. Moreover, Josiah's interference in northern affairs was according to them rather limited (2001, 347–53); cf. my criticisms in Albertz 2005, 27–32.

References

Albertz, R. 1994. *A History of Israelite Religion in the Old Testament Period*. 2 vols. OTL. Louisville, Ky.: Westminster John Knox.

Albertz, R. 2005. Why a Reform like Josiah's Must Have Happened. Pages 27–46 in *Good Kings and Bad Kings*. Edited by L. L. Grabbe. JSOTSup 393; ESHM 5. London: T&T Clark International.

Albertz, R. 2007. Social History of Ancient Israel. Pages 347–67 in *Understanding the History of Ancient Israel*. Edited by H. G. M. Williamson. Proceedings of the British Academy 143. Oxford: Oxford University Press.

Albertz, R. 2009. Israel in der offiziellen Religion der Königszeit. Pages 39–57 in *Die Identität Israels. Entwicklungen und Kontroversen in alttestamentlicher Zeit*. Edited by H. Irsigler. Herders Biblische Studien 56. Freiburg: Herder.

Bae, H.-S. 2005. *Vereinte Suche nach JHWH: Die Hiskianische und Josianische Reform in der Chronik*. BZAW 355. Berlin: de Gruyter.

Barstad, H. 1998. The Strange Fear of the Bible: Some Reflections on the "Bibliophobia" in Recent Ancient Israelite Historiography. Pages 120–27 in *Leading Captivity Captive: "The Exile" as History and Ideology*. Edited by L. L. Grabbe. JSOTSup 279; ESHM 2. Sheffield: Sheffield Academic.

Becker, U. 1997. *Jesaja—Von der Botschaft zum Buch*. FRLANT 179. Göttingen: Vandenhoeck & Ruprecht.

Blum, E. 1996/97. Jesajas prophetisches Testament: Beobachtungen zu Jes 1–11. *ZAW* 108:547–68 and 109:12–29.

Cahill, J. M. 2003. Jerusalem at the Time of the United Monarchy: The Archaeological Evidence. Pages 13–80 in Vaughn and Killebrew, eds., 2003.

Claessen, H. J. M., and P. Skalník. 1978. *The Early State*. New Babylon 32. The Haag: Mouton.

Dever, W. G., and S. Gitin, eds. 2003. *Symbiosis, Symbolism, and the Power of the Past: Canaan, Ancient Israel, and Their Neighbors from the Late Bronze Age through Roman Palestina. Proceedings of the Centennial Symposium W. F. Albright Institute of Archaeological Research and American School of Oriental Research Jerusalem, May 29–31, 2000*. Winona Lake: Eisenbrauns.

Dietrich, W. 2002. *Die frühe Königszeit in Israel: 10. Jahrhundert v. Chr. Biblische Enzyklopädie 3*. Stuttgart: Kohlhammer.

Finkelstein, I. 2003. City States to States: Polity Dynamics in the 10th–9th Centuries B.C.E. Pages 75–83 in Dever and Gitin, eds., 2003.

Finkelstein, I. 2007. King Solomon's Golden Age: History or Myth? Pages 107–16 in Finkelstein and Mazar, eds., 2007.

Finkelstein, I., and A. Mazar, eds. 2007. *The Quest for the Historical Israel: Debating Archaeology and the History of Early Israel*. SBLSS 17. Atlanta: SBL.

Finkelstein, I., and N. A. Silberman. 2001. *The Bible Unearthed: Archaeology's New Vision of Ancient Israel and the Origin of Its Sacred Texts*. New York: Free Press.

Grabbe, L. L. 2000. Writing Israel's History at the End of the Twentieth Century. Pages 203–18 in *Congress Volume, Oslo 1998*. Edited by A. Lemaire and M. Saebø. VTSup 80. Leiden: Brill.

Grabbe, L. L. 2007. *Ancient Israel: What Do We Know and How Do We Know It?* London: T&T Clark International.

Hardmeier, C. 1990. *Prophetie im Streit vor dem Untergang Judas. Erzählkommunikative Studien zur Entstehungssituation der Jesaja- und Jeremiaerzählungen in II Reg 18–20 und Jer 37–40*. BZAW 187. Berlin: de Gruyter.

Herzog, Z., and L. Singer-Avitz. 2004. Redefining the Centre: The Emergence of State in Judah. *Tel Aviv* 31:209–44.

Kottsieper, I. 1998. Die Inschrift vom Tell Dan und die politischen Beziehungen zwischen Aram–Damaskus und Israel in der 1. Hälfte des 1. Jahrtausends vor Christus. Pages 475–500 in *Und Mose schrieb dieses Lied auf': Studien zum Alten Testament und zum Alten Orient*. Edited by M. Dietrich and I. Kottsieper. FS O. Loretz. AOAT 250. Münster: Ugarit-Verlag.

Lehmann, G. 2003. The United Monarchy in the Countryside: Jerusalem, Judah, and the Shephela during the Tenth Century B.C.E. Pages 117–62 in Vaughn and Killebrew, eds., 2003.

Liss, H. 2003. *Die unerhörte Prophetie: Kommunikative Strukturen prophetischer Rede im Buch Yesha'yahu*. Arbeiten zur Bibel und ihrer Geschichte 14. Leipzig: Evangelische Verlagsanstalt.

Mayer, W. 1995. *Politik und Kriegskunst der Assyrer*. ALASPM 9. Münster: Ugarit-Verlag.

Mazar, A. 2007. The Search for David and Solomon: An Archaeological Perspective. Pages 117–39 in *The Quest for the Historical Israel: Debating Archaeology and the History of Early Israel*. Edited by I. Finkelstein and A. Mazar. SBLSS 17. Atlanta: SBL.

Na'aman, N. 2006. The Contribution of the Amarna Letters to the Debate on Jerusalem's Political Position in the Tenth Century. Pages 1–17 in *Ancient Israel's History and Historiography: Collected Essays*. Vol. 3, *The First Temple Period*. Winona Lake, Ind.: Eisenbrauns.

Reich, R., E. Shukron and O. Lernau. 2007. Recent Discoveries in the City of David, Jerusalem. *IEJ* 57:153–69.

Steck, O. H. 1982a. Beiträge zum Verständnis von Jesaja 7,10–17 und 8,1–4. Pages 187–203 in Steck 1982c.

Steck, O. H. 1982b. Rettung und Verstockung: Exegetische Bemerkungen zu Jesaja 7,3–9. Pages 171–86 in Steck 1982c.

Steck, O. H. 1982c. *Wahrnehmungen Gottes: Gesammelte Studien*. ThB 70. Munich: Chr. Kaiser.

Steiner, M. 2003. Expanding the Borders: The Development of Jerusalem in the Iron Age. Pages 68–79 in *Jerusalem in Ancient History and Tradition*. Edited by T. L. Thompson (with the collaboration of S. K. Jayyusi). JSOTSup 381; CIS 13. London: T&T Clark International.

Ussishkin, D. 2003. Jerusalem as a Royal and Cultic Centre in the 10th–8th Centuries B.C.E. Pages 529–38 in Dever and Gitin, eds., 2003.

Vaughn, A. G., and A. E. Killebrew, eds. 2003. *Jerusalem in Bible and Archaeology: The First Temple Period*. SBLSS 18. Atlanta: SBL.

Weippert, M. 1978. Israel und Juda. *RLA* 5:200–208.

Part 3

Case Study:
The Question of the Reform under Josiah

Introduction to Part 3

The essays in this section focus on the case of Josiah and his alleged reform. This is one of the main events of the history of Judah in the long seventh century (the period between the fall of Samaria c. 720 and the fall of Jerusalem c. 587/586 BCE). The Annotated Bibliography makes a number of suggestions about references that cover other events in this long century, but the reform of Josiah well illustrates the historical problems arising at this time. A number of the events of this century are well documented, including the invasion of Sennacherib in 701 BCE, some of the activities of Manasseh (who is mentioned in the Assyrian inscriptions) and the events surrounding the last couple of decades of the Southern Kingdom.

A further issue is the beginnings of the biblical text, especially Deuteronomy and the Deuteronomistic History (Joshua to 2 Kings). The origin of Deuteronomy has traditionally been ascribed to the late eighth century (perhaps following the fall of Samaria, with northern priests coming to Jerusalem) or the seventh century (perhaps being written by a Jerusalem temple scribe). The school that produced Deuteronomy continued and (later, though this is debated) wrote the Deuteronomistic History by editing pre-existing traditions (such as found in 1 and 2 Samuel) or writing new stories (that may have drawn on earlier traditions). Thus, many see the seventh and sixth centuries (and going on into the fifth century) as a time of major activity as far as writing various sections of the Bible is concerned. (See further some of the items in the Annotated Bibliography.)

What makes the reform of Josiah so controversial is the fact that Josiah has no mention in any extra-biblical sources. Although several Judahite kings are recorded, either by name or at least by office, Josiah is completely absent from the Assyrian texts so far, in spite of his alleged importance for Judah. Extant Egyptian records do not record Josiah's death, even though Pharaoh Necho II is well known from both Egyptian and Mesopotamian sources. We are thrown back on the biblical text and archaeology for information about Josiah's rule and his supposed religious activities. There is also the central question of the law book allegedly found in the Jerusalem temple and shown to Josiah. Since archaeology does not seem to give us a great deal of help, we rely more on the text than we would like, and a number of scholars are sceptical of the text's story. The main representative here is PHILIP R. DAVIES who makes a trenchant case for doubting the story in 2 Kings 22–23 (and 2 Chronicles 34–35). RAINER ALBERTZ responded directly to

DAVIES, arguing that such a reform had to take place. There were others who joined in the debate, both pro and con (though space prevented their reprinting here). These included a position similar to DAVIES on the part of Niels Peter Lemche and Herbert Niehr.[1] Yet CHRISTOPH UEHLINGER in a classic article argued why the report of some sort of a religious reform can be extracted from the text. In this he was joined by Christof Hardmeier.[2]

Thus, Josiah's law book and religious reform serves as an excellent case study for trying to evaluate the picture given in the biblical text. However, as I have noted in the final essay (Part 5) the biblical text generally presents a more credible picture, the later the event in the history of Israel. In the final days of Judah, we can reconstruct some of the major events almost year by year, which is certainly not the case in most of the rest of Israel and Judah's history. Even though there is reason to doubt some aspects of Josiah's reign as portrayed in the biblical description, it seems *a priori* unlikely that the basic outline of his reign is simply a fictional creation.

Summary of Papers

22. **PHILIP R. DAVIES** ('Josiah and the Lawbook') engages with two colleagues in the Seminar, Nadav Na'aman and Rainer Albertz. After an appreciative summary of Na'aman's paper,[3] he asks whether the latter goes far enough in criticism of the biblical text. Even the most critical can easily fall into the trap of a 'rationalistic midrash' of the text rather than treating its data in a fully critical way. If we start from the picture well demonstrated by Na'aman—that Josiah is an idealized figure—we have to ask whether the text is any more reliable about internal events than the external. Why should we accept the picture of a religious reform? One might reply with the question, Why would a writer invent such a story? Yet a reason has already been given for why Josiah was not pictured by the sources as subservient to the Assyrians. Was he righteous because he initiated a reform, or was he pictured as carrying a purge of the cult because that is what 'righteous'

---

[1] See Lemche, 'Did a Reform Like Josiah's Happen?', in Philip R. Davies and Diana V. Edelman (eds), *The Historian and the Bible: Essays in Honour of Lester L. Grabbe*, LHBOTS 530 (New York and London: T&T Clark International, 2010), 11–19. The essay by Niehr is cited in the Annotated Bibliography below.

[2] Hardmeier, 'King Josiah in the Climax of the Deuteronomic History (2 Kings 22–23) and the Pre-Deuteronomic Document of a Cult Reform at the Place of Residence (23.4-15): Criticism of Sources, Reconstruction of Literary Pre-Stages and the Theology of History in 2 Kings 22–23', in Lester L. Grabbe (ed.), *Good Kings and Bad Kings: The Kingdom of Judah in the Seventh Century BCE*, JSOTSup 393 = European Seminar in Historical Methodology 5 (London/New York: T&T Clark International, 2005), 123–63

[3] Na'aman, 'Josiah and the Kingdom of Judah', in Grabbe (ed.), *Good Kings and Bad Kings*, 189–247.

kings do? This ideological creation has already been argued for Hezekiah. The key to resolving the question seems to be the law book (which is where interaction with Albertz comes in). It (or its core) needs to be dated, but since there is no hint of it in Jeremiah or Zephaniah or any independent sources, we are forced back on internal criteria. Since almost all accept that parts of Deuteronomy date from different periods, the focus will be on Deuteronomy 12–26. A number of important features can be isolated and questions asked about the social situation presupposed by them:

(1) *The nature of 'Israel':* There was no Israel in the time of Josiah, only Judah. It is difficult to find a time when both Judah and Samaria were called Israel, though possibly Elephantine letter 30-32 might be an example. (2) *'The nations':* Deuteronomy does not refer to the Canaanites, but 'the nations' is used in two senses, as all nations other than Israel and as nations dispossessed from the land. This usage does not fit the age of Josiah, but it fits usage found in Nehemiah. (3) *'The covenant':* Garbini points out that the notion of a covenant of a people with the deity is unusual: normal ancient Near Eastern practice was a covenant between the deity and the king. It is in Nehemiah that a public covenant ceremony with the people is enacted. The Torah as an organ of personal religion (rather than a body of social teaching upheld by the state) belongs to the post-exilic age rather than the time of the monarchy. (4) *Role and function of the king:* Deuteronomy 17.14-15 refers to a foreign king ruling over Israel, which was not true while Judah had a monarchy but was true in the Persian period. 17.16-20 abolishes the main roles of the king, which are to provide security and justice. These functions were taken over by the high priest no later than the Ptolemaic period. 28.36 has the king go into exile. (5) *Centralization of the cult:* The temple played a prominent role in the Persian period, whereas we don't know its status in the exilic period.

The important point being made is that there is no compelling reason to put Deuteronomy in Josiah's time. We cannot show a Josianic date for Deuteronomy on the basis of its contents, so we do not know that any reform took place. What we cannot show, we do not know. No special claim is being made for the fifth century BCE at this point, though that does seem to fit well for all the features. Deuteronomy fits the context of an immigrant population, based around a temple, in conflict with some of the indigenous population as well as with Samaria, and encouraged to live and exercise their control by means of a written law.

23. **RAINER ALBERTZ** ('Why a Reform Like Josiah's Must Have Happened') gives a critique of Philip Davies's paper (above) and responds to his specific arguments. The first argument concerns the dating of Deuteronomy 12–26 which Davies places in the fifth century BCE. It is incorrect to assert that Judah being called 'Israel' is only a late development. Passages that call Judah 'Israel' also refer to 'Israel and Judah', showing that one cannot distinguish between them traditio-historically. The trauma of the split in the kingdom is still obvious in 1 Kings 12 and Isa. 7.17. The Persian period is not the most likely setting for

'Israel' to be used of Judaeans since Nehemiah does not have this usage but wants to exclude the Northern Kingdom from God's people. The citation of Deut. 23.4 in Neh. 13.1-2 suggests that the latter was composed long after the former. Contrary to Davies the shape of the covenant in Deuteronomy is quite different from that in Ezra-Nehemiah. Deuteronomy 17.14-20 is not very applicable to the Persian period since there was no restoration of the monarchy in the post-exilic period; neither is all authority conferred on the priests, but a constitutional monarchy is envisaged. The second argument relates to the dating of the Deuteronomistic History (DtrH). If the earliest parts of Deuteronomy are dated to the fifth century, the DtrH cannot be earlier than the beginning of the fourth century BCE. Yet the dating of DtrH to the exilic period is indicated by a number of arguments. Recent studies have argued that 2 Kings 22–23 arose in the exilic period.[4]

The release of Jehoiachin by Amel-Marduk makes the DtrH post-562; on the other hand, none of the significant Persian-period events is reflected in it nor is there any knowledge of the end of the exile or the fall of Babylon. It most likely preceded Cyrus's conquest of Lydia in 547–546 BCE. Only two passages in the DtrH move beyond this date: Deut. 4.25-32 and 30.1-10. Both are part of a hopeful frame around Deuteronomy and thus a part of a deliberate redaction of DtrH. This means that the account of the Josianic reform was only 50–75 years after the event. Yet that reform does not fit DtrH's ideology since it should have averted the captivity. Thus, DtrH has to invent a horrible apostasy under Manasseh to account for the exile. The third argument concerns the historical evidence. Following H. Niehr (see Annotated Bibliography) and N. Na'aman,[5] Davies argues that there was no time when Judah was free, since the Assyrian hegemony was replaced by the Egyptian without a break. But this is less than certain, being a general reconstruction rather than testimony of a specific source. Isaiah 8.23–9:6 suggests that the Assyrian withdrawal was seen as a great victory. In any case, Egyptian hegemony would not necessarily prevent a cultic, social, and even national reform. There might even have been limited expansion into the northern hill country. There are few sources for Josiah's reform, apart from 2 Kings 22–23. Archaeology really gives nothing decisive. On the other hand, Jeremiah does know of the reform (cf. Jer. 3.22–4.2; 5.4-6; 8.7-8; 31.2-6), in spite of frequent statements to the contrary, and his preaching against syncretism was only against the North (2.4–4.2) but not the Judaeans (4.3–6.30). Ideally, the evidence would have been better, but on balance the arguments for the traditional hypothesis of Josiah's reform seem to outweigh those of Philip Davies.

24. **CHRISTOPH UEHLINGER** ('Was There a Cult Reform under Josiah? The Case for a Well-Grounded Minimum') argues that historical reconstruction must depend fundamentally on primary sources; we cannot allow our picture to be dominated by secondary sources such as the Bible: the 'sub-Deuteronomism'

---

[4] See note 2.
[5] See note 3.

that M. Weippert warns about. In this Uehlinger is a 'minimalist', though there is more than one way to practise minimalism. The historian of Israel and Judah's religion should focus on F. Braudel's *histoire conjoncturelle* or social time. Granted, there are at present no direct primary sources for Josiah's reform, but that is not justification for simply dismissing it. It is important not to be too narrow: a complete picture of the religious world in the Iron IIC period from the primary sources is needed. Two pieces of primary evidence once thought to support Josiah's reform are no longer valid as evidence: the Tell es-Seba' II horned altars and the removal of a holy place and burial of altars between Arad VIII and VI. On the other hand, the fact that the shrine of Arad was not rebuilt together with the fortress in stratum VII requires an explanation. Uehlinger takes it as one aspect of an on-going process, contributing as much as being subject to Jerusalem's growing centrality. Glyptic imagery and epigraphy can provide additional context and background information. The astral imagery of the late eighth and seventh centuries has disappeared from seals and seal impressions of the Jerusalem elite by the early sixth. Also, the blessing and salvation functions of Yhwh's 'Asherah', known from several inscriptions, have been absorbed by Yhwh by the time of the Lachish and Arad ostraca. Similarly, Yhwh seems to have taken over functions of the sungod and the underworld, as indicated by amulets from Ketef Hinnom in Jerusalem.

As for 2 Kings 22–23, two sorts of measures are mentioned—cult centralization and cult purification—but most scholarly attention has gone toward the former. Measures for cult purification are more plausible than programmatic centralization. The 'reform notes' of 23.4-20 has been thought to be relatively independent of 2 Kings 22 which recounts the discovery of the law book. They make no reference to the finding of the law book and do not use Deuteronomistic language (except for a few passages which are probably late additions). Are there measures in the 'reform notes' that are probable in Josiah's time? At least two measures seem to be against cult practices and institutions that began with the Assyrian expansion and are tied to the Assyro-Aramaic astral cults of the late eighth and early seventh centuries: the removal of the horses and chariots of the sun(god) and the *kĕmārîm*. The sungod became the chief deity of divination in the Sargonid period; only under Sennacherib were these rituals carried out before a chariot. The Jerusalem temple was the residence of the sungod (Ezek. 8.16), though it is not clear whether the initiative for this came from the Judaean or the Assyrian side. But they would have lost meaning by the time of Josiah and would have been removed as a new orientation of the cult (not as an anti-Assyrian measure). The *kĕmārîm* were not just those priests outside Jerusalem but a specific class of priests functioning exclusively for astral deities. They are present in Jerusalem (not outside it) because of Aramaic influence. The altars on the roof (23.12, with pre-Deuteronomic information) are poorly attested in the primary sources, representing neither Assyrian nor Aramaic practice, but their removal would go along with the other two measures of cult removal. All three measures would most plausibly have the 'axial age' of the seventh century for their background. Whether they all fell at the same time cannot be stated, but they form a coherent group: all three eliminate practices that had lost significance in the changed political orientation after the withdrawal of the Assyrians, and all three are concentrated on Jerusalem and do not affect cults outside the capital. There was no real programme of reform but a more limited removal of obsolete rituals from the Jerusalem state cult.

The correlation of primary and secondary sources is notoriously difficult. Nevertheless, our picture of the religion is incomplete if we use exclusively the archaeological primary sources. No serious historian can renounce the secondary sources when the primary are inadequate. For example, if we put forward a hypothesis that the horses and chariots of the sun were removed by Josiah, what is the probability of confirming this through primary sources? We know relatively little about the past and should take the trouble to interpret adequately that little. On the other hand, historical reconstruction should only be based on secondary sources whose plausibility has been established by the primary sources. An example of the correlation of primary and secondary evidence is the removal of the Asherah in 2 Kgs 23.6. The seal owners of the early sixth century seem to give no value to Asherah symbols. Asherah has disappeared from the traditional greeting formulae. Neither primary nor secondary sources indicate the further existence of an Asherah in the Jerusalem temple after Josiah.

Annotated Bibliography

A number of books and essay collections for the history of Israel to the fall of Samaria were given in the previous section. This section lists some of the studies that address the period from the fall of Samaria (c. 720 BCE) to the fall of Jerusalem (c. 587/586 BCE), including the beginnings of the biblical literature. For general background on the period, see also the histories of Israel (Part I).

Dubovský, Peter, Dominik Markl, and Jean-Pierre Sonnet (eds) (2016), *The Fall of Jerusalem and the Rise of the Torah*, FAT 107 (Tübingen: Mohr Siebeck).
   This collection of essays on the origin of the Pentateuch provides orientation on the main historical, archaeological, and literary issues relating to the sources and compilation of the Pentateuch.

Finkelstein, Israel, and Neil Asher Silberman (2001), *The Bible Unearthed: Archaeology's New Vision of Ancient Israel and the Origin of the Sacred Texts* (New York: Free Press).
   This is a sort of history of Israel, with a focus on archaeology. Although the authors are archaeologists (especially Finkelstein) they bring in much information from the text. They tend to put a good deal of emphasis on developments in the seventh century BCE, which they see as the main period for compilation of the traditions found in the Bible.

Grabbe, Lester L. (2003), '*Like a Bird in a Cage*': *The Invasion of Sennacherib in 701 BCE*, JSOTSup 363 = European Seminar in Historical Methodology 4 (Sheffield: Sheffield Academic Press).

Grabbe, Lester L. (2005) *Good Kings and Bad Kings: The Kingdom of Judah in the Seventh Century BCE*, JSOTSup 393 = European Seminar in Historical Methodology 5 (London/ New York: T&T Clark International).

These two collections of essays cover some of the main events in the history of Israel between the fall of Samaria and the fall of Jerusalem. The 2005 volume is the more wide-ranging one, with a long survey essay on this whole period and then individual essays on a number of the Judahite rulers, especially Manasseh and Josiah, throughout this period of more than a century. The 2003 volume is more narrowly focused on Sennacherib's invasion, though it comments on the reign of Hezekiah before 701 BCE.

Lipschits, Oded (2005), *The Fall and Rise of Jerusalem: Judah under Babylonian Rule* (Winona Lake, IN: Eisenbrauns).

As the title suggests, this discusses the end of Jerusalem and the Kingdom of Judah at the beginning of the Neo-Babylonian period and the rise of Jerusalem and the province of Judah at the beginning of the Persian period. The archaeology of the late seventh century, the sixth century, and into the fifth century is discussed in detail. Also, on pp. 272–304 there is a good discussion of recent scholarship on the Deuteronomistic History and other Deuteronomistic traditions relating to the end of Judah.

Niehr, Herbert (1995), 'Die Reform des Joschija: Methodische, historische und religions-geschichtliche Aspekte', in Walter Gross (ed.), *Jeremia und die 'deuteronomistische Bewegung'*, BBB 98 (Beltz: Athenäum), 33–55.

He finds a double problem in 2 Kings 22–23, a problem of context (especially the historical and religious history aspects) and a problem of text (especially relating to the literary critical analysis and to the dating of sources). There are no primary sources for Josiah's reign. The 'minimalist approach' commends itself to the historian as a means of avoiding wide-ranging, uncontrolled speculation. The proposed massive expansion of Josiah's kingdom can no longer be supported (though it is possible that he annexed Bethel). The oldest piece of information on Josiah's actions is 2 Kgs 23:8a, but this bald statement says only that Josiah profaned the altars. One can explain the measures as part of the centralization of administration going on since the late eighth century, and also part of the judicial reform. One cannot say more than that, except that there is no indication of religious motives, as is shown by our knowledge of the succeeding kings where no evidence of a religious reform is found. The prophets also give no indication: Zephaniah and Jeremiah are silent. There is also nothing in the small finds or forms of artistic expression to provide evidence of a religious reform under Josiah.

Pury, Albert de, Thomas Römer, and Jean-Daniel Macchi (eds) (2000), *Israel Constructs its History: Deuteronomistic Historiography in Recent Research*, JSOTSup 306 (Sheffield: Sheffield Academic Press); ET of *Israël construit son histoire: L'historiographie deuté-ronomiste à la lumière des recherches récentes*, Le Monde de la Bible 34 (Geneva: Labor et Fides, 1996).

This essay collection covers some of the main issues relating to the traditions associated with the Deuteronomistic History. Especially important and helpful is the introductory essay by the editors Römer and de Pury which surveys the history of research and the main issues of debate relating to the subject. The essays in the volume well illustrate the diversity of opinion about the growth and development of the Deuteronomistic History. The student and non-specialist would probably best begin with the essay by Römer and de Pury and the volume below (Römer 2005) before tackling the rest of the essays in this collection.

Römer, Thomas C. (2005), *The So-Called Deuteronomistic History: A Sociological, Historical and Literary Introduction* (London and New York: T&T Clark International).
This is probably the clearest and most well-argued presentation of the issues on the origins and compilation of the Deuteronomistic History. It is probably the best place to begin for the student and person new to the subject. After it, one could then move on to Pury/Römer/Macchi 2000 above.

Sweeney, Marvin (2001), *King Josiah of Judah: The Lost Messiah of Israel* (Oxford: Oxford University Press).
Much of this wide-ranging study is literary analysis, devoted to a detailed exegesis of biblical passages, but it also attempts to draw some historical conclusions as well. Sweeney argues that Josiah sought to be anointed king (messiah) of a restored united kingdom of Israel with Jerusalem and the temple at its centre. Josiah's experiment failed with his death at Megiddo; nevertheless, his dream was remembered and left its mark on a variety of books and passages in the Bible, including Zephaniah, Nahum, Jeremiah, First Isaiah, Hosea, Amos, Micah, Habakkuk, and especially the Deuteronomistic History. He became the model for a restored Davidic monarchy, yet his failure meant that some were already abandoning the idea of a restored monarchy even before the time of Zerubbabel.

Josiah and the Law Book

Philip R. Davies

Josiah's Ambitions

The various historical questions surrounding Josiah have been very thoroughly covered elsewhere in this volume, and my own contribution is conceived largely as a methodological one, in which I shall engage with two of my colleagues in the Seminar. My starting point is Nadav Na'aman's study on the politics of the kingdom of Judah under Josiah (Na'aman 1992), which offers a very fine critique of scholarship on the reign of Josiah, summarized as follows.

The first part of Na'aman's study argues that the town lists of Judah and Benjamin in Joshua 15 and 18 reflect, despite some editorial enhancement, the situation in seventh-century Judah. The second part deals with the chronology of the decline of Assyrian power, often thought to have occurred suddenly in the early part of Josiah's reign, prompting a policy of Judaean expansion over adjacent territory. Na'aman shows this proposed scenario to be unlikely; on the contrary, the Assyrians seem to have ceded control over Palestine in a more or less orderly way to Egypt, so that the Judaean king had little or no opportunity for the exercise of political independence; in short, there was no 'power vacuum'. In connection with the death of Josiah, Na'aman argues that Necho marched through Palestine (rather than sailing his army to a Phoenician port, the more usual procedure) not to do battle with Babylonia but in order to receive the pledge of loyalty from the local kings that required to be renewed on the accession of a new sovereign pharaoh. Noting that nothing is said in 2 Kings of a battle with Josiah, Na'aman deduces that Josiah died not in battle but by assassination or execution for some reason, possibly a suspicion of disloyalty on Necho's part; thus Josiah's visit to Megiddo may have been in response to a summons to pledge his loyalty personally before the new pharaoh.

What might have provoked Josiah's execution? Although Na'aman allows that effective control of Palestine passed to Egypt as Assyrian power declined, Josiah might nevertheless have enjoyed (or felt he had) some freedom to 'unify' and 'crystallise' (1992: 41) his kingdom, while the efforts of the Egyptians were, as usual, concentrated on the coastal and valley districts. Only a limited expansion of borders, however, could have been even contemplated, let alone achieved; no grand design for extensive territorial gains.

This reconstruction makes sense of a death that otherwise, as Miller and Hayes (1986: 402) remark, 'remains a mystery'. While 2 Kgs 23.29 possibly hints at military confrontation in its use of לקראתו and its comment וירכבה ועבדיו (chariot and, perhaps 'soldiers'), military confrontation is not explicitly mentioned; and קרא does not necessarily mean 'meet in battle', nor are עבדים necessarily 'soldiers'. Nor is the chariot an inappropriate way to transport a royal corpse even in peacetime. The account of Josiah's death is tantalizingly vague, even mysterious—and perhaps deliberately so. At any rate, the hint of a military defeat allows 2 Chron. 35.20-24 to show the pious king dying of battle-wounds in Jerusalem, in turn encouraging most modern scholars to conclude that Josiah went into battle, even though it leaves them puzzled over the motives for such a suicidal venture.[1]

Even if Na'aman is not correct over Josiah's manner of death, his analysis of the political situation is well-grounded in the evidence. The often-asserted expansion of Judah under Josiah did not, and could not, take place. Statements such as 'He [Josiah] attempted to restore the kingdom or empire of David in all detail' (Cross 1973: 283) Na'aman dismisses as 'built on shaky foundations'; there are, he says (1992: 44), 'no grounds for the assumption that Josiah attempted to conquer the entire north and to impose his reforms throughout the territory of Palestine'—a conclusion already anticipated by a few earlier historians.[2]

There remains, however, some apparent epigraphic evidence to the contrary in letters from Arad and Meṣad Ḥashavyahu. Arad ostraca 1–18, dated to the reign of Josiah or his successor, belong to a collection sent to Eliashib, a military commander, and most give instructions for the provisioning of troops. However, these instructions are not necessarily evidence of Judaean military resurgence or of Judaean refortification of Arad. Under Egyptian jurisdiction Josiah would have been permitted or required to take responsibility for providing garrisons (Greeks, 'Kittim', are especially mentioned) and agricultural workers in adjacent areas, following the practice reflected much earlier in the Amarna correspondence. From Meṣad Ḥashavyahu the complaint from a worker (possibly from the time of Josiah or his successor) points rather to Judaeans obliged to work in the vicinity of the fortress (see Davies 1991: 76-77 [Meṣad Ḥashavyahu]; 11-16 [Arad]; for a convenient discussion, Smelik 1991: 93-115) The evidence of these ostraca is entirely consistent with known Egyptian practice during its periods of rule over Palestine and does not contradict Na'aman's reconstruction.

---

[1] Two motives that have been suggested are obedience to a treaty or understanding with Babylonia, against which Necho was marching; and a defence of Josiah's newly won territories. The biblical reports, perhaps significantly, state no motive for such an engagement.

[2] Cf. Miller and Hayes 1986: 401: 'It is highly doubtful, however, that Josiah extended Judean borders...except in the case of Bethel'; Ahlström 1993: 764: '[I]t is unrealistic to think that Josiah could have extended his kingdom in this period to include the Assyrian province of Samerina, perhaps also Magidu and Gal'aza, territories of the former kingdom of Israel, as well as part of the coast, as is often maintained'.

The conclusion of Na'aman's arguments is that 'The picture of Josiah's reign, as reflected in this discussion, is far removed from the description of those years as reflected in the book of Kings, and no less distant from the sketch of his period presented in modern historiography' (Na'aman 1992: 55). This points to a not unfamiliar state of affairs; a misleading biblical portrait further distorted by the speculations of biblical scholarship; in this case the thesis of a golden period of Josian *Wiederaufbau*. That portrait has to be redrawn—but not just in respect of territorial ambition or achievement, but also for other aspects of his reign.

The presentation of Josiah in 2 Kings is, then, misleading, and modern scholars have often magnified the distortion. But let us not be too arrogant about this; it can be extremely easy to fall back on seemingly innocent biblical details as historical data. Thus, Na'aman himself reports at the beginning of his essay what he says we *know* about Josiah: that he succeeded Amon, 'who had been murdered by his courtiers; the rebellion was quashed and the conspirators executed; Josiah was crowned at the age of 8 and was supported by his mother and by those circles which had ensured his accession'; Josiah then 'assumed full authority only upon reaching maturity' (Na'aman 1992: 3). But compare the text of 2 Kings, where the support of Josiah's mother is not mentioned: merely her name is given. And as for when Josiah assumed 'full authority'—we are told only that he issued an order at the age of 18. So here too Na'aman is drawn into saying things about Josiah that we do not really know, however minor these details may be! The value of a regular seminar of historians is that we can alert each other to our lapses, 'keep each other honest', as far as we can. More, rather than less, skepticism is needed if we are interested in historical knowledge, as distinct from scriptural testimony.

Josiah's 'Reform'

I now wish to pick up Na'aman's baton and run a little further with it. Does the account of Josiah's reform also belong to the idealization evident in respect of his territorial ambition? In modern scholarship, Josiah's assumed policy of expanding a newly independent Judah into territory formerly of the kingdom of Israel is founded, after all, on the report of his religious reform; or, the other way round, the reform is commonly explained as part of his measures to signal, or consolidate, his political independence. But if that independence could never have been achieved, only at best a modest acquisition of territory beyond the Judaean border, then the modern explanation given for Josiah's reform does not hold. Indeed, we are left unclear as to what it *was* intended to achieve. Religious reforms at the beginning of a king's reign are not uncommon: they serve to commend the new monarch to his subjects and deity. But this reform was not undertaken until well into his reign.

The account in 2 Kings does not in fact portray Josiah as expanding his territory; it takes his control over the erstwhile kingdom of Israel for granted, conveniently erasing (from the time of Hezekiah onwards) any hint of Assyrian domination. Na'aman has suggested that Josiah could not have been portrayed as subservient to Assyria because he was a just king, as Hezekiah before him. This is plausible, and both Hezekiah (2 Kgs 18) and Josiah are credited with a religious reform; but, according to the scheme of 2 Kings, any good king following a bad king would *have* to undertake religious reform and freedom from Assyrian influence is required to make this plausible. Given this theo-logic, whether either king actually did perform the Deuteronomistic requirement is really not easy to affirm. The historical reality of Hezekiah's resistance—as debated in an earlier seminar (Grabbe [ed.] 2003)—is that he lost most of his territory and paid off Sennacherib with a large fortune. The mere fact that Jerusalem was not taken and that the Assyrian king departed has permitted Hezekiah to be accorded the rank of a righteous king. The case of Josiah is more interesting. What qualified *him* for the same status? Was it his 'heroic' death? Or was it, indeed, some seemingly pious act? Was Josiah credited with a reform because his status required it, or was his status prompted by some Deuteronomistically approved deed that he accomplished? I shall try and arrive at an answer, if only provisionally.

The reform story falls into three episodes: the discovery and verification of the law book, followed by the covenant (22.3–23.3); and the destruction of religious objects and places (23.4-20). A third episode (23.21-24), comprising the celebration of the Passover and removal of certain religious practitioners, refers again to the law book. Whether the second episode is intrinsically connected to the first is unclear; the literary structure of 2 Kings 22–23 remains disputed and there is a possibility either that the law book motif was inserted into a reform narrative or a reform narrative developed after a story of the discovery of a law book (see Lohfink 1985). It should also be noted that Josiah's reforming activities are confined to Judah and its immediate environs, notably Bethel—with the exception of a single brief notice about the territory of Samaria (2 Kgs 23.19). What other evidence have we for either? We should begin (as have many previous scholars) by seeking allusions to a reform or echoes of it (or lack of either), in other biblical texts. Then the nature of the law book itself requires analysis.

The Impact of Josiah's Reform

There seems little or no hint of any reform in other biblical literature that might be assigned to the period, for instance the books of Jeremiah or Zephaniah. Albertz (1994: 200) points to Jer. 8.7-8, suggesting a written law in the hands of priests. But this text does not mention any *reform*. He also mentions Jer. 22.15, 31.2-6 and 44.18 as offering some support for the idea of a 'climate of reform'. But there is no clear or direct indication in the book—whose hero is a contemporary of Josiah and which has received substantial Deuteronomic editing—that a major religious reform has taken place. Sweeney (2001: 129-313) has more recently analyzed a wider range of prophetic texts (Zephaniah, Nahum, Jeremiah, Isaiah, Hosea, Amos, Micah and Habakkuk), concluding that 'Prophets who were contemporary with Josiah actively addressed aspects of his reform program and frequently point to aspects that are not evident in the DtrH account of his reign' (p. 310). Space does not, unfortunately, permit a detailed appraisal of Sweeney's lengthy discussion. But those texts that he cites in support pointing to the centrality of Jerusalem hardly indicate unambiguously the time of Josiah rather than a later period; several texts are said to refer to aspects of the reform not mentioned in 2 Kings (and so cannot in fact corroborate it!); and several other texts are said to have provided legitimation for the reforms, including the re-unification of the divided kingdoms, but do not necessarily presuppose it. Having assessed Sweeney's evidence and arguments, I have not found any convincing reference to a reform as described in 2 Kings 22–23, and very little that suggests any religious reform at all at this time, with one important exception, to which I shall return presently—and which does not involve a law book. I maintain, then, that we do not have any text that, in the absence of 2 Kings 22–23, would lead us to suggest a religious reform. This must be required of any independent corroboration. A few texts *might* refer to such a thing, *if it had happened*, but do not entail it having happened. In short, Sweeney's arguments (the fullest panoply yet assembled) depend on the assumption that there was a reform, and do not provide adequate evidence that there was one. Such absence is significant if not conclusive.[3]

This conclusion brings us, then, to the question of the law book. As is well-known, de Wette can be credited with having bequeathed to us the realization that Josiah's law book was the book of Deuteronomy, or some form of it. This identification provided him with a vital key to detaching the law from the Mosaic origins of Judaism, and thus to developing a critical reconstruction of the history of Israel's and Judah's religion. (It is, however, worth recalling that de Wette regarded D as the *latest* of the Pentateuchal sources, and that his identification of the law book as Deuteronomy has not been universally accepted to the present.[4]) Yet it takes no genius to see that the identification of Deuteronomy with the Josianic law book is precisely what the author of 2 Kings 22 intends. The language and ideology of the framework of 2 Kings is Deuteronomistic, and even before Noth's theory of the 'Deuteronomistic History' it could have been realized

---

[3] I cannot refrain from commenting here on the oft-quoted dictum that 'absence of evidence is not evidence of absence'. True, but as a principle it cannot cope with cases of extra-terrestrial abduction, charges of wife-beating or fairies in my garden. It allows anything to be true that is not contradicted. Not surprisingly, those who invoke this principle seem to confine it to the Bible and keep it well away from real life!

[4] This opinion has from time to time been challenged, though usually in terms of an *exilic* date (e.g. Hölscher 1922; Würthwein 1976). For a review of the history of scholarship on Deuteronomy, see Kaiser 1978: 113-20.

that any *Deuteronomistic* account of the finding of a law book would present that law book as *Deuteronomy* (rather than, say, Leviticus or the 'Covenant Code' of Exodus). The writer of the law book story wishes to make it clear that in the days of the kings of Judah, the scroll of Deuteronomy, which had been lost temporarily, was recovered and used as the basis of a religious reform, and with the full authority of a Davidic king, no less. Albertz's comment that 'it is only possible to assess Josiah's cultic reform more precisely when the identity of the law book which provided its basis has been established' (1994: 198-99) misses the point. We *know* what the law book of the story was: but we do *not* know if the story of its 'discovery' (or some modern rationalization, like a deliberate planting of the scroll soon after composition) is true! Our question now is: Is a seventh-century origin (or perhaps earlier) for Deuteronomy likely? Is it a plausible Josian law book?

Dating the Law Book

The method of dating Deuteronomy has to proceed entirely on internal evidence, interpreted in the light of what little we know of the history of Judah, its society and its religion, during the entire period in which Deuteronomy may have been written, which includes the monarchic period, the exilic period and the Second Temple period. For simplicity I will assume ben Sira's early second-century reference to the 'scroll of the covenant of El Elyon, the law that Moses commanded us' (24.23) as the *terminus ad quem*. In asking about the date of Deuteronomy, I am not trying to reopen a debate: that debate has never stopped (for an excellent account of the history of discussion, see Lohfink 1985).

Obviously a brief discussion paper cannot cover the range of themes and topics in Deuteronomy that would need to be addressed in order to arrive at a sound theory. The following represent a small selection of the most significant topics. Before commencing, it is important to accept that many parts of the book may have originated at a time different from the law collection itself. The first introduction (1.1–4.40) and the final chapters (chs. 27–34) are widely understood as arising from a subsequent editing process; we must therefore not seek to date the presumed 'law-book' on the basis of any material in these chapters. I shall also exclude the second introduction in 4.44–11.32 and concentrate only on the legal material, chs. 12–26.

In this core legal material (for convenience I shall treat it as a 'document') we find a sketch of a society that reflects some historical circumstances but is essentially utopian, and in some parts impractical. Its utopian character is expressed through a fictional past setting in which the utopia remains a future possibility: when 'Israel' comes into 'the land Yahweh your god is giving you as a possession' (12.1; 15.4, etc.). The key question for its dating is: What purpose does such a document serve, and in what kind of historical and social context would its definition of 'Israel' have any meaning or impact? These questions will be considered (very briefly) with respect to the definition of 'Israel', the 'nations', the 'covenant', the role and function of the king, and the centralization of the cult.

The Definition of 'Israel'

In the legal core of Deuteronomy, 'Israel' designates a society, and its members are called בני־ישראל. What this 'Israel' consists of is not specified in much detail. The double mention of the 'tribe' of Levi might indicate a tribal structure for the whole, but no other 'tribe', or set of tribes, is mentioned, nor does a tribal structure have any organizational role. The repeated mention of 'the land' implies a territorial dimension to 'Israel', and the acquisition of this land is by military conquest (19.1; 20.16). The laws concerning the king (ch. 17) also imply a territorial state. Yet (see below), the role of the monarch is in fact virtually ceremonial.

Deuteronomy's 'Israel' is scarcely historical. In the monarchic period, there existed two kingdoms, one called 'Judah' and the other sometimes known as 'Israel'. The results of recent Iron Age archaeology in central Palestine strongly suggest that the areas later represented by the two kingdoms underwent separate settlement. The biblical claim that they were united under David and Solomon (and a few years under Rehoboam) is equally without any archaeological support, and indeed, there are strong indications to the contrary (see Finkelstein and Silberman 2001 for an overview and archaeological reconstruction).

The notion of this 'Israel' acquiring the land through conquest and annihilation of the previous occupants is also utopian; indeed, the presentation of 'Israel' as coming from outside the land contradicts the archaeological evidence, which can reveal no non-indigenous population element in central Palestine in the centuries prior to the establishment of the two kingdoms (the Philistines did not settle in the highlands).

But utopias have a function; it is no good dismissing them as 'fiction', as if that resolved the most important question. In what historical context does such a utopian 'Israel' (something larger than Judah) have a role? The notion that Josiah wished to reunite Judah and the erstwhile kingdom of Israel has been discussed already; it is highly improbable, but a previously united 'Israel' is also improbable. In the kingdom of Israel itself, before 722 BCE, such an ambition might be entertained—and indeed many scholars have considered Deuteronomy to be an originally Israelite document, perhaps brought south in the wake of Samaria's destruction. But, apart from other considerations that exclude this (see below), such a theory does not explain the discovery and adoption of this document in late seventh-century Judah. How and to what effect could Josiah's Judah be represented in this 'Israel'? Indeed, even if Deuteronomy's origin lay in the kingdom of Israel, on what basis would Judah call itself by that name?

The 'Nations'

The legal section of Deuteronomy refers to 'Canaanites' once, in 20.17 ('Canaan' occurs only once in the whole book, in 32.49). But there are many references to 'the nations', which fall into two categories. In 14.2, 15.6, 17.4, 18.9, 14 and 26.19 the phrase refers to all other nations, undifferentiated. 'Israel' is to be quite distinct from these, creating the dichotomy Israel/nations that still persists in our modern use of the term 'gentiles'. The second category is 'the nations that you will dispossess': these are characterized as (a) occupying the land that 'Israel' has been promised and will take over, and (b) practising religious customs that are abhorrent to Yahweh and that 'Israel' is not to imitate.

Let us concentrate on the nations dispossessed. These are specified as seven in Deut. 7.1 and 20.17 ('Girgashites' is missing, probably accidentally, from 20.17) and are to be destroyed, along with their culture. What kind of social and political background gives rise to this notion of two nations of entirely different cultures in the same space, one indigenous, the other immigrant? Is this a historical reality or, again, a utopian one? That nation and culture are synonymous is an important principle in Deuteronomy, for 'Israel' itself is defined by its culture—specifically its covenant-determined religion. 'Canaanite is as Canaanite does' we might say; and the same for 'Israel'.

While it can be argued that some cultural difference existed between population elements in early Iron Age Palestine—for instance, between highland farmers and those living under a city-state regime—the stark animosity towards the Canaanite 'nations' that Deuteronomy betrays probably does not belong to Iron Age history, because the kingdom of Israel (if not Judah) was evidently composed of several population elements, among whom there was a widely shared set of religious practices. Religious persecution, let alone genocide, as ordained by Deuteronomy, thus translates into civil war, which monarchs and ruling elites on the whole do not seek to provoke. Certainly, religion can be used to promote chauvinistic sentiments and practices, which can aid a monarch; but Deuteronomy's remedy would be disastrous for a monarchic state. Even if we translate 'nations of Canaan' into 'enemies of the royal cult', Deuteronomy's ideology appears over-enthusiastic. What, precisely, would a call to wage war on 'Canaanites' achieve—even supposing one could identify a 'Canaanite' in the first place?

Deuteronomy's 'war' is, of course, not physical or even military but ideological: the framers of the document do not intend that 'Canaanites' shall be wiped out. But the issue might well be of rightful ownership of the land, of membership of 'Israel', of proper worship of the deity; and it might involve conflict between indigenous and immigrant populations. Such a context *can* be postulated in the history of Judah. But not for the seventh century.

The 'Covenant'

Garbini (2003: 65) makes the point that the notion of a covenant between deity and people is quite startling. He claims that:

> For all Near Eastern peoples a 'covenant' between a god and his people simply made no sense: the covenant concerned only the king and his dynastic god and the king was legitimate just because of this direct relationship with the god. It was through it that the king could grant the prosperity of his people and legitimated his own function. This is clear even from the Biblical text, where it is written, just about Josiah: 'And the king stood by a pillar and made a covenant (*wayyikrot 'et ha-b^{e}rit*) before Yahweh' (2 Kgs 23,3). The question was never posed why this book, which supposedly guided the steps of the pious Josiah, does not contain any mention of covenant rites or pillars of this kind. The same ceremony, besides, was said to have been celebrated at the time of Solomon, as it is clear from the narrative of 1 Kings 8, in spite of all Deuteronomistic amplifications. Consecrating the temple, Solomon made a covenant (8,23) with Yahweh, god of the dynasty (8,25), invoking his protection on the people, especially in the hard moments of war and famine.

This point can, however, be put more positively, as it has been by Geller in an essay on the role of Deuteronomy in the history of monotheism (Geller 2000: 300). He describes Deuteronomy as a 'radically new type of association of individuals... Israel is, in the deuteronomic formulation of covenant, ultimately each Israelite'. (This phenomenon, of the direct bond between the god and every individual, is of course strengthened rhetorically by the use of the singular 'you' in large sections of the book.) Geller further notes the denial of collective responsibility for sins in Deuteronomy 34. Deuteronomy marks the beginning of a personal definition of 'Israelite' religion—one might even say the fount of Judaism. In short, we have here, as Geller implies, a stage on the development of 'torah' into an organ of personal religiosity and not a body of social teaching upheld by a state institution (be that the monarchy or the priesthood).

How such a notion arose in the first place is an intriguing question. What sort of conditions prompted the emergence of a religion that was both social and individual? But again, the key question is: How does this personal character of Deuteronomy's covenant make sense in a small monarchic state? What is the goal and effect of such a redefinition of religion? And again, one does not have to reply that Deuteronomy is simply 'utopian'; it is necessary to suggest a context in which this vision makes sense, among a community that had formed itself, or wished to, into a community of such a kind that membership entailed individual responsibilities, especially religious ones.

Weinfeld (1972: 59-157), among others, has argued, in defence of a Josianic date for Deuteronomy, that the Assyrian vassal-treaty form (exemplified by those of Esarhaddon) supplies a model for Deuteronomy. But to be valid, this argument has to show that knowledge of such literary forms vanished at a certain point. However, the influence of Assyria on the diplomatic rhetoric and literature (as well as the imagination) of the ancient Near East persisted for several centuries. A seventh-century *terminus a quo* for Deuteronomy is not particularly indicative. More pertinent, again, is the question: Under what circumstances would a suzerainty treaty inspire a new theory of religion as a covenant between a deity and a nation, both corporately and individually conceived? And under what circumstances would such a concept acquire currency?

The Role and Function of the King

The king of 'Israel' appears in only two texts in the legal material of Deuteronomy. The first (17.14-15) runs:

> When you come to the land which Yahweh your God is giving you, and possess it, and inhabit it, and say, 'I will set a king over me, like all the nations that are about me', you shall in any case make king over you one whom Yahweh your God will choose: one from among yourselves you shall make king over you, and not put a foreigner over you, one who is not your own kin.
>
> He shall not multiply horses to himself, nor cause the people to return to Egypt, in order to multiply horses: for Yahweh has said unto you, 'You shall from now on return no more that way'. Nor shall he take many wives, or else his heart will turn away: nor shall he accumulate silver and gold. And when he sits on the throne of his kingdom, he shall write for himself a copy of this law in the presence of the levitical priests. It shall remain with him, and he shall read it all the days of his life: that he may learn to fear Yahweh his god, observing all the words of this law and these statutes. Thus he will not exalt himself above his fellows, nor turn not aside from the commandment, either to right or left, so that he may prolong his days in his kingdom, he, and his descendants, in the midst of Israel.

It is unlikely that the threat of a foreign king was substantial in the monarchic period (the canonized texts do not relate that this ever happened or was even threatened); even under the Assyrians and Babylonians, there was a native king on the throne—but this is a trivial matter. The major issue is this: two of the main functions of a king (according to both modern sociology and also ancient monarchs themselves) are security and justice; the former protects the people from external threats and the latter from internal exploitation. Both contribute to social order. Without these functions, the role of a king is redundant. The passage quoted proposes to abolish the role of monarch; to replace his right to be the fount of justice and to have a cavalry force. Elsewhere, Deuteronomy prescribes the rules for war (ch. 20) from which the king is entirely absent. There, as here, authority is conferred exclusively on the priests. The king is subject to the law that they hold and they, not he, dictate its contents. The king becomes a constitutional monarch.

The same question returns, but with rather more force: at what point in the history of Judah does such a political revolution make sense, even as a utopian ideal? When might the rule of a Judaean monarch be replaced by a book of laws? There is no parallel at all in the monarchic period for any such notion, and indeed it is an absurd idea for such a time. The ancient law codes of Mesopotamia have, like the Assyrian suzerainty treaty, undoubtedly served as one model for the book of Deuteronomy, but in a complete reversal from the ancient tradition whereby the king issues his law code, as representative of the god.

There are no plausible explanations why a king should accept a reform that deprives him of the essential powers of monarchy, justice and warfare. To suggest that Josiah was very young at the time and that the document is an attempt on the part of priests to control royal power is naive. Would the priests have the power to do this, against the opposition of all those retainers whose privilege depended precisely on the preservation of the power of the monarchy? The notion that such reform was instigated by the *'am ha-'aretz*, as Albertz also suggests (Albertz 1994: 201), is contradicted by the fact that these people would hardly have transferred authority over warfare or justice to the *priesthood*.

In short, the belief of most biblical scholars that a scroll depriving the monarch of all real powers (and in effect destroying the institution of monarchy) is a plausible product of seventh-century Judah is astonishing and can only be explained by assuming that such scholarship is taking the fact for granted and thus either ignoring the absurdity or fabricating an implausible rationalization for it.

Centralization of the Cult

Albertz rightly dismisses the idea of Würthwein (1976) that the centralization of the cult in Deuteronomy indicates the exilic period, asserting that 'there was no longer any conflict over the centralization of the cult in the early post-exilic period' (1994: 199-200), on the grounds that it is presupposed by Deutero-Isaiah and Ezekiel. But he cannot be thinking of the realities of life in Judah during the neo-Babylonian period, when the capital was at Mizpeh. We do not know whether Jerusalem had any kind of sanctuary at this time, but evidence does suggest that several sanctuaries in the vicinity of Mizpah functioned: Gibeon, Mizpah itself, and especially Bethel. How, and when, Jerusalem was reinstated as capital is not clear; the process of building the Persian period temple is itself unclear, and it is unthinkable that the change of capital from Mizpeh to Jerusalem was achieved without some resentment, nor the reinstatement of Jerusalem as the central sanctuary. Indeed, the replacement of Bethel by Jerusalem as the chief sanctuary of Judah in the mid-fifth century explains a great deal about the Josiah tradition, as I shall now suggest.

What Did Josiah Do?

Once the 2 Kings account of a Josianic reform is put into question rather than assumed, there seem to be no compelling, even cogent reasons, for thinking that a text such as Deuteronomy (specifically the legal material) comes from this time. On the contrary, for every single topic discussed there are more plausible contexts. I have not set out here to argue in detail for a fifth-century date, but I have noted that all of the features discussed fit well with such a period. Deuteronomy fits the context of an immigrant population, based around a temple, in conflict with some of the indigenous population as well as with Samaria, and encouraged to live and exercise their control by means of a written law, controlled by the priesthood.

But if such a date provides a better context for the core of Deuteronomy, we still need to account for the story of Josiah's reform as a later legend; but this follows fairly easily. Those population elements claiming to be the true 'Israel' (against the indigenous 'dispossessed nations') would require that the document on which their position depended was not ancient. Even better: that its imputed origin replicated the present situation: 'Israel' seeing itself threatened by the 'people of the land'. But the document requires further authentication: it must have been known, as a written source, and been authorized by a legitimate Judaean king. Why Josiah? This brings us back to another question already raised: Was Josiah commemorated for having done anything to earn the reputation?

The core element of the story of Josiah's reform (2 Kgs 23) concerns his destruction of Bethel, and this act is echoed in 1 Kgs 12.25–13.34 (cf. 2 Kgs 10.29) as well as in Exodus 32 (see Blenkinsopp 1998, 2003). If Josiah were executed for some offence against the pharaoh, the destruction of Bethel, signalling Judaean control over an area adjacent to Jerusalem itself, might have constituted such an act. Over a century later, when Jerusalem was being reinstated as the major sanctuary of the Persian province of Judah, perhaps at the expense of Bethel (see Blenkinsopp 2003), such an act would easily have identified Josiah as a righteous figure, and provided the context for the retrospective introduction of Deuteronomy into the earlier history of Judah. Indeed, the 'Deuteronomic reform' of 2 Kings 22–23 should then be seen, not as a historical event, but as a disguise for a new Jerusalem-centred community to seek to impose its definition of 'Israel', its god and its religion, and specifically its written law, on an 'idolatrous' indigenous population.

In short, the fifth century BCE provides a plausible context for both the law book of Deuteronomy and the story of Josiah's reform—in a number of ways. That case will, of course, have to be argued in more detail, but I suggest that even in the brief outline given here, it offers a better account of things than the idea of a 'Deuteronomic reform' under Josiah. The king's assault on Bethel earned him a reputation as a Deuteronomic champion, but the real 'reform' took place nearly two centuries later, and, as often happens, history was rewritten to give that reform the necessary authentication.

Bibliography

Ahlström, G. 1993. *The History of Ancient Palestine from the Palaeolithic Period to Alexander's Conquest* (JSOTSup, 146; Sheffield: Sheffield Academic Press).

Albertz, R. 1994. *A History of Israelite Religion in the Old Testament Period* (trans. John Bowden; OTL; Louisville, KY: Westminster/John Knox Press; London: SCM Press [German edn Göttingen, 1992]).

Blenkinsopp, J. 1998. 'The Judean Priesthood during the Neo-Babylonian and Achaemenid Periods: A Hypothetical Reconstruction', *CBQ* 60: 25-43.

Blenkinsopp, J. 2003. 'Bethel in the Neo-Babylonian Period', in O. Lipschits and J. Blenkinsopp (eds.), *Judah and the Judean in the Neo-Babylonian Period* (Winona Lake, IN: Eisenbrauns): 93-107.

Cross, F.M., Jr. 1973. *Canaanite Myth and Hebrew Epic: Essays in the History of the Religion of Israel* (Cambridge, MA: Harvard University Press).

Davies, G. 1991. *Ancient Hebrew Inscriptions* (Cambridge: Cambridge University Press).

Finkelstein, I., and N.A. Silberman. 2001. *The Bible Unearthed: Archaeology's New Vision of Ancient Israel and the Origin of its Sacred Texts* (New York and London: Simon & Schuster).

Garbini, G. 2003. *Myth and History in the Bible* (JSOTSup, 362; Sheffield: Sheffield Academic Press).

Geller, S.A. 2000. 'The God of the Covenant', in B.N. Porter (ed.), *One God or Many? Concepts of Divinity in the Ancient World* (Transactions of the Casco Bay Assyriological Institute, 1; Chebeague, ME: Casco Bay Assyriological Institute): 273-319.

Grabbe, L.L. (ed.). 2003. *'Like a Bird in a Cage': The Invasion of Sennacherib in 701 BCE* (JSOTSup, 363; ESHM, 4; London and New York: Sheffield Academic Press).

Hölscher, G. 1922. 'Komposition und Ursprung des Deuteronomiums', *ZAW* 40: 161-255.

Kaiser, O. 1978. *Einleitung in das Alte Testament* (Gütersloh: Gerd Mohn, 4th edn).

Lohfink, N. (ed.). 1985. 'Zur neueren Diskussion über 2 Kön 22–23', in *idem* (ed.), *Das Deuteronomium. Entstehung, Gestalt und Botschaft* (BETL, 68; Leuven: Peeters): 24-48.

Miller, J.M., and J.H. Hayes. 1986. *A History of Ancient Israel and Judah* (Philadelphia: Westminster Press).

Na'aman, N. 1992. *The Kingdom of Judah Under Josiah* (Tel Aviv Reprint Series, 9: Tel Aviv: Institute of Archaeology).

Smelik, K.A.D. 1991. *Writings from Ancient Israel: A Handbook of Historical and Religious Documents* (Edinburgh: T. & T. Clark).

Sweeney, M. 2001. *King Josiah of Judah: The Lost Messiah of Israel* (Oxford: Oxford University Press).

Weinfeld, M. 1972. *Deuteronomy and the Deuteronomic School* (Oxford: Clarendon Press).

Würthwein, E. 1976. 'Die Josianische Reform und das Deuteronomium', *ZTK* 73: 365-423.

Why a Reform Like Josiah's Must Have Happened

Rainer Albertz

1. The Role of the Josianic Period for Israel's Religious and Political History

In his contribution to the present volume (pp. 65-77 [reprinted as pp. 391–403, above]), Philip R. Davies cited a statement that I made about ten years ago: 'The most important decision in the history of Israelite religion is made with a dating of an essential part of Deuteronomy in the time of Josiah' (Albertz 1994: I, 199). I had become aware that any reconstruction of Israel's religion decisively depends on whether you—in accordance with W.M.L. de Wette—equate the core of Deuteronomy with Josiah's law book (2 Kgs 22.8, 11), dating it in the last third of the seventh century, or whether you dissolve this connection and—in company with Hölscher (1922) and Kaiser (1984: 132-34)—shift the date of Deuteronomy to the postexilic period. Since the date or even the existence of the Pentateuchal sources J and E have been heavily questioned, the dating of Deuteronomy constitutes the last fixed point in Old Testament literary history. So, giving up the seventh-century dating of Deuteronomy would have far-reaching consequences: not only important features of Israel's religion like monotheism, exclusivism, and brotherhood would have to be dated much later, but also most of the Deuteronomic reform ideas like the centralisation of cult or the subordination of all the state to the law would lose any connection to societal reality. In the Persian province of Yehud there was only one temple and there existed no king, thus there were no need for centralisation and subordination any longer. As a result of this, an important turning point in the development of Israel's religious history would disappear.

Recently it was shown that Josiah's reform became the decisive fixed point for the reconstruction of Israel's political history as well. In their recent book, Finkelstein and Silberman (2001)[1] developed their new view of the history of Israel and Judah, which they claimed to be based mainly on archaeological findings

---

[1] The title of the German edition (2002) is more aggressive: *No Trumpets before Jericho: The Archaeological Truth about the Bible.*

and not on the biblical text, whose historicity in their opinion is largely to be doubted. According to their view there was no United Monarchy under David and Solomon, and the Davidic empire never existed. The two states Israel and Judah came into existence independently, the state of Israel during the ninth, the state of Judah not before the eighth century. Nevertheless, in spite of this rather minimalistic view Finkelstein and Silberman do believe in the historicity of Josiah's reform. Moreover, they title their chapter on it 'A Great Reformation' and even call it a 'revolution' (Finkelstein and Silberman 2001: 275, 285, 288). The authors praise Josiah's reign as 'the climax of Israel's monarchic history' (Finkelstein and Silberman 2001: 275). And they add: 'During his thirty-one-year reign over the kingdom of Judah, Josiah was recognized by many as the greatest hope for national redemption, a genuine messiah who was destined to reform the fallen glories of the house of Israel' (Finkelstein and Silberman 2001: 275-76). According to the authors Josiah was not only the key figure of a 'new religious movement', but also created a new Israelite identity by attempting to unify the Judaeans with the people of the former northern state. In their view, vast parts of the biblical literature, not only Deuteronomy and the first edition of the Deuteronomistic History (DtrH) but also the stories of the Patriarchs, the Exodus, the Conquest, and the Judges were written during this great religious and national upheaval.[2] Even the stories about David and Solomon and their empire must be understood as reflections of the national hopes raised under Josiah and projected back into the past (cf. Finkelstein and Silberman 2001: 144). In 'Appendix F' of the book, which curiously enough was not included in the German edition, Finkelstein and Silberman admit on the grounds of archaeological considerations, however, that Josiah was possibly not able to realize his plans of a united monarchy to any large extent (cf. Finkelstein and Silberman 2001: 347-53).

One may ask what caused two scholars, who are inclined towards a minimal position, to reconstruct a vast religious and national movement under King Josiah that goes even beyond a scenario which 'conservative maximalists' like me would venture to draw? All methodical restrictions they made seemed to be forgotten: there are no, or no unambiguous, archaeological data which could verify Josiah's reform. The biblical text, which includes the report given by the DtrH in 2 Kings 22–23, is suddenly taken to be reliable. If we ask in amazement how that could happen, in my opinion the answer will be easy: Finkelstein and Silberman feel obliged to create a substitute for the United Monarchy that they denied. If it is right that pre-state Israel emerged from different populations and was organized in separate tribes, if it is right that the states of Israel and Judah 'represent two sides of ancient Israel's experience, two quite different societies with different attitudes

---

[2] Cf. Finkelstein and Silberman 2001: 45-46, 68-71, 95, 120-22; in their early dating of the DtrH Finkelstein and Silberman are still following F.M. Cross. That they date awkwardly many of the sources of DtrH in the same years as the DtrH itself, which levels all distinctions of literary analysis, does not seem to trouble them.

and national identities' (Finkelstein and Silberman 2001: 24), then it must be explained how the unifying concept of 'Israel' was born, which included all tribes and all the people from both states. Since the unifying concept is spread throughout all the exilic Prophets[3] and is present throughout the book of Deuteronomy,[4] the reform of Josiah—accepting the traditional dating—is the latest opportunity that would explain such a development to some extent. Therefore it was taken up by Finkelstein and Silberman and stressed so heavily. In their view the 'great reformation' of Josiah in the late seventh century not only gave birth to Israel's unique religion, but also to Israel's new identity as a united nation under Judaean leadership. From this example we learn that we cannot just deal with the historicity of one period, but we are forced to observe the interdependency between the assessments of different periods and must somehow bring them into balance.

Compared with Finkelstein and Silberman Philip Davies is more radical. In his article he is questioning the historicity of Josiah's reform,[5] even though he has denied the existence of the Davidic and Solomonic empire as well (cf. Davies 1992: 67-70). For the former, his main arguments are the following: first, at the time of Josiah there existed no political vacuum after the decline of the Assyrian empire. Davies shares the suggestion of Na'aman (1991: 39-41),[6] that the Assyrians ceded control over Palestine 'in a more or less orderly way' to Egypt in return for its military assistance against the Medes and Babylonians. Therefore 'the Judaean king had little or no opportunity for the exercise of political independence' (see p. 65, below [391, present volume]). Second, since the report of 2 Kings 18–23 does not mention any Assyrian dominance over Judah after Hezekiah's revolt in 701 BCE, which contrasts sharply with the historical evidence drawn from the extrabiblical sources, there is no reason to believe that it is more reliable on what it tells about the internal political conditions of Judah, including also Josiah's cultic measures. Third, since the book of Deuteronomy, even in its core, does not belong to the late seventh century but is better dated to the fifth century, there is no legislation that could serve as a base for Josiah's reform. Davies is not quite sure about the fifth-century date; however his negative result is clear: 'Once the 2 Kings account of a Josianic reform is put into question rather than assumed, there seem to be no compelling, even cogent reasons, for thinking that a text such as Deuteronomy (specifically the legal material) comes from this time. On the contrary, for every single topic discussed there are more plausible contexts. I have not set out here to argue in detail for a fifth-century date, but I have noted that all of the features discussed fit well with such a period' (see p. 75, below [402, present volume]). In contrast to Finkelstein and Silberman the

---

[3] Isa. 11.11-16; Jer. 30.3; 31.2-6, 15-22; Ezek. 37.15-22, etc.
[4] As also stated by Philip R. Davies in his contribution to the present volume (pp. 65-77 [reprinted as pp. 391–403, above]), but with different consequences.
[5] Cf. already Davies 1992: 40-41.
[6] See also Na'aman's contribution to the present volume (pp. 189-247, below).

question of how the unifying concept of the 'biblical Israel' could emerge does not bother Philip Davies. In his opinion, it was just an idealized myth of the past, invented by the post-exilic Golah-society of Yehud (1992: 87-93).[7]

Thus, Davies' argument has to do with the historical assessment of the international political situation during the reign of Josiah, the reliability of the DtrH, especially in the book of Kings, and the chronological setting of the Deuteronomic legislation in Deuteronomy 12–26. I would like to respond to that in the opposite sequence.

2. Dating Deuteronomy 12–26

I think Philip Davies is absolutely right when he states that any dating of Deuteronomy 12–26 must be done without the use of de Wette's hypothesis that the law book found by Josiah (2 Kgs 22–23) can be identified with it (see pp. 69-70, below [395–96, present volume]). Even if it is probable, that the Deuteronomistic Historian wanted his readers to believe that the law book was nothing else than the Deuteronomic law, which he had then included in his work,[8] this identification could be a misleading invention. Methodologically, inner-Deuteronomic observations have to decide whether a Josianic dating of the Deuteronomic law can be accepted or not.

2.1. Davies rightly notes that the name given to the society for which Deuteronomy legislates is 'Israel' (see p. 71, below [397, present volume]). One can add: the Deuteronomic legislation even stresses the concept that Israel constitutes a unity, where all members are brothers. It does not know any divisions concerning north or south; even a division into tribes is not mentioned in the core of Deuteronomy, where Israel is conceptualized as 'the people of God'.[9] The alternative concept of Israel as a nation composed of twelve tribes, which is so prominent in the Patriarchal Narratives and the Priestly Source, occurs only on the fringe of the book of Deuteronomy, in Deuteronomy 33, and has there only peripheral importance.

However, Davies' argument that this Deuteronomic concept of Israel would be historically problematic in the late seventh century and excludes such a dating is not convincing. It would be convincing only if one shares the historical and terminological reconstruction of Philip Davies: that there was no United Monarchy, that there existed only two different kingdoms, Judah and Israel, and that the meaning of the term 'Israel' in its historical sense must be restricted to the Northern

---

[7] The fact that the concept occurs already in the books of the exilic prophets (Ezekiel, Deutero-Isaiah, see above) conflicts with this solution and forces us to date these later likewise.

[8] Cf. the identical expression ספר התורה in 2 Kgs 22.8, 11 and Deut. 28.61; 29.20; 31.26 (cf. 31.24) and the scene, where Moses writes down the Deuteronomic law in Deut. 31.9-13.

[9] The assumptions Philip R. Davies made in this context are not fully correct, see pp. 71-72 [398, present volume], below.

Kingdom. If one takes those presuppositions for granted, the outcome that at the end of the seventh century Deuteronomy 12–26 should use only the name of the Northern Kingdom, which had perished a century before, for Judaean society would indeed be astonishing. But the presuppositions are questionable.

My first point is that already on the level of semantics the strict division that Davies made between the historical 'Israel', restricted to the Northern Kingdom, and the so-called 'biblical Israel', envisaging the ideal concept of a unified nation, is not true. I investigated the term 'Israel' in detail many years ago (Albertz 1987) and found that the name has an exclusive and an inclusive meaning. In its exclusive meaning it denotes the territory of Eshbaal (2 Sam. 2.9-10; 3.12, 21), the ten tribes of the middle and northern Palestinian hill country (2 Sam. 19.42-44), and later the Northern Kingdom (1 Kgs 12–2 Kgs 17). In its inclusive meaning it denotes all the tribes including Judah, so the 'men of Israel' (2 Sam. 15.13; 16.15, 18; 17.14, 24, etc.) and the 'elders of Israel' (2 Sam. 17.4, 15, etc.) during the Absalom revolt, when the northern and the southern tribes formed an alliance, or the united kingdom of David and Solomon (2 Sam. 5.12; 6.20-21; 8.15; 19.23; 1 Kgs 1.34; 4.1; 11.42), that could also be called 'Israel and Judah' (2 Sam. 5.5; 11.11; 1 Kgs 1.35; 4.20). Since the exclusive and inclusive meaning are often alternating confusingly in one and the same literary unit (e.g. 2 Sam. 5.5, 12; 1 Kgs 1.34, 35), it seems to me extremely difficult to divide them diachronically and to assign them to an old historical or a late ideological level. If Davies' thesis was right, all narratives and reports on David and Solomon would have to be dated into the post-exilic period, when according to him the inclusive concept of 'biblical Israel' was invented (cf. 1992: 87-93). But even though the dating of the David narratives varies in the recent discussion,[10] there still remains one passage that clearly contradicts Davies' hypothesis: in Isa. 8.17 the prophet Isaiah could call the Southern and Northern Kingdom 'both houses of Israel'. Here the term 'Israel' explicitly embraces the two states (בתים). This means that unless one wants to question Isaiah's preaching during the Syro-Ephraimite crisis 734–732 BCE, the inclusive meaning of the name 'Israel' is already common during the eighth century. Therefore, it is still likely that the expansion of the term took place much earlier. In my view, 'Israel' denoted in the pre-state period a coalition of tribes in the middle and northern Palestinian hill country and was expanded in order to include the southern tribes during the late pre-state and the early monarchic period.[11] Accordingly, the fact that Deuteronomy

---

[10] The date of the Succession Narrative (2 Sam. 9–1 Kgs 2*) varies from the time of Solomon (L. Rost) to the post-exilic period (J. van Seters), but even very critical scholars such as D.M. Gunn ('several centuries after the events') and O. Kaiser ('between Hezekiah and Jehoiakim') defended a pre-exilic dating; see the discussion in Dietrich and Naumann 1995: 213-16.

[11] Since not only 1 Kgs 12 but also Isa. 7.17 testify to the separation of the northern tribes from Judah, there must have existed some kind of United Monarchy under David and Solomon. Two independent and trustworthy sources cannot so easily be denied, not even by possible negative archaeological evidence. It must be taken into account that for the prophet Isaiah in the eighth century the separation of the north is still the most traumatic event in the history of Judah.

uses the name 'Israel' in a definitely inclusive sense is in no way astonishing and does not rule out a seventh-century date. On the contrary, the course of history in which the Northern Kingdom was destroyed and many refugees from the north joined the Judaean society in the late eighth century makes it comprehensible that the Deuteronomic legislators could easily appropriate the name 'Israel' for the Judaean society and stress—admittedly in archaic diction—the unity of the people without any tribal subdivisions.

Philip Davies suggested that the Persian period would be the most likely setting for the usage of the name 'Israel' in Deuteronomy. I have my serious doubts about this suggestion. The Nehemiah Memoir,[12] which we can date with a high degree of probability in the second part of the fifth century, does not lay any emphasis on the term 'Israel'. It uses 'Israel' only four times, two times for the people of the past (Neh. 1.6; 13.26) and just two times for those of the present (2.10; 13.18). Much more prominent is the usage of the term 'Jews', mostly with the article 'the Jews' (ה/יהודים), which appears ten times (1.2; 2.16; 3.33, 34; 4.6; 5.1, 8, 17; 6.6; 13.23) and denotes all descendants of the inhabitants of the former kingdom of Judah wherever they live, whether in the province Yehud, in other territories of Palestine or in Babylonia or Persia. This new linguistic usage accords with Nehemiah's policy to strengthen the independence of Yehud by excluding all the non-Jewish from the community, especially the descendants of the former northern tribes in the province Samaria. For such a policy the term 'Israel', which originally had denoted and always had included the northern tribes, would be counter-productive. In the rest of the books of Ezra and Nehemiah the term 'Israel' is more prominent, but it does not include the whole people, but is mostly restricted to the emigrants of the Babylonian Golah.[13] Thus it seems to me extremely difficult to explain the inclusive usage of the term 'Israel' in Deuteronomy from a fifth-century background.

Progressing from the terminology to the cultural background, it must be stated that the inclusive use of the name 'Israel' was not a pure fiction but mirrors a social reality. In spite of all political differences, the members of the northern and southern tribes had the feeling that they shared common moral and religious values. 'No such thing ought to be done in Israel', said the Judaean princess Tamar to Amnon who wanted to rape her in Jerusalem. The God Yhwh is always named the 'God of Israel',[14] never the God of Judah,[15] even when he was venerated in

---

[12] Neh. 1.1–7.5a; 12.21-32, 37-40; 13.4-31; probably without 7.1b; 13.24a, 30a. Cf. Mowinckel 1923: 278-322; Kellermann 1967: 4-56; Rudolph 1949: xxiv; Williamson 1985: xxiv-xxviii; Gunneweg 1987: 176-80; Blenkinsopp 1988: 46-47; Karrer 2001: 128-213; Reinmuth 2002.

[13] Cf. Ezra 2.2, 5, 59, 70; 3.1; 6.21; Neh. 9.2; the expression עם ישראל/ה in Ezra 2.2; 9.1; Neh. 7.7 does not appear in Deuteronomy.

[14] Altogether 202 times in the Hebrew Bible from Judg. 5.3, 5 to Mal. 2.16.

[15] This result is statistically significant; the expression אלהי ירושלם occurs in the Hebrew Bible only in 2 Chron. 32.19 and probably in the inscription A of Khirbet Bet Lei. Here it is stated, that the hills of Judah belong to Yhwh, who is also called אלהי כל ארץ; see Renz and Röllig 1995: 245.

Jerusalem.[16] Therefore the authors of Deuteronomy could combine religious and legal traditions from the north and the south when they stressed the ethnic, moral and religious unity of 'Israel'.

2.2. Philip Davies thinks that the sharp distinction between Israel and the foreign nations presented by Deuteronomy would make no sense in a reform under a king whose subjects include a plurality of cultures or population elements (see p. 72, below [397, present volume]). Interpreted as a contrast between the immigrants and the indigenous population it would fit much better in the conflict between the returnees and the 'people of the land' in the Persian period. It can be admitted that there are material parallels between the concepts of Deuteronomy and Ezra/Nehemiah. Nevertheless, there is the problem that the terminology in Deuteronomy and in Ezra/Nehemiah is completely different: the foreign nations, who would seduce Israel and whom Israel should expel, are called in Deuteronomy 12–26 generally (eighteen times) גוים, 'nations' or 'many nations', 'big nations', 'strong nations', and so on,[17] but only four times is עמים used.[18] But in Ezra/Nehemiah the term גוים is used hardly at all; it occurs only once in the expression גוי הארץ ('people of the land', Ezra 6.21) and several times in the older Nehemiah Memoir for non-Jewish people elsewhere in the world.[19] In Ezra/Nehemiah the groups, from which the Golah-community should separate itself, are called עמי הארץ/הארצות ('people of the land' or 'people of the lands').[20] The same expression עמי הארץ is used in Deut. 28.10 and in the DtrH (Josh. 4.24; 1 Kgs 8.43, 53, 60) with the total different meaning 'the nations of the world', like simple עמים in Deuteronomy 12–26 and its admonitory frame.[21] Thus it is not possible to bring Deuteronomy and Ezra–Nehemiah into a literary coherence. In contrast, to date Deuteronomy to a similar time as Ezra/Nehemiah, one must suppose that both literary works emerge in two totally separated groups whose terminologies had no mutual influence. Such a suggestion would not be totally impossible, though a little bit difficult, if we take the small size of the province Yehud into account. But if we become aware that the editors of Ezra/Nehemiah cited explicitly the law of Deut. 23.4 from 'the book of Moses' as authoritative (Neh. 13.1-2), it will be more likely that the Deuteronomic legislation preceded the writing of Ezra/Nehemiah by a long time. That would not completely exclude a Persian date but would limit it to the early Persian period.

---

[16] Cf. the expression 'The Holy One of Israel' coined by Isaiah, Isa. 5.19, 24; 30.11, 12, 15; 31.1.
[17] Deut. 7.1, 17, 22; 8.20; 9.1, 4, 5; 11.23; 12.2, 29, 30; 15.6; 17.14; 18.9, 14; 19.1; 20.15; 26.19.
[18] Deut. 6.14; 17.14, 19; 20.16.
[19] Neh. 5.8, 9, 17; 6.6, 16; 13.26.
[20] Ezra 3.3; 9.1, 2; 10.2, 11; Neh. 9.24, 30; 10.29, 31; cf. גוי הארץ, Ezra 6.21.
[21] Deut. 4.6, 9; 6.14; 7.6, 7, 14, 16; 10.15; 13.8; 14.2; 28.10, 37, 64; 30.3; 32.8.

Davies' doubts that the sharp distinction between Israel and the former inhabitants of the land would not be useful for a reform in the seventh century can perhaps be dispelled. Whatever different people had formed the people of Israel and Judah during a long historical process, their differences had fused for the most part in the late seventh century. Under those conditions, the Deuteronomic demand to expel the indigenous population from the land and keep apart from their horrible customs can be understood as an attempt to denounce specific Judaean and Israelite beliefs and practices as dangerous foreign influences that must be radically removed. The Deuteronomic reformers wanted to implant a new feeling of being a particular, 'holy people'[22] in Judaean society. Such a target would fit well the conditions of the seventh century, after Judah had suffered a century of Assyrian domination.

2.3. In his analysis, Philip Davies followed S.A. Geller (2000: 273-319) who stated that Deuteronomic legislators support an individual concept of covenant that would constitute a close parallel to the book of Nehemiah. Geller thinks that a new examination of Deuteronomy would conclude 'that the collectivity of the covenant community barely masks the fact that it is a radically new type of association of individuals' (2000: 300). Geller and Davies have rightly pointed out that many laws of Deuteronomy stress the responsibility of the individual, like Deut. 13.7-12. But their assessment that it 'negates the doctrine of collective responsibility for sin' can be questioned in this generality, because the rule of Deut. 24.16 that a son should not be punished for the sins of his father and vice versa is only valid for human jurisdiction. If God's jurisdiction is involved, then Deuteronomic legislators know a collective responsibility for appeasing God's anger (e.g. Deut. 21.1-9). And the same is valid for the Deuteronomic concept of covenant: in all passages where it is unfolded in some detail (Deut. 26.16-19; 28.69–29.28) it is always a collective 'you' who enters into the covenant with YHWH.[23] This collective shape of the Deuteronomic concept is a heritage of the Assyrian vassal-treaties, which gave the model. A closer comparison between the shapes of covenant in Deuteronomy and Ezra/Nehemiah reveals a decisive difference: what had been a collective covenant in accordance with the vassal-treaties in Deuteronomy became in Ezra 10 and Nehemiah 10 an individual commitment according to private contracts; no longer God but only the community made the agreement, and all leaders of the families of the different groups of society signed personally that they were going to commit themselves to specific moral and religious duties.[24]

---

[22] Deut. 7.6; 14.2, 21; 26.19.
[23] The same is true for the covenant of Josiah in 2 Kgs 23.1-3. It was the king as the representative of the people who made the covenant, the people only entered into it collectively, of course.
[24] I owe this insight to Dr Ralf Rothenbusch, with whom I co-operated in the 'Sonderforschungsbereich 493' in Münster.

Not by chance does a different terminology for such a self-commitment (עמנה instead of ברית) occur in Neh. 10.1. These differences in the covenant concepts are so fundamental that it is unlikely that both could come from the same post-exilic period. In my view, the parallels between the Deuteronomic concept of covenant and the Assyrian vassal-treaties make a dating in the seventh or at latest in the sixth century more probable.[25]

2.4. Philip Davies reflects on the somewhat utopian character of the law of kings (Deut. 17.14-20) in order to undermine the traditional seventh-century dating. Here he is in good company with G. Hölscher, who argued likewise that 'the ideological character of the Deuteronomic legislation' demonstrates 'that it could not have emerged in the pre-exilic Judah, but belongs to the period after the destruction' (1922: 228). Davies mainly pointed out that the radical limitations of monarchical power made in 17.16-20 were completely unrealistic: 'There are no plausible explanations why a king should accept a reform that deprives him of the essential powers of monarchy, justice and warfare' (see p. 74, below [401, present volume]). Admittedly, the law of kings sounds unrealistic to us; the question remains whether a later date would make its utopian concept more realistic. Moreover, there is no hint in the text that its author was looking forward to the restoration of an idealized kingship (cf. Nelson 2002: 223), in contrast to many exilic and postexilic prophetic texts.[26] Every attempt to date Deut. 17.14-20 in the Persian period is confronted with the problem that this law still held on to the divine election of the king according to the Davidic theology (Ps. 89.4, 20), whereas the Davidides disappeared from the political stage after the failure of Zerubbabel 519/518 BCE. After him, Nehemiah would be in accordance with that law in some way: a pious, selfless ruler, one who was obedient to God's law, as he presented himself (Neh. 5). And there were some people who wanted to make this Persian governor a king (6.6-7). Anyhow, he was no Davidide; therefore he and persons like him possibly did not influence the concept of Deut. 17.14-20.[27] So there are good reasons for dating the Deuteronomic law of kings during a period when Davidic kings were still on the throne.

Philip Davies overstates a little the radicalism of that law. As Nelson rightly points out, 'it does not forbid characteristic royal activities, but rather thoroughly limits them' (Nelson 2002: 222). That the king, who traditionally had been the supreme judge and legislator in the ancient Near East, is subjected to that law must be seen as the intended consequence of all Deuteronomic legislation: Moses as mediator of the divine law is promoted in order to replace the king as legislator (cf.

---

[25] Cf. also the close material parallels between Deut. 28.20-44 and the vassal treaties of Esarhaddon pointed out by Steymans 1995.
[26] Cf. Isa. 11.1-5; Jer. 23.1-7; Ezek. 34.23-24; 37.24-25; Mic. 5.1-5; Zech. 9.9-10, etc.
[27] The same would be true for Gedaliah, who otherwise would be also a good candidate for the ideal of a ruler with limited power.

Albertz 1997: 124-30). In reality that does not mean that 'authority is conferred exclusively on the priests', as Davies suggested (see p. 74, below [400–1, present volume]). According to Deut. 17.8-13 the supreme legal authority is conferred on a kind of upper court in Jerusalem, which consists of priests and laymen (v. 9). In the matters of warfare again priests and lay officials are provided with authority (20.1-9), but the functions of the king as military leader are not excluded (17.16).[28] What the Deuteronomic legislators intended with their radical law was nothing else than the creation of what was called later a 'constitutional monarchy'. The measures may have been impractical to some degree and somewhat utopian like other archaic reform models of the ancient world,[29] but the goal was very concrete and—as we can see in the later history of humankind—with other measures definitely realizable. But why should such a far reaching constitutional reform be conceptualized at a time when the legal limitation of monarchic power was completely irrelevant for Judah? In my view, the most probable period for dating the Deuteronomic law of kings are the reigns of Jehoiakim and Zedekiah, when the alliances with Egypt became a new threat for Judah (17.16) and when the Shaphanide scribes, who are the best candidates for having written the Deuteronomic law, resisted the ruling kings (Jer. 26.24; 36.9-26).[30]

2.5. Finally Philip Davies suggested that the centralization of the cult was a problem of the early Persian period, when after the reconstruction of the Jerusalem temple its claim to be the only authorized temple of YHWH had to be carried through against the claim of other cult places like that in the former capital Mizpeh. These suggestions are highly speculative. Whether there existed any YHWH-temple in Mizpeh during the period of exile is totally uncertain. The בית יהוה of Jer. 41.5, sometimes taken as a piece of evidence (cf. Veijola 1982: 190-210), probably refers to the temple in Jerusalem.[31] No archaeological evidence has been found. It seems that the sanctuary in Bethel played a role during

---

[28] Thus Davies' criticism of my thesis that the עם הארץ was the promoter of the Josianic reform falls short twice. First, his statement 'that these people would hardly have transferred authority over warfare or justice to the *priesthood*' (see p. 75, below [401, present volume]) does describe the intention of the Deuteronomic legislation correctly. Second, in my opinion a broad coalition promoted the Josianic reform, consisting not only of the עם הארץ but also of scribal circles like the Shaphanides, priestly circles like the Hilkiades, and prophets like Huldah and Jeremiah, cf. Albertz 1994: 201-203.

[29] Cf. Rüterswörden 1987: 102-105, who pointed out that the deprivation of the king's power as seen in Deut. 17 has some similarities in the Greek history of polity.

[30] The strange prohibition of bringing back the people to Egypt in order to multiply horses motivated by an oracle of YHWH (Deut. 17.16aβb), which seems to be inserted into its context, can easily have reference to the military alliance between Zedekiah and Psammetichus II in the years between 594 and 591 BCE. That alliance probably included the supply of Judaean mercenaries for Egypt, cf. Albertz 2002: 27. If this reference is accepted, we would have a *terminus ad quem* for the Deuteronomic law of kings.

[31] Not only in the tale of Jeremiah's woe (Jer. 38.14), but always in the book of Jeremiah the expression denotes the Jerusalem temple.

the exilic and early post-exilic period (cf. 2 Kgs 17.24-34a; cf. Albertz 1994: II, 525), but its legitimacy was heavily questioned. Again no temple has been found, so it is difficult to assess what really happened. We can only state, that in none of the post-exilic books of the Hebrew Bible—neither in Haggai and Zechariah nor in Ezra and Trito-Isaiah—is there any hint of a dispute on the question of whether any other sanctuary than Jerusalem should be reconstructed or put into operation. On the contrary, the prophet Haggai presupposed that no other sanctuary existed apart from the Jerusalem temple that could bring about the blessing over the land (Hag. 1.7-11). Thus, we cannot rule out that there were again rivalries between different YHWH sanctuaries in the post-exilic time,[32] but we can say that cult centralization was no serious problem of that period.

Thus we can conclude: None of Davies' arguments that Deuteronomy 12–26 should be better dated into the fifth century is convincing. There might be some doubts on a seventh century dating, but the Deuteronomic legislation fits rather less well the socio-political conditions and the literature of the Persian period.

3. Dating the Deuteronomistic History

Since 2 Kings does not know any Assyrian hegemony during the seventh century, Philip Davies questioned the historicity of the DtrH altogether. That seems to be appropriate in so far as Davies assigns a very late date to the DtrH. He has not dealt with it explicitly in the present article, but if he thinks of a fifth-century date for the earliest pieces of Deuteronomy, then the DtrH, which also included most of its later parts, cannot have emerged before the beginning of the fourth century. A History that is separated from Josiah's reform by more than 200 years can be of doubtful reliability. But the question must be raised: Is such a late dating of the DtrH possible at all?

The suggestion that the report of Josiah's reform was contemporary with the events, which is advocated by most scholars of the Cross school, has led I. Finkelstein and N.A. Silberman, among others, to believe that the DtrH is completely reliable on this point. But recently Th. Römer, who sympathizes with the Cross school, has shown convincingly that 2 Kings 22–23 'should be dated from the exilic period' (Römer 1997: 10).[33] What is true for this report is also true for

---

[32] The temple of YHW in Elephantine seems to be simply disregarded by the officials of Jerusalem, cf. Cowley 1923: 31.18-19. According to Lemaire 2002: 149-56, there existed a temple or shrine of YHW (בית יהו) in Idumaea during the fourth century. But the idea that somewhere in remote southern Palestine should have existed a proper cult centre where not only YHWH, but also the Babylonian God Nabû, and the Arabic Goddess 'Uzza were venerated, sounds to me very unlikely. Since the *Gattung* of text 283 is a cadaster, perhaps the names should be better interpreted as personal names of the land owners.

[33] Römer points to the Huldah oracle, which presupposes the exile (cf. 2 Kgs 22.16-17), and other features (1997: 6). As Hardmeier (2000: 81-145) has shown, the report must be seen as a mostly

the whole DtrH, whose climax it constitutes. Other evidence comes from 1 Kgs 8.46-53, where Solomon's prayer refers explicitly to the exile. Since it can be shown that this passage is no later addition but belongs to the Deuteronomistic edition of the chapter (8.1, 9, 14-30, 44-53, 55-61), which includes an older prayer in 8.31-43,[34] the exilic dating of DtrH becomes unavoidable. The last piece of evidence comes from the end of the DtrH (2 Kgs 25.27-30), which reports the release of Jehoiachin by Amel-Marduk in the year 562 BCE. Leaving apart the question to what extent the Deuteronomistic Historians used older material, it becomes likely that the years after 562 are the first possible date for the DtrH, as M. Noth (1957: 91) has already proposed. If one is not tied to the model of the Cross-school, the *terminus a quo* 562 BCE will be relatively certain.

The uncertainty concerns the *terminus ad quem*. Since several scholars are inclined to date the DtrH partly or completely into the Persian period (cf., among others, Würthwein 1994: 1-11; Römer 1997: 10-11), the question arises whether it is possible to define a latest possible date. Taking into consideration some older text- and literary-critical studies of A. Rofé (1985, 1987) and E. Tov (1985, 1986), R.F. Person (2002: 31-63) recently pleaded for a longer genesis of the DtrH, starting during the period of exile and coming to an end not before the time of Ezra. Person draws a vivid picture of what he called the 'Deuteronomic School' that he imagined as a scribal guild: after it had come home from Babylonia it supported Zerubbabel, but disillusioned with his failure and a later Persian supported administration, it developed an increasingly eschatological critique. Finally, Ezra's mission and the introduction of a new law led to its demise (Person 2002: 121-22, 135, 152). Whether that all happened, we do not know, but if we ask more concretely what passages would derive from the year 520 onwards, Person can name only a small number and mostly no others than those which have often been seen to be the latest.[35] Sometimes the historical setting given by Person remains obscure; for example, Person dates Deut. 30.1-14 during both the time of Zerubbabel and the period after him. Moreover, it remains strange that in none of the passages can we find an allusion to any event that we know from the period between Zerubbabel and Ezra: neither the reconstruction of the temple, nor the reconstruction of the Jerusalem wall is mentioned. So Person's results are not

---

coherent literary unit, which included in 2 Kgs 23.4-15 an older arrangement of cultic reform measures (*waw-perfect* sentences). Only a few verses are probably later additions: 23.15*, 16-18, 19-20, 24a.

[34] 1 Kgs 8.46-53 belongs to the same literary layer as 8.44-45 (cf. ושמעת השמים in vv. 45, 49 in distinction from the expressions used in the *Vorlage*, cf. vv. 32, 34, 36, 39, 43; and the use of דרך in the sense 'towards' in vv. 44, 48, etc.); both passages are bound to the Deuteronomistic introduction (cf. v. 44 and 18.19; vv. 48 and 16). The Deuteronomistic reworking can be seen by the fact that vv. 44-45 is a doublet of vv. 33-34. Moreover, the passage 8.46-53 contains many parallels to other Deuteronomistic texts, especially to Deut. 4 and 30.1-11.

[35] So Deut. 4.29-31; 30.1-14; 1 Kgs 8; 2 Kgs 17; 25.27-30 and some others: Josh. 1.1-11; Judg. 3.1-6; 17.6; 21.25; 1 Sam. 16–18; 2 Sam. 7.1-17; 23.1-7; 1 Kgs 21.1-20.

really convincing. There might have been smaller additions and limited alterations as the differences between the text traditions (MT, LXX, Samaritanus) show, but they are less substantial and may be even later than Person thinks. Rather, his investigation demonstrates that the Persian period, apart from its very beginning (539–520 BCE), did not leave any clear footprint in the DtrH.[36] The substantial redactions of DtrH seem to have happened earlier.

In this connection, it is of crucial importance that, apart from a few exceptions that will be discussed below, DtrH reveals no knowledge that the exile would ever come to an end. That can be demonstrated by 1 Kgs 8.46-50, one of the passages that clearly reflect the experience of the exilic period. According to vv. 49-50 God is asked to hear the prayers of the exiles in order to forgive them 'and grant them mercy before those who have taken them captive so that they may show them mercy'. In this passage, there is no hint of knowledge that the mighty Babylonian empire could ever collapse, there are no expectations that God would liberate the exiles and bring them home. The only hope is the wish to find mercy in the eyes of the Babylonian officials, to whose despotism they are hopelessly subjected.[37] What is meant more concretely can be demonstrated by the parallel passage in Jer. 42.12: the wish that the Babylonian king would not also punish all Judaeans for the murder of Gedaliah but would spare those who were loyal to him. The Deuteronomistic Historians describe a similar event at the very end of their work (2 Kgs 25.27-30): the Babylonian king Amel-Marduk released Jehoiachin from prison and restored his position of an honoured vassal. Probably Nebuchadnezzar had sentenced him to be his hostage because of the murder of Gedaliah by a member of the royal family.[38] When after his accession Amel-Marduk reprieved Jehoiachin, he actually 'showed him mercy' in accordance with the prayer of 2 Kgs 8.49-50.

Thus, 1 Kgs 8.46-50 and 2 Kgs 25.27-30 share the same horizon of hope and probably belong to the same literary layer. Both do not expect the downfall of the Babylonian empire, but a better treatment under the Babylonian government. Thus, these texts cannot have been written after 539 BCE, when the Babylonian empire was destroyed. Since there is no hint of a major political change, it is very probable that these passages emerged before Cyrus' impressive victory over Lydia in 547/46 BCE. As 2 Kgs 25.27-30 constitutes the compositional ending of the DtrH, therefore most of that history can be dated between 562 and 547 BCE.

---

[36] Römer (1997: 11) admitted this fact, when he wrote: 'We may still ask why are there no direct allusions to the Persian period in DH?' But his answer, that the Deuteronomistic Historians—like modern ones—avoided including their own present, is not convincing. The present can be excluded or not, but in every historical work, whether ancient or modern, the reader can find out from what temporal perspective it was written.
[37] Cf. the same expression נתן רחמים לפני in Gen. 43.14; Jer. 42.12; Neh. 1.11; Ps. 106.46; Dan. 1.9.
[38] For the historical reconstruction of this event and its far reaching consequences, see Albertz 2001: 63-64, 89-91.

There are only two passages in the present DtrH that move beyond this glimmer of hope. The first is Deut. 4.25-32, the second Deut. 30.1-10. All of the long sermon of Deut. 4.1-40 is an addition to its context, which presupposes the introduction to DtrH (Deut. 1–3),[39] but is still not known by it. Nevertheless, its shape is Deuteronomistic in style and theology. Within 4.25-32, which bends the listener's eyes to the future, vv. 29-31 seem to be again a later addition (cf. Nelson 2002: 62, 68). After giving a grim portrayal of the exile in vv. 25-28, the text turns abruptly to a positive viewpoint:

> You will seek Yhwh your God from there and you will find him, if only you search for him with all your heart and all your being. In your distress when all these things have happened to you, in the days to come[40] you will return to Yhwh your God and obey him. For a merciful God is Yhwh your God. He will not desert or destroy you. He will not forget the covenant with your ancestors that he swore them.[41] (Deut. 4.29-31)

In this passage there is still no hope for a return to the homeland, though its author expects a drastic change between God and his people. Yhwh will become attainable again for his people, and the people will return to its God. Israel will no longer be confronted with Yhwh's jealous anger, but will experience his mercy again. The same kind of hope expressed by a very similar wording can be found in Jer. 29.10-14a.[42] As I could show elsewhere, this passage belongs to the second edition of the Deuteronomistic book of Jeremiah (JerD²).[43] This edition can probably be dated during the years 545–540, just before the downfall of the Babylonian empire.[44] During the same years the anonymous prophetical group whom we call Deutero-Isaiah proclaimed that the period of God's wrath was over and a new period of God's mercy would begin (Isa. 40.1-2). So it is highly probable that a Deuteronomistic Historian—by adding Deut. 4.29-31—actualized the DtrH during those years when a drastic change in the Near Eastern history could be foreseen.

---

[39] Cf. Deut. 4.3-4 and 3.29; 4.21-22 and 3.23-28. The chs. 1–3 of Deuteronomy do not prepare for the sermon. With regard to the content, Deut. 4 interprets Deut. 5.
[40] The term באחרית הימים has nothing to do with eschatology as Person (2002: 125-26) suggests, but means a just and fairer future like in Gen. 49.1; Num. 24.14; Deut. 31.29; Jer. 30.24.
[41] The translation is taken from Nelson 2002: 58-59.
[42] Jer. 29.14bβ does not occur in LXX and is a later addition.
[43] Albertz 2001: 326-55; in my opinion the second edition consists of Jer. 1–45* without the book of consolation (Jer. 30–31) and its narrative transition (Jer. 32–35).
[44] Jer. 29.10 reckons a 70-year duration of the Babylonian dominion. The most probable solution to identify the beginning of that period can be seen in Nebuchadnezzar's accession to the throne in 605 or his first regnal year 604 BCE (cf. Schmid 1996: 224-25). Then the 70-years period would end in the years 535 or 534. Since the collapse of the Babylonian empire happened some years earlier, the passage must have been written before the year 539.

The second passage, Deut. 30.1-10, has so many significant features in common that it may have been written by the same author.[45] However, R.D. Nelson (2002: 348) is right to state that '30.1-11 goes a step further than 4.29-31 to envision the return home from the exile'. Along with that, God promised to multiply his people and make them prosperous again (v. 5). The wide horizon of hope reminds one of the promises of salvation made in the 'Book of Consolation' (Jer. 30–31), although it is still less detailed. In my view, those belong to the third edition of the Deuteronomistic book of Jeremiah (JerD³).[46] Likewise the hope that God would circumcise the heart of his people (Deut. 30.6) and by this would restore the broken relationship from his side has its closest parallels in JerD³ (Jer. 31.31-33; 32.37-41; cf. Jer. 4.4 and Deut. 10.16). JerD³ can be dated with some probability in the years between 525 and 521/0 BCE, after Cambyses' campaign against Egypt focused the Persian interest on the southwest of the empire, including Palestine, and before Darius conquered Babylon, which rebelled against him.[47] Thus, it is very probable that Deut. 30.1-10 also has to be dated in these dramatic years when, after the Gaumata rebellion and the usurpation of Darius, the Judaean minority got the first chance of repatriation. Both passages, Deut. 4.29-31 and 30.1-10, constitute a hopeful frame around the book of Deuteronomy. Thus, their insertion is part of a deliberate redaction of the DtrH. The time when that took place cannot be determined exactly, but it is improbable that it happened much later than the year 520 BCE, when after the return of Zerubbabel and Joshua the restoration in Judah was started. Since the discernible latest passages of the DtrH belong still in the late sixth and not in the fifth century as R.F. Person suggested, its *terminus ad quem* can probably be fixed around the year 520 BCE. However, the concept and most of the text of that history was largely drafted before the rise of Cyrus in 547 BCE.

In the event that the DtrH emerged largely between 562 and 547 and its later parts followed until the year 520, then several conclusions can be drawn which are of some importance for the assessment of the Josianic reform. First, we get another important confirmation that the book of Deuteronomy could not have emerged in the later Persian period but must have been written earlier. Since Deuteronomy 4 presupposes not only the Deuteronomic core in chs. 12–26, but also includes its admonitory frame in Deut. 4.44–30.20, the book of Deuteronomy must have been largely finished by 540. Second, since most of the DtrH was

---

[45] So Nelson 2002: 348. The phrase שוב עד־יהוה—with the preposition עד instead of normal אל—occurs within the DtrH only in Deut. 4.30 and 30.2, and is extremely infrequent in the Hebrew Bible (Hos. 14.2; Isa. 19.22; Lam. 3.40); the parallelism of returning to YHWH and hearing his voice occurs in 4.30 and 30.2; cf. 30.8, 10, the phrase 'with all your heart and all your being' in 4.29 and 30.2, 6, 10, etc.

[46] Cf. Jer. 30.18-22; 31.10-14, 21-22, 23-26; 32.37-44; 50.17-20, 33-34; 51.34-37. In my view, JerD³ consists of Jer. 1–51*, including the book of consolation and the oracles against foreign nations, cf. Albertz 2001: 255-60.

[47] Cf. the last oracle of the book of Jeremiah (51.58), which expects the occupation of Babylon.

composed during the 15 years following the release of Jehoiachin (562), their authors were not too far away from the period when Josiah's reform was carried through (622–609 BCE). The time covers just the range of 47 to 75 years.[48] This would mean that the Deuteronomistic Historians had to be aware that there were still some eye-witnesses alive and that there were a lot of people among their audience whose fathers or grandfathers had participated in Josiah's government. So they could not invent fabulous fairy tales, whatever religious ideology they wanted to promote. They could overstate some measures and they could ignore others—and they did both: they generalized the cult reform, but they ignored the social and national reform attempts—nevertheless, they could not lie. This means that the reliability of the DtrH for the events of the late seventh and early sixth century can be assessed as good, if we take its ideology into account. For example, as it is obvious that the Deuteronomistic Historians shared a nationalistic view and therefore praised revolts against the Assyrian dominance (2 Kgs 17.2-4; 18.5-6), there is no wonder that they ignored the re-establishment of the Assyrian domination under Manasseh.[49] As far as reliability is concerned, we cannot extrapolate conclusions from their treatment of foreign policy to that of domestic policy, as Philip Davies did.[50]

Apart from the temporal proximity, there is another strong argument that excludes the suggestion of a pure invention. The Josianic reform does not really fit the DtrH. According to the theological concept of the Deuteronomistic Historians, Josiah's exceptional cult reform that met YHWH's demands as never before should have opened Judah to a wonderful future. At least, it should have averted the catastrophe, the destruction of Judah and the deportations of major parts of its inhabitants. The historians had a great deal of trouble, to bring the course of history in line with the Josianic reform: they actually invented(!) a period of horrible apostasy under Manasseh, claimed that this provoked YHWH to decide on destruction (2 Kgs 21.10-15), and explained that this decision could not be removed by Josiah's reform, but only delayed (23.25-27). The concept of such an unchangeable destiny contradicts their effort to show God's morality in history. Their will to keep the Josianic reform and to defend its correctness forced the Deuteronomistic Historians to distort their own theology in some way. So it must have been such an important event for them that they could not deny it.

---

[48] Handy (1995: 252-75) rightly points out that the report of Josiah's reform is not contemporary, but 'cannot have been written prior to the sixth century' (p. 259). But when he concludes that the report cannot be reliable, because it would have been written 'a century or more' after the events of Josiah's reign (p. 275), then it becomes apparent, that he has no clear idea about the *terminus ad quem* of the DtrH.
[49] They were also forced to do so by incorporating the nationalistic Isaiah narrative (2 Kgs 18.9-10; 18.13–19.37*) into their history, which asserted the departure of the Assyrians; cf. Hardmeier 1989. The Deuteronomistic Historians also ignored that Jehu became a vassal of Assyria as can be seen and read on the 'Black Obelisk' of Shalmanesar III.
[50] See pp. 65-77, below [391–403, present volume].

4. The Historical Evidence

Finally, Philip Davies argued that the basic historical conditions during the late seventh century did not admit any significant reform movement. In his view, after the decline of the Assyrian power in Palestine, Egypt took over the hegemony directly. After having been a vassal of Assyria, Josiah became immediately an Egyptian vassal and did not have the scope of action for any bigger changes. In this assessment, Davies agrees with H. Niehr, who stated: 'All of these statements result in a picture of Josiah as an Egyptian vassal, unable to establish an enlarged kingdom or to pursue independent politics'.[51]

However, it must be remembered that such a historical reconstruction, which has now become more popular,[52] is not attested by any source but is a conclusion of more general considerations. Neither the archaeological results of Meṣad Ḥashavyahu nor the mysterious death of Josiah at Megiddo convey a clear picture.[53] How Assyrian rule collapsed in Judah, Samaria, and the other Palestinian provinces, and when and to what degree it was replaced by Egyptian rule, we do not know exactly. Biblical sources rather suggest a break and a certain vacuum of power until the Egyptians established their hegemony over Palestine in the year 609 BCE. In Isa. 8.23b–9.6 the withdrawal of the Assyrian armies could be compared with a great victory and is experienced as liberation.[54] And according to Jer. 2.36-37 influential groups of the population of the former Northern Kingdom obviously believed that the Egyptians could help them to restore their political independence, possibly against Josiah's national ambitions (cf. Albertz 2003: 228-30). Perhaps Josiah's strange interference in Megiddo has to do with such competing political interest. There seemed to be unsettled political conditions in Judah and Israel for some years, which could raise very different expectations and options.

---

[51] 'Aus allen diesen Angaben ergibt sich das Bild eines ägyptischen Vasallen Joschija, der keineswegs ein Großreich etablieren und eine eigenständige Politik verfolgen konnte' (Niehr 1995: 44).

[52] Cf. Miller and Hayes 1986: 383-91; Na'aman 1991: 40-41, 52-53; Ahlström 1993: 763-67, 778-79.

[53] See the interpretation of Na'aman, referred to by Davies (pp. 65-67, below [391–93, present volume]). Miller and Hayes 1986: 388, draw from Jer. 2.16-18, 36-37 the conclusion that in Palestine 'there was a hegemony shared between the Nile and Mesopotamian superpowers'. But this interpretation is very doubtful. Jer. 2.4–4.2 is addressed to Israel, the people of the former Northern Kingdom (2.4). The first passage, Jer. 2.14-18, does not deal with the present but with the past (cf. *waw* consecutive imperfect in v. 15), when the Northern Kingdom pursued its ruinous seesaw politics between Assyria and Egypt (cf. Hos. 5.12-14). On the contrary, Jer. 2.36-37 (and also the actualizing verse, 2.16) deals with present dangers and warns the northern brethren to place their hope in Egypt because they will fail, as their hope of Assyria had failed in the past. It can be suggested that—after becoming free from Assyrian rule—the population in the North hoped to win the restoration of their state with the help of Egypt. Thus, during the late-seventh century Egypt clearly succeeded Assyria in Palestine; cf. Albertz 2003.

[54] That Isa. 8.23b–9.6 is to be dated in the late seventh century and refers to the young king Josiah was convincingly shown by Barth 1977: 141-77.

Whatever concrete scenario one might imagine, however, it is interesting to notice that even most of those scholars who think that the domination over Palestine passed uninterrupted from the Assyrians to the Egyptians do not want to deny the possibility of the Josianic reform. According to N. Na'aman the emphasis of the Egyptian rule 'was placed on control of the valley districts and the coast, whereas the mountain areas were considered of secondary importance' (1991: 40). So, in his view the Egyptian vassalage of Josiah was of a more nominal kind. The same is true for Finkelstein and Silberman who restricted the Egyptian interest 'mainly to the coast' and saw the path 'open for a final fulfilment of Judahite ambitions' (2001: 283). Thus, in any case the change of hegemony in Palestine during the last third of the seventh century opened a space where a cultic, social, and national reform could take place in Judah. Even a limited expansion of Judah to the north on the hill country is conceivable under such international conditions.[55]

Admittedly, apart from the report in 2 Kings 22–23, other sources for the Josianic reform are rather scarce. The archaeologists could not provide anything essential for it.[56] Only a little bit more did the biblical scholars! The often repeated argument that contemporary texts like the book of Jeremiah[57] do not know anything of the reform is not correct. The passages of Jer. 5.4-6 and 8.7-8 refer explicitly to a law of YHWH that should give advice to the people, especially to the learned and wealthy upper class, but was neglected after Josiah's death. In Jer. 3.22–4.2; 31.2-6 the Israelites of the former Northern Kingdom are invited to come to Jerusalem and worship YHWH there, in accordance with Josiah's national policy. And a closer reading of Jeremiah 2–6 reveals that the accusation against syncretism, which played a prominent role in Jeremiah's preaching to the brethren in the north (2.4–4.2), does not appear in his preaching to the Judaeans at all (4.3–6.30), which could testify to the results of Josiah's reform indirectly. Sometimes it is said that the different kinds of syncretism and foreign cult practices in the accusation in Ezek. 8.7-18 contradicted any Josianic reform; but this event belongs to a much later period (593/2 BCE), 29 years after the cult reform (622 BCE). Moreover, it must be taken into account that Ezekiel could easily misunderstand or overstate a rumour from Jerusalem that he heard in Babylonia.[58]

---

[55] Heltzer (2000) thinks that the seventh-century bulla of the Shlomo Moussaieff Collection would testify that Josiah annexed even such a northern place like 'Arubboth in the vicinity of Taanach as early as 630/629 BCE from the Assyrians. But the evidence remains doubtful.

[56] Cf. Finkelstein and Silberman 2001: 287-88. The little that was found was partly made unusable by improper excavation; cf. the unclear closure or abandonment of the temple in Arad. The only possible evidence is provided by the seal impressions of the late seventh century, which include only names, sometimes decorated with some floral ornaments, but are lacking the religious, often astral icons, in contrast to the seals before, cf. Uehlinger 1995: 67-70, as well as his contribution to the present volume (pp. 279-316 [reprinted as pp. 425–64, below]). But they also can mean just a higher level of literate persons or simply a new fashion.

[57] So again Kaiser 1984: 134.

[58] Why Ezekiel personally charged with apostasy a member of the Shaphan family (Ezek. 8.12) who had been one of the promoters of the reform remains obscure.

Thus, the body of evidence that the Josianic reform happened during the late seventh century could have been much better. Often we possess only clues, not hard facts. Philip Davies is to be commended for not only denying the Josianic reform and pushing the book of Deuteronomy into any later period but also trying to give reasons for a fifth-century dating. But in my view, the evidence given by him is rather less convincing than that of the traditional hypothesis.

Bibliography

Ahlström, G.W. 1993. *The History of Ancient Palestine from the Palaeolithic Period to Alexander's Conquest* (JSOTSup, 146; Sheffield: Sheffield Academic Press).

Albertz, R. 1987. 'Israel I: Altes Testament', in *Theologische Realenzyklopädie* XVI: 368-79.

Albertz, R. 1994. *A History of Israelite Religion in the Old Testament Period* (OTL; 2 vols.; Louisville, KY: Westminster/John Knox Press).

Albertz, R. 1997. 'Die Theologisierung des Rechts im Alten Israel', in *idem* (ed.), *Religion und Gesellschaft. Studien zu ihrer Wechselbeziehung in den Kulturen des Antiken Vorderen Orients* (Alter Orient und Altes Testament, 248; Münster: Ugarit-Verlag): 115-32.

Albertz, R. 2001. *Die Exilszeit, Das 6. Jahrhundert v. Chr.* (Biblische Enzyklopädie, 7; Stuttgart: Kohlhammer).

Albertz, R. 2002. 'Die Zerstörung des Jerusalemer Tempels 587 v. Chr.: Historische Einordnung und religionspolitische Bedeutung', in J. Hahn (ed.), *Zerstörungen des Jerusalemer Tempels: Geschehen—Wahrnehmung—Bewältigung* (Wissenschaftliche Untersuchungen zum Neuen Testament, 147; Tübingen: Mohr Siebeck): 23-39.

Albertz, R. 2003. 'Jer 2–6 und die Frühzeitverkündigung Jeremias', in *idem, Geschichte und Theologie: Studien zur Exegese des Alten Testaments und zur Religionsgeschichte Israels* (ed. I. Kottsieper and J. Wöhrle; BZAW, 326; Berlin: W. de Gruyter): 209-38 (orig. *ZAW* 94 [1982]: 20-27).

Barth, H. 1977. *Die Jesaja-Worte in der Josiazeit: Israel und Assur als Thema einer produktiven Neuinterpretation der Jesajaüberlieferung* (WMANT, 48; Neukirchen-Vluyn: Neukirchener Verlag).

Blenkinsopp, J. 1988. *Ezra–Nehemiah: A Commentary* (OTL; Philadelphia: Westminster Press).

Cowley, A. 1923. *Aramaic Papyri of the Fifth Century B.C.* (Oxford: Clarendon Press).

Davies, P.R. 1992. *In Search of 'Ancient Israel'* (JSOTSup, 148; Sheffield: Sheffield Academic Press).

Dietrich, W., and Th. Naumann. 1995. *Die Samuelbücher* (Erträge der Forschung, 287; Darmstadt: Wissenschaftliche Buchgesellschaft).

Finkelstein, I., and N.A. Silberman. 2001. *The Bible Unearthed: Archaeology's New View of Ancient Israel and the Origin of Its Sacred Texts* (New York: Free Press).

Finkelstein, I., and N.A. Silberman. 2002. *Keine Posaunen vor Jericho. Die archäologische Wahrheit über die Bibel* (Munich: Beck).

Geller, S.A. 2000. 'The God of the Covenant', in B.N. Porter (ed.), *One God or the Many: Concepts of Divinity in the Ancient World* (Transactions of the Casco Bay Assyriological Institute, 1; New York: The New Yorker Collection): 273-319.

Gross, W. (ed.). 1995. *Jeremia und die 'deuteronomistische Bewegung'* (BBB, 98; Weinheim: Beltz Athenäum).

Gunneweg, A.H.J. 1987. *Nehemia* (KAT, XIX, 2; Gütersloh: Gütersloher Verlagshaus).
Handy, L.K. 1995. 'Historical Probability and the Narrative of Josiah's Reform in 2 Kings', in S.W. Holloway and L.K. Handy (eds.), *The Pitcher is Broken: Memorial Essays for Gösta W. Ahlström* (JSOTSup, 190; Sheffield: Sheffield Academic Press): 252-75.
Hardmeier, Chr. 1989. *Prophetie im Streit vor dem Untergang Judas. Erzählkommunikative Studien zur Entstehungssituation der Jesaja- und Jeremiaerzählungen in II Reg 18–20 und Jer 37–40* (BZAW, 187; Berlin: W. de Gruyter).
Hardmeier, Chr. 2000. 'König Joschia in der Klimax des DtrG (2Reg 22f.) und das vordtr Dokument einer Kultreform am Residenzort (23,4-15*)', in R. Lux (ed.), *Erzählte Geschichte: Beiträge zur narrativen Kultur im Alten Israel* (Biblisch-Theologische Studien, 40; Neukirchen-Vluyn: Neukirchener Verlag): 81-145.
Heltzer, M. 2000. 'Some Questions Concerning the Economic Policy of Josiah, King of Judah', *IEJ* 50: 105-108.
Hölscher, G. 1922. 'Komposition und Ursprung des Deuteronomiums', *ZAW* 40: 161-255.
Kaiser, O. 1984. *Einleitung in das Alte Testament: Eine Einführung in Ergebnisse und Probleme* (Gütersloh: Gütersloher Verlagshaus, 5th edn): 132-34.
Karrer, Chr. 2001. *Das Ringen um die Verfassung Judas. Eine Studie zu den theologisch-politischen Vorstellungen im Esra–Nehemia–Buch* (BZAW, 308; Berlin: W. de Gruyter).
Kellermann, U. 1967. *Nehemia. Quellen, Überlieferung, Geschichte* (BZAW, 102; Berlin: W. de Gruyter).
Lemaire, A. 2002. *Nouvelle inscriptions araméennes d'Idumée*, II (Transeuphratène, Supplement, 9; Paris: J. Gabalda).
Miller, J.M., and J.H. Hayes. 1986. *A History of Ancient Israel and Judah* (Philadelphia: Westminster Press).
Mowinckel, S. 1923. 'Die vorderasiatischen Königs- und Fürsteninschriften. Eine stilistische Studie', in H. Schmidt (ed.), *Eucharisterion* (Festschrift H. Gunkel; FRLANT, 36; Göttingen: Vandenhoeck & Ruprecht): 278-322.
Na'aman, N. 1991. 'The Kingdom of Judah under Josiah', *TA* 18: 3-71.
Nelson, R.D. 2002. *Deuteronomy: A Commentary* (OTL; Louisville, KY: Westminster/John Knox Press).
Niehr, H. 1995. 'Die Reform des Joschija: Methodische, historische und religionsgeschichtliche Aspekte', in Gross (ed.) 1995: 33-52.
Noth, M. 1957 [1943]. *Überlieferungsgeschichtliche Studien* (Tübingen: Max Niemeyer, 2nd edn).
Person, Jr, R.F. 2002. *The Deuteronomic School: History, Social Setting, and Literature* (Studies in Biblical Literature, 2; Atlanta: Society of Biblical Literature).
Reinmuth, T. 2002. *Der Bericht Nehemias. Zur literarischen Eigenart, traditionsgeschichtlichen Prägung und innerbiblischen Rezeption des Ich-Berichts Nehemias* (OBO, 183; Fribourg: Universitätsverlag).
Renz, J., and W. Röllig. 1995. *Handbuch der althebräischen Epigraphik*, I,1 (Darmstadt: Wissenschaftliche Buchgesellschaft).
Rofé, A. 1985. 'The Monotheistic Argumentation in Deuteronomy 4.32-40: Content, Composition, and Text', *VT* 35: 434-45.
Rofé, A. 1987. 'The Battle of David and Goliath: Folklore, Theology, Eschatology', in J. Neusner, A. Levine and E.S. Frerichs (eds.), *Judaic Perspectives on Ancient Israel* (Philadelphia: Fortress Press): 117-51.
Römer, Th.C. 1997. 'Transformations in Deuteronomistic and Biblical Historiography: On the "Book-Finding" and Other Literary Strategies', *ZAW* 109: 1-11.

Rudolph, W. 1949. *Esra und Nehemia* (HAT, I, 20; Tübingen: J.C.B. Mohr).
Rütersworden, U. 1987. *Von der politischen Gemeinschaft zur Gemeinde. Studien zu Dt 16,18–18,22* (BBB, 65; Frankfurt/Bonn: Peter Hanstein Verlag).
Schmid, K. 1996. *Buchgestalten des Jeremiabuches: Untersuchungen zur Redaktions- und Rezeptionsgeschichte von Jer 30–33 im Kontext des Buches* (WMANT, 72; Neukirchen-Vluyn: Neukirchener Verlag).
Steymans, H.U. 1995. *Deuteronomium 28 und die Adê zur Thronbesteigung Asarhaddons: Segen und Fluch im Alten Orient und Israel* (OBO, 145; Fribourg: Universitätsverlag).
Tov, E. 1985. 'The Composition of I Samuel 16–18 in the Light of the Septuagint Version', in J. Tigay (ed.), *Empirical Models for Biblical Criticism* (Philadelphia: University of Pennsylvania Press): 97-130.
Tov, E. 1986. 'The Nature of Differences between MT and LXX', in D. Barthélemy *et al.* (eds.), *The Story of David and Goliath: Textual and Literary Criticism* (OBO, 73; Fribourg: Universitätsverlag): 19-46.
Uehlinger, Chr. 1995. 'Gab es eine joschijanische Kultreform? Plädoyer für ein begründetes Minimum', in Gross (ed.) 1995: 57-89.
Veijola, T. 1982. *Verheißung in der Krise. Studien zur Literatur und Theologie der Exilszeit anhand des 89. Psalms* (Annales Academiae Scientiarum Fennicae, Series B, 220; Helsinki: Suomalainen Tiedeakatemia).
Williamson, H.G.M. 1985. *Ezra, Nehemiah* (WBC, 16; Waco, TX: Word Books).
Würthwein, E. 1994. 'Erwägungen zum sog. deuteronomistischen Geschichtswerk: Eine Skizze', in *idem, Studien zum Deuteronomistischen Geschichtswerk* (BZAW, 277; Berlin: W. de Gruyter): 1-11.

Was There a Cult Reform under King Josiah? The Case for a Well-Grounded Minimum*

Christoph Uehlinger

Preliminary Remarks

The original version of the following article, which was published in German in 1995, originated as an invited response to a paper presented by Herbert Niehr at a conference on Jeremiah and Deuteronomism held in Frankfurt on the Main by Catholic biblical scholars (Gross [ed.] 1995).[1] Although the present version has been partly rewritten in order to stand as an autonomous study, it still follows the outlines of the original paper. As a rule, responses cannot address a topic in its full complexity, but concentrate instead on a limited number of issues. In the present instance, these include basic considerations on historical concepts and methodology, discussions of selected archaeological material whose interpretation may or may not elucidate our understanding of Josiah's reform, and an historical evaluation of selected aspects of the so-called 'reform notices' (*Reformnotizen*) preserved in 2 Kings 23. In spite of its peculiar character as a literary tradition preserved for religious purposes, the biblical text remains the most relevant source when we deal with 'Josiah's cult reform'—as long as no other, extrabiblical document closer to the time of Josiah refers to anything resembling measures of cultic realignment. 'Josiah's reform', regardless of whether exposed by 'maximalists' or 'minimalists', is essentially a scholarly construct built upon the biblical tradition; without that tradition no one would look out for a 'cult reform' when studying the archaeology of Judah of the Iron Age II C.

---

* Bruce Wallace (Emory University) is to be credited for the draft translation of the original German paper into English, and Lester Grabbe (University of Hull) for his unfailing editorial support.
[1] Cf. Niehr 1995; Uehlinger 1995.

Ideally, therefore, the quest for the historical reality that may have given rise to the literary traditions about 'Josiah's reform'[2] should start with an independent examination of the biblical text and its own redactional history, as far as it can be reconstructed by historical-critical argument. Our first task would thus be to ascertain the text which is at the basis of our literary tradition.[3] Neither this nor the ensuing literary- and redaction-critical analysis can be accomplished here.[4] As for the other side of the argument, selected evidence collected from the archaeological, epigraphical, and iconographical record, my presentation will summarize much that has been laid out in greater detail in a book co-authored in 1992 with O. Keel.[5]

What sense does it make to repeat an argument more than ten years after its inception? New material has surfaced since, and long-known material appears in another light as a result of renewed analysis.[6] A mass of secondary literature on Josiah's reform published since 1994 has added to the multiplicity of views and the complexity of issues.[7] While I have tried to take stock occasionally of new evidence and arguments, doing so systematically would have required me to write a completely different article. The fact that the original paper continues over the years to be referred to regularly in the secondary literature, however, may justify its updated translation here.

* * *

The question of the extent, meaning, purpose and main actors of King Josiah's cultic reform is discussed in Old Testament scholarship as a problem not only of biblical exegesis but also of Israelite and Judahite religious history. Almost 200

---

[2] Note that I do not address the Chronicler's version of the story, which appears in 2 Chron. 34–35, nor later works of Jewish historiography.

[3] See now Schenker 2004: 34-84 for detailed comparisons of the Hebrew and Greek textual traditions.

[4] After the original version of this paper had been published, several authors, approaching the biblical tradition from a very different angle, arrived at conclusions which considerably overlap those defended here regarding reform measures that might be considered historical. Cf. Hardmeier 2000, a translated and revised version of which appears in this volume, above pp. 123-63; Arneth 2001: 189-216.

[5] *GGG*; *GGIG* (English translation of *GGG* 3rd edn). I shall refer to the English version (henceforth abbreviated *GGIG*) except for the 'Anhang' (*GGG* §§251-62), which was written for the German 4th edition and not yet available to the English translation.

[6] Especially the shrine located in the Judahite fortress of Arad, for which see below, Section 2.1, but also finds from neighbouring areas which put evidence from Judah into proper perspective. The presence of first class forgeries among recently published glyptic and epigraphic material requires even more circumspection than before when critically considering unprovenanced data.

[7] Cf., *inter alia*, Dever 1994; Rainey 1994; Einykel 1995 (for which see my review, Uehlinger 1997); Toloni 1998; Sweeney 2001: 40-51; Barrick 2002; Fried 2002; and studies mentioned above, n. 4.

years ago, W.M.L. de Wette identified the 'Torah Scroll' (ספר־התורה, 2 Kgs 22.8, 11) or 'Scroll of the Covenant' (ספר־הברית, 23.2, 21), which according to 2 Kings 22 was found in the Jerusalem Temple in the eighteenth year of Josiah, with the original scroll of Deuteronomy.[8] Ever since this identification, the reform itself has continued to be regarded as *the* key datum not only for Pentateuchal criticism but also for the religious history of pre-exilic Judah, as 'the event which, despite all uncertainties, is our firmest point of orientation' in the realm of the 'deuteronomistic phenomenon' (Lohfink 1987: 460).[9] In recent years, however, the historicity of the reform and the reliability of our sources have been thoroughly called into question by a number of biblical scholars. Among the most radical critics, C. Levin has advocated a *Grundschicht* within 2 Kings 22–23, which, for a few verse fragments left to the historian, would reduce the cult reform to a mere fantasy.[10] Taking Levin's minimal *Grundschicht* as a starting-point for his own religio-historical evaluation, H. Niehr (1995) has equally minimalized the reform's extent and significance on the basis of a sharp distinction between so-called 'primary' and 'secondary' sources.[11] Others have argued the lack of independent archaeological evidence that could substantiate the claim of a significant cultic and/or administrative reform under King Josiah.[12]

As a result, what we thought to be a firm point of orientation only a decade ago has turned into a long series of question marks: Was there a cult reform at all during the reign of king Josiah, or should we understand the report of 2 Kings 22–23, a 'secondary source' at best, as merely a literary fiction? Was the reform—however its contours are to be sketched in detail—part of the *mainstream* history of seventh-century (or 'pre-exilic') Judahite state religion, or just a convenient invention of a small group of later ('exilic' or even 'post-exilic') Deuteronomists?[13] If there was a reform in the time of Josiah, did it include, as 2 Kings 23 contends, a complex set of cult-political measures carried out quite systematically beyond the Jerusalem Temple, with dramatic consequences for local sanctuaries (במות) all over Judah and even in regions that had formerly belonged to the Northern Kingdom (esp. Bethel)?[14] Or did it merely consist of the diversion to Jerusalem of taxes that had hitherto benefited some local shrines of the Judean countryside?[15] Should one, then, speak of an actual *cult* reform at all?[16] Was it not, rather, an

---

[8] But cf. Paul 1985.
[9] Cf. Lohfink 1985; 1991a: 210.
[10] Levin 1984.
[11] For a more recent exposition of his methodological and material position, see Niehr 1999.
[12] Most recently Fried 2002 (with references to earlier literature).
[13] On the sociological contours of 'Deuteronomism', cf. Albertz 1992: 304-66, 390-97 (English translation Albertz 1994); and Lohfink 1995.
[14] On this, see Lopasso 1999.
[15] A thesis advocated long ago by Claburn 1973; cf. more recently, Zwickel 1999.
[16] Cf. Hjelm 1999.

economically and politically motivated effort to centralize and consolidate the power of the Judahite state administration in Jerusalem, without any genuinely religious aim and purpose, but merely related to religion in terms of cult-economy, undoubtedly a major preoccupation for a ancient Near Eastern state's policy and legitimacy? Admittedly, if an independent cult reform cannot be singled out (which is the main thesis advocated by H. Niehr[17]), it becomes more difficult for the historian to deal with specifically *religious* and *cult-related* aspects of Josiah's reform.[18]

Niehr's objective was 'to investigate the parameters that must be considered in current research if one wants to find a basis for something else than mere assertions and declarations'.[19] In this article, I shall therefore address questions of method and terminology (Section 1) before discussing specific details of Josiah's reform (Sections 2-4).[20]

1. Prerequisites

1.1. Primary and Secondary Sources

In a ground-breaking and important essay on historiography and historical method,[21] E.A. Knauf has established the necessity of prioritizing so-called *primary sources* over *secondary sources*.[22] Following this distinction and accor-

---

[17] Cf. Niehr 1995: 51.

[18] It will become clear in the following investigation that I do not aim at gathering indications of a cult reform driven by 'purely religious' interests, with no economic motives and consequences. To interpret Josiah's reform in such a way would result in a gross anachronism. The sacrificial and tithing system of ancient Judah must be understood in analogy to taxation in the realm of political economics, which conversely did not function independently from religion. The measures described or implied by Deuteronomy, for instance, liberalizing domestic meat consumption while at the same time diverting taxes to the central shrine, demonstrate how deeply political, economic and religious issues were interrelated in antiquity. Consequently, Niehr's conjecture that the set of measures described in 2 Kgs 23.8a (the removal of priests from the cities of Judah and the desecration of local shrines, which Niehr holds for the only historical kernel) could have been executed without any genuinely *religious* motivation is anachronistic and inadequate.

[19] Quote translated from a private communication (19 July 1993) preceding the Frankfurt meeting mentioned in the preliminary remarks.

[20] Secondary literature on the reform abounds; when preparing my paper, I consulted Lowery 1991: esp. 190-209; Laato 1992: esp. 37-68; Reuter 1993; cf. also Zwickel 1990: 210-33; Weinfeld 1991: 65-84; and literature refered to in the preceding and following notes.

[21] See Knauf 1991a: esp. 46-47, 51, on 'primary' and 'secondary evidence', and cf. also Ahlström 1991.

[22] The term 'source' is taken here in a broad, conventional sense (as in German *Quelle*) and does not imply the intention of preserving and communicating memory on behalf of original authors (as would be the case for a 'document'). While it may be useful to distinguish between 'data', 'remains', 'monuments' and 'documents' on the side of evidence, it is the historians who through inquiry and

ding to the definitions given by Knauf, the Hebrew Bible contains only secondary (and tertiary, quarternary, etc.) sources. Indeed, every historian who works with biblical texts will concede with Knauf that 'we simply do not have the documents; all we can do is in some cases reasonably assume that we may have copies of copies' (Knauf 1991a: 47 n. 1). This material lack of original documents (and not the issue of the sources' reliability) is the decisive reason why we cannot speak of primary sources when addressing the Bible (Uehlinger 2001: 31-36). Another well-known fact also mentioned by Knauf, namely that biblical representations of history all belong to the class of texts 'that were produced after the events in an attempt to clarify for future generations how things were thought to have happened' (Knauf 1991a: 46), is of related significance but comparatively less distinctive. As a matter of fact, the same evaluation would apply to ancient Near Eastern royal inscriptions, that is, primary sources: they were not only designed as propaganda for the gods and for contemporary society but explicitly present themselves again and again as documents written in view of later generations. In the interest of distinctiveness, we should therefore concentrate on two *formal* criteria when defining the concept of primary sources, and do without qualifications regarding their content and credibility:

1. Primary sources are documents that can be *dated* on the material basis of *archaeological* criteria (context of the find, typical classification, style, palaeography, or the like) with relative accuracy (criterion of *being dateable*).
2. Primary sources originated during or shortly after[23] the reported events (criterion of *temporal proximity*).

In my view, the distinction between primary, secondary, tertiary sources, etc. does not imply an *a priori* judgment regarding *historical reliability*. Reliability does not automatically follow from temporal proximity. It can only be critically assessed by evaluating the function of a document, which (regardless of whether it is a text or a picture) is generally related to its *genre*, and by comparing it to other documents wherever available. Primary sources can offer tendentious, concocted history, while tertiary sources may well pass down historically reliable information. Still, it must be obvious to anyone that the difficulty of documenting the past grows with increasing temporal distance from the events that should be related.

---

interpretation give any of them the character of a 'source'. I would not object to the concept of 'data' as long as it is not misconstrued in a positivistic sense, as if history could work on *bruta facta* without ever interpreting them. The English term 'evidence' is notoriously misleading, at least to a non-native speaker, but will also be deployed in the present discussion for the sake of convenience.

[23] Knauf's definition for primary sources, namely 'texts that were produced in the course of the events as they were happening' (1991a: 46), is in my opinion too narrow and would require knowledge about the exact circumstances of text production which remains exceptional even in well-documented instances (such as the redaction of Assyrian annals).

Hence, secondary and tertiary sources always suffer from a deficit of experience and relative lack of documentation when compared with primary sources, a deficit for which they usually seek to compensate through outside information that can no longer be verified by the author, and/or through recourse to an author's own experience. Belonging however to another period and context, the latter generally cannot make up the deficit. Increasing temporal distance from past events therefore leads to anachronisms, generally unintended but quite unavoidable; growing cultural distance produces analogous distortions. Hence, any historical reconstruction interested in matters of historicity must take the primary sources as its starting point.[24]

1.2. Braudelian Times

It has become fashionable in recent years for Bible scholars to refer to the work of the French historian Fernand Braudel[25] and his differentiation between *histoire événementielle* and *histoire de la longue durée*. That this distinction was introduced into the fields of Palestinian archaeology and the 'history of Israel'[26] scarcely three decades ago is symptomatic of a field characterized by considerable lack or bias of methodological reflection (cf. M. Weippert 1993: 103).[27] As it happens, belated reception is often rather superficial, and fashionable scholarship trademarked by the redundant use of slogans and catchwords (in our case, *longue durée*) instead of actual theoretical refinement.[28]

---

[24] The terminology, of course, implies hierarchy and a value judgment—which is precisely its heuristic function. That the biblical texts should in an *historical* inquiry be examined as *secondary* sources only, whenever primary evidence is available, will irritate not a few exegetes. In this regard, the requirements of historical method contradict the theological *a priori* of the Bible's normative character as Scripture (most exegetes and 'biblical historians' are first of all trained as theologians). They also contradict the current practice in 'histories of Israel' of postulating a general reliability of biblical texts as a historical source only because it represents the *only* available source for much that is written in the Bible. From a methodological standpoint, the fact that a text may be our only available source does not prejudice its character and quality as a reliable source. Apart from that, many 'history of Israel' textbooks are almost blind to archaeology and iconography, which limits their use for historical research.

[25] In addition to Braudel's classic *La Méditerranée et le monde méditerranéen à l'époque de Philippe II* (1990 [first published 1949]), one may refer to the essay 'Histoire et sciences sociales, la longue durée' (1958). H. and M. Weippert have accurately referred to A. Alt as a proponent of a *longue durée* approach *avant la lettre* (1991: 371).

[26] Notably by Coote and Whitelam 1987: 8-9, 15-16, 21, etc.; H. and M. Weippert 1991: 369-81; Knauf 1991a: 42-44, and Ahlström 1993: 23-24, among others, also have recourse to Braudel.

[27] Considering the generation-long debate on the status of archaeology for biblical history (W.F. Albright, M. Noth, R. de Vaux), it is more appropriate to speak of a bias rather than a lack of methodological reflection. Still, the debate evolved within an intellectual province of its own called 'biblical archaeology', a paradigm long dominated by theology-related preoccupations.

[28] But see Brandfon 1987 for the rather complex state of the problem.

It is ironic to note that H. Niehr's re-evaluation of Josiah's reform should reduce the chain of events to a minimum, a single event if any, and at the same time claim that scholars must consider the reform in a *longue durée* perspective. What reform should we consider at all, if the sources scarcely allow us to reconstruct its main features? How should we relate a few bits and pieces of event history (*histoire événementielle*) with the realm of actual longue durée? I doubt whether the *longue durée* provides the adequate background for dealing with an historical phenomenon like Josiah's reform. We better recall that Braudel not only distinguished between two kinds of history, the events and the *longue durée*; he also described an intermediate level, which is frequently overlooked in discussions of the history of Palestine/Israel: the *histoire conjoncturelle*.

For Braudel (1990: 13-14), each of his three levels of history relates to a particular kind or concept of time and historical awareness:

I. History by events (*histoire événementielle*) is most readily experienced by individuals and can be described in terms of individual time: this is 'traditional history, if one likes, the history not of the general human dimension, but of the individual dimension'. This level operates for any of us in our own biography; to Braudel—whose ultimate subject is the Mediterranean sea—it appears like 'a mere agitation of the surface'.

II. History as shaped by large collective destinies and a confluence of factors of change or 'conjunctures' (*histoire conjoncturelle*) is related to social time: 'a slowly rhythmical history; one would readily say, if the expression had not been deprived of its full meaning, a social history, that of groups and social movements'.

III. Long-term history (*histoire de la longue durée*), shaped by natural environment and geography, relates to geographical time: this is 'an almost motionless history, that of the human race in its relationship with the environment that surrounds it; a history that flows slowly, is transformed slowly, often creates constant, renewable patterns, cycles started anew without ceasing'.[29]

There can be no doubt that the *histoire de la longue durée* would deserve more attention than it has received up to now in the realm of religious history, in Palestine as elsewhere. Among other benefits, a *longue durée* perspective could relativize not a few theological debates on exclusive or distinctive *propria* of biblical creeds and beliefs, a debate that is too often fed by confessional prejudices and historical ignorance. The most appropriate level for the religious history of Israel and Judah, however, and surely for the discussion of a topic such as Josiah's reform, is the *histoire conjoncturelle*. Throughout the short existence of

---

[29] Such realities or 'structures' are normally beyond human reach, except when it comes to communication between places along roadways that generally follow rules imposed by topography.

Israel and Judah as states, their history was influenced by political developments in Egypt and Mesopotamia and by fluctuations between these major centres of power, prestige, and learning. While an event or chain of events such as Josiah's reform first represents a phenomenon on the level of the *histoire événementielle*—regardless of whether one thinks of the reform as an historical fact or as a literary projection—the contextual conditions that would have prepared and shaped it, and perhaps also its consequences, certainly belong to the realm of the *histoire conjoncturelle*.

This intermediate level is also the favourite realm for archaeology, which in recent years has come to be considered the first and foremost 'data pool' for critical history-writing. It is archaeology that provides the primary data and allows us to analyse and interpret historical processes that lie between single events on the one hand (level I), and the structures of geography, whose changes count in millennia (level III), on the other. When dealing with a topic such as Josiah's reform, we should therefore concentrate on the *histoire conjoncturelle* (level II) and address the relevant archaeological record.

1.3. Methodological Minimalism

Knauf has described the concept of a 'minimalist approach' as an alternative to the 'maximalist approach' generally followed by textbooks on the 'history of Israel' (Knauf 1991b: 171), terms that have since become commonplace and are sometimes used with a rather polemical overtone. I suspect that between the maximalist approach ('everything in the sources that could not be proved wrong has to be accepted as historical', in the words of Knauf) and a minimalist approach *stricto sensu* ('everything which is not corroborated by evidence contemporary with the events to be reconstructed is dismissed') there remains a broad spectrum of 'third ways', or, at least, various possibilities to practise and adapt methodological minimalism to specific data.[30] Since I agree with Knauf that only primary sources, that is, dateable archaeological finds, should be the *starting-point* for a religious history of Israel and Judah,[31] I am inclined to follow some kind of minimalist approach. However, 'methodological minimalists' should not take their task too easily. Measures possibly taken under King Josiah in order to redesign the Judahite state cult cannot simply be dismissed because they are not explicitly mentioned as such in primary sources: such a conclusion would proceed from an *argumentum e silentio* which should be inadmissible for maximalists and minimalists alike. Arguments of that kind—seldom proved but regularly disproved by new archaeological data—should be avoided, whether in

---

[30] The qualification, 'corroborated by evidence contemporary with the events' obviously needs further argument.
[31] See above, Section 1.1, and n. 24.

a minimalist or in any other approach. As a historical procedure, even a 'minimalist' approach should take stock of a maximum of available sources, however critically scrutinized.

The crucial question, then, is which kind of data or 'evidence' should be considered as primary sources when addressing a topic such as King Josiah's reform?

1.4. Which Are the Primary Sources to be Considered When Looking for Josiah's Reform?

History of *religion*, as any other attempt at critical history writing, must start from the primary sources. Histories of the religion(s) of Israel and Judah that take the biblical texts as their starting-point always run the risk of projecting 'exilic' and 'post-exilic' agendas and concepts back into the two kingdoms' 'pre-exilic' history. Such is the case with many textbooks on the 'History of Israel'[32] when they address matters of religion. Their perspective has aptly been characterized as 'sub-deuteronomistic history-writing' by M. Weippert (1993: 73).[33] Considering the eminent place of 2 Kings 22–23 in the Deuteronomistic History, the risk of writing 'sub-deuteronomistic history' is particularly acute with our topic, Josiah's reform.

In order not to allow our agenda to be dictated by secondary or tertiary sources, we should broaden our focus beyond isolated features that might be related to some detail of the biblical scenario. When examining developments in Judahite religion during the seventh century, we should certainly address the finds that previous research has hypothetically correlated with Josiah's reform (see below, Section 2.1), and we should certainly consider cultic structures that a definition based on biblical texts would identify as *bamôt* shrines (Nakhai 2001: 161-200; Fried 2002 with divergent conclusions). But we must not limit our view to these. Otherwise, we would still be methodologically prejudiced and proceed within a more subtle variant of 'sub-deuteronomism'—or, for that matter, *e silentio* argument. On methodological grounds, one should preferably start from an overall picture of Judahite religion at the end of the Iron Age II C as it can be ascertained from a maximum of primary sources.[34] Comparing this picture with documented finds from earlier and later periods may allow us to formulate hypotheses about

---

[32] Many publications on the *religious* history of Israel and Judah could equally be characterized in this way; correspondingly, the boundary between religious history and theology often remains unclear in these works.

[33] Even Ahlström's massive *History of Ancient Palestine* (1993) still follows these lines to a large extent, despite the programmatic beginning in the Palaeolithic period and numerous critical corrections of the biblical tradition.

[34] See Holladay 1987; H. Weippert 1988; *GGG*, *GGIG*; and now Zevit 2001, especially Chapters 2–5.

conjunctures and *developments* within Judahite religion from the eighth to the sixth century. Once these have been ascertained, we can examine whether one or several aspects or features might be related to Josiah's reform.

* * *

Having clarified my methodological point of departure, the remaining parts of this paper will proceed in three steps: in Section 2, I shall first examine salient items from the primary documentation that are or have been thought to be directly relevant for interpreting the religious history of Judah during the seventh century BCE. Attention will then be drawn very selectively to a few archaeological finds which demonstrate that Yahwistic religion had indeed a *history* in seventh-century Judah and that *changes* are discernible during that period alongside aspects of continuity.[35] In Section 3, I shall turn to the biblical tradition and consider selected features of Josiah's reform as described in 2 Kings 23. The last section will address the problem of correlating archaeological data and biblical sources.

2. Selected Primary Evidence from Seventh/ Sixth-Century Judah

2.1. Finds of Questionable Evidence: The Arad Shrine and Other Cult Places

Two finds that only a generation ago served as the principle archaeological evidence for Hezekiah's or Josiah's reform, or for both,[36] can no longer be used for that purpose: the disassembly of the great horned altar at Tell es-Seba' some time during the second half of the eighth century BCE,[37] and the (supposed) removal of the shrine of Arad in two stages during the Iron Age II C.[38] Tell es-Seba' must not retain us for long, since the relevant features are chronologically too far removed from Josiah's reform. Stones that had once belonged to a monumental, ashlar-built horned altar were found reused as constructional material in the wall of a pillared storehouse of Str. II and under the Str. II glacis. While the destruction of

---

[35] I do not assert that such changes must automatically be ascribed to Josiah's reform. Strictly speaking, the reform—as Josiah himself—is not for the time being a subject of primary sources. For this reason, it was only mentioned in passing in *GGIG* (§215).

[36] Cf. the reserved construal of both finds and their interpretation by Keel and Küchler 1982: 205-208, 227-33; Conrad 1979: 28-32; Laato 1992: 47-49; Rainey 1994.

[37] For various summaries, cf. Holladay 1987: 255-56, 294 and n. 128; H. Weippert 1988: 623-24; Reuter 1993: 203-208; Zevit 2001: 171-74.

[38] Cf. Holladay 1987: 256-57, 294 n. 128; H. Weippert 1988: 624; Reuter 1993: 193-202; Zevit 2001: 156-71, with both a presentation of the *communis opinio* and a detailed critique already informed by first sketches of Z. Herzog's revision (cf. above, p. 289).

Str. II provides a *terminus ante quem*, which may be connected with the campaign of Sennacherib (701 BCE),[39] it is impossible to ascertain the date of the altar's disassembly, even less its date of construction, beyond a very general date during the second half of the eighth century BCE. While the dismantling of the original altar may well have occurred during the reign of Hezekiah, we do not even know whether it occurred in the town of Str. III or just preceding the construction of the Str. II public defenses. Hence it is impossible positively to ascribe the inferred event at Tell es-Seba' to a putative cult reform under Hezekiah.[40] In any case, Tell es-Seba' cannot contribute to the debate on Josiah's reform. Strictly speaking, we do not even know for sure whether the considerably smaller settlement of Str. I belonged to Josiah's kingdom.[41]

The situation is much more complicated at Tel Arad. Over the last two decades the archaeological interpretation of the finds has undergone fundamental revisions resulting from refined pottery analysis, various observations concerning the architectural remains, and a thorough reconsideration of the Iron Age stratigraphy. The following comments by Z. Herzog, who is entrusted with the final publication of the dig, are illuminating from a methodological point of view. Having defended Aharoni's interpretation of the site's history over many years against all sorts of scholarly criticism, Herzog thoroughly re-examined all the available documentation and arrived at conclusions that now depart quite radically from Aharoni's. According to Herzog, former interpretations of the archaeological evidence at Arad had suffered from relying too heavily on putative biblical parallels:

> A strong impact of the 'biblical archaeology' paradigm directed both Yohanan Aharoni and his crew members [among which Herzog himself] to look for a simplistic correlation between the archaeological data and biblical references. This method, now viewed as oversimplified, is considered a most disturbing and misleading approach… The present reassessment of the temple in Arad negates most of the correlations with the biblical account suggested in previous treatments of the site. (Herzog 2001: 158, 175)

Y. Aharoni's attempt to interpret the history of the Arad shrine in close correlation with 2 Kgs 18.4 and 23.8, the two texts relating cultic reforms under Kings Hezekiah and Josiah in the Judean countryside, did find many followers among scholars and tourists alike until recently. According to Aharoni, the earliest cult place had been established by local Kenites in the twelfth century BCE, and the temple's foundation went back to King Solomon. The building's ritual organization

---

[39] Knauf considers a date during the reign of Manasseh (2002: 181-95).

[40] See Na'aman 1995; 2002: esp. 593-95; Fried 2002: 447-48. Fom a different angle, Swanson 2002.

[41] Ostracon no. 3 from Arad Str. VI (early sixth century BCE) mentions Beersheba as a place in the jurisdiction of the administrator Elishab, who was stationed at Arad (*AHI* no. 2.003, lines 3-4). However, whether this and the biblical town should be sought at Tell es-Seba' or at Bir es-Seba', as suggested long ago by A. Alt, remains disputed.

underwent two major modifications in Str. VIII and VI, which Aharoni dated to the late eighth and seventh centuries: first, the courtyard and sacrificial altar were suppressed and the area leveled out, a measure that Aharoni related to a cult reform under King Hezekiah;[42] second, the shrine itself was dismantled and built over in Str. VI by a casemate wall, which Aharoni dated to the time of Josiah. Defended by the Arad publication team over many years (Herzog *et al.* 1984), this interpretation had been repeatedly questioned by a number of scholars, among them D. Ussishkin (1988) who suggested that the shrine first came into existence with Str. VII, that is, as late as the seventh century, and remained in use until the early decades of the sixth century BCE, that is, well beyond the time of Josiah. According to Ussishkin, 'The dating of the shrine…means that its construction and destruction can hardly be related in any way to the religious reforms conducted in Judah by Hezekiah and Josiah' (1988: 156). Surprisingly, it has taken more than a decade until this theory met with substantial criticism. One suspects that it took so long because of the rather precarious state of stratigraphic documentation of the Arad excavations, which did not allow for an easy rebuttal.[43]

Starting from 1997, however, Z. Herzog has presented the long-awaited reinterpretation of the Arad 'evidence' in a series of articles and an expanded interim report.[44] According to the new scenario, the shrine was built together with the solid-walled fortress of Str. X in the mid-eighth century BCE. It remained in use during Str. IX, which Herzog dates to the second half of the eighth century, but did not exist longer than Str. IX. At some time towards the end of the eighth century, the shrine was dismantled and covered with a thick layer of earth that would have hidden any trace of the ancient sanctuary. According to Herzog, this measure affected the altar, the open courtyard and the actual shrine at one and the same time. It remains unclear to me whether the temple's cancellation should be attributed to the people stationed at the fortress at the end of Str. IX (Fried 2002: 447) or to those who designed the subsequent Str. VIII fortress, when secular (administrative) buildings were erected over the area, taking no notice of the former sanctuary buried underneath.[45] Following Herzog's reinterpretation, the shrine's cancellation should have occurred during the reign of Hezekiah, since either Str. IX or VIII may have been destroyed by Sennacherib.[46]

---

[42] For arguments against this, cf. the studies mentioned above, n. 40.
[43] Cf. Herzog 2001: 156-57; Na'aman 2003: 588-89.
[44] Herzog 1997: 174-76; 2001; 2002: esp. 21-72.
[45] Note that Na'aman (2003: 587-89) has criticized Herzog's division of walls and loci between Str. IX and VIII and thinks that the temple continued to be used during Str. VIII, albeit with a modified access to its cella. According to his view, 'the layers of earth that the members of the Arad publication team interpreted as a deliberate burial of the courtyard are the destruction level of Stratum VIII and the earth used for leveling the ground by the builders of Stratum VII', which Na'aman attributes to Manasseh (p. 592).
[46] As already noted, Knauf prefers a date during the reign of Manasseh for the destruction of both Arad VIII and Beersheba II; cf. above, n. 39.

Both Ussishkin and Herzog reduce the duration of the shrine's existence to merely two instead of Aharoni's four or five occupational strata. They diverge in their dating because they attribute the building to either Str. VII–VI (Ussishkin's late dating) or X–XI (Herzog's early dating). To the best of my understanding, this surprising contradiction is due to the precarious state of published documentation and to the relative paucity of clearly datable finds from the temple proper. The attribution of the shrine's two occupational phases to either Str. X–XI (VIII) or VII–VI ultimately rests on the absolute height of floor and wall levels rather than on a strictly stratigraphical argument.[47] Herzog's new theory is supported by L. Singer-Avitz's refined pottery analysis (2002) and will probably outrule Ussishkin's late dating, although the shrine's status in Str. VIII remains to be clarified (see Na'aman 2003: 587-92).

Regardless of whether one follows Ussishkin's or Herzog's phasing and interpretation, however, it is impossible to relate the archaeological evidence to the biblical testimony about Josiah's reform. The shrine's cancellation is characterized by Herzog as an emphatically careful treatment of cultic paraphernalia within the building proper: two horned incense altars[48] and a massebah were all laid on their sides at their respective positions, a measure which seems to indicate an intention to preserve and not to destroy them. It is rarely noticed that the shrine has apparently produced rather meagre finds in terms of pottery and small objects, particularly with regard to Str. IX (Herzog 2002: 66).[49] The sanctuary could not have functioned with only a handful of jars and bowls,[50] and this may be another indication of the shrine's precautious cancellation by those who had run it for the Judahite state administration. While we cannot know the precise reasons of the cancellation, protective measures at a time when the southern border of Judah came under military pressure and Judahite defensive control could not be guaranteed anymore to provide the most reasonable scenario.[51] This

---

[47] This has led to continuous debate on whether certain 'strata' should actually be regarded as such or rather as sub-phases within a given stratum; cf. Zimhoni 1985; Mazar and Netzer 1986; Ussishkin 1988, who all considered 'Strata' X–VIII and VII–VI as merely two distinct strata which they dated to the eighth-to-seventh centuries and to the early sixth century respectively. The reinterpretation of the remains by Herzog, who introduces a clear distinction between Str. IX and VIII, attributing features to Str. IX that were formerly considered belonging to Str. VIII, has prompted immediate criticism by N. Na'aman. Clearly it is difficult to speak in stratigraphical terms when no sections have been recorded.

[48] For these, cf. Zwickel 1990: 116-17.

[49] Interestingly enough, several Judahite pillar figurines were apparently found in the temple; cf. Kletter 1996: 63, 108 with fig. 35. To the best of my knowledge they had never been mentioned in earlier reports.

[50] See Str. IX pottery published in Singer-Avitz 2002: figs. 30 and 33.10-14, all from the courtyard. Str. X finds including an (Assyrian) lion weight and two inscribed bowls are slightly more impressive, cf. Herzog 2002: 58.

[51] But see Knauf's contribution to the present volume (above, pp. 164-88) for a rather imaginative alternative.

may have occurred during the years of Hezekiah's revolt against Sennacherib, although other explanations are equally valid.⁵² In Herzog's view, 'In any case, the careful burial of the symbolic objects expresses the desire or hope for a restoration of cultic activities in the future' (2002: 66).⁵³ This interpretation certainly does not fit the biblical report of a violent defilement of high places throughout the country—whether such a defilement took place under Hezekiah, or Josiah, or both. While we cannot exclude for the time being that the precautionary measures observed at Arad were taken during the reign of King Hezekiah, there is simply no common denominator between them and the flash notice in 2 Kgs 18.4—not even the abstract notion of 'reform'.⁵⁴ Interpreting the Arad evidence in terms of Hezekiah's reform therefore is an unnecessary hypothesis and looks like still another version of 'biblical archaeology', an outdated scholarly procedure based upon doubtful methodology.

According to N. Na'aman, the decision not to rebuild the Arad shrine in the Str. VII fortress was part of a general pattern that can be observed at other abandoned cult places in Israel and Judah. He suggests

> that it was a royal decision not to restore the sacred sites, which reflected the efforts of rulers to centralize power in their hands and to strength [sic] their hold over the districts and towns of their kingdoms. Local shrines must have enjoyed prestige, achieved a certain degree of independence and competed with the royal court for economic gains. The king was considered responsible for their maintenance and restoration and had reasons for trying to reduce their number. (Na'aman 2002: 596)

However, such an explanation is not entirely satisfactory in the case of Arad. The Arad shrine of Str. X–XI (VIII) was *not* a 'local shrine' but had been founded by royal decision in a state garrison built for administrative and defensive purposes. The issue at stake is therefore a different one, and concerns a change within state religion. Under what conditions and for what reasons would a monarch refrain from repairing a state sanctuary? Various explanations are possible, among them the need to minimize the dispersal of economic resources. After a certain gap of occupation, the Str. VII fortress at Arad went on again collecting taxes from the area, but Yahweh, instead of being served immediately, would henceforth get his share in his Jerusalem Temple only. Should we label this reaffectation of sacrificial dues from one place to another, from a provincial outpost to the capital

---

⁵² According to Knauf (see above, n. 39), eighth- and seventh-century destructions in the Negev should not be attributed to Sennacherib's campaign. Knauf would date the precautionary measures in the days of Manasseh, but I see no compelling evidence for this hypothesis.

⁵³ As mentioned above (n. 45), Na'aman has raised doubts against this scenario. He thinks that the incense altars were deliberately used as part of a wall blocking the cella's east entrance, and that the entrance to the cella was then shifted south. This hypothesis raises a new difficulty: Why should the incense altars be taken out of function and used as building material for the wall the cella, if the latter—and according to Na'aman, the whole temple—continued to function as before?

⁵⁴ *Pace* Herzog 2002: 66-67.

city a religious 'reform'? The parallel with Deuteronomic cult centralization may be stunning on first sight, but it can also be thoroughly misleading. What Deuteronomy and 2 Kings 22–23 present as a divine commandment and a programmatic effort on behalf of an idealized king—paradigmatic literature, if anything—may well, in historical terms, reflect a process that took a generation or two in order to materialize. Consider Arad Str. VIII in ruins: Manasseh would first take hold again of the area and reinstall the taxation system. We do not know (*pace* Na'aman) whether it was he who built the Str. VII fortress already in the first half of the seventh century, or whether that fortress was rebuilt only later under Josiah. Who of Hezekiah, Manasseh or Josiah was responsible for the centralization of the Judahite state cult in Jerusalem? All three, each in his own way, and probably none of the three with an explicitly 'deuteronomistic' agenda in mind![55] What matters most in the perspective of critical medium-term history is not the individuals anyway, but the process which reflects the growing centrality of Jerusalem in the religious and political administration of the Judahite kingdom. Arad Str. VII was a result of and a contribution to this process.

Arad and Tell es-Seba' have played the main roles in the scholarly discussions about cult reforms and archaeology because evidence from these two sites had been emphatically related to the biblical tradition by their excavator.[56] Other Israelite and Judahite sites and features had at best an occasional share in the debate. They have been recently surveyed by Lisbeth S. Fried, who concluded that 'there is no archaeological evidence consistent with the assumption that Josiah removed cult sites from the Iron Age II cities of Judah, Samaria, Megiddo, or the Negev... Neither the reforms of Josiah nor those of Hezekiah against the *bāmôt* should be considered historical' (Fried 2002: 460).[57] It thus

---

[55] At this point, I disagree with Na'aman who writes as a 'sub-Deuteronomist' when it comes to Josiah's reform. Note the following: 'By what means did the king and his followers justify their moves and explain to the elite and the populace the cultic reform that contradicted in many ways their ancestral traditions? Josiah must have cited the laws of the Book of Deuteronomy and claimed that his acts were the restoration of former glory... The work describing the history of Israel from the wandering in the wilderness to the time of Josiah (the Deuteronomistic History) was also written as part of the reform, and was composed in order to supply a solid historical basis for the act of reform' (2003: 173). This assessment can hardly be reconciled with the redactional complexity of the biblical sources.

[56] Y. Aharoni was highly esteemed among critical biblical scholars, particularly in Germany where the paradigms established by A. Alt and M. Noth long went unchallenged. He held a much more nuanced position than his opponent Y. Yadin in the debate on the so-called Israelite *Landnahme* and entertained close relations with a whole generation of German biblical scholars who studied in the 1960s and early 1970s, with some of them actively participating in Aharoni's digs in southern Judah and the Negev.

[57] There is a strange hiatus between the fully documented discussion of archaeological evidence for Judahite cult places and the rather conservative treatment of biblical traditions about Hezekiah's and Josiah's reforms in Zevit's *Religions of Ancient Israel* (2001), where obvious tensions between the archaeological data and the biblical record do not seem to get an adequate treatment.

seems that conventional ways of looking at the problem of archaeology and cult reforms have for the time being exhausted their potential.[58] It may be worthwile to examine other avenues.

2.2. Glyptic

Representations of Assyrian deities are rare on seals from Iron Age II Palestine/Israel; they occur almost exclusively on imported material, mostly cylinder seals which must have belonged to Assyrian officials who occupied administrative functions in provincial outposts (*GGIG* §§168-71). Locally produced glyptic of the eighth and early seventh centuries shows however a stark tendency to portray astral symbolism, a tendency that is clearly related to growing Assyro-Aramean influence (*GGIG* §§172-88). Through this striking astral imagery, deities of the night with the moon god of Harran at their pinnacle entered the foreground in a way scarcely known before. This is all the more remarkable since astral imagery, to the best of my knowledge, has no continuation in sixth-century glyptic from Judah.

Several groups of Judahite seals and bullae have been published in recent years. They form a reference corpus of hundreds of documents. Most of them can be dated fairly precisely between the last third of the eighth and the first quarter of the sixth century, although we still lack criteria for a clear subdivision within the seventh century. Data known up to 1993 were collected by N. Avigad and B. Sass in their *Corpus of West Semitic Stamp Seals* (1997b [hereafter *WSS*]),[59] which includes excavated and unprovenanced material side by side. Since 1993, new catalogues of unprovenanced seals and sealings from the antiquities market and private collections appeared almost every year, most of them compiled by the same author-editor who has almost created a new genre.[60] At the very moment when 'biblical archaeology' is fading away, it is superseded by a new kind of 'biblical collectorship'. Both the pace of publication and the apparent competition engaged between several prestigious private collectors has created a somewhat uneasy situation for critical scholarship: Should we simply ignore material whose provenance cannot be ascertained, or should we with all due caution consider this material as a significant enlargement of our database? Is it possible and reasonable to look for procedures that take stock of the new material without however giving it undue weight in the scholarly argument? How can we minimize the risks of

---

[58] Note however that if 'archaeological evidence indicates only four cult sites among all the cities, towns, and villages of eighth-century Judah' (Fried 2002: 450), one is forced to conclude that this cannot reasonably represent the whole reality and that archaeology has still missed dozens of places where ancient Judahites practised their cults during the Iron Age.

[59] Cf. my review, Uehlinger 1998.

[60] See Deutsch and Heltzer 1994, 1995, 1997, 1999; Deutsch 1999, 2003a, 2003b; Deutsch and Lemaire 2003, all published by Archaeological Center Publications at in Tel Aviv-Jaffa. See further Lemaire 1999; Avigad, Heltzer and Lemaire 2000.

affecting historical research by fakes and forgeries? A reasonable way of dealing with the situation, in my opinion, is to practise one's research and build up one's theory in concentric circles: much as we deal with primary, secondary and tertiary sources, we should consider excavated material first, and it is certainly legitimate to consider it exclusively. Still, it is also legitimate to test it with additional material once we have established a working hypothesis, without however giving undue weight to material belonging to the second (unprovenanced objects with clear parallels in excavated material), third (unprovenanced objects without parallels) or fourth circle (doubtful material). Any opportunity to put unprovenanced material to the test of science (e.g. by thermoluminescence analysis) should be taken. And valid historical hypothesis should proceed, if at all, from the inner to the outer circles but *never* vice versa.

According to these principles, the group of 49 bullae excavated in a well-stratified context in Area G of Y. Shiloh's 'City of David' excavations in Jerusalem obviously occupies a first-rank position.[61] These bullae probably represent the remains of a family archive recording real estate transactions extending over two or three generations until the city's conflagration in 587 BCE.[62] Among the 40 or 41 individuals represented in the archive, only three used an uninscribed seal; they were probably people from elsewhere, since their seal designs are typical for the Shephelah (dove and twig impressed with a bone seal), the Philistine coast or Egypt (sphinx and scarab), and North Syria (a moon crescent of Harran impressed with a conical seal). In contrast, local seals display a conspicuous reservation towards iconic designs and merely use decorative features and space fillers. A twig or a star may occasionally serve as an additional identity marker—but what kind of identity: family, club, or professional guild? Clearly enough, neither iconic design in general nor astral symbolism in particular were *en vogue* among the literate Jerusalemites represented in the 'House of the Bullae' archive.

A second group of 211 unprovenanced bullae ('Tell Beit Mirsim' or Jerusalem?) published by N. Avigad almost twenty years ago (1986) presents a rather different picture. First, there is a greater variety in decorative designs; second, a number of bullae display architectural and vegetal or floral motifs which can be related tentatively to temple and/or fertility symbolism (*GGIG* §208). One bulla even shows a worshipper. In neither of the two groups, however, would one find an anthropomorphic portrayal of a deity—neither Assyrian nor Syro-Palestinian—or such conspicuous astral symbols as the crescent moon or stars of earlier periods.[63] Some of the Avigad sealings clearly go back to late eighth- and early seventh-century seals. These, as other seals and sealings of earlier periods, are less uniform

---

[61] Shiloh 1986; Shiloh and Tarler 1986; Shoham 1994, 2000. *WSS* (pp. 167-68) provides a useful concordance.

[62] Since only a few bullae show sealings from identical seals, the archive cannot result from regular business transactions.

[63] Cf. *GGIG* §§187-88 with §§206-207; Sass 1993: 239-40.

than the designs of the late seventh and early sixth centuries.[64] Two instances of an enthroned (lunar?) god depicted on Judahite seals[65] are especially noteworthy. A *dea nutrix* presenting her breasts is known on an eighth-century anepigraphical seal from Lachish (*GGIG* fig. 323).[66] Globally speaking, Israelite and Judahite glyptic of the eighth century were relatively open and receptive to anthropomorphic and theriomorphic representations (deities and genies, sphinxes, scarabs, uraei, etc.). During the seventh century, some Judahite workshops seem to have adopted at least occasionally the astral symbolism which was *en vogue* at that time,[67] while others developed remarkable skills in vegetal and floral decoration. In contrast, late pre-exilic seals and sealings are clearly reluctant to use anthropomorphic and theriomorphic representations and concentrate instead on calligraphy and geometric decorum. One may conclude from such comparisons that astral symbolism may have affected part of the earlier Judahite glyptic but was clearly not (no longer?) fashionable among the Jerusalem elite in c. 600 BCE.[68]

We should not draw hasty conclusions with regard to Josiah's reform. First of all, let us recall that the cult reform is reported in 2 Kings 23 as a series of events and thus typically belongs to the *histoire événementielle*; in contrast, the seals testify to developments on the level of *histoire conjoncturelle*. Moreover, only rarely can seals be dated so precisely that we could assign them, for instance, to the reign of Josiah but not of Jehoiakim, or vice versa. The sensitive handling of sources requires that we respect the limits of what they can tell. Still, when we consider the overall picture of Judahite glyptic from the eighth to the sixth centuries, we may discern a clear evolution of preferences characterized by the rarefaction of iconic and otherwise deity-related seal designs.

Another aspect of the problem has only recently come to my attention.[69] If one considers the evolution of the glyptic repertoires all over Palestine during the seventh century BCE, it is striking to see the strong impact of Twenty-Sixth-Dynasty Egypt from Philistia and the Beersheba area in the south, to the Jezreel plain, the Beth-Shean Valley, the Galilee and the coastal cities in the north, particularly during the long reign of Psammetichus I (664–610 BCE). To this, one should add Egyptian small finds of various kind, such as bronze statuary or even cultic vessels and utensils. Clearly Egypt was back in these areas during the second

---

[64] As a rule, Northwest Semitic inscribed stamp seals prefer worshippers to anthropomorphic portrayals of deities; cf. Ornan 1993; Uehlinger 1993: 262-65.
[65] *GGIG* figs. 305c and 306a; Sass 1993: 232-34 Motif F6.
[66] A frontally placed, nude female(?) figure flanked by two falcons appears on the seal of a certain Ahaz published by Deutsch and Lemaire 2003: no. 15.
[67] Compare, e.g., Deutsch and Lemaire 2003: nos. 41, 45, 71, 84.
[68] Differences are also notable when we compare Judahite glyptic of the seventh and sixth centuries with contemporaneous seals from Moab and Ammon. Eggler 2003 stresses the different iconographic profiles of inscribed vs. uninscribed seals from Moab. Still, astral symbolism is common to both categories.
[69] See Uehlinger 2001: 61-71, with references to the primary sources.

half of the century, following the retreat of the Assyrian administration, and entertained close economic, political and cultural ties with the region.⁷⁰ However, Judah did not completely participate in this broad general conjuncture. In comparison with lowland developments, Judahite glyptic shows an almost traditionalist character—traditionalist in the sense of clear focus on established local repertoire. Seal-cutting workshops in Jerusalem do not seem to have been even slightly affected by the resurgence of *Aegyptiaca* (of which a few items made their way to the Judahite capital). Considering the admittedly narrow evidence of sealings and a sherd from Ramat Raḥel displaying human figures, costume among the Judahite elite remained unchanged, that is, indebted to previous Assyro-Aramean fashion.⁷¹ There are a few seals and sealings that are reminiscent of Egypt-related symbolism, some of which may have belonged to people with pro-Egyptian sympathies who undoubtedly had their place in Jerusalem, too. But on the whole, Judahite symbolism of the late seventh and early sixth centuries was remarkably parochial and rather conservative—a picture which fits rather nicely the general cultural profile of the reign of Josiah as we perceive it from the biblical record.

2.3. Epigraphical Sources

Epigraphical sources may yield more distinctive results than seals for our purpose, especially when they can be dated with more precision. If we limit ourselves to Hebrew inscriptions from the time of Hezekiah to the end of the monarchy, they seem to reflect a development that one may generally label as an expansion of Yahweh's divine authority, which *eo ipso* implies a transfer of authority from other deities or divine entities and thus their relative deprivation of power.⁷²

Hebrew and particularly Judahite inscriptions make it probable that between c. 700 and 587 Yahweh took over specific functions as provider of blessing and salvation from 'his Asherah'. That several inscriptions on the pithoi from Kuntilet 'Ajrud contain blessings *lyhwh* X *wl'šrth* is well known and does not need to be commented on here, since the inscriptions dated c. 800 BCE are Israelite rather

---

⁷⁰ Na'aman 1991 has clearly demonstrated that no power vacuum existed in Palestine at the time of Josiah; cf. also Na'aman's article in the present volume (pp. 189-247).
⁷¹ On this and the influence of politics on vestimentary fashion among the elite, see Uehlinger 1996.
⁷² Texts in the book of Jeremiah suggest that in the course of the seventh century Yahweh was promoted to a creator god, but there are currently no clear primary sources to document this development; cf. H. Weippert 1981. A fragmentary inscription from Jerusalem (*AHI* no. 4.201) has been thought to refer to a deity *'lqn'rṣ* (H. Weippert 1981: 16; cf. *GGIG* §§180 and 200 for tentative pictorial correlations), but this seems doubtful in the light of the inscription's fuller treatment by Renz 1995: 198. The syntagma *yhwh 'lhy kl h'rṣ* in inscription A from Khirbet Beit Lei may emphatically designate Yahweh as 'God of the *whole* land' (*AHI* no. 15.005 = [!] 15.006), which would make equal sense in the face of an Assyrian attack or shortly after the exclusion of the Shephelah and the Negev following Sennacherib's campaign, rather than 'God of the whole earth' (*GGIG*, p. 312; Renz 1995: 246). A very different reading is defended by Zevit 2001: 417-27.

than Judahite. Suffice it to say that the blessings of Kuntilet 'Ajrud represent a standard epistolary greeting formula.[73] Roughly a century later, similar notions about blessing and salvation were expressed in a cave inscription near Khirbet el-Kom, apparently commissioned by a certain Uriah.[74] According to line 3, Yahweh had saved him 'from his adversaries "through" (or "for the sake of") his Asherah' (*wmṣryh l'šrth hwš'lh*). A slightly different reading has been suggested by A. Lemaire (1977), who believes that the syntagma *l'šrth*, which appears two more times below, was erroneously displaced and should be read in sequence with the preceding line, where he reconstructs a blessing that would parallel the formulae known from Kuntilet 'Ajrud: 'Blessed be/is Uriah through (or "on behalf of") Yahweh and through ("on behalf of") his Asherah'. Whether one follows Lemaire's suggestion or not, it is clear that the author of the inscription regarded Yahweh's Asherah as a major instance of salvation and/or blessing. In contrast, more recent greeting formulas found in letters from Arad (Str. VI) and Lachish (Str. II), that is, in contexts that are roughly contemporaneous with the above-mentioned bullae from Jerusalem, do not mention Asherah (anymore?).[75] While the primary sources do not explain to us the reasons behind this change, that it occurred in such a tradition-bound context as greeting and blessing is remarkable.[76] To put it squarely, something must have happened to Yahweh's Asherah between roughly 700 and 587 BCE.

The inscriptions on the two silver amulets from Ketef Hinnom in Jerusalem[77] are famed for their variations of the priestly blessing known through Num. 6.24-26. More interesting for our concern, they seem to count on the effectiveness of Yahweh even in the underworld, which would again imply a remarkable extension of Yahweh's power. The blessing of the second, smaller amulet directly addresses dead Oniyahu ([*ʾt]h brw[kʾ]nyhw*, II.1-2). The corresponding lines are missing from the larger amulet, but there would have been enough space for a similar formula. Amulet I reads, 'Indeed/for through him [Yahweh] is salvation; indeed/for Yahweh brings light back to us' *(ky bw gʾlh ky yhwh [y]šybnw* [xʾ] *ʾwr*, I.11-14).[78] Salvation through Yahweh is here metaphorized with the notion that Yahweh brings back light: this recalls the common Near Eastern concept of the sun-god who travels through the underworld during the night and literally 'brings back light' in the morning.

---

[73] On this cf. *GGIG* §§134, 143; cf. Müller 1992: esp. 21-23, 35-37.

[74] *AHI* no. 25.003; Renz 1995: 202-11; *GGIG* §141; cf. Zevit 2001: 359-70 (with a different interpretation of *ʾšrth*).

[75] Cf. *GGIG* §209.

[76] The authors of inscriptions B and C from Khirbet Beit Lei (*AHI* nos. 15.007 and 15.008; Renz 1995: 248-49; Zevit 2001: 426, 429) also apparently expect salvation from Yahweh only; however, their 'quick prayers' are not of the same genre.

[77] Barkay 1992; *GGIG* §210.

[78] *AHI* no. 4.301]*šynmw* [] *kwr* follows the reading by Barkay; a look at the photo and drawing shows its difficulty, cf. Yardeni 1991: 178-79 with fig. 1.

As O. Keel and I have argued elsewhere (1994), Yahweh originally came to Jerusalem as a typical storm god. As the patron deity of the Davidic dynasty, Yahweh increasingly took over aspects and functions of other deities, among them the former city god who had probably solar characteristics. From the end of the eighth century onwards, Yahweh himself was to a large extent perceived as a royal solar deity.[79] Another step in the integration of divine roles opened the way towards the netherworld, to which Yahweh had not been related before. The two amulets from Ketef Hinnom, originally made for living persons and not specifically for the dead,[80] document an advanced stage of this development. One could probably buy such amulets in the vicinity of the Jerusalem Temple, maybe choose from a repertoire of blessing formulae and have one's own name put on them. When their owners died, the amulets were placed with them in the grave. Once the idea developed that Yahweh could be active in the grave and netherworld and preserve the dead from evil, too, some sort of competition between the main deity of Jerusalem and other gods who were traditionally related to the netherworld (among them, *mlk*?) became inevitable.

If a cult reform ever took place under King Josiah, it must be plausibly situated within the religio-historical context implied by the afore-mentioned developments.

3. Notes on Selected Reform Measures Mentioned in 2 Kings 23[81]

Let us now turn to the 'secondary source' on Josiah's reform as preserved in 2 Kings 23—still our best 'source' for that matter. Scholars have long noted the differences in style and divergences in content which distinguish the so-called 'reform report' (*Reformbericht*, 2 Kgs 23.4-20) from the report on the scroll's discovery and ensuing covenant ceremony (2 Kgs 22.3–23.3, 21-24).[82] The reform report never refers to the scroll found in ch. 22; conversely, that chapter contains only a single reference to inappropriate cultic behaviour (v. 17), which clearly stems from a late deuteronomistic hand and offers no motive for the particular reform efforts described in ch. 23.[83] Hence not only the correlation between the

---

[79] In an important investigation of the iconography of the Hebrew name-inscribed seals, B. Sass observed that in the realm of astral motifs, the solar symbolism was clearly dominant while portrayals of the moon and other stars appear only occasionally (1993: 238-40). This stands in sharp contrast to the glyptic of (Ammonite and) Moabite name seals (cf. above, n. 68) and must be connected with the different orientation of the respective state deities.

[80] In I.8, *mškb* ('resting place') does not necessarily mean the grave; the word could just as well denote 'a place for the night'; cf. Beuken 1993: 1310-11.

[81] For overviews of recent research, cf. Lohfink 1985; Preuss 1993: 246-50; Gieselmann 1994.

[82] Cf. Hardmeier's article in the present volume (above, pp. 123-63).

[83] 2 Kgs 22.17, where the reasons are given for the disaster with which Yahweh threatens *Jerusalem*, concerns the *inhabitants of the city* who have fallen away from Yahweh: 'because *they* have

reform report and the book of Deuteronomy,[84] but the thematic and chronological relationship between the reform report and the 'scroll' are open to debate. In the present context of an approach aiming at critical minimalism, I shall limit my discussion to some selected features mentioned in the reform report.[85] Since my demonstration will be focused on particular measures and the quest for relevant primary sources, I shall use the term 'reform notices' (*Reformnotizen*) when addressing them individually. This terminology does not imply that I consider the 'reform report' as it stands a planless piece of atomized notices, but the literary analysis of the chapter as a whole is far beyond the subject of this study.[86]

3.1. Centralization or Purification of the Cult? Literary Criticism and Critical Minimalism

Even a superficial examination of the reform-notices allows one to distinguish two kinds of measures which are usually designated by the keywords 'centralization' vs. 'purification' of the cult. Centralization has received greater scholarly attention because it could be more easily correlated with Deuteronomic requirements (cf. Deut. 12). In contrast, the purification measures or purges mentioned in 2 Kings 23 are less easily related to Deuteronomic law.[87] Many authors, among

---

left me and *offered incense to other deities*, in order to anger me through all the pitiful work of their hands'. Nothing in ch. 23 relates to this diagnosis. Only cults practised in the capital would have come into question, such as those mentioned in v. 5b, where *burning incense* for other deities is again mentioned. However, v. 5 is not concerned with the inhabitants of Jerusalem in general but with the כמרים, a particular group of priests (see below, Section 3.3); not Yahweh, but 'Baal, the sun, the moon, the constellations and the entire host of heaven' are named as the addressees of their cult. On the basis of its phraseology, 22.17 belongs to the literary horizon of Jer. 1.16; 19.4 (קטר לאלהים אחרים with עזב את יהוה), 44.3, 5, 8, 15 (only קטר לאלהים אחרים) and 25.6, 7; 32.20; 44.8 respectively (for כעס את יהוה במעשה ידים; see also Deut. 31.29; 1 Kgs 16.17) (cf. Tagliacarne 1989: 129-30, 377-78). Like the first part of the Huldah oracle in general, the verse is directed at the capture and destruction of Jerusalem in 2 Kgs 25 and justifies this through the cultic offences named there. It should not be used as a historical source for cult practices observed in seventh-century Jerusalem.

[84] Doubts about the correlation between the reform and Deuteronomy have been expressed time and again, for example by Ahlström 1993: 774-77. Tagliacarne's careful investigation concludes that 'the connections to Deuteronomy are conspicuously less than one would suppose from the literature'. Substantially more themes connect with Jeremiah.

[85] More attention than usual should be paid to the fact that the Old Greek (OG) seems to have relied on a Hebrew *Vorlage* which considerably differed from the Masoretic text (MT). Schenker (2004: 34-74) has defended the priority of a pre- and proto-MT closer to OG than MT. Within the limits of this article, I shall comment on his arguments only as far as they concern the particular reform measures discussed below.

[86] I may refer to Hardmeier's and Arneth's studies (above, n. 4) in addition to Lohfink 1987: 460-65; Sweeney 2001: 40-45.

[87] Deuteronomy mentions neither כמרים priests and their burning incense for divine heavenly bodies (v. 5) nor a Tophet (v. 10); neither chariots nor horses of the sun-god (v. 11), and no roof altars (v. 12). These cult practices and their equipment could be subsumed under Deuteronomy's generally

them Niehr and Levin, think that cult centralization was the main if not the only purpose of Josiah's reform and that the various notices on purges were added by later deuteronomistic redactors. Others, in contrast, reconstruct a reform report which contains no reference to centralization.[88] As will be shown below, a number of purgative measures are more plausibly explained as late seventh-century features than cult centralization in Jerusalem, which, at least as far as state cult is concerned, did not require particular impetus at the time of Josiah. Provided Herzog's interpretation of Arad is correct, the lack of a new shrine in the fortress of Str. VII indicates that Jerusalem was at that time the uncontested centre of Judahite state religion, a situation which may well have prevailed since the very days of Manasseh.

Niehr assumes that the notices on purges are, on the whole, post-exilic additions and thus irrelevant to the religious policy of King Josiah. Such an extensive, deliberately self-imposed rejection of source material is amazing. Instead of providing an argument, Niehr simply refers to the authority of C. Levin, who is known for his rather radical literary-critical approach. In an essay published 20 years ago, Levin had tackled 2 Kings 22–23 and postulated a torso-like *Grundschicht* consisting of merely six verses (22.1-2; 23.8a, 25a [up to מלך], b, 28-30).[89] According to Levin, 'whoever believes he or she cannot do without additional Old Testament material [on Josiah's reform] does not write history but passes on legends'.[90] Levin's literary-critical impetuousness may be excused, since his reading of 2 Kings 22–23 disclosed to him a text 'of unprecedented corruption', indeed the '*cloaca maxima* of the Old Testament' (1984: 356-57 = 2003: 201-202). Such judgments may accommodate with radical minimalism, but they can hardly be regarded as unbiased.[91] Why should history of religion be based on such an eccentric viewpoint—especially since Levin shows little if any interest in actual historical questions and accordingly, primary sources? Whoever thinks that critical history writing should limit itself to the hypothetical reconstruction of putative 'original sources' embedded in secondary, tertiary or quaternary tradition, ignores the full heuristic potential of tradition and redaction history. Considering later, secondary texts as essentially unreliable is doubtful methodology. Even if a number of measures described in 2 Kings 23 may not belong to the *Grundschicht* of the text, it would not follow automatically that they must be irrelevant for the

---

formulated rejection of astral cults (Deut. 17.3), fire cults (18.10) or foreign cults in general, but in contrast to the reform-notices, they do not represent a *specific* problem in Deuteronomy.

[88] Among others, Würthwein 1976: 415-18; Hollenstein 1977: 330-35; cf. Hardmeier's article in the present volume (pp. 123-63).

[89] Levin 1984: 358-63 (= 2003: 205-208).

[90] Levin 1984: 364 (= 2003: 209): 'Wer auf das übrige alttestamentliche Material nicht glaubt verzichten zu können, schreibt nicht Geschichte, sondern tradiert Legende'.

[91] Let alone that, as every archaeologist knows, sewers and cesspools can be unimaginably rich in information about the daily life of an epoch. Synchronic analyses demonstrate 2 Kgs 22–23 is far less 'corrupt' than Levin thought; cf. Hoffmann 1980: 208-52; Tagliacarne 1989 and others.

historical quest of Josiah's reform. Such a conclusion would require a reciprocal argument, namely that the assumption of a later, deuteronomistic or post-deuteronomistic addition is intrinsically more plausible and provides a more coherent explanation within a later historical context.[92]

Within the limits of this article, we may cut down the historical problem to the following question: Does 2 Kings 23 list measures that are most plausibly understood against the background of the political and religious situation of Judah during the latter part of the seventh century BCE than at any other period?[93] At least two measures appear to be directed against cult practices or institutions whose introduction in Judah must have been originally connected with the Assyrian expansion and the accompanying reception of Assyro-Aramean traditions of astral cults: the removal of the horses and chariots of the sun-god (v. 11*) and the suppression of the כמרים priests (v. 5*). Both measures are reported in similar terminology (X את והשבית/וישבת).[94] The purged cult practices are said to have

---

[92] Needless to say, good reasons must be available if literary, secondary texts are to be declared historically reliable. But the matter should not be considered closed without discussion.

[93] Concerning the general political climate at the time of Josiah, we may again refer to Na'aman 1991, cf. also his article in the present volume (above, pp. 189-247).

[94] The use of *waw* conjunctive + Perfect in the reform report (seven occurrences: vv. 4b, 5, 8b, 10, 12b, 14a, 15b) is an old crux that cannot be resolved here. Hoffmann (1980: 215-16) and Tagliacarne (1989: 171 n. 355) avoid the problem. A thorough discussion of all the evidence but no plausible solution is presented by Spieckermann 1982: 120-30. Spieckermann is criticized by M. Weippert (1990), who argues for a '(proto-) middle Hebraic crystal embedded in an old Hebraic text' and 'a reworking' of the relevant verses (p. 453) without following the consequences of this thesis in any detail. To postulate a common literary origin for all seven occurrences (Hollenstein 1977; Würthwein 1976: 414-15: post-Chr!) may be elegant but too simple because the corresponding passages vary starkly in content. W. Von Soden (1991) and K. Koch (1992) independently postulated a specific function, which they call 'habitative', for *waw* conjunctive + Perfect constructions. In contrast to simple narrative, this tense would characterize actions or events which are meant to have durable effects. While this suggestion allows for a more subtle perception of the text, it does not dispense us from literary-critical considerations. A new, detailed analysis is provided by Barrick (2002: 64-105), who concludes that three occurrences (vv. 5, 8b, 10) are 'intrusive in the larger context of the pericope', four (vv. 4b, 5, 10, 12b) should be seen as 'doublets or echoes of material in the "original" report', while two (vv. 12b, 14a) should be considered as 'editorial "fine-tuning"' (2002: 104). Regarding v. 5, however, its excision from the original report is argued by Barrick on the sole ground that the mention of 'the cities in Judah' in v. 5a does not fit a Jerusalem-based context (2002: 3). Barrick makes no attempt at diachronic analysis within v. 5. He can consider v. 5a a doublet of v. 8a + 9 because he does not differentiate between כמרים and כהנים priests (2002: 67-70; but see below, Section 3.3), while v. 5a is merely 'a doublet (of a sort)' of v. aab' (2002: 72). I cannot find all this very convincing, particularly since in the final run, Barrick is left wondering from where the putatively late redactor could have taken his apparently quite specific knowledge and terminology (כמרים, מזלות): 'Presumably this information is not completely imaginary, but has some basis in the realities known to the author-compiler responsible for the items to be comprehensible to his intended audience' (2002: 105). While I cannot prove that the כמרים passage as understood in the following paragraph is original, I hope to show that seventh-century realities provide the most plausible background to v. 5*.

been 'introduced by the kings of Judah' (אשר נתנו מלכי יהודה).⁹⁵ Although this last remark may go back to a late redactor,⁹⁶ the two measures thus glossed may well be considered to be historically reliable.

3.2. The Horses and Chariots of the Sun(-God) (2 Kings 23.11)

The removal of the horses and chariots of the sun is a measure that, in my opinion, can be traced back to Josiah with great probability.⁹⁷ The statement is so detailed that even Levin concedes that it could have 'a concrete cult practice in view' (1984: 361 n. 38 = 2003: 206)⁹⁸—albeit not one dating to the seventh century.⁹⁹

H. Spieckermann has not only rightly underscored the absence of deuteronomist phraseology in v. 11* (1982: 107) but also pointed out that the סריס, in whose chamber at the entrance to the Yahweh Temple the horses were supposed to have been stationed, bore not a religious but a civic title of Assyrian provenance, which led him to ask 'whether an apparent political functionary in the Temple might not have exercised some sort of surveillance in relation to the cult' (1982: 109). In any case, the man bore the title of an Assyrian government official, and he was not a priest. As for the horses, the Masoretic text does not consider them as inanimate votive statues or cult symbols but as living animals,¹⁰⁰ which explains why they had to be cared for by a civil official. The listing of horses and chariots next to each other suggests chariot horses.

---

⁹⁵ This is also said of the altars on the roof (of the Temple; v. 12* with עשה instead of נתן, because it deals with objects; so again in v. 19 for the high places of Samaria). Note that OG ascribes the installation of altars on the roofs [sic] to King Ahaz. Schenker (2004: 72-73) is among those who favour this reading.

⁹⁶ The statement has a compensatory character. Lacking a clear reference in the previous chapters (a helpful table is provided by Hoffmann 1980: 253) or other sources, the historiographer is not in the position to ascribe the vile cult practice to a particular king.

⁹⁷ *GGIG* §199; Taylor 1993: 176-82; and see now Arneth 2001: 196-201.

⁹⁸ Cf. also Würthwein 1976: 417.

⁹⁹ One should be aware, however, that the Masoretic and the Greek text (especially the Antiochene tradition) show considerable disagreement about the realia involved: According to the Antiochene text, Josiah '*burned* the horses *consecrated* to the sun by the kings of Judah...and he burned the chariot [*sg.*!] of the sun in fire *in the house/temple of Bethôn* (בית און), *which the kings of Israel had built as a high place for Baal and all the Host of Heaven*'. In other words, this text views the horses as votive statues, which could explain the emphasis on their locale, whereas the MT clearly thinks of *living* horses. And it reserves a separate treatment to the chariot which had to be moved to Beth On prior to its destruction. This text form is preferred by Schenker (2004: 67-72) although it requires considerable reconstructive efforts with limited support by Lucifer of Cagliari's Old Latin version. It seems preferable to consider it as a midrashic expansion and to retain the MT for the purpose of our historical inquiry.

¹⁰⁰ Hence, the late-deuteronomistic glossator uses the verb נתן instead of עשה, as with the כמרים priests of v. 5 (see above, n. 95).

Except for attributing the horses to the sun(-god), the laconic note in v. 11 does not allow one to specify their function with certainty. Spieckermann's interpretation (1982: 245-51) is based on a neo-Assyrian *tāmītu* ritual of the seventh century (*KAI* 218). In this ritual, a horse is carefully chosen through an oracular procedure by Adad and Shamash to serve with a divine chariot. This function gives the animal itself almost sacred status: 'Binding and loosing are given to you as to a god' (v. 6). The horse is believed capable of intercession: 'Concerning NN,... the governor (*šakkanaku*), speak good about him, speak up for him!' (vv. 7-8). To have the horse do this in the desired way, one must whisper an incantation in its left ear and offer him a sacrifice, 'as to the gods' (*kīma ilāni*, v. 11). Currently, this text is the only first-millennium witness for the cultic use of living chariot horses, beyond that of pulling divine chariots. Since it is methodologically difficult to fill out our sketchy knowledge about the 'horses of the sun' expelled by Josiah with a *tāmītu* from Assur, especially since no duplicate of this text is known from other cities, we cannot simply accept that the horses of the sun in Jerusalem also had an intercessory function (Spieckermann 1982: 252). But the Assyrian text gives at least a possible direction for further investigation.[101]

Both horses and chariots are assigned to the sun or sun-god in 2 Kgs 23.11. Spieckermann would like to identify this god with Assyro-Babylonian Shamash. A consideration of iconography might support this assertion. The connection between horse and sun-god has no tradition in Palestine itself but is typical of Assyria, especially during the late eighth and early seventh century (the time of Sargon and Sennacherib), when the horse was repeatedly represented as the symbolic animal of the sun-god (Seidl 1989: 234-35; Schroer 1987: 282-300). Furthermore, the all-knowing sun-god is known to have acted in the time of Sargon as a major deity addressed by the diviners, along with Adad, particularly for concerns of state security (Starr 1990). At the same time period, however, and indeed *only* under Sennacherib, are divination rituals before divine (albeit unharnassed) chariots represented on palace reliefs, a custom that was apparently felt to be obsolete at the time of Ashurbanipal.[102] Against this background, one might understand the horses and chariot of the sun-god supervised by a סריס (2 Kgs 23.11) as standard equipment for Assyrian divination practices which may have been introduced in the time of Sennacherib, presumably under King Hezekiah.[103]

---

[101] Cf. Weinfeld 1972: esp. 151 on horse donations during the neo-Assyrian era.

[102] Cf. Pongratz-Leisten, Deller and Bleibtreu 1992. The standards, always portrayed in pairs, do not represent the sun-god but Adad and Nergal (or Ninurta) as patrons of the Assyrian military campaigns. In textually attested divination rituals, however, Adad and Shamash are consulted.

[103] That the Assyrian sun-god had a chariot can be concluded indirectly from the epithets *rākib narkabti* ('chariot driver') and *mukīl appāti* ('rein-holder') of two subordinate gods attending Shamash; cf. Cogan 1974: 85 n. 106.

From among the great Assyrian divinities, why should Shamash in particular be worshipped or be asked an oracle? The likely coincidence that the Jerusalem Temple was regarded as the residence of a solar deity may have favoured such a plausible arrangement (cf. also Ezek. 8.16). In the history of Near Eastern religions, we can observe time and again that the functions and roles of deities had a stronger local inertia than even their names, which could be combined, exchanged, grouped genealogically, and brought into line with political and economic shifts. Yahweh, the weather god, had taken the place of a local sun-god in Jerusalem during the tenth century, and during the reign of Hezekiah he was likely perceived as a solar king divine. Once Assyria distinguished itself as an irresistible power, what would be more logical than to install horses and a chariot in the temple of Jerusalem's solar deity in accordance with Assyrian custom? We do not know whether this goes back to an Assyrian or a Judahite initiative.[104] Nor do we know whether and how Judahites mastered the techniques of horse divination or whether the horses only served as draught animals for the sun-god's processional chariot. At any rate, the perpetuation of this somewhat obsolete and rather expensive institution was no longer sensible in the second half of Josiah's reign, when politics and religion were no longer conditioned by Assyria's symbol system.[105] The arrangement of Sîn-shar-ishkun with Psammetich I (around 625 BCE) had consecrated a territorial order firmly established during the preceding decade. From that time at the very latest, Judah was no longer a vassal state of Assyria but again part of an Egypt-ruled region.[106] However, in Egyptian symbolism as in local Jerusalem symbolism neither horses nor chariots had a place in the vicinity of the sun-god.

The measure thus mirrors an economically and politically conditioned reorientation of the cult practised at the royal shrine of Jerusalem. The burning of the chariots gives it considerable emphasis, but I do not think one should explain the event as an anti-Assyrian demonstration. Assyria was gone, and time was ripe to come back to local custom.

---

[104] Religious pressure from Assyria is neither suggested by the text nor attested as a usual Assyrian practice; cf. *GGIG* §167 and Cogan (1993: 403-14) who concludes: 'No Assyrian text states or implies that conquered peoples were required to worship the gods of Assyria... But in the end, it was a new cultural and technological *koine*, Assyro-Aramean in derivation, that ultimately dominated the entire region' (pp. 412-13). In the case of Jerusalem's 'horses of the sun', one should probably think of a more or less 'voluntary accommodation to the institutions of the sovereign' (Würthwein 1976: 417) of the now uncontested superpower.

[105] The fact that only a סריס, but no priest or oracle specialist, is mentioned, a man who bears the telling name נתנמלך, may indicate that the institution was no longer in practise anyway, now that Judah had no more contact with Assyria. I am sceptical whether this נתנמלך should be identified with the 'servant of the king' Nathan-melech whose seal was impressed on a recently published unprovenanced bulla. Cf. Deutsch 1999: 73-74 n. 9; McCarter 1999: 146.

[106] Cf. above, Section 2.2.

3.3. The *kêmārîm* (2 Kings 23.5*)

The priestly title כמרים is not attested in Israel/Judah before Hosea (10.5) and disappears from biblical vocabulary after Zephaniah (1.4). Hence, it was probably just as rare in Judah as it was typical for the seventh century. It is not originally Assyrian (akk. *kumru* is not attested in first-millennium cuneiform texts), but of North Syrian provenance (Spieckermann 1982: 85).[107] The title is attested in Aramaic on two funerary steles from seventh-century Neirab that were set up by priests of the moon god (*kmr šhr*).[108] Both inscriptions conjure punishment not only by the moon god, but also Shamash (only *KAI* 225), Nikkal, and Nusku upon him who would desecrate the graves. Nikkal is the bride, Nusku the son of the moon god. Thus, all the gods mentioned belong to the astral realm. Against this background and the strong astral symbolism documented in seventh-century glyptic from Palestine (see above 2.2.), the association of the כמרים with astral cults in 2 Kgs 23.5 is thoroughly plausible.

Nonetheless, the verse in its present form is rather muddled. The use of the problematic *wĕ-qāṭal* should perhaps express the definitive elimination of the כמרים.[109] The sentence must have originally read:

והשית את הכמרים
(or., אשר נתנו מלכי יהודה לקטר*)[110]
המקטרים
[...][111] לשמש ולירח ולמזלות ולכל צבא השמים

which would yield the following translation: 'He (Josiah) removed (permanently) the כמרים priests, who burned incense to the sun(-god), the moon(-god), the fixed stars/constellations, and the entire heavenly host'.

---

[107] Albertz (1992: 297, 308 n. 2) and Koch (1992: 84 n. 11) maintain that the כמרים were experts in astral divination. As far as I know, the only piece of evidence for this is the mention of the מצלות in 2 Kgs 23.5 (on which see Spieckermann 1982: 271-73).

[108] *KAI* 225 and 226.

[109] See above, n. 94. Unlike the regular priests (כהנים), 'The *hakumarīm* are removed completely, without mention of an "afterwards" regarding them (cf. v. 9a-b); in the estimation of Josiah (and the transmitter of the text), they thus represent a more wicked group' (Tagliacarne 1989: 179). A scholarly way of doing away with the כמרים is to prefer the OG and conjecture כהנים for the original text (Schenker 2004: 63-66).

[110] The subordinate clause אשר נתנו מלכי יהודה is probably a late-deuteronomistic addition (see above, n. 96). The entire sentence from ויקטר through ירשלם is a continuation of the subordinate clause. The following ויקטר makes best sense if one applies it with RaDaQ to every single Judahite king *except* Josiah or to an unspecified subject ('each and everyone') who burned incense all over Judah and in the greater Jerusalem area, but it cannot then concern specifically the כמרים. To conjecture לקטר on the basis of Greek and Vulgate is a *lectio facilior* (Tagliacarne 1989: 169-70). Since המקטרים can hardly designate a profession, the participle must have originally specified the cultic activity of the כמרים.

[111] The absence of a copula before לשמש reveals לבעל to be a later insertion (in view of Jer. 7.9; 11.13, 17; 32.29; cf. Tagliacarne 1989: 182; *pace* Arneth 2001: 201).

Levin, considering the entire v. 5 a mess of secondary or tertiary additions, simply takes the כמרים for 'priests not from Jerusalem', whom he identifies with the כהנים of vv. 8-9.[112] Practised on such premises, history of religion becomes superfluous. In contrast, we should maintain that the כמרים represent a *specific* priestly group whose cultic activities seem to have been exclusively directed towards astral deities, and whose existence in Judah and/or Jerusalem in the seventh century probably go back to Aramean influence.[113] Note that, if correctly reconstructed, our text concerns measures within Jerusalem, close to the temple or actually in the temple area (Spieckermann 1982: 84). Regardless of whether the dissolution[114] of the כמרים by Josiah was a success or whether they could hold on for a while (Zeph. 1.4!), they are absent from cultic law and the books of Jeremiah and Ezekiel, books that seem to have been most concerned with ritual matters during the 'exilic' and 'post-exilic' periods. Apparently, כמרים no longer practised in Judah after the exile. It is therefore scarcely conceivable that their dissolution by King Josiah was only an invention of a post-exilic redactor.

3.4. Roof Altars (2 Kings 23.12*)

Let us examine a third measure: the destruction of the altars that the kings of Judah had set up 'on the roof of the upper chamber of Ahaz'.[115] Again, it is probable that the narrator relies on outside information with a pre-deuteronomistic kernel. The roof altars may well belong to the context of seventh-century astral cult practices, since nocturnal worship addressed to the gods of the night and the stars of heaven fits very well a setting on the roofs. Unfortunately, however, no primary sources support this hypothesis. Offering sacrifices on the roofs does not seem to be an Assyrian or Aramean custom. Spieckermann's assertion that 'Assyrian influence is obvious' (1982: 109)[116] is surely overstated. A piece of evidence from the Ugaritic Kirtu epic (*KTU* 1.14 II 20-27, IV 3-8) is too remote to offer any help. Zephaniah

---

[112] Levin 1984: 360 (= 2003: 205) with a thoughtless quote from Budde in n. 35: 'The כמרים are undoubtedly the same people as the כהנים of the high places from all the cities of Judah'. Similarly Barrick 2002: 67-70, but see above, n. 94.

[113] A characteristic class of seventh-century stamp seals made of dark brown limestone show a new type of individuals, some of them lyre and double-flute players, worshipping astral symbols or cult symbols of astral deities. These seals have been found at various places in Palestine/Israel, including Jerusalem, but they are not specifically limited to Judah (cf. *GGIG* §176).

[114] Not extermination, unless one prefers the Greek text with Schenker (2004: 66-67), who has the idolatrous priests burned as their Samarian colleagues of v. 20. השבית only implies the cessation of activity and permanent dissolution of the institution, *pace* Levin 1984: 360 (= 2003: 205).

[115] The 'upper chamber of Ahaz' (עלית אחז) is often considered a gloss by modern commentators. In contrast, the Antiochene Greek text speaks of 'the roofs of the upper chambers of *King* Ahaz', cf. Schenker 2004: 72-75. According to Schenker, who again favours the Greek text, these upper chambers were probably meant to be situated within the temple compound.

[116] R. Borger, Spieckermann's mentor and expert resource for Assyriological matters, would have pointed to roof altars if they were known from Assyrian texts.

1.5 and Jer. 19.13 (cf. 32.29) mention incense offerings presented to the 'host of heaven' on the roofs of Jerusalem. The roof altars of 2 Kgs 23.12* must have served the same purpose. However, whereas in Zephaniah and Jeremiah private (household?) cult is envisioned, as shown by the plural הגגות ('roofs', 2 Kgs 23.12*) seems to presuppose cult practices in the precincts of the Temple.[117] The passages quoted from the books of Zephaniah and Jeremiah, which assume that worship on the roofs continued after Josiah's reform, therefore do not contradict the historicity of Josiah's measures, since they remained confined to the temple and, again, affected a *specific* cult practice, namely sacrifice.[118]

* * *

To sum up, the end of the seventh century, quite an 'axial age' in the history of the region, still offers the most plausible religious-historical background for the three reform measures discussed above, albeit with a different degree of certainty for each. We do not know if all three purges occurred at the same period of time. Obviously, 2 Kings 23 does present the reforms in a chronological order (Lohfink 1991a: 219-21). Still, a certain coherence may be discerned:

1. All three purges are concerned with the elimination of practices that have lost their plausibility in view of the changed political climate with its new economic and cultural orientation and significantly lessened contacts with northern Syria and Assyria. Also, their upkeep costs (horses, a society of priests, roof-sacrifice) perhaps no longer stood in a realistic relationship to projected benefits and usefulness.
2. All three concentrated on the Jerusalem Temple, that is, on the royal shrine and the state cult, and did not affect cults outside of the capital, not even guild and family cults practised in the city. In this respect, their profile is, for example, clearly different from the desecration of the Tophet in the Valley of Hinnom (2 Kgs 23.10), whose historicity can be doubted in view of the continued polemic of much later times (Jer. 7.31-32; 19.5-6, 11-13; cf. 32.35; Ezek. 16.21; 20.26, 31; Lev. 18.21; 20.2-4).[119]
3. All three concern some kind of astral worship, which may be considered the hallmark of the seventh century, a period of strong Assyro-Aramean influence.[120]

---

[117] Cf. n. 115.
[118] Indeed, altars, not observatories, are the topic here, and thus it is doubtful whether 'a religious interpretation of astronomical phenomena' in the technical sense was the concern *(pace* Spieckermann 1982: 109; Lowery 1991: 205). Note that מזלות are mentioned, typically enough, in v. 5, but neither in v. 12 nor, for that matter, in Zeph. 1.5; Jer. 19.13; 32.29. Cf. Taylor 1993: 168-72.
[119] But cf. Dearman 1996.
[120] Cf. *GGIG*, Chapter VIII (pp. 283-372); Barrick 2002: 159-64.

Whether Josiah's purging of the Jerusalem state cult or royal shrine from rituals that had become obsolete should be called a 'religious reform' is debatable. A reform implies an agenda, but the actual motives behind those of Josiah's purges that can be historically substantiated are far from clear. The biblical sources present Josiah's reform as a 'new religious beginning' (Lohfink 1991a: 225), while modern scholars have sometimes construed it as a political-religious declaration of independence with anti-Assyrian tendencies.[121] Neither of these two rather far-reaching agendas seem to fit the more confined picture based on critical historical research.

4. Correlations between Primary and Secondary Sources? On the Removal of the Jerusalem Asherah (2 Kings 23.6)

The observations presented thus far have sought entry into the religious history of Judah and Jerusalem from two sides. Looking back, I realize that to a large extent the two paths run off quite independently one from another. Methodologically, this has the advantage of avoiding biblicist or historicist short circuits. The last section has also demonstrated, however, that our picture of the religious history of Judah remains incomplete if we base ourselves exclusively on the archaeological primary sources. No serious historian should dismiss secondary sources on the sole argument that they cannot be confirmed with utter precision. On the other hand, we must of course endeavor to build only upon such secondary sources that plausibly fit the primary framework based on primary sources.

The correlation of primary and secondary sources is a notoriously difficult business that in many respects can only be practised as a fragile, hypothetical combination of circumstantial evidence. A catchword like *minimalist approach* does not help much. The *minimalist approach* becomes extremely *maximalist* when it approaches the sources with inappropriate expectations, just to drop them as soon as they do not respond to gross questions. Take my hypothesis that the removal of the horses and chariots of the sun-god from the precincts of the Temple did in fact happen under Josiah: to see these measures confirmed through primary sources would be extremely unlikely. What kind of sources should we

---

[121] Cf. Lohfink 1987: 466-68; Ahlström 1993: Chapter 18; and most recently Arneth 2001: 208, 216. Two remarks are in order: first, the motives of the historical measures may have differed from those of the biblical reform report, a point acknowledged by Arneth who firmly postulates an anti-Assyrian tendency for the literary report only. Second, however, I can see no overtly anti-Assyrian stance in the report. Arneth himself seems to be hesitating on that matter, sliding from opposition against Assyria to one against 'Assyrian-influenced institutions' in his conclusions (p. 216). Asherah certainly cannot be counted among these.

expect? An ostracon with instructions for the Nathanmelek, a dated receipt from the royal stable master for having received a number of horses to be trained for military service? Chariot fittings with solar symbols in the Kidron Valley? There is no purpose in drawing up the agenda for forgers of 'biblical antiquities'. We can know so little about the past, that we should endeavor to interpret adequately what little we have.

Still, there is *one* correlation which may supplement the picture of Josiah's reform efforts as we have sketched them thus far. 2 Kings 23.6 reports that Josiah removed the Asherah from the Temple of Yahweh to the Kidron Valley, had it burned there and the dust thrown on the graves of the common people. Many consider this report, which doubtlessly responds to 2 Kgs 21.7, particularly suspect of deuteronomistic prejudice. Yet, consider the omission of '*šrth* in the later Judahite blessing formulae; consider that those of the Jerusalem elite who possessed seals appear to have placed no importance whatsoever on specific Asherah symbolism; consider the long- and medium-term transfer of divine roles and competences to Yahweh: you may then hesitate to hold Josiah's removal of Asherah from the Jerusalem Temple as a mere invention. As far as I can see, there are neither primary nor secondary sources that attest to the existence of Asherah in the Jerusalem Temple (be it as a cult symbol or as a statue of a goddess) after Josiah.[122] It may well be that the removal of personified 'evil' towards Shinar in Zechariah's sixth vision (Zech. 5.5-11) concerns the banning of a goddess, formerly worshipped 'in the entire land' (v. 6). But the text is enigmatic enough and does not provide evidence for a continued worship of Asherah in the pre-exilic temple of Jerusalem.[123]

Let us stop here, before removing ourselves too far from likelihood towards sheer possibility, which would go beyond the limits of sensible historical work. Still other reform efforts mentioned in 2 Kings 23 could well go back to the historical Josiah, though the current lack of sources prevents us from evaluating these reforms with probability comparable to that offered in the cases above.[124]

---

[122] A stamped terracotta relief applied on a sixth-century vessel from En-Gedi, portraying an enthroned man with a raised hand before a stylized tree (*GGIG* fig. 348), may come close to the idea of a royal Asherah cult. However, it can scarcely be correlated unambiguously with the Jerusalem Temple, and is probably a Phoenician product.

[123] *GGIG* §227; Uehlinger 1994: 93-103.

[124] In contrast to Hollenstein (1976: 327-30) and Würthwein (1976: 417; but see 1984: 452-53, 456), I do not consider the destruction of the cult utensils in 2 Kgs 23.4 to be part of Josiah's historical measures. The controversy over the proper cult utensils occurred in the early post-exilic period, cf. Ackroyd 1972: 166-81. On a literary and ideological level, Josiah's destruction of all utensils used in foreign cults is the premise for the concept that only pure utensils were carried off to Babylon (2 Kgs 25.14; Jer. 27.18, 21-22, note the discrepancies between the MT and OG!). Those returning from exile could use this argument to legitimate their claims to control the Second Temple.

5. Conclusion

The last thirty years or so of Old Testament scholarship has witnessed a strong general trend towards a late dating of biblical sources to the 'late pre-exilic', 'exilic' or 'post-exilic' period. At the same time, ever increasing weight has been placed on the importance of archaeological primary sources for the reconstruction of the history of Israel and Judah. Recently, archaeology has in turn come in the maelstrom of 'down-dating' with the important debate on I. Finkelstein's 'Low chronology' proposal. From the point of view of historiography and its methodological awareness, the trend towards the primary sources can only be welcomed. Nothing remains for exegetes interested in historical research but to take note of the new methodological hierarchy which implies the necessary subordination of non-archaeological, secondary documentation, including the biblical texts, to primary data.

A secondary effect of this development, however, could be the drifting apart of history and theology—a process obvious since the advent of post-modernism but engaged for the past two and a half centuries at least. Lessing's assertion, 'The accidental truths of history can never become the proof of necessary truths of reason', has become just as questionable today as the *a priori* of dialectical theology, that the truth of history stands in glaring contrast to the (deceptive) truth of myth, and that (salvation) history alone may bear revelation. These are some of the deep roots of latent 'sub-deuteronomism' of most text books on the 'history of Israel', in addition to the unquestionably difficult state of the sources that makes it easier to write a 'history' that retells the Bible rather than to get involved with the more arduous business of archaeology.

The time of Josiah and his successors until the capture of Jerusalem and the destruction of the 'First' Temple represents an 'axial age', for the religious history of Judah just as much as for the history of Old Testament theology. Though highly stylized as a time of de-connection by the deuteronomistic historians, it is also an age that provides the necessary *link* between Old Testament theology and its ancient Judahite (and ultimately 'Canaanite') roots. In the interest both of historical and theological research, we should therefore neither overstrain this link with historicist or biblicist naiveté, nor simply leap over the gap with dismissively minimalist assumptions.

Bibliography

Ackroyd, Peter R. 1972. 'The Temple Vessels: A Continuity Theme', in G.W. Anderson *et al.* (eds.), *Studies in the Religion of Ancient Israel* (VTSup, 23; Leiden: E.J. Brill, 1972): 166-81.

Aharoni, Miriam. 1993. 'Arad: The Israelite Citadels', in E. Stern (ed.), *New Encyclopaedia of Archaeological Excavations in the Holy Land* (4 vols.; Jerusalem: Israel Exploration Society): I, 82-87.

Ahlström, Gösta W. 1991. 'The Role of Archaeological and Literary Remains in Reconstructing Israel's History', in Edelman (ed.) 1991: 116-41.

Ahlström, Gösta W. 1993. *The History of Ancient Palestine from the Palaeoloithic Period to Alexander's Conquest* (JSOTSup, 146; Sheffield: Sheffield Academic Press).

Albertz, Rainer. 1992. *Religionsgeschichte Israels in alttestamentlicher Zeit* (Altes Testament Deutsch Ergänzungsbände = Grundrisse zum Alten Testament, 8; Göttingen: Vandenhoeck & Ruprecht).

Albertz, Rainer. 1994. *A History of Israelite Religion in the Old Testament Period: From the Beginnings to the End of the Monarchy* (OTL; Louisville, KY: Westminster/John Knox Press).

Arneth, Martin. 2001. 'Die antiassyrische Reform Josias von Juda. Überlegungen zur Komposition und Intention von 2 Reg 23,4-15', *Zeitschrift für Altorientalische und Biblische Rechtsgeschichte* 7: 189-216.

Avigad, Nahman. 1986. *Hebrew Bullae from the Time of Jeremiah: Remnants of a Burnt Archive* (Jerusalem: Israel Exploration Society).

Avigad, Nahman, Michael Heltzer and André Lemaire. 2000. *West Semitic Seals: Eighth–Sixth Centuries BCE* (The Reuben and Edith Hecht Museum Collection, vol. B; Haifa: Reuben and Edith Hecht Museum).

Avigad, Nahman, and Benjamin Sass. 1997a. *Corpus of West Semitic Seals* (Jerusalem: Israel Academy of Sciences and Humanities).

Avigad, Nahman, and Benjamin Sass. 1997b. *Corpus of West Semitic Stamp Seals* (Jerusalem: Israel Exploration Society).

Barkay, Gabriel 1992. 'The Priestly Benediction on Silver Plaques from Ketef Hinnom in Jerusalem', *TA* 19: 139-92.

Barrick, W. Boyd. 2002. *The King and the Cemeteries: Toward a New Understanding of Josiah's Reform* (VTSup, 88; Leiden: E.J. Brill).

Beuken, W.A.M. 1993. 'משכב', in J. Botterweck *et al.* (eds.), *Theologisches Wörterbuch zum Alten Testament*, VII (Stuttgart: W. Kohlhammer): 1306-18.

Brandfon, Frederick R. 1987. 'Kinship, Culture and "Longue Durée" ', *JSOT* 39: 30-38.

Braudel, Fernand. 1990. *La Méditerranée et le monde méditerranéen à l'époque de Philippe II* (Paris: Armand Colin, 9th edn [first published 1949]).

Braudel, Fernand. 1958. 'Histoire et sciences sociales, la longue durée', *Annales. Économies, Sociétés, Civilisations* 13: 725-53; reprinted in F. Braudel, *Écrits sur l'histoire*, I (Champs, 23; Paris: Flammarion, 1984): 44-61.

Claburn, W. Eugene. 1973. 'The Fiscal Basis of Joasiah's Reforms', *JBL* 92: 11-22.

Cogan, Mordechai. 1974. *Imperialism and Religion: Assyria, Judah and Israel in the Eighth and Seventh Centuries B.C.E.* (SBLMS, 19; Missoula, MT: Scholars Press).

Cogan, Mordechai. 1993. 'Judah under Assyrian Hegemony: A Reexamination of Imperialism and Religion', *JBL* 112: 403-14.

Conrad, Diethelm 1979. 'Einige (archäologische) Miszellen zur Kultgeschichte Judas in der Königszeit', in A.H.J. Gunneweg and O. Kaiser (ed.), *Textgemäß. Aufsätze und Beiträge zur Hermeneutik des Alten Testaments* (Festschrift E. Würthwein; Göttingen: Vandenhoeck & Ruprecht): 28-32.

Coogan, M., J.C. Exum and L.E. Stager (eds.). 1994. *Scripture and Other Artifacts: Essays on the Bible and Archaeology in Honor of Philip J. King* (Louisville, KY: Westminster/John Knox Press).

Coote, Robert B., and Keith W. Whitelam. 1987. *The Emergence of Early Israel in Historical Perspective* (SWBA, 5; Sheffield: Sheffield Academic Press).

Dearman, John A. 1996. 'The Tophet in Jerusalem: Archaeology and Cultural Profile', *JNSL* 22: 59-71.

Deutsch, Robert. 1999. *Messages from the Past: Hebrew Bullae from the Time of Isaiah Through the Destruction of the First Temple* (Tel Aviv-Jaffa: Archaeological Center Publications).

Deutsch, Robert. 2003a. *Biblical Period Hebrew Bullae: The Josef Chaim Kaufman Collection* (Tel Aviv-Jaffa: Archaeological Center Publications).

Deutsch, Robert. 2003b. 'A Hoard of Fifty Hebrew Bullae from the Time of Hezekiah', in *idem* (ed.), *Shlomo: Studies in Epigraphy, Iconography, History and Archaeology in Honor of Shlomo Moussaieff* (Tel Aviv-Jaffa: Archaeological Center Publications): 45-98.

Deutsch, Robert, and Michael Heltzer. 1994. *Forty New [sic] Ancient West Semitic Inscriptions* (Tel Aviv-Jaffa: Archaeological Center Publications).

Deutsch, Robert, and Michael Heltzer. 1995. *New Epigraphic Evidence from the Biblical Period* (Tel Aviv-Jaffa: Archaeological Center Publications).

Deutsch, Robert, and Michael Heltzer. 1997. *Windows to the Past* (Tel Aviv-Jaffa: Archaeological Center Publications).

Deutsch, Robert, and Michael Heltzer. 1999. *West Semitic Epigraphic News of the 1st Millennium BCE. With a contribution by Gabriel Barkay* (Tel Aviv-Jaffa: Archaeological Center Publications).

Deutsch, Robert, and André Lemaire. 2003. *The Adoniram Collection of West Semitic Inscriptions* (Tel Aviv-Jaffa: Archaeological Center Publications).

Dever, William G. 1994. 'The Silence of the Text: An Archaeological Commentary on 2 Kings 23', in Coogan, Exum and Stager (eds.) 1994: 143-68.

Edelman, Diana V. (ed.) 1991. *The Fabric of History: Text, Artifact and Israel's Past* (JSOTSup, 127; Sheffield: Sheffield Academic Press).

Eggler, Jürg. 2003. 'Die eisen-II-zeitlichen Siegel und -abdrücke aus Grabungen in Moab', in F. Ninow (ed.), *Wort und Stein. Studien zur Theologie und Archäologie* (Beiträge zur Erforschung der antiken Moabitis [Ard el-Kerak], 4; Frankfurt: Peter Lang): 33-87.

Einykel, Erik. 1995. *The Reform of King Josiah and the Composition of the Deuteronomistic History* (OTS, 33; Leiden: E.J. Brill).

Fried, Lisbeth E. 2002 'The High Places (*BĀMÔT*) and the Reforms of Hezekiah and Josiah: An Archaeological Investigation', *JAOS* 122: 437-65.

Gieselmann, Bernd. 1994. 'Die sogenannte josianische Reform in der gegenwärtigen Forschung', *ZAW* 106: 223-42.

Gross, W. (ed.). 1995. *Jeremia und die 'deuteronomistische Bewegung'* (BBB, 98; Weinheim: Beltz Athenäum).

Hardmeier, Christof. 2000. 'König Joschija in der Klimax des DtrG (2Reg 22f.) und das vordtr Dokument einer Kultreform am Residenzort (23,4-15*). Quellenkritik, Vorstufenrekonstruktion und Geschichtstheologie in 2Reg 22f.', in R. Lux (ed.), *Erzählte Geschichte. Beiträge zur narrativen Kultur im alten Israel* (Biblisch-Theologische Studien, 40; Neukirchen-Vluyn: Neukirchener Verlag): 81-145.

Hardmeier, Christof (ed.). 2001. *Steine—Bilder—Texte. Historische Evidenz außerbiblischer und biblischer Quellen* (Arbeiten zur Bibel und ihrer Geschichte, 5; Leipzig: Evangelische Verlagsanstalt).

Herzog, Ze'ev. 1997. 'Arad: Iron Age Period', in E. Meyers (ed.), *The Oxford Encyclopedia of Archaeology in the Near East* (5 vols.; Oxford: Oxford University Press): I, 174-76.

Herzog, Ze'ev. 2001. 'The Date of the Temple at Arad: Reassessment of the Stratigraphy and the Implications for the History of Religion in Judah', in A. Mazar (ed.), *Studies in the Archaeology of the Iron Age in Israel and Jordan* (JSOTSup, 331; Sheffield: Sheffield Academic Press): 156-78.

Herzog, Ze'ev. 2002. 'The Fortress Mound at Tel Arad: An Interim Report', *TA* 29: 3-109.

Herzog, Ze'ev, Miriam Aharoni, Anson F. Rainey and Shmuel Moshkovitz. 1984. 'The Israelite Fortress at Arad', *BASOR* 254: 1-34.

Hjelm, Ingrid. 1999. 'Cult Centralization as a Device of Cult Control?', *SJOT* 13: 298-309.

Hoffmann, Hans-Detlef. 1980. *Reform und Reformen. Untersuchungen zu einem Grundthema der deuteronomistischen Geschichtsschreibung* (ATANT, 66; Zürich: TVZ).

Holladay, John S. 1987. 'Religion in Israel and Judah Under the Monarchy: An Explicitly Archaeological Approach', in Miller, Hanson and McBride (eds.) 1987: 249-99.

Hollenstein, Helmut. 1977. 'Literarkritische Erwägungen zum Bericht über die Reformmaßnahmen Josias 2 Kön. xxiii 4ff'., *VT* 27: 321-36.

Keel, Othmar, and Max Küchler. 1982. *Orte und Landschaften der Bibel. Ein Handbuch und Studienreiseführer*. II. *Der Süden* (Zürich: Benziger; Göttingen: Vandenhoeck & Ruprecht).

Keel, Othmar, and Christoph Uehlinger. 1992. *Göttinnen, Götter und Gottessymbole. Neue Erkenntnisse zur Religionsgeschichte Kanaans und Israels aufgrund bislang unerschlossener ikonographischer Quellen* (QD, 134; Freiburg: Herder [5th edn 2001]).

Keel, Othmar, and Christoph Uehlinger. 1994. 'Jahwe und die Sonnengottheit von Jerusalem', in W. Dietrich and M. Klopfenstein (eds.), *Ein Gott allein? JHWH-Verehrung und biblischer Monotheismus im Kontext der israelitischen und altorientalischen Religionsgeschichte* (OBO, 139; Freiburg: Universitätsverlag; Göttingen: Vandenhoeck & Ruprecht): 269-306.

Kletter, Raz. 1996. *Judaean Pillar-Figurines and the Archaeology of Asherah* (BAR International Series, 636; Oxford: Tempus Reparatum).

Knauf, Ernst Axel. 1991a. 'From History to Interpretation', in Edelman (ed.) 1991: 26-64.

Knauf, Ernst Axel. 1991b. 'King Solomon's Copper Supply', in E. Lipiński (ed.), *Phoenicia and the Bible* (Studia Phoenicia, 11; Orientalia Lovaniensia Analecta, 44; Leuven: Peeters): 167-86.

Knauf, Ernst Axel. 2002. 'Who Destroyed Beersheba II?', in U. Hübner and E.A. Knauf (eds.), *Kein Land für sich allein. Studien zum Kulturkintakt in Kanaan, Israel/Palästina und Ebirnâri für Manfred Weippert zum 65. Geburtstag* (OBO, 186; Freiburg: Universitätsverlag; Göttingen: Vandenhoeck & Ruprecht): 181-95.

Koch, Klaus. 1992. 'Gefüge und Herkunft des Berichts über die Kultreformen des Königs Josia. Zugleich ein Beitrag zur Bestimmung hebräischer "Tempora" ', in J. Hausmann and H.-J. Zobel (eds.), *Alttestamentlicher Glaube und Biblische Theologie* (Festschrift H.D. Preuss; Stuttgart: W. Kohlhammer): 80-92.

Koch, Klaus. 1999. 'Molek astral', in A. Lange, H. Lichtenberger and D. Römheld (eds.), *Mythos im Alten Testament und seiner Umwelt* (Festschrift H.-P. Müller; BZAW, 278; Berlin: W. de Gruyter): 29-50.

Laato, Antti. 1992. *Josiah and David Redivivus: The Historical Josiah and the Messianic Expectations of Exilic and Postexilic Times* (ConBOT, 33; Stockholm: Almqvist & Wiksell).

Lemaire, André. 1977. 'Les inscriptions de Khirbet el-Qôm et l'Ashérah de Yhwh', *RB* 84: 595-608.

Lemaire, André. 1999. 'New Palaeo-Hebrew Seals and Bullae', *ErIs* 26: 106*-15*.

Levin, Christoph. 1984. 'Joschija im deuteronomistischen Geschichtswerk', *ZAW* 96: 351-71; reprinted in C. Levin, *Fortschreibungen. Gesammelte Studien zum Alten Testament* (BZAW, 316; Berlin: W. de Gruyter, 2003): 198-216.

Lohfink, Norbert. 1985. 'Zur neueren Diskussion über 2 Kön 22–23', in *idem* (ed.) 1985: 24-48; reprinted in Lohfink 1991b: 179-207.

Lohfink, Norbert. 1987. 'The Cult Reform of Josiah of Judah: 2 Kings 22–23 as a Source for the History of Israelite Religion', in Miller, Hanson and McBride (eds.) 1987: 459-75.

Lohfink, Norbert. 1991a. 'Die Kultreform Joschijas von Juda. 2 Kön 22–23 als religionsgeschichtliche Quelle', in Lohfink 1991b: 209-27.

Lohfink, Norbert. 1991b. *Studien zum Deuteronomium und zur deuteronomistischen Literatur II* (Stuttgarter Bibilische Aufsatz-Bände, 12; Stuttgart: Katholisches Bibelwerk).

Lohfink, Norbert. 1995. 'Gab es eine deuteronomistische Bewegung?', in Gross (ed.) 1995: 313-82; reprinted in N. Lohfink, *Studien zum Deuteronomium und zur deuteronomistischen Literatur III* (Stuttgarter Bibilische Aufsatz-Bände, 20; Stuttgart: Katholisches Bibelwerk, 1996): 65-142.

Lohfink, Norbert (ed.). 1985. *Das Deuteronomium. Entstehung, Gestalt und Botschaft* (BETL, 68; Leuven: Peeters).

Lopasso, V. 1999. 'La riforma di Giosia nel Nord', *BeO* 41: 29-40.

Lowery, Richard H. 1991. *The Reforming Kings: Cult and Society in First Temple Judah* (JSOTSup, 120; Sheffield: Sheffield Academic Press).

Mazar, Amihai, and Ehud Netzer. 1986. 'On the Israelite Fortress at Arad', *BASOR* 263: 87-91.

McCarter, P. Kyle. 1999. 'The Bulla of Nathan-Melech, the Servant of the King', in P.H. Williams and Th. Hiebert (eds.), *Realia Dei* (Festschrift E.F. Campbell; Scholars Press Homage Series, 23; Atlanta: Scholars Press): 142-53.

Miller, P.D., P.D. Hanson and S.D. McBride (eds.). 1987. *Ancient Israelite Religion* (Festschrift F.M. Cross; Philadelphia: Fortress Press).

Müller, Hans-Peter. 1992. 'Kolloquialsprache und Volksreligion in den Inschriften von Kuntillet 'Aǧrūd und Kirbet el-Qōm', *ZAH* 5: 15-51.

Na'aman, Nadav. 1991. 'The Kingdom of Judah under Josiah', *TA* 18: 3-71.

Na'aman, Nadav. 1995. 'The Debated Historicity of Hezekiah's Reform in the Light of Historical and Archaeological Research', *ZAW* 107: 179-95.

Na'aman, Nadav. 1996. 'The Dedicated Treasures Buildings within the House of Yhwh where Women Weave Coverings for Asherah (2 Kings 23,7)', *BN* 83: 17-18.

Na'aman, Nadav. 2002. 'The Abandonment of Cult Places in the Kingdoms of Israel and Judah as Acts of Cult Reform', *UF* 34: 585-602.

Na'aman, Nadav. 2003. 'The Distribution of Messages in the Kingdom of Judah in Light of the Lachish Ostraca', *VT* 53: 169-80.

Nakhai, Beth Alpert. 2001. *Archaeology and the Religions of Canaan and Israel* (ASOR Books, 7; Boston, MA: American Schools of Oriental Research).

Niehr, Herbert. 1995. 'Die Reform des Joschija. Methodische, historische und religionsgeschichtliche Aspekte', in Gross (ed.) 1995: 33-55.

Niehr, Herbert. 1999. 'Auf dem Weg zu einer Religionsgeschichte Israels und Judas. Annäherungen an einen Problemkreis', in B. Janowski and M. Köckert (eds.), *Religionsgeschichte Israels. Formale und materiale Aspekte* (VWGTh, 15; Gütersloh: Gütersloher Verlagshaus): 57-78.

Ornan, Tallay. 1993. 'The Mesopotamian Influence on West Semitic Inscribed Seals: A Preference for the Depiction of Mortals', in Sass and Uehlinger (eds.) 1993: 52-73.

Paul, M.J. 1985. 'Hilkiah and the Law (2 Kings 22) in the 17th and 18th Centuries: Some Influences on W.M.L. de Wette', in Lohfink (ed.) 1985: 9-12.
Pongratz-Leisten, Beate, Karlheinz Deller and Erika Bleibtreu. 1992. 'Götterstreitwagen und Götterstandarten: Götter auf dem Feldzug und ihr Kult im Feldlager', *Baghdader Mitteilungen* 23: 291-356.
Preuss, Horst Dietrich. 1982. *Deuteronomium* (Erträge der Forschung, 164; Darmstadt: Wissenschaftliche Buchgesellschaft).
Preuss, Horst Dietrich. 1993. 'Zum deuteronomistischen Geschichtswerk', *TRu* 58: 229-64.
Rainey, Anson F. 1994. 'Hezekiah's Reform and the Altars at Beersheba and Arad', in Coogan, Exum and Stager (eds.) 1994: 333-54.
Renz, Johannes. 1995. *Die althebräischen Inschriften.* I. *Text und Kommentar* (Handbuch der althebräischen Epigraphik, 1; Darmstadt: Wissenschaftliche Buchgesellschaft).
Renz, Johannes. 2001. 'Der Beitrag der althebräischen Epigraphik zur Exegese des Alten Testaments und zur Profan- und Religionsgeschichte Palästinas. Leistung und Grenzen, aufgezeigt am Beispiel der Inschriften des (ausgehenden) 7. Jahrhunderts vor Christus', in Hardmeier (ed.) 2001: 123-58.
Reuter, Eleonore. 1993. *Kultzentralisation. Zur Entstehung und Theologie von Dtn 12* (BBB, 87; Frankfurt: Hain).
Sass, Benjamin. 1993. 'The Pre-Exilic Hebrew Seals: Iconism vs. Aniconism', in Sass and Uehlinger (eds.) 1993: 194-256.
Sass, Benjamin, and Christoph Uehlinger (eds.). 1993. *Studies in the Iconography of Northwest Semitic Inscribed Seals* (OBO, 125; Fribourg: University Press; Göttingen: Vandenhoeck & Ruprecht).
Schenker, Adrian. 2004. *Älteste Textgeschichte der Königsbücher. Die hebräische Vorlage der ursprünglichen Septuaginta als älteste Textform der Königsbücher* (OBO, 199; Fribourg: Academic Press; Göttingen: Vandenhoeck & Ruprecht).
Schroer, Silvia. 1987. *In Israel gab es Bilder. Nachrichten von darstellender Kunst im Alten Testament* (OBO, 74; Freiburg: Universitätsverlag; Göttingen: Vandenhoeck & Ruprecht).
Seidl, Ursula. 1989. *Die babylonischen Kudurru-Reliefs. Symbole mesopotamischer Gottheiten* (OBO, 87; Freiburg: Universitätsverlag; Göttingen: Vandenhoeck & Ruprecht).
Shiloh, Yigal. 1986. 'A Group of Hebrew Bullae from the City of David', *IEJ* 36: 16-38.
Shiloh, Yigal, and David Tarler. 1986. 'Bullae from the City of David: A Hoard of Seal Impressions from the Israelite Period', *BA* 49: 196-209.
Shoham, Yair. 1994. 'A Group of Hebrew Bullae from Yigal Shiloh's Excavations in the City of David', in H. Geva (ed.), *Ancient Jerusalem Revealed* (Jerusalem: Israel Exploration Society): 55-61.
Shoham, Yair. 2000. 'Hebrew Bullae', in D.T. Ariel (ed.), *Excavations in the City of David.* VI. *Inscriptions* (Qedem, 41; Jerusalem: Institute of Archaeology, Hebrew University): 29-57.
Singer-Avitz, Lily. 2002. 'Arad: The Iron Age Pottery Assemblages', *TA* 29: 110-214.
Spieckermann, Hermann. 1982. *Juda unter Assur in der Sargonidenzeit* (FRLANT, 129; Göttingen: Vandenhoeck & Ruprecht).
Starr, Ivan. 1990. *Queries to the Sungod: Divination and Politics in Sargonid Assyria* (SAA, 4; Helsinki: Helsinki University Press).
Swanson, Kristin A. 2002. 'A Reassessment of Hezekiah's Reform in Light of Jar Handles and Iconographic Evidence', *CBQ* 64: 460-69.
Sweeney, Marvin A. 2001. *King Josiah of Judah: The Lost Messiah of Israel* (New York and Oxford: Oxford University Press).

Tagliacarne, Pierfelice. 1989. *'Keiner war wie er'. Untersuchung zur Struktur von 2 Könige 22–23* (ATSAT, 31; St Ottilien: EOS).
Taylor, J. Glenn. 1993. *Yahweh and the Sun: Biblical and Archaeological Evidence for Sun Worship in Ancient Israel* (JSOTSup, 111; Sheffield: JSOT Press).
Toloni, G. 1998. 'Una strage di sacerdoti? Dalla storiografia alla storia in 2 Re 23,4b-5', *Estudios Bíblicos* 56: 41-60.
Uehlinger, Christoph. 1993. 'Northwest Semitic Inscribed Seals, Iconography and Syro-Palestinian Religions of Iron Age II: Some Afterthoughts and Conclusions', in Sass and Uehlinger (eds.) 1993: 257-88.
Uehlinger, Christoph. 1994. 'Die Frau im Efa (Sach 5,5-11): eine Programmvision von der Abschiebung der Göttin', *Bibel und Kirche* 49: 93-103.
Uehlinger, Christoph. 1995. 'Gab es eine joschijanische Kultreform? Plädoyer für ein begründetes Minimum', in Gross (ed.) 1995: 57-89.
Uehlinger, Christoph. 1996. 'Astralkultpriester und Fremdgekleidete, Kanaanvolk und Silberwäger. Zur Verknüpfung von Kult- und Sozialkritik in Zefanja 1', in W. Dietrich and M. Schwantes (ed.), *'Der Tag wird kommen'. Ein interkontextuelles Gespräch über das Buch des Propheten Zefanja* (Stuttgarter Bibel-Studien, 170; Stuttgart: Katholisches Bibelwerk): 49-83.
Uehlinger, Christoph. 1997. 'Review of Eynikel 1996', *BO* 57: 144-51.
Uehlinger, Christoph. 1998. 'Westsemitisch beschriftete Stempelsiegel: ein Corpus und neue Fragen', *Bib* 79: 103-19 (review of Avigad and Sass, *Corpus of West Semitic Seals*).
Uehlinger, Christoph. 2001. 'Bildquellen und "Geschichte Israels": grundsätzliche Überlegungen und Fallbeispiele', in Hardmeier (ed.) 2001: 25-77.
Ussishkin, David. 1988. 'The Date of the Judaean Shrine at Arad', *IEJ* 38: 142-57.
Von Soden, Wolfram. 1991. 'Gab es bereits im vorexilischen Hebräisch Aramaismen in der Bildung und der Verwendung von Verbalformen?', *ZAH* 4: 32-45.
Weinfeld, Moshe. 1972. 'The Worship of Molech and the Queen of Heaven and its Background', *UF* 4: 133-54.
Weinfeld, Moshe. 1991. *Deuteronomy 1–11* (AB, 5; Garden City, NY: Doubleday).
Weippert, Helga. 1981. *Schöpfer des Himmels und der Erde. Ein Beitrag zur Theologie des Jeremiabuches* (Stuttgarter Bibel-Studien, 102; Stuttgart: Katholisches Bibelwerk).
Weippert, Helga. 1988. *Palästina in vorhellenistischer Zeit* (Handbuch der Archäologie, Vorderasien II.1; Munich: Beck).
Weippert, Helga, and Manfred Weippert. 1991. 'Die Vorgeschichte Israels in neuem Licht', *TRu* 56: 341-90.
Weippert, Manfred. 1990. 'Die Petition eines Erntearbeiters aus Mᵉṣad Ḥăšavyāhū und die Syntax althebräischer erzählender Prosa', in E. Blum, C. Macholz and E.W. Stegemann (eds.), *Die Hebräische Bibel und ihre zweifache Nachgeschichte* (Festschrift R. Rendtorff; Neukirchen-Vluyn: Neukirchener Verlag): 449-66.
Weippert, Manfred. 1993. 'Geschichte Israels am Scheideweg', *TRu* 58: 71-103.
Whitelam, Keith. 1986. 'Recreating the History of Israel', *JSOT* 35: 45-70.
Würthwein, Ernst. 1976. 'Die joschijanische Reform und das Deuteronomium', *ZTK* 73: 395-423.
Würthwein, Ernst. 1984. *Die Bücher der Könige. I. 1. Kön. 17–2. Kön. 25* (ATD 11.2; Göttingen: Vandenhoeck & Ruprecht).
Yardeni, Ada. 1991. 'Remarks on the Priestly Blessing on Two Ancient Amulets from Jerusalem', *VT* 41: 176-85.

Zevit, Ziony. 2001. *The Religions of Ancient Israel: A Synthesis of Parallactic Approaches* (London and New York: Continuum).

Zimhoni, Ora. 1985. 'The Iron Age Pottery of Tel 'Eton and its Relation to the Lachish, Tell Beit Mirsim and Arad Assemblages', *TA* 12: 63-90; reprinted in Zimhoni 1997: 179-210.

Zimhoni, Ora. 1990. 'Two Ceramic Assemblages from Lachish Levels III and II', *TA* 17: 3-52; reprinted in Zimhoni 1997: 211-62.

Zimhoni, Ora. 1997. *Studies in the Iron Age Pottery of Israel: Typological, Archaeological and Chronological Aspects* (Tel Aviv Occasional Publications, 2; Tel Aviv: Institute of Archaeology, 1997).

Zwickel, Wolfgang. 1990. *Räucherkult und Räuchergeräte. Exegetische und archäologische Studien zum Räucheropfer im Alten Testament* (OBO, 97; Freiburg: Universitätsverlag; Göttingen: Vandenhoeck & Ruprecht).

Zwickel, Wolfgang. 1999. 'Die Wirtschaftsreform des Hiskia und die Sozialkritik der Propheten', *EvT* 59: 356-77.

Part 4

Case Study:
The Problem of Nehemiah's Wall

Introduction to Part 4

This final case study falls into the period of Israelite and Judahite history following the destruction of Jerusalem after 587/586 BCE. This period after the fall of Jerusalem has often been referred to as the 'exilic' and 'post-exilic' periods, though the tendency today is to use the terms 'Neo-Babylonian' and 'Persian' periods (though the Neo-Babylonian period of course begins earlier than the fall of Jerusalem, perhaps being mostly easily calculated from the fall of Nineveh in 612 BCE). This used to be a neglected period in Hebrew Bible studies, but in recent years it has become one of the most important fields of concentrated work, especially the Persian period.

In fact, the Persian period is problematic in many ways, mainly because of lack of information, in particular from the ancient Near Eastern perspective. Much of our documentation has come from Greek sources, especially the historians Herodotus, Thucydides, and Xenophon. In the twentieth century a good many Near Eastern sources were uncovered, including the Persepolis tablets and many late Assyrian, Neo-Babylonian, and Persian cuneiform tablets. Cuneiform tablets for these periods were found from an early time, but Assyriologists tended to specialize in the earlier periods. Now we have a number of cuneiform specialists who work primarily on the Neo-Babylonian and Persian texts.

The best overview of the Persian period is the massive work of Pierre Briant (2002). It may seem daunting to the newcomer, but it is well indexed and is encyclopaedic in its coverage. A collection of early sources has been produced by another Persian specialist, Amélie Kuhrt (2007). The 2004 volume by Grabbe covers the Persian period in the history of the Jewish people and Judaism. In addition to his 2005 (see Part 3 above) volume that overlaps the Neo-Babylonian and Persian periods, Oded Lipschits has edited or co-edited a number of volumes that address various aspects of the Neo-Babylonian and Persian periods.

With regard to the case study here, Nehemiah's wall, no better illustration can be found of the historical problems thrown up by the apparent conflict between archaeological and literary sources. The book of Nehemiah, especially ch. 3, is categorical that Nehemiah supervised the repair of the Jerusalem city wall, including rebuilding some parts of it. Yet there is little or no trace of such a wall so far in the archaeology. In a 2008 article ISRAEL FINKELSTEIN looked thoroughly at the archaeology and pointed out this lack of evidence.[1] He suggested

---

[1] Finkelstein (2008) 'Jerusalem in the Persian (and Early Hellenistic) Period and the Wall of Nehemiah', *JSOT* 32: 501-20.

several solutions, though the one he favoured was that no such building took place in Nehemiah's time. The article reprinted here is a revision and expansion of that original article. Yet, as pointed out in Part 1, Nadav Na'aman has rightly questioned whether archaeology can be the final arbiter in a case like this. Finkelstein's colleague, Oded Lipschits, recognizes the archaeological conundrum but nevertheless argues that the literary evidence is too strong to be dismissed. He suggests various ways as to why the archaeology should not be considered definitive in this case. Finally, we have the interesting essay by Nadav Na'aman (see Annotated Bibliography) who showed the discrepancy between the importance of several cities in the Late Bronze (as shown by the Amarna letters) and their archaeology so far found. Readers will have to weigh the issues and make up their own mind, but this will make them aware of some of the difficulties faced by historians of this period.

Summary of Papers

25. **ISRAEL FINKELSTEIN** ('Geographical Lists in Ezra and Nehemiah in the Light of Archaeology: Persian or Hellenistic?') examines the question of Jerusalem in the Persian Period and the Wall of Nehemiah. In his view, the archaeology of Jerusalem in the Persian (and Early Hellenistic) period—the size of the settlement and whether it was fortified—is crucial to understanding the history of the province of Yehud, the reality behind the book of Nehemiah and the process of compilation and redaction of certain biblical texts. It is therefore essential to look at the finds free of preconceptions (which may stem from the account in the book of Nehemiah) and only then attempt to merge archaeology and text. A considerable number of studies dealing with Jerusalem in the Persian period have been published in recent years. Although the authors were aware of the results of recent excavations, which have shown that the settlement was poor and limited to the eastern ridge (the City of David), they continued to refer to a meaningful, fortified 'city' with a relatively large population. All the scholars who dealt with the nature of Jerusalem in the Persian period based their discussion on the biblical text, mainly on the description of the reconstructed city-wall in Nehemiah 3. Intensive archaeological research in Jerusalem in the past 40 years has shown that:

1. The southwestern hill was part of the fortified city in the late Iron II and the Late Hellenistic periods.
2. The southwestern hill was not inhabited in the Persian and Early Hellenistic periods. The Persian and Early Hellenistic settlement should therefore be sought on the southeastern ridge—the City of David.

In the City of David, too, the evidence is fragmentary. Most finds from the Persian and Early Hellenistic periods were retrieved from the central part of the ridge, between Areas G and D of the Shiloh excavations. In the case of the City of David, too, the negative evidence is as important as the positive. No Persian or Early Hellenistic finds were retrieved in the southern tip of the ridge and from the area between the Temple Mount and Area G of the Shiloh excavations. The maximal size of the Persian and Early Hellenistic settlement was c. 240 (N-S) × 120 (E-W) m, that is, c. 20–25 dunams. Calculating the population according to the broadly accepted density coefficient of 20 people per one built-up dunam – a number which may be too high for what seems to have been a sparsely settled ridge – one reaches an estimated population of 400–500 people; that is, about 100 adult men.

Two finds in the field have been perceived as indications for the course of Nehemiah's city-wall: a wall excavated by Kenyon on the crest above the eastern slope of the City of David and a structure unearthed by Crowfoot on the western side of that ridge. Yet, both finds cannot be dated to the Persian period. Also, there is no indication for the renovation in the Persian period of the ruined late Iron II city wall. Therefore, there is no archaeological evidence for the city-wall of Nehemiah. Had it not been for the Nehemiah 3 account, no scholar would have argued for a Persian period city-wall in Jerusalem. Another clue that Nehemiah 3 does not reflect Persian period realities may be found in the archaeology of two of the three well-identified and excavated (rather than surveyed) sites mentioned in the list: Beth-zur and Gibeon. Beth-zur yielded only limited Persian period finds and Gibeon was not inhabited between the sixth century and the late-Hellenistic period.

So what is the historical reality behind the description of Nehemiah's rebuilding of the walls of Jerusalem? Scholars have noted the independent nature of the list in Nehemiah 3 as compared to the rest of the 'Nehemiah Memoir', but are divided on the question of whether Nehemiah used an earlier or a contemporary source that was kept in the Temple archives, or whether a later editor inserted the text into the Book of Nehemiah. Taking into consideration the archaeological evidence presented in this paper, an existing source from the Persian period, which described a genuine construction effort at that time, is not a viable option. We are left, therefore, with the following possibilities:

1. That the description in Nehemiah 3 is utopian; it was based on the geographical reality of the ruined Iron II city-wall but does not reflect actual work on the wall.
2. That a Persian period author used an early source, which described the late eighth-century construction or a pre-586 renovation of the Iron II city-wall and incorporated it into the Nehemiah text.
3. That the description was inspired by the construction of the Late Hellenistic, Hasmonaean city-wall.

26. **ODED LIPSCHITS** discusses 'Jerusalem between Two Periods of Greatness: The Size and Status of the City in the Babylonian, Persian and Early Hellenistic Periods'. His aim is to present the archaeological material from Jerusalem to consider its size and status in the sixth and fifth–fourth centuries, and in the Early Hellenistic period. In the years between 586 and 167 Judah was a small province under the rule of great empires. Jerusalem became again the *Birah* of the province only in the middle of the fifth century. In contrast with the rich and well-recognized architectural remains from the seventh as well as from the second centuries, not many building-remains from the Persian and early Hellenistic periods have been uncovered in Judah or Samaria. This is the case even in sites where abundant pottery sherds, stamp impressions, figurines and other typical Persian period finds were uncovered. Under the Assyrian, Babylonian and Persian rule there was a marked process of attenuation in urban life in Judah. The administrative and urban centres that survived those periods were small and weak in comparison with their state before the sixth century or after the second century. We should also accept Stern's claim that the scarcity of building-remains from the Persian period does not reflect the actual situation at that time, but is the outcome of incomplete archaeological data. The topographical nature of the southeastern hill in Jerusalem requires that buildings be built on bedrock, which requires previous buildings to be removed. This is why archaeological remains of the sixth–third centuries have been found mainly in pockets or dumps down the valley.

The 586 destruction of Jerusalem appears prominently in the excavations over the site. The force of the destruction and the degree of demographic decline with regard to the city are there to see. The city remained desolate and deserted for the next 50 years, evidently as a result of Babylonian policy. Although the Persians supported trade cities along the coast, they did not encourage urban centres in the hill country. Not many building-remains from the Persian period have been found in the boundaries of Yehud. As in many other sites, also in most of the excavated areas at the city of David many finds from the Persian period (pottery sherds and stamp impressions) were discovered. However, in most cases these finds were not linked to any clear stratum or architectural finds. The dating of the few finds on the Western Hill (especially the *yehud* stamp impressions) leads to the conclusion that it was uninhabited during the Persian and Early Hellenistic period. Most of the pottery sherds and stamp impressions from the City of David dated to the Persian period were discovered, however, during Kenyon and Shiloh's excavations along the eastern slope: in Area G, Area E, Area D, and in the excavations of Reich and Shukron south of Area D. Only area G of Shiloh's excavations revealed many finds from the Persian period that are also related to architectural remains. In this area, Shiloh identified a clear stratum (Stratum 9) on top of Stratum 10A (the stratum of the Babylonian destruction), and under Strata 8–7 that are dated to the Hellenistic period. In Area E three different stages of Stratum 9 were distinguished. The dating, the location and the long line along the eastern slope of the ridge of quarrying refuse are all indications of the missing Persian period wall. The finds on the ridge of the City of David and on the slopes provide evidence for a poor but existing settlement in the Persian period.

Despite the relatively massive finds, the information available to us about the Persian period is still very scant, and there is no possibility of characterizing the nature of this occupation. The major find uncovered outside of the line of fortification built on the rock at the top of the eastern slope and its stratigraphic context has not been proven. As against other assumptions it seems that the remains from the Persian period were spread all along the City of David, and the areas where these finds were not discovered are the areas where intensive building activities were conducted during the Hellenistic-Roman and later periods. This is also the case as regards the Ophel. In this large area between the Temple enclosure and the City of David very intensive building activities were conducted in later periods, and the area was cleaned to the bedrock more than once. The minimum built-up area in the Persian period should be calculated, therefore, as covering only the City of David, about 350 m from north to south and about 80–100 m from east to west (ca. 28–30 dunams). To this must be added the 20 dunams of the Ophel, as the main built-up area. If we will use the accepted density coefficient of 25 people per one built-up dunam, one reaches an estimated population of 1000–1250 people. Jerusalem did not become a real urban centre before the Hellenistic period: the 'return to Zion' was a slow and gradual process. In this case it is no wonder that no such wall was discovered and securely dated to the Persian period, but the absence of the find should not serve the argument that the story in Nehemiah is a fiction. This will be too hasty.

Annotated Bibliography

This bibliography lists some of the main volumes providing recent information on the Neo-Babylonian and Persian periods (though see also Lipschits 2005 in the Part 3 Annotated Bibliography).

Briant, Pierre (2002), *From Cyrus to Alexander: A History of the Persian Empire*, trans. Peter T. Daniels (Winona Lake, IN: Eisenbrauns); ET of *Histoire de l'empire perse de Cyrus à Alexandre: Volumes I–II*, Achaemenid History 10 (Leiden: Nederlands Instituut voor het Nabije Oosten, 1996 [originally published by Librairie Arthème Fayard, Paris]).
This is the definitive history of Persia in the Achaemenid period, encyclopaedic in scope and content. Because there is so much information, some may be put off consulting the volume, but there are good indexes and the notes also provide orientation on the sources used and also why the author has made certain choices in his reconstruction of Persian history. The volume of sources by Kuhrt (2007) listed below is a very useful companion.

Carter, Charles E. (1999), *The Emergence of Yehud in the Persian Period: A Social and Demographic Study*, JSOTSup 294 (Sheffield: Sheffield Academic Press).
This was one of the first archaeological histories of Judah in the Persian period. As a pioneer volume, some aspects of its conclusions have been criticized (e.g., the demography). Division of the archaeology into 'early' and 'late' Persian is not always as easily made as the study sometimes suggests, but the overall picture given remains widely accepted. One should compare his results with those of Lipschits (2005, listed in Part 3).

Grabbe, Lester L. (2004), *A History of the Jews and Judaism in the Second Temple Period 1: Yehud: A History of the Persian Province of Judah*, LSTS 47 (London/New York: T&T Clark International).

Grabbe, Lester L. (2008), *A History of the Jews and Judaism in the Second Temple Period 2: The Coming of the Greeks: The Early Hellenistic Period (335–175 BCE)*, LSTS 68 (London/New York: T&T Clark International).
These two volumes (of a projected four-volume history of the Jews and Judaism in the Second Temple Period) cover the all-important Persian period (from the end of the Neo-Babylonian period to the invasion of Alexander) and also the early part of the Hellenistic period, from Alexander to the rule of Antiochus IV. The historical sources are surveyed in detail, and the main historical issues and questions are addressed and a variety of solutions explored.

Kuhrt, Amélie (2007), *The Persian Empire: A Corpus of Sources from the Achaemenid Period* (London and New York: Routledge).
As the sub-title indicates this is a collection of historical literary sources in English translation. The main classical historians (Herodotus, Thucydides, Xenophon, Diodorus Siculus) are readily available in English translation, but excerpts from them are given, along with other Greek histories and some inscriptions. But it is especially valuable for gathering together Mesopotamian sources (Neo-Babylonian and Persian cuneiform texts, Persepolis Fortification and Treasury tablets, texts in Old Persian). It is divided according to historical period and sociological topic. The extracts of sources have introductions and notes. At more than a thousand pages this is a valuable volume for the history of this period and a very useful companion to Briant's above.

Lipschits, Oded, and Joseph Blenkinsopp (eds) (2003), *Judah and the Judeans in the Neo-Babylonian Period* (Winona Lake, IN: Eisenbrauns).

Lipschits, Oded, Gary N. Knoppers, and Rainer Albertz (eds) (2007), *Judah and the Judeans in the Fourth Century B.C.E.* (Winona Lake, IN: Eisenbrauns).

Lipschits, Oded, and Manfred Oeming (eds) (2006), *Judah and the Judeans in the Persian Period* (Winona Lake, IN: Eisenbrauns).
Lipschits organized a series of conferences on the Neo-Babylonian and Persian periods, and co-edited the volumes in which the papers from these conferences were published. They cover such topics as whether Palestine was an 'empty land' during the exilic period, the importance of Benjamin in the exilic and post-exilic periods, the question of whether the Aramaic documents in Ezra are authentic, the archaeology of this period, and the picture arising from the sources for the fourth century where few written texts survive.

Na'aman, Nadav (2010), 'Text and Archaeology in a Period of Great Decline: The Contribution of the Amarna Letters to the Debate on the Historicity of Nehemiah's Wall', in Philip R. Davies and Diana V. Edelman (eds), *The Historian and the Bible: Essays in Honour of Lester L. Grabbe*, LHBOTS 530 (New York and London: T&T Clark International), 20–30. Na'aman begins by noting that a primary literary source, one of the Elephantine letters, shows that Jerusalem was an important political and cultic site in the Persian period. A survey of the Amarna letters in comparison with the archaeology of the period shows that the actual importance of such cities as Shechem, Gezer and Lachish (as shown by the letters) is not necessarily matched by the archaeological finds so far discovered. The same applies to Jerusalem where hardly anything from the Late Bronze has been found. The type of wall erected by Nehemiah is likely to have been thin and fragmentary and would not have lasted for any length of time nor left much in the way of archaeological remains.

Geographical Lists in Ezra and Nehemiah in the Light of Archaeology: Persian or Hellenistic?

Israel Finkelstein

The geographical lists in Ezra and Nehemiah have served as the backbone for the reconstruction of the history of Yehud. But do they really represent the Persian period? Scholars took their dating for granted because this is what the text says. But with no extra-biblical sources to support this notion, this conventional wisdom is gripped by circular reasoning. The only way out of this trap is to consult archaeology. Yet, archaeology has never been systematically and independently utilized in order to verify the background of these lists. In what follows I wish to discuss two lists – the construction of the city-wall of Jerusalem in Nehemiah 3 and the List of Returnees in Ezra 2.1-67; Neh. 7.6-68 – in the light of archaeology.

The Wall of Nehemiah

Knowledge of the archaeology of Jerusalem in the Persian (and Early Hellenistic) period – the size of the settlement and whether it was fortified – is crucial to understanding the history of the province of Yehud, the reality behind the Book of Nehemiah and even the process of compilation and redaction of certain biblical texts (on the latter see, e.g. Schniedewind 2003; 2004: 165–78; Edelman 2005: 80–150). Indeed, a considerable number of studies dealing with Jerusalem in the Persian period have been published in recent years (e.g. Carter 1999; Eshel 2000; Stern 2001: 434–36; Edelman 2005; Lipschits 2005; 2006; Ussishkin 2006). Although the authors were aware of the results of recent excavations, which have shown that the settlement was limited to the eastern ridge (the City of David), they continued to refer to a meaningful, fortified 'city' with a relatively large population.

The Current View

Carter argued that Jerusalem grew from a built-up area of 30 dunams in the Persian I period to 60 dunams 'after the mission of Nehemiah' (1999: 200) and estimated the peak population to have been between 1,250 and 1,500 people (ibid.: 288).

Eshel (2000) reconstructed the history of Jerusalem in the Persian period almost solely according to the biblical texts, arguing that the 'Jerusalem of Nehemiah was a small town ... nevertheless it had eight gates ... much more than the real need of the town at that time' (ibid.: 341). Regarding the rebuilding of the walls, following Nehemiah 3, Eshel envisioned a major operation, which involved many groups of builders.

Stern began the discussion of the archaeology of Jerusalem in the Persian period with a sentence based solely on the biblical text: 'Persian period Jerusalem was bounded by walls erected by Nehemiah' (2001: 434). At the same time he acknowledged that 'only a few traces have survived of the city wall of Nehemiah along the course described in the Bible (ibid.: 435, referring to a segment of a city-wall which was dated by Kenyon to the Persian period (below)).

Edelman (2005) saw the construction of the walls by Nehemiah as a turning point in the history of Yehud – marking the transfer of the capital from Mizpah to Jerusalem. She described a major construction effort in Jerusalem under Persian auspices in the days of Artaxerxes I – an effort far greater than the reconstruction of the city-walls, that also included the Temple and a fort (2005: 344–48).

Ussishkin declared that 'the corpus of archaeological data should be the starting point for the study of Jerusalem ... This source of information should take precedence, wherever possible, over the written sources, which are largely biased, incomplete, and open to different interpretations' (2006: 147–48). Reviewing the archaeological data, he rightly concluded that the description in Nehemiah 3 must relate to the maximal length of the city-walls, including the western hill. But then, solely according to the textual evidence in Nehemiah 3, he accepted that the Persian period settlement was indeed fortified: 'When Nehemiah restored the city wall destroyed by the Babylonians in 586 B.C.E., it is clear ... that he restored the city wall that encompassed the Southwestern Hill, as suggested by the "maximalists" ' (Ussishkin 2006: 159; also 160).

Lipschits's reconstruction of the history of Jerusalem in the Persian period (2006) revolved around the rebuilding of the city-wall by Nehemiah. Though 'there are no architectural or other finds that attest to Jerusalem as an urban center during the Persian Period' (ibid.: 31), 'the real change in the history of Jerusalem occurred in the middle of the fifth century B.C.E., when the fortifications of Jerusalem were rebuilt. Along with scanty archaeological evidence, we have a clear description of this event in the Nehemiah narrative ...' (ibid.: 34). Lipschits described Jerusalem as a 'city' of 60 dunams, with a population of ca. 1,500 inhabitants (ibid.: 32; also 2003: 330–31; 2005: 212; see a different number, 3,000 people, in 2005: 271).

Obviously, all the scholars who dealt with the nature of Jerusalem in the Persian period based their discussion on the biblical text, mainly on the description of the reconstruction of the city-wall in Nehemiah 3.

The Finds

Intensive archaeological research in Jerusalem in the past 40 years has shown that:

1. The southwestern hill was part of the fortified city in the late Iron II and the Late Hellenistic periods (for the Iron II see Geva 2003b: 505–18; 2003c; Avigad 1983: 31–60; Reich and Shukron 2003; for the Late Hellenistic period see Geva 2003b: 526–34; Wightman 1993: 111–57).
2. The southwestern hill *was not* inhabited in the Persian and Early Hellenistic periods. This has been demonstrated by excavations in the Jewish Quarter (Avigad 1983: 61–63; Geva 2003b: 524; 2003c: 208), the Armenian Garden (Gibson 1987; Geva 2003b: 524–25), the Citadel (Amiran and Eitan 1970) and Mt Zion (Broshi 1976: 82–83). Apart from a few possible isolated finds (Geva 2003b: 525), there is no evidence of any activity in any part of the southwestern hill between the early sixth century and the second century BCE. The Persian and Early Hellenistic settlement should therefore be sought on the southeastern ridge – the City of David.

In the City of David, too, the evidence is fragmentary. Most finds from the Persian and Early Hellenistic periods were retrieved from the central part of the ridge, between Areas G and D of the Shiloh excavations (Shiloh 1984: 4). The Persian period is represented by Stratum 9, which fully appears, according to Shiloh (1984: 4, Table 2), in Areas D1 (Ariel, Hirschfeld and Savir 2000: 59–62), D2 and G (Shiloh 1984: 20), and which is partially represented in Area E1. But even in these areas the finds were meagre and poor; most of them came from fills and quarrying refuse. Persian-period sherds and a few seal impressions were found in Reich and Shukron's Areas A and B, located in the Kidron Valley and mid-slope respectively, ca. 200–250 m south of the Gihon Spring; they seem to have originated in the settlement located on the ridge (Reich and Shukron 2007).

Stratum 8 stands for the Early Hellenistic period. It is fully represented only in Area E2, partially represented in Areas E1 and E3, and scarcely represented in Areas D1 and D2 (Shiloh 1984: 4, Table 2). In this case, too, the finds are meagre. They are composed of three *columbaria* (De Groot 2004) and a structure that yielded the only assemblage of Early Hellenistic pottery from Jerusalem (in Area E1 – Shiloh 1984: 15).

In the case of the City of David, too, the negative evidence is as important as the positive. No Persian or Early Hellenistic finds were found in Area A on the southern tip of the ridge. It is significant to note that in Area A1, Early Roman remains were found over Iron II remains (De Groot, Cohen and Caspi 1992). In Kenyon's Site K, located on the southwestern side of the City of David, ca. 50 m to the north of the Siloan Pool, Iron II sherds were found on bedrock, superimposed by Late Hellenistic finds (Kenyon 1966: 84).[1]

As for the northern part of the ridge, the Persian and Early Hellenistic periods were not represented in B. and E. Mazar's excavations to the south of the southern wall of the Temple Mount, which yielded Late Hellenistic and mainly Early Roman finds superimposed over Iron II buildings (E. Mazar and B. Mazar 1989: XV–XVI). It is also significant that Persian and Early Hellenistic finds were not reported from B. Mazar's excavations near the southwestern corner of the Temple Mount (B. Mazar 1971). A few finds, but no architectural remains or in situ assemblages of pottery, were retrieved by Crowfoot in the excavation of the 'Western Gate' (Crowfoot and Fitzgerald 1929) and by Macalister and Duncan (1926) in the excavation immediately to the west of Shiloh's Area G. The 8–10 m thick dump-debris removed by Reich and Shukron on the eastern slope of the City of David, near the Gihon Spring (Reich and Shukron 2007; also 2004), yielded ceramic material from the Iron II and 'late Second Temple period', but no Persian and Early Hellenistic pottery. Reich and Shukron interpret this as evidence that Area G, located upslope from their dig, was uninhabited at that time. Finally, it is noteworthy that sifting of debris from the Temple Mount recovered almost no Persian period finds (compared to a significant number of finds from the Iron II and from the Hellenistic-Early Roman periods – Barkay and Zweig 2006).

Reich and Shukron (2007) also noted that 75 of the 85 *Yehud* seal impressions from the Shiloh excavations published by Ariel and Shoham (2000) originated from Areas B, D and E. They concluded that the settlement of the Persian and Early Hellenistic periods was restricted to the top of the ridge, south of Area G (see a somewhat similar view in Ariel and Shoham 2000: 138).

All this seems to indicate that:

1. In the Persian and Early Hellenistic periods activity on the Temple Mount was not strong (compare the Iron II finds to the south of the southern wall of the Temple Mount to the negative evidence for the Persian and Early Hellenistic periods and see Barkay and Zweig 2006), and in any event did not include intensively inhabited areas;
2. The northern part of the ridge of the City of David was uninhabited;
3. The southern part of the ridge was probably uninhabited as well.

---

[1] Shiloh's Area K, located on the ridge 90 m to the north of Area A, in roughly the same line as Kenyon's Site K, was excavated to bedrock. The earliest remains date to the Early Roman period. In this case a large-scale clearing operation, which could have destroyed the earlier remains, seems to have taken place in the Roman period (also Kenyon 1965: 14; 1966: 88 for her excavations nearby).

The Persian and Early Hellenistic settlement was confined to the central part of the ridge, between Shiloh's Area G (which seems to be located on the margin of the inhabited area) and Shiloh's Areas D and E. The settlement was located on the ridge, with the eastern slope outside the built-up area. Even in this restricted area, a century of excavations, by a number of archaeologists, failed to yield even a single (!) house or proper floor from the Persian period, and only one structure from the Early Hellenistic period was found. The idea that the settlement was eradicated because of later activity and erosion (e.g. De Groot 2004: 67) must be rejected in the light of the reasonable preservation of the Late Hellenistic and Iron II remains.

The maximal size of the Persian and Early Hellenistic settlement was therefore ca. 240 (N-S) × 120 (E-W), that is, ca. 20–25 dunams (contra to the idea of a 60-dunam settlement [excluding the Temple Mount] in Carter 1999: 200; Lipschits 2006: 32; and a 30-acre settlement [possibly including the Temple Mount] in Avigad 1993: 720). Calculating the population according to the broadly accepted density coefficient of 20 people per one built-up dunam (Finkelstein 1992 and bibliography)[2] – a number which may be too high for what seems to have been a sparsely settled ridge (ibid.) – one reaches an estimated population of 400–500 people; that is, ca. 100 adult men.[3] This stands in sharp contrast to previous, even minimal, estimates of 1,250, 1,500 or 3,000 inhabitants (Carter 1999: 288; Lipschits 2006: 32; 2005: 271; 'a few thousands' in Avigad 1993: 720), estimates which call for a large settlement of 75–150 dunams – more than the entire area of the City of David.[4]

These data fit well the situation in the immediate environs of Jerusalem, where the number of spots with archaeological remains dropped from 140 in the Iron II to 14 in the Persian period (Kloner 2003a: 28*; 2001: 92; 2003a: 30* for the Early Hellenistic period). They also fit the general demographic depletion in the entire area of the province of Yehud – a maximum of 20,000–30,000 people in the Persian period according to Carter (1999: 195–205) and Lipschits (2003: 364), ca. 15,000 according to my own calculations (Finkelstein forthcoming) – about a third or a fourth of the population of that area in the late Iron II (Carter 1999: 247 based on Broshi and Finkelstein 1992; Ofer 1993).

---

[2] This coefficient is based on ethno-archaeological and ethno-historical data, which stand against Zorn 1994. Zorn reached inflated numbers which do not fit the demographic data on premodern societies. His error may have stemmed from the assumption that all buildings at Tell Nasbeh were inhabited at the same time; the truth of the matter is that no stratigraphic sequence has been established for the settlement, which was inhabited continuously for centuries, throughout the Iron and Babylonian periods!

[3] King and Stager (2001: 389) are the only scholars to speak about a small settlement with 'a few hundred inhabitants'; at the same breath they accepted the description of the construction of the city-wall by Nehemiah as historical (see below).

[4] Not to mention Weinberg's estimate, based on his interpretation of the biblical text, of 15,000 people in Jerusalem and 150,000 in Yehud in the time of Nehemiah (1992: 43 and 132 respectively).

Nehemiah's Wall

Archaeologists have accepted the description of the reconstruction of the wall in Nehemiah 3 as a historical fact, and have been divided only about the course of the fortifications. The minimalists restricted them to the City of David, and the maximalists argued that the description included the southwestern hill (see summary in Ussishkin 2006). Two finds in the field have been perceived as indications for the course of Nehemiah's city-wall: one on the crest above the eastern slope of the City of David and the other on the western side of that ridge.

Kenyon (1974: 183–84) argued that because of the collapse of the late Iron II city-wall and buildings on the eastern slope of the ridge as a result of the Babylonian destruction, the city-wall of Nehemiah was built higher up, at the top of the slope. In her Square A XVIII (adjacent to Shiloh's Area G) she identified a short segment in the city-wall that had first been uncovered by Macalister and Duncan (1926) – a wall that was later unanimously dated to the Late Hellenistic period (see literature on the First Wall above) – as the city-wall built by Nehemiah. Her dating of this segment of the wall was based on pottery found in a layer dumped against its outer face; this pottery was dated by Kenyon (1974: 183) to the fifth to early third centuries BCE (the sixth to fifth centuries BCE in ibid.: caption to Pl. 79). Shiloh, too, argued – without any archaeological evidence – that the city wall was built 'on the bedrock at the top of the eastern slope' (1984: 29; also Avigad 1993: 720). Stern (2001: 435) accepted Kenyon's identification and dating of this segment as Nehemiah's wall. Ussishkin (2006: 160), on the other hand, suggested that Nehemiah reconstructed the Iron II wall, which runs on the lower part of the eastern slope of the City of David.

The only piece of information from the western side of the City of David comes from Crowfoot's 1927 excavations. A massive structure that had been founded on bedrock, under thick layers of later occupations and debris, was identified as a Bronze Age gatehouse that continued to be in use until Roman times (Crowfoot and Fitzgerald 1929: 12–23). Albright (1930–31: 167) identified Crowfoot's 'gatehouse' with the Dung Gate of Nehemiah 3.13, while Alt (1928) proposed equating it with the Valley Gate of Nehemiah 3.13.

Yet, both finds – the wall uncovered by Kenyon and the structure unearthed by Crowfoot – cannot be dated to the Persian period.

Kenyon's identification of Nehemiah's wall was based on (yet unpublished) pottery found in a small sounding, in a fill or a dump thrown against the outer face of the wall (1974: Pl. 79). As rightly argued by De Groot (2001: 78), such a layer cannot be used for dating a city-wall. This material could have been taken from any dump on the slope and put there in order to support the wall (for the same situation in the Outer Wall of Gezer, see Finkelstein 1994: 278). Excavations immediately to the west of this spot by E. Mazar (2007a) did not unearth architectural remains of the Persian and Early Hellenistic periods. But they made clear that this segment is part of the Late Hellenistic city-wall, first uncovered by Macalister and Duncan (1926; see in details Finkelstein et al. 2007).

Ussishkin (2006) has recently dealt in detail with the structure excavated by Crowfoot and identified by him as a gatehouse. Ussishkin has cast doubt on the identification of the structure as a gate, and convincingly argued that it probably dates to the Late Hellenistic or Early Roman period (2006: 159; see also Kenyon 1964: 13).

To sum up this issue, there is no archaeological evidence for the city-wall of Nehemiah. The wall in the east dates to the Late Hellenistic period and the structure in the west – regardless of its function – also post-dates the Persian period. Had it not been for the Nehemiah 3 account, no scholar would have argued for a Persian-period city-wall in Jerusalem. Three early city-walls are known in the City of David, dating to the Middle Bronze Age, the late Iron II and the Late Hellenistic period. All three have been easy to trace and have been found relatively well preserved. No other city-wall has ever been found and I doubt if this situation will change as a result of future excavations.[5]

One could take a different course and argue, with Ussishkin (2006), that Nehemiah merely rebuilt the ruined late-Iron II wall. Yet, in the many sections of the Iron II wall that have been uncovered – on both the southwestern hill and the southeastern ridge – there is no clue whatsoever for a renovation or reconstruction in the Persian period. In the parts of the late-Iron II city wall uncovered on the southwestern hill, the first changes and additions date to the Late Hellenistic period (Avigad 1983: 65–72; Geva 2003b: 529–32). No such reconstruction has been traced in the long line of the Iron II wall uncovered in several excavations along the eastern slope of the City of David south of the Gihon spring. Archaeologically, then, Nehemiah's wall is a *mirage*.

This should come as no surprise, judging from what we do know about the Persian period settlement systems in Yehud in particular and the entire country in general. To differ from the construction of the Iron II and Late-Hellenistic fortifications in Jerusalem – which represent a well-organized territorio-political entity with significant wealth and population, evidence for high-level bureaucracy and clear ideology of sovereignty – the small community of several hundred inhabitants of Persian-period Jerusalem (that is, not many more than 100 adult men), with a depleted hinterland and no economic base, could not have possibly engaged in the reconstruction of the ca. 3.5-km-long(!) Iron II city-wall with many gates (accepting Ussishkin's reconstruction) (2006). And why should the Persian authorities allow the reconstruction of the old, ruined fortifications and make Jerusalem the only fortified town in the hill country? The explanations of scholars who have dealt with this issue – that this was made possible because of the pressure of the Delian League on the Mediterranean coast, revolt in Egypt, etc. (summaries in Hoglund 1992: 61–4, 127–28; Edelman 2005: 334–40;

---

[5] Theoretically, one could argue that Nehemiah 3 relates to the walls of the Temple compound. Yet, the description of a city-wall with many gates and towers does not comply with this possibility.

Lipschits 2006: 35–8) – seem far-fetched, given the location of Jerusalem, distance from Egypt, international roads, coastal ports or other strategic locations (Lipschits, ibid.). Indeed, Persian-period fortifications are known only along the coastal plain (Stern 2001: 464–68).

The Reality behind Nehemiah 3

So what *is* the historical reality behind the description of Nehemiah's rebuilding of the walls of Jerusalem?

Scholars have noted the independent nature of the list in Nehemiah 3 as compared to the rest of the 'Nehemiah Memoir' (Torrey 1910: 225; Williamson 1985: 200; Blenkinsopp 1988: 231; Throntveit 1992: 74–5; Grabbe 1998: 157), but are divided on the question of whether Nehemiah used an earlier or a contemporary source that was kept in the Temple archives (Kellermann: 1967: 14–17; Williamson 1985: 201; Throntveit 1992: 75; Blenkinsopp 1988: 231), or whether a later editor inserted the text into the Book of Nehemiah (e.g., Torrey 1896; 37–8; 1910: 249, who identified the editor with the Chronist; Mowinckel 1964: 109–16, who opted for a post-chronist redactor). Taking into consideration the archaeological evidence presented in this paper, an existing source from the Persian period, which described a genuine construction effort at that time, is not a viable option. We are left, therefore, with the following possibilities:

1. That the description in Nehemiah 3 is utopian; it was based on the geographical reality of the ruined Iron II city-wall but does not reflect actual work on the wall. The text may describe a symbolic act rather than an actual work, similar to symbolic acts connected to the founding of Etruscan and Roman cities. And it may correspond to an ascriptive, ideal-type of a city that ought to include a wall (cf. Odyssey 6.6-10).[6]
2. That a Persian-period author used an early source, which described the late eighth-century construction or a pre-586 renovation of the Iron II city-wall and incorporated it into the Nehemiah text.
3. That the description was inspired by the construction of the Late Hellenistic, Hasmonaean city-wall.

The first possibility is difficult to accept. The detailed description of the construction of the city-wall and the prominence of the story of the wall throughout the Nehemiah Memoirs renders it highly unlikely. Moreover, the description in Nehemiah 3 – which includes reference to many gates, towers, pools and

---

[6] I am grateful to my colleague and friend Irad Malkin for drawing my attention to these possibilities.

houses – seems to refer to a true reality of a big city; in the light of what has already been said, the late Iron II and Hasmonaean periods are the only options.

The second possibility should probably be put aside: A) There is no evidence – historical or archaeological – of major work on the Iron II city-wall in the late seventh or early sixth centuries, and it is doubtful if a source from the late eighth century would have survived until the fifth or fourth centuries without being mentioned in any late-monarchic biblical source. B) Most names of gates, towers and pools in the list do not correspond to the many such names in late-monarchic biblical texts.[7]

The third option would put Nehemiah 3 with what scholars see as late redactions in Ezra and Nehemiah, which can be dated as late as the Hasmonaean period (Williamson 1985: xxxv; Wright 2004). The usage of words such as the province *Beyond the River* (עבר הנהר – Neh. 3.7), *pelekh* and פחת (Neh. 3.11) does not present difficulty for such a late dating, as they appear in late Jewish sources (for עבר הנהר see *1 Macc.* 7.8 – Rappaport 2004: 281; for *pelekh* in the rabbinical literature [without entering the discussion on the meaning of the word] see Kohut 1926: 346; Demsky 1983: 243; for פחת see Dan. 3.27).

Dating this text to the Hasmonaean period[8] may correspond to the importance given to the figure of Nehemiah in the first two chapters of *2 Maccabees* (as the builder of the Temple!), which Bergren (1997) interpreted as an attempt to bolster the figure of Judas Maccabaeus, the hero of *2 Maccabees*, by comparing him to Nehemiah – a prominent figure in the restoration, a builder, a political leader, a zealot for the law and a paradigm of piety (ibid.: 261–62).[9] Nehemiah could have been chosen as such a model for the Hasmonaeans because he represented a non-Davidide, non-Zadokite leadership.

Clues that Nehemiah 3 does not reflect Persian-period realities may be found in the archaeology of two of the three well-identified and excavated (rather than surveyed) sites mentioned in the list – Beth-zur and Gibeon.

The archaeology of Beth-zur (Neh. 3.16) in the Persian period has been debated. Funk (1993: 261), Paul and Nancy Lapp (1968: 70; P. Lapp 1968a: 29) and Carter (1999: 157), argued that the site was very sparsely, in fact, insignificantly inhabited in the Persian and Early Hellenistic periods. Funk noted that the 'interpretation of

---

[7] Except for the Tower of Hananel and the Horse Gate, mentioned in Jer. 31.38 and 31.40 respectively. The Fish Gate and the Valley Gate appear in 2 Chron. (33.14 and 26.9 respectively), but not in late-monarchic texts.

[8] According to Nehemiah 3, the population of Jerusalem included 3,044 men, a number which translates to a total of 12,000–15,000 inhabitants (Weinberg 2000: 316). If this number has any credibility, it fits a city of ca. 600 dunams – the size of Jerusalem in the late Iron II and the second century BCE.

[9] Ben Sira (49.13), an early second-century author, also emphasizes the role of Nehemiah as a builder. This reference may indicate the existence of a pre-Hasmonean tradition about Nehemiah as a builder; it cannot be used as a proof for the construction of a wall in the Persian period.

the Persian-Hellenistic remains at Beth-zur is dependent in large measure on the extant literary references ...' (1968: 9). Based on a single locus (!), Stern (2001: 437–38; see also 1982: 36) adhered to the notion of a significant activity at the site in the Persian period. Reich (1992) argued in the same line according to an architectural analysis. The published material from the excavations (Sellers 1933; Sellers et al. 1968) includes only a limited number of finds – sherds, vessels and coins – that can safely be dated to the Persian period (Stern 2001: 437), while most forms belonging to the Persian-period repertoire are missing altogether. Hence, though archaeology may have revealed traces of some Persian-period activity at the site, it is clear that it was an important place only in the late Iron II and the late Hellenistic periods. It should be noted that Beth-zur – supposedly the headquarters of half a district in the province of Yehud – did not yield even a single Yehud seal impression (over 530 have so far been recorded – Lipschits and Vanderhooft 2007b: 3).

It is noteworthy that during the wars of the Maccabees Beth-zur was located on the border of Judaea and seems to have changed hands several times. It was fortified by Judas Maccabaeus (*1 Macc.* 4.61), held by Lysias (*1 Macc.* 6.7), fortified by Bacchides (*1 Macc.* 9.52), besieged by Simeon (*1 Macc.* 11.65) and fortified by him (*1 Macc.* 14.33). One can argue that in the Persian period Beth-zur belonged to the province of Yehud and that it became a border stronghold in the early Hellenistic Period, but there is no evidence for such a change in any source and it seems highly unlikely.

Gibeon (Neh. 3.7) did not yield unambiguous Persian-period finds either. Without going into the debate over the dating of the Gibeon winery and inscriptions – late monarchic or sixth century (see summary in Lipschits 1989: 287–91) – the *mwsh* seal impressions and wedge-shaped and reed-impressed sherds found at the site (Pritchard 1964: Figs 32.7, 48.17) attest to a certain activity in the Babylonian or Babylonian/early Persian period. Yet, typical Persian-period pottery and Yehud seal impressions were not found (for the latter see Lipschits 2005: 180). Late Hellenistic pottery and coins dated to the days of Antiochus III and John Hyrcanus are attested at Gibeon (Pritchard 1962: 163). According to Pritchard, there is 'only scant evidence of occupation from the end of the sixth century until the beginning of the first century BCE' at Gibeon (1993: 513). Still, in an attempt to provide evidence for the Gibeon of Neh. 3.7 he argued that 'scattered and sporadic settlements' did exist there during the Persian and Hellenistic periods (Pritchard 1962: 163). Stern rightly interpreted the Gibeon finds as evidence for only sixth century and possibly early Persian period activity at the site (1982: 32–3; 2001: 433; Lipschits 2005: 243–45 – sixth century).[10]

---

[10] Three other sites in the list which are well identified yielded both Persian and Hellenistic finds: Jericho (Stern 1982: 38; Netzer 2001 respectively), Zanoah (Dagan 1992: 92) and Tekoa (Ofer 1993: Appendix IIA: 28). Keilah poses a problem, as thus far surveys of the site seem to have yielded only Persian-period pottery (Kochavi 1972: 49; Dagan 1992: 161).

Another clue for dating Nehemiah 3 may be found in the Yehud seal impressions. The distribution of Groups 1–12 (Vanderhooft and Lipschits 2007), which date to the Persian period, does not fit the territory described in this chapter.[11] In the highlands, these seal impressions are concentrated in Jerusalem and its surroundings, including Ramat Rahel, with only a few (six items) found in the highlands to the north of Jerusalem. No seal impression of this type was found south of Ramat Rahel. In the east, seal impressions of these types were retrieved at Jericho and En-Gedi (six items) – a reasonable reason for the inclusion of this area within the borders of Yehud.[12] Nehemiah 3 mentions the districts of Jerusalem and Beth-haccherem (most probably Ramat Rahel – Aharoni 1979: 418), Mizpah in the north, Beth-zur in the south and Keilah in the upper Shephelah, in the southwest. Therefore the two sources of information – the distribution of the Persian period Yehud seal impressions and Nehemiah 3 – describe different situations in the history of Yehud-Judea. If it indeed reflects realities of the Hellenistic period, it may be meaningful that it does not mention a district in the Gezer/Lod area, which implies that it predates the annexation of these cities to Judaea in the 140s BCE.

There are several problems regarding the Hasmonaean option for the background of Nehemiah 3. First, the toponyms in the description of the First Wall in Josephus's *War* 5, 4.2 – especially the 'gate of the Essenes' (as well as names of gates mentioned by Josephus elsewhere) – are different from the toponyms in Nehemiah 3. But the change may be assigned to post-Hasmonaean, mainly Herodian times. A more severe problem is the prominence of the story on the construction of the city-wall throughout the Nehemiah Memoirs. Accepting a Hasmonaean reality behind the city-wall account in Nehemiah would therefore call for a drastic new approach to the entire Book of Nehemiah.

The List of Returnees

Scholars have debated the relationship between the two versions of the list (Ezra 2.1-67; Neh. 7.6-68), the historical authenticity of this source, its date, whether it represents one wave of returnees or a summary of several immigrations, and its value for estimating the population of Yehud (for the latest discussions see Carter 1999: 77–8; Edelman 2005: 175–76; and especially Lipschits 2005: 158–68 with extensive bibliography).

---

[11] I refer to the main concentrations of the seal impressions. The presence or absence of a single item means nothing, as shown by the impressions found in Babylon and Kadesh-barnea (Vanderhooft and Lipschits 2007: 21 and 27 respectively).

[12] In the west they were found at Gezer and Tel Harasim in the western Shephelah (four items altogether) – places clearly outside the borders of Yehud until the expansion of the Hasmonaean state in the days of Jonathan and Simeon; none was found in the many sites of the upper Shephelah.

Twenty places are mentioned in the list. They are located in the highlands of Benjamin, the vicinity of Jerusalem (to Bethlehem in the south), and the areas of Lod in the west and Jericho in the east. The location of three of these places – Netophah, Nebo (Nob) and Senaah – is not sufficiently well established, while the rest are well (or reasonably well) identified and hence their archaeology can be consulted.

Sites Excavated

For *Jerusalem* and *Gibeon* see above. Gibeon is mentioned in late monarchic biblical sources – in the list of towns of Benjamin (Josh. 18.25), unanimously dated to the late seventh century BCE (Alt 1925; Na'aman 1991 with previous literature) and in the Book of Jeremiah (28.1; 41.16).

Bethel was fully settled in the late Iron II (Kelso 1968: 36–7). A wedge-shaped and reed-impressed sherd found at the site (Kelso 1968: Pl. 67,8) and a Babylonian seal bought from the villagers of Beitin (Kelso 1968: 37; Stern 1982: 31) seem to indicate that the site continued to be inhabited in the sixth century BCE (and see below for the reference in Zech. 7.2). Kelso (1968: 37, 38) suggested that the town was destroyed in the second half of the sixth century.

No unambiguous evidence for a Persian-period occupation was found at Bethel; there were no architectural remains, no pottery and no seal impressions. Moreover, the foundations of the Hellenistic walls penetrated into the Iron II remains (Kelso 1968: 36) with no Persian period layer in between. The excavators speculated that a Persian-period settlement may have been located under the built-up area of the village of Beitin, near the spring, in the southern part of the site (Kelso 1968: 38), but such a settlement should have left a clear ceramic imprint at the site. The only such clue is a tiny sherd identified by Illiff as part of a fifth-century BCE Greek lekythos (Kelso 1968: 80, Pl. 37, 10).[13]

A prosperous Hellenistic settlement was uncovered at Bethel (Kelso 1968: 36, 40, 52; Lapp 1968b).

Bethel is mentioned in a large number of late-monarchic biblical sources, such as the list of towns of Benjamin (Josh. 18.22) and the description of the days of Josiah (2 Kings 23). Papyrus Amherst 63 mentions deportees brought by the Assyrians, who were probably settled at Bethel (Steiner 1991). If the mention of Bethel in Zech. 7.2 refers to a place (e.g. Meyers and Meyers 1987: 382–83; and is not part of a name of a person – e.g. Ackroyd 1968: 207), it testifies to the fact that the site was inhabited in the late sixth century. Bethel is mentioned in the list of forts built by Bacchides (*1 Macc.* 9.50).

---

[13] I wish to thank Oren Tal for checking this sherd and confirming its date as suggested decades ago by Illiffe.

Hadid is safely identified in the mound of el-Haditheh northeast of Lod. Salvage excavations at the site indicate that the late Iron Age settlement extended over the main mound and its northwestern slope (Brand 1998: 27–9). The excavation yielded two seventh-century BCE Neo-Assyrian cuneiform tablets (Na'aman and Zadok 2000). The site was occupied in both the Persian and Hellenistic periods (Brand 1997; for the Hellenistic settlement see also Nagorsky 2005).

Hadid is mentioned in connection with the history of the Hasmonaeans; it was fortified by Simon (*1 Macc.* 12, 38; 13, 13; Jos., *Ant.* XIII, 203, 392).

Jericho. Tell es-Sultan was intensively settled in the seventh century BCE. Yehud seal impressions and attic vessels (Vanderhooft and Lipschits 2007; Stern 1982: 38 respectively) indicate that the site was inhabited in the Persian period. The late Hellenistic settlement was located at Tulul Abu el-Alayiq to the southwest of Tell es-Sultan (Netzer 2001).

Jericho is mentioned in the late-seventh century BCE list of towns of Benjamin (Josh. 18.21). It is referred to in various Hellenistic sources – the Zenon papyri, *1* and *2 Macc.*, Diodorus, and Strabo (Tsafrir, Di Segni and Green 1994: 143).

Lod. The mound of Lod has never been properly excavated; in fact, its exact extent under the Arab town is not very clear (see Gophna and Beit-Arieh 1997: 88). Still, enough finds have been unearthed to show that Lod was inhabited from Neolithic to Ottoman times (ibid.). Excavations at Neve Yarak, a neighbourhood of modern Lod situated near the ancient mound, yielded Iron II, Persian and Hellenistic finds (Rosenberger and Shavit 1993; Feldstein 1997; Khalaily and Gopher 1997; Arbel 2004). It is quite clear, then, that the site was inhabited in all three periods discussed in this paper.

Lod is mentioned in *1 Macc.* 11.34 as one of the three toparchies added to the Hasmonaean territory in 145 BCE.

Sites Surveyed

Bethlehem. The ancient mound occupies the eastern sector of the ridge overbuilt by the town of Bethlehem. It seems to have been fully occupied in the Iron II (see list of spots with Iron II finds in Prag 2000: 170–71). A recent survey of parcels of land still available for research to the east of the Church of Nativity revealed Iron II and Byzantine sherds (Prag 2000); no other period is mentioned.

The only quantitative survey at the site was conducted by Ofer (1993: Appendix IIA, 13), who collected 26 rims from the late Iron II, two rims from the Persian period, and one or two rims from the Hellenistic period. Beyond indicating periods of occupation, these data are insufficient for reconstructing the size of the site and the intensity of activity in the various periods of habitation.

Bethlehem is mentioned in the LXX version of the list of towns of Judah (Josh. 15.59a) which dates to the late seventh century BCE (Alt 1925; Na'aman 1991) and in the Book of Jeremiah (41.17).

Anathoth. Early studies did not locate pre-Roman remains at the village of Anata (Blair 1936; Albright 1936). Hence the location of biblical Anathoth was sought at two sites in the vicinity of the village.

Ras el-Kharubeh was both surveyed and excavated (for early research see Bergman 1936). The modern excavation yielded a small number of sherds (40 altogether) from the late Iron II, sherds from the Persian period (about 25 per cent of the material from the dig), and a large number of sherds from the late Hellenistic period. The site was found to be eroded and sparsely inhabited (Biran 1985: 209–11). A survey conducted at the site yielded Iron II and Hellenistic sherds, but no Persian-period finds (Dinur and Feig 1993: 358).

Another site suggested for the location of biblical Anathoth is Khirbet Deir es-Sidd, which was also excavated by Biran (1985: 211–13). It was strongly inhabited in the late-Iron II, but did not yield Persian-period finds. Only a few Hellenistic-Roman sherds were found. A survey conducted at the site yielded a large number of sherds, 70 per cent of which were dated to the Iron II. Persian-period sherds were found in a tomb. Hellenistic sherds were also present (Dinur and Feig 1993: 379).

A thorough, modern survey of the village of Anata (Dinur and Feig 1993: 359–60) has shown that it is built on an ancient site. Hence there is no reason to seek the location of Anathoth elsewhere. The survey yielded 242 sherds, 35 per cent of which date to the Iron II and 10 per cent to the Hellenistic period. The Persian period is not represented.[14]

The mention of Anathoth in the Book of Jeremiah attests to its being settled in late-monarchic times.

Azmaveth is safely identified with the village of Hizma northeast of Jerusalem. The site was surveyed twice. Kallai (1972: 185) reported sherds from the Roman period and later. A more thorough and modern survey was conducted by Dinur and Feig (1993: 372–73), who reported sherds from the Iron II, Persian and Hellenistic periods.

Kirjath-Jearim is safely identified in the mound of Deir el-'Azar, above the village of Abu-Ghosh. A large collection of pottery from the site, stored by the Antiquities Authority, was studied by the author in 1992. It includes 440 sherds, of which 310 date to the Iron II, 1 to the Persian period, 49 to the Persian or Hellenistic period, 23 to the Hellenistic period, and 11 to the Hellenistic or Roman period. The number of sherds collected at the site is sufficient to state that it was strongly inhabited in the late Iron II, very sparsely inhabited – if at all – in the Persian period and inhabited in the Hellenistic period.

Kirjath-Jearim is mentioned in the late seventh century BCE list of towns of Judah (Josh. 15.60; 18.14) and in the Book of Jeremiah (26.20).

---

[14] As an editor of the volume in which Dinur and Feig and Feldstein et al.'s surveys were published, the author went over the pottery of all sites. This includes the sites reported here, Anata, Hizma, Kh. el-Kafira, Kh. el-Burj, er-Ram, Jaba and Mukhmas.

Chephirah is safely identified with Kh. el-Kafira northwest of Jerusalem. The site was surveyed twice. Vriezen (1975) collected a large number of Iron II sherds and several Persian and Hellenistic sherds (ibid. Figs. 4: 23–25 and 5 respectively). Feldstein et al. (1993: 209–11) surveyed the site thoroughly and collected 243 sherds, of which 81 per cent date to the Iron II. A few sherds were tentatively dated to the Persian period and 13 per cent were assigned to the Hellenistic and Roman periods. It is clear from these data that the main period of occupation was the Iron II, that activity at the site in the Persian period was weak, and that occupation intensified in the Hellenistic period.

Chephirah is mentioned in the late seventh century BCE list of towns of Benjamin (Josh. 18.26).

Beeroth. The location of Beeroth was debated in the early years of research (summary in Yeivin 1971: 141–42), but was later safely fixed at the site of Khirbet el-Burj on the outskirts of the modern Jerusalem neighbourhood of Ramot (ibid.). The site was surveyed and partially excavated in a salvage operation.

Kallai (1972: 186–87) was the first to conduct a modern survey at the site. He reported Iron II pottery and a single wedge-shaped and reed-impressed sherd that should probably be dated to the sixth century BCE. Feldstein et al. (1993: 231–33) conducted a more modern and thorough survey at the site and collected 212 sherds, of which 74 per cent date to the Iron II, a few to the Persian period, 9 per cent to the Persian or Hellenistic period and 8 per cent to the Hellenistic period.

A salvage excavation was conducted at the site in 1992 (Onn and Rapuano 1994). Most of the finds belonged to medieval times, but evidence was revealed for a settlement that was occupied from the Iron Age through the Hellenistic period.

It is clear from this data that the settlement was at its peak in the Iron II, that activity in the Persian period was weak and that a certain recovery occurred in the Hellenistic period.

Beeroth appears in the late seventh century BCE list of towns of Benjamin (Josh. 18.25). It is possibly mentioned in *1 Macc.* 9.4 as Βερεα. (Jos. *Ant.* 12.422 writes Βεηρζεθ, but see discussion in Rappaport 2004: 233).

Ramah is unanimously identified with the village of er-Ram north of Jerusalem. Only one modern survey was conducted at the site – by Feldstein et al. (1993: 168–69). They collected a large number of 359 sherds, of which 20 per cent date to the Iron II, 2 per cent to the Persian period and 13 per cent to the Hellenistic period. This means that the site was strongly inhabited in the Iron II, that it declined in the Persian period, and that it recovered in the Hellenistic period.

Ramah appears in the list of towns of Benjamin (Josh. 18.25) and in the Book of Jeremiah (31.15; 40.1).

Geba is safely identified with the village of Jaba northeast of Jerusalem. The site was surveyed twice. Kallai (1972: 183) reported sherds from the Iron II and the Persian period. Feldstein et al. (1993: 177–79) conducted a more thorough survey at the site and collected 284 sherds, of which 23 per cent date to the Iron II and 22 per cent to the Hellenistic period. It seems, therefore, that the site was strongly inhabited in both the Iron II and the Hellenistic period. It was probably deserted (or very sparsely inhabited) in the Persian period.

Geba appears in the late seventh century BCE list of towns of Benjamin (Josh. 18.24).

Michmash is safely identified with the village of Mukhmas to the northeast of Jerusalem. The ancient site – Khirbet el-Hara el-Fauqa – is located on the northern edge of the village. The site was thoroughly surveyed by Feldstein et al. (1993: 185–86), who collected 643 sherds (!), of which 14 per cent date to the Iron II, 10 per cent to the Persian period and 19 per cent to the Hellenistic period. This means that the site was strongly inhabited in all three periods discussed here.

Michmash served for a while as the seat of Jonathan the Hasmonaean (*1 Macc.* 9.73; Jos. *Ant.* 13.34).

Ai of the List of Returnees is a riddle. The site of et-Tell was not inhabited after the Iron I. Assuming that there is a connection between the Ai of the Book of Joshua (as a name originally derived from an etiological story) and the Ai of the List of Returnees, the only sites which may provide an archaeological reality behind this place-name are the village of Deir Dibwan, or better (from the preservation of the name point of view) Khirbet el-Haiyan, located on the southern outskirts of Deir Dibwan.

Deir Dibwan is a large village that has never been properly surveyed. Feldstein et al. (1993: 183–84) managed to collect 20 sherds there, among them a single sherd from the Iron II and all the others from the Roman period and later. This is insufficient to reach conclusions regarding the settlement history of the site.

Khirbet el-Haiyan was both excavated and surveyed. Excavation at the site revealed evidence for occupation starting in the Roman period (Callaway and Nicol 1966: 19). Kallai (1972: 178–79) collected sherds from the Roman period and later. Feldstein et al. (1993: 183) retrieved 112 sherds at the site, of which 32 per cent were dated to the Hellenistic or Roman period.

These data are not sufficient for this discussion. It seems logical to suggest that Ai of the List of Returnees should be sought at Deir Dibwan.

Ono. Gophna, Taxel and Feldstein (2005) have recently shown that Ono cannot be identified with Kafr Ana, a site that was not occupied from the Chalcolithic to the Byzantine period. Instead, they suggested identifying Ono at the site of Kafr Juna, located 1 km to the northeast of Kafr Ana. Surveys conducted there yielded a large number of Iron II, Persian and Hellenistic sherds (ibid.).

Discussion

Table 2.1 summarizes the finds at the sites mentioned in the List of Returnees.

Table 2.1 Summary of periods represented at the sites mentioned in the List of Returnees, including intensity of occupation (V = evidence for activity, but data not sufficient to specify intensity of activity)

	Iron II	**Persian**	**Hellenistic**
Jerusalem	Strong	Weak	Strong
Bethlehem	V	Weak	Weak
Gibeon	Strong	— (except for sixth century)?	Weak
Anathoth	Strong	—	Medium
Azmaveth	V	V	V
Kirjath-Jearim	Strong	Weak	Medium
Chephirah	Strong	Weak	Weak
Beeroth	Strong	Weak	Medium
Ramah	Strong	Weak	Medium
Geba	Strong	—?	Strong
Michmash	Strong	Medium	Strong
Bethel	Strong	(except for sixth century)?	Strong
Ai (if Kh. Haiyan)	—	—	V?
(if Deir Dibwan)	V		
Lod	V	V	V
Hadid	V	V	V
Ono	Strong	Strong	Strong
Jericho	V	V	V

Three to five places mentioned in the list (including places which were thoroughly excavated), were not inhabited in the Persian period, and at other sites activity was meagre. Places which are not mentioned in the list are also worth mentioning. The best marker for importance of Judaean sites in the Persian period is the number of Yehud seal impressions found in the course of their excavations (I refer to Types 1–15 in Vanderhooft and Lipschits 2007, Types 13–15 may date to the early Hellenistic period). The sites with the largest number of such seal impressions are Ramat Rahel, Jerusalem, Mizpah, Nebi Samuel, Jericho and En Gedi. Mizpah, En Gedi and Beth-haccherem (most probably Ramat Rahel – Aharoni 1979: 418) do not appear in the list, and the list does not include any name which can fit the location of Nebi Samuel. In other words, four of the six sites with the largest number of Yehud seal impressions are absent from the list – another indication that the list does not fit the reality of the Persian period.

The concentration of Yehud seal impressions of Types 13–15 (Vanderhooft and Lipschits 2007) in the area north of Jerusalem is also noteworthy. In this area Impressions 13–14 mark a growth from ca. 5.5 per cent of the seal impressions in the early group (Types 1–12, of the Persian period), to 11 per cent in the middle group. This may indicate an expansion of the province, or at least of the Jewish population, to the north, to include the highlands around Mizpah, in the late-Persian/early Hellenistic period.

Finally, it is evident that the number of returnees which appear in the list (see discussion in Lipschits 2005: 161–62) – if taken as reflecting a real demographic reality – does not fit the depleted population of Yehud in the Persian period (for the latter see Carter 1999: 195–205; Lipschits 2005: 270; Finkelstein forthcoming).

All this is sufficient to argue that the list of returnees cannot be seen as an authentic record of the places where returnees settled in the Persian period. The archaeology of the list contradicts the ideas of both those who accept the list as genuinely representing the early settlement, immediately after the return (e.g. Galling 1951; Myers 1965: 14–17), or in the days of Nehemiah (Blenkinsopp 1988: 83), and those who see it as summarizing several waves of returnees up to the days of Nehemiah (summary in Lipschits 2005: 159–60, n. 91). Based on a demographic estimate for Persian-period Yehud, Lipschits (2005: 160–61) rejected the notions of large-scale deportations at the end of the Iron II and significant waves of returnees thereafter, and suggested that the list is a literary compilation that could have been based on several censuses that were undertaken during the Persian period (for other scholars who proposed a similar solution see references in ibid: 160, n. 92). The results of this investigation make this suggestion too untenable.

There are several ways to decipher the reality behind the List of Returnees. According to the first, it reflects a late Iron II situation, possibly focused on a vague memory of the main areas from which people were deported, or the main areas to which they returned in the sixth century BCE. Another possibility is that the list has no historical value at all, and simply mentions important settlements of the late Iron II, in areas that were included in the province of Yehud. A third explanation could be that the list was compiled in the late Hellenistic (Hasmonaean) period and reflects the settlement reality of that time, against the background of a vague memory of the territory of the province of Yehud with the addition of the area of Lod. The latter possibility would also fit the demographic reality hidden behind the list.

It is noteworthy that seven of the places in the list are mentioned in the Books of Maccabees, including important places in the history of the Hasmonaeans such as Beeroth, Michmash and Hadid. The appearance in the list of Lod, Hadid and Ono is also significant, as the district of Lod was added to Judea only in 145 BCE (*1 Macc.* 11.34) – another clue that the list may depict second century BCE realities.

Conclusion

Archaeology seems to indicate that Nehemiah 3 and the List of Returnees cannot be dated to the Persian period. Though there are several possibilities to decipher the reality behind these lists, dating them to the second century BCE seems the most logical and less difficult one.

Regarding Nehemiah 3, the archaeological finds indicate that in the Persian and Early Hellenistic periods Jerusalem was a small village with a depleted population, incapable of engaging in large-scale building operations. In addition, there is no archaeological evidence for any reconstruction or renovation of the Iron II fortifications in the Persian period. Taking these data into consideration, there are three ways to explain Nehemiah 3.1: (1) that it is a utopian list; (2) that it preserves a memory of an Iron Age construction or renovation of the city-wall; (3) that the list is influenced by the construction of the First Wall in the Hasmonaean period. The latter option seems to pose lesser difficulties.

Regarding the List of Returnees, several sites mentioned in it were not inhabited in the Persian period, or were very sparsely settled. Moreover, important Persian-period places are not mentioned in the list. This leaves two main options for understanding the reality behind the list. According to the first, it portrays a late Iron II situation. According to the second, it was compiled in the late Hellenistic (Hasmonaean) period and represents the settlement conditions of the time.

Dating the actuality behind Nehemiah 3 and the List of Returnees to the Hellenistic period calls for a re-evaluation of the date of the Books of Ezra and Nehemiah, but this is beyond the scope of this article.

Concluded October 2007

Acknowledgment

Oded Lipschits and David Ussishkin read parts of this manuscript and provided me with valuable comments; I am grateful to both of them. Needless to say, the responsibility for the ideas presented in the article rests with me only.

Bibliography

Ackroyd, P.R. 1968. *Exile and Restoration: A Study of Hebrew Thought of the Sixth Century BC* (London: SCM Press).
Aharoni, Y. 1979. *The Land of the Bible, A Historical Geography* (Philadelphia: Westminster).
Albright, W.F. 1930–31. 'Excavations at Jerusalem', *JQR* 21: 163-168.
———. 1936. 'Additional Note', *BASOR* 62: 25-26.
Alt, A. 1925. 'Judas Gaue unter Josia', *PJ* 21: 100-116.
———. 1928. 'Das Taltor von Jerusalem', *PJ* 24: 74-98.
Amiran, R., and A. Eitan. 1970. 'Excavations in the Courtyard of the Citadel, Jerusalem, 1968–1969 (Preliminary Report)', *IEJ* 20: 9-17.
Arbel, Y. 2004. 'Lod', *Excavations and Surveys in Israel* 116: 40*.
Ariel, D.T., H. Hirschfeld and N. Savir. 2000. 'Area D1: Stratigraphic Report', in D.T. Ariel (ed.), *Excavations at the City of David V: Extramural Areas* (*Qedem* 40; Jerusalem: The Hebrew University): 33-72.
Ariel, D.T., and Y. Shoham. 2000. 'Locally Stamped Handles and Associated Body Fragments of the Persian and Hellenistic Periods', in D.T. Ariel (ed.), *Excavations at the City of David 1978–1985 VI, Inscriptions* (*Qedem* 41; Jerusalem): 137-171.
Avigad, N. 1983. *Discovering Jerusalem* (Nashville: T. Nelson).
———. 1993. 'Jerusalem: The Second Temple Period', *The New Encyclopedia of Archaeological Excavations in the Holy Land* 2: 717-25.
Barkay, G., and Y. Zweig. 2006. 'The Temple Mount Debris Sifting Project: Preliminary Report', in E. Baruch, Z. Greenhut and A. Faust (eds.), *New Studies on Jerusalem* 11 (Ramat Gan: Bar Ilan University): 213-37 (Hebrew).
Bergman, A. 1936. 'Soundings at the Supposed Site of Old Testament Anathoth', *BASOR* 62: 22-25.
Bergren, T.A. 1997. 'Nehemiah in 2 Maccabees 1:10-2:18', *Journal for the Study of Judaism* 28: 249-70.
Biran, A. 1985. 'On the Identification of Anathoth', *Eretz-Israel* 18: 209-14 (Hebrew).
Blair, E.P. 'Soundings at 'Anata (Roman Anathoth)', *BASOR* 62: 18-21.
Blenkinsopp, J. 1988. *Ezra/Nehemiah: A Commentary* (Philadelphia: Westminster).
Brand, E. 1997. 'el-Haditha', *Excavations and Surveys in Israel* 19: 44*-46*.
———. 1998 *Salvage Excavation on the Margin of Tel Hadid, Preliminary Report* (Tel Aviv: Institute of Archaeology, Hebrew).
Broshi, M. 1976. 'Excavations on Mount Zion, 1971–1972 (Preliminary Report)', *IEJ* 26: 81-88.
Broshi, M., and I. Finkelstein. 1992. 'The Population of Palestine in Iron Age II', *BASOR* 287: 47-60.
Callaway, J.A., and M.B. Nicol. 1966. 'A Sounding at Khirbet Hayian', *BASOR* 183: 12-19.

Carter, C.E. 1999. *The Emergence of Yehud in the Persian Period: A Social and Demographic Study* (Sheffield: Academic Press).

Crowfoot, J.W., and G.M. Fitzgerald. 1927. *Excavations in the Tyropoen Valley, Jerusalem* (Palestine Exploration Fund Annual, 5; London: Palestine Exploration Fund).

De Groot, A. 2001. 'Jerusalem during the Persian Period', in A. Faust and E. Baruch (eds.), *New Studies on Jerusalem, Proceedings of the Seventh Conference* (Ramat Gan: Bar Ilan University): 77-82 (Hebrew).

———. 2004. 'Jerusalem in the Early Hellenistic Period', in E. Baruch and A. Faust (eds.), *New Studies on Jerusalem*, Vol. 10 (Ramat Gan: Bar Ilan University): 67-70 (Hebrew).

De Groot, A., D. Cohen, and A. Caspi 1992 'Area A1', in A. De Groot and D.T. Ariel (eds.), *Excavations at the City of David 1978–1985*. Vol. III, *Stratigraphic, Environmental, and Other Reports* (*Qedem* 33; Jerusalem: The Hebrew University): 1-29.

Demsky, A. 1983. '*Pelekh* in Nehemiah 3', *IEJ* 33: 242-44.

Dinur, U., and N. Feig. 1993. 'Eastern Part of the Map of Jerusalem', in I. Finkelstein and Y. Magen (eds.), *Archaeological Survey of the Hill Country of Benjamin* (Jerusalem: Israel Antiquities Authority): 339-427 (Hebrew).

Edelman, D. 2005. *The Origins of the 'Second' Temple: Persian Imperial Policy and the Rebuilding of Jerusalem* (London: Equinox).

Eshel, H. 2000. 'Jerusalem under Persian Rule: The City's Layout and the Historical Background', in S. Ahituv and A. Mazar (eds.), *The History of Jerusalem, The Biblical Period* (Jerusalem: Yad Ben Zvi): 327-44 (Hebrew).

Feldstein, A. 1997. 'Lod, Neve Yaraq (B)', *Excavations and Surveys in Israel* 19: 50*.

Feldstein, A., G. Kidron, N. Hanin, Y. Kamaisky, and D. Eitam. 1993. 'Southern Part of the Maps of Ramallah and el-Bireh and Northern Part of the Map of 'Ein Kerem', in I. Finkelstein and Y. Magen (eds.), *Archaeological Survey of the Hill Country of Benjamin* (Jerusalem: Israel Antiquities Authority): 133-264 (Hebrew).

Finkelstein, I. 1992. 'A Few Notes on Demographic Data from Recent Generations and Ethnoarchaeology', *PEQ* 122: 47-52.

———. 1994. 'Penelope's Shroud Unraveled: Iron II Date of Gezer's Outer Wall Established', *Tel Aviv* 21: 276-82.

———. Forthcoming. 'Notes on the Territorial Extension and Population of Yehud/Judea in the Persian and Early Hellenistic Periods'.

Finkelstein, I., Z. Herzog, L. Singer-Avitz, and D. Ussishkin. Forthcoming. 'Has King David's Palace been Found in Jerusalem?' *Tel Aviv* 34(2).

Funk, R.W. 1968. 'The History of Beth-zur with Reference to its Defenses', in O.R. Sellers *et al.* (eds.), *The 1957 Excavation at Beth-zur* (*AASOR* 38; Cambridge: American Schools of Oriental Research): 4-17.

———. 1993. 'Beth-zur', *The New Encyclopedia of Archaeological Excavations in the Holy Land* I: 259-61.

Galling, K. 1951. 'The "Gola-List" According to Ezra 2//Nehemiah 7', *JBL* 70: 149-58.

Geva, H. 2003a. 'Summary and Discussion of Findings from Areas A, W and X-2', in H. Geva *Jewish Quarter Excavations in the Old City of Jerusalem II* (Jerusalem: Israel Exploration Society): 501-52.

———. 2003b. 'Western Jerusalem at the End of the First Temple Period in Light of the Excavations in the Jewish Quarter', in A.G. Vaughn and A.E. Killebrew (eds.), *Jerusalem in the Bible and Archaeology: The First Temple Period* (Atlanta: Society of Biblical Literature): 183-208.

Gibson, S. 1987. 'The 1961–67 Excavations in the Armenian Garden, Jerusalem', *PEQ* 119: 81-96.

Gophna, R., and I. Beit-Arieh. 1997. *Archaeological Survey of Israel Map of Lod (80)* (Jerusalem: Israel Antiquities Authority).

Gophna, R., I. Taxel, and A. Feldstein. 2005. 'A New Identification of Ancient Ono', *Bulletin of the Anglo-Israel Archaeological Society* 23: 167-76.

Grabbe, L.L. 1998. *Ezra–Nehemiah* (London: Routledge).

Hoglund, K.G. 1992. *Achaemenid imperial administration in Syria-Palestine and the Missions of Ezra and Nehemiah* (Atlanta: Scholars Press).

Kallai, Z. 1972. 'The Land of Benjamin and Mt. Ephraim', in M. Kochavi (ed.), *Judaea, Samaria and the Golan, Archaeological Survey 1967–1968* (Jerusalem: Carta): 153-95 (Hebrew).

Kellermann, U. 1967. *Nehemia: Quellen Überlieferung und Geschichte* (Berlin: Alfred Töpelmann).

Kelso, J.L. 1968. *The Excavation of Bethel (1934–1960)* (AASOR, 39; Cambridge: American Schools of Oriental Research).

Kenyon, K.M. 1964. 'Excavations in Jerusalem, 1963', *PEQ* 96: 7-18.

———. 1965 'Excavations in Jerusalem, 1964', *PEQ* 97: 9-20.

———. 1966. 'Excavations in Jerusalem, 1965', *PEQ* 98: 73-88.

———. 1974. *Digging Up Jerusalem* (London: Ernest Benn).

King, P.J., and L.E. Stager. 2001. *Life in Biblical Israel* (Louisville: Westminster Press).

Khalaily, H., and A. Gopher. 1997. 'Lod', *Excavations and Surveys in Israel* 19: 51*.

Kloner, A. 2001. 'Jerusalem's Environs in the Persian Period', in A. Faust and E. Baruch (eds.), *New Studies on Jerusalem, Proceedings of the Seventh Conference* (Ramat Gan: Bar Ilan University): 91-96 (Hebrew).

———. 2003. *Archaeological Survey of Israel, Survey of Jerusalem: The Northwestern Sector, Introduction and Indices* (Jerusalem: Israel Antiquities Authority).

Kohut, A. 1926. *Aruch Completum* (Vienna: Hebräischer Verlag Menorah).

Lapp, P.W. 1968a. 'The Excavation of Field II', in O.R. Sellers *et al.* (eds.), *The 1957 Excavation at Beth-zur* (AASOR, 38; Cambridge: American Schools of Oriental Research): 26-34.

———. 1968b. 'Bethel Pottery of the Late Hellenistic and Early Roman Periods', in J.L. Kelso *The Excavation of Bethel (1934–1960)* (AASOR, 39; Cambridge: American Schools of Oriental Research): 77-80.

Lapp, P., and N. Lapp. 1968. 'Iron II—Hellenistic Pottery Groups', in O.R. Sellers *et al.* (eds.), *The 1957 Excavation at Beth-zur* (AASOR, 38; Cambridge: American Schools of Oriental Research): 54-79.

Lipschits, O. 1999. 'The History of the Benjaminite Region under Babylonian Rule', *Zion* 64: 271-310 (Hebrew).

———. 2003. 'Demographic Changes in Judah between the Seventh and the Fifth Centuries B.C.E.', in O. Lipschits and J. Blenkinsopp (eds.), *Judah and the Judeans in the New-Babylonian Period* (Winona Lake: Eisenbrauns): 323-76.

———. 2005. *The Fall and Rise of Jerusalem* (Winona Lake: Eisenbrauns).

———. 2006. 'Achaemenid Imperial Policy, Settlement Processes in Palestine, and the Status of Jerusalem in the Middle of the Fifth Century B.C.E.', in O. Lipschits and M. Oeming (eds.), *Judah and the Judeans in the Persian Period* (Winona Lake: Eisenbrauns): 19-52.

Lipschits, O., and D. Vanderhooft. 2007. 'Yehud Stamp Impressions: History of Discovery and Newly-Published Impressions', *Tel Aviv* 34: 3-11.

Macalister, R.A.S., and J.G. Duncan. 1926. *Excavation on the Hill of Ophel, Jerusalem, 1923–1925* (Palestine Exploration Fund Annual, 4; London: Palestine Exploration Fund).

Mazar, B. 1971. 'The Excavations in the Old City of Jerusalem near the Temple Mount – Second Preliminary Report, 1969–1970 Seasons', *Eretz-Israel* 10: 1-34 (Hebrew).

Mazar, E. 2007. *The Excavations in the City of David, 2005* (Jerusalem: Shoham, Hebrew).

Mazar, E., and B. Mazar. 1989. *Excavations in the South of the Temple Mount, The Ophel of Biblical Jerusalem* (Qedem, 29; Jerusalem: The Hebrew University).

Meyers, C.L., and E.M. Meyers. 1987. *Haggai, Zechariah 1–8* (Garden City: Doubleday).

Mowinckel, S. 1964. *Studien zu dem Buche Ezra-Nehemia* (Oslo: Universitetsforlaget).

Myers, J.M. 1965. *Ezra Nehemiah* (Garden City: Doubleday).

Na'aman, N. 1991. 'The Kingdom of Judah under Josiah', *Tel Aviv* 18: 3-71.

Na'aman, N., and R. Zadok. 2000. 'Assyrian Deportations to the Province of Samaria in the Light of the Two Cuneiform Tablets from Tel Hadid', *Tel Aviv* 27: 159-88.

Nagorsky, A. 2005. 'el-Haditha', *Excavations and Surveys in Israel* 117. http://www.hadashot-esi.org.il/reports_eng.asp?id=110

Netzer, E. 2001. *Hasmonean and Herodian Palaces at Jericho I* (Jerusalem: Israel Exploration Society).

Ofer, A. 1993. 'The Highland of Judah during the Biblical Period' (Ph.D. thesis; Tel Aviv University, Hebrew).

Onn, A., and Y. Rapuano. 1994. 'Jerusalem, Khirbet el-Burj', *Excavations and Surveys in Israel* 14: 88-90.

Prag, K. 2000. 'Bethlehem, A Site Assessment', *PEQ* 132: 169-81.

Pritchard, J.B. 1962. *Gibeon, Where the Sun Stood Still, The Discovery of the Biblical City* (Princeton: Princeton University Press).

———. 1964. *Winery, Defenses and Soundings at Gibeon* (Philadelphia: University Museum).

———. 1993. 'Gibeon', *The New Encyclopedia of Archaeological Excavations in the Holy Land* 2: 511-14.

Rappaport, U. 2004. *The First Book of Maccabees* (Jerusalem: Yad Ben Zvi, Hebrew).

Reich, R. 1992. 'The Beth-zur Citadel II – A Persian Residency?, *Tel Aviv* 19: 113-23.

Reich, R., and E. Shukron. 2003 'The Urban Development of Jerusalem in the Late Eight Century B.C.E.', in A.G. Vaughn and A.E. Killebrew (eds.), *Jerusalem in the Bible and Archaeology: The First Temple Period* (Atlanta: Society of Biblical Literature): 209-18.

———. 2004. 'The History of the Gihon Spring in Jerusalem', *Levant* 36: 211-23.

———. 2007. 'The Yehud Seal Impressions from the 1995–2005 Excavations in the City of David', *Tel Aviv* 34: 59-65.

Rosenberger, A., and A. Shavit. 1993. 'Lod, Newe Yaraq', *Excavations and Surveys in Israel* 13: 54*-56*.

Schniedewind, W. 2003. 'Jerusalem, the Late Judaean Monarchy and the Composition of the Biblical Texts', in A.G. Vaughn and A.E. Killebrew (eds.), *Jerusalem in the Bible and Archaeology: The First Temple Period* (Atlanta: Society of Biblical Literature): 375-94.

———. 2004. *How the Bible Became a Book: The Textualization of Ancient Israel* (Cambridge: Cambridge University Press).

Sellers O.R. 1933. *The Citadel of Beth-Zur* (Philadelphia: Westminster Press).

Sellers, O.R., R.W. Funk, J.L. McKenzie, P. Lapp, and N. Lapp. 1968. *The 1957 Excavation at Beth-zur* (*AASOR* 38; Cambridge: American Schools of Oriental Research).

Shiloh, Y. 1984. *Excavations at the City of David* I (Qedem, 19; Jerusalem: The Hebrew University).

Steiner, R.C. 1991. 'The Aramaic Text in Demotic Script, The Liturgy of a New Year's Festival Imported from Bethel to Syene by Exiles from Rash', *JAOS* 111: 362-63.

Stern, E. 1982. *Material Culture of the Land of the Bible in the Persian Period, 538–332 B.C.* (Warminster: Aris & Phillips).

———. 2001. *Archaeology of the Land of the Bible*. Vol. II, *The Assyrian, Babylonian, and Persian Periods (732–332 B.C.E.)* (New York: Doubleday).

Throntveit, M.A. 1992. *Ezra–Nehemiah* (Louisville: John Knox).

Torrey, C.C. 1896. *The Composition and Historical Value of Ezra–Nehemiah* (Giessen: J. Kicker'sche Buchhandlung).

———. 1910. *Ezra Studies* (Chicago: University of Chicago Press).

Tsafrir, Y., L. Di Segni, and J. Green. 1994. *Tabula Imperii Romani Judaea Palastina, Maps and Gazetteer* (Jerusalem: Israel Academy of Sciences and Humanities).

Ussishkin, D. 2006. 'The Borders and *De Facto* Size of Jerusalem in the Persian Period', in O. Lipschits and M. Oeming (eds.), *Judah and the Judeans in the Persian Period* (Winona Lake: Eisenbrauns): 147-66.

Vanderhooft, D., and O. Lipschits. 2007. 'A New Typology of the Yehud Stamp Impressions', *Tel Aviv* 34: 12-37.

Vriezen, K.J.H. 1975. 'Hirbet Kefire – eine Oberflächenuntersuchung', *ZDPV* 91: 135-58.

Weinberg, J. 1992. *The Citizen-Temple Community* (Sheffield: Academic Press).

———. 2000. 'Jerusalem in the Persian Period', in S. Ahituv and A. Mazar (eds.), *The History of Jerusalem, The Biblical Period* (Jerusalem: Yad Ben Zvi): 307-26 (Hebrew).

Wightman, G.J. 1993. *The Walls of Jerusalem: From the Canaanites to the Mamluks* (Sydney: Meditarch).

Williamson, H.G.M. 1985. *Ezra, Nehemiah* (Waco: Word Books).

Wright, J.L. 2004. *Rebuilding Identity: The Nehemiah Memoir and its Earliest Readers* (Berlin: Walter de Gruyter).

Yeivin, S. 1971. 'The Benjaminite Settlement in the Western Part of their Territory', *IEJ* 21: 141-54.

Zorn, J.R. 1994. 'Estimating the Population Size of Ancient Settlements: Methods, Problems, Solutions, and a Case Study', *BASOR* 295: 31-48.

Jerusalem between Two Periods of Greatness: The Size and Status of the City in the Babylonian, Persian and Early Hellenistic Periods

Oded Lipschits[1]

The history of Jerusalem between 586 and 167 BCE is an 'interlude' between two periods of greatness and political independence: the end of the first temple period on the one hand and the period of the Hasmoneans on the other. Between these two periods Jerusalem was a very small city and Judah was a small province under the rule of great empires.

According to both biblical and archaeological evidence, Jerusalem was destroyed in 586 BCE and left deserted by the Babylonians for a period of nearly 50 years (Lipschits 2005: 210–18, with further literature). Biblical accounts assert that the temple in Jerusalem was rebuilt at the beginning of the Persian period. During this period, the city once again became the centre of the Judahite cult. According to an account in Nehemiah, the fortifications of Jerusalem were rebuilt in the middle of the fifth century BCE. As a result, Jerusalem became a *Bîrāh*, replacing Mizpah, which had served as the capital of the newly established province of Yehud for 141 years, from 586 BCE (Lipschits 2001a), through the Neo-Babylonian period (Lemaire 2003: 292), until the time of Nehemiah (445 BCE, Blenkinsopp 1998: 42, n. 48; *cf.* Lemaire 1990: 39–40; 2003: 292).[2] The available archaeological data for the Persian period that might corroborate this biblical evidence is minimal, and scholars have assumed that the city did not become a large and important urban and administrative centre before the middle of the second century BCE.

---

[1] *Author Note*: This paper is a summary of ten years of research on Jerusalem between the seventh and fourth centuries BCE (Lipschits 1999a; 2001a; 2001b; 2003; 2005: 206–71; 2006; 2009; Lipschits and Vanderhooft 2007a; 2007b). A comprehensive methodological discussion and a detailed archaeological survey concerning Persian period finds in Jerusalem were published in Lipschits 2009.

[2] On the word *Bîrāh* and its optional interpretations, see: Grabbe 2009: 133–34, who suggested the option (p. 135) that Jerusalem became the central city of the province later than the time of Nehemiah.

The aim of this paper is to present the archaeological material from Jerusalem, dating between these two periods of greatness, and to consider its size and status in the sixth century BCE ('the period of the Babylonian Exile'), in the fifth to fourth centuries BCE ('the period of the return' and the time when Judah was a Persian province), and to add some observations regarding the history of the city in the Early Hellenistic period (third century BCE).

Jerusalem in the Babylonian, Persian and Early Hellenistic Periods – Some Methodological Notes[3]

During the late eighth and seventh, as well as during the second century BCE, the built-up area of Jerusalem expanded to the Western Hill of Jerusalem (the area of the modern-day Jewish and Armenian Quarters and the so-called Mount Zion) and was enclosed by strong fortifications. The Southeastern Hill (the 'City of David') was rebuilt and fortified as well. These two periods, together with the later Herodian period, became the most defined and easily recognizable in the historical and archaeological research of Jerusalem in the First and Second Temple Periods. In contrast, not many building remains from the intervening period, i.e. the Babylonian, Persian and Early Hellenistic periods, have been uncovered in Jerusalem. It is not a unique phenomenon to Jerusalem, but a well-known phenomenon in Judah and Samaria. Under the Assyrian, Babylonian and Persian rule, there was a marked process of attenuation in urban life in Judah (Lipschits 2006: 26–30, with further literature). No new cities were built, and the administrative and urban centres that survived the catastrophes of those periods were small and weak compared to their late eighth to seventh century or second century BCE counterparts. However, this scarcity of building remains from the Persian and Early Hellenistic periods does not fully reflect the actual, admittedly poor, situation at that time. Rather, it is the outcome of incomplete archaeological data (Stern 2001: 461–62), especially in the case of Jerusalem (Lipschits 2009).

Contrary to views that take the negative finds, especially in Jerusalem, as reflecting the actual situation in the city ('the negative is as important as the positive', Finkelstein 2008: 505), I have suggested that the Persian and Early Hellenistic period occupation levels, which were not as strong, imposing and big as in the glorious periods of independence before and after them, were severely damaged by intensive building activities conducted in the late Hellenistic, Roman, Byzantine and even later periods (Lipschits 2009). The situation

---

[3] For a detailed discussion on the methodological subject of the finds in Jerusalem from the Persian and Early Hellenistic periods see: Lipschits 2009.

in Jerusalem is not unique or exceptional, especially when dealing with hilltop sites, but it is much more dramatic because of the scope and grandeur of the subsequent building efforts, as well as the frequent destruction of the site. The religious, cultic and political status of Jerusalem probably motivated not only frequent political upheavals and destruction, but also a desire to remove previous political and religious structures, and to reshape the city. It seems that the main destructive force in Jerusalem is the efforts of people in later periods to build new buildings and leave their own impression in the city. Additionally, the topographical nature of the Southeastern Hill, which is very steep and narrow at the top, requires that buildings, especially the more prominent ones, be built on bedrock. This may explain why the remains from the intervening sixth to third centuries BCE were discovered mainly in 'pockets' between the late complexes, or in the dumps down in the valleys to the east and to the west of the hill. When discussing the meaning of the archaeological remains dated to the Babylonian, Persian and Early Hellenistic periods discovered in the city, one should be very careful about concluding that the city was empty or nearly empty throughout these periods. In this case, it is more difficult to assert that the absence of finds means that there was nothing there; explanations regarding the negative finds must be taken seriously.

Jerusalem in the 'Exilic' Period – Between Destruction and Restoration

The Assyrian's conquest of the Levant during the last third of the eighth century BCE caused heavy destructions upon most of the urban centres and a deportation of large parts of the population. We may assume that the Assyrian policy was to retain fortifications only in provincial capitals (Stern 2001: 50) and to build forts and Assyrian economic and military centres in strategic places all over the country (Lipschits 2006: 19–21). Most of the major towns were abandoned or only poorly rebuilt and most of the population in the Assyrian provinces, especially in the interior areas, used to live in farms and villages; there was a marked decline in the urban life.

The geopolitical and administrative character of the Levant did not change under Egyptian rule, during the last third of the seventh century BCE (Lipschits 2005: 31–5; 2006: 21–2), nor during the beginning of Babylonian rule which started with the military campaign conducted by Nebuchadrezzar in ïattu-Land between June 604 and January/February 603 BCE (Lipschits 2005: 37–42). Besides Ekron and Ashkelon, there is no reason to ascribe any other destruction to the Babylonian army during the first years of the Babylonian rule in Palestine: most of the country was arranged in a line of provinces that dated back to the Assyrian period. It seems that the Egyptian retreat left the country unopposed to the rule of Nebuchadrezzar.

The Babylonian policy in the region did not change even following Nebuchadrezzar's failed attempt to conquer Egypt, and the subsequent temporary weakening of Babylonian rule in the region (Lipschits 1999: 472–80; 2005: 49–52). However, the continued instability during the days of Psammetichus II (595–589 BCE), even more during the first years of Hophra (589–570 BCE), and the increasing threat by Egypt over the Babylonian rule in this region, caused Nebuchadrezzar to modify his policy (589 BCE): during the next years he conquered the small vassal kingdoms that remained close to the border with Egypt, annexed them and turned them into provinces (Lipschits 1998: 482–87; 2005: 62–8).[4]

The 586 BCE destruction of Jerusalem is one of the prominent archaeological finds to appear in the many years of excavations in the different parts of it. The excavations led by Avigad in the Jewish Quarter from 1969 to 1978 disclosed, adjacent to the late Iron age tower, the remains of a fire, and Scythian bronze triple-winged arrowheads (Avigad 1980: 52–4). In the excavations conducted by Kenyon on the eastern slope of the City of David in the 1960s, evidence was found of destruction of the wall from the end of the Iron age (phase 9) (Kenyon 1974: 170–71; Franken and Steiner 1990: 57). Excavations led by Yigal Shiloh in the City of David between 1978 and 1982 produced evidence of the destruction of all the buildings (including the wall) and of a fierce fire that sealed stratum X in areas D, E, and G (Shiloh 1984: 14, 18–19, 29). Remains of the Babylonian destruction were also found in excavations in the Citadel (Johns 1950: 130, Fig. 7, No. 1; Geva 1983: 56–8), and in part of the structures excavated by Eilat Mazar in the Ophel (Mazar 1993: 25–32).

The finds of the archaeological survey within the confines of the city of Jerusalem and its environs indicate the force of the destruction and the degree of demographic decline in and around the city (Lipschits 2003: 326–34; 2005: 210–18). Even at the zenith of the Persian period the settlement in Jerusalem was limited to a narrow extension of the historic City of David; settlement in the city and its surroundings amounted to about 15 per cent of what it had been on the eve of the destruction. The slight continuity reflected in the settlement patterns in this area calls for the assumption that previously, during the sixth century BCE, the condition of settlement and demography had been even worse (Lipschits 2003: 330–32; 2005: 215–18). The conclusion is that Jerusalem and its environs took a heavy blow from the Babylonians at the beginning of the sixth century BCE, and they were almost entirely depleted of their inhabitants.

---

[4] Judah was the first goal of the Babylonians. Afterwards, apparently in 585 BCE, they attacked Tyre and Sidon, putting a closure on Tyre that lasted for 13 years (until 572 BCE) (Katzenstein 1973: 330; 1994: 186; Weisman 1991: 235; Redford 1992: 465–66; Vanderhooft 1999: 100–102). Apparently during the years of siege against Tyre, the Babylonians also attacked Ammon and Moab (Lipschits 2004), and established their rule also over Gaza, Arwad and Ashdod. One may accept the idea, that the successful takeover of north Arabia by Nabunidus and his move to Tema (553–543 BCE) caused the disappearance of the kingdom of Edom and probably the integration of its territory within greater Arabia (Lemaire 2003: 290, and see also Briant 2002: 45).

The city remained desolate and deserted throughout the next 50 years (Lipschits 1999: 2001a: 129–42; 2005: 215–18). The laments that 'the roads to Zion mourn, for none come to the appointed feasts' (Lam. 1.4) and 'all who pass along the way clap their hands at you; they hiss and wag their heads at the daughter of Jerusalem: "Is this the city which was called the perfection of beauty, the joy of all the earth?"' (Lam. 2.15) faithfully reflect this historical reality. Nor is Jerusalem mentioned in the account of the rule of Gedaliah at Mizpah (2 Kings 25.22-26; Jer. 40.7–41.18) (Lipschits 2005: 304–47), and the events described encircle the city to the north (Mizpah and Gibeon) and to the south (around Bethlehem). In light of this, and in light of the archaeological data, it may be assumed that the systematic acts of destruction by Nebuzaradan, about four weeks after the conquest of the city, were accompanied by political instructions that created this situation and made it permanent (Cogan and Tadmor 1988: 319). This was the sight that met the earliest Returners to Zion (compare Zech. 1.12; 2.5-9), as well as the later (compare Neh. 2.13-17; 7.6).

No information exists on events in Jerusalem between the time immediately after the destruction and the restoration period. Nevertheless, the perception that the status of ritual in Jerusalem was a result of Babylonian policy requires the assumption that any change in this status would have to be connected with a change in policy.

The fate of Jerusalem was not exceptional. Unlike the fate of the political entities along the Phoenician coast, the consequence of the new Babylonian policy was destructive of the southern part of Palestine as well as of the Transjordanian kingdoms.[5] In all this area, Nebuchadrezzar created a buffer zone between Babylon and Egypt that consisted of devastated, diminished provinces (Lipschits 2006: 22–4). There is no evidence that the Babylonians invested any kind of effort in economic development in this region, and it seems that Nebuchadrezzar used the destruction of the region as a lever for rebuilding those parts of Babylonia that had been damaged during the long years of war, devastation and deportation caused by the Assyrians.[6]

---

[5] The Babylonians evinced a different attitude towards the kingdoms of Philistia and those on the Phoenician coast. The former were conquered and turned into Babylonian provinces. Although the fate of the latter is unclear, it appears that during most years of Babylonian rule, certainly during the Persian period, they were ruled by kings (Katzenstein 1994: 46–8). For an explanation for this different attitude, see Oppenheim 1967; Brown 1969: 101; Katzenstein 1994: 48; Lipschits 2006: 26–9.

[6] Total devastation of the southern part of Palestine was, however, against Babylonian interests, and the rural settlements all over the land continued to exist, even if on a much smaller scale (Lipschits 2004: 42–3; 2005: 212–61; 2006: 29–30). Since the Babylonians did not have any direct policy of developing and protecting such areas, especially in the peripheral regions of the south, many changes occurred there, apparently as a side effect of the collapse of the central systems and the infiltration of semi-nomadic groups (Lipschits 2005: 140–47; 227–40).

Jerusalem in the Persian Period: The Geopolitical Background

During the long years of the Persian rule in Palestine many geopolitical changes and administrative reorganizations were made, especially along the coast, but also in the hill country and in the southern areas of Cis- and Transjordan. The main evidence for this can be found in the rich and big urban and commercial centres that were established at the very beginning of the Achaemenid period along the Mediterranean coast, most of them well built and planned, some according to the Hippodamian plan (Kenyon 1960: 311–12; Stern 1990; 2001: 380–401; 461–64; Lipschits 2003: 347; 2006: 34).[7] In contrast with the rich and well-developed cities along the coast, not many Persian period building-remains have been uncovered within the borders of the province of Yehud, as well as within the borders of the province of Samaria (Lipschits 2001b; 2005: 214–16; 2006: 29–34). This settlement pattern is a continuation of the process that began during the Babylonian period, after the harsh blow the Babylonians dealt to the small kingdoms in the hill country west and east of the Jordan. Neither the Babylonians, nor the Persians had any interest in encouraging and developing urban centres in the rural hilly regions on both sides of the Jordan. The Achaemenids, like the Babylonians, were interested in the continued existence of the rural settlement in the hill country. It was an important source for agricultural supply, which was probably collected as tax. They had no interest in establishing urban centres in the hill country and in creating new social, political and economical local power structures.

Persian Period and Early Hellenistic Finds in the Western Hill of Jerusalem

Only a few pottery sherds and other small finds from the Persian period have been found in the many excavations conducted in the Western Hill of Jerusalem. In most cases, these finds were excavated in landfills from the Late Hellenistic and especially from the Roman period and with no clear stratigraphic context.[8]

---

[7] The Achaemenid regime had governmental, military and economic interests in basing its rule along the Mediterranean coast, stabilizing the political situation in this area and encouraging the maritime and continental trade. One of the major goals of the Persians was to secure the Via-Maris, as well as the roads in southern Palestine, as part of the military, administrative and economic effort to keep the way to Egypt open (Eph'al 1998: 117; Stern 2001: 371). Another interest was to establish a strong political, military and economic coalition against the Greeks. From the economic point of view, the Persian regime tried to develop and encourage the maritime trade, dominated by the Phoenicians (Briant 2002: 383, 489–90).

[8] For a detailed discussion of all Persian period archaeological finds from the Western Hill, see: Lipschits 2009.

The unavoidable conclusion is that throughout the Persian and Early Hellenistic periods, the Western Hill was entirely abandoned, and the area was only first resettled in the second century BCE.[9] This fact stands in agreement with the finds of *Yehud* stamp impressions, since according to the new typology developed by Vanderhooft and Lipschits (2007), no stamp impressions belonging to the early (late sixth and fifth century BCE) or middle types (fourth and third centuries BCE) were discovered in any of the excavated areas outside the limits of the City of David (Lipschits and Vanderhooft 2007a: 108–12). All the stamp impressions discovered on the Western Hill belong to the two late types (dated to the second century BCE, maybe even to the middle or second half of this century), and some of them came from clear Hasmonaean archaeological contexts, in some cases together with *yršlm* stamp impressions and other material dated to this period (Geva 2007a; Lipschits and Vanderhooft 2007a: 111–12).[10]

Persian Period Finds in the City of David

The northern part of the City of David, just below the Ophel, contains a significant number of Persian period finds. The fills in which these finds were found seem to have originated from the Ophel, just above this area to the north, and were laid before the late Hellenistic and Roman periods (Lipschits 2009).

The most important area where finds from the Persian period were discovered is the one excavated by Macalister and Duncan (1923–25), at the northern area of the City of David and just below the Ophel (Macalister and Duncan 1926: 49–51; Duncan 1931: 143).[11] Persian period finds were discovered a bit to the north of the Macalister and Duncan's Persian tower where Kenyon excavated her square AXVIII, and identified there part of 'Nehemiah's wall'.[12] Shiloh continued the

---

[9] This is the common view among scholars, and see, e.g., Kenyon 1974: 188–255; Tsafrir 1977: 36; Avigad 1983: 61–3; Geva 1983; 1994; 2000a: 24; 2000b: 158; 2003a: 113–14; 2003b: 524–26; Geva and Reich 2000: 42; Geva and Avigad 2000b: 218; Shiloh 1984: 23; Tushingham 1985: 85; Broshi and Gibson 1994; Chen, Margalit and Pixner 1994; Sivan and Solar 1994; Finkielstejn 1999: 28*; Lipschits 2005: 212–13; Lipschits and Vanderhooft 2007a: 108–12.

[10] See, for example, the six stamp impressions discovered in the Kenyon–Tushingham excavations in the Armenian Garden; all were excavated in a fill connected to the podium of Herod's palace, which includes a mixture of pottery from the First and Second Temple periods (Tushingham 1985: 37, Fig. 17: 18–23). Also in Amiran and Eitan's excavations in the Citadel a stamp impression was discovered in the fill of the podium of Herod's palace (Amiran and Eitan 1970: 13).

[11] The Persian period finds from this area include a lot of Persian period pottery sherds, as well as 54 *Yehud* and 6 lion stamp impressions.

[12] Kenyon (1963: 15; 1974: 183–84, 191–92, Pl. 77; cf. 1966: 83–4; 1967a: 69) observed that the tower was attached to an earlier wall that was built of large stones on a rock scarp about 7–8 metres high, dated the wall to the Persian period, and assigned its construction to Nehemiah. She dated the tower as part of the Hasmonaean fortification.

excavations in this area as part of his Area G,[13] and Eilat Mazar renewed the excavations in the same area in 2005.[14] In 2007, as part of the conservation project of the Hasmonaean northern tower, Mazar excavated the landfill under the tower, and discovered the same Persian period material previously exposed by Kenyon and Shiloh.[15] The fill in this spot contains finds only from the sixth–fifth centuries BCE, which seems to indicate that it was part of the cleaning of the area above it (in the northern edge of the city of David, just under the Ophel), which in turn indicates that that area was populated in the Persian period. E. Mazar suggested dating the tower and the wall attached to it (wall 27) to the fifth century BCE and identified it as a part of Nehemiah's wall (2007a: 49–60; 2007b: 17–21; 2008: 31–7).[16]

On the same line of the upper part of the City of David, but on its western slopes towards the Tyropoeon, some more Persian period finds, including one *Yehud* stamp impression, were discovered in Crowfoot and Fitzgerald's excavations (1927–28) at the 'western gate' of the City of David (Crowfoot and Fitzgerald 1929: 67). Pottery sherds dated to the Persian period, as well as another stamp impression, were excavated by Shukron and Reich, just a few metres to the north, in the Givati parking place (Shukron and Reich 2005: 8). These finds provide further evidence that the hill above this area – the Ophel and the northern part of the City of David – were settled during the Persian period.

Beside the upper part of the City of David, most of the Persian period pottery sherds and stamp impressions from the central and southern parts of the City of David were discovered in Shiloh's excavations along the eastern slope of the ridge, where three Strata were observed and dated to the period between the late sixth or early fifth and the second century BCE: Stratum 9 was dated to the Persian period, Stratum 8 to the Early Hellenistic period, and Stratum 7 to the second century BCE (Hasmonaean Period). Stratum 9, however, does not appear in all the excavated areas (Shiloh 1984: 4, Table 2). Finds attributed to this Stratum appeared in Area D1 (Ariel, Hirschfeld and Savir 2000: 59–62; De Groot 2001:

---

[13] Shiloh (1984: 20–21, and figs. 27, 28; *cf.* the photo in Mazar 2007a: 64) connected the northern tower to the first century BCE glacis that was already excavated by Kenyon. Its connection to Macalister's northern tower was well demonstrated.

[14] Mazar (2007a: 49–60; 2007b: 17–21) identified Kenyon's Persian wall as part of the northern Iron Age IIA fortification of what she called 'David's Palace'.

[15] According to Kenyon, this fill was connected to the tower that was built on the bedrock, and this is why she attempted to date it to the Persian period. Franken (Franken and Steiner 1990), however, presented the drawing of the cut of Kenyon's Square XVIII and demonstrated that this fill was not connected to the wall, as Macalister and Duncan had earlier presumed.

[16] The date of the landfill, where there are no indications for a late Persian material (including *yehud* stamp impressions) may indicate that it was laid before the landfill above it, discovered by Macalister and Duncan, but it is certainly not sufficient grounds to date the northern tower to the fifth century BCE or identify it as part of Nehemiah's wall.

77), Area D2 (Shiloh 1984: 8–9),[17] and in Area G (Shiloh 1984: 20).[18] Shiloh's finds from the Persian period were also partially represented in Area E1 (Shiloh 1984: 14; De Groot 2001: 77), and included some chalk vessels (Cahill 1992: 191–98, fig. 14). Sherds dated to the Persian period were discovered in the fills in Area H, to the east of the Siloam Pool, on the eastern slopes of Mount Zion (De Groot and Michaeli 1992: 50–51; De Groot 2001: 78).[19] Persian period sherds and seal impressions were discovered in Reich and Shukron's Areas A and B, above the Kidron Valley, ca. 200–250 m south of the Gihon spring (Reich and Shukron 1998: 2007). The finds from these areas probably come from the settlement on the ridge above.

The most significant finds from the Persian period were excavated in Area E, where three different stages from the Persian period Stratum 9 were distinguished (De Groot 2001: 77, and *cf.* Cahill 1992: 191–98, fig. 14). The early stage (9C) is a reuse of a large Iron Age building that was destroyed along with the rest of the city in 586 BCE, and should be dated to the end of the sixth and first half of the fifth century BCE (De Groot 2001: 77–8). A sloping level of quarrying refuse (composed of limestone chips with very little interspersed earth or pottery) was ascribed to the second stage (9b), and can be dated to the reconstruction of the city undertaken by Nehemiah in the middle of the fifth century BCE (De Groot 2001: 78; 2005: 82).[20] The Persian period date, the location of the works, and the long line along the eastern slope of the ridge, are all indications of the 'missing' wall of the Persian period.[21] A few terrace walls and some floors with ovens were attributed to the third stage (9C) of the late Persian period (Ariel, Hirschfeld and Savir 2000: 59).

---

[17] The finds assigned to Stratum 9 at Area D2 include a Lycian coin dated to 500–440 BCE (Ariel 1990: C1) and an ostracon (Naveh 2000: IN 16).

[18] In this area Kenyon also discovered Persian period finds (dated by her to the fifth–third centuries BCE) in the fill adjacent to the Northern tower, and this is the reason why she assigned this wall to Nehemiah's fortifications. See, however, the critique of De Groot 2001: 78.

[19] De Groot assumed that the finds from the Persian period are a proof that the Siloam pool was fortified during the Persian period.

[20] The same level of quarrying refuse appeared also in Area D1, 500 m to the south, and was dated to Stratum 9 (Ariel, Hirschfeld and Savir 2000: 59, and *cf.* Shiloh 1984: 7; De Groot 2001: 78). In some cases the levels of those chips were separated by thin layers of earth, without any coherent pattern. The quarrying activities above the eastern slope were documented in the excavations by Bliss and Dickie (1898), Weill (1920) and in Area K of the City of David excavations (Ariel and Magness 1992). It should be emphasized that the existence of such levels of quarrying refuse is an indication that the areas where it was discovered were outside the limits of the city (Ariel, Hirschfeld and Savir 2000: 59), but it also indicates that immediately above this area significant construction activity was undertaken.

[21] It can be assumed that the heavy destruction of the city in 586 BCE forced the late sixth and fifth century BCE settlers to move the wall to the upper part of the ridge, where there was a need for preparation-quarrying activity.

These Persian period finds may be combined with the observations of Ariel and Shoham (2000: 138) and Reich and Shukron (2007: 64) concerning the location of the *Yehud* stamp impressions,[22] and the conclusion that Persian and Early Hellenistic settlement was restricted to the top of the ridge, to the south of Area G (*cf.* Finkelstein 2008: 506). The problem with this assumption is that it relates to the area down the slopes of the settled area on the ridge, where above the Gihon spring and Area G of Shiloh's excavations, there were many more Persian period sherds and *Yehud* stamp impressions that were excavated by Macalister and Duncan (1926: 49–51; *cf.* Cook 1925). The actual significance of the distribution of the Persian period finds in this area is that the Gihon spring was not in use since the water flow in Hezekiah tunnel to the southern part of the City of David, and the spring itself, was blocked and covered, far below the limits of the city. The finds on the ridge of the City of David, as well as on the slopes of the hill are indications for a poor but existing settlement all along the narrow ridge of the City of David (Lipschits 2009).

Early Hellenistic Finds in the City of David, Yehud Stamp Impressions, and Settlement Processes in Jerusalem During the Fourth–Third Centuries BCE

The Early Hellenistic Stratum 8 is fully represented in the City of David only in Area E2 (Shiloh 1984: 4, Table 2 and *cf.* to p. 10; De Groot 2004: 67–9). This Stratum is also partially represented in Areas E1 (Shiloh 1984: 14–15) and E3 (*cf.* to pp. 10–11), and scarcely represented in Areas D1 (*cf.* to pp. 7–8) and D2 (*cf.* to pp. 8–9). In this case, too, the finds that can safely be attributed to this Stratum are meagre, and mainly consist of three *columbaria* (De Groot 2004: 67–8; 2005: 84) and a structure (in Area E1) that yielded a rich corpus of pottery dating to the third century BCE.[23] The excavators did not find *Yehud* stamp impressions of the late types, dated to the second century BCE, in either of these strata (Stratum 9 and 8). Most of the late types were discovered in Stratum 7 (Ariel and Shoham 2000, Table 1, and see also Reich 2003: 258–59 and Tables 7.1–7.2).

---

[22] Most of the *Yehud* stamp impressions from Shiloh's excavations originated in Areas B, D and E. Of the eight stamp impressions discovered by Reich and Shukron on the eastern slope of the Southeastern Hill of Jerusalem, five originated in Area A, located in the Kidron Valley, some 200–250 metres south of the Gihon spring, two in Area B, at the mid-slope of the hill, above Area A, and next to Shiloh's Areas B and D1. Only one *Yehud* stamp impression was retrieved in the areas excavated around the Gihon spring, where vast amounts of late Second Temple debris were excavated above a huge fill containing late Iron Age II pottery.

[23] This is the only pottery assemblage of a pre-Hasmonaean phase in the City of David (Shiloh 1984: 15).

The 27 *Yehud* stamp impressions discovered in different areas of the Western Hill are more than 30 per cent of the total finds of the late group of *Yehud* stamp impressions discovered in Jerusalem (59 more stamp impressions from the late group were discovered in the City of David). This proportion is much higher than the Rhodian stamp impressions, of which only 5 per cent of the finds were discovered on the Western Hill, and most of the rest were discovered in the City of David. The difference in the proportion of the two types of stamp impressions discovered on the Western Hill and in the City of David probably does not point to different population groups in these areas before the destruction of the Akra in 141 BCE by Simeon (*1 Macc.* 13.49-51), as assumed by Finkielsztejn (1999: 28*–31* with further literature, and see against this idea Ariel 1990: 25; 2000: 269, 276–80). Instead, this fact likely indicates that the settlement on the Western Hill did not start before the beginning of the second half of the second century BCE (Geva 1985: 30; Lipschits and Vanderhooft 2007a: 112), a period in which there was a sharp decline in the importation of wine from Rhodes (Ariel 1990: 21–5; 2000: 267–69). We can also assume that the settlement process of the Western Hill was a much slower and gradual process than described by some scholars (see, e.g., Finkielsztejn 1999: 28*).

Archaeological Finds, Demographical Processes and the History of Jerusalem between the Sixth and Second Centuries BCE

The archaeological finds from Jerusalem can only be interpreted as evidence of a meagre settlement, confined to the City of David, between the late Iron Age and the Hasmonaean period (early sixth to second centuries BCE).[24] The settlement in the Persian and Early Hellenistic periods concentrated on the upper part of the ridge, in a very narrow north to south strip, with an average width of no more than 80–100 metres, and along the edge of the ridge, about 350 metres from north to south (Lipschits 2009). The settlement on the ridge included a settled area of about 28–30 dunams. However, since the area in the northern part of the ridge of the City of David is the richest with Persian period finds (with more than 75 per cent of the finds from this period), and the finds in this area were mostly discovered in earth fills that probably originated from the area above it; namely, the Ophel hill, this area should be considered as an important settled area during this period (Lipschits 2009). The importance of the 20 dunams of the Ophel hill, between the

---

[24] This is an observation shared by all scholars dealing with Persian period finds in Jerusalem (Kenyon 1963: 15; Carter 1999: 285; Eshel 2000: 341; Lipschits 2003: 330–31; 2005: 212; 2006: 32; Lipschits and Vanderhooft 2007a; Schniedewind 2003; 2004: 165–78; Grabbe 2004: 25; Geva 2007b: 56–7; Finkelstein 2008: 501–04).

ascension of the hill towards the Temple Mount and the northern part of the City of David, as the main built-up area in the Persian period, was never discussed in the archaeological and historical research. However, this is the only flat, easy to settle area in the Persian and Early Hellenistic Jerusalem. Its closeness to the Temple Mount on the one hand and the easy option to fortify it on the other, made it the preferable option for settlement in the Persian and Early Hellenistic periods.

The settled area of Jerusalem during the Persian and Early Hellenistic periods included an area of about 50 dunams. The population of Jerusalem did not include more than between 1,000 and 1,250 people.[25] In light of this clear archaeological evidence, we should interpret the 'Return to Zion' as a slow and gradual process, that did not leave its imprint on the archaeological data. Even if a real change in the history of Jerusalem occurred in the middle of the fifth century BCE, with the rebuild of the fortifications of Jerusalem, with all its dramatic implication on its status, it did not change the actual demographic situation of the city. Jerusalem did not become a real urban centre until the Hellenistic period.

Bibliography

Amiran, R., and A. Eitan. 1970. 'Excavations in the Courtyard of the Citadel, Jerusalem, 1968–1969 (Preliminary Report)'. *IEJ* 20: 9-17.

Ariel, D.T. 1990. 'Imported Stamped Amphora Handles'. In D.T. Ariel (ed.), *Excavations at the City of David 1978–1985 Directed by Yigal Shiloh. Vol. II, Imported Stamped Amphora Handles, Coins, Worked Bone and Ivory, and Glass* (Qedem 30). Jerusalem: 13-98.

Ariel, D.T. (ed.). 2000. *City of David Excavations: Final Report V* (Qedem 40). Jerusalem.

Ariel, D.T. 2003. 'Imported Greek Stamped Amphora Handles'. In H. Geva (ed.), *Jewish Quarter Excavations in the Old City of Jerusalem Conducted by Nahman Avigad, 1969–1982. Vol. I, Architecture and Stratigraphy: Areas A, W and X-2. Final Report*. Jerusalem: 267-83.

Ariel, D.T., H. Hirschfeld, and N. Savir. 2000. 'Area D1: Stratigraphic Report'. In D.T. Ariel (ed.), *Excavations at the City of David V: Extramural Areas* (Qedem 40). Jerusalem: 33-72.

Ariel, D.T., and J. Magness. 1992. 'Area K'. In A. De Groot and D.T. Ariel (eds.), *Excavations at the City of David 1978–1985. Vol. III, Stratigraphic, Environmental, and Other Reports* (Qedem 33). Jerusalem: 63-97.

Ariel, D.T., and Y. Shoham. 2000. 'Locally Stamped Handles and Associated Body Fragments of the Persian and Hellenistic Periods'. In D.T. Ariel (ed.), *Excavations at the City of David 1978–1985, Directed by Yigal Shiloh. Vol. 6, Inscriptions* (Qedem 41). Jerusalem: 137-69.

Avigad, N. 1972. 'Excavations in the Jewish Quarter of the Old City of Jerusalem, 1971'. *IEJ* 22: 193-200.

Avigad, N. 1975. 'Excavations in the Jewish Quarter of the Old City, 1969–1971'. In Y. Yadin, (ed.), *Jerusalem Revealed: Archaeology in the Holy City 1968–1974*. Jerusalem: 38-49.

---

[25] This population estimate is very close to the accepted estimations in research in the last years – these of Carter (1999: 288) and Lipschits (2005: 271; 2006: 32) – of about 60 dunams and 1,250–1,500 people respectively, or that of Geva (2007b: 56–7) of a settled area of 60 dunams and population estimate of about 1,000 people.

Avigad, N. 1980. *The Upper City of Jerusalem*. Jerusalem (Hebrew).
Avigad, N. 1983. *Discovering Jerusalem*. Nashville.
Blenkinsopp, J. 1998. 'The Judean Priesthood during the Neo-Babylonian and Achaemenid Periods: A Hypothetical Reconstruction'. *CBQ* 60: 25-43.
Bliss, F.J., and A.C. Dickie. 1898. *Excavations at Jerusalem 1894–1897*. London.
Briant, P. 2002. *From Cyrus to Alexander: A History of the Persian Empire*. Trans. Peter T. Daniels. Winona Lake. English translation of 1996 *Histoire de l'empire perse de Cyrus à Alexandre: Volumes I–II*. Achaemenid History 10. Leiden.
Broshi, M., and S. Gibson. 1994. 'Excavations along the Western and Southern Walls of the Old City of Jerusalem'. In H. Geva (ed.), *Ancient Jerusalem Revealed*. Jerusalem: 147-55.
Brown, J.P. 1969. *The Lebanon and Phoenicia I*. Beirut.
Cahill, J.M. 1992. 'The Chalk Assemblages of the Persian/Hellenistic and Early Roman Periods'. In A. De Groot and D.T. Ariel (eds.), *Excavations at the City of David 1978–1985. Vol. III, Stratigraphic, Environmental, and Other Reports* (Qedem 33). Jerusalem: 190-274.
Cahill, J.M., and D. Tarler. 1994. 'Excavations Directed by Yigal Shiloh at the City of David, 1978–1985'. In H. Geva (ed.), *Ancient Jerusalem Revealed*. Jerusalem: 31-45.
Carter, C.E. 1999. *The Emergence of Yehud in the Persian Period – A Social and Demographic Study* (JSOT Supplement Series 294). Sheffield.
Chen, D., S. Margalit, and B. Pixner. 1994. 'Mount Zion: Discovery of Iron Age Fortifications below the Gate of the Essens'. In H. Geva (ed.), *Ancient Jerusalem Revealed*. Jerusalem: 76-81.
Cogan, M., and H. Tadmor. 1988. *II Kings*. New York.
Cook, S.A. 1925. 'Inscribed Jar Handle'. *PEFQST* 57: 91-95.
Crowfoot, J.W., and G.M. Fitzgerald. 1929. *Excavations in the Tyropoeon Valley, Jerusalem 1927* (Palestine Exploration Fund Annual 7). London.
De Groot, A. 2001. 'Jerusalem during the Persian Period'. In A. Faust and E. Baruch (eds.), *New Studies on Jerusalem, Proceedings of the Seventh Conference*. Ramat Gan: 77-82 (Hebrew).
De Groot, A. 2004. 'Jerusalem in the Early Hellenistic Period'. In E. Baruch and A. Faust (eds.), *New Studies on Jerusalem, Proceedings of the Tenth Conference*. Ramat Gan: 67-70 (Hebrew).
De Groot, A. 2005. 'Excavations in the South of the City of David – Reinterpretation of Former Excavations'. *Qadmoniot* 130: 81-86 (Hebrew).
De Groot, A., D. Cohen, and A. Caspi. 1992. 'Area A1'. In A. De Groot and D.T. Ariel. *Excavations at the City of David 1978–1985. Vol. III, Stratigraphic, Environmental, and Other Reports* (Qedem 33). Jerusalem: 1-29.
De Groot, A., and D. Michaeli. 1992. Area H – Stratigraphic Report'. In A. De Groot and D.T. Ariel. *Excavations at the City of David 1978–1985. Vol. III, Stratigraphic, Environmental, and Other Reports* (Qedem 33). Jerusalem: 35-53.
Duncan, J.G. 1931. *Digging Up Biblical History I–II*. London.
Eph'al, I. 1998. 'Changes in Palestine During the Persian Period in Light of Epigraphic Sources'. *IEJ* 38: 106-19.
Eshel, H. 2000. 'Jerusalem Under Persian Rule: The City's Layout and the Historical Background'. In S. Ahituv and A. Mazar (eds.), *The History of Jerusalem, The Biblical Period*. Jerusalem: 327-44 (Hebrew).
Finkelstein, I. 2008. 'Jerusalem in the Persian (and Early Hellenistic) Period and the Wall of Nehemiah'. *JSOT* 32.4: 501-20.

Finkielsztejn, G. 1999. 'Hellenistic Jerusalem: The Evidence of the Rhodian Amphora Stamps'. In A. Faust and E. Baruch (eds.), *New Studies on Jerusalem. Proceedings of the Fifth Conference*. Ramat Gan: 21-36.

Franken, H.J., and M.L. Steiner. 1990. *Excavations in Jerusalem 1961–1967. Vol. II, The Iron Age Extramural Quarter on the South-East Hill*. Oxford.

Geva, H. 1983. 'Excavations in the Citadel of Jerusalem, 1979–1980: Preliminary Report'. *IEJ* 33: 55-71.

Geva, H. 1985. 'The "First Wall" of Jerusalem during the Second Temple Period – An Architectural-Chronological Note'. *Eretz-Israel* 18: 21-39 (Hebrew).

Geva, H. 1994. 'Excavations at the Citadel of Jerusalem, 1976–1980'. In H. Geva (ed.), *Ancient Jerusalem Revealed*. Jerusalem: 156-67.

Geva, H. 2000a. 'General Introduction to the Excavations in the Jewish Quarter'. In H. Geva (ed.), *Jewish Quarter Excavations in the Old City of Jerusalem Conducted by Nahman Avigad, 1969–1982. Vol. I, Architecture and Stratigraphy: Areas A, W and X-2. Final Report*. Jerusalem: 1-31.

Geva, H. 2000b. 'Excavations at the Citadel of Jerusalem'. In H. Geva (ed.), *Ancient Jerusalem Revealed* (Reprinted and Expanded Edition). Jerusalem: 156-67.

Geva, H. 2003a. 'Hellenistic Pottery from Areas W and X-2'. In H. Geva (ed.), *Jewish Quarter Excavations in the Old City of Jerusalem Conducted by Nahman Avigad, 1969–1982, Volume II, The Finds from Areas A, W and X-2, Final Report*. Jerusalem: 113-75.

Geva, H. 2003b. 'Summary and Discussion of Findings from Areas A, W and X-2'. In H. Geva (ed.), *Jewish Quarter Excavations in the Old City of Jerusalem Conducted by Nahman Avigad, 1969–1982. Volume II, The Finds from Areas A, W and X-2, Final Report*. Jerusalem: 501-52.

Geva, H. 2007a. 'A Chronological Reevaluation of *yehud* Stamp Impressions in Paleo-Hebrew Script, Based Upon Findings from the Jewish Quarter Excavations in the Old City of Jerusalem'. *TA* 34.1: 92-103.

Geva, H. 2007b. Estimating Jerusalem's Population in Antiquity: A Minimalist View. *Eretz Israel* 28: 50-65 (Hebrew).

Geva, H., and N. Avigad. 2000a. 'Area W – Stratigraphy and Architecture'. In H. Geva (ed.), *Jewish Quarter Excavations in the Old City of Jerusalem Conducted by Nahman Avigad, 1969–1982. Vol. I, Architecture and Stratigraphy: Areas A, W and X-2. Final Report*. Jerusalem: 131-97.

Geva, H., and N. Avigad. 2000b. 'Area X2 – Stratigraphy and Architecture'. In H. Geva (ed.), *Jewish Quarter Excavations in the Old City of Jerusalem Conducted by Nahman Avigad, 1969–1982. Vol. I, Architecture and Stratigraphy: Areas A, W and X-2. Final Report*. Jerusalem: 199-240.

Geva, H., and R. Reich. 2000. 'Area A – Stratigraphy and Architecture IIa: Introduction'. In H. Geva (ed.), *Jewish Quarter Excavations in the Old City of Jerusalem Conducted by Nahman Avigad, 1969–1982. Vol. I, Architecture and Stratigraphy: Areas A, W and X-2. Final Report*. Jerusalem: 37-43.

Grabbe, L.L. 2004. *A History of the Jews and Judaism in the Second Temple Period. Volume I: Yehud: A History of the Persian Province of Judah*. London and New York.

Grabbe, L.L. 2009. 'Was Jerusalem a Persian Fortress?' In G.N. Knoppers, L.L. Grabbe, and D.N. Fulton (eds.), *Exile and Restoration Revisited – Essays on the Babylonian and Persian Periods in Memory of Peter R. Ackroyd*. New York: 128-37.

Johns, C.N. 1950. 'The Citadel, Jerusalem (A Summary of Work Since 1934)'. *QDAP* 14: 121-90.

Katzenstein, H.J. 1973. *A History of Tyre*. Jerusalem.

Katzenstein, H.J. 1994. 'Gaza in the Neo-Babylonian Period (626–539 B.C.E.)'. *Transeuphratène* 7: 35-49.
Kenyon, K.M. 1960. *Archaeology in the Holy Land.* London.
Kenyon, K.M. 1963. 'Excavations in Jerusalem, 1962'. *PEQ* 95: 7-21.
Kenyon, K.M. 1966. 'Excavations in Jerusalem, 1965'. *PEQ* 98: 73-88.
Kenyon, K.M. 1967a. *Jerusalem: Excavating 3000 Years of History.* London.
Kenyon, K.M. 1967b. 'Excavations in Jerusalem, 1966'. *PEQ* 99: 65-71.
Kenyon. K.M. 1974. *Digging Up Jerusalem.* London.
Lemaire, A. 1990. 'Populations et territoires de Palestine à l'époque perse'. *Transeuphratène* 3: 31-74.
Lemaire, A. 1991. 'Le royaume de Tyre dans le second moitie du IV av. J.C.' *Atti del II Congresso Internationale di Studi Fenici e Punici.* Vol. I. Rome: 132-49.
Lemaire, A. 2003. 'Nabonidus in Arabia and Judah in the Neo-Babylonian Period'. In O. Lipschits and J. Blenkinsopp (eds.), *Judah and the Judeans in the Neo-Babylonian Period.* Winona Lake: 285-98.
Levine, L.I. 2002. *Jerusalem, Portrait of the City in the Second Temple Period (538 BCE – 70 CE).* Philadelphia.
Lipschits, O. 1999. 'Nebuchadrezzar's Policy in "Hattu-Land" and the Fate of the Kingdom of Judah'. *Ugarit-Forschungen* 30: 467-87.
Lipschits, O. 2001a. 'Judah, Jerusalem and the Temple (586–539 B.C.)'. *Transeuphratène* 22: 129-42.
Lipschits, O. 2001b. 'The Policy of the Persian Empire and the Meager Architectural Finds in the Province of Yehud'. In A. Faust and E. Baruch (eds.), *New Studies in Jerusalem* (Proceedings of the Seventh Conference). Ramat-Gan: 45-76 (Hebrew).
Lipschits, O. 2003. 'Demographic Changes in Judah between the 7th and the 5th Centuries BCE'. In O. Lipschits and J. Blenkinsopp (eds.), *Judah and the Judeans in the Neo-Babylonian Period.* Winona Lake: 323-76.
Lipschits, O. 2004. Ammon in Transition from Vassal Kingdom to Babylonian Province. *Bulletin of the American Schools of Oriental Research* 335: 37-52.
Lipschits, O. 2005. *The Fall and Rise of Jerusalem: The History of Judah under Babylonian Rule.* Winona Lake.
Lipschits, O. 2006. 'Achaemenid Imperial Policy, Settlement Processes in Palestine, and the Status of Jerusalem in the Middle of the Fifth Century BCE'. In O. Lipschits and M. Oeming (eds.). *Judah and the Judeans in the Persian (Achaemenid) Period.* Winona Lake: 19-52.
Lipschits, O. 2009. 'Persian Period Finds from Jerusalem: Facts and Interpretations'. *Journal of Hebrew Scriptures* 9: Article 20.
Lipschits, O. Forthcoming. 'Persian Period Finds from Jerusalem: Facts and Interpretations'. *JHS.*
Lipschits, O., and D. Vanderhooft. 2007a. 'Jerusalem in the Persian and Hellenistic Periods in Light of the Yehud Stamp Impressions'. *Eretz Israel – Archaeological, Historical and Geographical Studies* (Tedi Kolek's volume). Jerusalem: 106-15 (Hebrew).
Lipschits, O., and D. Vanderhooft. 2007b. 'Yehud Stamp Impressions of the Fourth Century BCE: A Time of Administrative Consolidation?' In O. Lipschits, G.N. Knoppers, and R. Albertz (eds.), *Judah and the Judeans in the 4th Century BCE.* Winona Lake: 75-94.
Macalister, R.A.S., and J.G. Duncan. 1926. *Excavations on the Hill of Ophel, Jerusalem 1923–1925.* London.
Mazar, B. 1969. *The Excavations in the Old City of Jerusalem. Preliminary Report of the First Season 1968.* Jerusalem.
Mazar, B. 1972. 'Excavations Near the Temple Mount'. *Qadmoniot* 19-20: 74-90 (Hebrew).

Mazar, E. 1993. 'Excavations in the Ophel – The Royal Quarter of Jerusalem during the First Temple Period'. *Qadmoniot* 26 (101-102): 25-32 (Hebrew).

Mazar, E. 2007a. *Excavations at the City of David 2005 – Visiting Center (Preliminary Publication)*. Jerusalem (Hebrew).

Mazar, E. 2007b. 'Excavations at the City of David – Visiting Center (2006–2007)'. In E. Baruch, A. Levy-Reifer, and A. Faust (eds.), *New Studies on Jerusalem* (vol. 13). Ramat-Gan: 7-26 (Hebrew).

Mazar, E. 2008. 'The Steppe Stone Structure in the City of David in Light of the New Excavations in Area G'. In E. Baruch, A. Levy-Reifer, and A. Faust (eds.), *New Studies on Jerusalem* (vol. 14). Ramat-Gan: 25-40 (Hebrew).

Mazar, E., and B. Mazar. 1989. *Excavations in the South of the Temple Mount, the Ophel of Biblical Jerusalem* (Qedem 29). Jerusalem.

Naveh, J. 2000. 'Hebrew and Aramaic Inscriptions'. In D.T. Ariel (ed.), *Excavations at the City of David, 1978–1985. Directed by Yigal Shiloh.* VI, *Inscriptions* (Qedem 41). Jerusalem: 1-14.

Oppenheim, A.L. 1967. 'Essay on Overland Trade in the First Millennium B.C.' *JCS* 21: 236-54.

Redford, D.B. 1992. *Egypt, Canaan, and Israel in Ancient Times*. Princeton.

Reich, R. 1994. 'The Ancient Burial Ground in the Mamilla Neighborhood, Jerusalem'. In H. Geva (ed.), *Ancient Jerusalem Revealed*. Jerusalem: 111-18.

Reich, R. 2003. 'Local Seal Impressions of the Hellenistic Period'. In H. Geva (ed.), *Jewish Quarter Excavations in the Old City of Jerusalem Conducted by Nahman Avigad, 1969–1982. Volume II, The Finds from Areas A, W and X-2, Final Report*. Jerusalem: 256-62.

Reich, R., and E. Shukron. 1998. 'Jerusalem, the City of David'. *Excavations and Surveys in Israel* 18: 91-92.

Reich, R., and E. Shukron. 2007. 'The Yehud Seal Impressions from the 1995–2005 Excavations in the City of David'. *Tel Aviv* 34 (1): 59-65.

Ryle, H.E. 1907. *Ezra and Nehemiah*. Cambridge.

Schniedewind, W. 2003. 'Jerusalem, the Late Judaean Monarchy and the Composition of the Biblical Texts'. In A.G. Vaughn and A.E. Killebrew (eds.), *Jerusalem in the Bible and Archaeology: The First Temple Period*. Atlanta: 375-94.

Schniedewind, W. 2004. *How the Bible Became a Book: The Textualization of Ancient Israel*. Cambridge.

Shiloh, Y. 1984. *Excavations in the City of David, I* (Qedem 19). Jerusalem (Hebrew).

Shiloh, Y. 1990. 'Stratigraphical Introduction to Parts I and II'. In D.T. Ariel (ed.), *Excavations at the City of David 1978–1985 Directed by Yigal Shiloh. Vol. II, Imported Stamped Amphora Handles, Coins, Worked Bone and Ivory, and Glass* (Qedem 30). Jerusalem: 1-12.

Shukron, E., and R. Reich. 2005. Jerusalem, City of David, the Giv'ati Car Park. *Hadashot Arkheologiot – Excavations and Surveys in Israel* 117: 7-9 (http://www.hadashot-esi.org.il/report_detail_eng.asp?id=250&mag_id=110).

Sivan, R., and G. Solar. 1994. 'Excavations in the Jerusalem Citadel, 1980–1988'. In H. Geva (ed.), *Ancient Jerusalem Revealed*. Jerusalem: 168-76.

Stern, E. 1982. *Material Culture of the Land of the Bible in the Persian Period, 538–332 B.C.* Warminster.

Stern, E. 1990. 'The Dor Province in the Persian Period in the Light of the Recent Excavations at Dor'. *Transeuphratène* 2: 147-55.

Stern, E. 2001. *Archaeology of the Land of the Bible. Vol. II, The Assyrian, Babylonian and Persian Periods 732–332 B.C.E.* New York.

Tsafrir, Y. 1977. 'The Walls of Jerusalem in the Period of Nehemiah'. *Cathedra* 4: 31-42 (Hebrew).

Tushingham, A.D. 1967. 'Armenian Garden'. *PEQ* 99: 71-73.

Tushingham, A.D. 1985. *Excavations in Jerusalem, 1961–1967. Vol. I, Excavations in the Armenian Garden, on the Western Hill*. Toronto.

Vanderhooft, D.S. 1999. *The Neo-Babylonian Empire and Babylon in the Latter Prophets*. Atlanta.

Vanderhooft, D.S., and O. Lipschits. 2007. 'A New Typology of the Yehud Stamp Impressions'. *Tel Aviv* 34.1: 12-37.

Weisman, D.J. 1991. 'Babylonia 605–539 B.C.' *The Cambridge Ancient History* (Second Edition), Vol. III/2: 229-51.

Zwickel, W. 2008. 'Jerusalem und Samaria zur Zeit Nehemias. Ein Vergleich'. *Biblische Zeitschrift* 52.2: 201-22.

Part 5

Conclusions

Introduction to Part 5

The concluding essay here is self-contained and serves to provide a conclusion both to the volume in which originally appears and the present volume. It summarizes some of the main points of historical methodology to be applied in researching the history of Israel.

Seventeen Years of the European Seminar in Historical Methodology: The Results*

Lester L. Grabbe

This final essay in our final volume from the European Seminar on Methodology in Israel's History is a chance to describe our work as a Seminar over 17 years, to sum up some of the things we accomplished, and to reflect on proper historical methodology as it relates to writing the history of ancient Israel/Palestine/ Southern Levant.

Founding of the Seminar

In the early 1990s there was quite a flurry of activity relating to the history of ancient Palestine. I knew a number of those involved in the debate. I would see statements by some of the so-called minimalists and by their critics, and kept thinking, 'Someone needs to organize a forum where these issues can be debated, instead of this posturing and talking past one another.' I was already trying to be a historian, though my own research had related mainly to the history of Second Temple Jews and Judaism; however, for a number of years I had taught a History of Israel course. I cannot remember if I suggested a forum to anyone, but then it suddenly dawned on me that I knew many of the historians in Europe and could be advised on others I did not know personally: I was in a good position to organize something. I suggested the idea to several people, who were encouraging and also gave me names of scholars I did not know who might participate.

I wanted it to be a European seminar, partly because this is where some of the major researchers were working. But also I did not know much about what was being done in Israel, and I thought that we might be overwhelmed if we included North America (from which I had been away for more than a decade). So in the

---

* Adapted slightly from my article, 'Seventeen Years of the European Seminar in Historical Methodology: The Results', in Lester L. Grabbe (eds), *'Not Even God Can Alter the Past': Reflections on 17 Years of the European Seminar in Historical Methodology*, LHBOTS 663; European Seminar in Historical Methodology 11 (London and New York: Bloomsbury T&T Clark, 2018), 215–31.

end I wrote to everyone I knew or whose name was suggested to me as working in the history of Israel/Palestine in Europe (by Europe I hasten to say I include the UK—though some British people, especially after Brexit, would not). Except for a few retired scholars who were no longer active, I believe every scholar working on the history side was invited to participate. Most replied and most accepted, although some of those accepting the invitation then did not take part. As it turned out, only about a dozen of those who originally accepted my invitation were active in the Seminar, but I freely invited guests to join us for specific topics and periodically invited new members, with the result that we had not only new Europeans as members but also some Israelis—and even a few North Americans who met with us regularly.

The name of the Seminar was the European Seminar on Methodology in Israel's History. This name was not changed, though we often used a shortened form for convenience (European Seminar in Historical Methodology, as in the title of the present essay).[1] I emphasize this because Professor William G. Dever somehow inferred that the name was changed from the former to the latter (Dever 2016: 9), which he interpreted negatively. Also, I always made it clear that some would prefer to think of 'Palestine' or 'Southern Levant' rather than 'Israel' in their own work and writings, and I always interpreted our task as including all the nations of the region, not just Israel and Judah. But the Seminar focus on the history of Israel did not change, and I often cited the full name of the Seminar when introducing sessions or when describing it. Dever was incorrect in thinking the title was changed.

Our first meeting was in Dublin in 1996, with the International Society of Biblical Literature. In addition to the Seminar members, we had observers filling the room and flowing out into the hall, indicating that history was once again a subject of interest to biblical scholars. The proceedings of this conference were published as the first book of the Seminar, *Can a History of Israel Be Written?* I have since been told that it made an impact. It went into paperback and continues to sell briskly now 20 years later. Even Professor Dever liked parts of it. Although he initially criticized it publicly at the SBL meeting where it first went on sale, he later wrote to me—after he had finally read it!—that he liked a number of essays, especially Hans Barstad's.

As we began, I naively thought that with time and discussion, the members of the Seminar might draw closer together in our views. Not a chance! Well, perhaps I exaggerate. I think there may have been a meeting of the minds in certain subtle ways. We learned from each other—or at least some of us did. But I think above all that we came to understand the issues better, even if our individual approaches

---

[1] This shortened title was also used as the title of the monograph sub-series in the JSOT Supplements (the name of the main series later changed to Library of Hebrew Bible/Old Testament Studies). Again, it was matter of convenience, not a change of aim or intent.

to them may have differed considerably. Above all, in our volumes we carried the debate to a much wider audience. In 17 years we produced 11 published volumes (counting the present one). Also, as well as the debates on methodology we issued volumes on certain more narrow topics that provided important and useful information on specific periods in the history of Israel, including Sennacherib's invasion, the Omri dynasty, and the last century of the kingdom of Judah.

Because I did not know how long the Seminar would last, we tended to plan only a year or two ahead. But I did have the goal that we would one day tackle the 10th century, if we did not disband first. Finally, I got research council funding for a project that included the transition period from the Late Bronze to the Iron IIA, or about 1250–850 BCE. I then discussed conferences with various individuals. When I suggested a conference on the 10th century to my Tel Aviv friend Nadav Na'aman, he groaned: 'It's been done to death. We have had numerous conferences on the subject to the point that no new ideas are coming forth. Each participant just repeats arguments and positions already taken.' Well, he may have been right about things in the Israeli context, but it is surprising how little public discussion there has been of the 10th century in the Anglo-German environment. Despite Nadav's reaction, I went ahead and planned two conferences, one involving archaeologists and one a regular meeting of the European Seminar.

Getting archaeologists to come was difficult only to the extent that the funding decision came somewhat late in the planning process, and a number of those invited were not free at the times planned. But when I put the proposal to my colleagues in the European Seminar, I was astonished at the opposition. Other historical periods had not caused any problem, but when the era of David and Solomon was on the agenda, a number of my colleagues were against this as a topic of debate. The reasons given seemed to me to be specious—and still seem to be. The real reason seems to me—and perhaps I'm just prejudiced—to be a reluctance on the part of some to discuss this period seriously as possibly containing historical data. I could not help thinking of an essay by Hans Barstad in our second published volume (Barstad 1998; reprinted here in Part 1).

One regret I have is that more women did not participate. This was not through lack of invitation. For example, Helge Weippert was invited, as was Josette Elay who works in the Persian period. Both expressed an interest, but neither ever attended, even though they remained on the mailing list for a number of years. Diana Edelman did attend for several years, and other female scholars contributed articles to our volumes. However, the purpose of the seminar was to encourage those actually working in history to dialogue with one another, not to be an example of political correctness. The fact is that when we began the Seminar, few men worked seriously in history, and even fewer women. I would like to think that the situation is changing, but I am not really clear that this is the case.

Another small regret is that we only made a couple of forays into Second Temple Jewish history. My original proposal included the history of Israel up to about 100 CE, but we did only one volume on the Hellenistic period in general, and a session on the Maccabean period did not lead to publication (though several essays from it were published in the final volume). However, the majority of our participants were specialists in earlier history and not in the period after Alexander the Great. We did have one session on the Persian period, but it was too diffuse, and so much is being done on the Persian period that I gave up trying to produce a volume on it.

There have been various views from outsiders as to what sort of seminar it was, and I need to correct some mistaken descriptions. Some have characterized it as a minimalist seminar. Before the founding of the Seminar, Philip Davies and some others such as Niels Peter Lemche and Thomas Thompson were labelled 'minimalists'. The term 'minimalist' was apparently invented by William Hallo—or so he claims (see the discussion in the next section). I do not know who applied it to 'the Copenhagen School', but they seem to have embraced the designation, though I have never heard Davies call himself a minimalist and am not sure he likes the title. In any case, Rainer Albertz—who is no minimalist—found it totally misleading, as did I. (One journalist who wrote a book on the debate, and consulted me about some points, nevertheless stated that the European Seminar was the same as the Copenhagen Seminar, which is completely wrong.) I wish to stress that the members, as well as guests invited for individual sessions, had a range of views. It is safe to say that ultra-conservatives were not a part of it. This was because I felt that all who participated had to be genuinely critical scholars, whereas fundamentalists and many conservative evangelicals would be unable to engage in a useful dialogue on the issues. I appreciate that some evangelical scholars these days are able to take part in critical discussion of the Bible, but during the period of the Seminar none came to my personal attention or was suggested to me by others as a possible Seminar member. This did not prevent a range of views, from conservative to radical, being expressed on individual issues.

Similarly, some years ago while reading a paper on history at the Society of Biblical Literature conference, a North American scholar referred to the 'European School', apparently with the European Seminar in mind. I think the members of the Seminar, as well as those who have been observers at our discussions, would have been quite surprised to hear this. The term 'school' usually implies a common view or perspective. The common perspective of the Seminar was, I believe, two-fold: (a) that we thought the subject of history and ancient Israel was one worth spending time on and debating, and (b) that there was no quick and easy answer to the issue of Iron Age Palestine's history or of its relationship to the contents of the biblical text. Beyond this common interest, however, there was a great variety of viewpoints and also some sharp exchanges and vociferous disagreements over the 17 years that we met. I think we would all agree that the term 'school' was entirely inappropriate. We sat around the same table, and we published papers between the same set of covers, but the papers—far from taking a unified position—in fact formed a vigorous debate.

What we did have, however, was unique at the time. We were not aware of another group trying to thresh out questions of historical methodology in a forum which took in a diversity of views. This is a pity, since many biblical scholars and archaeologists think the subject of the Bible and history is important, yet there was little formal discussion on the subject. Polemics there were aplenty, not to mention sermonizing to the converted. What was lacking was genuine discussion. The Seminar was not a partisan exercise but an attempt to have the proper face-to-face debate that seemed to be lacking elsewhere. Perhaps things have changed to some extent—perhaps the Seminar helped in that—but I think there is still a great need for more dialogue on the question of history.

I even heard our Seminar characterized once or twice as 'postmodernist', though only orally, to the best of my knowledge, and not in print. To me—no fan of postmodernism—this was a rather repugnant label. More will be said on postmodernism and history in the next section, but we were decidedly not a postmodern seminar of any kind. I cannot speak for all members of the Seminar, especially since some of them did and do some of their work in a postmodernist context. Nevertheless, I can say that the Seminar as such was not postmodernist, and some members of the Seminar would wholeheartedly reject the term 'postmodernist' as applied to themselves. In the first volume of papers coming from the Seminar, Hans Barstad discussed in detail the implications of postmodernism (among other trends) for historical research (Barstad 1997). He pointed out that postmodernist study has some relevant contributions to make to the debate (with which I agree), but he certainly did not recommend that the postmodernist agenda (some postmodernists would reject the concept of having an agenda!) should be whole-heartedly embraced. On the contrary, he suggested, on the one hand, that it was already being superseded and, on the other hand, that older questions and issues were still very much in the picture.

Two of those most likely to be labelled 'postmodernist' were Lemche and Thompson. I confess that some of Thompson's later writings have seemed almost surreal to me, but whether they should be labelled 'postmodernist' is for him and others to say. Yet Thompson wrote an article some 20 years ago in which he considered his general position (Thompson 1995: especially 696-97). Perhaps his tongue was slightly in his cheek when he applied the term 'Neo-Albrightean' to what he, Lemche, and some others were doing, but the historical work he referred to was definitely in the modernist mould. And ours was definitely a modernist seminar, with its roots in the Enlightenment, not postmodernist.

Among historians there is at present no uniform answer to the question of the value—or not—of postmodernism in historical study. Therefore, it would hardly be surprising if different members of the Seminar chose varying approaches to the question. But the fact is that different participants were likely to have quite divergent views on the question, and as a collective we were definitely *not* a 'postmodern seminar' (see the next section for a further discussion of postmodernism and history).

Principles of Writing History

I have laid out my principles on writing history, both in books on Second Temple Judaism (especially the Persian volume) and on ancient Israel (Grabbe 2004; 2017). What I propose to do now is list some of the criteria or principles on which I attempt to write critical history. I think all of my colleagues in the Seminar would agree on some of the points, though perhaps only some would follow me on all of them. In any case, I speak only for myself at this point:

1. Moving Beyond the 'Minimalist'/'Maximalist' Dichotomy

The unfortunate dichotomy of 'minimalist' versus 'maximalist' has bedevilled the debates in our field. The terms get thrown around a lot in contemporary discussions about the history of ancient Israel. It seems to me that they are often employed inappropriately, if we accept a widely used definition of the terms. William W. Hallo claims to have coined the terms.[2] Here are his comments in the context of a discussion about Sennacherib's invasion:

> What, then, is the general methodological lesson we can learn from the case of Jerusalem under Hezekiah? The simple test of the minimalists, that the biblical version of events must have extra-biblical, preferably contemporaneous, verification before it can be regarded as historical, is an impossible demand even in the best of circumstances as here, where the events loom so large in Assyrian royal inscriptions and art, but are presented in such a widely divergent manner. However, the maximalist willingness to accept the biblical version until falsified by extra-biblical sources, preferably contemporaneous and bearing on the same matters, also lacks a rational basis, given the randomness of these sources and their accidental discovery. Because Mesopotamian references to Jerusalem by name were confined to the single reign of Sennacherib and his contemporary Hezekiah, we cannot treat the absence of conflicting sources about Jerusalem in other periods as confirmation of every biblical statement about the city. The task of the biblical historian thus remains as before: to weigh the comparative evidence point by point in order to discover, if possible, the nature of its convergence with the biblical data and the reasons for its divergence. (Hallo 1999)

I am not happy with his term 'biblical historian', since we are historians of a place and/or period of time, not of a book. That is, we are historians of ancient Israel, ancient Palestine, the Assyrian empire, the Iron II period, or the like. Just as most now eschew the term 'biblical archaeologist', we should no longer speak of 'biblical historian'. But Hallo's basic point is well taken. In the actual execution of reconstructing history, we might well evaluate the specific details rather differently, but I believe a number of us in the Seminar would agree with the general sentiment of his summary statements.

---

[2] Hallo 2005: 50 (citing Hallo 1980: 3-5, nn. 4, 11, 12, 23, 55).

E. A. Knauf defined the 'minimalist approach' as 'everything which is not corroborated by evidence contemporary with the events to be reconstructed is dismissed' and 'the maximalist approach which implies that everything in the sources that could not be proved wrong has to be accepted as historical' (Knauf 1991: 171). By that description, only a few minimalists exist and hardly any maximalists, at least in mainstream scholarship.

In my view the only maximalist history is the Provan, Long and Longman's *A History of Biblical Israel* (2003). Even John Bright (1980) was not a maximalist according to the formal definition, which is someone who accepts the biblical account unless it can be disproved. On the other hand, minimalism has had a considerable influence. Thomas Thompson's book (1974), along with some help from John Van Seters (1975), killed off the patriarchal period, while Niels Peter Lemche (1985) contributed to the change of view on the settlement with his lengthy critique of Norman Gottwald. Philip Davies' *In Search of 'Ancient Israel'* (1992), while not claiming originality, was nevertheless highly original in making various scholarly ideas accessible to students—and biblical scholars, who tend to be simple-minded individuals. For a generation of students it was Philip's book rather than Thomas's or Niels Peter's that made them aware of the problems with the old histories. The influence of minimalism cannot be over-estimated. (On the position of the minimalists, see further below.)

2. Use of the *Longue Durée*

I often see the term "*longue durée*" used to mean a lengthy period of political or national history. As I understand it, this is actually an incorrect usage from the point of view of Fernand Braudel. I haven't read as much Braudel as I should have, but I believe he uses the term to refer to natural history: the landscape, geology, geography, the climate. We are talking about the ground on which human history is enacted, and the long-term evolution of geology, flora, fauna, and the all-important climate (Braudel 1980: 25-54). If I understand him correctly, he uses the term *histoire conjoncturelle* to refer to longer trends in human history on the social and economic level. One of the first things that struck me about Palestine was the difference in fertility between the area that became the Kingdom of Israel and that which became the Kingdom of Judah. The Northern Kingdom had most of the natural resources, it seemed to me, and I have often seen this remarked on in subsequent years.

3. The Basic Reliance on Primary Sources

I am often struck in reading books on history about how little is said about sources. Perhaps it is unnecessary in some cases because readers will already be aware of the sources available, but I think it also often leads to muddled thinking, with the writer not being clear in his or her own mind the differences between sources. It is basic method to go the primary sources first, which means those close in time and distance to the events they describe. This usually means inscriptions, documents, and the few eye-witness accounts. It also means the all-important archaeology. As a textual person I long gave lip service to archaeology without really appreciating its centrality. It was as I came to wrestle with various periods in the history of Israel, especially in the context of the Seminar, that I came to appreciate how important archaeology was. This is why, when I wrote the first volume of my *History of the Jews and Judaism in the Second Temple Period* (2004) and especially my book on *Ancient Israel* (first edition, 2007), that I gave priority to archaeology.

I have seen some argue against the importance of primary sources, usually by noting that primary sources can be biased, inaccurate, and so on. Of course, this is the case: primary sources are not perfect, and some can be very flawed. Also, a late secondary source might depend heavily on an early primary source. Thus, Arrian's *Anabasis of Alexander* is a first-rate historical source, even though very late and secondary, because Arrian made use of important primary sources that have since been lost. And the primary source of archaeology requires interpretation. But to make no distinction between primary and secondary sources is often a trick used by those who want to favour the biblical text.[3] In spite of some necessary qualifications, a basic rule of historical research is that one should go first and most vigorously to primary sources.

4. All Sources Should Be Considered

This is where many part company with the minimalists. Most of us have taken a pop at the minimalists at some point, and that includes me. Yet the minimalists have done a service to scholarship by making us justify our positions by argument, rather than taking them for granted. Some years ago I was asked to give a response to a minimalist paper at a conference. In my evaluation, I made the comment that I did not think the minimalists were much interested in history. Niels Peter Lemche took me to task for that statement, and quite rightly: minimalism as a philosophical position can be found in a variety of disciplines, from music to art to architecture. Furthermore, almost all of us biblical scholars are minimalists for some periods in Israel's history, because most of us reject the text for certain periods. There are few who now defend the patriarchal narratives. Likewise, few would give much credence to Joshua's picture of the settlement now, though when I was a PhD student in the early '70s, the opposite was true, at least in North America. In that sense, the minimalists have won—and deserve to win. For that reason, I find it ironic that they sometimes adopt the mantel of victimhood, as if everyone is against them. On the contrary, they have won an important victory!

---

[3] For example, I can refer to *A Biblical History of Israel*, by Provan, Long, and Longman (see my review and their response in Part 1).

But where they are wrong, in my opinion, is in throwing out the baby with the bath water. Or, to put it more academically, in relying dogmatically on a methodology that has been shown to be inadequate. This is the case—as I think I have demonstrated on many occasions—with the biblical text. Biblical minimalism rejects the biblical text unless it is confirmed by a reliable source, which means that the biblical text can never give us usable data on its own. This seems to me absurd. It is simply not the way historians work. We make decisions on the basis of probability, and these decisions are subjective: what I think is credible may not seem so to you, and vice versa. We have to put forward our arguments and see whether we convince others. But we do not exclude sources that have demonstrably contained usable historical data just because they are sometimes wrong or even fictional in places.

There are many cases in which the biblical text has been shown to contain historical data even when this has not been confirmed by other sources. Indeed, our years of discussion of the range of Israelite history has brought one thing home to me. This is that in general the later one moves in the Israelite monarchy, the more reliable the biblical account is. We have better information in the Bible on the 8th century than the 10th, and quite good information on the 7th century, to the point that in the last part of the 7th century we know what was happening almost year by year. This is only a broad generalization of course: there are black spots in every century, and some early biblical passages seem to be based on good sources. Nevertheless, a dogmatic minimalism can reject helpful data and become just another fundamentalism that impedes proper historical research.

5. Classical Historians Serve as a Good Model

I have learned a lot from classical historians. Strangely, in the UK 'ancient history/historians' means Greek and Roman history/historians, which makes those of us who work in the ancient Near East slightly irritated. Yet historians of ancient Palestine hardly face new or unprecedented problems. On the contrary, most of the problems exercising us already challenged historians of Greece and Rome long ago. For example, histories of ancient Rome draw on archaeology, inscriptions, coins, and literary works, but they still depend heavily on narrative history. Writers such as Polybius, Livy, Tacitus and Cassius Dio were in some cases writing hundreds of years after the events described, often drawing on unknown sources or sources of indifferent quality. Writers such as Julius Caesar were telling their own story, with the dangers of self-justification and personal bias, as well as the benefits of being eye witnesses to many events.

But many of the Greek and Roman sources are of the same sort and have the same problems as the biblical sources. When we look at Herodotus and Livy and even Tacitus, we often find problematic scenarios. This does not stop classical historians from using them to reconstruct history. One of the main ancient historians I wrestle with is Josephus. He is often misinformed, credulous, uncritical, biased, and even downright duplicitous. This frequently makes it difficult to evaluate his data. But he is also extremely important and useful. The same applies to 1 and 2 Kings and some other sections of the Bible. True, I give little weight to Joshua and Judges, yet here and there...[4] In the final analysis, I feel I have learned a lot from classical historians and classical history.

6. The Contribution of Postmodernism

Although I have read a couple of conventional historians arguing for thorough postmodernism, most of the historians I know or have read about have not embraced the movement. Yet the debate about postmodernism continues in a vigorous fashion among professional historians, at least in some parts of the Academy in English-speaking scholarship.[5] One of the main advocates for a postmodern perspective in history, Keith Jenkins,[6] has recently produced a 'postmodernist reader' that tries to bring together some of the most influential articles in the debate (Jenkins [ed.] 1997). In a long introduction he tries to lay out the main issues, with a defence of his own approach. One can find a similar advocacy of postmodernism, though perhaps less flamboyantly presented, by Alun Munslow (1997). But the past few years have been especially characterized by a strong resistance movement against postmodernism. Joyce Appleby, Lynn Hunt, and Margaret Jacob (1994) produced a book which might appear at first to have a postmodern agenda in its assault on the way 'outsiders' (women and other minorities) have been excluded or neglected.[7] Yet a good part of their text is a strong attack on such postmodern gurus as Foucault and Derrida. A book achieving wide-spread circulation in the UK is Evans's *In Defence of History* (1997), which was written for a non-technical readership. It actually tries to explain clearly the different approaches of recent writers on historiography and is not just an assault on the postmodern, but it ultimately rejects it as the way forward even if the relevance of some aspects of postmodernism is accepted.

A wide-ranging attack on a number of recent trends in history-writing, as the title *The Killing of History* already makes quite plain, has been carried out by Keith Windschuttle (1997). He covers more than postmodernism, and such figures as Derrida are mentioned mainly in passing; however, he has a long chapter

---

[4] On this see the essays by Knauf (Knauf 2010a, 2010b) in Part 2.

[5] How to definite or characterize 'postmodernism' as it applies to history is not an easy task since postmodernists themselves often seem to avoid a positive statement of their historical method. For example, the Introduction to Keith Jenkins' recent 'postmodernist reader' (Jenkins [ed.] 1997) spends a lot of time defining the way most historians do history, but then treats postmodernism only as a critique of this.

[6] See, for example, his *Re-Thinking History* (Jenkins 1991); also most recently, *Why History?* (Jenkins 1999) (my thanks to the late Professor Carroll for drawing my attention to this latter work).

[7] See the extensive reviews by Martin et al. (1995: 320-39).

attacking Foucault whom he sees as the main culprit in undermining traditional study of history. Although the title and style might suggest an irresponsible blunderbuss attack on ill-defined targets, the book makes some effective points despite some shortcomings.[8] C. B. McCullagh (1998) has tried to steer a middle way by recognizing that the critics have not always presented the arguments of the postmodernists fairly and by himself giving due weight to the postmodernist positions; nevertheless, taking into consideration the valid points about subjectiveness and the place of language in reality, he still concludes that historical knowledge is possible. Interestingly, this debate comes at a time when Collingwood's major work on the philosophy of history, a manuscript left at his death and thought destroyed, has recently surfaced and has now been published (Collingwood 1999).

The basic problem is that postmodernism is essentially a-historical or even anti-historical. Even the so-called 'New Historicism' is essentially a literary movement (Hens-Piazza 2002; cf. Grabbe 2003). Most of us who work as historians are still modernists and set our roots in the Enlightenment. Yet even the critics of postmodernism recognize that historical method can benefit from aspects of postmodernism, as noted above. I would draw two prime considerations from postmodernism: first, the subjective nature of our enterprise; secondly, the fact that any position has to be argued for.

On the first point, the days of pure positivism are long since passed. History cannot be reduced to a set of rules like one of the sciences. Historical reconstruction requires a making of decisions by the historian at every turn, especially with regard to ancient history. This means that two serious and solid historians can disagree substantially on certain points. This leads to our second point: the need to present evidence, meaning data and arguments, for any position taken. Naturally, we all appeal to the consensus at times: life is too short to argue everything from first principles. But we should expect to be challenged—or to issue our own challenge—on even fundamental issues. How much of the 1970 consensus on the history of Israel still stands unaltered today? Whether it is the patriarchs, the settlement, the Persian period, or even much in the period of the two monarchies, things have a much different structure and feel than when I began my graduate studies.

Yet this does not mean that everything is subjective. Many would now argue for a limited objectivity, even if complete objectivity is an impossibility. The reason is that everything needs to be tested against the data. Granted, data do not necessarily 'speak for themselves', even if some still insist that they do; they have to be dissected, interpreted, arranged into some sort of intelligent order. This requires a historical mind and historical method. But the data limit interpretation; they exclude certain hypotheses; they point more toward some possibilities than others. To take archaeology as an example: of course, it has to be interpreted, and

---

[8] See the review of Gordon (1999).

archaeologists will disagree on some things about the 'facts' of this dig or that. But some historical reconstructions become difficult or even impossible when the archaeology is considered. And, yes, contrary to the oft-quoted mantra, 'absence of evidence can sometimes be evidence of absence'!

Conclusions

I have tried to present some of the history of the European Seminar on Methodology in Israel's History over its 17 years of work. This is my take on what we did, but other participants will have their own view, which you can read for yourself. I have also attempted here to give my own major principles which I try to exercise when writing history and to apply when reconstructing the history of ancient Israel. Again, readers will have to judge for themselves whether the principles are adequate and whether I apply them adequately.

As we sing our swan song, or to use the technical term, *Schwannengesang*, I think we made a worthwhile contribution to developments in the discipline of the history of ancient Palestine, not only individually but collectively. Many of us will continue to plough the odd furrow in the field, though perhaps the main task is now being shifted on to a younger generation. I am encouraged by new groups of younger scholars that have arisen both in Europe and in North America. I wish them well. It is not my desire to stand over them and try to tell them how to do their job but only to encourage them to push ahead. If they attack and/or overturn what we have done, that will no doubt be for the benefit of the field. On the other hand, as we move from being radical young turks to conservative old fogeys (yes, I include even you, Thomas), I for one feel that our Seminar has made a useful contribution to developing scholarship in the field.

Bibliography

Appleby, Joyce, Lynn Hunt, and Margaret Jacob. 1994. *Telling the Truth about History* (New York: Norton).

Barstad, Hans M. 1997. 'History and the Hebrew Bible', in *Can a 'History of Israel' Be Written?*, ed. Lester L. Grabbe, JSOTSup 245 = ESHM 1 (Sheffield: Sheffield Academic Press, 1997): 37–64.

Barstad, Hans M. 1998. 'The Strange Fear of the Bible: Some Reflections on the "Bibliophobia" in Recent Ancient Israelite Historiography', in *Leading Captivity Captive: 'The Exile' as History and Ideology*, ed. Lester L. Grabbe, JSOTSup 278 = ESHM 2 (Sheffield: Sheffield Academic Press, 1998): 120–27.

Braudel, Fernand. 1980. *On History*, trans. Sarah Matthews (London: Weidenfeld & Nicolson). ET of *Écrits sur l'histoire* (Paris: Flammarion, 1969).

Bright, John. 1980. *A History of Israel*. 3rd ed. (Philadelphia: Westminster Press).

Collingwood, R. G. 1999. *The Principles of History and Other Writings in Philosophy of History*, ed. with an introduction by W. H. Dray and W. J. van der Dussen (Oxford: Oxford University Press).
Davies, Philip R. 1992. *In Search of 'Ancient Israel'*, JSOTSup 148 (Sheffield: JSOT Press).
Dever, William G. 2016. 'History from Things: On Writing New Histories of Ancient Israel', in *Le-ma'an Ziony: Essays in Honor of Ziony Zevit*, ed. Frederick E. Greenspahn and Gary A. Rendsburg (Eugene, OR: Wipf & Stock): 3–20.
Evans, Richard J. 1997. *In Defence of History* (London: Granta Books, 1997).
Grabbe, Lester L. 2003. Review of Gina Hens-Piazza, *The New Historicism*, *RBL* 8/16/2003.
Hallo, William W. 1980. 'Biblical History in its Near Eastern Setting: The Contextual Approach', in *Scripture in Context: Essays on the Comparative Method*, ed. Carl D. Evans, William W. Hallo, and John B. White, Pittsburgh Theological Monograph Series 34 (Pittsburgh, PA: Pickwick): 1–26.
Hallo, William W. 1999. 'Jerusalem under Hezekiah: An Assyriological Perspective', in *Jerusalem: Its Sanctity and Centrality to Judaism, Christianity, and Islam*, ed. Lee I. Levine (New York: Continuum; Poole: Cassell): 36–50.
Hallo, William W. 2005. 'The Kitchen Debate: A Context for the Biblical Account', *BAR* 31, no. 4: 50–51.
Hens-Piazza, Gina. 2002. *The New Historicism*, OTG (Minneapolis: Fortress Press).
Jenkins, Keith. 1991. *Re-Thinking History* (London/New York: Routledge, 1991).
Jenkins, Keith. 1999. *Why History? Ethics and Postmodernity* (Abingdon/New York: Routledge).
Jenkins, Keith. ed. 1997. *The Postmodern History Reader* (London/New York: Routledge).
Knauf, Ernst Axel. 1991. 'King Solomon's Copper Supply', in *Phoenicia and the Bible*, ed. E. Lipiński, Studia Phoenicia 11, OLA 44 (Leuven: Peeters): 167–86.
Lemche, Niels Peter. 1985. *Early Israel: Anthropological and Historical Studies on the Israelite Society Before the Monarchy*, VTSup 37 (Leiden: Brill).
McCullagh, C. Behan. 1998. *The Truth of History* (London/New York: Routledge).
Martin, Raymond, Joan W. Scott, and Cushing Strout. 1995. Reviews of Joyce Appleby, Lynn Hunt, and Margaret Jacob, *Telling the Truth about History*, *History and Theory* 34: 320–39.
Munslow, Alun. 1997. *Deconstructing History* (London/New York: Routledge, 1997).
Provan, Iain, V. Philips Long, and Tremper Longman III. 2003. *A Biblical History of Israel* (Louisville/London: Westminster John Knox Press).
Thompson, Thomas L. 1974. *The Historicity of the Patriarchal Narratives: The Quest for the Historical Abraham*, BZAW 133 (Berlin/New York: W. de Gruyter).
Thompson, Thomas L. 1995. 'A Neo-Albrightean School in History and Biblical Scholarship?', *JBL* 114: 683–98.
Van Seters, John. 1975. *Abraham in History and Tradition* (New Haven: Yale University Press).
Windschuttle, Keith. 1997. *The Killing of History: How Literary Critics and Social Theorists Are Murdering our Past* (New York: The Free Press).

Index of References

HEBREW BIBLE/ OLD TESTAMENT		*Exodus*		*Leviticus*	
		1–23	129	16	131
		1–15	174, 186-87,	18.21	454
Genesis			201, 202	20.2-4	454
1–11	19	1	201		
1	19, 20	1.1–24.8	130	*Numbers*	
6–9	131	1.11	186, 187, 193	1.46	142
10	123	2.3-5	199	2.32	142
11	9, 122	5–13	131	6.24-26	444
11.1-9	123	12.37	142, 200, 197	10.21	142
11.26–12.4	131	13.17-18	197	13.21	259
12	9, 122, 123	13.18	199	13.29	243
12.10-20	131	13.20	197	14.39-45	288
12.10	123	14	131, 199	21.4-9	129
14	132	14.1-2	201	24.14	417
14.19	308	14.9	201	32.34-36	211
16	123	15	132	33.45-46	303
17.9-14	271	15.22-26	129	34.1-12	206, 208
19	123	15.22-24	130		
20	123	15.22	199	*Deuteronomy*	
21	123	15.26	129	1–3	417
21.22-34	287	17.8-16	288	1.1–4.40	396
26	123, 131	19	130	3.23-28	417
26.23-33	287	20	130	3.29	417
28.10-22	68	23	130	4	415, 417
29–30	276	23.1–24.8	130	4.1-40	417
29.15-28	279	23.20–24.8	130	4.3-4	417
38	131	23.21	129, 130	4.6	410
41.50	191	24.4	130	4.9	410
43.14	416	24.7	130	4.21-22	417
45.10	174	24.12	130	4.25-32	386, 417
46.28-34	195	25.1–31.11	298	4.25-28	417
46.34	174	32	402	4.29-31	415, 417, 418
47.1-10	195	34.4-6	130		
47.6	197	34.27-29	130	4.29	418
47.11	186, 194, 197	35.4–40.33	298	4.30	418
49.1	417	40.17	298	4.44–30.20	418
				4.44–11.32	396

Index of References

5	417	20	399	9	207, 208
6.10-12	144	20.1-9	413	10	175, 204, 210
6.14	410	20.15	410		
7.1	397, 410	20.16	397, 410	10.1-14	175, 205
7.6	410, 411	20.17	397	10.12-13	175, 205
7.7	410	21.1-9	411	10.13	175, 206, 282, 307
7.12-15	130	23.4	386, 410		
7.14	410	24.16	411	10.40-42	207
7.16	410	26.16-19	411	10.40	142
7.17	410	26.19	397, 410, 411	11.10	205, 332
7.22	410	27–34	396	11.13	145
8.20	410	28.10	410	11.16-23	207
9.1	410	28.20-44	412	11.16-20	142
9.4	410	28.36	385	11.16	142
9.5	410	28.37	410	11.22	238
10.15	410	28.61	407	11.23	143
10.16	418	28.64	410	12	175, 204
11.23	410	28.69–29.28	411	12.16	207
12–26	385, 396, 407, 410, 414, 418	29.20	407	12.22	208
		30.1-14	415	13–19	143, 276, 294, 341
		30.1-11	415, 418		
12	446	30.1-10	386, 417, 418	13–14	340
12.1	396			13	175, 204, 210, 211
12.2	410	30.2	418		
12.29	410	30.3	410	13.1-7	143
12.30	410	30.5	418	14–15	208
13.7-12	411	30.6	418	14	175, 204
13.8	410	30.8	418	14.1-6	207
14.2	397, 410, 411	30.10	418	14.6-15	208
14.21	411	31.9-13	407	14.15	143
15.4	396	31.24	407	15–19	208
15.6	397, 410	31.26	407	15.1-20	210, 340
17	397, 413	31.29	417, 446	15.9	175, 205
17.3	447	32.8-9	308	15.13-19	208
17.4-15	399	32.8	410	15.14	203
17.4	397	34	398	15.20–18.1	175, 204, 207, 210
17.8-13	413				
17.9	413	*Joshua*		15.20-62	207
17.14-20	300, 386, 412	1–11	175, 204	15.20-44	207
		1–10	276	15.21-44	340
17.14-15	385	1.1-11	415	15.28	287
17.14	410	1.4	210	15.45-47	208
17.16-20	385	2	207	15.45	144
17.16	413	4.24	410	15.47	144
17.19	410	6–11	175, 204	15.48-62	207, 340
18.9	397, 410	6	150, 175, 204, 210	15.55	286
18.10	447			15.60	488
18.14	397, 410	7–8	207	15.63	144, 175, 206, 246
19.1	397, 410	8.17	207		

Joshua (cont.)

16–19	340	1.1–3.11	213	16.25-30	238		
16.10	175, 206	1.8	246	17–21	213		
17.1-6	206	1.18	238	17–18	208, 219		
17.2	175, 205	1.21	246	17.6	415		
17.11-13	175, 206	1.22-26	214, 218, 219	18.12	218, 219		
17.11	206	2.18	228	18.28	246, 259		
17.14-18	207	3–9	213	19–21	218, 219		
17.14-17	144	3.1-6	415	19	123		
17.14	175, 205	3.11	214	19.12	52		
18–19	175, 204	3.12-30	176, 215, 219	20.1	287		
18.1	214	3.13	176, 215	21.25	415		
18.2–19.48	208	3.15	215				
18.14	488	3.22-23	176	*Ruth*			
18.15	175, 205	3.22	215	1.1	123		
18.20-28	207	3.23	215				
18.21-28	207	4–5	176, 215	*1 Samuel*			
18.21	487	4	176	1–3	276		
18.22	486	5	132, 211, 215, 216	1	275, 331		
18.24	490			1.19-27	229		
18.25	489	5.2-30	219	3.20	287		
18.28	144, 246	5.3	409	4–6	35		
19.1-8	207	5.4-5	307	4.1	275		
19.2	287	5.5	409	5.8	238, 271, 287		
19.10-14	206	5.20-21	307	5.11	238, 287		
19.15	206	6–8	216	6.4	287		
19.17-21	206	6.2-6	216	6.12	287		
19.23-31	294	6.2-5	219	6.16	287		
19.25-30	206	6.3	288	6.17	238, 271		
19.25-29	206	6.11-32	214, 219	6.18	287		
19.35-38	206	6.25-32	216	7–14	276		
19.37	206	6.33	288	7.14	238		
19.40-46	207	7.1–8.3	216	7.16-17	231		
19.43	144, 238	7.12	288	8	177, 227, 253, 275		
20–22	175, 204	7.17-18	216				
20.7	208	8.3-21	176, 217	9–11	377		
21	208	8.4-28	219	9.1–10.16	177, 227, 231		
21.32	208	8.4-27	216				
21.41-43	143	8.10	176, 217	9.1-10	243, 251		
22	208	8.13-17	176, 217	9.1	177, 230, 234		
23	143, 175, 204	9	176, 217, 219	9.4-5	231		
23.1	214			9.15-17	231		
24	175, 204, 209	10.10	79	9.16	230, 243, 251, 289		
		11.33	217, 219				
		12	213	9.21	234		
Judges		12.7	213	9.23	243, 251		
1–19	214	13–16	218, 219	9.27–10.1	231		
1	111	13.25	218, 219	10	372, 377		

Index of References

10.1	227	17.48	280	22.1-2	274, 285, 325
10.11-12	177, 229	17.50	280	22.1	283
10.16	231	17.51-53	280	22.6	243, 249
10.21	234	17.52	238	22.10	280
11.1-15	243, 251	17.55	325	22.20-23	281
11.1-11	227	18	271, 278, 285	22.20	246
11.1-3	237			23	280
11.14-15	227	18.1-5	228, 279	23.1-13	271
11.15	227	18.1	249	23.1-5	280-84, 286, 325
12	275	18.6-7	280		
13–14	227, 289, 325, 331	18.7	177, 229, 249, 278, 281	23.6-13	280
13.1	227, 243			23.6	281
13.2–14.52	243, 251	18.8-9	278, 280	23.13	285
13.2–14.46	227	18.10-11	280	23.15-18	228
13.3	285	18.12-16	280	23.16-18	249
13.7	342	18.16-30	228	23.17	273
13.17-18	285	18.17-30	271, 279	23.19	228, 286
13.19-22	240, 241	18.17-27	249, 251, 279	23.24-26	286
13.19-21	178, 239, 240			23.24	286
		18.17	278	23.27	271, 285, 286
14	286	18.18	278		
14.1	285	18.19	278	23.28	271
14.3	331	18.21	279	24	277
14.42	228	18.23	279	24.2	271, 286
14.46	177, 230	18.25	271, 279	24.20	273
14.47-48	227, 229, 266, 278	18.27	271, 279	24.23	283
		18.28-29	279	25	285, 286, 307
14.50-52	325	18.30	279		
14.52	285	19.1-7	228	25.2-43	336
15	275, 288	19.8-25	228	25.3	288
16–18	285, 415	19.8	271	25.13	285
16	270	19.11-17	250	25.30	273
16.1-13	249, 251	19.24	177, 229	25.39-43	282
16.13	227	20.1-21	228	26	277
16.14–17.58	228	20.12-17	249	26.1	286
16.14-23	249, 251, 285	21	325, 344	26.19-20	277
		21.2–23.15	228	26.19	273
17–18	280	21.7	281	27	271, 281, 287, 325
17	227, 249, 251, 271, 279	21.9	280		
		21.11-16	271, 273, 274, 281	27.1	273, 277, 282
17.1-6	280	21.11	239	27.2-4	239
17.1	285	21.12	177, 229, 249	27.2-3	274
17.4	271			27.2	281, 285
17.25	279	21.13	239	27.3	281, 282
17.26	271	22	331	27.4-12	336
17.34-47	280	22.1-5	282, 336	27.4	282
17.36	271			27.5	282

1 Samuel (cont.)		1.19-27	177, 271,	5.17-25	244, 262,
27.6-12	307		282		263, 266,
27.6	281, 282,	1.20	271, 282,		272, 283,
	288		289		289, 290,
27.7	281	1.24	234		325, 326,
27.8-12	274, 282	2–5	377		336
27.8-9	286, 288	2.1-4	288, 336	5.17-23	284
27.10	288	2.1-3	266	5.17-21	282, 286
27.11	239	2.4-7	272	5.17	282, 283
28–31	230	2.4	227, 235,	5.18	283, 285
28.1	274		338, 373	5.20	262
28.2	274	2.6-8	206	5.21	289
29	271, 278,	2.8-32	289	5.22-25	282
	281, 282,	2.8-9	234	5.22	283, 285
	325	2.8	266	5.25	244, 263,
29.1-5	274	2.9-10	408		326, 336,
29.1	277, 282	2.9	177, 230,		344
29.2	277, 282,		243, 251,	6	35
	287		325	6.10-12	290
29.3-10	277	2.10	232	6.10	271
29.3-5	277	2.11	326	6.11	271
29.5	249, 281	2.12–3.1	177, 232	6.14	281
29.6-10	277	2.12-17	289, 336	6.20-21	408
29.6	287	2.12-13	232	7	275
29.7	287	2.18-32	336	7.1-17	415
29.8	274	3.2-5	257	7.1	272
29.11	277, 282	3.12-16	250	8	245, 271,
30	275, 278,	3.12-13	338		284, 289
	286, 288,	3.12	408	8.1-2	336
	307, 336	3.14	271, 272	8.1	244, 263,
30.1-25	288	3.18	272, 289,		272, 289,
30.1-20	286		290		290
30.10	285	3.21	408	8.2-14	290
30.26-31	274, 288	4.3	271	8.2	264
31	278, 282,	4.4	232	8.3	259, 260
	325	5	282	8.5-6	260
31.1	227	5.1-6	227	8.6	245, 290,
31.2	231	5.1-3	283, 338,		339
31.4	271		339	8.7	263
31.11-13	272	5.3	227	8.9-10	263
		5.4-5	326	8.12	259, 260,
2 Samuel		5.5	408		272
1	177, 206,	5.6-10	283	8.13-14	264
	227, 278,	5.6-9	246, 248,	8.15	408
	282		266	8.16-18	257
1.1-10	275	5.7	282	8.17	246, 257
1.13-16	278	5.9	282	8.18	326
1.17-27	278	5.12	408	9–20	271
1.18	282, 307	5.14-16	257	9	336, 408

10–12	263	19.9-41	377	24.15	292		
10	290	19.10	271	24.17	79		
10.1–11.1	245	19.23	408	24.20-23	246		
10.1-19	290	19.42–20.22	377	27.2	271		
10.1-14	336	19.42-44	408	27.3	271		
10.6-7	260	20–24	271	27.4	271		
10.16	260	20.1-22	335, 336	27.11	271		
11	279	20.6	281				
11.1	290	20.14-15	281	*1 Kings*			
11.11	408	20.23-26	257	1–11	252, 297, 298, 303		
12.8	373	20.24	335				
12.20	330	20.25	246, 257	1–2	271, 298, 303, 304, 307, 326		
12.26-31	245, 290, 336	21–24	275, 276				
		21	284, 372				
12.29-30	263	21.1-14	177, 232, 233	1	206		
12.30	263			1.34	408		
13.12	377	21.4-5	234	1.35	408		
13.15-19	377	21.6	233	2	275, 408		
15–19	283, 335	21.11	271	2.39-40	245, 326		
15	283	21.13	271	2.39	239, 287		
15.1–19.16	337	21.14	325, 331	3–11	294, 299		
15.13	408	21.15-22	325	3–8	328		
15.18-22	245, 271, 272, 283, 290	21.15-21	284	3	327		
		21.15	272, 284	3.1	332		
		21.16-21	272	3.4–4.1	299, 307		
15.18	272, 283, 326	21.16	284	3.4-5	303		
		21.17	271	3.4	233		
15.19-20	284	21.18	284	3.15	303		
15.19	283, 284	21.19	271, 280, 284, 285	3.16-28	300		
15.20	284			4–10	180, 300		
15.21-22	283	21.20	284	4	230, 327, 335		
15.22	283	21.22	272				
15.24-29	283	22.15-22	336	4.1	303, 408		
15.32-37	283	23	283, 284	4.2-6	257		
16.1-13	283	23.1-7	415	4.3	257		
16.3	373	23.8-39	257, 325, 336	4.5	338		
16.5-14	377			4.6	335		
16.7-8	338	23.8-17	286	4.7-19	181, 329, 335-38, 340–43, 347, 348		
16.8	273	23.9-17	284				
16.15	408	23.9-12	272				
16.18	408	23.9-10	325				
17.4	408	23.11-12	325	4.7	337, 339		
17.11	287	23.11	284	4.8-19	180, 303		
17.14	408	23.13-17	272, 325	4.9-19	257		
17.15	408	23.13-14	283	4.9	337, 339		
17.24	408	23.13	284, 285	4.10	337-39		
17.27-29	336	23.14	284	4.12	338		
18.2	271, 272	24	270, 330	4.13	338, 339		
19	335	24.2	287	4.14	338, 339		

1 Kings (cont.)

Ref	Pages
4.18 LXX	342
4.19	303, 338, 342
4.19 LXX	180
4.20	408
5–7	197, 296
5	294, 327
5.1	292, 300, 301, 333
5.1 LXX	294, 340, 350, 351
5.4	300, 333
5.5	287, 292
5.7	339
5.9-14	299
5.15	351
5.15 MT	294
5.15-32	300, 327
5.17	330
5.20-32	335
5.20	294, 334
5.22-24	294
5.25	294
5.27-29	296
5.27-28	300
5.27	300
5.28	294
5.30	300
5.32	303
6–7	4, 180, 298, 303
6	303, 328
6.1–9.9	328
6.1	298
6.34	303
6.37-38	298
7	295, 296
7.1-12	328
7.13–8.66	328
7.13-14	294
7.46	298, 308, 309
7.47	296, 300
8–9	330
8	206, 415
8.1	415
8.9	415
8.12-13	19, 304, 307, 330
8.13 LXX	282
8.14-30	415
8.15	330
8.17-21	329
8.17	330
8.18	330
8.19	329, 330
8.20	330
8.24-26	330
8.31-43	415
8.32	415
8.33-34	415
8.34	415
8.36	415
8.39	415
8.43	410, 415
8.44-53	415
8.44-45	415
8.44	415
8.45	415
8.46-53	415
8.46-50	416
8.48	415
8.49-50	416
8.49	415
8.53	410
8.53 LXX	307
8.55-61	415
8.60	410
9.1-9	328
9.4-5	330
9.9	339
9.10-28	328
9.10-14	294, 328, 340, 344, 351
9.11	294
9.14	294
9.15-23	335
9.15-19	332
9.15-18	333
9.15	257, 318, 320, 328, 332, 339, 346
9.16-18	298, 304
9.16-17	306
9.16	306, 328, 332, 350, 351
9.17-19	318, 320, 328, 339, 346
9.17-18	257, 306, 333
9.17	328
9.19	180, 333
9.20-22	300, 328, 333
9.22	333
9.23	300, 328
9.24	328, 332
9.25	328
9.26-28	294, 328, 334
10	327, 328
10.1-13	299, 328, 351
10.14-29	299, 328, 351
10.14	334
10.22-29	299
10.26	300
10.28-29	334
10.28	304
11–12	375
11	266, 374
11.1-13	299, 300, 375
11.1-8	327, 350
11.9-13	327
11.13	375
11.14-28	327
11.14-25	299
11.14	339
11.26	374, 376
11.27-28	182, 374
11.27	374
11.28	335, 374
11.29-43	327
11.29-39	182, 375, 376
11.32-36	375
11.38	375

11.39	375	*2 Kings*		18.17–19.10	371
11.40	326, 349,	2	377	18.17–19.9	78
	374, 376	2.11	298	18.36	79
11.41	299, 326	2.18	238	19–35	78
11.42	326, 408	3	4, 8, 103–5	19.4	79
11.43	374	3.4-28	48	19.6	79
12	275, 333,	8	398	19.7	78
	336, 339,	8.23	398	19.9	94
	345, 385,	8.25	398	19.16	79
	408	8.46-50	416	19.22	79
12.1-19	374, 376	8.49-50	416	19.23	79
12.1	182, 374	10.29	402	19.28	79
12.2	374, 376	11	344	19.32	371
12.3-14	182, 374	11.5	453	19.34	81
12.3	374	11.8-9	453	19.35-37	85
12.12	374	11.23-24	260	19.35	80, 83
12.15	374	11.42	298	19.36-37	78
12.16	182, 374	12.17	262	19.36	94, 371
12.17	374	12.18	287	19.37	80
12.18-19	182, 374	14.7	179, 245,	20.12-13	351
12.18	374		264	20.20	48
12.19	374, 376	14.13	61	21.7	455
12.20	374, 376	14.19	344	21.10-15	419
12.21	373	15.6-11	108	21.24	344
12.25–13.34	402	15.21-26	108	22–23	383, 386,
12.33	375	15.29-30	107		387, 389,
14.19-20	326	15.31-36	108		394, 395,
14.21	307, 350	16.5-9	276		402, 405,
14.25-28	48, 257, 306	16.5	61		407, 414,
14.25-26	306, 350	17	81, 408, 415		421, 427,
14.25	306, 348,	17.2-4	419		433, 439,
	349	17.4-6	276		447
14.26	306	17.24-34	414	22	387, 395,
14.29	326	17.25-28	70		427, 445
14.31	350	18–23	406	22.1-2	447
15.9	41	18–19	8, 82, 101	22.3–23.3	394, 445
15.25	41	18	394	22.4	113
15.33	41	18.4	435, 438	22.8	404, 407,
16	110	18.5-6	419		427
16.17	446	18.7	79, 81	22.11	404, 407,
16.27	110	18.9-12	78, 80		427
17–19	214	18.9-10	419	22.16-17	414
18.16	415	18.13–19.37	77, 419	22.17	445, 446
18.19	415	18.13-16	78, 101, 371	23	402, 425,
20.31	373	18.13	78		427, 434,
21.1-20	415	18.14-15	82		445–48, 454,
22.48-49	302	18.15-16	79		455, 486
		18.17–19.37	78, 79	23.1-3	411

2 Kings (cont.)

23.2	427
23.3	398
23.4-20	387, 394, 445
23.4-15	415
23.4	448, 455
23.5	446, 448, 449, 452, 454
23.6	388, 450, 455
23.7-8	450
23.8	389, 428, 435, 447, 448
23.9	448, 452
23.10	446, 448
23.11	446, 448-50
23.12	387, 446, 448, 449, 453, 454
23.14	448
23.15	415, 448
23.16-18	415
23.17	445
23.19-20	415
23.19	394, 449
23.20	453
23.21-24	394, 445
23.21	427
23.22	84
23.24	415
23.25-27	419
23.25	447
23.28-30	447
23.29	301, 392
24–25	5, 28, 29
24	20
24.3	81
24.7	301
24.12	81
24.20	79
25	446
25.14	455
25.18	113
25.22-26	503
25.27-30	81, 415, 416

1 Chronicles

1–10	276
2	208
8.29-40	177, 232, 233
8.33-40	231, 233
9.33-44	177, 232
9.39-44	231
10.1–12.4	377
11–29	270
11.13	270
11.14	270
11.15	270
11.16-17	374
11.18	270
12.19	270
12.20	270
13.4-12	377
14.8-16	262
14.8	270
14.9	270
14.10	270
14.11	262
14.13	262, 270
14.15	270
14.16	262, 270
16.39	331
17	330
18.1	270, 289
18.11	270
18.13	260
20.4-8	284
20.4	270
20.5	270

2 Chronicles

10.2	374
15.1-7	84
19.35	83
26.6	238, 262
26.9	483
29–32	83-85
29–31	83
31.20	83
32.1-23	75, 82, 84
32.1	83, 84
32.5	61
32.7-8	84
32.10	83
32.13	84
32.19	409
32.20	84
32.21	83
32.23	79
32.30	48
33.14	483
34–35	383, 426
35.18	84
35.20-24	392
35.20	84
36	19

Ezra

1.2-4	19
2.1-67	475, 485
2.2	409
2.5	409
2.28	66
2.55	208
2.59	409
2.70	409
3.1	409
3.3	410
4.9-10	67
6.2-5	19
6.21	409, 410
9.1	409, 410
9.2	410
10	411
10.2	410
10.11	410

Nehemiah

1.1–7.5	409
1.2	409
1.6	409
1.11	416
2.10	409
2.13-17	503
2.16	409
3	476, 477, 481–83, 485, 493
3.1-32	60
3.1	493
3.7	483, 484
3.8	61
3.11	483

3.13	480	5.24	410	19.13	454	
3.16	483	6–8	376	22.15	394	
3.33	409	6.1–8.19	375	23.1-7	412	
3.34	409	7.1-17	182, 375	25.6	446	
4.6	409	7.1	61	25.7	446	
5	412	7.17	375, 376,	25.20	238, 261,	
5.1	409		385, 408		305, 488	
5.8	409, 410	8.14	373, 377	25.24	305	
5.9	410	8.17	408	26.24	413	
5.17	409, 410	8.23–9.6	420	27.18	455	
6.6-7	412	9.7-20	377	27.21-22	455	
6.6	409, 410	11.1-5	412	28.1	486	
6.15	63	11.11-16	406	29.10-14	417	
6.16	410	11.15	200	29.14	417	
7.1	409	19.22	418	30–31	418	
7.6-68	475, 485	28.21	262	30.3	406	
7.6	503	30.11	410	30.18-22	418	
7.7	409	30.12	410	30.24	417	
7.31	66	30.15	410	31.2-6	386, 394,	
9.2	409	31.1	410		406, 421	
9.24	410	36–37	78	31.10-14	418	
9.30	410	36.1–37.38	78	31.15-22	406	
10	411	40.1-2	417	31.15	489	
10.1	412			31.21-22	418	
10.29	410	*Jeremiah*		31.23-26	418	
10.31	410	1–51	418	31.31-33	418	
11.31	66	1–45	417	31.38	483	
12.21-32	409	1.16	446	31.40	483	
12.37.40	409	2–6	421	32.20	446	
12.38-39	61	2.4–4.2	386, 420,	32.29	452, 454	
13.1-2	386, 410		421	32.35	454	
13.4-31	409	2.14-18	420	32.37-44	418	
13.18	409	2.15	420	32.37-41	418	
13.23	409	2.16-18	420	36.9-26	413	
13.24	409	2.26	373	38.14	413	
13.26	409, 410	2.36-37	420	38.17-23	81	
13.30	409	3.22–4.2	386, 421	40.1	489	
		4.3–6.30	386, 421	40.7–41.8	503	
Psalms		4.4	418	41.5	413	
89.4	412	5.4-6	386, 421	41.16	486	
89.20	412	5.11	373	41.17	487	
106.46	416	7.31-32	454	41.34-37	418	
151	270	8.7-8	386, 394,	42.12	416	
151.1-5	270		421	44.3	446	
151.6-7	270	11.13	452	44.5	446	
		11.17	452	44.8	446	
Isaiah		19.4	446	44.15	446	
5.7	377	19.5-6	454	44.18	394	
5.19	410	19.11-13	454	50.17-20	418	

Jeremiah (cont.)		*Amos*		9.50	486
50.33-34	418	1.7-8	261	9.52	484
51.58	418	1.13	245	9.73	490
52.3	79			10.84	239
		Micah		11.4	239
Lamentations		1	80	11.34	487, 493
1.4	503	5.1-5	412	11.65	484
2.15	503	5.1-4	344	12.38	487
3.40	418			13.13	487
5.9	216	*Zephaniah*		13.49-51	509
		1.4	452, 453	14.33	484
Ezekiel		1.5	454		
8.7-18	421	2.4	261	BABYLONIAN TALMUD	
8.12	421			*Sanhedrin*	
8.16	387, 451	*Haggai*		94a	84
16.3	206	1.7-11	414		
16.21	454	2.7-9	79	Josephus	
17.11-21	81			*Antiquities*	
17.16	79	*Zechariah*		10.1-23	75, 86
20.26	454	1.12	503	10.18-23	85
20.31	454	2.5-9	503	12.422	489
27.12-24	295	5.5-11	455	13.34	490
27.17	295	5.6	455	13.203	487
34.23-24	412	7.2	65, 215, 486	13.392	487
37.15-22	182, 376, 406	9.5-6	261		
		9.9-10	412	*War*	
37.22	376			5.4.2	485
37.24-25	412	*Malachi*		5.386-88	75, 86
		2.16	409	5.404-8	82, 86
Daniel				5.404-408	75
1–6	42	NEW TESTAMENT		5.405	79
1.9	416	*Luke*			
3.27	483	2.1	42	CLASSICAL AND ANCIENT CHRISTIAN WRITINGS	
7–12	42				
		Acts		Cicero	
Hosea		8.34	10	*De Oratore*	
1.4	373			2.9.36	110
5.8	64	APOCRYPHA			
5.12-14	420	*Ecclesiasticus*		Herodotus	
5.12	373	24.23	396	*History*	
5.14	373	46.4-8	270	1.105	112
9.9	64	49.13	483	2.104	112
10.5	452			2.158	187, 191, 200
10.9	64	*1 Maccabees*			
10.28-32	64	4.61	484	3.5.91	112
14.2	418	6.7	484	4.39	112
		7.8	483	4.71-75	26
		9.4	489	7.89	112

Homer
Iliad
2.819   287

Odyssey
6.6-10   482

PAPYRI
Papyrus Amherst
63   67, 486

ANCIENT NEAR EASTERN SOURCES
AHI
2.3, lines 3-4   435
4.301   444
15.5   443
15.6   443
15.7   444
15.8   444
25.3   444

Ash. Nin. A
V 40-VI 1   300

EA
237   325
244-46   325
249-50   325
252-53   325
255   325
263   325
280   325
287   325
289   325

Hinnon amulet
line 8   445
lines 11-14   444
lines 1-2   444

KAI
218   450
225   452
226   452

KTU
1.14 II 20-27   453
1.14 IV 3-8   453

Mesha inscription
lines 10-21   299
lines 10-11   342

OTHER SOURCES
Book of Mormon
1 Nephi
4.9   150, 151
16.18   150, 151
18.25   148

2 Nephi
5.14-15   150, 151
24.19   151

3 Nephi
3.22   149

Alma
3.6-10   148
17.37   150, 151
20.6   149
43.13   148
47.35   148
57.33   150, 151

Ether
1–6   147
7.9   150, 151
9.19   150
14–15   147

Jarom
1.8   150, 151

Mosiah
9.9   148

Index of Authors

Abdulfattah, K. 313
Achenbach, R. 291
Ackroyd, P. R. 66, 84, 456, 457, 494
Aharoni, M. 457, 460
Aharoni, Y. 134, 317, 439, 485, 492, 494
Ahlström, G. W. 16–18, 20, 108, 124, 235, 312, 317, 326, 340, 349, 392, 403, 420, 422, 428, 430, 433, 446, 455, 458
Akenson, D. H. 99
Albertz, R. 301, 373, 377, 378, 394, 396, 401, 403, 404, 408, 413, 414, 416–18, 420, 422, 427, 452, 458, 472
Albright, W. F. 64, 116, 188, 480, 488, 494
Alt, A. 64, 111, 116, 291, 320, 345, 486, 487, 494
Alter, R. 121
Amiran, R. 477, 494, 505, 510
Amit, Y. 84, 218, 220
Andersen, F. I. 64
Andersen, N. E. 125
Appleby, J. 530, 532
Arbel, Y. 487, 494
Ariel, D. T. 353, 357, 477, 478, 494, 506–10
Arneth, M. 426, 449, 452, 455, 458
Arnold, P. M. 231, 233
Ash, M. 147, 151, 154
Ash, P. S. 341, 342
Attridge, H. W. 125
Auld, A. G. 216, 220, 322, 329
Avi-Yonah, M. 53
Avigad, N. 440, 441, 458, 477, 479–81, 494, 502, 505, 510–12

Bae, H.-S. 377, 378
Bahn, P. 313, 339
Balcer, J. M. 125
Bär, J. 17
Bar-Efrat, S. 278
Bardtke, H. 291

Barkay, G. 354, 359, 444, 458, 478, 494
Barrick, W. B. 426, 448, 453, 454, 458
Barstad, H. M. 29, 113, 132, 368, 378, 523, 525, 532
Barth, H. 420, 422
Barthélemy, D. 263, 267
Bartl, K. 316, 327
Bartlett, J. R. 53
Becker, U. 376, 378
Beckerath, J. von 306
Becking, B. 73, 183, 291, 479
Beit-Arieh, I. 487, 496
Ben Barak, Z. 227
Ben Zvi, E. 77, 78, 80, 81, 95, 113
Ben-Ami, D. 247
Bergman, A. 488, 494
Bergran, T. A. 483, 494
Beuken, W. A. M. 445, 458
Bickerman, E. J. 264, 267
Bieberstein, K. 18
Bienkowski, P. 316
Bierbrier, M. L. 306, 349
Bietak, M. 192–95, 199
Bimson, J. 54
Binford, L. 312
Biran, A. 107, 316, 488, 494
Blair, E. P. 488, 494
Bleibtrau, E. 450, 462
Blenkinsopp, J. 63, 66, 67, 216, 220, 232, 304, 325, 331, 402, 403, 409, 422, 472, 482, 492, 494, 499, 511
Bliss, F. J. 507, 511
Block, D. I. 125, 126
Bloedhorn, H. 18
Blum, E. 136, 214, 220, 261, 267, 375, 378
Boaretto, E. 241
Borger, R. 76
Bowersock, G. W. 54
Boyd, K. 139, 154

Brand, E. 487, 494
Brandfon, F. R. 430, 458
Bratt, K. D. 125
Braudel, F. 312, 430, 431, 458, 527, 532
Braun, R. L. 122
Breisach, E. 139, 154
Breuer, S. 327, 339
Briant, P. 467, 471, 504, 511
Bright, J. 193, 527, 532
Brodie, F. M. 153, 154
Bron, F. 259, 267, 300
Brooker, C. H. 295
Broshi, M. 477, 479, 494, 505, 511
Brown, J. P. 503, 511
Bunimovitz, S. 112, 316, 324
Burstein, M. B. 265, 267

Cahill, J. M. 248, 319, 332, 371, 378, 507, 511
Callaway, J. A. 490, 494
Caminos, R. A. 175
Campbell, A. F. 35
Cancik, H. 125
Carena, O. 26
Carlson, R. A. 228
Carter, C. E. 472, 475, 476, 479, 483, 485, 492, 495, 509–11
Caspi, A. 478, 495, 511
Cazelles, H. 193, 199–201
Chadwick, J. R. 151, 154
Chen, D. 505, 511
Childs, B. S. 78, 102, 119
Christensen, D. L. 281, 287
Claburn, W. E. 427, 458
Claessen, H. J. M. 373, 378
Clements, R. E. 54, 78
Cogan, M. 102, 450, 451, 458, 503, 511
Cohen, A. 313
Cohen, C. 68, 322, 344, 478
Cohen, D. 495, 511
Cole, S. W. 70
Collingwood, R. G. 531, 533
Connor, W. R. 124, 125
Conrad, D. 434, 458
Conroy, C. 284
Coogan, M. 458
Cook, S. A. 508, 511
Coote, R. B. 15, 33, 300, 304, 315, 430, 459
Cowley, A. 414, 422

Crawford, H. 27
Cross, F. M. 392, 403
Crowfoot, J. W. 478, 480, 495, 506, 511
Crüsemann, F. 291
Crüsemann, N. 327

Davies, G. I. 64, 198–201, 392, 403
Davies, P. R. 12, 19, 20, 67, 98, 217, 220, 237, 256, 267, 406–8, 412, 422, 527, 533
De Groot, A. 353, 357, 478–80, 495, 506–8, 511
Dearman, J. A. 299, 303, 454, 459
Deist, F. 27
Deller, K. 450, 462
Demsky, A. 233, 483, 495
Deutsch, R. 440, 442, 451, 459
Dever, W. G. 34, 66, 317, 318, 320, 350, 361, 378, 426, 459, 522, 533
Di Segni, L. 487, 498
Dickie, A. C. 507, 511
Dietrich, W. 239, 240, 244, 249, 253, 273, 275, 277, 280, 281, 283, 286, 287, 289, 377, 378, 408, 422
Dinur, U. 488, 495
Dion, P. E. 78
Donner, H. 51, 64, 294, 312, 317, 324, 330
Dostal, W. 343
Dothan, T. 239, 287
Drews, R. 265, 267, 316
Driver, S. R. 263, 267
Dubovský, P. 388
Duncan, J. G. 478, 480, 496, 505, 508, 511, 513
Dyck, J. 85

Earle, T. K. 339
Edelman, D. 54, 58, 73, 74, 133, 224, 227, 230, 243, 244, 297, 304, 325–27, 331, 340, 459, 475, 476, 481, 485, 495
Eggler, J. 459
Ehrlich, A. S. 284, 287
Einykel, E. 426, 459
Eissfeldt, O. 116, 122
Eitam, D. 495
Eitan, A. 477, 494, 505, 510
Elayi, J. 88–90
Eliyahu-Behar, A. 241
Elliger, K. 262, 267
Eph'al, I. 259, 267, 300, 504, 511

Eran, M. 56
Eshel, H. 63, 475, 476, 495, 509, 511
Eshel, I. 353
Evans, R. J. 139, 154, 530, 533
Exum, J. C. 458

Fahr, H. 125
Fales, F. M. 27
Fehling, D. 26
Feig, N. 359, 488, 495
Feldman, L. H. 86
Feldstein, A. 487, 489, 490, 495, 496
Feller, B. 327
Finkelstein, I. 34, 62, 66, 112, 133, 134, 183, 184, 217, 220, 237, 239, 241, 242, 248, 251, 287, 288, 296, 298, 316–18, 320, 326, 351, 361, 371, 372, 377, 378, 388, 397, 403–6, 421, 422, 467, 479, 480, 492, 494, 500, 508, 511
Finkielsztejn, G. 505, 509, 512
Fischer, A. A. 288
Fitzgerald, G. M. 478, 480, 495, 506, 511
Flanagan, J. 133
Fokkelman, J. P. 284
Forrer, E. 259, 267
Frahm, E. 76, 89, 90
Frame, G. 73
Frankel, R. 340
Franken, H. J. 309, 353, 358, 502, 506, 512
Freedman, D. N. 64, 315
Frevel, C. 12
Fried, L. S. 426, 427, 433, 435, 436, 439, 459
Fried, M. H. 327, 332, 339
Friedman, R. E. 125
Frisch, B. 309
Fritz, V. 237, 287, 307, 336
Fuchs, A. 73, 262, 267
Funk, R. W. 483, 484, 495, 497

Gal, Z. 340
Galil, G. 276, 291
Gallagher, W. R. 76, 89, 90
Galling, K. 116, 242, 492, 495
Ganor, S. 291, 292
Garbini, G. 121, 124, 126, 256, 267, 306, 322, 328, 334, 350, 399, 403
Gardiner, A. H. 188, 189, 193, 194, 196, 197
Garfinkel, Y. 291, 292

Gauthier, H. 196
Gelinas, M. M. 322
Geller, S. A. 399, 403, 411, 422
George, A. R. 69, 70
Gese, H. 308
Geva, H. 62, 353, 354, 359, 364, 477, 481, 495, 505, 509, 510, 512
Gibson, J. C. L. 103, 477, 505
Gibson, S. 495, 511
Giercke-Ungermann, A. 286
Gieselmann, B. 445, 459
Gilboa, A. 361
Gill, C. 26
Gitin, S. 239, 378
Goldwasser, O. 258, 267
Gomes, J. F. 65, 67
Gonçalves, F. J. 78
Gopher, A. 487, 496
Gophna, R. 487, 490, 496
Gordon, D. 531
Gottlieb, Y. 240, 241
Gottwald, N. 12, 119
Grabbe, L. L. 12, 27, 28, 113, 139, 153, 154, 156–70, 173, 184, 237, 246, 247, 252, 297, 367–73, 378, 389, 394, 403, 467, 472, 482, 496, 499, 509, 512, 521, 526, 528, 531, 533
Graf, D. F. 315
Gray, J. 340
Grayson, A. K. 26, 82, 92
Green, J. 487, 498
Greenspahn, F. E. 68
Gross, W. 422, 425, 459
Guillaume, P. 13, 213, 216, 218, 220
Gunkel, H. 116
Gunn, D. 122
Gunneweg, A. H. J. 409, 423

Hallo, W. W. 27, 69, 125, 138, 155, 526, 533
Halpern, B. 126, 227, 289
Hamblin, W. J. 147, 149, 155
Hammershaimb, E. 267
Handy, L. 136, 419
Handy, L. K. 308, 423
Hanin, N. 495
Hanson, P. D. 461
Haran, M. 265, 267
Hardmeier, C. 78, 379, 384, 414, 419, 423, 426, 459

Hartog, F. 125
Hauer, C. E. 158
Hausleitner, A. 217, 220
Hawkins, D. J. 261, 267
Hayes, J. H. 12, 13, 33, 51, 54, 122, 124, 132, 235, 300–302, 305, 312, 325, 348, 392, 420
Heinz, M. 327
Helck, W. 190, 195
Helm, P. R. 125
Heltzer, M. 421, 423, 440, 459
Hens-Piazza, G. 531, 533
Herr, L. G. 20
Herrmann, S. 192, 193, 195
Herzog, Z. 371, 379, 435–38, 460, 495
Hirsch, S. W. 125
Hirschfeld, H. 477, 494, 506, 507, 510
Hjelm, I. 460
Hodder, I. 312, 313
Hoffmann, H.-D. 460
Hoffmann, Y. 66, 447–49
Hoglund, K. G. 481, 496
Holladay, J. S. 66, 190, 198, 320, 433, 434, 460
Hollenstein, H. 447, 456, 460
Hölscher, G. 403
Hölscher, L. 87, 97, 395, 404
Hooker, P. K. 235, 348
Hopkins, D. C. 314
Horn, S. 263, 267
Hornung, E. 349
Houtman, C. 68
Howie, J. G. 26
Hrouda, B. 300
Hübner, U. 295, 316, 350
Huddlestun, J. R. 199
Hunt, L. 530, 532
Hurowitz, V. A. 68, 70
Hurvitz, A. 25
Hütteroth, W. D. 313
Hyatt, J. P. 66

Iggers, G. G. 139, 155
Immerwahr, H. R. 125
Isserlin, B. S. J. 318

Jacob, M. 530, 532
Jacobsen, T. 27, 69

Jamieson-Drake, D. W. 17, 126, 256, 265, 267, 268, 297, 317, 321
Janowski, B. 331
Japhet, S. 83
Jenkins, A.K. 73
Jenkins, K. 72, 530, 533
Jeremias, J. 64, 331
Jirku, A. 305, 349
Jobling, D. 121, 228, 273, 274
Johns, C. N. 512
Jones, G. H. 333

Kaiser, O. 303, 395, 403, 404, 421, 423
Kalimi, I. 84, 95
Kallai, Z. 488–90, 496
Kamaisky, Y. 495
Karrer, C. 409, 423
Katzenstein, H. J. 503, 512, 513
Kearney, P. J. 232
Keel, O. 18, 205, 211, 314, 330, 331, 334, 345, 426, 434, 445, 460
Kellenberger, E. 284
Kellermann, U. 409, 423, 482, 496
Kelm, G. L. 318
Kelso, J. L. 66, 486, 496
Kenyon, K. M. 356, 478, 480, 481, 496, 502, 504, 505, 509, 513
Khalaily, H. 487, 496
Kidron, G. 495
Killebrew, A. E. 237, 247, 379
King, P. J. 495, 496
Klein, J. 274
Kletter, R. 437, 460
Kloner, A. 479, 496
Knapp, A. B. 295
Knauf, E. A. 13, 16, 18–21, 66, 67, 117, 126, 138, 155, 205–7, 211, 212, 215–18, 220, 236, 252, 256, 258, 267, 268, 295–99, 303–5, 308, 309, 312, 317, 322, 325–28, 330, 334, 342, 344, 349–51, 354, 428–30, 432, 435, 460, 527, 530, 533
Knight, D. A. 54
Knoppers, G. 224
Knoppers, G. N. 472
Kobayashi, Y. 263, 268
Koch, K. 448, 452, 460
Kochavi, M. 134, 313, 317, 484
Koenen, K. 65, 69
Kohata, F. 136

Köhlmoos, M. 65
Kohut, A. 483, 496
Komoróczy, G. 265, 268
Kooij, G. van der 17
Kopp, H. 343
Kottsieper, I. 67, 373, 379
Kramer, C. 343
Kraus, H.-J. 21, 22
Kuan, J. K. 294, 327, 340, 350
Küchler, M. 314, 334, 434, 460
Kuhrt, A. 26, 27, 265, 268, 467, 471, 472

LaBianca, Ø. S. 316
Laato, A. 78, 92, 428, 434, 460
Lambert, W. G. 69, 70
Lamprecht, K. 312
Lamprichs, R. 17
Lang, B. 127
Langlamet, F. 283
Laperrousaz, E.-M. 303
Lapp, N. 64, 483, 496, 497
Lapp, P. W. 64, 483, 486, 496, 497
Lehmann, G. 314, 340
Lehmann, R. G. 22, 315, 371, 379
Leiman, S. Z. 119
Lemaire, A. 205, 212, 258–60, 265, 267, 268, 293, 294, 299, 300, 302, 414, 423, 440, 442, 444, 459, 460, 499, 513
Lemche, N. P. 16, 100, 104, 106, 110–12, 114, 124, 132, 136, 256, 268, 296, 315–17, 343, 384, 527, 533
Lenzen, C. J. 309
Leonard, A. 316
Lernau, O. 60, 373, 379
Levin, C. 427, 447, 449, 453, 461
Levine, L. D. 73, 76
Levine, L. I. 513
Levy, T. E. 173, 185
Lieberman, S. J. 265, 268
Lipschits, O. 66, 220, 389, 467, 472, 475, 479, 482, 484, 485, 487, 492, 496, 498–505, 508–10, 513
Lipton, D. 68
Liss, H. 376, 379
Liverani, M. 73, 86, 125, 313, 315, 316
Lloyd, A. B. 200
Lohfink, N. 394, 396, 403, 427, 445, 446, 454, 455, 461
London, G. 316

Long, B. O. 118, 132
Long, V. P. 4, 10, 155, 156, 170, 527, 528, 533
Longman, T. 4, 10, 155, 156, 527, 528, 533
Lopasso, V. 427, 461
Lowery, R. H. 428, 454, 461
Luckenbill, D. D. 76

MacDonald, B. 190
Macalister, R. A. S. 478, 480, 496, 505, 508, 513
Madden, R. 240
Maeir, A. M. 237, 238, 241, 287
Magen, Y. 215, 221
Magness, J. 507, 510
Malamat, A. 122
Mallowan, M. E. L. 69
Mansfeld, G. 295, 309
Marfoe, L. 315
Margalit, S. 505, 511
Martin, R. 74, 87, 530, 533
Maxwell-Hyslop, K. R. 240
May, H. G. 198
Mayer, W. 17, 371, 379
Mays, J. L. 64
Mazar, A. 54, 184, 251, 316, 318–20, 329, 332, 354, 361, 371, 372, 378, 379, 437, 461
Mazar, B. 134, 306, 349, 354, 478, 497, 513, 514
Mazar, E. 247, 354, 480, 497, 506, 514
Mazuel, J. 199
McBride, S. D. 461
McCarter, P. K. 35, 283, 336, 451, 461
McCullagh, C. B. 531, 533
McGovern, P. E. 114
McKenzie, J. L. 497
McKenzie, S. 224
Megill, A. 140, 155
Mettinger, T. 227, 340
Meyers, C. 54, 132, 486
Meyers, C. L. 497
Meyers, E. M. 486, 497
Michaeli, D. 507, 511
Michalowski, P. 125
Michel, E. 261, 268
Middell, M. 312
Middlemas, J. 66, 67
Milgrom, J. 123

Millard, A. R. 82, 317, 327
Miller, J. M. 12, 13, 16, 22, 31, 35, 36, 51, 54, 122, 124, 132, 133, 231, 300–302, 305, 312, 322, 325, 328, 392, 420, 423
Miller, P. D. 35, 461
Milne, A. A. 135
Milson, D. 318
Miscall, P. D. 274
Mishaqa, M. 215, 221
Mitscherlich, A. 301
Mitscherlich, M. 301
Mittmann, S. 215, 221, 263, 268
Momigliano, A. 264, 268
Montet, P. 193, 196
Montgomery, J. A. 108
Moore, M. B. 170
Moran, W. L. 350, 360, 361
Morenz, S. 327
Moshkovitz, S. 460
Mowinckel, S. 409, 423, 482, 497
Muhly, J. D. 240, 295, 309, 322
Mulder, M. J. 317
Müller, H. P. 316, 444, 461
Munslow, A. 530, 533
Myers, J. M. 492, 497

Na'aman, N. 58, 61, 65, 67, 73, 81, 89, 184, 207, 212, 237, 238, 245, 252, 257, 262, 268, 316, 317, 325, 340, 379, 384, 391–93, 406, 420, 421, 423, 435–39, 443, 461, 473, 486, 487, 497
Nakhai, B. A. 433, 461
Naumann, Th. 408, 422
Naveh, J. 107, 239, 259, 267, 300, 316, 507, 514
Naville, E. H. 87, 89, 195–97, 199–201
Nelson, R. D. 412, 417, 418, 423
Netzer, E. 437, 461, 487, 497
Neusner, J. 120, 121, 129
Ngo, R. 248
Nicol, M. B. 490, 494
Niehr, H. 331, 389, 420, 423, 425, 427, 428, 461
Nielsen, E. 116
Nielsen, F. A. J. 26
Niemann, A. M. 238, 240, 244, 292, 312, 314, 315, 317, 319, 325, 327, 328, 331–35, 337, 338, 340, 341, 350
Nimms, C. F. 67

Nissen, H. J. 296, 329
Noort, E. 237, 316, 319
Norman, V. G. 147–49, 155
North, R. 35
Noth, M. 116, 306, 326, 349, 415, 423

Oded, B. 87
Oden, R. A. 125
Odorico, M. de 90, 91
Oeming, M. 220, 472
Ofer, A. 313, 320, 321, 325, 479, 484, 487, 497
Onn, A. 489, 497
Oppenheim, A. I. 265, 268, 503
Oppenheim, A. L. 514
Oren, E. D. 237
Ornan, R. 442, 461
Ortiz, S. M. 287
Otto, E. 350
Ottoson, M. 20

Parpola, S. 265, 268
Parr, P. J. 217, 221
Paul, M. J. 462
Paul, S. M. 261, 268, 427
Perks, R. 140, 155
Person, R. F. 415, 417, 423
Peterson, J. L. 288
Pfeiffer, H. 65
Piasetzky, E. 217, 220
Pixner, B. 505, 511
Polzin, J. 274
Pomian, K. 27
Ponchia, S. 262, 268
Pongratz-Leisten, B. 450, 462
Porten, B. 63
Portugali, Y. 339
Postgate, J. N. 27
Prag, K. 353, 359, 487, 497
Preuss, H. D. 445, 462
Price, B. J. 305, 339
Pritchard, J. A. 233
Pritchard, J. B. 54, 298, 322, 328, 484, 497
Pritchett, W. K. 26
Propp, W. H. C. 173, 185
Provan, I. 4, 10, 16, 78, 140, 155, 156, 527, 528, 533
Puech, E. 262, 268
Pury, A. de 67, 389

Rabinowitz, P. 225
Rainey, A. F. 426, 434, 460, 462
Rappaport, A. 483, 489, 497
Rapuano, Y. 489, 497
Rast, W. E. 317
Redford, D. B. 73, 111, 188–94, 197, 198, 201, 202, 203, 212, 265, 268, 514
Reich, R. 60, 248, 319, 353, 354, 357, 358, 361, 373, 379, 477, 478, 484, 497, 505, 506, 508, 512, 514
Reinmuth, T. 409, 423
Renfrew, C. 313, 339
Renz, J. 17, 409, 423, 443, 444, 462
Reuter, E. 428, 434, 462
Richter, W. 305
Rivkin, E. 123
Roberts, J. J. M. 35
Robinson, P. 125
Rochberg-Halton, F. 125
Rofé, A. 67, 415, 423
Rogerson, J. 54, 122, 126, 305
Röllig, W. 17, 409, 423
Römer, T. C. 390, 414–16, 423
Roper, M. 151, 155
Rose, M. 136
Rosen, B. 314, 315
Rosenberger, A. 487, 497
Rost, L. 35
Rothenberg, B. 334
Rudman, D. 78, 82
Rudolph, W. 64, 409, 424
Rupprecht, K. 330
Ruprecht, K. 303
Russell, J. M. 90, 93
Rütersworden, U. 327, 340, 413, 424
Ryle, H. E. 514

Sader, H. S. 262, 268
Sallaberger, W. 70
Sammler, S. 312
Sancisi-Weerdenburg, H. 125
Sandars, N. K. 315
Sanders, J. 119
Sanders, P. 291
Särkiö, P. 312
Sass, B. 440–42, 445, 458, 462
Sasson, J. M. 36, 231
Savir, N. 477, 494, 506, 507, 510
Schäfer-Lichtenberger, C. 318, 324

Schenker, A. 426, 446, 449, 452, 453, 462
Schley, D. G. 328
Schley, D. R. 304, 334
Schmid, H. H. 136, 417
Schmid, K. 213, 221, 424
Schmidt, L. 231
Schmitt, R. 126
Schneider, T. 191, 185
Schniedewind, W. 475, 497, 509, 514
Schroer, S. 450, 462
Schulte, H. 125
Schunck, K.-D. 325, 326, 331
Schwartz, J. 67
Scott, J. W. 533
Seidl, U. 450, 462
Seitz, C. R. 78, 80
Sellers, O. R. 484, 497
Service, E. R. 332, 339
Shafer-Elliott, C. 241
Shai, I. 287
Shalit, A. 292
Shalom Brooks, S. 243, 249
Sharon, I. 361
Shavit, A. 497
Shavit, Y. 56, 487
Shea, W. H. 72
Sheppard, T. 119
Sherratt, A. 312, 327
Sherratt, S. 327
Shiloh, Y. 319, 353, 356, 358, 363, 441, 462, 477, 480, 497, 505–8, 514
Shilstein, S. 241
Shirts, K. A. 149, 155
Shoham, Y. 441, 462, 478, 494, 508, 510
Shukron, E. 60, 353, 357, 358, 373, 379, 477, 478, 497, 506–8, 514
Silberman, N. A. 287, 288, 361, 372, 377, 378, 388, 397, 403–6, 421, 422
Simons, J. 306, 349
Sinclair, L. A. 64, 66
Singer, I. 205, 212, 241
Singer-Avitz, L. 66, 371, 379, 462, 495
Sivan, R. 505, 514
Skalnik, P. 373, 378
Smelik, K. A. D. 392, 403
Soggin, J. A. 13, 51, 122, 124, 126, 132, 312, 317, 328, 350
Solar, G. 505, 514
Sommerfeld, W. 70

Sorenson, J. L. 148–50, 155
Spieckermann, H. 448–50, 452–54, 462
Stager, L. E. 205, 212, 272, 315, 316, 320, 458, 479, 495, 496
Starr, I. 450, 462
Stech-Wheeler, T. 240
Steck, O. H. 376, 379
Steele, C. S. 294
Steiner, M. 248, 355, 357, 358, 360, 362, 364, 371, 379, 502, 512
Steiner, M. L. 319, 353
Steiner, R. C. 67, 249, 486, 497, 506
Stern, E. 221, 498, 514
Stern, M. 98, 215, 475, 476, 480, 482, 484, 486, 500, 501, 504
Steymans, H. U. 424
Stiebing, W. H. 315
Stone, E. C. 70
Streck, B. 327
Strout, C. 533
Swanson, K. A. 435, 462
Sweeney, M. A. 78, 390, 395, 403, 426, 446, 462

Tadmor, H. 77, 78, 87, 90, 102, 125, 503, 511
Tagliacarne, P. 446–48, 452, 463
Tanner, H. A. 288
Tappy, R. E. 320
Tarler, D. 319, 332, 441, 462, 511
Taxel, I. 490, 496
Taylor, J. G. 449, 454, 463
Tertel, H. J. 83
Thiel, W. 336
Thiele, E. 235
Thiele, W.-R. 309
Thomasson, G. C. 151, 155
Thompson, T. L. 13, 15, 33, 111, 117, 122–25, 131, 132, 233, 256, 267, 268, 525, 527, 533
Thomson, A. 140, 155
Thorarson, F. 26
Throntveit, M. A. 482, 498
Tigay, J. H. 308
Timm, S. 300, 302, 316
Toloni, G. 426, 463
Torrey, C. C. 482, 498
Tov, E. 415, 424
Trompf, G. W. 125

Tsafrir, Y. 487, 498, 505, 515
Tucker, G. M. 54
Tushingham, A. D. 353, 505, 515

Uehlinger, C. 205, 211, 314, 421, 424–26, 429, 440, 442, 443, 456, 460, 463
Ullendorff, E. 310
Ungnad, A. 259, 268
Uphill, E. P. 191
Ussishkin, D. 57, 61, 65, 90, 318, 320, 354, 371, 436, 437, 463, 475, 476, 480, 481, 498
Uziel, J. 238, 292

Van Seters, J. 13, 26, 54, 76, 86, 111, 124, 125, 128, 132, 136, 193, 194, 200, 245, 264, 272, 322, 328, 527, 533
Vanderhooft, D. 484, 485, 487, 492, 496, 498, 499, 505, 509, 513, 515
Vaughn, A. G. 64, 359, 379
Vaux, R. de 116
Veijola, T. 66, 67, 276, 280, 283, 324, 330, 345, 413, 424
Vermeylen, J. 78
Vernus, P. 258, 268
Veyne, P. 125
Vleeming, S. P. 67
Von Soden, W. 448, 463
Vorländer, H. 136
Vriezen, K. J. H. 489, 498

Wagner, V. 287
Wallerstein, I. 294
Weidner, E. F. 28
Weinberg, J. 479, 483, 498
Weiner, S. 241
Weinfeld, M. 68, 125, 400, 403, 428, 450, 463
Weippert, H. 17, 18, 117, 124, 298, 300–302, 305, 309, 316, 319, 320, 327, 329, 331, 332, 430, 433, 434, 443, 463
Weippert, M. 18, 21, 124, 125, 262, 268, 299, 300, 305, 308, 334, 373, 379, 430, 433, 448, 463
Weisman, D. J. 515
Wellhausen, J. 19, 116
Welten, P. 109, 122, 334
Wesselius, J. W. 67
Westenholz, J. G. 69, 70

Whitelam, K. W. 15, 33, 205, 212, 300, 304, 315, 316, 332, 334, 430, 463
Whybray, R. N. 121, 124
Wightman, G. J. 320, 498
Willi-Plein, I. 215, 221, 278, 279
Williamson, H. G. M. 61, 63, 85, 122, 409, 424, 482, 483, 498
Wilson, J. A. 175
Winckler, H. 259, 268
Windschuttle, K. 530, 533
Wiseman, T. P. 26
Wolff, H. W. 64, 261, 268
Wright, J. L. 483, 498
Würthwein, E. 217, 221, 296, 303, 322, 328, 330, 333, 334, 395, 401, 403, 415, 424, 447–49, 451, 456, 463
Wüst, M. 294

Yadin, Y. 317
Yahalom-Mack, N. 241
Yardeni, A. 444, 463
Yeivin, S. 489, 498
Young, I. 25
Younger, K. L. 162
Younker, R. W. 316
Yurco, F. J. 72, 73

Zaccagnini, C. 313
Zadok, R. 67, 487, 497
Zagorin, P. 72, 74
Zevit, Z. 433, 434, 439, 443, 444, 464
Zimhoni, O. 464
Zorn, J. R. 479, 498
Zukerman, A. 241
Zweig, Y. 478, 494
Zwickel, W. 62, 427, 428, 437, 464, 515

Index of Subjects

'Abdi-Ḫeba 372
Abimelech 51, 176, 217, 221, 299, 304–5
Abraham 13, 45, 47, 111, 118, 123, 128, 136, 153, 169, 293, 533
Adad 450
Adam 42, 153, 169
administration 18, 140, 175, 206, 211, 258, 267, 297, 313, 337, 389, 415, 428, 437, 439, 443, 496
administrators 265
Aegean 272, 279
Aeolic 364
Agade 27
agriculturalists 52
Ahab 8, 16, 18, 28, 32, 47–48, 103–4, 106, 170, 180–81, 184, 220, 300, 320–21, 348, 369, 375
Ahaz, 28, 61, 84, 442, 449, 453
Ai 35, 50, 146, 156–57, 159, 161, 163–65, 170, 204, 490–91
Ajrud 443–44
Akko 340
altar 387, 389, 434–36, 438, 446, 449, 453–54, 462
Amalekites 243, 278, 286, 288
Amarna 7, 47, 58–59, 234, 259, 286, 323, 350, 357, 360–61, 379, 392, 468, 473
Amaziah 179, 245, 264
Ammon 245, 305, 316, 442, 502, 513
Ammonites 112, 179, 217, 227, 229, 245, 260, 263, 267, 278–79, 290
Amon 393
Amorites 342
amphictyony 46
amphora 353, 510, 512, 514
Amun 194
Amurru 91
Anat 302, 308

Anatolia 22, 25
angels 40, 219
aniconism 462
Annales school 180, 222, 312
Anthropology 3, 5, 7, 15, 54, 147, 151, 173, 305, 312, 327, 339
'Apiru 246, 251
Aphek 35, 275, 277
Arab 53, 184, 207–8, 217, 487
Arabah 180, 295, 309–10
Arabia 54, 174, 196, 198, 200, 258, 268, 290, 295, 305, 343, 502, 513
Arad 204, 245, 320, 387, 392, 421, 426, 434–36, 438–39, 444, 447, 457, 460–64
Aram 61, 260, 262–63, 267–68, 287, 290, 332, 368, 379
Aramaeans 67, 112, 170, 179, 245
Arbel 487, 494
architecture 178, 182, 238, 247, 254, 302, 308, 317–19, 353, 369, 510, 512, 528
Aroer 217, 220, 288
Ashdod 208, 238, 261–62, 318–19, 502
Asherah 302, 307–8, 387–88, 443–44, 455–56, 460–61
Ashkelon 208, 238, 258, 261, 282, 501
ashlar 303, 364
Ashur 261
Ashurbanipal 67, 265, 450
Ashurnasirpal 300
Asia 47, 73, 111, 114, 202, 295, 306, 349
Assyria 26–27, 48, 73, 79–81, 83, 85, 87–91, 93–94, 97, 100–101, 117, 170, 180, 265, 268, 300, 394, 400, 419–20, 450–51, 454–55, 458, 462
Assyrians 40, 52, 78, 80, 85–86, 92, 101–2, 104, 121, 170, 176, 179, 183, 206, 213, 215, 259, 267, 276, 302, 366, 377, 384, 388, 391, 400, 406, 419, 421, 486, 503

Astarte 295
astral 387, 421, 440–42, 445, 447–48, 452–54, 460
Athaliah 211
Atum 187–93, 198
Avaris 192–94, 199
Azariah 19–20, 113

Baal 47, 201, 210, 214, 216–17, 262, 446, 449
Babylon 28, 48, 68–71, 73, 82, 378, 386, 418, 456, 485, 503, 515
Babylonian 7, 16, 19, 23, 42, 45, 48, 57, 65–71, 80–82, 85, 107–9, 117, 121–22, 136, 201, 209, 218, 233, 265, 267, 275, 358, 368, 389, 400–401, 403, 406, 409, 414, 416–17, 450, 467, 470–72, 476, 479–80, 484, 486, 496, 498–504, 511–15
bamah 303
Baruch 494–96, 511–14
Bashan 204, 342
Batash 318
Bathsheba 252
Beersheba 59, 61, 179, 207, 241, 287, 292, 302, 314, 435–36, 442, 460, 462
Beit Lei 443–44
Beit Mirsim 441, 464
Bel 73
Benjamin 7, 37, 51, 64, 66, 144, 177, 205, 207, 211, 215–17, 234, 243, 246, 314, 325–26, 331, 336, 344, 353–54, 358, 391, 458, 462, 472, 486–87, 489–90, 495–96
Benjaminites 207, 234, 246, 283, 336
Berossus 85, 236, 265–68
Beth-Shean 114, 442
Beth-Shemesh 61
Beth-Zur 469, 483–85, 495–97
Bethel 7, 65–71, 164, 205, 207, 212, 214–15, 218, 220, 241, 253, 288, 389, 392, 394, 401–3, 413, 427, 486, 491, 496–97
Bethlehem 280, 283–85, 344, 486–87, 491, 497, 503
Bichrome 292, 318, 320–21, 350
bulla 421, 441, 451, 461
bullae 60, 373, 440–41, 444, 458–60, 462
bureaucracy 481
burial 227, 353–54, 359, 387, 436, 438, 514

Burnt Archive 458
Byblos 125, 298
bytdwd 373

calendar 41, 339
Canaan 31, 34, 46, 48, 50, 52, 54, 58–59, 111–12, 133–34, 141, 143, 162, 184, 186, 198, 205, 208, 212, 258, 268, 314, 316, 318, 350, 357, 361, 378, 398, 461, 514
Canaanites 112, 142, 144–45, 162, 207, 244, 385, 398, 498
Carmel 333
chief 48, 52, 179, 181, 187, 196–97, 246, 285–86, 288–89, 305, 323, 338–39, 344, 387, 401
chiefdom 178, 180–81, 305, 307, 311, 318, 332, 335, 338–39, 341, 347
chronicle 75, 82, 105, 107–8, 179, 182, 228, 258, 260, 262–64, 266, 299, 301, 374
chronicles 5, 7, 19, 21, 42–43, 48, 73–75, 77, 79–87, 91–92, 94–96, 108–10, 113, 122, 124, 126, 128, 136, 214, 233, 265, 267, 270, 298–99, 368, 377, 383
chronology 20, 37, 48, 53, 56, 73, 104, 126, 128, 142, 176, 190, 191, 203, 212, 217, 231, 235, 247, 276, 298–99, 305, 348, 354, 361, 365–66, 372, 391, 457
Cisjordan 226, 234
cisterns 145
citadel 362–64, 371, 457, 477, 494, 497, 502, 505, 510, 512, 514
city 7, 27–28, 35, 46–51, 54, 58–65, 68–71, 77–79, 81–83, 88–90, 92–94, 97, 100–103, 114, 142, 144–47, 153, 155, 164, 174–75, 179, 181, 182, 186–91, 193–97, 199–201, 204–6, 208, 214–15, 231–34, 238, 245–48, 253–54, 261–62, 272–75, 281–82, 284, 286–92, 295, 298, 303, 305–7, 314–15, 318–19, 323, 325, 330–34, 336–37, 341, 344–46, 348, 350, 352–66, 371–72, 378–79, 398, 428, 439–42, 445, 448, 450, 453–54, 462–63, 467–71, 473, 475–83, 485, 493–95, 497, 499–514, 526
clan 51, 175–76, 181, 205, 212, 215, 217, 323, 330, 335, 337–38, 344–45
clans 51, 181, 206, 208, 233, 254

climate 3, 368, 394, 448, 454, 527
copper 19–21, 150, 155, 176, 180, 217, 220, 241, 257, 268, 293, 295–97, 299, 301, 303, 305, 307–10, 312, 317, 322, 326–28, 330, 334, 342, 349–51, 460, 533
cubit 61
cult(s) 7, 66–71, 83, 123, 136, 180, 215, 246, 281, 331, 384–88, 397–98, 401, 404, 413–14, 419, 421, 425, 427–29, 431–43, 445–49, 451–57, 459–61, 463, 499
Cyprus 89, 180, 309

Dab'a 186, 192–94
Dagan 484
Damascus 32, 245, 259–60, 262–64, 287, 290, 305, 323, 332, 368
Dan 27, 78, 107, 126, 144, 178–79, 182, 207, 218–19, 259, 268, 287, 292, 302–3, 316, 345–46, 368, 373, 379, 416, 483, 513
David 8, 20, 35, 40, 46, 48, 51–52, 57, 60–62, 64, 78, 95, 107, 111–12, 122, 126, 133, 142, 155, 173–76, 178–83, 205–7, 217–18, 227–29, 231–32, 236–39, 242–94, 298–99, 301–5, 307, 316–19, 322–26, 329–39, 341, 344–48, 350, 352–65, 372–73, 375, 377, 379, 392, 397, 405, 408, 423–24, 441, 460, 462–63, 468–71, 475, 477–81, 494–95, 497, 500, 502, 505–11, 514, 523
Debir 145, 204
Deborah 132, 176–77, 212, 215, 220
deities 387, 440, 442–43, 445–46, 451, 453
Deuteronomist 81, 133, 136, 144, 179, 227, 255, 274–75, 375, 427, 439, 449
Deuteronomistic History 5, 19, 26, 28, 46, 78, 179, 182, 232, 236, 258, 273, 275, 365–66, 375, 383, 386, 389–90, 395, 405, 414, 433, 439, 459
divination 125, 387, 450–52, 462
divinities 451
Documentary Hypothesis 45
Dor 205–6, 361, 514

Ebla 47
economy 15, 27, 50, 60, 71, 85, 217, 240, 292, 294, 296, 314, 428

Edom 21, 103, 179, 189, 245, 264, 268, 290, 295, 304–5, 316, 334, 502
Edomite 21, 50, 179, 208, 245, 264, 278, 299, 309
Edrei 206
Eglon 145, 176, 204, 215, 219–20
Egypt 6, 22, 25, 46–48, 51, 54, 67, 80, 98, 102, 111–12, 130, 142, 154, 169, 173, 179, 180, 184, 186–95, 197–98, 201–2, 207–8, 226, 254, 257–58, 265, 268, 292, 295, 300–301, 313, 322–23, 327, 333, 336, 347, 350–51, 373–74, 391, 400, 406, 413, 418, 420, 432, 441–43, 451, 481–82, 502–4, 514
Egyptians 88, 98, 111, 113–14, 182, 186, 234, 321, 351, 391, 420–21
Ehud 72, 74, 76, 78, 80, 82, 84, 86, 88, 90, 92, 94, 96, 98, 113, 176, 215, 219, 461
Ekron 65, 88, 91, 102, 144, 151, 207–8, 238–39, 254, 261, 287, 289, 501
'El 307–8, 494, 497
Elam 70
Elephantine 63, 207–8, 385, 414
Eliashib 392
Elijah 214, 216
elites 220, 398
Elyon 84, 396
empire(s) 8, 42, 51, 65, 68, 70, 86–88, 107, 111–12, 122, 125, 132, 174, 180, 254, 300–301, 310, 316–18, 322–24, 343, 348, 366, 372–73, 392, 405–6, 416–18, 470–72, 499, 511, 513, 515, 526
En-gedi 283, 286, 456, 485
Ephraim 15, 51–52, 61, 134, 205, 208, 231, 234, 243, 325, 340, 374–75, 496
Ephraimite 64, 177, 234, 276, 314, 373, 375, 408
epigrapher 302
epigraphy 47, 52, 211, 221, 387, 459
Eretria 259
Esarhaddon 400, 412
Eshbaal 215, 230, 232, 302, 325, 340, 408
Ethiopia 310
ethnicity 121, 206, 271
Euphrates 51, 179, 180, 260, 292, 300, 322, 336

exile 8, 45, 48, 57, 66–67, 77, 79, 85, 91, 111–13, 123, 130, 134, 208, 275, 301, 378, 385–86, 413–18, 453, 456, 494, 497, 500, 512, 532
exilic 7, 21–22, 25, 45, 52, 61, 67, 69, 113, 121, 123, 128–29, 131–32, 136–37, 175–76, 202, 207, 209, 213–14, 226, 233, 268, 275, 294, 307–8, 368, 375–76, 385–86, 395–96, 401, 406–8, 412, 414–16, 427, 433, 442, 447, 453, 456–57, 460, 462, 467, 472, 501
exodus 8, 20, 33, 45–46, 48, 54–55, 98, 110–11, 123, 127, 129–30, 132, 136, 142, 169, 173–75, 184, 186–89, 191–202, 204, 207, 276, 396, 402, 405
Ezekiel 42, 136, 376, 401, 407, 421, 453
Ezra 8, 19, 42, 61, 63, 66–68, 111, 113, 122, 124, 126, 128, 136, 208, 264, 267, 386, 409–11, 414–15, 422, 424, 468, 472, 475, 477, 479, 481, 483, 485, 487, 489, 491, 493–98, 514

figurines 437, 460, 470
food 150, 195, 292, 339
forgeries 426, 441
fortifications 61–62, 65, 188, 192, 247, 332, 339, 346, 355–56, 361–62, 364, 371, 476, 480–82, 493, 499–501, 507, 510–11
frontier(s) 19–20, 35, 87, 192, 195, 201, 314, 316
fundamentalism 157, 171, 297, 529

Gad 112, 180, 210–11, 216, 303, 342
Galilee 32, 134–35, 206–8, 216–18, 314, 322–23, 332, 340, 442
garrison(s) 114, 245, 339, 392, 438
gateway 320
Gath 178–79, 237–39, 241, 244–45, 254, 261–62, 271–74, 281–84, 286–92
Gaza 91, 208, 238, 258, 261, 323, 502, 513
Geba 233, 490–91
Gedaliah 301, 412, 416, 503
genealogies 208
Genesis 4, 9, 19–21, 33, 42–43, 45, 50, 68–69, 116, 122–23, 125–28, 131–32, 135, 169, 195, 209, 214, 237, 301, 415
Gerizim 208, 215, 217, 221

Gezer 56, 58–59, 145, 181, 204, 206, 249, 258, 262, 284, 306, 318, 320–21, 326, 328, 332–34, 336, 339, 341, 344, 346, 348, 350–51, 362, 372, 473, 480, 485, 495
Gibeon 50, 175–77, 181, 205, 217, 232–35, 244, 262, 289, 302–4, 325–26, 331, 336, 344–45, 401, 469, 483–84, 486, 491, 497, 503
Gibeonites 232–34
Gideon 176, 214, 216–17, 220, 231, 305
Gihon 48, 181, 248, 353, 355, 357, 360–61, 373, 477–78, 481, 497, 507–8
Gilead 51, 133, 213, 227, 243, 272, 304, 325, 342
Girgashites 398
goddess 289, 414, 456
gods 70, 87, 108, 130, 193–94, 273, 308, 429, 445, 450–53
Goliath 228, 241–42, 251, 270–71, 279–80, 285, 287, 292, 423–24
Goshen 174, 194–98, 201–2
government 70, 234, 313, 329, 335, 341, 416, 419, 449
governor(s) 63, 271, 273–74, 323, 336–37, 339, 341, 346, 412, 450
grain 246
Greek 25–26, 46, 48, 53, 98, 124–25, 129, 187, 196, 200, 218, 226, 236, 242, 245–46, 268, 270, 272, 287, 297, 392, 413, 426, 446, 449, 452–53, 467, 472, 486, 504, 510, 529

Hadad 259, 299, 327
Hadadezer 179, 245, 259–60, 263, 268
Hamath 183, 259–64
Hammurabi 69
Haran 265, 267
Harasim 485
Harran 76, 440–41
Hatti 76–77
Hazael 179, 238, 245, 259–60, 262, 267–68, 287, 300, 373
Hazor 59, 145, 181, 204–6, 249, 298, 305, 317–18, 320, 328, 332–34, 339, 346, 362, 372

Hebrew 5–6, 16, 21, 24–25, 27–38, 41–42, 45, 47, 54–56, 62–63, 66–68, 77, 80, 82, 84, 86, 98, 100, 103, 106, 109, 111–12, 119–20, 125, 163, 178, 194, 199, 203, 206, 212, 214, 216–18, 220, 225, 235, 240, 246, 257–58, 267, 270, 284, 286, 291, 294, 297, 305, 307–8, 319, 353–54, 357, 359, 364, 368–70, 372–73, 403, 409, 414, 418, 426, 429, 443, 445–46, 458–60, 462, 467, 494–98, 511–15, 522, 532

Hebron 135, 145, 204, 232, 266, 280, 288, 299, 304, 306, 320, 325, 344, 347

Herodotus 3, 5, 25–26, 85, 112, 124–25, 187, 191, 200, 236, 467, 472, 529

Hezekiah 7, 28, 48, 61, 64, 73, 77–86, 89–94, 96–97, 100–102, 107, 182, 301, 305, 317, 342, 348, 351, 359–60, 365, 371, 375, 377, 385, 389, 394, 406, 408, 434–36, 438–39, 443, 450–51, 459, 461–62, 508, 526, 533

hieratic 178, 182, 257–58, 267

highlands 7, 58, 65, 68, 147, 173, 178, 183, 241, 243, 250, 255, 298, 313–14, 316–17, 319, 321, 326–27, 332–34, 336, 343–44, 397, 485–86, 492

Hilkiah 113, 462

Hinnom 387, 444–45, 454, 458

histoire événementielle 430–32, 442

historiography 5–6, 8–11, 13, 18, 24–27, 29, 38, 40, 54–57, 65, 67, 72, 75, 89, 98, 108, 110, 116–17, 119, 121–25, 127–29, 131–35, 137, 139, 148, 154–55, 159–61, 165, 167–68, 170, 224, 227, 235–36, 244, 258, 261, 266, 268–69, 275, 293, 298, 322, 340, 367, 369, 378–79, 389, 393, 423, 426, 428, 457, 530, 532

Hittite(s) 22, 47 214–15, 240, 254, 267

Hoshea 28

Huldah 413–14, 446

Ḥumri 8, 16

Hyksos 193–94, 203

iconography 18, 206, 430, 445, 450, 459, 462–63

ideology 7, 16, 18, 20, 27, 40, 53, 68–70, 77, 79, 84–86, 88–89, 92–93, 97, 113, 121, 124–26, 128–30, 132, 136, 157, 207, 216, 267, 306, 308, 322, 328, 334, 349–50, 370, 378, 386, 395, 398, 419, 481, 532

Ikausu 287

Ilu-bi'di 183

inscription(s) 4, 8, 16–17, 23, 27, 32, 47–49, 70, 73, 76, 87, 89–90, 92, 94, 103–4, 106–7, 109, 178, 182, 183, 188, 189, 191-94, 206, 212, 217, 220, 236, 239, 256, 258–63, 267, 287, 289, 291, 295, 298–300, 303, 308, 316, 342, 353, 368–69, 371, 373, 383, 387, 403, 409, 443–44, 452, 459–60, 462, 472, 484, 494, 510, 514, 526, 528–29

Iran 125, 343

Iranian 26, 125

iron 7, 9, 24, 26, 30, 32–38, 49, 52, 54, 59–62, 64, 66, 68–69, 108, 112, 114, 117, 133–35, 150, 170, 175–76, 181–82, 184–85, 205–6, 211, 213, 217, 226, 233–34, 238, 240–43, 245, 247–49, 254, 258, 265, 291–92, 295, 298, 304, 309–10, 312, 314–22, 324, 333–34, 340, 343, 352–61, 363–66, 371, 379, 387, 397–98, 425, 433–35, 439–40, 460, 462–64, 468–69, 477–84, 486–96, 502, 506–9, 511–12, 523–24, 526

Isaac 45, 47, 153, 169, 287

Isaiah 42, 64–65, 75, 78–79, 82, 84, 96, 101–2, 136, 214, 262, 371, 375–76, 386, 390, 395, 401, 408, 410, 414, 417, 419, 459

Ishbosheth 243

Isin 27

Jaffa 323, 440, 459

jar(s) 37, 233, 437, 462, 511

Jebusite(s) 175, 206, 246–48, 356, 363

Jehoiachin 28–29, 48, 81, 386, 415–16, 419

Jehoiakim 82, 84–85, 408, 413, 442

Jehoram 302

Jehu 28, 32, 206, 419

Jephthah 51, 213, 217–18

Jeremiah 42, 82, 84, 214, 301, 385–86, 389–90, 394–95, 413, 417–18, 421, 425, 443, 446, 453–54, 458, 486–89

Jericho 50, 56, 145–46, 150, 163–65, 176, 204, 211, 216, 404, 422, 484–87, 491–92, 497

Jeroboam 5, 19–20, 41, 123, 176, 194, 196, 206, 215, 217, 235, 298–99, 301, 306, 322, 326–27, 342, 348–49, 373–75

Jerusalem 5, 7, 12, 18–19, 27–28, 34, 40–42, 48–49, 51, 54, 56–64, 67–68, 70–71, 78–85, 89–90, 92, 94, 96–98, 100–103, 107, 111–12, 117, 121, 123, 126, 129–30, 133–34, 141, 144, 148, 174–76, 178, 180–83, 195, 204–8, 210–11, 216–18, 220, 232–33, 238, 245–49, 251–52, 254, 256–58, 265–68, 272, 282–84, 287, 289–92, 294, 297–99, 302–4, 306–10, 313–16, 318–23, 325–26, 329–34, 338–41, 344–66, 371–73, 377–79, 383, 387–90, 392, 394–95, 401–2, 409–10, 413–15, 421, 427–28, 438–39, 441–48, 450–60, 462–63, 467–71, 473, 475–77, 479, 481–83, 485–86, 488–505, 507–15, 526, 533
Jezreel 59, 135, 177, 235, 244, 277, 305, 314, 320–21, 332, 340, 442
Joash 28, 61
Job 339, 532
Jokneam 205
Jonah 81
Jonathan 177, 227–29, 232, 240, 250, 274–75, 289, 485, 490
Joram 302
Jordan 123, 143–44, 162, 177, 208, 211, 215, 234, 243, 249, 251, 290, 294, 299, 308–9, 313, 316, 336, 460, 504
Joseph 47, 107, 151, 153–54, 194–95, 207, 214, 374, 472
Josephus 7, 48, 50, 53, 73–75, 79, 82–83, 85–87, 94–95, 97–98, 297, 485, 529
Joshua 4, 11, 20, 46, 48, 111, 123, 141–45, 153, 162–64, 170, 173, 175, 203–5, 207–11, 213–14, 236, 268, 332, 383, 391, 418, 490, 528, 530
Josiah 70, 84–85, 113, 207, 212, 220, 288, 299–301, 308, 317, 326, 342, 348, 351, 360, 376–78, 381, 383–97, 399, 401–7, 409, 411, 413–15, 417, 419–21, 423, 425–29, 431–39, 441–43, 445, 447–63, 486, 497
Judges 8, 11, 20, 46, 111–12, 117, 123, 132, 141–43, 162–63, 170, 173, 175–77, 204, 212–15, 217, 219–21, 228, 230, 237, 246, 276, 405, 530

Karnak 217
Kemosh 103
Kenites 288, 435
Ketef Hinnom 387, 444–45, 458
Khirbet 35–36, 220, 241, 245, 280, 291–92, 409, 443–44, 460, 488–90, 494, 497
Kinneret 206, 211
Kittim 392
Kurkh 369

Lab'aya 372
Lachish 16, 58–59, 61, 73, 90, 94, 100–101, 123, 145, 204, 249, 267, 318, 371, 387, 442, 444, 461, 464, 473
law 40, 74, 111, 129, 237, 278–80, 285, 291, 306, 323, 338, 383–85, 387, 391, 393–97, 399–404, 407, 410–13, 415, 421, 439, 446, 453, 462, 483
Lebanon 32, 112, 143–44, 221, 259, 322, 333, 511
Lebo-hamath 259
Levant 25, 103, 111, 218, 240–41, 251, 275, 292, 316, 361, 497, 501, 521–22
Levi 397
Libyan 341, 346, 350
literacy 127
Lod 485–87, 491, 493–97
longue durée 3, 16, 313, 372, 430–31, 458, 527

Maccabees 483, 493–94, 497
Mamilla 354, 514
Manasseh 15, 28, 81, 91, 206–7, 383, 386, 389, 419, 435–36, 438–39, 447
Manetho 98, 265–66
Marduk 68–70, 386, 415–16
Mari 290, 504
Maskhuta 174, 186-93, 195, 198–200
Masoretic 446, 449
maximalists 10, 138, 148, 158, 367, 405, 425, 432, 476, 480, 527
Medes 406
Mediterranean 13, 60, 200–201, 226, 236, 238, 240, 294–95, 309–10, 312–13, 322, 327, 431, 481, 504
Megiddo 50, 56, 176, 181, 205–6, 215, 220, 235, 241, 249, 298, 305, 318, 320–21, 328, 332–34, 339, 346, 362, 372, 390–91, 420, 439

Menahem 28
Menorah 496
Merneptah 32, 47, 49, 175, 188–90, 192, 195, 205, 210, 212, 369
Merodach 73
Meṣad Ḥashavyahu 392, 420
Mesha 4, 8, 20, 32, 48, 103–5, 176, 179, 211, 215, 235, 245, 263–64, 298–99, 303, 342, 368
Mesopotamia 6–7, 22, 25, 27, 47, 69–70, 86, 125, 227, 265, 267–68, 313, 347, 401, 432
Mesopotamians 17
Midianites 217
minimalism 387, 432, 446–47, 527–29
Miqne 65, 238, 287
Mizpah 67, 218, 253, 401, 476, 485, 492, 499, 503
Moab 4, 8, 21, 48, 103–6, 176, 179, 215, 218–19, 245, 264, 298–300, 303–5, 316, 368, 442, 459, 502
Moabites 21, 50, 103, 112, 179, 264, 278
monotheism 45, 105, 127, 399, 404
Moses 20, 45, 48, 98, 105, 111, 130, 200, 276, 396, 407, 410, 412

Nabonidus 66, 76, 82, 513
Nabopolassar 68
Nahas 220
Nasbeh 479
Nebo 176, 215, 486
Nebuchadnezzar 4, 7, 12, 28, 70, 82, 107, 113, 141, 416–17
Nebuzaradan 113, 503
Necho 174, 191, 192, 200, 383, 391–92
Negev 135, 241, 243, 256, 274–75, 278, 288, 298, 336, 438–39, 443
Nergal 450
Nile 60, 191–92, 197–98, 200, 208, 420
Nimrud 215, 221
Nineveh 73, 90, 102, 107, 467
Nob 284, 331, 486
nomadism 112, 184, 268, 313–14, 316–17, 320, 339–40
nomads 286, 288, 298
Nuzi 313

Og 112, 170, 342, 446, 449, 452, 456
Omri 5, 8, 18, 20, 28, 32, 47–48, 103–4, 107, 110, 177, 180, 184, 206, 217, 220, 235, 252, 298–99, 301–3, 305, 317, 342, 372–73, 523
Omrides 16, 298, 306, 322
Ophel 182, 319, 353–54, 357–59, 364, 471, 496–97, 502, 505–6, 509, 513–14
Ophir 328
Ophrah 220
oracle 103, 281–82, 375–76, 413–14, 418, 446, 451
oral 116–17, 128, 140, 155, 256, 258, 268, 341, 357–58, 361
ostraca 17, 48–49, 206, 212, 257, 387, 392, 461

Palestine 4, 6–7, 9, 12, 15–18, 20, 22, 24, 26, 28–30, 32–33, 36, 46–52, 54, 56, 64, 78, 101–3, 106–8, 111–15, 117, 121–22, 124, 126, 130, 133, 137, 167, 170, 173, 183, 195, 202, 224, 241, 268, 286, 293–96, 298, 300, 304–7, 309–10, 312–18, 322–26, 340, 344–49, 361, 368, 391–92, 397–98, 403, 406, 409, 414, 418, 420–22, 431, 433, 440, 442–43, 450, 452–53, 458, 472, 494–96, 501, 503–4, 511, 513, 521–22, 524, 526–27, 529, 532
pantheon 69–70, 308
Passover 84, 394
patriarchs 19, 45–46, 110, 117, 405, 531
Pekah 28, 61
Pentateuch 45–46, 116, 123–25, 128, 130, 202, 388
Perez, 72, 74
Persians 53, 66, 470, 504
pharaoh 40, 47–48, 106, 113, 176, 189, 191, 193, 197, 210, 254, 306, 328, 332, 341, 348–50, 360, 383, 391, 402
Philistia 51, 60, 143, 205, 218, 239, 241, 262, 271, 273, 281, 287, 292, 305, 313, 442, 503
Philistines 35–36, 88, 101, 112, 143, 173–74, 177–79, 198, 229–30, 234, 236–37, 239–45, 252, 254, 261–63, 266, 270–92, 296, 316, 318, 325–26, 397

Phoenicia 19, 88–89, 102, 155, 205, 268, 293–94, 304–5, 308–9, 312–13, 332, 361, 460, 511, 533
Phoenicians 143, 180, 302, 335, 340, 504
Pithom 174, 187–93, 195, 198–202
populations 145, 314, 340, 398, 405, 513
postmodernism 72, 140, 525, 530–31
priest 63, 113, 246, 249, 252–53, 281, 283, 331, 385, 449, 451
priesthood 45, 66–67, 331, 399, 401–3, 413, 511
priestly 45, 201, 246, 252–53, 296, 301, 407, 413, 444, 452–53, 458, 463
priests 19, 53, 63, 70–71, 232, 246, 383, 386–87, 394, 400–401, 413, 428, 446, 448–49, 452–54

Qadesh-barnea 268
Qantir 186, 193, 197–98
Qarqar 16, 176, 217, 220, 300, 369
Qôm 460

Rabshakeh 8, 78, 82, 101–3
Raddana 35, 241
radiocarbon 57, 165, 220, 291, 361
rainfall 183, 304, 314
Ramat Rahel 485, 492
Rameses 174, 186–87, 193–95, 197–99, 201–2
Ras Shamra 47
Rehoboam 180, 182, 257, 298–99, 301, 306–7, 326, 333, 335, 341–42, 345, 348–50, 374, 397
religion 12, 18, 67, 70–71, 106, 111, 116, 120, 202, 220, 271, 302, 308, 316, 331, 345, 352, 378, 385, 387–88, 395–96, 398–400, 402–4, 406, 422, 427–28, 433–34, 438–39, 447, 451, 453, 457–58, 460–61, 463–64
Rephaim 262, 282–83
revolt 12, 50, 83, 104, 335, 406, 408, 419, 438, 481
Rezin 61

sacrifice(s) 67, 103, 214, 233, 450, 453–54
Saite 174, 189–91, 197, 202, 245
Sam'al 267

Samaria 9, 18–19, 32, 48, 50, 53, 56, 62, 73, 101, 107, 110, 117, 121, 126, 129–30, 134–35, 176, 181, 183, 206–7, 209–10, 215, 243, 276, 295, 303, 313, 317, 320, 359, 374, 377, 383, 385, 388–89, 394, 397, 402, 409, 420, 439, 449, 470, 496–97, 500, 504, 515
Samarians 216, 377
Samerina 67, 392
Samson 213, 218, 237
Sargon 27, 72–73, 82, 87, 89, 183, 215, 261, 267–68, 450
scarabs 49, 60, 442
scribes(s) 17, 19, 62, 87, 108, 126, 179, 203, 205, 212, 217, 256–58, 260, 262–63, 265, 267–68, 297, 317, 321, 383, 413
scroll 49, 67, 284, 396, 401, 427, 445–46
seal(s) 17–18, 20, 49, 60, 64, 235, 295, 387–88, 421, 440–43, 445, 451, 453, 456, 458, 460–63, 477–78, 484–87, 492, 497, 507, 514
sedentary 50
Semites 184
Semitic 17, 20, 28, 103, 126, 170, 212, 220, 279, 287, 303, 308, 440, 442, 458–59, 461–63
Sennacherib 4, 7–8, 72–94, 96–98, 100–102, 107, 371, 383, 387, 389, 394, 403, 435–36, 438, 443, 450, 523, 526
settlement(s) 4, 7, 12, 15, 31–36, 49, 52, 54, 56, 58–59, 65, 68, 70–71, 111, 114, 133–35, 141, 162, 165, 167, 173, 181–84, 207–11, 215, 233, 241, 243, 246–47, 249, 275–76, 292, 297, 313–14, 316–18, 320, 334, 353–57, 359–61, 363–64, 366, 371, 397, 435, 468–69, 471, 475–79, 481, 484, 486–87, 489–90, 492–93, 496, 498, 502–4, 507–10, 513, 527–28, 531
Shalmaneser 32, 182–83, 259, 369
Shalom 243, 249
Shaphan 421
Sheba 298–99, 310, 322, 345, 377
Shechem 58–59, 176, 209–10, 217, 299, 304, 306, 349, 372, 374, 473
Shephelah 216, 241, 243, 245, 284, 371, 441, 443, 485
Sheva 68, 70, 320

Shiloh 35–36, 182, 209, 319, 331–32, 345, 353, 355–58, 360–64, 375, 441, 462, 469–70, 477–80, 497, 502, 505–8, 510–11, 514
Shoham 247, 441, 462, 478, 494, 497, 508, 510
Shoshenq 174, 180–81, 252, 297, 302, 305–7, 309–10, 349
Siloam 48, 357, 507
Simeon 207, 484–85, 509
Sin 18, 76, 79, 81, 83, 92, 110, 130, 148, 399, 411
Sinai 40, 188–89, 195–98
sociology 3, 5, 7, 12, 15, 39, 47, 50, 54, 173, 184, 400
Solomon 8, 19–21, 40–41, 48, 51–52, 84, 95–96, 107, 111–12, 123, 132, 141, 155, 174, 181, 178, 180–82, 184, 195, 205–6, 208, 211, 233, 245, 247–48, 252, 254–58, 264–66, 268, 275, 292–313, 315–52, 354–55, 361–63, 365, 372–75, 377–79, 397, 399, 405, 408, 415, 435, 460, 523, 533
statehood 304, 317, 377
States 50, 58–59, 82, 107, 112, 114, 117, 121, 145, 149, 158, 164, 177, 205, 217, 234–35, 237, 244, 267, 290, 292, 294, 299, 302, 304–5, 316, 318, 322–23, 325, 329, 333, 336, 356, 363, 368, 372, 378, 405–8, 432, 451
steppe 314, 514
Stepped Stone Structure 182, 247–48, 319, 355, 361–64
Syria 22, 47–48, 112, 143, 215, 262, 303, 313–16, 332, 336–37, 347, 441, 454, 496
Syrian 47, 103, 309, 313, 452

Taanach 56, 205–6, 240, 421
Taharqa 73
Tash 262, 268
taxation 428, 439
Tema 220, 502
temple 12–13, 18–19, 21, 61–63, 67–70, 76, 79, 82, 95–96, 101, 117, 178, 180–81, 187–93, 195, 198, 203, 208, 215, 221, 232–33, 238–39, 247, 251–52, 254–55, 257, 264–66, 293, 295, 298, 303–4, 307–8, 317, 319, 326, 328–31, 339, 346, 350, 353–54, 358–59, 364, 379, 383, 385, 387–88, 390, 396, 399, 401–2, 404, 413–15, 421, 427, 435–38, 441, 445, 449, 451, 453–57, 459–61, 469, 471–72, 476, 478–79, 481–83, 494–95, 497–500, 505, 508, 510, 512–14, 521, 523, 526, 528
terracing 360–63
Tiglath-pileser 32, 261–62
Timnah 102, 144, 180, 318
Tirhakah 94
tombs 359
Torah 19, 111, 119, 207, 385, 388, 399, 427
trade 52, 147, 176–77, 180, 191, 200, 216–17, 234, 244, 254, 290, 294–95, 299, 302, 304, 309, 313, 327–29, 332, 334–35, 338, 351, 470, 504, 514
Transjordan 54, 177, 205, 208, 215, 217, 235, 245, 252, 260, 313, 316, 345, 504
Transjordanians 208
tribalism 163, 206
tribes 12–13, 32–34, 37, 49–51, 134, 143, 176, 178, 182, 189, 205, 216, 218, 220, 244, 255, 279, 288, 294, 365–66, 374, 376, 397, 405–9
Tyre 88–92, 293–94, 334–35, 340, 350–51, 502, 512–13

Ugarit 17, 47, 211–12, 217, 220, 238, 245, 379, 422, 513
Ugaritic 453
Ur 27, 125, 224, 266
urban 56, 58–59, 69, 71, 181, 181–82, 267, 305, 325, 331, 336, 344–45, 348, 355, 357, 360–61, 363–66, 470–71, 476, 497, 499–501, 504, 510
Uriah 279, 345, 444
Uzziah 19–20, 317, 322, 348

vassalage 334, 421
vassals 102, 113, 260, 300, 306
village(s) 33–36, 49–50, 52, 59, 62–63, 70, 77, 112, 114, 177, 182, 215, 218, 249, 271, 278, 287–88, 322, 343, 354–55, 359, 364, 366, 371, 440, 486, 488–90, 493, 501
vineyard 144–45

Wadi 180, 188, 190–92, 195, 197–201, 309–10
Warren's shaft 353, 357
weight(s) 11, 76, 152, 160, 163, 209, 239, 257, 313, 327, 437, 440–41, 457, 530–31
wine 234, 509

Yahu 379
Yhwh 7, 143–44, 227–28, 242, 253–54, 263, 271, 273, 278–79, 284, 289–90, 317, 329–31, 346, 375, 387, 443–44, 460–61
Zayit 340
Zedekiah 7, 19–20, 28, 80–82, 84–85, 107, 298, 413
Ziph 286